Further Pure 2 & 3

Hugh Neill and Douglas Quadling

Series editor Hugh Neill

CAMBRIDGE
UNIVERSITY PRESS

CAMBRIDGE UNIVERSITY PRESS
Cambridge, New York, Melbourne, Madrid, Cape Town, Singapore,
São Paulo, Delhi, Dubai, Tokyo, Mexico City

Cambridge University Press
The Edinburgh Building, Cambridge CB2 8RU, UK

www.cambridge.org
Information on this title: www.cambridge.org/9780521548991

First published 2005
6th printing 2010

Printed in the United Kingdom at the University Press, Cambridge

A catalogue record for this publication is available from the British Library

ISBN 978-0-521-54899-1 Paperback

Cover image © Digital Vision

Contents

Introduction

Cambridge Advanced Level Mathematics has been written especially for the OCR modular examination. It consists of one book or half-book corresponding to each module. This book combines the last two Pure Mathematics modules, FP2 and FP3. The OCR specification does not require that FP2 is taken before FP3. In this book, the modules are almost independent, and large parts of FP3 can be tackled before FP2.

The books are divided into chapters roughly corresponding to syllabus headings. Some sections include work which goes beyond the examination specification. These sections are marked with an asterisk (*) in the section heading.

Occasionally within the text paragraphs appear in a grey box. These paragraphs are usually outside the main stream of the mathematical argument, but may help to give insight, or suggest extra work or different approaches.

References are made throughout the text to previous work in modules C1 to C4. It is expected that students still have access to these books in the classroom, even if they do not have a copy for their personal use.

Numerical work is presented in a form intended to discourage premature approximation. In ongoing calculations inexact number appear in decimal form like 3.456... signifying that the number is held in a calculator to more places than are given. Numbers are not rounded at this stage; the full display could be, for example, 3.456 123 or 3.456 789. Final answers are then stated with some indication that they are approximate, for example '3.46 correct to 3 significant figures'.

There are plenty of exercises, and each chapter contains a Miscellaneous exercise which includes some questions of examination standard. There are also two Revision exercises for each module, with many questions taken from OCR examination papers, and two practice examination papers for each module.

The authors thank Lawrence Jarrett and Richard Davies, who read the book very carefully and made many extremely useful comments, and OCR and Cambridge University Press, in particular Rufus Curnow, for their help in producing this book. However, the responsibility for the text, and for any errors, remains with the authors.

Module FP2

Further Pure 2

1 Differentiating inverse trigonometric functions

Throughout the course you have gradually been increasing the number of functions that you can differentiate and integrate. This chapter extends this development to inverse trigonometric functions. When you have completed it, you should

- know the derivatives of $\tan^{-1} x$, $\sin^{-1} x$ and $\cos^{-1} x$
- know the integrals corresponding to these derivatives
- be familiar with other inverse trigonometric functions and relations between them
- use these relations to differentiate other inverse trigonometric functions.

1.1 The inverse tangent

The simplest of the inverse trigonometric functions to differentiate is $\tan^{-1} x$. You can do this directly from the definition, that $y = \tan^{-1} x$ is the number such that

$$\tan y = x \quad \text{and} \quad -\tfrac{1}{2}\pi < y < \tfrac{1}{2}\pi.$$

You know, from a general result about inverse functions (see C3 Section 2.9) that its graph is the reflection in the line $y = x$ of the part of the graph of $y = \tan x$ for which $-\tfrac{1}{2}\pi < x < \tfrac{1}{2}\pi$.

This is shown in Fig. 1.1.

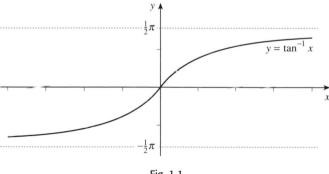

Fig. 1.1

The equation $\tan y = x$ is not in the form $y = \ldots$, but it can be differentiated using the method for curves defined implicitly described in C4 Chapter 8. The derivative with respect to x of $\tan y$ is $\sec^2 y \dfrac{dy}{dx}$, and the derivative of x is 1, so

$$\tan y = x \quad \Rightarrow \quad \sec^2 y \frac{dy}{dx} = 1$$

$$\Leftrightarrow \quad \frac{dy}{dx} = \frac{1}{\sec^2 y}.$$

But this isn't really satisfactory. When you differentiate $y = \tan^{-1} x$, you expect an answer in terms of x, not y. However, this is easily dealt with. Since $\sec^2 y = 1 + \tan^2 y$, and $\tan y = x$,

$$\sec^2 y = 1 + x^2,$$

so $$\frac{dy}{dx} = \frac{1}{1 + x^2}.$$

$$\frac{d}{dx} \tan^{-1} x = \frac{1}{1 + x^2}.$$

It is interesting that the derivative of $\tan^{-1} x$ is not any sort of trigonometric function, but a rational function. This may remind you of what happens with $\ln x$, whose derivative $\dfrac{1}{x}$ doesn't involve logarithms or exponentials.

Notice that, since $1 + x^2 \geqslant 1$, the gradient of the graph in Fig. 1.1 is less than or equal to 1 throughout its length.

Example 1.1.1
Differentiate with respect to x (a) $\tan^{-1} \frac{1}{3} x$,   (b) $\tan^{-1} x^2$.

Both derivatives can be found by using the chain rule.

(a) $$\frac{d}{dx} \tan^{-1} \tfrac{1}{3} x = \frac{1}{1 + \left(\frac{1}{3} x\right)^2} \times \tfrac{1}{3} = \frac{\frac{1}{3}}{1 + \frac{1}{9} x^2}.$$

To write this more simply, multiply top and bottom of the fraction by 9, to get

$$\frac{d}{dx} \tan^{-1} \tfrac{1}{3} x = \frac{9 \times \frac{1}{3}}{9 \left(1 + \frac{1}{9} x^2\right)} = \frac{3}{9 + x^2}.$$

(b) $$\frac{d}{dx} \tan^{-1} x^2 = \frac{1}{1 + (x^2)^2} \times 2x = \frac{2x}{1 + x^4}.$$

Example 1.1.2
Find $\displaystyle\int \tan^{-1} x \, dx$

In C4 Example 2.1.3, $\displaystyle\int \ln x \, dx$ was found by writing the integrand as $\ln x \times 1$ and using integration by parts. This works because the derivative of $\ln x$ is a rational function of x, and doesn't involve a logarithm.

You can find $\displaystyle\int \tan^{-1} x \, dx$ in a similar way, and for the same reason.

Writing $u = \tan^{-1} x$ and $\dfrac{dv}{dx} = 1$, so that $v = x$,

$$\int \tan^{-1} x \, dx = \tan^{-1} x \times x - \int \frac{1}{1 + x^2} \times x \, dx.$$

You should recognise this last integral, $\int \dfrac{x}{1+x^2}\,dx$, as a constant multiple of the form $\int \dfrac{f'(x)}{f(x)}\,dx$, which is $\ln|f(x)| + k$ (see C4 Section 2.4). So

$$\int \frac{x}{1+x^2}\,dx = \tfrac{1}{2}\int \frac{2x}{1+x^2}\,dx = \tfrac{1}{2}\ln(1+x^2) + k.$$

So $\int \tan^{-1} x\,dx = x\tan^{-1}x - \tfrac{1}{2}\ln(1+x^2) - k.$

1.2 Inverse sine and cosine

The method of differentiating $\sin^{-1}x$ and $\cos^{-1}x$ is similar to that for $\tan^{-1}x$, but there are some small complications. The easier and more important is $\sin^{-1}x$, so begin with this.

The definition is that $y = \sin^{-1}x$ is the number such that

$$\sin y = x \quad\text{and}\quad -\tfrac{1}{2}\pi \leqslant y \leqslant \tfrac{1}{2}\pi.$$

Its graph is shown in Fig. 1.2. The domain of the function is $-1 \leqslant x \leqslant 1$.

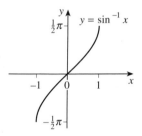

Fig. 1.2

Differentiating this equation by the implicit method gives

$$\sin y = x \quad\Rightarrow\quad \cos y\,\frac{dy}{dx} = 1$$
$$\Leftrightarrow\quad \frac{dy}{dx} = \frac{1}{\cos y}.$$

Again this derivative has to be expressed in terms of x, and this time the relation you want is $\cos^2 y + \sin^2 y = 1$, so that $\cos y = \pm\sqrt{1 - \sin^2 y}$, which is $\pm\sqrt{1 - x^2}$. But should the sign be $+$ or $-$?

To answer this, look at the graph in Fig. 1.2. You can see that the gradient of the graph is always positive, so the $+$ sign must be chosen. So replacing $\cos y$ by $\sqrt{1 - x^2}$,

$$\frac{dy}{dx} = \frac{1}{\sqrt{1 - x^2}}.$$

Example 1.2.1

Find the domains, and the derivatives with respect to x, of

(a) $\sin^{-1}\frac{1}{5}x$,   (b) $\sin^{-1}(1-x)$.

(a) The domain of $\sin^{-1}x$ is $-1 \leqslant x \leqslant 1$, so the numbers in the domain of $\sin^{-1}\frac{1}{5}x$ must satisfy the inequalities $-1 \leqslant \frac{1}{5}x \leqslant 1$. The domain is therefore $-5 \leqslant x \leqslant 5$.

Using the chain rule,

$$\frac{d}{dx}\sin^{-1}\tfrac{1}{5}x = \frac{1}{\sqrt{1 - \left(\frac{1}{5}x\right)^2}} \times \tfrac{1}{5}$$

$$= \frac{1}{5\sqrt{1 - \frac{1}{25}x^2}}$$

$$= \frac{1}{\sqrt{25\left(1 - \frac{1}{25}x^2\right)}}$$

$$= \frac{1}{\sqrt{25 - x^2}}.$$

(b) The numbers in the domain of $\sin^{-1}(1-x)$ must satisfy the inequalities $-1 \leqslant 1-x$ and $1-x \leqslant 1$, that is $x \leqslant 2$ and $x \geqslant 0$. The domain is therefore $0 \leqslant x \leqslant 2$.

Using the chain rule,

$$\frac{d}{dx}\sin^{-1}(1-x) = \frac{1}{\sqrt{1 - (1-x)^2}} \times (-1)$$

$$= \frac{-1}{\sqrt{1 - (1 - 2x + x^2)}}$$

$$= \frac{-1}{\sqrt{2x - x^2}}.$$

You can find the derivative of $\cos^{-1}x$ using the same method as for $\sin^{-1}x$. This is left for you to do for yourself in Exercise 1A Question 7. But there is an even easier way.

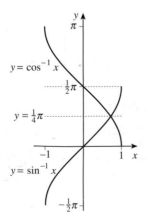

Fig. 1.3

Figure 1.3 shows the graphs of $y = \sin^{-1} x$ and $y = \cos^{-1} x$ drawn using the same axes. You can see that the graphs are reflections of each other in the line $y = \frac{1}{4}\pi$. So, for each value of x, the gradient of $y = \cos^{-1} x$ is minus the gradient of $y = \sin^{-1} x$. That is,

$$\frac{d}{dx} \cos^{-1} x = -\frac{d}{dx} \sin^{-1} x = -\frac{1}{\sqrt{1 - x^2}}.$$

If $-1 < x < 1$,
$$\frac{d}{dx} \sin^{-1} x = \frac{1}{\sqrt{1 - x^2}} \quad \text{and} \quad \frac{d}{dx} \cos^{-1} x = -\frac{1}{\sqrt{1 - x^2}}.$$

The derivatives of $\tan^{-1} x$, $\sin^{-1} x$ and $\cos^{-1} x$ are important and you should remember them.

You may be surprised that the derivatives of $\sin^{-1} x$ and $\cos^{-1} x$ are stated for $-1 < x < 1$, and not for the whole domain $-1 \leqslant x \leqslant 1$. It is easy to see why from Fig. 1.3. When $x = -1$ and $x = 1$ the tangents to the graphs are parallel to the y-axis, so that the gradient is undefined. Also of course $\dfrac{1}{\sqrt{1 - x^2}}$ has no meaning for these values of x.

Exercise 1A

1 Find the derivatives of the following with respect to x.

(a) $\tan^{-1} 2x$ (b) $\sin^{-1} \frac{1}{3} x$ (c) $x \tan^{-1} x$ (d) $(\sin^{-1} x)^2$

(e) $\sin^{-1} \sqrt{x}$ (f) $\tan^{-1}(x\sqrt{x})$ (g) $\sin^{-1} \sqrt{1 - x^2}$

2 Find the minimum point of the graph of $y = x^2 - 4 \tan^{-1} x$.

3 State the natural domain (that is, the largest possible domain) of the function $f(x) = 5x - 3 \sin^{-1} x$. Find the turning points on the graph of $y = f(x)$, and sketch the graph. Hence find the range of the function.

4 Repeat Question 3 for the function $f(x) = 5x - 4 \sin^{-1} x$.

5 The tangent to $y = (\tan^{-1} x)^2$ at the point where $x = 1$ cuts the y-axis at the point P. Find the y-coordinate of P.

6 Find the maximum value of $f(x) = (\sin^{-1} x)^2 \cos^{-1} x$ in the interval $0 < x < 1$.

7 Find $\dfrac{d}{dx} \cos^{-1} x$ by the method used in Section 1.2 to find $\dfrac{d}{dx} \sin^{-1} x$.

1.3 The corresponding integrals

The derivatives in Sections 1.1 and 1.2 can also be interpreted as integrals. From $\frac{d}{dx}\tan^{-1}x = \frac{1}{1+x^2}$ it follows that

$$\int \frac{1}{1+x^2}\,dx = \tan^{-1}x + k.$$

And from $\frac{d}{dx}\sin^{-1}x = \frac{1}{\sqrt{1-x^2}}$ you can deduce

$$\int \frac{1}{\sqrt{1-x^2}}\,dx = \sin^{-1}x + k.$$

You could also use $\frac{d}{dx}\cos^{-1}x = -\frac{1}{\sqrt{1-x^2}}$ to obtain $\int \frac{1}{\sqrt{1-x^2}}dx = -\cos^{-1}x + k'$, but there is no point in using two different forms for the same integral, and $\sin^{-1}x + k$ is simpler. What is the connection between k and k'?

Example 1.3.1

Find $\int_0^1 \frac{1}{1+x^2}\,dx.$

$$\int_0^1 \frac{1}{1+x^2}\,dx = \left[\tan^{-1}x\right]_0^1$$
$$= \tan^{-1}1 - \tan^{-1}0$$
$$= \tfrac{1}{4}\pi - 0$$
$$= \tfrac{1}{4}\pi.$$

Use a graphic calculator to display the graph of $y = \frac{1}{1+x^2}$ for $0 \leqslant x \leqslant 1$, and identify the area represented by the integral in Example 1.3.1. It is interesting that the number π appears in calculating an area which has nothing to do with a circle.

Example 1.3.2

Find $\int_0^1 \frac{1}{\sqrt{1-x^2}}\,dx.$

This integral needs a little more care. Notice that the integrand $\frac{1}{\sqrt{1-x^2}}$ is not defined when $x = 1$, because $\sqrt{1-1^2} = 0$. So this is an improper integral, and it must be calculated as a limit.

Use a graphic calculator to display the graph of $y = \frac{1}{\sqrt{1-x^2}}.$

Begin by finding, for a number s such that $0 < s < 1$,

$$\int_0^s \frac{1}{\sqrt{1-x^2}}\, dx = \left[\sin^{-1} x\right]_0^s$$
$$= \sin^{-1} s - \sin^{-1} 0$$
$$= \sin^{-1} s.$$

The graph of $y = \sin^{-1} x$ in Fig. 1.2 shows that, as $x \to 1$, $\sin^{-1} x \to \frac{1}{2}\pi$. So

$$\int_0^1 \frac{1}{\sqrt{1-x^2}}\, dx = \lim_{s\to 1} \int_0^s \frac{1}{\sqrt{1-x^2}}\, dx$$
$$= \lim_{s\to 1}(\sin^{-1} s)$$
$$= \tfrac{1}{2}\pi.$$

You will find that you often want to find integrals like those at the beginning of this section in a slightly more general form, as $\int \dfrac{1}{a^2+x^2}\, dx$ or $\int \dfrac{1}{\sqrt{a^2-x^2}}\, dx$, where a is a positive number.

It is easy to do this by using the substitution $x = au$. Then $\dfrac{dx}{du} = a$, so

$$\int \frac{1}{a^2+x^2}\, dx = \int \frac{1}{a^2+a^2u^2} \times a\, du$$
$$= \int \frac{a}{a^2(1+u^2)}\, du$$
$$= \frac{1}{a} \int \frac{1}{1+u^2}\, du$$
$$= \frac{1}{a}\tan^{-1} u + k$$
$$= \frac{1}{a}\tan^{-1}\frac{x}{a} + k,$$

and

$$\int \frac{1}{\sqrt{a^2-x^2}}\, dx = \int \frac{1}{\sqrt{a^2-a^2u^2}} \times a\, du$$
$$= \int \frac{a}{\sqrt{a^2(1-u^2)}}\, du$$
$$= \frac{a}{a} \int \frac{1}{\sqrt{1-u^2}}\, du$$
$$= \sin^{-1} u + k$$
$$= \sin^{-1}\frac{x}{a} + k.$$

You will need to remember these results, either in the forms given at the beginning of the section or in these more general forms.

If $a > 0$,

$$\int \frac{1}{a^2+x^2}\, dx = \frac{1}{a}\tan^{-1}\frac{x}{a} + k, \qquad \int \frac{1}{\sqrt{a^2-x^2}}\, dx = \sin^{-1}\frac{x}{a} + k.$$

Example 1.3.3

Figure 1.4 shows the graph of $y = \dfrac{1}{\sqrt{4 + x^2}}$ for $-2 \leqslant x \leqslant 2$. Find the volume of the solid formed when the region bounded by this curve and parts of the lines $x = -2$, $x = 2$ and the x-axis is rotated though a complete revolution about the x-axis.

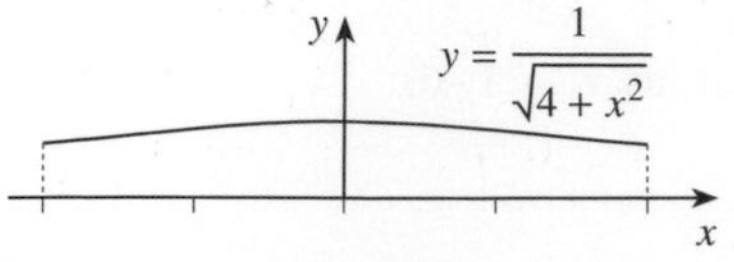

Fig. 1.4

The volume is given by the integral

$$\int_{-2}^{2} \pi y^2 \, dx = \pi \int_{-2}^{2} \frac{1}{4 + x^2} \, dx$$

$$= \pi \left[\tfrac{1}{2} \tan^{-1} \frac{x}{2} \right]_{-2}^{2}$$

$$= \tfrac{1}{2}\pi \left(\tan^{-1} 1 - \tan^{-1}(-1) \right)$$

$$= \tfrac{1}{2}\pi \left(\tfrac{1}{4}\pi - (-\tfrac{1}{4}\pi) \right)$$

$$= \tfrac{1}{2}\pi \times \tfrac{1}{2}\pi = \tfrac{1}{4}\pi^2.$$

The volume of the solid is $\tfrac{1}{4}\pi^2$.

Example 1.3.4

Find $\displaystyle\int \frac{1}{\sqrt{a^2 - b^2 x^2}} \, dx$, where a and b are positive constants.

If bx is written as au, then $\sqrt{a^2 - b^2 x^2}$ becomes $\sqrt{a^2 - a^2 u^2}$, which simplifies to $a\sqrt{1 - u^2}$. So, substituting $x = \dfrac{au}{b}$,

$$\int \frac{1}{\sqrt{a^2 - b^2 x^2}} \, dx = \int \frac{1}{a\sqrt{1 - u^2}} \times \frac{a}{b} \, du = \frac{1}{b} \int \frac{1}{\sqrt{1 - u^2}} \, du$$

$$= \frac{1}{b} \sin^{-1} u + k = \frac{1}{b} \sin^{-1} \frac{bx}{a} + k.$$

Example 1.3.5

Find $\displaystyle\int_{-1}^{1} \frac{1}{9x^2 + 6x + 5} \, dx$.

Since $9x^2 + 6x + 5 = (3x + 1)^2 + 4$, substitute $3x + 1 = 2u$. Then $\dfrac{dx}{du} = \tfrac{2}{3}$; also when $x = -1$ and 1, $u = -1$ and 2 respectively. So the integral becomes

$$\int_{-1}^{2} \frac{1}{4u^2 + 4} \times \tfrac{2}{3} \, du = \tfrac{1}{6} \int_{-1}^{2} \frac{1}{u^2 + 1} \, du = \tfrac{1}{6} \left[\tan^{-1} u \right]_{-1}^{2}$$

$$= \tfrac{1}{6}(\tan^{-1} 2 - \tan^{-1}(-1)) = \tfrac{1}{6}(\tan^{-1} 2 + \tan^{-1} 1).$$

If you want a numerical answer, don't forget to put your calculator into radian mode. The value is 0.315, correct to 3 decimal places.

Exercise 1B

1 Evaluate the following definite integrals. Give each answer as an exact multiple of π if possible; otherwise give the answer correct to 3 significant figures.

(a) $\displaystyle\int_{-1}^{1} \frac{1}{\sqrt{4-x^2}}\, dx$

(b) $\displaystyle\int_{0}^{5} \frac{1}{25+x^2}\, dx$

(c) $\displaystyle\int_{1}^{3} \frac{1}{4+x^2}\, dx$

(d) $\displaystyle\int_{1}^{3} \frac{1}{3+x^2}\, dx$

(e) $\displaystyle\int_{0}^{1} \frac{1}{\sqrt{2-x^2}}\, dx$

(f) $\displaystyle\int_{-4}^{-3} \frac{1}{\sqrt{25-x^2}}\, dx$

2 Find the following infinite integrals.

(a) $\displaystyle\int_{1}^{\infty} \frac{1}{1+x^2}\, dx$

(b) $\displaystyle\int_{0}^{\infty} \frac{1}{9+x^2}\, dx$

(c) $\displaystyle\int_{-\infty}^{\infty} \frac{1}{100+x^2}\, dx$

3 Find the following improper integrals.

(a) $\displaystyle\int_{0}^{5} \frac{1}{\sqrt{25-x^2}}\, dx$

(b) $\displaystyle\int_{-3}^{3} \frac{1}{\sqrt{9-x^2}}\, dx$

(c) $\displaystyle\int_{1}^{2} \frac{1}{\sqrt{4-x^2}}\, dx$

4 Use a substitution of the form $x = cu$ for a suitable value of c to find the following indefinite integrals.

(a) $\displaystyle\int \frac{1}{9+4x^2}\, dx$

(b) $\displaystyle\int \frac{1}{\sqrt{4-9x^2}}\, dx$

(c) $\displaystyle\int \frac{1}{\sqrt{1-4x^2}}\, dx$

(d) $\displaystyle\int \frac{1}{1+9x^2}\, dx$

(e) $\displaystyle\int \frac{1}{2+3x^2}\, dx$

(f) $\displaystyle\int \frac{1}{\sqrt{4-5x^2}}\, dx$

5 By completing the square and then using a substitution of the form $x = a + bu$, find the following indefinite integrals.

(a) $\displaystyle\int \frac{1}{x^2+2x+2}\, dx$

(b) $\displaystyle\int \frac{1}{x^2+6x+13}\, dx$

(c) $\displaystyle\int \frac{1}{4x^2-12x+25}\, dx$

(d) $\displaystyle\int \frac{1}{\sqrt{5-4x-x^2}}\, dx$

(e) $\displaystyle\int \frac{1}{\sqrt{8+6x-9x^2}}\, dx$

(f) $\displaystyle\int \frac{1}{\sqrt{10x-x^2}}\, dx$

6 Evaluate the following definite integrals. Give your answers to 3 significant figures. In some parts you may need to use one of the methods described in Question 4 and Question 5.

(a) $\displaystyle\int_{0}^{2} \frac{1}{x^2+25}\, dx$

(b) $\displaystyle\int_{1}^{3} \frac{1}{1+16x^2}\, dx$

(c) $\displaystyle\int_{-1}^{1} \frac{1}{x^2-6x+25}\, dx$

(d) $\displaystyle\int_{0}^{\infty} \frac{1}{9+25x^2}\, dx$

(e) $\displaystyle\int_{1}^{2} \frac{1}{\sqrt{9-x^2}}\, dx$

(f) $\displaystyle\int_{0}^{1} \frac{1}{\sqrt{16-9x^2}}\, dx$

(g) $\displaystyle\int_{-1}^{1} \frac{1}{\sqrt{3+2x-x^2}}\, dx$

(h) $\displaystyle\int_{-0.5}^{0.5} \frac{1}{\sqrt{1-4x^2}}\, dx$

(i) $\displaystyle\int_{1}^{2} \frac{1}{\sqrt{4x-x^2}}\, dx$

7 Find $\displaystyle\int \frac{1}{a^2+b^2x^2}\, dx$, where a and b are positive constants.

8 Show that the rule $\displaystyle\int \frac{1}{a^2+x^2}\, dx = \frac{1}{a}\tan^{-1}\frac{x}{a} + k$ remains true if $a < 0$, but that

$\displaystyle\int \frac{1}{\sqrt{a^2-x^2}}\, dx = \sin^{-1}\frac{x}{a} + k$ doesn't.

1.4* Other inverse trigonometric functions

This section is optional. You may omit it if you wish, and go straight on to the Miscellaneous exercise at the end of the chapter.

In C3 Section 6.2 the trigonometric functions sec, cosec and cot (short for secant, cosecant and cotangent) were introduced, with definitions

$$\sec x = \frac{1}{\cos x}, \quad \operatorname{cosec} x = \frac{1}{\sin x}, \quad \cot x = \frac{1}{\tan x} = \frac{\cos x}{\sin x}.$$

These also have inverses $\sec^{-1}$, $\operatorname{cosec}^{-1}$ and $\cot^{-1}$, but they are not very important, because they can be expressed in terms of the inverse functions you already know.

Take $\sec^{-1}$ as an example. To define this you have to restrict the domain of the function sec to make it one-one. Figure 1.5 shows that this can be done in the same way as for cos (except that sec is not defined at $\frac{1}{2}\pi$), and the graphs of the inverse functions are then as shown in Fig. 1.6.

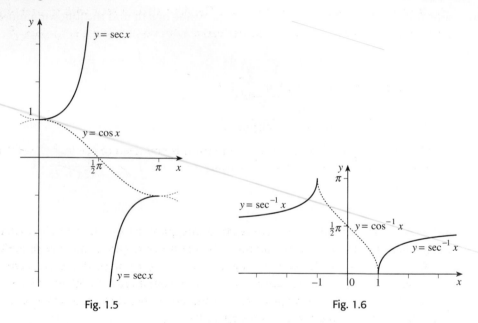

Fig. 1.5   Fig. 1.6

Notice that $\cos^{-1}$ has domain $-1 \le x \le 1$, and $\sec^{-1}$ has a domain combining the two intervals $x \le -1$ and $x \ge 1$. Both have range $0 \le x \le \pi$, except that the range of $\sec^{-1}$ excludes $\frac{1}{2}\pi$.

But there is a closer connection between these functions, since

$$y = \sec^{-1} x \quad \Leftrightarrow \quad \sec y = x \quad \Leftrightarrow \quad \cos y = \frac{1}{x} \quad \Leftrightarrow \quad y = \cos^{-1} \frac{1}{x}.$$

This means that, for any x in the domain of $\sec^{-1}$,

$$\sec^{-1} x = \cos^{-1} \frac{1}{x}.$$

You can find for yourself similar relations connecting $\csc^{-1}$ with $\sin^{-1}$, and $\cot^{-1}$ with $\tan^{-1}$. If you restrict the domains of cosec and cot in the same way as for sin and tan, to the interval $-\frac{1}{2}\pi \leqslant x \leqslant \frac{1}{2}\pi$ (except that neither cosec nor cot is defined at 0), you obtain:

> **Reciprocal rules**
>
> $$\sec^{-1}x = \cos^{-1}\frac{1}{x}, \quad \csc^{-1}x = \sin^{-1}\frac{1}{x}, \quad \cot^{-1}x = \tan^{-1}\frac{1}{x}.$$

Example 1.4.1

Differentiate $\sec^{-1}x$ with respect to x.

You can do this either by the same method as you used to differentiate $\tan^{-1}x$ and $\sin^{-1}x$ or by using the reciprocal rule and the chain rule. Whichever method you prefer, care has to be taken to get the correct sign for the derivative when x is negative.

Method 1 If $y = \sec^{-1}x$, then $\sec y = x$. The derivative of $\sec y$ with respect to y is $\sec y \tan y$ (see C4 Section 1.4), so its derivative with respect to x is $\sec y \tan y \dfrac{dy}{dx}$.

So

$$\sec y = x \quad \Rightarrow \quad \sec y \tan y \frac{dy}{dx} = 1$$

$$\Leftrightarrow \quad \frac{dy}{dx} = \frac{1}{\sec y \tan y}.$$

This has to be expressed in terms of x, and for this you need to use $\tan^2 y = \sec^2 y - 1$, so $\tan y = \pm\sqrt{\sec^2 y - 1} = \pm\sqrt{x^2 - 1}$. Therefore

$$\frac{dy}{dx} = \pm\frac{1}{x\sqrt{x^2 - 1}}.$$

Should the sign be $+$ or $-$? You can see from the graph of $y = \sec^{-1}x$ in Fig. 1.6 that the gradient is always positive, whether x is positive or negative. But this doesn't mean that you should choose the $+$ sign, since the right side contains the factor x in the denominator. (The other factor, $\sqrt{x^2 - 1}$, is of course always positive if $|x| > 1$.) So, to make the right side always positive, you should choose the $+$ sign when x is positive, and the $-$ sign when x is negative. That is,

$$\frac{dy}{dx} = \begin{cases} +\dfrac{1}{x\sqrt{x^2 - 1}} & \text{when } x > 1, \\[2mm] -\dfrac{1}{x\sqrt{x^2 - 1}} & \text{when } x < -1. \end{cases}$$

This can be written more simply by using modulus notation, as

$$\frac{dy}{dx} = \frac{1}{|x|\sqrt{x^2 - 1}} \qquad \text{when } |x| > 1.$$

Method 2   Since $\sec^{-1} x = \cos^{-1} \dfrac{1}{x}$,

$$\frac{d}{dx} \sec^{-1} x = \frac{d}{dx} \cos^{-1} \frac{1}{x}$$

$$= -\frac{1}{\sqrt{1 - \dfrac{1}{x^2}}} \times \left(-\frac{1}{x^2}\right)$$

$$= \frac{1}{\sqrt{\dfrac{x^2 - 1}{x^2}}} \times \frac{1}{x^2}$$

$$= \sqrt{\frac{x^2}{x^2 - 1}} \times \frac{1}{x^2}$$

$$= \frac{\sqrt{x^2}}{\sqrt{x^2 - 1}} \times \frac{1}{x^2}.$$

At this point it is tempting to write $\sqrt{x^2}$ as x, but this is only true if x is positive. The correct way to proceed is to write $\dfrac{\sqrt{x^2}}{x^2}$ as $\dfrac{1}{\sqrt{x^2}}$, and then to use $\sqrt{x^2} = |x|$ (see C3 Section 7.7). This gives

$$\frac{d}{dx} \sec^{-1} x = \frac{1}{|x|\sqrt{x^2 - 1}}.$$

Notice that, as with $\sin^{-1} x$ and $\cos^{-1} x$, the values $x = \pm 1$ have to be excluded; Fig. 1.6 shows that the tangent to the graph is parallel to the y-axis at $(1, 0)$ and $(-1, \pi)$. So the expression for the derivative is valid for $x > 1$ and $x < -1$, that is, for $|x| > 1$.

Another set of relations between inverse trigonometric functions can be derived from the symmetries of the graphs.

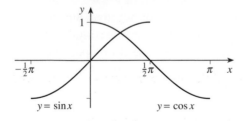

Fig. 1.7

Figure 1.7 shows the graphs of $\sin x$ from $-\tfrac{1}{2}\pi$ to $\tfrac{1}{2}\pi$ and $\cos x$ from 0 to π. If you reflect the sine graph in the y-axis and then translate the result by $\tfrac{1}{2}\pi$ in the x-direction you get the cosine graph. The effect on the x-coordinates is to transform x first to $-x$, then to $\tfrac{1}{2}\pi - x$. So, for $-\tfrac{1}{2}\pi \leqslant x \leqslant \tfrac{1}{2}\pi$ (so $0 \leqslant \tfrac{1}{2}\pi - x \leqslant \pi$),

$$\cos\left(\tfrac{1}{2}\pi - x\right) = \sin x.$$

This can also be interpreted in terms of the inverse functions shown in Fig. 1.8. (You have already seen this as Fig. 1.3.) The equivalent equation is

$$\cos^{-1} x = -\sin^{-1} x + \tfrac{1}{2}\pi, \quad \text{or} \quad \cos^{-1} x + \sin^{-1} x = \tfrac{1}{2}\pi.$$

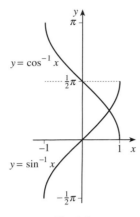

Fig. 1.8

This is called a 'complement rule' (since angles which add up to $\frac{1}{2}\pi$ are said to be complementary).

Using this in combination with the reciprocal rules gives

$$\sec^{-1} x + \operatorname{cosec}^{-1} x = \cos^{-1} \frac{1}{x} + \sin^{-1} \frac{1}{x} = \tfrac{1}{2}\pi.$$

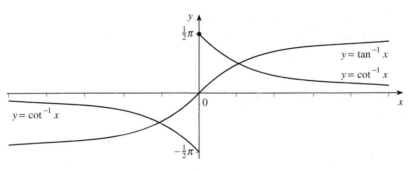

Fig. 1.9

The corresponding result for $\tan^{-1}$ and $\cot^{-1}$ is a little more complicated. You can see from the graphs in Fig. 1.9 that

$$\tan^{-1} x + \cot^{-1} x = \tfrac{1}{2}\pi \text{ if } x \geqslant 0, \quad \tan^{-1} x + \cot^{-1} x = -\tfrac{1}{2}\pi \text{ if } x < 0.$$

Complement rules

$$\cos^{-1} x + \sin^{-1} x = \tfrac{1}{2}\pi, \quad \sec^{-1} x + \operatorname{cosec}^{-1} x = \tfrac{1}{2}\pi,$$

$$\tan^{-1} x + \cot^{-1} x = \tfrac{1}{2}\pi \text{ if } x \geqslant 0, \quad \tan^{-1} x + \cot^{-1} x = -\tfrac{1}{2}\pi \text{ if } x < 0.$$

Example 1.4.2

Find $\dfrac{d}{dx} \operatorname{cosec}^{-1} x$.

Using the complement rule,

$$\frac{d}{dx} \operatorname{cosec}^{-1} x = \frac{d}{dx} \left(\tfrac{1}{2}\pi - \sec^{-1} x \right)$$

$$= 0 - \frac{1}{|x|\sqrt{x^2 - 1}},$$

from Example 1.4.1. Therefore

$$\frac{d}{dx} \operatorname{cosec}^{-1} x = -\frac{1}{|x|\sqrt{x^2 - 1}},$$

Exercise 1C*

1 State the values of

   (a) $\sec^{-1}(-2)$,   (b) $\operatorname{cosec}^{-1}(\tfrac{2}{3}\sqrt{3})$,   (c) $\cot^{-1} 1$,   (d) $\cot^{-1}(-\sqrt{3})$.

2 Find the derivatives of the following with respect to x.

   (a) $\sec^{-1} 3x$ (b) $\cot^{-1} x$ (c) $\cot^{-1}(1 - x)$

   (d) $\operatorname{cosec}^{-1}(\sec x)$ (e) $\cot^{-1} \dfrac{1 + x}{1 - x}$ (f) $\sec^{-1} \sqrt{x^2 + 1}$

3 Evaluate $\displaystyle\int_1^2 \frac{1}{x\sqrt{x^2 - 1}}\, dx$.

4 (a) If $\sec^{-1} x = a$, express $\sin^{-1} \dfrac{1}{x}$ in terms of a.

   (b) If $\tan^{-1} y = b$, express $\cot^{-1} \dfrac{1}{y}$ in terms of b.

5 Write an equation connecting x and y not involving trigonometric functions if

   (a) $\sec^{-1} x = \operatorname{cosec}^{-1} y$,   (b) $\cot^{-1} x = \tan^{-1} y$,   (c) $\sin^{-1} x = \sec^{-1} y$.

6 Use the addition formula for tangents to show that $\tan(\tan^{-1} a + \tan^{-1} x) = \dfrac{a + x}{1 - ax}$.

   Hence show that $\tan^{-1} a + \tan^{-1} x = \tan^{-1} \dfrac{a + x}{1 - ax} + k\pi$, where k is an integer. What is the value of k

   (a) when $a = 2$ and $x = 3$,   (b) when $a = \tfrac{1}{2}$ and $b = \tfrac{1}{3}$?

   Use this result to find $\dfrac{d}{dx} \tan^{-1} \dfrac{a + x}{1 - ax}$.

7 Use a method similar to that in Question 6 to show that $2 \tan^{-1} x = \tan^{-1} \dfrac{2x}{1 - x^2} + k\pi$,

   where k is an integer. Hence find $\dfrac{d}{dx} \tan^{-1} \dfrac{2x}{1 - x^2}$.

8 Use the equations in Questions 6 and 7 to express in the form $\tan^{-1} x$

   (a) $2 \tan^{-1} \tfrac{1}{5}$,   (b) $4 \tan^{-1} \tfrac{1}{5}$,   (c) $4 \tan^{-1} \tfrac{1}{5} - \tfrac{1}{4}\pi$.

Miscellaneous exercise 1

1 Find the area under the graph of $y = \dfrac{1}{\sqrt{25 - x^2}}$ from $x = 3$ to $x = 4$. Check your answer by calculating a one-interval trapezium rule approximation.

2 Find $\dfrac{d^2 y}{dx^2}$ if
   (a) $y = (\tan^{-1} x)^2$,   (b) $y = (\sin^{-1} x)^2$.

3 A curve passes through $(0, 1)$ and satisfies the differential equation $\dfrac{dy}{dx} = \sqrt{4 - y^2}$. Find its equation and sketch its graph.

4 Find the general solution of the differential equation $\dfrac{dy}{dx} = 1 + y^2$ and sketch some typical solution curves.
   Find where the solution curve through $(2, 1)$ cuts the axes.

5 Find the solution of the differential equation $\sqrt{4 - x^2}\, \dfrac{dy}{dx} = \sqrt{4 - y^2}$ for which $y = -1$ when $x = 1$. Express your answer in a form not involving trigonometric functions.

6 Sketch the graph with equation $y = \sqrt{4 - \dfrac{1}{x^2}}$. Find the area of the region in the first quadrant bounded by the curve, the axes and the line $y = s$, where $s < 2$. Investigate whether this area tends to a finite limit as $s \to 2$.

7 Sketch the graph with equation $y = \sqrt{\dfrac{1}{x^2} - 4}$. Find the volume of the solid of revolution formed by rotating about the y-axis the region bounded by the curve, the x-axis and the line $y = r$. Investigate whether this volume tends to a finite limit as $r \to \infty$.

8 Find the point of intersection of the graphs of $y = \tan^{-1} x$ and $y = \cos^{-1} x$.
   Find the gradient of each graph at this point of intersection.

9 Find the integral $\displaystyle\int \sin^{-1} x \, dx$ by substituting $x = \sin u$ and using integration by parts.
   Check your answer by differentiation.

10 A rugby goal has posts erected at A and B. A point C lies on AB produced so that $AC = a$ and $BC = b$. A player wishes to place the ball at the point P on the straight line through C perpendicular to AB, so that the angle APB is a maximum.
   Show that, if $CP = y$ and angle $APB = \theta$, then $\theta = \tan^{-1}\dfrac{y}{b} - \tan^{-1}\dfrac{y}{a}$, and deduce that the maximum value of θ occurs when $y^2 = ab$.   (OCR, adapted)

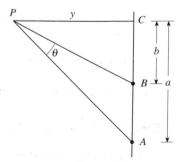

11 Given that $y = x - \sqrt{1 - x^2}\sin^{-1}x$, show that $\dfrac{dy}{dx} = \dfrac{x\sin^{-1}x}{\sqrt{1-x^2}}$. Hence evaluate

$\displaystyle\int_0^{\frac{1}{4}\sqrt{3}} \dfrac{2x\sin^{-1}2x}{\sqrt{1-4x^2}}\,dx$, giving your answer in terms of π and $\sqrt{3}$. (OCR)

12 Given that x and y satisfy the equation $\tan^{-1}x + \tan^{-1}y + \tan^{-1}(xy) = \frac{11}{12}\pi$, prove that, when $x = 1$, $\dfrac{dy}{dx} = -1 - \frac{1}{2}\sqrt{3}$. (OCR)

2 Rational functions

This chapter takes partial fractions on from C4 Chapter 6. When you have completed it, you should

- be able to put a rational function into partial fractions when one of the factors is a quadratic which is the sum of squares
- be able to put a rational function into partial fractions when the degree of the numerator is greater than or equal to the degree of the denominator.

2.1 Partial fractions

In C4 Chapter 6, you learned how to split rational functions of the forms

$$\frac{ax+b}{(px+q)(rx+s)} \quad \text{and} \quad \frac{ax^2+bx+c}{(px+q)(rx+s)^2}$$

into partial fractions.

Neither of these types includes a form such as $\dfrac{3x+7}{(x-1)(x^2+4)}$, where the quadratic factor x^2+4 in the denominator is the sum of two squares and hence has no real factors.

In this case, you would certainly expect to write

$$\frac{3x+7}{(x-1)(x^2+4)} \equiv \frac{A}{x-1} + \frac{\text{something}}{x^2+4}.$$

But what is the 'something'? Multiply by $x-1$, and put $x=1$ in the subsequent identity.

$$\frac{3x+7}{(x^2+4)} \equiv A + \frac{(\text{something})(x-1)}{x^2+4} \text{ with } x=1 \text{ gives } A = \frac{10}{5} = 2.$$

Therefore $\dfrac{3x+7}{(x-1)(x^2+4)} \equiv \dfrac{2}{x-1} + \dfrac{\text{something}}{x^2+4}.$

You can now find what the 'something' is by subtraction, since

$$\begin{aligned}
\frac{\text{something}}{x^2+4} &\equiv \frac{3x+7}{(x-1)(x^2+4)} - \frac{2}{x-1} \\
&\equiv \frac{3x+7-2(x^2+4)}{(x-1)(x^2+4)} \\
&\equiv \frac{3x+7-2x^2-8}{(x-1)(x^2+4)} \\
&\equiv \frac{-(2x^2-3x+1)}{(x-1)(x^2+4)} \\
&\equiv \frac{-(2x-1)(x-1)}{(x-1)(x^2+4)} \\
&\equiv \frac{-(2x-1)}{(x^2+4)} \equiv \frac{-2x+1}{(x^2+4)}.
\end{aligned}$$

The 'something' has the form $Bx + C$.

The method shown in the example above will be called the **substitution and algebraic method**, with the change that $Bx + C$ will be used in place of 'something'.

Here are two other methods which you can use.

If you write $\dfrac{3x + 7}{(x - 1)(x^2 + 4)} \equiv \dfrac{A}{x - 1} + \dfrac{Bx + C}{x^2 + 4}$ initially, you can multiply the identity by $(x - 1)(x^2 + 4)$, and simplify the resulting numerator on the right side to get a quadratic. You can then equate the coefficients of x^0, x^1 and x^2 to get three equations, and solve them for A, B and C. This is the **equating coefficients method**.

Or you can multiply $\dfrac{3x + 7}{(x - 1)(x^2 + 4)} \equiv \dfrac{A}{x - 1} + \dfrac{Bx + C}{x^2 + 4}$ by $x - 1$ and put $x = 1$ as before to get $A = 2$, and then equate coefficients to find B and C. This is the **substitution and equating coefficients method**.

The two examples which follow show these three methods of getting the partial fractions. Use whichever method you find easiest.

Method 1 has the advantage that it is self-checking. If the fraction just before the final result does not cancel, you have made a mistake. If it cancels, there is probably no mistake.

Method 2 is in many ways the most straightforward, but involves solving three equations for A, B and C.

In Method 3 the coefficients of x^2 and x^0 are used to get the values of B and C. This is because they give the simplest equations. You will usually find that the highest and lowest powers give the simplest equations in these situations. However, you should be aware that equating the coefficients of x^0 has the same result as putting $x = 0$; you get no extra information.

A rational function of the form $\dfrac{px + q}{(rx + s)(x^2 + a^2)}$ can be split into

partial fractions in the form $\dfrac{A}{rx + s} + \dfrac{Bx + C}{x^2 + a^2}$.

Example 2.1.1

Split $\dfrac{5x - 4}{(x + 2)(x^2 + 3)}$ into partial fractions.

As $x^2 + 3 \equiv x^2 + (\sqrt{3})^2$ it is the sum of two squares.

Substitution and algebraic method

Write $\dfrac{5x - 4}{(x + 2)(x^2 + 3)} \equiv \dfrac{A}{x + 2} + \dfrac{Bx + C}{x^2 + 3}$.

Multiply by $x + 2$ to get $\dfrac{5x - 4}{(x^2 + 3)} \equiv A + \dfrac{(Bx + C)(x + 2)}{x^2 + 3}$, and put $x = -2$. Then
$\dfrac{5 \times (-2) - 4}{(-2)^2 + 3} = A$, so $A = -2$.

Then
$$\begin{aligned}
\frac{Bx + C}{x^2 + 3} &\equiv \frac{5x - 4}{(x + 2)(x^2 + 3)} - \frac{-2}{x + 2} \\
&\equiv \frac{5x - 4 - (-2)(x^2 + 3)}{(x + 2)(x^2 + 3)} \\
&\equiv \frac{2x^2 + 5x + 2}{(x + 2)(x^2 + 3)} \\
&\equiv \frac{(x + 2)(2x + 1)}{(x + 2)(x^2 + 3)} \\
&\equiv \frac{2x + 1}{x^2 + 3}.
\end{aligned}$$

So $\dfrac{5x - 4}{(x + 2)(x^2 + 3)} \equiv \dfrac{-2}{x + 2} + \dfrac{2x + 1}{x^2 + 3}$.

Equating coefficients method

Write $\dfrac{5x - 4}{(x + 2)(x^2 + 3)} \equiv \dfrac{A}{x + 2} + \dfrac{Bx + C}{x^2 + 3}$.

Multiply by $(x + 2)(x^2 + 3)$ to get $5x - 4 \equiv A(x^2 + 3) + (Bx + C)(x + 2)$, which you can write as

$$5x - 4 \equiv (A + B)x^2 + (2B + C)x + 3A + 2C.$$

The three equations which you get by equating coefficients of x^0, x^1 and x^2 are

$$3A + 2C = -4, \quad 2B + C = 5 \quad \text{and} \quad A + B = 0.$$

Solving these equations gives $A = -2$, $B = 2$ and $C = 1$, so

$$\frac{5x - 4}{(x + 2)(x^2 + 3)} \equiv \frac{-2}{x + 2} + \frac{2x + 1}{x^2 + 3}.$$

Substitution and equating coefficients method

Write $\dfrac{5x - 4}{(x + 2)(x^2 + 3)} \equiv \dfrac{A}{x + 2} + \dfrac{Bx + C}{x^2 + 3}$.

Multiply by $x + 2$ to get $\dfrac{5x - 4}{x^2 + 3} \equiv A + \dfrac{(Bx + C)(x + 2)}{x^2 + 3}$, and put $x = -2$. Then
$\dfrac{5 \times (-2) - 4}{(-2)^2 + 3} = A$, so $A = -2$.

Multiplying both sides of the identity $\dfrac{5x - 4}{(x + 2)(x^2 + 3)} \equiv \dfrac{-2}{x + 2} + \dfrac{Bx + C}{x^2 + 3}$ by $(x + 2)(x^2 + 3)$ and equating the coefficients in the result gives

$$5x - 4 \equiv -2(x^2 + 3) + (Bx + C)(x + 2),$$

which you can write as

$$5x - 4 \equiv (-2 + B)x^2 + (2B + C)x - 6 + 2C.$$

Equating the coefficients of x^2 gives $-2 + B = 0$, so $B = 2$.

Equating the coefficients of x^0 gives $-4 = -6 + 2C$, so $C = 1$.

Checking the x-coefficient: on the left side 5; on the right $2B + C = 2 \times 2 + 1 = 5$.

Therefore $\dfrac{5x - 4}{(x + 2)(x^2 + 3)} \equiv \dfrac{-2}{x + 2} + \dfrac{2x + 1}{x^2 + 3}$.

Example 2.1.2

Find $\displaystyle\int_2^3 \dfrac{x + 1}{(x - 1)(x^2 + 1)}\,dx$.

To integrate you need to put $\dfrac{x + 1}{(x - 1)(x^2 + 1)}$ into partial fractions.

Substitution and algebraic method

Write $\dfrac{x + 1}{(x - 1)(x^2 + 1)} \equiv \dfrac{A}{x - 1} + \dfrac{Bx + C}{x^2 + 1}$.

Multiplying by $x - 1$ and putting $x = 1$ gives $A = 1$.

Calculating $\dfrac{x + 1}{(x - 1)(x^2 + 1)} - \dfrac{1}{x - 1}$ to find the other fraction on the right gives

$$
\begin{aligned}
\frac{x + 1}{(x - 1)(x^2 + 1)} - \frac{1}{x - 1} &\equiv \frac{x + 1 - (x^2 + 1)}{(x - 1)(x^2 + 1)} \\
&\equiv \frac{-(x^2 - x)}{(x - 1)(x^2 + 1)} \\
&\equiv \frac{-x(x - 1)}{(x - 1)(x^2 + 1)} \\
&\equiv -\frac{x}{x^2 + 1}.
\end{aligned}
$$

Therefore $\dfrac{x + 1}{(x - 1)(x^2 + 1)} \equiv \dfrac{1}{x - 1} - \dfrac{x}{x^2 + 1}$. Then

$$
\begin{aligned}
\int_2^3 \frac{x + 1}{(x - 1)(x^2 + 1)}\,dx &= \int_2^3 \left(\frac{1}{x - 1} - \frac{x}{x^2 + 1} \right) dx \\
&= \left[\ln(x - 1) - \tfrac{1}{2}\ln(x^2 + 1) \right]_2^3 \\
&= \left(\ln 2 - \tfrac{1}{2}\ln 10 \right) - \left(\ln 1 - \tfrac{1}{2}\ln 5 \right) \\
&= \ln 2 - \tfrac{1}{2}(\ln 10 - \ln 5) \\
&= \ln 2 - \tfrac{1}{2}(\ln 2) \\
&= \tfrac{1}{2}\ln 2.
\end{aligned}
$$

Example 2.1.3

Calculate $\displaystyle\int_{-2}^{2} \frac{x^2 + x}{(x - 4)(x^2 + 4)}\,dx$.

Putting $\dfrac{x^2 + x}{(x - 4)(x^2 + 4)}$ into partial fractions gives $\dfrac{x^2 + x}{(x - 4)(x^2 + 4)} \equiv \dfrac{1}{x - 4} + \dfrac{1}{x^2 + 4}$.

So $\displaystyle\int_{-2}^{2} \frac{x^2 + x}{(x - 4)(x^2 + 4)}\,dx = \int_{-2}^{2} \left(\frac{1}{x - 4} + \frac{1}{x^2 + 4} \right) dx$

$$= \int_{-2}^{2} \frac{1}{x - 4}\,dx + \int_{-2}^{2} \frac{1}{x^2 + 4}\,dx.$$

The first of these integrals is $\left[\ln |x - 4| \right]_{-2}^{2} = \ln 2 - \ln 6 = \ln \tfrac{1}{3} = -\ln 3$.

The second integral is also a standard form (Section 1.3).

$$\int_{-2}^{2} \frac{1}{x^2 + 4}\,dx = \left[\tfrac{1}{2} \tan^{-1} \tfrac{1}{2}x \right]_{-2}^{2}$$

$$= \left(\tfrac{1}{2} \times \tfrac{1}{4}\pi \right) - \left(\tfrac{1}{2} \times \left(-\tfrac{1}{4}\pi \right) \right)$$

$$= \tfrac{1}{4}\pi.$$

Thus $\displaystyle\int_{-2}^{2} \frac{x^2 + x}{(x - 4)(x^2 + 4)}\,dx = -\ln 3 + \tfrac{1}{4}\pi = \tfrac{1}{4}\pi - \ln 3$.

Example 2.1.4

Find the binomial expansion of $\dfrac{5x - 4}{(x + 2)(x^2 + 3)}$ up to and including the term in x^2.

The strategy is to begin by splitting $\dfrac{5x - 4}{(x + 2)(x^2 + 3)}$ into partial fractions. This was done in Example 2.1.1 which showed that $\dfrac{5x - 4}{(x + 2)(x^2 + 3)} \equiv \dfrac{-2}{x + 2} + \dfrac{2x + 1}{x^2 + 3}$.

So it remains to find the expansion of $\dfrac{-2}{x + 2} + \dfrac{2x + 1}{x^2 + 3}$.

Dealing with the terms separately, and neglecting terms in x^3 and higher,

$$\frac{-2}{x + 2} = \frac{-2}{2\left(1 + \tfrac{1}{2}x\right)}$$

$$= -\left(1 + \tfrac{1}{2}x\right)^{-1}$$

$$\approx -\left(1 + \frac{(-1)}{1} \times \tfrac{1}{2}x + \frac{(-1)(-2)}{1 \times 2} \times \left(\tfrac{1}{2}x\right)^2\right)$$

$$= -1 + \tfrac{1}{2}x - \tfrac{1}{4}x^2.$$

$$\frac{2x + 1}{x^2 + 3} = \frac{2x + 1}{3\left(1 + \tfrac{1}{3}x^2\right)}$$

$$= \tfrac{1}{3}(1 + 2x)\left(1 + \tfrac{1}{3}x^2\right)^{-1}$$

$$\approx \tfrac{1}{3}(1 + 2x)\left(1 + \frac{(-1)}{1} \times \tfrac{1}{3}x^2\right)$$

$$\approx \tfrac{1}{3} + \tfrac{2}{3}x - \tfrac{1}{9}x^2.$$

So, combining the two expansions,

$$\frac{-2}{x+2} + \frac{2x+1}{x^2+3} \approx \left(-1 + \tfrac{1}{2}x - \tfrac{1}{4}x^2\right) + \left(\tfrac{1}{3} + \tfrac{2}{3}x - \tfrac{1}{9}x^2\right)$$

$$= -\tfrac{2}{3} + \tfrac{7}{6}x - \tfrac{13}{36}x^2.$$

The next example deals with a denominator of the form $(x^2 + a^2)(x - p)^2$, where the linear factor is squared.

Example 2.1.5

(a) Express $\dfrac{2x^3}{(x^2 + 1)(x - 1)^2}$ in partial fractions.

(b) Hence find $\displaystyle\int \frac{2x^3}{(x^2 + 1)(x - 1)^2}\,dx.$

(a) **Substitution and algebraic method**

Using the work of C4 Section 6.5 together with this section suggests that you try finding the constants to make

$$\frac{2x^3}{(x^2+1)(x-1)^2} \equiv \frac{Ax+B}{x^2+1} + \frac{C}{(x-1)^2} + \frac{D}{x-1}.$$

Multiplying by $(x - 1)^2$ gives the identity

$$\frac{2x^3}{x^2+1} \equiv \frac{(Ax+B)(x-1)^2}{x^2+1} + C + D(x-1).$$

Putting $x = 1$ gives $C = 1$.

So, putting this result back in the original identity gives

$$\frac{2x^3}{(x^2+1)(x-1)^2} \equiv \frac{Ax+B}{x^2+1} + \frac{1}{(x-1)^2} + \frac{D}{x-1},$$

which on rearranging gives

$$\frac{2x^3}{(x^2+1)(x-1)^2} - \frac{1}{(x-1)^2} \equiv \frac{Ax+B}{x^2+1} + \frac{D}{x-1}.$$

Interchanging the sides of this identity and simplifying the new right side gives

$$\frac{Ax+B}{x^2+1} + \frac{D}{x-1} \equiv \frac{2x^3}{(x^2+1)(x-1)^2} - \frac{1}{(x-1)^2}$$

$$\equiv \frac{2x^3 - (x^2+1)}{(x^2+1)(x-1)^2}$$

$$\equiv \frac{2x^3 - x^2 - 1}{(x^2+1)(x-1)^2}$$

$$\equiv \frac{(x-1)(2x^2 + x + 1)}{(x^2+1)(x-1)^2}$$

$$\equiv \frac{2x^2 + x + 1}{(x^2+1)(x-1)}.$$

Now, multiplying by $x - 1$ gives

$$\frac{2x^2 + x + 1}{x^2 + 1} \equiv \frac{(Ax + B)(x - 1)}{x^2 + 1} + D,$$

and putting $x = 1$ gives $D = \dfrac{4}{2} = 2.$

Finally,

$$\begin{aligned}
\frac{Ax + B}{x^2 + 1} &\equiv \frac{2x^2 + x + 1}{(x^2 + 1)(x - 1)} - \frac{2}{x - 1} \\
&\equiv \frac{2x^2 + x + 1 - 2(x^2 + 1)}{(x^2 + 1)(x - 1)} \\
&\equiv \frac{2x^2 + x + 1 - 2x^2 - 2}{(x^2 + 1)(x - 1)} \\
&\equiv \frac{x - 1}{(x^2 + 1)(x - 1)} \\
&\equiv \frac{1}{x^2 + 1}.
\end{aligned}$$

Putting all this together gives

$$\frac{2x^3}{(x^2 + 1)(x - 1)^2} \equiv \frac{1}{x^2 + 1} + \frac{1}{(x - 1)^2} + \frac{2}{x - 1}.$$

(b) It is now easy to use this form to carry out the integral.

$$\begin{aligned}
\int \frac{2x^3}{(x^2 + 1)(x - 1)^2} \, dx &= \int \left(\frac{1}{x^2 + 1} + \frac{1}{(x - 1)^2} + \frac{2}{x - 1} \right) dx \\
&= \tan^{-1} x - \frac{1}{x - 1} + 2 \ln |x - 1| + k.
\end{aligned}$$

Here is a summary of the results of this section.

To put rational functions of the forms

$$\frac{ax + b}{(px^2 + q)(rx + s)} \quad \text{and} \quad \frac{ax^2 + bx + c}{(px^2 + q)(rx + s)^2}$$

into partial fractions write them in the forms

$$\frac{Ax + B}{px^2 + q} + \frac{C}{rx + s} \quad \text{and} \quad \frac{Ax + B}{px^2 + q} + \frac{C}{(rx + s)^2} + \frac{D}{rx + s} \quad \text{respectively.}$$

Exercise 2A

1 Express each of the following in partial fractions.

(a) $\dfrac{x^2 + x}{(x - 1)(x^2 + 1)}$

(b) $\dfrac{2x - 1}{x(x^2 + 1)}$

(c) $\dfrac{2x^2 + x - 3}{(x + 3)(x^2 + 3)}$

(d) $\dfrac{3x^2 + 4x - 28}{(2x - 1)(x^2 + 25)}$

(e) $\dfrac{x^2 - x - 20}{(3x + 2)(x^2 + 9)}$

(f) $\dfrac{2x^2}{(x + 2)(x^2 + 4)}$

2 Find the values of A, B and C such that

(a) $\dfrac{10x^2 - 8x + 7}{(2x - 3)(3x^2 + 2)} \equiv \dfrac{A}{2x - 3} + \dfrac{Bx + C}{3x^2 + 2}$,

(b) $\dfrac{12x}{(2x - 3)(4x^2 + 9)} \equiv \dfrac{A}{2x - 3} + \dfrac{Bx + C}{4x^2 + 9}$,

(c) $\dfrac{17x + 3}{(3x - 2)(4x^2 + 3)} \equiv \dfrac{A}{3x - 2} + \dfrac{Bx + C}{4x^2 + 3}$,

(d) $\dfrac{1 - 3x}{(x - 1)(x^2 + 1)} \equiv \dfrac{A}{x - 1} + \dfrac{Bx + C}{x^2 + 1}$.

3 Express each of the following in partial fractions.

(a) $\dfrac{8x^2}{(4x^2 + 9)(3 + 2x)}$

(b) $\dfrac{-3x}{(2 + x)(2 + x^2)}$

4 Find the values of the following definite integrals.

(a) $\displaystyle\int_1^2 \dfrac{2 + 3x^2}{x(x^2 + 2)} \, dx$

(b) $\displaystyle\int_0^1 \dfrac{1 - 2x - x^2}{(1 + x)(1 + x^2)} \, dx$

(c) $\displaystyle\int_2^3 \dfrac{8 + 3x - x^2}{(x - 1)(x^2 + 4)} \, dx$

(d) $\displaystyle\int_0^1 \dfrac{x^2 - 3x}{(x + 3)(9 + x^2)} \, dx$

5 Find the binomial expansions up to and including the term in x^2 of the following expressions.

(a) $\dfrac{2x^2 - x + 1}{(x - 1)(x^2 + 1)}$

(b) $\dfrac{-x + 3x^2}{(1 + x)(1 + x^2)}$

(c) $\dfrac{5 + 9x - 5x^2}{(1 + 3x)(1 + 4x^2)}$

(d) $\dfrac{10 - x}{(3 + x)(4 + x^2)}$

6 Express $\dfrac{x^3 + 2x^2 + 5x}{(x^2 + 1)(x + 1)^2}$ in partial fractions and hence differentiate it.

2.2 Improper fractions

So far all the rational functions you have seen have been 'proper' fractions. That is, the degree of the numerator has been less than the degree of the denominator.

Rational functions such as $\dfrac{x^2 - 3x + 5}{(x + 1)(x - 2)}$ and $\dfrac{x^3}{x^2 + 1}$, in which the degree of the numerator is greater than or equal to the degree of the denominator, are called **improper fractions**.

Improper fractions are often not the most convenient form to work with; it is frequently better to express them in a different way.

For example, you cannot find $\displaystyle\int \dfrac{6x}{x - 1} \, dx$ with the integrand in its present form, but it is quite straightforward to integrate the same expression as $\displaystyle\int \left(6 + \dfrac{6}{x - 1}\right) dx$. You get

$$\int \left(6 + \dfrac{6}{x - 1}\right) dx = 6x + 6\ln|x - 1| + k.$$

Similarly, if you wish to sketch the graph of $y = \dfrac{6x}{x - 1}$, although you can see immediately that the graph passes through the origin, other features are much clearer in the form $y = 6 + \dfrac{6}{x - 1}$. This idea will be taken further in Chapter 5.

You may find it helpful to think about an analogy between improper fractions in arithmetic and improper fractions in algebra. Sometimes in arithmetic it is more useful to think of the number $\frac{25}{6}$ in that form; at other times it is better in the form $4\frac{1}{6}$. The same is true in algebra, and you need to be able to go from one form to the other.

In C4 Section 6.6, you learned how to divide one polynomial by another polynomial to get a quotient and a remainder.

When you divide the polynomial p(x) by the polynomial a(x) you will get a quotient q(x) and a remainder r(x) defined by

$$p(x) \equiv a(x)q(x) + r(x)$$

where the degree of the remainder r(x) is less than the degree of the divisor a(x).

If you divide the equation $p(x) \equiv a(x)q(x) + r(x)$ by a(x), you get

$$\frac{p(x)}{a(x)} = \frac{a(x)q(x) + r(x)}{a(x)}$$

$$\equiv q(x) + \frac{r(x)}{a(x)}.$$

This form, in which the degree of the numerator is less than that of the denominator, will be called **divided out form**. It is equivalent to the quotient and remainder form in C4 Section 6.6. Example 2.2.1 shows this in practice.

Example 2.2.1

Express $\dfrac{x^2 - 3x + 5}{(x + 1)(x - 2)}$ in the form $A + \dfrac{Px + Q}{(x + 1)(x - 2)}$, where A, P and Q are constants.

Writing $\dfrac{x^2 - 3x + 5}{(x + 1)(x - 2)} \equiv A + \dfrac{Px + Q}{(x + 1)(x - 2)}$ and multiplying both sides by $(x + 1)(x - 2)$ gives

$$x^2 - 3x + 5 \equiv A(x + 1)(x - 2) + Px + Q.$$

Equating coefficients of x^2 gives $1 = A$.

Equating coefficients of x gives $-3 = -A + P$, and since $A = 1$, $P = -2$.

Equating the constant terms gives $5 = -2A + Q$, and since $A = 1$, $Q = 7$.

Therefore

$$\frac{x^2 - 3x + 5}{(x + 1)(x - 2)} \equiv 1 + \frac{-2x + 7}{(x + 1)(x - 2)}.$$

You can see from the form $\dfrac{x^2 - 3x + 5}{(x + 1)(x - 2)} \equiv 1 + \dfrac{-2x + 7}{(x + 1)(x - 2)}$ that, for large values of x, the term $\dfrac{-2x + 7}{(x + 1)(x - 2)}$ on the right gets very small, so $\dfrac{x^2 - 3x + 5}{(x + 1)(x - 2)}$ gets very close to 1. This point is taken further in Chapter 5.

2.3 Improper fractions and partial fractions

You can now put together the work on improper fractions in Section 2.2 with the work on partial fractions in Section 2.1 and C4 Chapter 6.

For example, if you take the result from Example 2.2.1,

$$\frac{x^2 - 3x + 5}{(x + 1)(x - 2)} \equiv 1 + \frac{-2x + 7}{(x + 1)(x - 2)},$$

you can go further by putting the right side into partial fraction form using the standard method and getting

$$\frac{x^2 - 3x + 5}{(x + 1)(x - 2)} \equiv 1 - \frac{3}{x + 1} + \frac{1}{x - 2}.$$

Example 2.3.1

Split $\dfrac{2x^2 + 4x - 3}{(x + 1)(2x - 3)}$ into partial fractions.

Here are two methods you can use. You could go immediately into a partial fraction form and find the coefficients either by equating coefficients or by other methods. Or you could put it into divided out form first, and then use one of the standard methods for the remaining partial fractions.

Substitution method

Write $\dfrac{2x^2 + 4x - 3}{(x + 1)(2x - 3)}$ in the form $\dfrac{2x^2 + 4x - 3}{(x + 1)(2x - 3)} \equiv A + \dfrac{B}{x + 1} + \dfrac{C}{2x - 3}.$

Multiplying by $x + 1$ gives $\dfrac{2x^2 + 4x - 3}{2x - 3} \equiv A(x + 1) + B + \dfrac{C(x + 1)}{2x - 3}$, and then putting

$x = -1$ gives $\dfrac{2 \times (-1)^2 + 4 \times (-1) - 3}{2 \times (-1) - 3} = B$, so $B = 1$.

Multiplying instead by $2x - 3$ gives $\dfrac{2x^2 + 4x - 3}{x + 1} \equiv A(2x - 3) + \dfrac{B(2x - 3)}{x + 1} + C$, and

then putting $x = \frac{3}{2}$ gives $\dfrac{2 \times \left(\frac{3}{2}\right)^2 + 4 \times \left(\frac{3}{2}\right) - 3}{\frac{3}{2} + 1} = C$, so $C = 3$.

Therefore $\dfrac{2x^2 + 4x - 3}{(x + 1)(2x - 3)} \equiv A + \dfrac{1}{x + 1} + \dfrac{3}{2x - 3}.$

Putting $x = 0$ gives $A = 1$.

Therefore $\dfrac{2x^2 + 4x - 3}{(x + 1)(2x - 3)} \equiv 1 + \dfrac{1}{x + 1} + \dfrac{3}{2x - 3}.$

Substitution and algebraic method

If you divide out first, you start with the form

$$\frac{2x^2 + 4x - 3}{(x + 1)(2x - 3)} \equiv A + \frac{Px + Q}{(x + 1)(2x - 3)}.$$

By multiplying by $(x + 1)(2x - 3)$ and equating the coefficients of x^2, you find that $A = 1$.

Thus

$$\frac{2x^2 + 4x - 3}{(x + 1)(2x - 3)} \equiv 1 + \frac{Px + Q}{(x + 1)(2x - 3)},$$

so

$$\frac{2x^2 + 4x - 3}{(x + 1)(2x - 3)} - 1 \equiv \frac{Px + Q}{(x + 1)(2x - 3)}.$$

Simplifying the left side,

$$\frac{2x^2 + 4x - 3 - (x + 1)(2x - 3)}{(x + 1)(2x - 3)} \equiv \frac{2x^2 + 4x - 3 - (2x^2 - x - 3)}{(x + 1)(2x - 3)}$$

$$\equiv \frac{5x}{(x + 1)(2x - 3)}.$$

Any of the standard methods for partial fractions now shows that

$$\frac{5x}{(x + 1)(2x - 3)} \equiv \frac{1}{x + 1} + \frac{3}{2x - 3},$$

so

$$\frac{2x^2 + 4x - 3}{(x + 1)(2x - 3)} \equiv 1 + \frac{1}{x + 1} + \frac{3}{2x - 3}.$$

Use whichever method suits you best. Equating coefficients and solving the resulting equations always works, but it is not always the quickest method. You will see later that it can lead to a large number of simultaneous equations to solve.

In Example 2.3.1, the numerator $2x^2 + 4x - 3$ was a polynomial of the same degree as the denominator $(x + 1)(2x - 3)$, but the numerator could be a polynomial of higher degree than the denominator.

If the polynomial in the numerator of a fraction is of higher degree than the denominator, you need to find the difference in degree. That is, if you divide the numerator by the denominator to get a quotient and a remainder, what will the degree of your quotient be? The answer will tell you what polynomial to write in the divided out form.

Example 2.3.2

Split $\dfrac{3x^4 - 3x^3 - 17x^2 - x - 1}{(x - 3)(x + 2)}$ into partial fractions.

In this case, the degree of the numerator is 4 and the degree of the denominator is 2. This shows that the degree of the quotient polynomial when you divide the numerator by the denominator is $4 - 2 = 2$. Therefore write $\dfrac{3x^4 - 3x^3 - 17x^2 - x - 1}{(x - 3)(x + 2)}$ in the form

$$\frac{3x^4 - 3x^3 - 17x^2 - x - 1}{(x - 3)(x + 2)} \equiv Ax^2 + Bx + C + \frac{D}{x - 3} + \frac{E}{x + 2},$$

where the polynomial $Ax^2 + Bx + C$ has the degree $4 - 2 = 2$.

The process of multiplying by $x - 3$, and putting $x = 3$ in the resulting identity, as in Example 2.2.1, gives $D = 1$. Similarly, multiplying by $x + 2$, and then putting $x = -2$ in the resulting identity, as in Example 2.2.1, gives $E = -1$. Therefore

$$\frac{3x^4 - 3x^3 - 17x^2 - x - 1}{(x - 3)(x + 2)} \equiv Ax^2 + Bx + C + \frac{1}{x - 3} - \frac{1}{x + 2}.$$

It is best now to multiply both sides of the identity by $(x - 3)(x + 2)$ and to equate coefficients, choosing carefully which powers of x to use to minimise the work.

$$3x^4 - 3x^3 - 17x^2 - x - 1 \equiv (Ax^2 + Bx + C)(x - 3)(x + 2) + (x + 2) - (x - 3)$$

Equating the coefficients of x^4: $3 = A$.

Equating the coefficients of x^0: $-1 = -6C + 2 + 3$, so $C = 1$.

Equating the coefficients of x^1: $-1 = -6B - C + 1 - 1$, so $B = 0$.

Therefore $\dfrac{3x^4 - 3x^3 - 17x^2 - x - 1}{(x - 3)(x + 2)} \equiv 3x^2 + 1 + \dfrac{1}{x - 3} - \dfrac{1}{x + 2}.$

Example 2.3.3

Split $\dfrac{x^4}{(x^2 + 4)(x - 2)^2}$ into partial fractions, and hence differentiate it.

You want $\dfrac{x^4}{(x^2 + 4)(x - 2)^2}$ in the form

$$\frac{x^4}{(x^2 + 4)(x - 2)^2} \equiv A + \frac{Bx + C}{x^2 + 4} + \frac{D}{(x - 2)^2} + \frac{E}{x - 2}.$$

Multiplying both sides by $(x - 2)^2$ and putting $x = 2$ gives $D = \dfrac{2^4}{2^2 + 4} = 2.$

Then

$$\begin{aligned}
\frac{x^4}{(x^2 + 4)(x - 2)^2} - \frac{2}{(x - 2)^2} &\equiv \frac{x^4 - 2(x^2 + 4)}{(x^2 + 4)(x - 2)^2} \\
&\equiv \frac{x^4 - 2x^2 - 8}{(x^2 + 4)(x - 2)^2} \\
&\equiv \frac{(x^2 + 2)(x^2 - 4)}{(x^2 + 4)(x - 2)^2} \\
&\equiv \frac{(x^2 + 2)(x + 2)}{(x^2 + 4)(x - 2)}.
\end{aligned}$$

So $\dfrac{(x^2+2)(x+2)}{(x^2+4)(x-2)} \equiv A + \dfrac{Bx+C}{x^2+4} + \dfrac{E}{x-2}.$

Multiplying both sides by $x-2$ and putting $x=2$ gives $E = \dfrac{6\times 4}{8} = 3.$

Calculate

$$\dfrac{(x^2+2)(x+2)}{(x^2+4)(x-2)} - \dfrac{3}{x-2} \equiv \dfrac{(x^2+2)(x+2) - 3(x^2+4)}{(x^2+4)(x-2)}$$

$$\equiv \dfrac{x^3 + 2x^2 + 2x + 4 - 3x^2 - 12}{(x^2+4)(x-2)}$$

$$\equiv \dfrac{x^3 - x^2 + 2x - 8}{(x^2+4)(x-2)}$$

$$\equiv \dfrac{(x^2 + x + 4)(x-2)}{(x^2+4)(x-2)}$$

$$\equiv \dfrac{x^2 + x + 4}{x^2+4}.$$

So $\dfrac{x^2+x+4}{x^2+4} \equiv A + \dfrac{Bx+C}{x^2+4}.$

At this stage you can multiply by x^2+4 and equate coefficients, but you may notice that direct division gives

$$\dfrac{x^2+x+4}{x^2+4} \equiv \dfrac{(x^2+4)+x}{x^2+4}$$

$$\equiv 1 + \dfrac{x}{x^2+4}.$$

So $\dfrac{x^4}{(x^2+4)(x-2)^2} \equiv 1 + \dfrac{x}{x^2+4} + \dfrac{2}{(x-2)^2} + \dfrac{3}{x-2}.$

Therefore

$$\dfrac{\mathrm{d}}{\mathrm{d}x}\left(\dfrac{x^4}{(x^2+4)(x-2)^2} \right) = \dfrac{\mathrm{d}}{\mathrm{d}x}\left(1 + \dfrac{x}{x^2+4} + \dfrac{2}{(x-2)^2} + \dfrac{3}{x-2} \right)$$

$$= \dfrac{1 \times (x^2+4) - x \times 2x}{(x^2+4)^2} - 4(x-2)^{-3} - 3(x-2)^{-2}$$

$$= \dfrac{4 - x^2}{(x^2+4)^2} - \dfrac{4}{(x-2)^3} - \dfrac{3}{(x-2)^2}.$$

You can summarise the results of this section by:

To put into partial fractions a rational function of the form

$$\dfrac{f(x)}{(px+q)(rx+s)} \quad \text{or} \quad \dfrac{f(x)}{(px+q)(x^2+a^2)} \quad \text{or} \quad \dfrac{f(x)}{(px+q)^2(x^2+a^2)}$$

where $f(x)$ is a polynomial whose degree is greater than or equal to the degree of the denominator, begin by expressing the function in divided out form.

Exercise 2B

1 Express the following improper fractions in partial fraction form.

(a) $\dfrac{2x^2 + x + 1}{(x+1)(x-1)}$

(b) $\dfrac{x^2 + 1}{(x+3)(x-2)}$

(c) $\dfrac{7 - 5x + 2x^2}{(3-x)(1-2x)}$

(d) $\dfrac{6x^2 + 11x + 3}{(x+2)(2x-1)}$

(e) $\dfrac{4x^3 + 6x + 1}{(x+1)(2x-1)}$

(f) $\dfrac{2 + 9x + 6x^2 + x^3}{(3+x)(1+x)}$

(g) $\dfrac{32x^4}{(2x-1)(2x+1)}$

(h) $\dfrac{2x^4 + x^3 - 14x^2}{(x+3)(2x-3)}$

(i) $\dfrac{1 + x^4}{x(1+x^2)}$

2 Find the values of the following definite integrals.

(a) $\displaystyle\int_2^3 \dfrac{x^3 + x^2 + x - 1}{x(x^2 - 1)}\,dx$

(b) $\displaystyle\int_1^2 \dfrac{2 + 2x + 2x^2 + x^3}{x^2(1+x)}\,dx$

(c) $\displaystyle\int_0^1 \dfrac{6x^3 - 7x^2 - 11}{(2x-3)(x^2 + 1)}\,dx$

(d) $\displaystyle\int_0^2 \dfrac{8 - 2x - x^2 - x^4}{(x+2)(x^2 + 4)}\,dx$

3 Express the following improper fractions in partial fraction form.

(a) $\dfrac{2x^5}{(x^2 + 1)(x-1)^2}$

(b) $\dfrac{3x^4 + 6}{(x^2 + 2)(x+1)^2}$

(c) $\dfrac{24x^4 - 24}{(2x^2 + 1)(2x+1)^2}$

4 Express $\dfrac{2x^4 + 4x^3 - 3}{(2x^2 + 3)(x+1)^2}$ in partial fractions. Hence differentiate $\dfrac{2x^4 + 4x^3 - 3}{(2x^2 + 3)(x+1)^2}$, leaving your answer as the sum of two terms.

Miscellaneous exercise 2

1 Express the following in partial fractions.

(a) $\dfrac{1 + x}{x^2(1 - x)}$

(b) $\dfrac{6 + x - x^4}{(x+2)(x^2 + 2)}$

2 (a) Given that

$$\frac{2}{(x-1)^2(x^2 + 1)} \equiv \frac{A}{x-1} + \frac{B}{(x-1)^2} + \frac{Cx}{x^2 + 1},$$

find the values of the constants A, B and C.

(b) Show that

$$\int_2^3 \frac{2}{(x-1)^2(x^2 + 1)}\,dx = a + b\ln 2,$$

where a and b are constants whose values you should find.   (OCR)

3 (a) Find the values of A, B and C for which $\dfrac{x^2 - 2}{(x-2)^2} \equiv A + \dfrac{B}{x-2} + \dfrac{C}{(x-2)^2}$.

(b) The region bounded by the curve with equation $y = \dfrac{x^2 - 2}{(x-2)^2}$, the x-axis and the lines $x = 3$ and $x = 4$ is denoted by R. Show that R has area $(2 + 4\ln 2)$ square units.   (OCR)

4 (a) Express $\dfrac{2}{(x-1)(x-3)}$ in partial fractions, and use the result to express $\dfrac{4}{(x-1)^2(x-3)^2}$ in partial fractions.

The finite region bounded by the curve with equation $y = \dfrac{2}{(x-1)(x-3)}$ and the lines $x = 4$ and $y = \frac{1}{4}$ is denoted by R.

(b) Show that the area of R is $\ln \frac{3}{2} - \frac{1}{4}$.

(c) Calculate the volume of the solid formed when R is rotated through 2π radians about the x-axis. (OCR)

5 Evaluate $\displaystyle\int_0^1 \dfrac{x^2 + 6x - 4}{(x+2)(x^2+2)}\,dx.$

6 Calculate the exact value of $\displaystyle\int_0^{\frac{1}{2}} \dfrac{1 + x + x^2}{(1-x)^2}\,dx.$

7 Calculate the exact value of $\displaystyle\int_0^1 \dfrac{x^2 + x + 1}{(2x+1)(x+1)^2}\,dx.$

8 (a) Find the value of a such that a translation in the direction of the x-axis transforms the curve with equation $y = \dfrac{x^2 + ax - 1}{x^3}$ into the curve with equation $y = \dfrac{x^2 - 2}{(x-1)^3}$.

(b) Hence find the exact value of $\displaystyle\int_2^3 \dfrac{x^2 - 2}{(x-1)^3}\,dx.$ (OCR)

9 Find the value of the constants A and B such that

$$\dfrac{x^4 - 2x + 1}{(x^2 + 1)(x+1)^2} \equiv 1 - \dfrac{x+1}{x^2 + 1} + \dfrac{Ax + B}{(x+1)^2}.$$

Hence find the binomial expansion of $\dfrac{x^4 - 2x + 1}{(x^2 + 1)(x+1)^2}$ in ascending powers of x up to and including x^2.

3 Maclaurin series

You have already used series expansions in connection with geometric series and binomial expansions. In this chapter the idea is extended to other functions. When you have completed it, you should

- be able to find Maclaurin polynomials, and understand why they give good approximations to functions
- know the Maclaurin series for a number of functions
- understand what is meant by the interval of validity of a series
- be able to find expansions of composite functions
- know how to find expansions using integrals.

3.1 Agreement between functions

If $f(x)$ denotes the function $\sqrt{1+x}$, or $(1+x)^{\frac{1}{2}}$, then it can be expressed using the binomial expansion as

$$f(x) = 1 + \tfrac{1}{2}x - \tfrac{1}{8}x^2 + \tfrac{1}{16}x^3 - \dots.$$

Fig. 3.1, Fig. 3.2 and Fig. 3.3 show the graph of $f(x)$ compared with graphs of the polynomial functions

$$p_1(x) = 1 + \tfrac{1}{2}x,$$
$$p_2(x) = 1 + \tfrac{1}{2}x - \tfrac{1}{8}x^2,$$
$$p_3(x) = 1 + \tfrac{1}{2}x - \tfrac{1}{8}x^2 + \tfrac{1}{16}x^3.$$

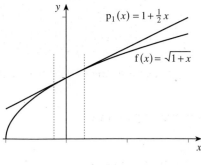

Fig. 3.1

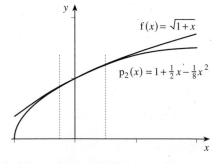

Fig. 3.2

The dotted lines indicate the intervals of values of x for which you can't distinguish the pairs of graphs by eye. You can see that the more terms of the expansion you take, the wider the interval over which the polynomial gives a good approximation to $\sqrt{1+x}$.

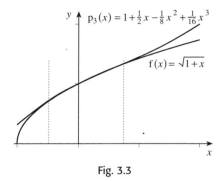

Fig. 3.3

The polynomial $p_1(x)$ has the same value as $f(x)$ when $x = 0$, and also the same gradient. Thus $f(0) = \sqrt{1+0} = 1$ and $p_1(0) = 1$. Also, since

$$f'(x) = \tfrac{1}{2}(1+x)^{-\frac{1}{2}} \quad \text{and} \quad p_1'(x) = \tfrac{1}{2},$$

you find that $f'(0) = p_1'(0) = \tfrac{1}{2}$.

The reason why $p_2(x)$ fits $f(x)$ better than $p_1(x)$ is that, by adding a term in x^2, the graph can be made to bend into a curve. The coefficient of x^2 has been chosen so that the two graphs bend at the same rate when $x = 0$; that is, their second derivatives are the same. Thus

$$f''(x) = -\tfrac{1}{4}(1+x)^{-\frac{3}{2}} \quad \text{and} \quad p_2''(x) = -\tfrac{1}{4},$$

so that $f''(0) = p_2''(0) = -\tfrac{1}{4}$.

The functions $p_3(x)$ and $f(x)$ agree even better, since they not only bend at the same rate at $x = 0$, but also their rates of bending are changing at the same rate. You can check for yourself that $f'''(0) = p_3'''(0) = \tfrac{3}{8}$.

The ideas above can be summarised with the help of a definition:

> **Definition** The functions f and g **agree to the nth degree** at $x = 0$ if
>
> $$f(0) = g(0), \quad f'(0) = g'(0), \quad f''(0) = g''(0), \quad \ldots, \quad f^{(n)}(0) = g^{(n)}(0);$$
>
> that is, if $f^{(r)}(0) = g^{(r)}(0)$ where r is an integer and $0 \leqslant r \leqslant n$.

Thus $f(x)$ and $p_1(x)$ agree to the first degree, $f(x)$ and $p_2(x)$ agree to the second degree and $f(x)$ and $p_3(x)$ agree to the third degree.

You can extend this idea to functions other than binomial expansions.

Example 3.1.1
Find a cubic polynomial which agrees with $\tan x$ to the third degree.

Writing $\tan x$ as $f(x)$, use the chain rule and the product rule to find

$$f'(x) = \sec^2 x, \quad f''(x) = 2 \sec x \times \sec x \tan x = 2 \sec^2 x \tan x,$$
$$f'''(x) = 4 \sec x \times \sec x \tan x \times \tan x + 2 \sec^2 x \times \sec^2 x$$
$$= 2 \sec^2 x \,(2 \tan^2 x + \sec^2 x).$$

Since $\tan 0 = 0$ and $\sec 0 = 1$,

$$f(0) = 0, \quad f'(0) = 1, \quad f''(0) = 0, \quad f'''(0) = 2.$$

If the cubic polynomial is $p(x) = a + bx + cx^2 + dx^3$, then

$$p'(x) = b + 2cx + 3dx^2, \qquad p''(x) = 2c + 6dx, \qquad p'''(x) = 6d.$$

So

$$p(0) = a, \quad p'(0) = b, \quad p''(0) = 2c, \quad p'''(0) = 6d.$$

For $p(x)$ and $f(x)$ to agree at $x = 0$, you need

$$a = 0, \quad b = 1, \quad 2c = 0, \quad 6d = 2.$$

Therefore $p(x) = x + \frac{1}{3}x^3$.

> It is interesting to plot the graphs of $\tan x$ and $p(x) = x + \frac{1}{3}x^3$ on a graphic calculator, and to suggest an interval over which you would consider that $p(x)$ is a good approximation to $\tan x$.

3.2 Maclaurin polynomials

You can generalise the argument in the last section to give polynomial approximations to any function $f(x)$ around $x = 0$, provided that all the derivatives of the function are defined.

The result is stated in the form of the following theorem.

Theorem The polynomial of degree n which agrees with $f(x)$ to the nth degree at $x = 0$ is

$$p_n(x) = f(0) + \frac{f'(0)}{1!}x + \frac{f''(0)}{2!}x^2 + \cdots + \frac{f^{(r)}(0)}{r!}x^r + \cdots + \frac{f^{(n)}(0)}{n!}x^n.$$

The polynomial $p_n(x)$ in the theorem is called the **Maclaurin polynomial for $f(x)$ of degree n**. In sigma notation it can be written as $\sum_{r=0}^{n} \frac{f^{(r)}(0)}{r!}x^r$. It is named after Colin Maclaurin, a Scottish mathematician who lived in the first half of the 18th century.

Before going on to prove the theorem, here is an example to show how it can be used.

Example 3.2.1
Find the Maclaurin polynomial of degree 4 for the function $f(x) = (1 + x)^{-3}$.

The first four derivatives are

$$f'(x) = -3(1 + x)^{-4}, \quad f''(x) = 12(1 + x)^{-5},$$
$$f'''(x) = -60(1 + x)^{-6}, \quad f^{(4)}(x) = 360(1 + x)^{-7}.$$

Therefore

$$f(0) = 1, \quad f'(0) = -3, \quad f''(0) = 12, \quad f'''(0) = -60, \quad f^{(4)}(0) = 360.$$

This gives

$$p_4(x) = 1 + \frac{(-3)}{1!}x + \frac{12}{2!}x^2 + \frac{(-60)}{3!}x^3 + \frac{360}{4!}x^4$$
$$= 1 - 3x + 6x^2 - 10x^3 + 15x^4.$$

You can check that this is the same as the binomial expansion of $(1+x)^{-3}$ up to and including the term in x^4.

Before giving the proof of the theorem, it will be useful to establish two mini-theorems (or 'lemmas'). These are set out in a general notation, but if you have difficulty following this, try writing the equations out for yourself in full using values such as $r = 3$ and $n = 5$.

Mini-theorem   If $g(x) = x^r$, where $r \in \mathbb{N}$, then $g^{(r)}(0) = r!$ and $g^{(i)}(0) = 0$ if $i < r$ or $i > r$.

> **Proof**   Generalising from $g'(x) = rx^{r-1}, \quad g''(x) = r(r-1)x^{r-2}, \ldots$ you get
>
> $$g^{(i)}(x) = r(r-1)(r-2)\ldots(r-(i-1))x^{r-i},$$
>
> provided that $i \leqslant r$. If $i < r$, the power of x is positive, so that $g^{(i)}(0) = 0$. But when $i = r$, so that $r - i = 0$, $g^{(i)}(x)$ has the constant value
>
> $$g^{(r)}(x) = r(r-1)(r-2)\ldots 1 = r!.$$
>
> The formula for $g^{(i)}(x)$ no longer holds when $i > r$. Since $g^{(r)}(x)$ is constant, $g^{(r+1)}(x) = 0$ and all subsequent derivatives are 0 for all x.
>
> So $g^{(i)}(0) = 0$ for $i > r$.

Example 3.2.2

If $g(x) = x^5$, state the values of   (a) $g'''(0)$,   (b) $g^{(5)}(0)$,   (c) $g^{(8)}(0)$.

> (a) $i = 3$ and $r = 5$, so $i < r$ and $g'''(0) = 0$.
>
> (b) $i = 5$ and $r = 5$, so $i = r$ and $g^{(5)}(0) = 5! = 120$.
>
> (c) $i = 8$ and $r = 5$, so $i > r$ and $g^{(8)}(0) = 0$.

The next mini-theorem extends this result to a polynomial of degree n. To do this it is convenient to use a new notation for the coefficients of a polynomial, denoting the coefficient of the term in x^r by a_r so that

$$p(x) = a_0 + a_1 x + a_2 x^2 + \cdots + a_r x^r + \cdots + a_n x^n.$$

The term $a_r x^r$ is called the **general term** of $p(x)$. You can use sigma notation to abbreviate this equation to

$$p(x) = \sum_{r=0}^{n} a_r x^r.$$

Mini-theorem   If $p(x) = \sum_{r=0}^{n} a_r x^r$, $p^{(r)}(0) = a_r r!$ for $0 \leqslant r \leqslant n$.

Proof   When you find the rth derivative of $p(x)$, all the terms of the form $a_i x^i$ with $i < r$ and $i > r$ have rth derivatives which are 0 when $x = 0$, by the previous mini-theorem. Only the term $a_r x^r$ has an rth derivative which is not 0 when $x = 0$, and the value of this derivative is $a_r r!$.

Example 3.2.3

If $p(x) = 3 - 5x^2 + 4x^3 + 2x^4 - 7x^6 + x^7$, find $p^{(4)}(0)$.

The coefficient $a_4 = 2$, so $p^{(4)}(0) = 2 \times 4! = 48$.

You now have everything you need to prove the main result.

Proof of the main theorem   Denoting $p_n(x)$ by $\sum_{r=0}^{n} a_r x^r$ you require $p_n^{(r)}(0) = f^{(r)}(0)$ for $0 \leqslant r \leqslant n$. By the previous mini-theorem, $p_n^{(r)}(0) = a_r r!$. Therefore $a_r r! = f^{(r)}(0)$, so that $a_r = \dfrac{f^{(r)}(0)}{r!}$ for $0 \leqslant r \leqslant n$.

That is,

$$p_n(x) = f(0) + \frac{f'(0)}{1!}x + \frac{f''(0)}{2!}x^2 + \cdots + \frac{f^{(r)}(0)}{r!}x^r + \cdots + \frac{f^{(n)}(0)}{n!}x^n.$$

Example 3.2.4

Find the Maclaurin polynomial of degree 4 for $f(x) = \cos x$.

Differentiating four times in succession,

$$f'(x) = -\sin x, \quad f''(x) = -\cos x, \quad f'''(x) = \sin x, \quad f^{(4)}(x) = \cos x.$$

So

$$f(0) = 1, \quad f'(0) = 0, \quad f''(0) = -1, \quad f'''(0) = 0, \quad f^{(4)}(0) = 1.$$

From the theorem, with $n = 4$, the Maclaurin polynomial is

$$p_4(x) = 1 + \frac{0}{1!}x + \frac{-1}{2!}x^2 + \frac{0}{3!}x^3 + \frac{1}{4!}x^4$$

$$= 1 - \tfrac{1}{2}x^2 + \tfrac{1}{24}x^4.$$

Use a graphic calculator to display the graphs of $y = \cos x$ and $y = p_4(x)$ with the same axes. Over what interval would you say that $p_4(x)$ is a good approximation to $\cos x$?

Exercise 3A

1 For the following expressions $f(x)$ write down the binomial expansions as far as the term in x^3. Denoting this expansion by $p_3(x)$, verify that $f(x)$ and $p_3(x)$ agree to the third degree at $x = 0$. Display graphs of $f(x)$ and $p_3(x)$ on a graphic calculator, and estimate the interval over which you cannot distinguish between the graphs.

(a) $(1 + x)^{\frac{3}{2}}$ (b) $(1 - x)^{-\frac{3}{2}}$ (c) $(1 + 2x)^{-3}$ (d) $(1 + x^2)^{\frac{1}{2}}$

2 For the following expressions $f(x)$ find the Maclaurin polynomial $p_n(x)$ of the given degree n. Illustrate your answers by comparing the graphs of $f(x)$ and $p_n(x)$.

(a) $\sin x, \quad n = 5$ (b) $\sin 2x, \quad n = 5$ (c) $e^x, \quad n = 4$

(d) $e^{-3x}, \quad n = 4$ (e) $\sin^2 x, \quad n = 3$ (f) $\cos^2 x, \quad n = 3$

(g) $\ln(1 - x), \quad n = 4$ (h) $\dfrac{1}{\sqrt{1 - 2x}}, \quad n = 3$ (i) $e^{-\frac{1}{2}x^2}, \quad n = 4$

(j) $\ln(1 + x^2), \quad n = 4$

3 Show that it is possible to find numbers a and b such that $ax + bx^2$ and $e^x \ln(1 + x)$ agree to degree 2 at $x = 0$.

4 Show that it is possible to find numbers a and b such that $a + bx^2$ and $\sec x$ agree to degree 3 at $x = 0$.

5 Show that it is possible to find numbers a and b such that $ax + bx^3$ and $\dfrac{e^x - 1}{e^x + 1}$ agree to degree 3 at $x = 0$.

6 Find the Maclaurin polynomial of degree 4 for $(1 + x)^m$, where m is not a positive integer. Verify that this agrees with the first five terms of the binomial expansion of $(1 + x)^m$.

7 Show that $\dfrac{d}{dx}(f(ax)) = af'(ax)$, and that $\dfrac{d}{dx}(f(x^2)) = 2xf'(x^2)$. Hence show that

(a) if $f(x)$ and $g(x)$ agree to degree 3 at $x = 0$, then $f(ax)$ and $g(ax)$ agree to degree 3;

(b) if $f(x)$ and $g(x)$ agree to degree 2 at $x = 0$, then $f(x^2)$ and $g(x^2)$ agree to degree 4.

3.3 Maclaurin series and intervals of validity

The expression

$$f(0) + \frac{f'(0)}{1!}x + \frac{f''(0)}{2!}x^2 + \cdots + \frac{f^{(r)}(0)}{r!}x^r + \cdots,$$

continued indefinitely, is called the **Maclaurin expansion** of $f(x)$. By cutting off the expansion after the second, third, fourth, . . . terms you get a sequence of Maclaurin polynomials $p_1(x), p_2(x), p_3(x), \ldots$.

Fig. 3.1, Fig. 3.2 and Fig. 3.3 showed how such a sequence of polynomials can give better and better approximations to $f(x)$ for certain values of x. In such cases you can say that $f(x)$ is the limit of the sequence of polynomial values as n tends to infinity.

This can be written as a **Maclaurin series**

$$f(x) = \lim_{n \to \infty} p_n(x) = \lim_{n \to \infty} \sum_{r=0}^{n} \frac{f^{(r)}(0)}{r!} x^r, \text{ or } \sum_{r=0}^{\infty} \frac{f^{(r)}(0)}{r!} x^r.$$

It means that, by taking n large enough, you can (for a particular value of x) make $p_n(x)$ as close as you like to $f(x)$.

> The terms 'Maclaurin expansion' and 'Maclaurin series' have almost the same meaning. It would be normal to use the word 'series' when you are concerned with the convergence to a limit as $n \to \infty$, and 'expansion' to suggest that you can go on calculating terms as far as you want to, but will stop when you think you have enough. But there is no hard and fast distinction between them.

For many functions this is true for some but not all values of x. For example, if $f(x) = \ln(1 + x)$, then

$$f'(x) = (1 + x)^{-1}, \quad f''(x) = -(1 + x)^{-2}, \quad f'''(x) = 2(1 + x)^{-3}, \ldots,$$

so that

$$f'(0) = 1, \quad f''(0) = -1, \quad f'''(0) = 2, \ldots.$$

The general term is positive when r is odd and negative when r is even. It is not difficult to check that

$$f^{(r)}(x) = (-1)^{r-1}(r - 1)!(1 + x)^{-r},$$

so that

$$\frac{f^{(r)}(0)}{r!} = \frac{(-1)^{r-1}(r - 1)!}{r!} = (-1)^{r-1} \frac{1}{r}.$$

The Maclaurin series is therefore

$$\ln(1 + x) = x - \tfrac{1}{2}x^2 + \tfrac{1}{3}x^3 - \tfrac{1}{4}x^4 + \ldots.$$

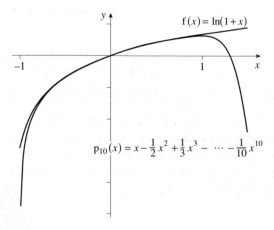

Fig. 3.4

Figure 3.4 shows a comparison of the graphs of $\ln(1 + x)$ and the 10th Maclaurin polynomial, ending with the term $-\frac{1}{10}x^{10}$. It is striking how closely the Maclaurin polynomial follows the function from just above -1 to just below 1, but that beyond 1 the two functions separate very sharply. However many terms you take, you can never get $p_n(x)$ to come close to $\ln(1 + x)$ for $x > 1$.

Contrast this with the function $f(x) = \sin x$. Since the derivatives are successively

$$\cos x, -\sin x, -\cos x, \sin x, \ldots$$

and then repeat through the same cycle, the values of $f^{(r)}(0)$ are successively

$$1, 0, -1, 0, 1, 0, \ldots .$$

Also $f(0) = 0$. The Maclaurin expansion is therefore

$$\sin x = \frac{x}{1!} - \frac{x^3}{3!} + \frac{x^5}{5!} - \frac{x^7}{7!} \cdots .$$

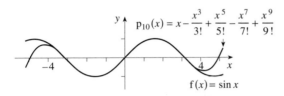

$$p_{10}(x) = x - \frac{x^3}{3!} + \frac{x^5}{5!} - \frac{x^7}{7!} + \frac{x^9}{9!}$$

$$f(x) = \sin x$$

Fig. 3.5

Figure 3.5 shows a comparison of the graphs of $\sin x$ and the 10th Maclaurin polynomial. (The last non-zero term of $p_{10}(x)$ is $\frac{x^9}{9!}$, because $f^{(10)}(0) = 0$.) You can see that already the graphs cannot be distinguished from each other by eye between about -4 and $+4$. And in fact, by taking enough terms, you can get a Maclaurin polynomial which fits the $\sin x$ graph over as wide an interval as you like.

The set of values of x for which the Maclaurin series can be made to fit a function, provided that enough terms are taken, is called the **interval of validity** of the series. For the function $\ln(1 + x)$ the interval of validity is $-1 < x \leqslant 1$; the series for $\sin x$ is valid for all real values of x, so its interval of validity is $\mathbb{R}$.

The only condition for a function to have a Maclaurin series is that $f(0)$ and all the derivatives $f^{(r)}(0)$ must be defined. So $\operatorname{cosec} x$ and $\ln x$ do not have Maclaurin series, because they are not defined when $x = 0$; and $|x|$ does not have one, since $\frac{d}{dx}|x|$ is not defined when $x = 0$.

But many of the standard functions do have Maclaurin series, and the most important ones are listed in the blue box. Before reading on, you should check these for yourself; it is worth remembering the first few terms of each expansion, but not the expression for the general term. You will have to take the intervals of validity on trust, but you could try using a computer or a graphic calculator to produce graphs like Figs. 3.4 and 3.5.

Maclaurin expansions for standard functions

$e^x = 1 + \dfrac{x}{1!} + \dfrac{x^2}{2!} + \dfrac{x^3}{3!} + \cdots + \dfrac{x^r}{r!} + \ldots,$ for $x \in \mathbb{R}$.

$\sin x = \dfrac{x}{1!} - \dfrac{x^3}{3!} + \dfrac{x^5}{5!} - \dfrac{x^7}{7!} + \cdots + (-1)^r \dfrac{x^{2r+1}}{(2r+1)!} + \ldots,$ for $x \in \mathbb{R}$.

$\cos x = 1 - \dfrac{x^2}{2!} + \dfrac{x^4}{4!} - \dfrac{x^6}{6!} + \cdots + (-1)^r \dfrac{x^{2r}}{(2r)!} + \ldots,$ for $x \in \mathbb{R}$.

$\ln(1 + x) = x - \tfrac{1}{2}x^2 + \tfrac{1}{3}x^3 - \tfrac{1}{4}x^4 + \cdots + (-1)^{r-1}\dfrac{1}{r}x^r + \ldots,$ for $-1 < x \leqslant 1$.

$(1 + x)^n = 1 + nx + \dfrac{n(n-1)}{2!}x^2 + \dfrac{n(n-1)(n-2)}{3!}x^3 + \cdots$

$\qquad + \dfrac{n(n-1)(n-2)\ldots(n-(r-1))}{r!}x^r + \ldots,$ for $x \in \mathbb{R}$ if $n \in \mathbb{N}$,

otherwise for $-1 < x < 1$ (and, in some cases, also for $x = -1$ or $x = 1$).

Example 3.3.1

Find the values of e and $\dfrac{1}{e}$, correct to 4 decimal places.

You can evaluate these by substituting $x = 1$ and $x = -1$ in the expansion for e^x:

$$e = 1 + \frac{1}{1!} + \frac{1}{2!} + \frac{1}{3!} + \frac{1}{4!} + \ldots,$$

$$\frac{1}{e} = 1 - \frac{1}{1!} + \frac{1}{2!} - \frac{1}{3!} + \frac{1}{4!} - \ldots.$$

The calculation is very simple, since $(r + 1)! = (r + 1)r!$, so that you can find $\dfrac{1}{(r+1)!}$ by dividing $\dfrac{1}{r!}$ by $r + 1$.

Table 3.6 lists values of $\dfrac{1}{r!}$ up to $r = 9$.

$1 = 1$	$\dfrac{1}{1!} = 1$
$\dfrac{1}{2!} = 0.5$	$\dfrac{1}{3!} = 0.166\ 667$
$\dfrac{1}{4!} = 0.041\ 667$	$\dfrac{1}{5!} = 0.008\ 333$
$\dfrac{1}{6!} = 0.001\ 389$	$\dfrac{1}{7!} = 0.000\ 198$
$\dfrac{1}{8!} = 0.000\ 025$	$\dfrac{1}{9!} = 0.000\ 003$
$1.543\ 081$	$1.175\ 201$

Table 3.6

So $e \approx 1.543\ 081 + 1.175\ 201 \approx 2.7183,$

$\dfrac{1}{e} \approx 1.543\ 081 - 1.175\ 201 \approx 0.3679,$ correct to 4 decimal places.

Exercise 3B

1 Use Maclaurin expansions to find, correct to 4 decimal places, the values of

(a) $\sqrt{e}$,   (b) $\sin 1$,   (c) $\sqrt[3]{0.9}$,   (d) $\cos 20°$,

(e) $\ln 0.95$,   (f) $\ln 2.25$,   (g) $\cos 3$.

2 Find the Maclaurin series for $\ln \dfrac{1+x}{1-x}$, and state its interval of validity. By choosing a suitable value for x, calculate the value of $\ln 3$, correct to 3 decimal places.

Why can't you find $\ln 3$ directly from the Maclaurin series for $\ln(1 + x)$?

3 Use the standard expansions to find the first two non-zero terms in the expansion of $x \cos x - \sin x$. Hence find the limit, as $x \to 0$, of $\dfrac{x \cos x - \sin x}{x^3}$.

4 Use the method of Question 3 to find the limit, as $x \to 0$, of

(a) $\dfrac{e^x - e^{-x}}{x}$,

(b) $\dfrac{1 - \cos x}{x^2}$,

(c) $\dfrac{\ln(1 + x)}{x}$,

(d) $\dfrac{\ln(1 + x) - x}{x^2}$.

5 Show that, if you assume that a function can be differentiated by differentiating each term of its Maclaurin expansion, you get correct results for

(a) $\dfrac{d}{dx} e^x$,

(b) $\dfrac{d}{dx} \sin x$,

(c) $\dfrac{d}{dx} \ln(1 + x)$,

(d) $\dfrac{d}{dx} \sqrt{(1 + x)}$.

6 An approximate value for π can be found by putting $x = \frac{1}{2}\pi$ in the Maclaurin expansion of $\cos x$ and neglecting all the terms of degree greater than 4, and then solving a quartic polynomial equation for π. To how many significant figures is the approximation accurate?

An alternative method is to use the substitution $x = \frac{1}{3}\pi$. To how many significant figures is the resulting approximation accurate?

Which method gives the better approximation? Suggest a reason why.

7* Prove that, if $x = 10$, the terms of the Maclaurin expansion for $\cos x$ decrease in absolute value from $\dfrac{x^{12}}{12!}$ onwards. Deduce that the errors in replacing $\cos 10$ by its Maclaurin polynomials $p_{30}(10)$ and $p_{40}(10)$ are less than $\dfrac{10^{32}}{32!}$ and $\dfrac{10^{42}}{42!}$ respectively in absolute value. Evaluate these expressions correct to 1 significant figure, and explain why your answers suggest that the expansion is valid for $x = 10$.

By generalising this argument, say what this suggests about the interval of validity of the Maclaurin expansion for $\cos x$.

3.4 Maclaurin expansions for composite functions

If you want to find the Maclaurin expansion for a function such as $\sin 5x$ or $\ln(1 + x^2)$, you could use the general expression at the beginning of Section 3.3 with $f(x) = \sin 5x$ or $f(x) = \ln(1 + x^2)$. This is quite easy for $\sin 5x$, since the derivatives are successively $5 \cos 5x$, $-5^2 \sin 5x$, $-5^3 \cos 5x, \ldots$, whose values for $x = 0$ are $5, 0, -5^3, \ldots$. It is easy to see how this continues. The Maclaurin expansion then begins

$$\frac{5}{1!}x - \frac{5^3}{3!}x^3 + \frac{5^5}{5!}x^5 - \cdots.$$

You can write this as

$$\frac{(5x)}{1!} - \frac{(5x)^3}{3!} + \frac{(5x)^5}{5!} - \cdots,$$

which is (as you would probably expect) what you would get by simply replacing x by $5x$ in the Maclaurin expansion of $\sin x$.

Differentiating $\ln(1+x^2)$ several times is a lot more difficult, and you might not recognise the general pattern. But, just as you could with $\sin 5x$, you can find the Maclaurin expansion by substitution, in this case by simply replacing x by x^2 in the Maclaurin expansion of $\ln(1+x)$. This gives

$$\ln(1+x^2) = (x^2) - \tfrac{1}{2}(x^2)^2 + \tfrac{1}{3}(x^2)^3 - \tfrac{1}{4}(x^2)^4 + \cdots$$
$$= x^2 - \tfrac{1}{2}x^4 + \tfrac{1}{3}x^6 - \tfrac{1}{4}x^8 + \cdots .$$

Since the series for $\ln(1+x)$ is valid when $-1 < x \leqslant 1$, this series is valid when $-1 < x^2 \leqslant 1$, that is when $-1 \leqslant x \leqslant 1$.

The methods described can be justified by generalising the results in Exercise 3A Question 7.

Sometimes it is worth using some special property of the function before finding the Maclaurin expansion, as in the following example.

Example 3.4.1
Find Maclaurin expansions for (a) $\sin\left(x + \tfrac{1}{4}\pi\right)$,   (b) $\ln(2 - 4x)$.

(a) By the addition formula, $\sin\left(x + \tfrac{1}{4}\pi\right) = \sin x \cos\tfrac{1}{4}\pi + \cos x \sin\tfrac{1}{4}\pi$.

Since $\sin\tfrac{1}{4}\pi = \cos\tfrac{1}{4}\pi = \dfrac{1}{\sqrt{2}}$,

$$\sin\left(x + \tfrac{1}{4}\pi\right) = \frac{1}{\sqrt{2}}(\sin x + \cos x)$$
$$= \frac{1}{\sqrt{2}}\left(\left(\frac{x}{1!} - \frac{x^3}{3!} + \frac{x^5}{5!} - \cdots\right) + \left(1 - \frac{x^2}{2!} + \frac{x^4}{4!} - \cdots\right)\right)$$
$$= \frac{1}{\sqrt{2}}\left(1 + x - \frac{x^2}{2!} - \frac{x^3}{3!} + \frac{x^4}{4!} + \frac{x^5}{5!} - \cdots\right).$$

(b) Use the multiplication rule of logarithms to write

$$\ln(2 - 4x) = \ln 2 + \ln(1 - 2x).$$

Then use the Maclaurin series for $\ln(1+x)$, replacing x by $-2x$, to get

$$\ln(2 - 4x) = \ln 2 + (-2x) - \tfrac{1}{2}(-2x)^2 + \tfrac{1}{3}(-2x)^3 - \tfrac{1}{4}(-2x)^4 - \cdots$$
$$= \ln 2 - 2x - 2x^2 - \tfrac{8}{3}x^3 - 4x^4 - \cdots .$$

This expansion is valid if $-1 < -2x \leqslant 1$, that is if $\dfrac{(-1)}{(-2)} > x \geqslant \dfrac{1}{(-2)}$, or $-\tfrac{1}{2} \leqslant x < \tfrac{1}{2}$.

Sometimes you want to find a Maclaurin expansion for a function which is the product of two simpler functions. Although you could do this by the usual Maclaurin method, finding the derivatives by the rule for differentiating a product, it is often simpler to expand the two functions separately as far as is needed and then to multiply the two resulting polynomials together. (Exercise 3C Question 6 indicates how this can be justified.) The next example compares the two methods.

Example 3.4.2

Find the Maclaurin expansion, as far as the term in x^4, of $f(x) = e^{2x} \cos 3x$

(a) by direct application of the Maclaurin expansion formula,

(b) by multiplying together the expansions of the separate factors.

(a) Differentiating four times in succession, using the product rule,

$$f'(x) = 2e^{2x} \cos 3x + e^{2x}(-3 \sin 3x)$$
$$= e^{2x}(2 \cos 3x - 3 \sin 3x);$$

$$f''(x) = 2e^{2x}(2 \cos 3x - 3 \sin 3x) + e^{2x}(-6 \sin 3x - 9 \cos 3x)$$
$$= e^{2x}(-5 \cos 3x - 12 \sin 3x);$$

$$f'''(x) = 2e^{2x}(-5 \cos 3x - 12 \sin 3x) + e^{2x}(15 \sin 3x - 36 \cos 3x)$$
$$= e^{2x}(-46 \cos 3x - 9 \sin 3x);$$

$$f^{(4)}(x) = 2e^{2x}(-46 \cos 3x - 9 \sin 3x) + e^{2x}(138 \sin 3x - 27 \cos 3x)$$
$$= e^{2x}(-119 \cos 3x + 120 \sin 3x).$$

So $f(0) = 1, \quad f'(0) = 2, \quad f''(0) = -5, \quad f'''(0) = -46, \quad f^{(4)}(0) = -119.$

The Maclaurin expansion, as far as the term in x^4, is therefore

$$1 + \frac{2}{1!}x + \frac{-5}{2!}x^2 + \frac{-46}{3!}x^3 + \frac{-119}{4!}x^4$$
$$= 1 + 2x - \tfrac{5}{2}x^2 - \tfrac{23}{3}x^3 - \tfrac{119}{24}x^4.$$

(b) Using the standard expansions for e^x and $\cos x$, with x replaced by $2x$ and $3x$ respectively, gives

$$e^{2x} = 1 + \frac{(2x)}{1!} + \frac{(2x)^2}{2!} + \frac{(2x)^3}{3!} + \frac{(2x)^4}{4!} + \dots$$
$$= 1 + 2x + 2x^2 + \tfrac{4}{3}x^3 + \tfrac{2}{3}x^4 + \dots,$$

and

$$\cos 3x = 1 - \frac{(3x)^2}{2!} + \frac{(3x)^4}{4!} - \dots$$
$$= 1 - \tfrac{9}{2}x^2 + \tfrac{27}{8}x^4 - \dots.$$

So

$$e^{2x} \cos 3x = \left(1 + 2x + 2x^2 + \tfrac{4}{3}x^3 + \tfrac{2}{3}x^4 + \dots\right)\left(1 - \tfrac{9}{2}x^2 + \tfrac{27}{8}x^4 - \dots\right)$$
$$= 1 + 2x + \left(2 - \tfrac{9}{2}\right)x^2 + \left(\tfrac{4}{3} - 2 \times \tfrac{9}{2}\right)x^3 + \left(\tfrac{27}{8} - 2 \times \tfrac{9}{2} + \tfrac{2}{3}\right)x^4 + \dots$$
$$= 1 + 2x - \tfrac{5}{2}x^2 - \tfrac{23}{3}x^3 - \tfrac{119}{24}x^4,$$

as far as the term in x^4.

Example 3.4.3

Find the first three non-zero terms of the Maclaurin expansion of $\dfrac{\ln(1+2x)}{\sqrt{1+x}}$.

In algebra multiplication is simpler than division, so it is best to begin by writing f(x) as $(1+x)^{-\frac{1}{2}}\ln(1+2x)$.

The first factor can be expanded by the binomial formula, as

$$(1+x)^{-\frac{1}{2}} = 1 + \frac{\left(-\frac{1}{2}\right)}{1!}x + \frac{\left(-\frac{1}{2}\right)\times\left(-\frac{3}{2}\right)}{2!}x^2 + \frac{\left(-\frac{1}{2}\right)\times\left(-\frac{3}{2}\right)\times\left(-\frac{5}{2}\right)}{3!}x^3 + \dots$$
$$= 1 - \tfrac{1}{2}x + \tfrac{3}{8}x^2 - \tfrac{5}{16}x^3 + \dots .$$

For the second factor, replace x by $2x$ in the expansion of $\ln(1+x)$, which gives

$$\ln(1+2x) = \frac{(2x)}{1} - \frac{(2x)^2}{2} + \frac{(2x)^3}{3} - \frac{(2x)^4}{4} + \dots$$
$$= 2x - 2x^2 + \tfrac{8}{3}x^3 - 4x^4 + \dots .$$

So

$$f(x) = \left(1 - \tfrac{1}{2}x + \tfrac{3}{8}x^2 - \tfrac{5}{16}x^3 + \dots\right)\left(2x - 2x^2 + \tfrac{8}{3}x^3 - 4x^4 + \dots\right)$$
$$= 2x + \left(-2 - \tfrac{1}{2}\times 2\right)x^2 + \left(\tfrac{8}{3} + \tfrac{1}{2}\times 2 + \tfrac{3}{8}\times 2\right)x^3 + \dots .$$

> Once you have reached this stage it is obvious that none of the coefficients are zero, so there is no need to find the coefficient of x^4. This means that it wasn't necessary to find the fourth terms, $-\tfrac{5}{16}x^3$ and $-4x^4$, in the separate expansions. But you can never be sure!

The first three terms in the expansion of $\dfrac{\ln(1+2x)}{\sqrt{1+x}}$ are therefore $2x - 3x^2 + \tfrac{53}{12}x^3$.

Example 3.4.4

Find the Maclaurin polynomials of degree 4 for (a) $\ln\cos x$, (b) $e^{\cos x}$, (c) $x\operatorname{cosec} x$.

> The functions in this example each involve two expansions. The work can be eased by discarding powers of x higher than x^4 as you go along, but you need to be careful in (c) where division is involved.

(a) $\ln\cos x = \ln\left(1 - \dfrac{x^2}{2!} + \dfrac{x^4}{4!} - \dots\right)$

$= \ln\left(1 + \left(-\tfrac{1}{2}x^2 + \tfrac{1}{24}x^4 - \dots\right)\right)$

$= \left(-\tfrac{1}{2}x^2 + \tfrac{1}{24}x^4 - \dots\right) - \tfrac{1}{2}\left(-\tfrac{1}{2}x^2 + \tfrac{1}{24}x^4 - \dots\right)^2 + \dots$

$= \left(-\tfrac{1}{2}x^2 + \tfrac{1}{24}x^4\right) - \tfrac{1}{2}\left(\tfrac{1}{4}x^4\right)$ to degree 4

$= -\tfrac{1}{2}x^2 + \left(\tfrac{1}{24} - \tfrac{1}{8}\right)x^4$

$= -\tfrac{1}{2}x^2 - \tfrac{1}{12}x^4.$

(b) If you try to use a method similar to that in (a), writing $e^{\cos x}$ as $\exp\left(1 - \dfrac{x^2}{2!} + \dfrac{x^4}{4!} - \ldots\right)$ and expanding this as

$$1 + \frac{\left(1 - \dfrac{x^2}{2!} + \dfrac{x^4}{4!} - \ldots\right)}{1!} + \frac{\left(1 - \dfrac{x^2}{2!} + \dfrac{x^4}{4!} - \ldots\right)^2}{2!} + \ldots,$$

then you run into a problem. However far you continue with the exponential expansion, every term is of the form $\dfrac{\left(1 - \dfrac{x^2}{2!} + \dfrac{x^4}{4!} - \ldots\right)^r}{r!}$, which when expanded contributes to the constant term and the terms in x^2 and x^4 of the expansion. The way round this is to begin by using the multiplication rule for indices to write the expansion as

$$\exp(1) \times \exp\left(-\frac{x^2}{2!}\right) \times \exp\left(\frac{x^4}{4!}\right) \times \ldots.$$

The dots at the end of this product represent factors like $\exp\left(-\dfrac{x^6}{6!}\right)$ which when expanded contribute only the first term, 1, to the powers of x of degree up to 4. Then

$$e^{\cos x} = e \times \left(1 + \frac{1}{1!}\left(-\frac{x^2}{2}\right) + \frac{1}{2!}\left(-\frac{x^2}{2}\right)^2 + \ldots\right) \times \left(1 + \frac{1}{1!}\left(\frac{x^4}{24}\right) + \ldots\right) \times \ldots$$

$$= e\left(1 - \tfrac{1}{2}x^2 + \tfrac{1}{8}x^4 - \ldots\right) \times \left(1 + \tfrac{1}{24}x^4 + \ldots\right) \times \ldots$$

$$= e\left(1 - \tfrac{1}{2}x^2 + \left(\tfrac{1}{24} + \tfrac{1}{8}\right)x^4\right) \text{ to degree 4}$$

$$= e\left(1 - \tfrac{1}{2}x^2 + \tfrac{1}{6}x^4\right).$$

(c) The first step is to write $x \csc x$ as $\dfrac{x}{\sin x}$ and to replace $\sin x$ by its Maclaurin expansion. There will then be factors of x in both numerator and denominator, which will cancel out. So you have to keep the x^5 term in the $\sin x$ expansion, which will become x^4 after cancellation.

$$x \csc x = \frac{x}{\sin x} = \frac{x}{\left(x - \dfrac{x^3}{3!} + \dfrac{x^5}{5!} - \ldots\right)} = \frac{1}{1 - \dfrac{x^2}{6} + \dfrac{x^4}{120} - \ldots}$$

$$= \left(1 - \left(\tfrac{1}{6}x^2 - \tfrac{1}{120}x^4 + \ldots\right)\right)^{-1}.$$

Now replace u in the binomial expansion $(1 - u)^{-1} = 1 + u + u^2 + \ldots$ by $\tfrac{1}{6}x^2 - \tfrac{1}{120}x^4 + \ldots$ to obtain

$$x \csc x = 1 + \left(\tfrac{1}{6}x^2 - \tfrac{1}{120}x^4 + \ldots\right) + \left(\tfrac{1}{6}x^2 - \ldots\right)^2 + \ldots$$

$$= 1 + \tfrac{1}{6}x^2 + \left(-\tfrac{1}{120} + \tfrac{1}{36}\right)x^4 \text{ to degree 4}$$

$$= 1 + \tfrac{1}{6}x^2 + \tfrac{7}{360}x^4.$$

There is no easy way of knowing the interval of validity of these composite expansions because you don't have an expression for the general term. The value of the expansions lies in their use as polynomial approximations to the functions when x is small.

Exercise 3C

1 Each of the following expressions $f(x)$ can be written as $g(h(x))$, where g is one of the functions whose Maclaurin expansion is listed on page 42. Expand $f(x)$ as far as the term in x^4 by two methods: (i) by finding $f^{(r)}(x)$ for $r = 1, 2, 3, 4$ and using the general formula for a Maclaurin expansion, and (ii) by substituting $h(x)$ in place of x in the expansion of $g(x)$. Verify that both methods give the same answer.

(a) $f(x) = (1 + 2x)^{\frac{3}{2}}$

(b) $f(x) = e^{-2x}$

(c) $f(x) = \ln(1 + x^3)$

(d) $f(x) = \sin x^3$

2 Write the Maclaurin expansion of the following, giving the first three non-zero terms, an expression for the general term and the interval of validity.

(a) e^{3x}

(b) $\cos \frac{1}{2}x$

(c) $\sqrt{x} \sin \sqrt{x}$

(d) $\ln(1 - x)$

(e) $\ln(1 + 2x)$

(f) e^{1+x}

(g) $\cos^2 x$

(h) $\ln(e + x)$

(i) $\cos(1 + x)$

3 Find the Maclaurin expansions of the following functions as far as the term in x^4.

(a) $e^{-x} \sin x$

(b) $\sqrt{1 - x} \cos x$

(c) $\dfrac{e^x}{1 + x}$

(d) $(1 + x)^2 \ln(1 + x)$

(e) $e^{-2x} \ln(1 + 3x)$

(f) $\ln(1 - 2x) \sin 3x$

4 Find the Maclaurin polynomials of degree 4 for the following.

(a) $e^{(1+x)^2}$

(b) $e^{\sqrt{1+x}}$

(c) $\cos(\sin x)$

(d) $\sin(\cos x)$

(e) $\sec x$

(f) $\dfrac{x^2}{\ln(1 + x^2)}$

(g) $\tan x$

(h) $\ln(1 + e^x)$

(i) $\sqrt{\dfrac{1 + x}{1 - x}}$

5 Find functions whose Maclaurin expansions are

(a) $1 + \dfrac{x^2}{1!} + \dfrac{x^4}{2!} + \cdots + \dfrac{x^{2r}}{r!} + \cdots,$

(b) $1 + \dfrac{x^2}{2!} + \dfrac{x^4}{4!} + \cdots + \dfrac{x^{2r}}{(2r)!} + \cdots,$

(c) $1 + \dfrac{x}{2!} + \dfrac{x^2}{4!} + \cdots + \dfrac{x^r}{(2r)!} + \cdots.$

6 If $f(x) = g(x) \times h(x)$, express $f'(0)$ and $f''(0)$ in terms of the functions g and h. Hence show that, if the Maclaurin expansions of $g(x)$ and $h(x)$ are multiplied together, then the terms of the product as far as the term in x^2 are the same as the terms of the Maclaurin expansion of $f(x)$ as far as the term in x^2.

Extend your proof to include the term in x^3.

3.5   Integrals as functions

You know that $\displaystyle\int_a^b f(x)\,dx$ can be calculated as $I(b) - I(a)$, where $I(x)$ is a function such that $I'(x) = f(x)$. Changing the notation, you can say that $\displaystyle\int_a^x f(t)\,dt$ can be calculated as $I(x) - I(a)$.

Notice that the variable in the integrand has been changed from x to t. When you write a definite integral it doesn't matter what letter you use in the integrand. Thus $\int_1^4 x^2 \, dx$ has the value 21, and so does $\int_1^4 u^2 \, du$ and $\int_1^4 t^2 \, dt$. But it confuses the issue to use the same letter in the integrand as you have used for one of the limits of integration. The variable t here is another example of a dummy variable.

Now $\int_a^x f(t) \, dx$ is itself a function of x; for each value of x the integral has a unique value. If it is denoted by $F(x)$, then

$$F(x) = \int_a^x f(t) \, dt = I(x) - I(a), \text{ so that } F'(x) = I'(x) = f(x).$$

This can be summarised in the important result:

$$\frac{d}{dx} \int_a^x f(t) \, dt = f(x).$$

From this you can derive a theorem which is useful in obtaining expansions in some cases when Maclaurin's result is difficult to apply directly.

Theorem If two functions $f(x)$ and $g(x)$ agree to the nth degree at $x = 0$, then
$$F(x) = \int_0^x f(t) \, dt \quad \text{and} \quad G(x) = \int_0^x g(t) \, dt \quad \text{agree to the } (n+1)\text{th degree.}$$

Proof Notice first that $F(0) = G(0) = 0$. Also $F'(x) = f(x)$ and $G'(x) = g(x)$, so that $F^{(r+1)}(x) = f^{(r)}(x)$ and $G^{(r+1)}(x) = g^{(r)}(x)$. Therefore, since $f(0) = g(0)$ and $f^{(r)}(0) = g^{(r)}(0)$ for $1 \leqslant r \leqslant n$, it follows that $F^{(r+1)}(0) = G^{(r+1)}(0)$ for $0 \leqslant r \leqslant n$. That is, $F^{(r)}(0) = G^{(r)}(0)$ for $1 \leqslant r \leqslant n+1$.

Suppose now that $g(x)$ is the Maclaurin polynomial of $f(x)$ of degree n. This theorem then shows that the Maclaurin polynomial of $\int_a^x f(t) \, dt$ of degree $n+1$ can be found by integrating the Maclaurin polynomial g from 0 to x.

Also, since this holds for any n, you can find the expansion of $\int_a^x f(t) \, dt$ (continued indefinitely) by integrating the terms of the Maclaurin expansion of $f(x)$.

Example 3.5.1
Find the expansion of $\tan^{-1} x$.

Since $\int_0^x \frac{1}{1+t^2} \, dt = \left[\tan^{-1} t\right]_0^x = \tan^{-1} x - \tan^{-1} 0 = \tan^{-1} x$, you can find the expansion of $\tan^{-1} x$ by integrating the terms of the binomial expansion for $(1+t^2)^{-1} = 1 - t^2 + t^4 - t^6 + \ldots$ from 0 to x.

That is,

$$\tan^{-1} x = x - \tfrac{1}{3}x^3 + \tfrac{1}{5}x^5 - \tfrac{1}{7}x^7 + \ldots$$
$$= \sum_{r=0}^{\infty} (-1)^r \frac{1}{2r+1} x^{2r+1}.$$

It can be proved that when you integrate an expansion in this way, the interval of validity of the result is at least as wide as that of the original expansion. In Example 3.5.1, the binomial expansion is valid for $-1 < x < 1$, but the $\tan^{-1} x$ expansion is also valid when $x = \pm 1$. The value $x = 1$ produces the delightful (but not very useful) result

$$\tfrac{1}{4}\pi = 1 - \tfrac{1}{3} + \tfrac{1}{5} - \tfrac{1}{7} + \dots .$$

Example 3.5.2

Find the value of $\dfrac{1}{\sqrt{2\pi}} \displaystyle\int_{-1}^{1} e^{-\frac{1}{2}t^2}\, dt$.

> This integral is important in probability. It gives the probability that a normal random variable takes a value within one standard deviation of the mean.

Integrating the expansion $e^{-\frac{1}{2}t^2} = 1 - \dfrac{1}{1!}\dfrac{t^2}{2} + \dfrac{1}{2!}\left(\dfrac{t^2}{2}\right)^2 - \dots$ gives

$$\int_0^x e^{-\frac{1}{2}t^2}\, dt \approx \left[t - \frac{1}{2}\frac{t^3}{3} + \frac{1}{8}\frac{t^5}{5} - \frac{1}{48}\frac{t^7}{7} + \frac{1}{384}\frac{t^9}{9} - \frac{1}{3840}\frac{t^{11}}{11} + \dots \right]_0^x,$$

which, evaluating at $x = 1$,

$$= 1 - \tfrac{1}{6} + \tfrac{1}{40} - \tfrac{1}{336} + \tfrac{1}{3456} - \tfrac{1}{42\,240} + \dots = 0.855\,62\dots .$$

Since $e^{-\frac{1}{2}t^2}$ is an even function, the integral from -1 to 1 is double the integral from 0 to 1. The probability required is therefore

$$\frac{1}{\sqrt{2\pi}} \times 2 \times 0.855\,62\dots \approx 0.683, \text{ correct to 3 decimal places.}$$

Exercise 3D

1 Use the property $\sin^{-1} x = \displaystyle\int_0^x \frac{1}{\sqrt{1-t^2}}\, dt$ to find the Maclaurin expansion of $\sin^{-1} x$. Hence find the expansion of $\cos^{-1} x$. By taking $x = \tfrac{1}{2}$, use your Maclaurin expansion to find the value of π, correct to 4 decimal places.

2 In Exercise 1C Question 8 you showed that $4\tan^{-1}\tfrac{1}{5} - \tfrac{1}{4}\pi = \tan^{-1}\tfrac{1}{239}$. Use this, with the Maclaurin expansion of $\tan^{-1} x$, to find a 5 decimal place approximation to π.

3 A function called the *sine integral* is defined by $\mathrm{Si}\,(x) = \displaystyle\int_0^x \frac{\sin u}{u}\, du$. Find the Maclaurin expansion of $\mathrm{Si}\,(x)$, and use this to obtain the graph of $y = \mathrm{Si}\,(x)$ for $x > 0$.

4 Find the Maclaurin expansion of $\displaystyle\int_0^x \frac{e^t - 1}{t}\, dt$. Hence evaluate $\displaystyle\int_0^{\frac{1}{2}} \frac{e^t - 1}{t}\, dt$, correct to 3 decimal places.

5 Use the sum of the geometric series $1 - u + u^2 - \dots + (-1)^{n-1}u^{n-1}$ to find an expression for the error in using the Maclaurin polynomial of degree n as an approximation to $\ln(1 + x)$.

6 The following construction is suggested to trisect a given angle θ. Make a triangle ABC with angle BAC equal to θ and angle ABC a right angle. Divide the side BC into three equal parts at X and Y, so that $BX = XY = YC$. Then angle XAY is approximately $\frac{1}{3}\theta$. Prove that angle XAY is exactly $\tan^{-1}\left(\frac{2}{3}\tan\theta\right) - \tan^{-1}\left(\frac{1}{3}\tan\theta\right)$. Find the Maclaurin polynomial of degree 3 for this function, and use this to estimate the greatest value of θ for which the construction is accurate to within 5%.

7 Prove that the difference between $\tan^{-1}x$ and the first n non-zero terms of its Maclaurin expansion has absolute value $\displaystyle\int_{0}^{|x|} \frac{t^{2n}}{1+t^2}\, dt$, and show that this is less than $\dfrac{|x|^{2n+1}}{2n+1}$.
Use this to estimate the largest number of terms of the $\tan^{-1}x$ expansion that you might need to use to compute $\tan^{-1}0.2$ with an error of less than 10^{-10}.

Miscellaneous exercise 3

1 Find the first three non-zero terms of the Maclaurin series for $\dfrac{e^{2x}}{(1-2x)^2}$.

2 Find the first four derivatives of $\ln(1+\cos x)$ with respect to x. Hence write down its Maclaurin expansion as far as the term in x^4.

Check your answer by writing $1 + \cos x$ as $2\cos^2\frac{1}{2}x$ and using the result of Example 3.4.4 (a).

3 Express $\cos^2 x$ in terms of $\cos 2x$. Hence write down the Maclaurin series for $\cos^2 x$ as far as the term in x^6.

Check your answer by squaring the expansion for $\cos x$.

4 Obtain the first three terms in the Maclaurin series for $\ln(3+x)$.   (OCR)

5 Show that, if x is small, $e^{-\frac{1}{2}x} - \dfrac{1}{\sqrt{1+x}} \approx ax^2$ where the value of the constant a should be stated.   (OCR)

6 It is given that the series expansions of $(1+x)^p$ and $1 + \ln(1+qx)$ are identical, up to and including the terms in x^2. Find the values of the non-zero constants p and q.   (OCR)

7 The function $f(x)$, defined by $f(x) = x(1+4x)^p + q\ln(1+x)$, where p and q are constants, is expanded in ascending powers of x. It is given that the coefficient of x^2 in the expansion of $f(x)$ is zero. Show that $q = 8p$.

It is also given that the coefficient of x in the expansion of $f(x)$ is 13. Find the numerical value of the coefficient of x^3 in the expansion of $f(x)$.   (OCR)

8 Find the values of the constants A, B and C such that the series expansion of $A\cos x + Be^x + C$ is the same as the series expansion of $4\sqrt{1+x}$, given that x is so small that terms in x^3 and higher powers of x may be neglected.   (OCR)

9 Find the Maclaurin series of $e^{\sin x}$ up to and including the term in x^2. Show that, when $x = 0.5$, the relative error in the approximation obtained is 0.6%, correct to 1 significant figure.   (OCR)

10 Use the Maclaurin series for $\ln(1 + x)$ and $\ln(1 - x)$ to show that, for small values of x,
$$\ln\left(\frac{1+x}{1-x}\right) \approx 2\left(x + \tfrac{1}{3}x^3\right).$$

It is desired to use the approximation to find an estimate for $\ln 1.25$. Find the appropriate value for x, and hence find the estimate for $\ln 1.25$ giving your answer to 6 decimal places.

(OCR)

11 *PMQ* is a minor arc of a circle with centre O and radius r. M is the mid-point of the arc PQ and the angle MOQ is θ radians. The lengths of the chords MQ and PQ are denoted by a and b respectively. In the series for $\sin x$, put x equal to θ and $\tfrac{1}{2}\theta$ in turn, to find approximations for a and b in terms of r and θ, up to the terms in θ^5. Deduce the series expansion of $\tfrac{1}{3}(8a - b)$ up to the term in θ^5. Hence show that $\tfrac{1}{3}(8a - b)$ is approximately equal to the length of the arc *PMQ*, and give an estimate of the error in terms of r and θ.

Calculate the percentage error when $\theta = \tfrac{1}{6}\pi$, giving your answer to two significant figures.

Write down a formula, in terms of a, b and r, which gives an approximation to the area of the sector *POQ*.

(OCR)

12 By expanding $(1 - 4x^2)^{-\frac{1}{2}}$ and integrating term by term, find the series expansion for $\sin^{-1} 2x$ when $|x| < \tfrac{1}{2}$ as far as the term in x^7.

(MEI)

13 Show that, if q and r are natural numbers, then $(q + r)! \geqslant q! \times (q + 1)^r$. Show further that the symbol $\geqslant$ can be replaced by $>$ if $r > 1$. Hence show that

$$\frac{q!}{(q + 1)!} + \frac{q!}{(q + 2)!} + \frac{q!}{(q + 3)!} + \ldots < \frac{1}{q}.$$

Suppose that e is a rational number $\dfrac{p}{q}$, where p and q are natural numbers. Deduce that $q!\,$e is a natural number. Also, by using the Maclaurin expansion of e^x, deduce that $q!\,$e is not a natural number. What conclusion can you draw from this contradiction?

4 Hyperbolic functions

Hyperbolic functions are a link between the exponential function e^x and trigonometric functions. When you have completed the chapter, you should

- know how to express a function as the sum of an even and an odd function
- know the definitions of $\cosh x$, $\sinh x$ and other hyperbolic functions
- know and be able to apply properties of hyperbolic functions and their inverses analogous to those of trigonometric functions
- understand the relation of hyperbolic functions to the rectangular hyperbola.

4.1 Even and odd functions

In C1 Section 3.3 you met the idea of even and odd functions. An **even function** is one such that, for all real numbers x in its domain, $f(x) = f(-x)$. An **odd function** has $f(x) = -f(-x)$. Notice that, for these definitions to be valid, the domain D of f has to be symmetrical about 0: if $x \in D$, then $-x \in D$. A real domain with this property will be called a **symmetrical domain**.

Not all functions are even or odd. For example, $f(x) = x(x + 1)$ is not. But you can write $f(x)$ as $x^2 + x$, which is the sum of the even function $g(x) = x^2$ and the odd function $h(x) = x$. In fact, every function with a symmetrical domain can be split up in this way.

Theorem Any function f with a symmetrical domain can be written as the sum of an even function g and an odd function h.

> **Proof** The proof is in two parts. First, suppose that the theorem is true and find the forms that g and h must take; then show that these functions g and h do have the required properties.
>
> If $f(x)$ is written as $g(x) + h(x)$, where g is even and h is odd, then $f(-x)$ must be equal to $g(-x) + h(-x)$, where $g(-x) = g(x)$ and $h(-x) = -h(x)$. So $g(x)$ and $h(x)$ must be chosen to satisfy the two equations
>
> $$g(x) + h(x) = f(x) \quad \text{and} \quad g(x) - h(x) = f(-x).$$
>
> Adding and subtracting these equations gives
>
> $$2g(x) = f(x) + f(-x) \quad \text{and} \quad 2h(x) = f(x) - f(-x).$$
>
> These equations define the functions g and h in terms of the function f.
>
> To complete the proof, you have to show that
>
> $$g(x) = \tfrac{1}{2}(f(x) + f(-x)) \quad \text{and} \quad h(x) = \tfrac{1}{2}(f(x) - f(-x)),$$
>
> whose sum is $f(x)$, are respectively even and odd.

That is,

$$g(-x) = \tfrac{1}{2}(f(-x) + f(x)) = \tfrac{1}{2}(f(x) + f(-x)) = g(x),$$

and $\qquad h(-x) = \tfrac{1}{2}(f(-x) - f(x)) = -\tfrac{1}{2}(f(x) - f(-x)) = -h(x).$

Example 4.1.1

Express $f(x) = \dfrac{1}{1+x}$ as the sum of an even and an odd function.

Since the natural domain of f does not include -1, and the domain of f has to be symmetrical, it must exclude both -1 and 1.

The theorem shows that the even function is

$$g(x) = \tfrac{1}{2}\left(\frac{1}{1+x} + \frac{1}{1-x}\right) = \tfrac{1}{2}\left(\frac{1-x+1+x}{(1+x)(1-x)}\right) = \frac{1}{1-x^2},$$

and the odd function is

$$h(x) = \tfrac{1}{2}\left(\frac{1}{1+x} - \frac{1}{1-x}\right) = \tfrac{1}{2}\left(\frac{1-x-(1+x)}{(1+x)(1-x)}\right) = \frac{-x}{1-x^2}.$$

You can see that, although 1 is not excluded from the natural domain of f, the natural domains of g and h both exclude 1 and -1.

It is interesting to illustrate this result by displaying the graphs of $f(x)$, $g(x)$ and $h(x)$ together using the same axes.

Much the most important application of the theorem is when f is taken to be the exponential function e^x. The functions g and h are then called **hyperbolic functions**, and are denoted by the symbols cosh and sinh (pronounced 'shine'). Thus:

$$\cosh x = \tfrac{1}{2}\left(e^x + e^{-x}\right) \quad \text{and} \quad \sinh x = \tfrac{1}{2}\left(e^x - e^{-x}\right).$$

The reasons for using a notation formed by adding 'h' (for 'hyperbolic') to the symbols cos and sin will become clear in Section 4.2. The connection with the hyperbola is explained in Section 4.9.

You can almost certainly get values of $\cosh x$ and $\sinh x$ directly with your calculator, and you should find out how to do this. Since e^x has domain $\mathbb{R}$, $\cosh x$ and $\sinh x$ are defined for all real x. Their graphs are drawn in Figs. 4.1 and 4.2.

Other points which you should notice are:

- When x is a large positive number, e^{-x} is very small, so that $\cosh x \approx \tfrac{1}{2}e^x$ and $\sinh x \approx \tfrac{1}{2}e^x$. When x is negative and $|x|$ is large, $\cosh x \approx \tfrac{1}{2}e^{-x}$ and $\sinh x \approx -\tfrac{1}{2}e^{-x}$. These approximations are illustrated by the graphs shown dotted in Fig. 4.1 and Fig. 4.2.

- The range of the sinh function is $\mathbb{R}$. However, the graph of $\cosh x$ has a minimum of 1 when $x = 0$, so that the range of cosh is $y \in \mathbb{R}$, $y \geqslant 1$.

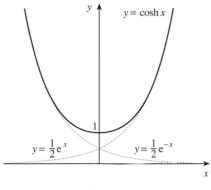

Fig. 4.1

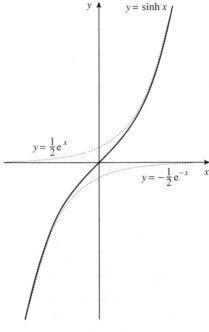

Fig. 4.2

4.2 Hyperbolic and trigonometric functions

It is not at all obvious from the graphs that there is any similarity between $\cosh x$ and $\cos x$, $\sinh x$ and $\sin x$. One of the most important properties of the trigonometric functions is their periodicity, and Figs. 4.1 and 4.2 are certainly not periodic graphs.

However, when you start to investigate the algebraic properties of cosh and sinh, and to differentiate and integrate them, there is a remarkable resemblance to the properties of cos and sin. This makes them easy to remember, though you have to be careful to notice where the signs are different.

In the proof of the theorem in Section 4.1 the functions g and h were found from the equations

$$g(x) + h(x) = f(x) \quad \text{and} \quad g(x) - h(x) = f(-x).$$

With $f(x) = e^x$, $g(x) = \cosh x$ and $h(x) = \sinh x$ these equations take the form

$$\cosh x + \sinh x = e^x \quad \text{and} \quad \cosh x - \sinh x = e^{-x}.$$

Using these equations (or, more properly, identities) is often the simplest way of obtaining properties of the hyperbolic functions.

The basic identity

Since $\cosh x + \sinh x \equiv e^x$ and $\cosh x - \sinh x \equiv e^{-x}$,

$$(\cosh x + \sinh x)(\cosh x - \sinh x) \equiv e^x e^{-x} = e^0 = 1.$$

This gives the basic identity for hyperbolic functions:

$$\cosh^2 x - \sinh^2 x \equiv 1.$$

This will remind you of the Pythagoras identity $\cos^2 x + \sin^2 x \equiv 1$. But note that, while $\cos^2 x$ is replaced by $\cosh^2 x$, $\sin^2 x$ is replaced by $-\sinh^2 x$.

You will often want to use this identity in one of the alternative forms

$$\cosh^2 x \equiv 1 + \sinh^2 x \quad \text{or} \quad \sinh^2 x \equiv \cosh^2 x - 1.$$

Addition formulae

In C3 Chapter 6 several important identities were obtained from the addition formula

$$\cos(A + B) = \cos A \cos B - \sin A \sin B.$$

This was proved by a geometrical argument, combining the cosine rule with the coordinate formula for distance.

There is a similar formula for $\cosh (A + B)$, but A and B no longer stand for angles, so it can't be proved geometrically. Instead, you use the definition of cosh and sinh in terms of exponentials.

Expressions for $\cosh (A + B)$ and $\sinh (A + B)$ can be obtained from

$$e^{A+B} \equiv e^A e^B \equiv (\cosh A + \sinh A)(\cosh B + \sinh B)$$

and $e^{-(A+B)} \equiv e^{-A} e^{-B} \equiv (\cosh A - \sinh A)(\cosh B - \sinh B).$

So $\cosh(A + B) \equiv \frac{1}{2}\left(e^{A+B} + e^{-(A+B)}\right)$

$$\equiv \frac{1}{2}\left(\begin{array}{l}(\cosh A + \sinh A)(\cosh B + \sinh B) \\ \qquad + (\cosh A - \sinh A)(\cosh B - \sinh B)\end{array}\right)$$

$$\equiv \frac{1}{2}\left(\begin{array}{l}\cosh A \cosh B + \sinh A \cosh B + \cosh A \sinh B + \sinh A \sinh B \\ + \cosh A \cosh B - \sinh A \cosh B - \cosh A \sinh B + \sinh A \sinh B\end{array}\right)$$

$$\equiv \frac{1}{2}(2\cosh A \cosh B + 2\sinh A \sinh B),$$

and $\sinh(A + B) \equiv \frac{1}{2}\left(e^{A+B} - e^{-(A+B)}\right)$

$$\equiv \frac{1}{2}\left(\begin{array}{l}(\cosh A + \sinh A)(\cosh B + \sinh B) \\ \qquad - (\cosh A - \sinh A)(\cosh B - \sinh B)\end{array}\right)$$

$$\equiv \frac{1}{2}\left(\begin{array}{l}\cosh A \cosh B + \sinh A \cosh B + \cosh A \sinh B + \sinh A \sinh B \\ - \cosh A \cosh B + \sinh A \cosh B + \cosh A \sinh B - \sinh A \sinh B\end{array}\right)$$

$$\equiv \frac{1}{2}(2\sinh A \cosh B + 2\cosh A \sinh B),$$

giving the addition formulae:

$$\cosh(A + B) \equiv \cosh A \cosh B + \sinh A \sinh B,$$
$$\sinh(A + B) \equiv \sinh A \cosh B + \cosh A \sinh B.$$

Notice that the formula for $\sinh(A+B)$ carries over directly from that for $\sin(A+B)$, but that in comparing $\cosh(A+B)$ with $\cos(A+B)$ there is a change of sign, $-\sin A\sin B$ being replaced by $+\sinh A\sinh B$.

The easiest way to find formulae for $\cosh(A-B)$ and $\sinh(A-B)$ is to write $A-B$ as $A+(-B)$ and use the even and odd properties $\cosh(-B)=\cosh B$ and $\sinh(-B)=-\sinh B$. This gives:

$$\cosh(A-B)\equiv\cosh A\cosh B-\sinh A\sinh B,$$
$$\sinh(A-B)\equiv\sinh A\cosh B-\cosh A\sinh B.$$

From the addition formula you can obtain other formulae corresponding to the double angle formulae in trigonometry.

If you put $B=A$ in the formulae for $\cosh(A+B)$ and $\sinh(A+B)$ you get

$$\cosh(A+A)\equiv\cosh A\cosh A+\sinh A\sinh A\equiv\cosh^2 A+\sinh^2 A,$$

and $\sinh(A+A)\equiv\sinh A\cosh A+\cosh A\sinh A\equiv 2\sinh A\cosh A.$

You can write the expression $\cosh^2 A+\sinh^2 A$ in terms of $\cosh A$ or $\sinh A$ alone, using the basic identity in one of the alternative forms given above.

In this way you get hyperbolic analogues of the double angle formulae:

$$\cosh 2A\equiv\cosh^2 A+\sinh^2 A\equiv 1+2\sinh^2 A\equiv 2\cosh^2 A-1,$$
$$\sinh 2A\equiv 2\sinh A\cosh A.$$

You often, especially in integration, need these in their backwards forms:

$$2\cosh^2 A\equiv 1+\cosh 2A,\qquad 2\sinh^2 A\equiv\cosh 2A-1,$$
$$2\sinh A\cosh A\equiv\sinh 2A.$$

Example 4.2.1
Write as simply as possible

(a) $\sinh 1-\cosh 1,$

(b) $\sqrt{\cosh^2 x-1},$

(c) $\sinh(A+B)-\sinh(A-B),$

(d) $\sinh x\cosh^3 x+\sinh^3 x\cosh x.$

(a) Since $\cosh x-\sinh x\equiv e^{-x}$,

$$\sinh 1-\cosh 1=-(\cosh 1-\sinh 1)=-e^{-1}=-\frac{1}{e}.$$

(b) The identity $\cosh^2 x-\sinh^2 x\equiv 1$ can be rearranged as $\cosh^2 x-1\equiv\sinh^2 x$, so

$$\sqrt{\cosh^2 x-1}\equiv\sqrt{\sinh^2 x}.$$

But beware! Since $\sinh x \geqslant 0$ when $x \geqslant 0$ but $\sinh x < 0$ when $x < 0$, $\sqrt{\sinh^2 x}$ is equal to $\sinh x$ when $x \geqslant 0$ but to $-\sinh x$, which is $\sinh(-x)$, when $x < 0$. So

$$\sqrt{\cosh^2 x - 1} = \sinh|x|.$$

(c) Using the expansions for $\sinh(A + B)$ and $\sinh(A - B)$

$$\sinh(A + B) - \sinh(A - B)$$
$$\equiv (\sinh A \cosh B + \cosh A \sinh B) - (\sinh A \cosh B - \cosh A \sinh B)$$
$$\equiv 2 \cosh A \sinh B.$$

(d) Begin by taking out the common factor $\sinh x \cosh x$, which is $\frac{1}{2} \sinh 2x$.

$$\sinh x \cosh^3 x + \sinh^3 x \cosh x \equiv \sinh x \cosh x (\cosh^2 x + \sinh^2 x)$$
$$\equiv \tfrac{1}{2} \sinh 2x \times \cosh 2x.$$

Now, using the identity $\sinh 2A \equiv 2 \sinh A \cosh A$ with $2x$ in place of A,

$$2 \sinh 2x \cosh 2x \equiv \sinh 4x.$$

So $\sinh x \cosh^3 x + \sinh^3 x \cosh x \equiv \frac{1}{4} \sinh 4x.$

Exercise 4A

1 Use the definitions of $\sinh x$ and $\cosh x$ to evaluate the following. Check your answers by using the hyperbolic function keys on your calculator.

(a) $\cosh 2$ (b) $\sinh \pi$ (c) $\cosh(-e)$ (d) $\sinh(\ln 3)$

(e) $\sinh(-\sqrt{2})$ (f) $\cosh 1 + \sinh 1$ (g) $\cosh 2 - \sinh 2$ (h) $\cosh(-2\ln 2)$

2 Write the following in as simple a form as possible.

(a) $\sqrt{1 + \sinh^2 A}$ (b) $\sqrt{\cosh^2 2 - 1}$

(c) $\sinh^2 1 + \cosh^2 1$ (d) $\sinh^2 1 - \cosh^2 1$

(e) $\cosh(A + B) + \cosh(A - B)$ (f) $\cosh 2x + \sinh 2x$

(g) $\sinh 1 \cosh 2 + \cosh 1 \sinh 2$ (h) $\sinh x \sinh y - \cosh x \cosh y$

3 Find and prove the property of hyperbolic functions corresponding to each of the following properties of trigonometric functions.

(a) $2 \sin A \cos B \equiv \sin(A + B) + \sin(A - B)$ (b) $2 \sin x \sin y \equiv \cos(x - y) - \cos(x + y)$

(c) $\sin 3x \equiv 3 \sin x - 4 \sin^3 x$ (d) $8 \sin^4 u \equiv 3 - 4 \cos 2u + \cos 4u$

4 Find the roots of the following equations in terms of u.

(a) $x^2 - 2x \cosh u + 1 = 0$ (b) $x^2 + 2x \sinh u - 1 = 0$

(c) $x^2 - 2x \cosh u + \sinh^2 u = 0$ (d) $x^2 \sinh 2u + 2x - \sinh 2u = 0$

5 Prove that $\cosh x - 1 \equiv \frac{1}{2}\left(e^{\frac{1}{2}x} - e^{-\frac{1}{2}x}\right)^2$. Deduce that $\cosh x \geqslant 1$ for all real x.

6 Express the following in terms of hyperbolic functions as simply as possible.

(a) $\dfrac{2}{e^x}$ (b) $\sqrt{(e^x + e^{-x})^2 - 4}$ (c) $\dfrac{e^x}{1 + e^{2x}}$ (d) $\dfrac{e^x + 1}{e^x - 1}$

7* Express each of the following functions as the sum of an even function and an odd function. State the domain over which the relation holds.

(a) $\dfrac{1}{x(2 - x)}$ (b) $\dfrac{1}{(1 + x)^2}$ (c) $\dfrac{1}{1 + e^x}$ (d) $\dfrac{1}{2 + \sinh x}$

(e) $\dfrac{\cos x}{1 + \sin x}$ (f) $\dfrac{x + 3}{x^2 + x - 2}$ (g) $\dfrac{x - 3}{x^2 - x + 2}$ (h) $\dfrac{e^x}{1 + e^{2x}}$

4.3 Differentiation and integration

The derivatives of $\cosh x$ and $\sinh x$ can be found directly from the definitions. Since

$$\frac{d}{dx}e^x = e^x \quad \text{and} \quad \frac{d}{dx}e^{-x} = -e^{-x},$$

$$\frac{d}{dx}\cosh x = \frac{d}{dx}\left(\tfrac{1}{2}(e^x + e^{-x})\right) = \tfrac{1}{2}(e^x - e^{-x}),$$

and $\quad \dfrac{d}{dx}\sinh x = \dfrac{d}{dx}\left(\tfrac{1}{2}(e^x - e^{-x})\right) = \tfrac{1}{2}(e^x + e^{-x}).$

That is:

$$\frac{d}{dx}\cosh x = \sinh x, \quad \frac{d}{dx}\sinh x = \cosh x.$$

These derivatives are even easier to remember than their trigonometric counterparts, since there are no minus signs to worry about.

As with the trigonometric functions, you can immediately deduce the corresponding integrals:

$$\int \sinh x\, dx = \cosh x + k, \quad \int \cosh x\, dx = \sinh x + k.$$

Example 4.3.1

If $x = a\sinh 3t + b\cosh 3t$, where a and b are constants, show that $\dfrac{d^2x}{dt^2} = 9x$.

Differentiating,

$$\frac{dx}{dt} = a \times 3\cosh 3t + b \times 3\sinh 3t$$
$$= 3a\cosh 3t + 3b\sinh 3t.$$

So $\quad \dfrac{d^2x}{dt^2} = 3a \times 3\sinh 3t + 3b \times 3\cosh 3t$
$$= 9(a\sinh 3t + b\cosh 3t) = 9x.$$

Example 4.3.2
Show that the area under the graph of $y = \sinh 2x$ from $x = 0$ to $x = a$ is $\sinh^2 a$.

The area is

$$\int_0^a \sinh 2x \, dx = \left[\tfrac{1}{2}\cosh 2x\right]_0^a$$
$$= \tfrac{1}{2}(\cosh 2a - 1)$$
$$= \tfrac{1}{2}((1 + 2\sinh^2 a) - 1)$$
$$= \tfrac{1}{2}(2\sinh^2 a) = \sinh^2 a.$$

4.4 Maclaurin expansions

The definitions of $\cosh x$ and $\sinh x$, combined with the Maclaurin expansions (see Section 3.3)

$$e^x = 1 + \frac{x}{1!} + \frac{x^2}{2!} + \frac{x^3}{3!} + \frac{x^4}{4!} + \frac{x^5}{5!} + \frac{x^6}{6!} + \frac{x^7}{7!} + \cdots$$

and

$$e^{-x} = 1 - \frac{x}{1!} + \frac{x^2}{2!} - \frac{x^3}{3!} + \frac{x^4}{4!} - \frac{x^5}{5!} + \frac{x^6}{6!} - \frac{x^7}{7!} + \cdots,$$

give $\cosh x = \tfrac{1}{2}(e^x + e^{-x})$

$$= 1 + \frac{x^2}{2!} + \frac{x^4}{4!} + \frac{x^6}{6!} + \cdots$$

and $\sinh x = \tfrac{1}{2}(e^x - e^{-x})$

$$= \frac{x}{1!} + \frac{x^3}{3!} + \frac{x^5}{5!} + \frac{x^7}{7!} + \cdots.$$

The expansions differ from those given in Section 3.3 for $\cos x$ and $\sin x$ only in having all the signs positive.

Exercise 4B

1 Differentiate these functions with respect to x.

(a) $\cosh 4x$ (b) $\sinh 5x$ (c) $\sinh x \cosh x$ (d) $\sinh^2 x$

(e) $\sqrt{\cosh x}$ (f) $\ln(\sinh x + \cosh x)$ (g) $\dfrac{1}{\sinh x + 2\cosh x}$ (h) $\dfrac{1 + \sinh x}{x + \cosh x}$

(i) $\dfrac{\cosh x + \sin x}{\cos x + \sinh x}$ (j) $e^x \cosh x$

2 Find and prove the property of hyperbolic functions corresponding to each of the following properties of trigonometric functions.

(a) $\dfrac{d}{dx}\cos^2 x = -\sin 2x$ (b) $\dfrac{d}{dt}\sin^3 t = 3\sin^2 t \cos t$

(c) $\displaystyle\int \cos 2x \, dx = \tfrac{1}{2}\sin 2x + k$ (d) $\displaystyle\int \sin^2 u \, du = \tfrac{1}{2}(u - \sin u \cos u) + k$

3 Find the following indefinite integrals.

(a) $\displaystyle\int \sinh 3x \, dx$ (b) $\displaystyle\int \sinh x \cosh x \, dx$ (c) $\displaystyle\int \cosh^2 x \, dx$

(d) $\displaystyle\int x \sinh x \, dx$ (e) $\displaystyle\int x^2 \cosh 2x \, dx$ (f) $\displaystyle\int e^x \cosh x \, dx$

4 Evaluate the following definite integrals, correct to 3 significant figures.

(a) $\displaystyle\int_0^1 \cosh 4x \, dx$ (b) $\displaystyle\int_0^{\ln 2} \sinh 4x \, dx$ (c) $\displaystyle\int_{-\ln 3}^{\ln 5} \cosh 2x \, dx$

(d) $\displaystyle\int_0^2 \sinh^2 x \, dx$ (e) $\displaystyle\int_1^2 x \cosh 2x \, dx$ (f) $\displaystyle\int_0^1 \sinh^2 x \cosh x \, dx$

5 Show that the graph of $y = \cosh x$ intersects the line $y = 1.25$ at the points where $x = \pm \ln 2$. Find the area of the region bounded by parts of the line and the curve.

6 Find the volume of the solid of revolution formed by rotating the graph of $y = \cosh x$ over the interval $-2 \leqslant x \leqslant 2$ about the x-axis.

7 Find $\displaystyle\int \cosh 3x \sinh 2x \, dx$,

(a) by expressing the integrand as $\frac{1}{2}(\sinh(3x + 2x) - \sinh(3x - 2x))$,

(b) by expressing the integrand in exponential form.

Show that your two expressions for the integral are equivalent.

8 Use the Maclaurin series to evaluate

(a) cosh 1, correct to 5 decimal places,

(b) sinh 5, correct to the nearest whole number.

9 Find the Maclaurin expansions of each of the following functions, giving the terms as far as x^6 and an expression for the general term.

(a) $\cosh 2x$ (b) $\sinh^2 x$ (c) $\cosh^3 x$ (d) $\sinh^4 x$

4.5 Other hyperbolic functions

The analogy with trigonometric functions can be carried further by defining hyperbolic functions corresponding to tan, sec, cot and cosec. In practice the important ones are

$$\operatorname{sech} x = \frac{1}{\cosh x} \quad \text{and} \quad \tanh x = \frac{\sinh x}{\cosh x} \quad \text{(pronounced 'tanch' or 'than').}$$

Note that $\operatorname{sech}(-x) = \dfrac{1}{\cosh(-x)} = \dfrac{1}{\cosh x} = \operatorname{sech} x,$

and $\tanh(-x) = \dfrac{\sinh(-x)}{\cosh(-x)} = \dfrac{-\sinh x}{\cosh x} = -\tanh x,$

so that sech is an even function and tanh is an odd function.

Since $\cosh x \geqslant 1$ for all x, values of $\operatorname{sech} x$ always have $0 < \operatorname{sech} x \leqslant 1$, and $\operatorname{sech} x$ tends to 0 as $x \to \pm\infty$. The graph is drawn in Fig. 4.3.

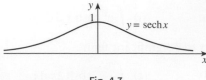

Fig. 4.3

You can express $\tanh x$ in terms of exponentials by noting that $\cosh x$ and $\sinh x$ can be written as

$$\tfrac{1}{2}e^{-x}(e^{2x} \pm 1), \text{ or } \tfrac{1}{2}e^{x}(1 \pm e^{-2x}), \text{ so } \tanh x = \frac{e^{2x} - 1}{e^{2x} + 1} = \frac{1 - e^{-2x}}{1 + e^{-2x}}.$$

For $x > 0$, $0 < e^{-2x} < 1$, so that $0 < \tanh x < 1$. Also, since e^{-2x} tends to 0 as $x \to \infty$, $\tanh x$ tends to $\dfrac{1 - 0}{1 + 0} = 1$. Corresponding properties for $x < 0$ follow by noting that $\tanh$ is an odd function. The graph is drawn in Fig. 4.4.

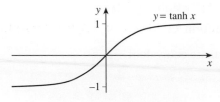

Fig. 4.4

The basic identity $\cosh^2 x - \sinh^2 x \equiv 1$ can be adapted by dividing by $\cosh^2 x$, to give

$$1 - \frac{\sinh^2 x}{\cosh^2 x} \equiv \frac{1}{\cosh^2 x},$$

which is:

$$1 - \tanh^2 x \equiv \operatorname{sech}^2 x.$$

The derivatives of $\tanh x$ and $\operatorname{sech} x$ can be found from the definitions by using the quotient rule and the chain rule respectively.

$$\begin{aligned}
\frac{d}{dx} \tanh x &= \frac{d}{dx} \frac{\sinh x}{\cosh x} \\
&= \frac{\cosh x \times \cosh x - \sinh x \times \sinh x}{\cosh^2 x} \\
&= \frac{\cosh^2 x - \sinh^2 x}{\cosh^2 x} \\
&= \frac{1}{\cosh^2 x} = \operatorname{sech}^2 x \quad (\text{since } \cosh^2 x - \sinh^2 x \equiv 1).
\end{aligned}$$

$$\frac{d}{dx}\operatorname{sech} x = \frac{d}{dx}\frac{1}{\cosh x}$$

$$= -\frac{1}{\cosh^2 x} \times \sinh x$$

$$= -\frac{1}{\cosh x} \times \frac{\sinh x}{\cosh x}$$

$$= -\operatorname{sech} x \tanh x.$$

These are very similar to the corresponding rules for trigonometric functions except for the minus sign in the derivative of $\operatorname{sech} x$. You would expect this from the graph of $y = \operatorname{sech} x$ in Fig. 4.3, whose gradient is positive when $x < 0$ and negative when $x > 0$.

$$\frac{d}{dx}\tanh x = \operatorname{sech}^2 x, \quad \frac{d}{dx}\operatorname{sech} x = -\operatorname{sech} x \tanh x.$$

Example 4.5.1

For $x > 0$, find the maximum value of $f(x) = \dfrac{\sinh x}{\cosh^2 x}$.

You could find $f'(x)$ by using the quotient rule for differentiation, but it is a little simpler to write

$$f(x) = \frac{\sinh x}{\cosh x} \times \frac{1}{\cosh x} = \tanh x \times \operatorname{sech} x$$

and to use the product rule. Then

$$f'(x) = \operatorname{sech}^2 x \times \operatorname{sech} x + \tanh x \times (-\operatorname{sech} x \tanh x)$$

which can be written as

$$f'(x) = \operatorname{sech} x((1 - \tanh^2 x) - \tanh^2 x)$$

$$= \operatorname{sech} x(1 - 2\tanh^2 x).$$

Since $\operatorname{sech} x$ is never zero (see Fig. 4.3), $f'(x) = 0$ when $\tanh^2 x = \frac{1}{2}$. Since $x > 0$, $\tanh x > 0$, so the stationary point on the graph is where

$$\tanh x = \frac{1}{\sqrt{2}}.$$

To check that this is a maximum, note that $\operatorname{sech} x$ is always positive, and that $\tanh x$ is an increasing function (see Fig. 4.4). So $(1 - 2\tanh^2 x)$ is positive for points to the left of $\tanh^{-1}\dfrac{1}{\sqrt{2}}$, and negative to the right. Therefore $f'(x)$ changes sign from $+$ to $-$ as x increases through the stationary point.

You could use a calculator to find the value of x, but this isn't necessary. When $\tanh x = \dfrac{1}{\sqrt{2}}$,

$$\text{sech}^2\, x = 1 - \tanh^2 x$$
$$= 1 - \left(\frac{1}{\sqrt{2}}\right)^2$$
$$= \tfrac{1}{2},$$

so that $\text{sech}\, x = \dfrac{1}{\sqrt{2}}$ (since $\text{sech}\, x$ is always positive).

The maximum value of $f(x) = \tanh x \times \text{sech}\, x$ is therefore $\dfrac{1}{\sqrt{2}} \times \dfrac{1}{\sqrt{2}} = \tfrac{1}{2}$.

The other two hyperbolic functions are

$$\text{cosech}\, x = \frac{1}{\sinh x} \quad \text{and} \quad \coth x = \frac{1}{\tanh x} = \frac{\cosh x}{\sinh x}.$$

Notice that neither of these is defined when $x = 0$, where $\sinh x = \tanh x = 0$. You are asked to investigate properties of these functions in Exercise 4C Questions 4 and 5.

Exercise 4C

1 Copy the table and fill in the missing entries in rows (a) to (d).

	$\cosh x$	$\sinh x$	$\tanh x$	$\text{sech}\, x$
(a)	$\frac{13}{5}$			
(b)		$2\sqrt{2}$		
(c)			$\frac{1}{2}$	
(d)				$\frac{4}{5}$

2 Evaluate the following, and check your answers with a calculator.

(a) $\tanh(\ln 3)$ (b) $\text{sech}(\ln 5)$ (c) $\text{cosech}(-\ln 2)$ (d) $\coth(\ln 7)$

3 Find an identity connecting $\text{cosech}\, x$ and $\coth x$.

4 For the function $f(x) = \text{cosech}\, x$,

(a) sketch the graph,   (b) state the range,   (c) find the derivative.

5 Repeat Question 4 for the function $f(x) = \coth x$.

6 Find the derivatives with respect to x of the following functions.

(a) $\ln(\text{sech}\, x)$ (b) $\ln\!\left(\tanh \tfrac{1}{2}x\right)$ (c) $\text{cosech}\, x \coth x$

(d) $\text{sech}^2 x$ (e) $\tanh^2 x$ (f) $\tan^{-1}(e^x)$

7 Prove the following identities.

(a) $\tanh(x + y) \equiv \dfrac{\tanh x + \tanh y}{1 + \tanh x \tanh y}$ (b) $\dfrac{\text{sech}\, x}{1 - \tanh x} \equiv \dfrac{1 + \tanh x}{\text{sech}\, x}$

8 Find the following indefinite integrals.

(a) $\displaystyle\int \coth x \, dx$ (b) $\displaystyle\int \text{sech}^2 x \, dx$ (c) $\displaystyle\int \text{cosech}\, x \coth x \, dx$

9 Find $\displaystyle\int \tanh^n x \, dx$, for

(a) $n = 1$,   (b) $n = 2$,   (c) $n = 3$,   (d) $n = 4$.

10 For $x > 0$ and $n \geqslant 1$, prove that the maximum value of $\tanh x \operatorname{sech}^n x$ is $\dfrac{n^{\frac{1}{2}n}}{(n+1)^{\frac{1}{2}(n+1)}}$.

4.6 Inverse hyperbolic functions

You can see from Fig. 4.2 that sinh is a one–one function with domain and range $\mathbb{R}$, so there is no complication in defining the inverse function $\sinh^{-1}$, also with domain and range $\mathbb{R}$.

However, Fig. 4.1 shows that the function cosh is not one–one.

To define $\cosh^{-1}$ you have to begin by restricting the domain of cosh so as to make the function one-one. The obvious way to do this is to remove the parts of the cosh graph in Fig. 4.1 for which x is negative, that is, define $\cosh^{-1}$ as the inverse of the function $x \mapsto \cosh x$ with domain $\mathbb{R}$, $x \geqslant 0$, and range $\mathbb{R}$, $y \geqslant 1$. The inverse function $x \mapsto \cosh^{-1} x$ then has domain $\mathbb{R}$, $x \geqslant 1$, and range $\mathbb{R}$, $y \geqslant 0$. Fig. 4.5 shows its graph.

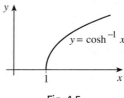

Fig. 4.5

The most important property of these inverse functions is that they can be calculated as logarithms. If $y = \sinh^{-1} x$, then $\sinh y = x$, so

$$\cosh^2 y = 1 + \sinh^2 y = 1 + x^2.$$

Now $\cosh y$ is always positive, so it follows that $\cosh y = \sqrt{1 + x^2}$. Therefore

$$e^y = \sinh y + \cosh y = x + \sqrt{1 + x^2},$$

giving

$$y = \ln(x + \sqrt{1 + x^2}).$$

By a similar argument, if $y = \cosh^{-1} x$, then $\cosh y = x$, so

$$\sinh^2 y = \cosh^2 y - 1 = x^2 - 1.$$

Now by definition $\cosh^{-1} x$ is positive or zero, and since $y \geqslant 0$ then $\sinh y \geqslant 0$. Therefore $\sinh y = \sqrt{x^2 - 1}$, so

$$e^y = \cosh y + \sinh y = x + \sqrt{x^2 - 1},$$

giving

$$y = \ln(x + \sqrt{x^2 - 1}).$$

These are important results, which you should remember.

> For all x, $\sinh^{-1} x = \ln(x + \sqrt{1 + x^2}\,)$.
> For $x \geqslant 1$, $\cosh^{-1} x = \ln(x + \sqrt{x^2 - 1}\,)$.

Example 4.6.1
Prove that $\cosh^{-1} 3 = 2 \sinh^{-1} 1$.

>**Method 1**   The formulae give
>$$\cosh^{-1} 3 = \ln(3 + \sqrt{8}) = \ln(3 + 2\sqrt{2}) \quad \text{and} \quad \sinh^{-1} 1 = \ln(1 + \sqrt{2}).$$
>So $2\sinh^{-1} 1 = 2\ln(1 + \sqrt{2}) = \ln(1 + \sqrt{2})^2$
>$$= \ln(1 + 2\sqrt{2} + 2) = \ln(3 + 2\sqrt{2}) = \cosh^{-1} 3.$$
>**Method 2**   If $A = \sinh^{-1} 1$, then $\cosh 2A = 1 + 2\sinh^2 A = 1 + 2 \times 1^2 = 3$.
>So $\cosh^{-1} 3 = 2A = 2\sinh^{-1} 1$.

> Try using your calculator to check this result numerically.

You can also express $\tanh^{-1} x$ as a logarithm, using the exponential form for $\tanh x$ in Section 4.5.

If $y = \tanh^{-1} x$, then $x = \tanh y = \dfrac{e^{2y} - 1}{e^{2y} + 1}$.

So $xe^{2y} + x = e^{2y} - 1$,

giving $1 + x = (1 - x)e^{2y}$,

and thus

$$e^{2y} = \frac{1 + x}{1 - x}.$$

For the right side to be positive, x must lie between -1 and 1. This you should expect; Fig. 4.4 shows that values of $\tanh$ always lie between -1 and 1. Then

$$2y = \ln \frac{1 + x}{1 - x}.$$

> For $-1 < x < 1$, $\tanh^{-1} x = \tfrac{1}{2} \ln \dfrac{1 + x}{1 - x}$.

Example 4.6.2
Find the Maclaurin expansion of $\tanh^{-1} x$, and its interval of validity.

>You know the Maclaurin series for $\ln(1 + x)$,
>$$\ln(1 + x) = x - \tfrac{1}{2}x^2 + \tfrac{1}{3}x^3 - \tfrac{1}{4}x^4 + \tfrac{1}{5}x^5 - \dots \text{ for } -1 < x \leqslant 1.$$

Replacing x by $-x$ gives

$$\ln(1-x) = -x - \tfrac{1}{2}x^2 - \tfrac{1}{3}x^3 - \tfrac{1}{4}x^4 - \tfrac{1}{5}x^5 - \ldots \text{ for } -1 < -x \leqslant 1,$$

that is $-1 \leqslant x < 1$.

Since $\tanh^{-1} x = \tfrac{1}{2}\ln\dfrac{1+x}{1-x}$, you get by subtraction and halving

$$\tanh^{-1} x = x + \tfrac{1}{3}x^3 + \tfrac{1}{5}x^5 + \ldots.$$

The interval of validity is the set of points common to the intervals $-1 < x \leqslant 1$ and $-1 \leqslant x < 1$, that is $-1 < x < 1$.

Compare this with the expansion of $\tan^{-1} x$ found in Section 3.5.

4.7 Differentiating inverse hyperbolic functions

You can find the derivatives of the inverse functions in two ways. One is to adapt the method used for $\tan^{-1}$ and $\sin^{-1}$ in Sections 1.1 and 1.2. For example, if $y = \sinh^{-1} x$, then $\sinh y = x$, so $\cosh y \dfrac{dy}{dx} = 1$,

and
$$\frac{dy}{dx} = \frac{1}{\cosh y} = \frac{1}{\sqrt{1 + \sinh^2 y}} = \frac{1}{\sqrt{1 + x^2}}.$$

There is no ambiguity about the sign of the square root, since $\cosh y$ is always positive.

Alternatively, you can find the derivatives from the logarithmic forms above. For example,

$$\frac{d}{dx}\cosh^{-1} x = \frac{d}{dx}\ln\left(x + \sqrt{x^2 - 1}\right) = \frac{1}{x + \sqrt{x^2 - 1}} \times \left(1 + \frac{x}{\sqrt{x^2 - 1}}\right)$$

$$= \frac{1}{x + \sqrt{x^2 - 1}} \times \left(\frac{\sqrt{x^2 - 1} + x}{\sqrt{x^2 - 1}}\right) = \frac{1}{\sqrt{x^2 - 1}},$$

and
$$\frac{d}{dx}\tanh^{-1} x = \frac{d}{dx}\left(\tfrac{1}{2}(\ln(1+x) - \ln(1-x))\right) = \tfrac{1}{2}\left(\frac{1}{1+x} + \frac{1}{1-x}\right) = \frac{1}{1-x^2}.$$

$$\frac{d}{dx}\cosh^{-1} x = \frac{1}{\sqrt{x^2 - 1}}, \qquad \frac{d}{dx}\sinh^{-1} x = \frac{1}{\sqrt{1 + x^2}}, \qquad \frac{d}{dx}\tanh^{-1} x = \frac{1}{1 - x^2}.$$

More generally, if a is a positive constant,

$$\frac{d}{dx}\cosh^{-1}\frac{x}{a} = \frac{1}{\sqrt{\left(\dfrac{x}{a}\right)^2 - 1}} \times \frac{1}{a} = \frac{1}{\sqrt{x^2 - a^2}},$$

and similarly

$$\frac{d}{dx}\sinh^{-1}\frac{x}{a} = \frac{1}{\sqrt{a^2 + x^2}}.$$

These results are especially important in their integral forms.

> If $a > 0$,
>
> $$\int \frac{1}{\sqrt{x^2 - a^2}}\,dx = \cosh^{-1}\frac{x}{a} + k, \qquad \int \frac{1}{\sqrt{a^2 + x^2}}\,dx = \sinh^{-1}\frac{x}{a} + k.$$

Example 4.7.1

Evaluate $\displaystyle\int_0^4 \frac{1}{\sqrt{9 + x^2}}\,dx$, giving the answer as a logarithm.

The integrand is of the form $\dfrac{1}{\sqrt{a^2 + x^2}}$ with $a = 3$, so

$$\int_0^4 \frac{1}{\sqrt{9 + x^2}}\,dx = \left[\sinh^{-1}\frac{x}{3}\right]_0^4$$
$$= \sinh^{-1}\tfrac{4}{3}.$$

In logarithmic form this can be expressed as

$$\ln\left(\tfrac{4}{3} + \sqrt{1 + \left(\tfrac{4}{3}\right)^2}\right) = \ln\left(\tfrac{4}{3} + \sqrt{\tfrac{25}{9}}\right)$$
$$= \ln\left(\tfrac{4}{3} + \tfrac{5}{3}\right)$$
$$= \ln 3.$$

So $\displaystyle\int_0^4 \frac{1}{\sqrt{9 + x^2}}\,dx = \ln 3.$

Example 4.7.2

Find the indefinite integral $\displaystyle\int \frac{1}{\sqrt{x^2 + x}}\,dx.$

The integrand is not in one of the standard forms, but it can be converted to a standard form by a substitution. Begin by completing the square,

$$x^2 + x = \left(x + \tfrac{1}{2}\right)^2 - \tfrac{1}{4},$$

so that the integral becomes

$$\int \frac{1}{\sqrt{\left(x + \tfrac{1}{2}\right)^2 - \left(\tfrac{1}{2}\right)^2}}\,dx.$$

This suggests the substitution $x + \tfrac{1}{2} = u$, or $x = u - \tfrac{1}{2}$. Since $\dfrac{dx}{du} = 1$,

$$\int \frac{1}{\sqrt{\left(x + \tfrac{1}{2}\right)^2 - \left(\tfrac{1}{2}\right)^2}}\,dx = \int \frac{1}{\sqrt{u^2 - \left(\tfrac{1}{2}\right)^2}} \times 1\,du$$
$$= \cosh^{-1}\frac{u}{\tfrac{1}{2}} + k$$
$$= \cosh^{-1}(2x + 1) + k.$$

Exercise 4D

1 Use the logarithmic forms to evaluate the following. Check your answers by using the inverse hyperbolic function keys on your calculator.

(a) $\cosh^{-1} 1.25$ (b) $\sinh^{-1} 2$ (c) $\tanh^{-1}\left(-\frac{1}{4}\right)$ (d) $\sinh^{-1}(-0.7)$

2 Evaluate the following exactly, and check your answers with a calculator.

(a) $\tanh(\ln 3)$ (b) $e^{\sinh^{-1} 2.4}$ (c) $\tanh\left(\sinh^{-1}\frac{3}{4}\right)$ (d) $\sinh\left(\tanh^{-1}\frac{4}{5}\right)$

3 Solve these equations for x giving your answer in exact form.

(a) $\sinh^{-1} x = 2\cosh^{-1} 2$

(b) $\mathrm{sech}^{-1}x = \cosh^{-1} 2$

(c) $\sinh^{-1} x = \coth^{-1} 3$

(d) $\cosh^{-1}(2x) = \sinh^{-1}x$

(e) $\mathrm{sech}^{-1}x = \cosh^{-1}(x+1)$

(f) $\sinh^{-1}\left(x - \frac{1}{2}\right) = \cosh^{-1}x$

4 Prove that, if $y = \sinh^{-1} x$, then $(e^y)^2 - 2xe^y - 1 = 0$. Solve this quadratic equation for e^y, and hence obtain the expression for $\sinh^{-1} x$ in logarithmic form. Investigate the significance of the second root of the quadratic equation.

Find the expression for $\cosh^{-1} x$ in logarithmic form by a similar method.

5 Use the implicit differentiation method to prove that $\dfrac{\mathrm{d}}{\mathrm{d}x} \cosh^{-1} x = \dfrac{1}{\sqrt{x^2 - 1}}$ and

$\dfrac{\mathrm{d}}{\mathrm{d}x} \tanh^{-1} x = \dfrac{1}{1 - x^2}$.

6 Obtain $\dfrac{\mathrm{d}}{\mathrm{d}x} \sinh^{-1} x$ by differentiating the logarithmic form for $\sinh^{-1} x$.

7 Find the derivatives with respect to x of the following functions.

(a) $\sinh^{-1} \sqrt{x}$ (b) $\cosh^{-1} \sqrt{1 + x^2}$ (c) $\tanh^{-1}\left(\dfrac{1 - x}{1 + x}\right)$

8 Sketch the graphs of $\sinh^{-1} x$ and $\tanh^{-1} x$.

9* Explain why $\mathrm{sech}^{-1}x = \cosh^{-1}\dfrac{1}{x}$, and write similar definitions for $\mathrm{cosech}^{-1}x$ and $\coth^{-1}x$. For each of these functions,

(a) state the domain and range,   (b) sketch the graph,

(c) find the derivative with respect to x,   (d) find an expression as a natural logarithm.

10 Evaluate the following integrals, giving your answers as logarithms.

(a) $\displaystyle\int_0^1 \frac{1}{\sqrt{x^2 + 1}}\,\mathrm{d}x$

(b) $\displaystyle\int_{10}^{17} \frac{1}{\sqrt{x^2 - 64}}\,\mathrm{d}x$

(c) $\displaystyle\int_{-1}^1 \frac{1}{\sqrt{x^2 + 4x + 5}}\,\mathrm{d}x$

(d) $\displaystyle\int_3^4 \frac{1}{\sqrt{(x + 4)(x - 2)}}\,\mathrm{d}x$

(e) $\displaystyle\int_1^2 \frac{1}{x\sqrt{1 + x^2}}\,\mathrm{d}x \quad \left(\text{try } x = \frac{1}{u}\right)$

(f) $\displaystyle\int_{\frac{1}{2}}^1 \frac{1}{x\sqrt{(3 + 4x)(3 - 2x)}}\,\mathrm{d}x$

11 Use integration by parts to find the following integrals.

(a) $\displaystyle\int \tanh^{-1} x\,\mathrm{d}x$

(b) $\displaystyle\int \sinh^{-1} x\,\mathrm{d}x$

12 Prove that, if $0 < x < \frac{1}{2}\pi$, $\cosh^{-1}(\sec x) = \ln(\sec x + \tan x)$. Find similar expressions for

(a) $\ln(\sec x - \tan x)$ if $0 < x < \frac{1}{2}\pi$,   (b) $\ln(\sec x + \tan x)$ if $-\frac{1}{2}\pi < x < 0$.

13 Use $\sinh^{-1} x = \displaystyle\int \frac{1}{\sqrt{1 + x^2}}\,dx$ to find the expansion of $\sinh^{-1} x$ as the sum of powers of x, giving the first three terms and an expression for the general term.

14* Find $\displaystyle\int \frac{1}{\sqrt{x^2 - 1}}\,dx$ when $x < -1$. Hence evaluate $\displaystyle\int_{-2}^{-1} \frac{1}{\sqrt{x^2 - 1}}\,dx$. Illustrate your answers graphically.

4.8   Independent methods

Although results for hyperbolic functions are often best obtained by comparison with those for trigonometric functions, this does not always work, or it doesn't pay to use it.

One example is the integral of $\operatorname{sech} x$. You can find $\displaystyle\int \sec x\,dx$ by noticing that

$$\frac{d}{dx}\ln(\sec x + \tan x) = \frac{1}{\sec x + \tan x} \times (\sec x \tan x + \sec^2 x)$$
$$= \frac{\sec x\,(\tan x + \sec x)}{\sec x + \tan x} = \sec x.$$

But if you try differentiating the corresponding hyperbolic function,

$$\frac{d}{dx}\ln(\operatorname{sech} x + \tanh x) = \frac{1}{\operatorname{sech} x + \tanh x} \times (-\operatorname{sech} x \tanh x + \operatorname{sech}^2 x)$$
$$= \frac{\operatorname{sech} x(-\tanh x + \operatorname{sech} x)}{\operatorname{sech} x + \tanh x},$$

you do not get a common factor in the numerator and denominator.

However, with hyperbolic functions an alternative method is always available: to go back to the exponential definition. In this example,

$$\int \operatorname{sech} x\,dx = \int \frac{2}{e^x + e^{-x}}\,dx$$
$$= \int \frac{2}{e^{2x} + 1}e^x\,dx.$$

The substitution $e^x = u$ can now be used to express this as

$$\int \frac{2}{u^2 + 1}\frac{du}{dx}\,dx = \int \frac{2}{u^2 + 1}\,du$$
$$= 2\tan^{-1} u + k.$$

Therefore

$$\int \operatorname{sech} x\,dx = 2\tan^{-1} e^x + k.$$

Example 4.8.1

(a) Solve $7 \sinh x + 3 \cosh x = 9$. (b) Find $\int \dfrac{1}{7 \sinh x + 3 \cosh x - 9}\, dx$.

In exponential form,

$$7 \sinh x + 3 \cosh x - 9 = \tfrac{7}{2}(e^x - e^{-x}) + \tfrac{3}{2}(e^x + e^{-x}) - 9$$
$$= 5e^x - 2e^{-x} - 9,$$

which can be written as

$$e^{-x}(5e^{2x} - 9e^x - 2) = e^{-x}(5e^x + 1)(e^x - 2).$$

(a) It is possible to use a method similar to that for the comparable trigonometric equation, writing $7 \sinh x + 3 \cosh x$ as $R \sinh(x + a)$ with $R \cosh a = 7$ and $R \sinh a = 3$, so that $R^2(\cosh^2 a - \sinh^2 a) = 49 - 9$, $R = \sqrt{40}$. But it is simpler to put the equation into exponential form

$$e^{-x}(5e^x + 1)(e^x - 2) = 0.$$

Since e^{-x} and $5e^x + 1$ cannot be 0, the only solution is $e^x = 2$, $x = \ln 2$.

(b) Using the exponential form,

$$\int \frac{1}{7 \sinh x + 3 \cosh x - 9}\, dx = \int \frac{e^x}{(5e^x + 1)(e^x - 2)}\, dx.$$

The substitution $e^x = u$ transforms this to

$$\int \frac{1}{(5u + 1)(u - 2)}\, du = \int \frac{1}{11}\left(\frac{-5}{5u + 1} + \frac{1}{u - 2}\right) du$$
$$= \tfrac{1}{11}(-\ln|5u + 1| + \ln|u - 2|) + k$$
$$= \tfrac{1}{11} \ln\left|\frac{e^x - 2}{5e^x + 1}\right| + k.$$

4.9* The rectangular hyperbola

This section gives a reason why cosh and sinh are called hyperbolic functions. You may omit it if you wish.

The functions cos and sin are often called the circular functions because of their links with the circle. The circle with centre O and radius a, shown in Fig. 4.6, can be described by parametric equations

$$x = a \cos t, \quad y = a \sin t,$$

where $0 \leqslant t < 2\pi$. You obtain the usual cartesian equation from these by noting that

$$x^2 + y^2 = a^2 \cos^2 t + a^2 \sin^2 t = a^2(\cos^2 t + \sin^2 t) = a^2 \times 1 = a^2,$$

using one of Pythagoras' identities.

If A is the point on the circle with parameter 0 and Q the point with parameter q, then the angle AOQ is equal to q. As the parameter t increases from 0 to q, the point $(a\cos t, a\sin t)$ moves round the circle from A to Q, and the radius sweeps out the region OAQ shown shaded in Fig. 4.6. You know that the area of this region is $\frac{1}{2}a^2q$.

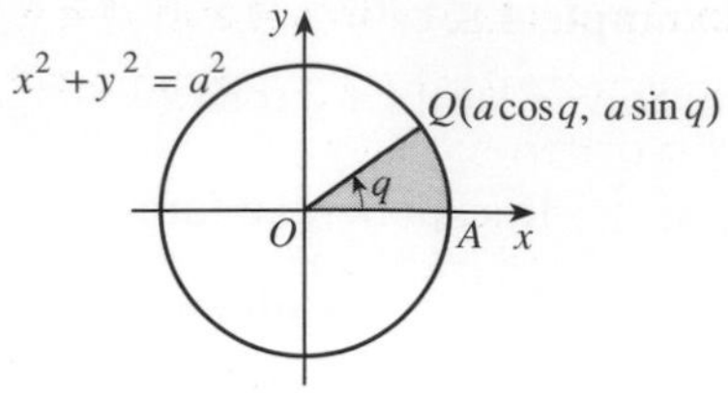

Fig. 4.6

Replacing the circular functions by hyperbolic functions leads to similar results for a rectangular hyperbola, which is the curve shown in Fig. 4.7. Starting with parametric equations $x = a\cosh t, y = a\sinh t$, where $t \in \mathbb{R}$, it follows that

$$x^2 - y^2 = a^2\cosh^2 t - a^2\sinh^2 t = a^2(\cosh^2 t - \sinh^2 t) = a^2 \times 1 = a^2,$$

using the basic identity for hyperbolic functions. The cartesian equation is therefore

$$x^2 - y^2 = a^2.$$

Notice, though, that there is a mismatch between the parametric and cartesian equations. Since y and x appear squared in the cartesian equation, the curve is symmetrical about both the x- and y-axes. It therefore represents a curve in two parts (called 'branches'). But since $\cosh t$ is always positive, the parametric equations give only the branch of the rectangular hyperbola for which $x > 0$, shown in Fig. 4.8. Points for which $t > 0$ lie in the first quadrant, and points for which $t < 0$ lie in the fourth quadrant.

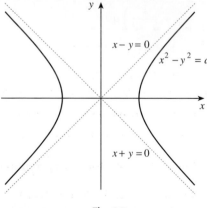

Fig. 4.7

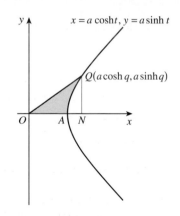

Fig. 4.8

Since $x - y = a\cosh t - a\sinh t = ae^{-t}$, $x - y$ tends to 0 as $t \to \infty$. This shows that the curve approaches the line $x - y = 0$ when t is large and positive. Similarly, since $x + y = a\cosh t + a\sinh t = ae^t$, the curve approaches the line $x + y = 0$ when t is negative and $|t|$ is large. The lines $x - y = 0$ and $x + y = 0$ are called asymptotes of the hyperbola. (You will meet many more examples of asymptotes in Chapter 5.) The reason for describing the hyperbola as 'rectangular' is that these two asymptotes are at right angles to each other.

In Fig. 4.8 the points A and Q have parameters 0 and q respectively, and N is the foot of the perpendicular from Q to the x-axis, with coordinates $(a \cosh q, 0)$. The region ANQ under the curve then has area

$$\int_a^{a\cosh q} y\,dx.$$

Substituting $x = a \cosh t$, $y = a \sinh t$ transforms this integral into

$$\int_0^q a \sinh t \frac{dx}{dt}\,dt = \int_0^q a \sinh t \times a \sinh t\,dt,$$

which can be found as

$$\tfrac{1}{2}a^2 \int_0^q 2\sinh^2 t\,dt = \tfrac{1}{2}a^2 \int_0^q (\cosh 2t - 1)dt$$
$$= \tfrac{1}{2}a^2 \left[\tfrac{1}{2}\sinh 2t - t\right]_0^q = \tfrac{1}{2}a^2 (\sinh q \cosh q - q).$$

Also, the area of the triangle ONQ is $\tfrac{1}{2}a \cosh q \times a \sinh q = \tfrac{1}{2}a^2 \sinh q \cosh q$. It follows that the area of the shaded sector OAQ is

$$\tfrac{1}{2}a^2 \sinh q \cosh q - \tfrac{1}{2}a^2 (\sinh q \cosh q - q) = \tfrac{1}{2}a^2 q.$$

So the parameter can be given exactly the same interpretation for the circle and the rectangular hyperbola, as $q = \dfrac{2\,(\text{area of sector } OAQ)}{a^2}.$

Exercise 4E

1 Find the indefinite integrals

(a) $\displaystyle\int \frac{1}{25\cosh x + 7 \sinh x}\,dx,$ (b) $\displaystyle\int \frac{1}{25\sinh x + 7 \cosh x}\,dx.$

2 Solve the equations $f(x) = a$ for the following functions $f(x)$ and constants a, using the method in Example 4.8.1. Illustrate your solutions with sketch graphs of the functions.

(a) $f(x) = 5\cosh x - 4\sinh x,\quad a = 3$ (b) $f(x) = 6\cosh x - \sinh x,\quad a = 6$

(c) $f(x) = 5\sinh x - 8\cosh x,\quad a = 8$ (d) $f(x) = 3\sinh x + 11\cosh x,\quad a = 16$

3 For the functions and constants in Question 2, find expressions for $\displaystyle\int \frac{1}{f(x) - a}\,dx.$

4 Express each of the functions in Question 2 in one or other of the forms $R\sinh(x+\alpha)$, $R\cosh(x+\alpha)$ (where R may be positive or negative), and hence solve the equations by another method.

5* Show that, for the rectangular hyperbola $x^2 - y^2 = a^2$ in Section 4.9, alternative parametric equations to $x = a\cosh t$, $y = a\sinh t$ are $x = a\sec u$, $y = a\tan u$. What interval of values of u gives the positive branch of the hyperbola shown in Fig. 4.8?

If $\sinh t = \tan u$, express $\cosh t$ and $\tanh t$ in terms of u. Find expressions for $\dfrac{dt}{du}$ in terms of u, and for $\dfrac{du}{dt}$ in terms of t. Use your answers to find

(a) $\displaystyle\int \sec u\,du,$ (b) $\displaystyle\int \operatorname{sech} t\,dt.$

Match your answer to part (b) with the expression for the integral given in Section 4.8.

Miscellaneous exercise 4

1 Find the coordinates of the points at which $\dfrac{d^2y}{dx^2} = 0$ on the graph of $y = \operatorname{sech} x$.

2 Find the area of the region bounded by the graphs of $y = \tanh x$, $y = \operatorname{sech} x$ and $x = 0$.

3 Find the coordinates of the maximum point on the graph of $y = \operatorname{sech} x + \lambda \tanh x$, where λ is constant. Illustrate your answer with sketches of the graph when

   (a) $\lambda > 0$,   (b) $\lambda < 0$.

4 Show that $\dfrac{d}{dx} \sin^{-1}(\tanh x) = \operatorname{sech} x$.   (MEI)

5 A curve has equation $y = x \sinh^{-1} x$. Show that $\dfrac{d^2y}{dx^2} = \dfrac{2 + x^2}{(1 + x^2)^{\frac{3}{2}}}$.   (OCR, adapted)

6 Show that $\displaystyle\int_5^6 \dfrac{1}{\sqrt{25x^2 - 576}}\, dx = \tfrac{1}{5} \ln \tfrac{3}{2}$.   (MEI)

7 Evaluate $\displaystyle\int_0^4 \dfrac{1}{\sqrt{9x^2 + 4}}\, dx$ giving your answer in terms of a natural logarithm.   (OCR)

8 Show that $\displaystyle\int_0^{\frac{1}{2}} \tanh^{-1} x\, dx = \tfrac{1}{4} \ln \tfrac{27}{16}$.   (MEI)

9 Find $\displaystyle\int \dfrac{1}{a^2 - x^2}\, dx$, where $0 < x < a$,

   (a) by substituting $x = a \tanh t$,   (b) by using partial fractions.

   Show algebraically that your solutions are equivalent.   (OCR)

10 Draw sketches with the same axes of the graphs of $y = \operatorname{sech} x$ and $y = \dfrac{1}{1 + x^2}$. Show that the areas of the regions under the two graphs are equal.

   The graphs are rotated through a complete revolution about the x-axis to form surfaces of revolution. Which encloses the larger volume?

11 The function $f(x)$ is defined to be $f(x) = 13 \cosh x + 5 \sinh x$.

   (a) For the curve with equation $y = f(x)$, show that the area under the curve between $x = -a$ and $x = a$ (where $a > 0$) is $\tfrac{13}{5}(f(a) - f(-a))$.

   (b) By first expressing $f(x)$ in terms of e^x and e^{-x}, find the minimum value of $f(x)$.

   (c) Solve the equation $f(x) = 20$, giving the answers as natural logarithms.

   (d) Differentiate $\tan^{-1}\left(\tfrac{3}{2}e^x\right)$ with respect to x. Hence find $\displaystyle\int \dfrac{1}{f(x)}\, dx$.   (MEI)

12* Find expressions for the indefinite integral $\displaystyle\int \dfrac{1}{\cosh x + a \sinh x}\, dx$ distinguishing various possibilities for the value of the constant a.

13 If $f(x) = \cosh x \cos x$, prove that $f^{(4)}(x) = -4f(x)$. Hence expand $f(x)$ as a Maclaurin series, giving the first three non-zero terms and an expression for the general term.

14 Apply the binomial theorem and the definition of cosh x to prove that

$$\cosh^3 x \equiv \tfrac{1}{4}\cosh 3x + \tfrac{3}{4}\cosh x.$$

Use a similar method to express the following in a similar form.

(a) $\sinh^3 x$ (b) $\cosh^4 x$ (c) $\sinh^6 x$ (d) $\sinh^2 x \cosh^3 x$

15 Explain why

$$(\cosh x + \sinh x)^5 \equiv \cosh 5x + \sinh 5x \quad \text{and} \quad (\cosh x - \sinh x)^5 \equiv \cosh 5x - \sinh 5x.$$

Hence show that $\cosh 5x \equiv \cosh^5 x + 10\cosh^3 x \sinh^2 x + 5\cosh x \sinh^4 x$.

Use this to obtain an expression for $\cosh 5x$ in terms of $\cosh x$ alone.

Use a similar method to find expressions for

(a) $\sinh 5x$ in terms of $\sinh x$ alone,

(b) $\cosh 6x$ in terms of $\cosh x$ alone.

5 Graphs of rational functions

This chapter is about sketching graphs of rational functions without using a calculator. When you have completed it, you should

- be able to sketch graphs of rational functions in which the denominator is linear
- know the meaning of the term 'asymptote' and be able to find vertical, horizontal and oblique asymptotes
- be able to sketch graphs of rational functions in which the denominator is linear or quadratic
- be able to use an algebraic method to determine 'forbidden' regions of some rational functions.

5.1 Functions with linear denominators

In previous modules you have learned how to sketch graphs of various forms: straight lines and circles, and trigonometric, exponential and logarithmic functions. In this chapter this sequence of graphs is taken forward to include rational functions.

The form $y = \dfrac{k}{x-a}$

The key to sketching the graph $y = \dfrac{k}{x-a}$, where k and a are constants, is knowing the shape of the graph $y = \dfrac{1}{x}$. From C1 Section 10.1, the graph of $y = \dfrac{1}{x-a}$ is the graph of $y = \dfrac{1}{x}$ translated by a in the positive x-direction. The graph of $y = \dfrac{k}{x-a}$ is a stretch of factor k in the y-direction of the graph of $y = \dfrac{1}{x-a}$.

Figure 5.1 shows graphs of $y = \dfrac{1}{x}$ and $y = \dfrac{2}{x+1}$ to illustrate these remarks.

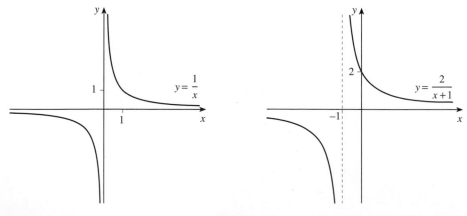

Fig. 5.1

For many purposes a sketch, rather than a carefully drawn graph, is all that is required. If so you do not need to put in an enormous amount of detail. You should mark important points, and show the general behaviour of the graph, but it is not necessary to plot the graph on graph paper, or to do a pseudo-plot on lined paper using the distance between the lines as a unit for an approximate square.

Notice the vertical lines $x = 0$ on the graph of $y = \dfrac{1}{x}$ and $x = -1$ on the graph of $y = \dfrac{2}{x+1}$. These lines are examples of vertical **asymptotes**. In fact, all vertical asymptotes are lines of the form $x = $ constant, where the constant is the value of x excluded from the domain of the function whose graph you are drawing. Thus $y = \dfrac{1}{x}$ is not defined for $x = 0$, and $x = 0$ is an asymptote; similarly, $y = \dfrac{2}{x+1}$ is not defined when $x = -1$, and $x = -1$ is an asymptote.

In the previous paragraph, the word 'vertical' was used to mean 'parallel to the y-axis'. It is convenient, although strictly incorrect, to do this, and to use the word 'horizontal' to mean 'parallel to the x-axis'.

The graphs of $y = \dfrac{1}{x}$ and $y = \dfrac{2}{x+1}$ also have the same horizontal asymptote as each other, namely $y = 0$. It is easy to see that when x is large, each of the graphs becomes close to $y = 0$.

Example 5.1.1

Sketch the function $f(x) = \dfrac{3}{2-x}$, and give the equation of the vertical asymptote.

Write $\dfrac{3}{2-x}$ in the form $\dfrac{-3}{x-2}$ so that $f(x) = \dfrac{-3}{x-2}$ is in the form $\dfrac{k}{x-a}$ with $k = -3$ and $a = 2$.

The graph of $y = \dfrac{-3}{x-2}$ is then the graph of $y = \dfrac{1}{x}$ translated by 2 units in the positive x-direction, and then stretched by a factor of -3 in the y-direction, which involves a reflection in the x-axis. The graph is shown in Fig. 5.2.

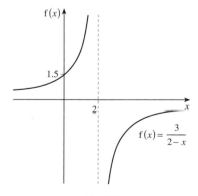

Fig. 5.2

The vertical asymptote is the line with equation $x = 2$.

The form $y = \dfrac{cx - d}{x - a}$

The key to sketching a graph with this form of equation, as will be the case in much of this chapter, is to start by putting the right side of equation into divided out form (or, later, into partial fraction form). The equation then takes the form $y = c + \dfrac{k}{x - a}$, which you should recognise as being the graph of $y = \dfrac{k}{x - a}$ translated by c in the y-direction. An example will help you to see what is happening.

Example 5.1.2

Sketch the curve with equation $y = \dfrac{2x + 1}{x + 1}$. Give the equations of the asymptotes.

Begin by writing $\dfrac{2x + 1}{x + 1} \equiv A + \dfrac{B}{x + 1}$, and finding $A = 2$ and $B = -1$.

Then $y = 2 + \dfrac{-1}{x + 1}$.

This is the graph of $y = \dfrac{1}{x + 1}$, reflected in the x-axis, and then translated by 2 units in the positive y-direction. The graph is shown in Fig. 5.3.

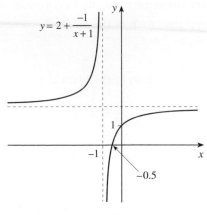

Fig. 5.3

The vertical asymptote is $x = -1$ and the horizontal asymptote is $y = 2$. As a final check, note that $y = 0$ when $x = -0.5$, and $y = 1$ when $x = 0$.

The form $y = \dfrac{cx^2 + dx + e}{x - a}$

Once again, you should use the divided out form to turn an equation of the form $y = \dfrac{cx^2 + dx + e}{x - a}$ into the form $y = Ax + B + \dfrac{C}{x - a}$. An example will clarify how you can obtain information from an expression of this form.

Example 5.1.3

Sketch the curve with equation $y = \dfrac{x^2 - 3x + 3}{x - 2}$, and identify the asymptotes.

Write the equation of the curve in divided out form as $y = x - 1 + \dfrac{1}{x - 2}$.

You can then see that the graph has a vertical asymptote at $x = 2$.

When x is just greater than 2, y is very large and positive. When x is just less than 2, $|y|$ is very large and y is negative.

It also looks as though the graph has an oblique asymptote. You can check this by letting $x \to \infty$. The part of the equation $\dfrac{1}{x - 2}$ then becomes very small and the graph approaches the straight line with equation $y = x - 1$.

When $|x|$ is large and x is positive, y is just greater than $x - 1$; similarly, when $|x|$ is large and x is negative, y is just less than $x - 1$. These pieces are shown in Fig. 5.4.

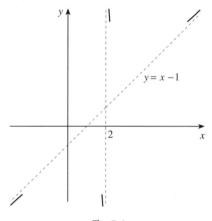

$y = x - 1$

Fig. 5.4

To check for maxima and minima, note that the domain of definition of $x - 1 + \dfrac{1}{x - 2}$ is $\mathbb{R}$, $x \neq 2$.

Then $\dfrac{dy}{dx} = 1 - \dfrac{1}{(x - 2)^2}$.

This is defined for all x except $x = 2$, and is 0 when $(x - 2)^2 = 1$, that is when $x = 3$ and $x = 1$, with corresponding y-values $y = 3$ and $y = -1$. Thus there are turning values at $(3, 3)$ and $(1, -1)$. Also $\dfrac{d^2y}{dx^2} = \dfrac{2}{(x - 2)^3}$, which is positive when $x = 3$ and negative when $x = 1$, showing that $(3, 3)$ is a minimum and $(1, -1)$ is a maximum.

The graph is completed in Fig. 5.5.

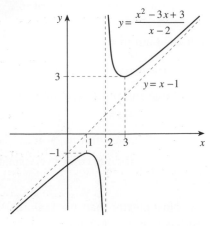

Fig. 5.5

The asymptotes are $x = 2$ and $y = x - 1$.

Example 5.1.4

You are given that the straight line $y = x + 2$ is an oblique asymptote to the curve
$y = \dfrac{2x^2 + ax + 4}{2x - 3}$. Find the value of a.

If $y = x + 2$ is an asymptote of $y = \dfrac{2x^2 + ax + 4}{2x - 3}$, then the two graphs must approach one another when $|x|$ is large.

Consider $\dfrac{2x^2 + ax + 4}{2x - 3} - (x + 2) = \dfrac{2x^2 + ax + 4 - (2x^2 + x - 6)}{2x - 3} = \dfrac{x(a - 1) + 10}{2x - 3}$.

If the right side is small for large values of $|x|$, then the coefficient of x, namely $a - 1$, must be 0. Hence $a = 1$.

Here is a summary of the methods you can use for sketching graphs of rational functions. You will see that for some of the processes it is better to have the equation of the graph with a common denominator, while for others the partial fraction form is more helpful.

> Look for the places where the graph crosses the axes, and mark them.
>
> Look for vertical asymptotes, and check the behaviour of the curve on each side of the asymptote.
>
> Look for horizontal asymptotes, and investigate how the curve approaches the asymptote.
>
> Look for any oblique asymptotes.
>
> Find any maxima and minima.

Exercise 5A

1 For each of the following graphs, write down the equations of the vertical and horizontal asymptotes, and draw a sketch.

(a) $y = \dfrac{2}{x}$ (b) $y = \dfrac{1}{x-1}$ (c) $y = \dfrac{3}{x+2}$ (d) $y = \dfrac{5}{2x-1}$

(e) $y = 1 + \dfrac{2}{x}$ (f) $y = 3 - \dfrac{2}{x+1}$ (g) $y = 4 + \dfrac{3}{x+2}$ (h) $y = 3 - \dfrac{5}{2x-1}$

(i) $y = \dfrac{1+x}{x}$ (j) $y = \dfrac{x-1}{x}$ (k) $y = \dfrac{2-x}{1-x}$ (l) $y = \dfrac{2+3x}{2+x}$

2 For each of the following graphs, find the equations of any vertical, horizontal and oblique asymptotes. Draw diagrams similar to Fig. 5.4, and join up the pieces to sketch the graph.

(a) $y = x + \dfrac{1}{x}$ (b) $y = x + 1 - \dfrac{1}{x}$ (c) $y = 3x - 2 - \dfrac{1}{x-1}$

(d) $y = x - 3 + \dfrac{1}{x-2}$ (e) $y = \dfrac{x^2 - 2}{x}$ (f) $y = \dfrac{x^2 - 2x - 1}{x - 1}$

(g) $y = \dfrac{x^2 + 3x + 1}{x + 2}$ (h) $y = \dfrac{2x^2 + x}{x + 1}$ (i) $y = \dfrac{3 + x - 2x^2}{1 + 2x}$

3 For each of the following graphs, find the coordinates of any maxima and minima, and distinguish between them.

(a) $y = x + \dfrac{4}{x}$ (b) $y = x + 1 + \dfrac{1}{1+x}$ (c) $y = 8x + 3 + \dfrac{1}{1+2x}$

4 For each of the following graphs, find the equations of any asymptotes, find the coordinates of the points where the graphs cross the coordinate axes, find the coordinates of any maxima and minima, and sketch the curve.

(a) $y = x - \dfrac{1}{x}$ (b) $y = x + \dfrac{1}{x}$ (c) $y = 3 + 2x + \dfrac{1}{2x}$

(d) $y = x - 1 - \dfrac{1}{2x-1}$ (e) $y = \dfrac{9x^2 - 5x - 3}{x - 1}$ (f) $y = \dfrac{2x^2}{2x-1}$

5 One of the two asymptotes of the curve $y = \dfrac{2x^2 + kx + 3}{x + 2}$ is $y = 2x + 4$. Find k.

6 Find the equations of all the asymptotes of the curve $y = \dfrac{x^2 + a^2}{x - a}$, where $a \neq 0$.

7 If $y = ax + b$ is an asymptote to the curve with equation $y = \dfrac{px^2 + qx + r}{ax + b}$ where $a \neq 0$, what can you say, if anything, about the values of p, q and r in terms of a and b?

5.2 Functions with quadratic denominators which factorise

If the denominator of $y = \dfrac{px^2 + qx + r}{ax^2 + bx + c}$ has factors $dx - e$ and $fx - g$, then the expression can be transformed by division and partial fractions into the form $y = A + \dfrac{B}{dx - e} + \dfrac{C}{fx - g}$, as described in Section 2.3.

You will find the summary of the methods of producing a sketch at the end of section 5.1 useful for the following examples, and for Exercise 5B.

Example 5.2.1

Sketch the graph of $y = \dfrac{x^2 - x - 2}{(x - 1)(x - 3)}$.

It is useful first to do some preliminary detective work with the equation in this form. By solving the equation $x^2 - x - 2 = 0$ you can see that the graph crosses the x-axis at $x = -1$ and $x = 2$.

The graph crosses the y-axis when $x = 0$, that is at $\left(0, -\frac{2}{3}\right)$.

The vertical asymptotes are $x = 3$ and $x = 1$.

When you divide out and use partial fractions, writing the equation as
$y = 1 + \dfrac{1}{x - 1} + \dfrac{2}{x - 3}$, you can see that, as $x \to \infty$, $y \to 1$, so $y = 1$ is a horizontal asymptote. What is more, when $|x|$ is large and x is positive, y is just greater than 1, so the graph approaches the asymptote $y = 1$ from the positive side. When $|x|$ is large and x is negative, y is just less than 1, so the graph approaches the asymptote $y = 1$ from the negative side.

Now look at what happens to the graph at each side of the vertical asymptotes. When x is just less than 1, the term $\dfrac{1}{x - 1}$ has large modulus and is negative, but when x is just greater than 1, the term $\dfrac{1}{x - 1}$ is large and positive. Around $x = 1$ the term $\dfrac{1}{x - 1}$ dominates the other terms, 1 and $\dfrac{2}{x - 3}$.

Similarly, when x is just less than 3, the term $\dfrac{2}{x - 3}$ has large modulus and is negative, but when x is just greater than 3, the term $\dfrac{2}{x - 3}$ is large and positive. Around $x = 3$ the term $\dfrac{2}{x - 3}$ dominates the terms 1 and $\dfrac{1}{x - 1}$.

As you go along, you can put these pieces in a diagram as shown in Fig. 5.6.

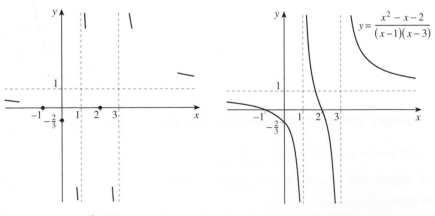

Fig. 5.6   Fig. 5.7

Now check for maxima and minima. When $y = 1 + \dfrac{1}{x-1} + \dfrac{2}{x-3}$,

$\dfrac{dy}{dx} = -\dfrac{1}{(x-1)^2} - \dfrac{2}{(x-3)^2}$. The value of $\dfrac{dy}{dx}$ is always negative, since perfect squares are always positive or zero, so there are no maxima or minima, and the gradient always slopes down from left to right. You can fill in the remainder of the graph as in Fig. 5.7.

Example 5.2.2

Sketch the graph of $y = \dfrac{x^2 - 7x + 14}{(x-1)(x-3)}$.

Attempting to solve the equation $x^2 - 7x + 14 = 0$ shows that the graph does not cross the x-axis. The graph crosses the y-axis when $x = 0$, that is at $\left(0, 4\frac{2}{3}\right)$.

The vertical asymptotes are $x = 3$ and $x = 1$.

Dividing out and using partial fractions, $y = 1 - \dfrac{4}{x-1} + \dfrac{1}{x-3}$. As $x \to \infty$, $y \to 1$, so $y = 1$ is a horizontal asymptote. When x is large and positive, y is just less than 1, so the graph approaches the asymptote $y = 1$ from the negative side. When $|x|$ is large and x is negative, y is just greater than 1, so the graph approaches the asymptote $y = 1$ from the positive side.

When x is just less than 1, the term $-\dfrac{4}{x-1}$ is large and positive, but when x is just greater than 1, the term $-\dfrac{4}{x-1}$ has large modulus and is negative.

Similarly, when x is just less than 3, the term $\dfrac{1}{x-3}$ has large modulus and is negative, but when x is just greater than 3, the term $\dfrac{1}{x-3}$ is large and positive.

As you go along, you can put these pieces in a diagram as shown in Fig. 5.8. (Note that different scales have been used for the x- and y-axes.)

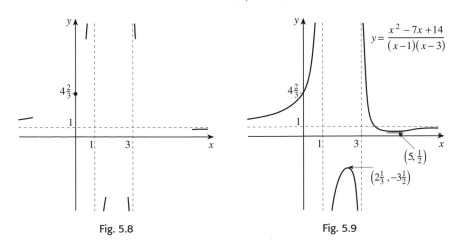

Fig. 5.8   Fig. 5.9

Before you fill in the gaps, you need information about maxima and minima. From the pieces in Fig. 5.8, it looks as though there is a maximum between $x = 1$ and $x = 3$, and a minimum when x is greater than 3.

When $y = 1 - \dfrac{4}{x-1} + \dfrac{1}{x-3}$, $\dfrac{dy}{dx} = \dfrac{4}{(x-1)^2} - \dfrac{1}{(x-3)^2}$. For maxima and minima, $\dfrac{dy}{dx} = 0$, so $\dfrac{4}{(x-1)^2} - \dfrac{1}{(x-3)^2} = 0$, or $\dfrac{4}{(x-1)^2} = \dfrac{1}{(x-3)^2}$. Therefore $2(x-3) = \pm(x-1)$, giving $x = 5$ and $2\frac{1}{3}$. The corresponding y-values are $\frac{1}{2}$ and $-3\frac{1}{2}$. Also $\dfrac{d^2y}{dx^2} = \dfrac{-8}{(x-1)^3} + \dfrac{2}{(x-3)^3}$, which is positive when $x = 5$ and negative when $x = 2\frac{1}{3}$, showing that $\left(5, \frac{1}{2}\right)$ is a minimum and $\left(2\frac{1}{3}, -3\frac{1}{2}\right)$ a maximum. You can fill in the details and obtain Fig. 5.9.

Example 5.2.3

Sketch the graph of $y = \dfrac{x}{(x-1)^2}$.

The graph passes through the origin, and doesn't meet either axis again.

The only vertical asymptote is at $x = 1$. Since $(x-1)^2 \geqslant 0$, the value of y is positive when x is positive, and negative when x is negative. So, on both sides of the asymptote $x = 1$, y is positive.

When $|x|$ is large, y approaches 0, so $y = 0$, the x-axis, is an asymptote. The remark about the sign of y in the previous paragraph tells you that when x is negative it approaches $y = 0$ from below, and when x is positive it approaches $y = 0$ from above.

To find any maxima or minima, differentiate to get

$$\frac{dy}{dx} = \frac{(x-1)^2 \times 1 - x \times 2(x-1)}{((x-1)^2)^2}$$

$$= \frac{(x-1)(x-1-2x)}{(x-1)^4}$$

$$= \frac{-(1+x)}{(x-1)^3}.$$

As $\dfrac{dy}{dx} = 0$ when $x = -1$ there is a stationary point when $x = -1$. Also, when $x = -1$, $y = \dfrac{-1}{((-1)-1)^2} = -\frac{1}{4}$.

When $x < -1$, $\dfrac{dy}{dx}$ is negative; when $x > -1$, $\dfrac{dy}{dx}$ is positive. There is therefore a minimum at $x = -1$. (See C1 Section 11.2.)

As you go along, you can put these pieces in a diagram as shown in Fig. 5.10.

Fig. 5.11 shows the complete sketch.

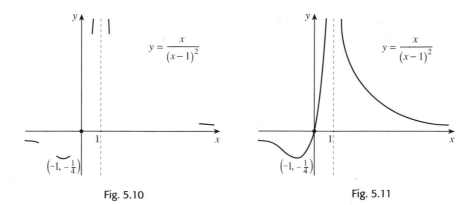

Fig. 5.10   Fig. 5.11

5.3   Functions with quadratic denominators which do not factorise

An important feature of graphs of functions with quadratic denominators which do not factorise is that, as there are no values for which the denominator is zero, there are no points for which the function is undefined, and there are no vertical asymptotes. The curve therefore has no breaks.

Example 5.3.1

Sketch the curve with equation $y = \dfrac{1}{x^2 + 2x + 2}$.

The denominator does not factorise, and completing the square (see C1 Section 4.4) shows that $x^2 + 2x + 2 = (x + 1)^2 + 1$. It is therefore always positive, so y is always positive. The minimum value of the denominator is 1 when $x = -1$, so the value of y has a maximum of 1 when $x = -1$.

For values of x with large modulus, both positive and negative, the denominator is very large, so $y \to 0$.

You can fill in the details to get the graph shown in Fig. 5.12.

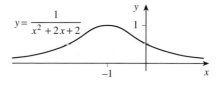

Fig. 5.12

Example 5.3.2

Sketch the curve with equation $y = \dfrac{x}{x^2 + 1}$.

The denominator is always positive, so y is positive when x is positive and negative when x is negative. In fact, $\dfrac{x}{x^2 + 1}$ is an odd function, and so its graph is symmetrical about the origin.

For values of x with large modulus, both positive and negative, you can see by writing the equation in the form $y = \dfrac{\frac{1}{x}}{1 + \frac{1}{x^2}}$ that $y \to 0$ as $x \to \infty$ and as $x \to -\infty$.

To look for maxima and minima, $\dfrac{dy}{dx} = \dfrac{1 - x^2}{(x^2 + 1)^2}$, so $\dfrac{dy}{dx} = 0$ when $x = \pm 1$.

The corresponding y-values are $\frac{1}{2}$ and $-\frac{1}{2}$. To verify whether these are maxima or minima it is easiest to look at the sign of $\dfrac{dy}{dx}$. If $|x| < 1$, $\dfrac{dy}{dx} > 0$, and if $|x| > 1$, $\dfrac{dy}{dx} < 0$. This shows that $\left(1, \frac{1}{2}\right)$ is a maximum and $\left(-1, -\frac{1}{2}\right)$ is a minimum.

You can fill in the details and obtain Fig. 5.13.

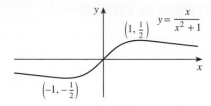

Fig. 5.13

Example 5.3.3

Sketch the curve with equation $y = \dfrac{x^2 - 7x + 6}{x^2 + 1}$.

With the equation in the form $\dfrac{(x - 1)(x - 6)}{x^2 + 1}$, you can see that the graph cuts the x-axis at $x = 1$ and $x = 6$, and the y-axis at $y = 6$.

For values of x with large modulus, both positive and negative, it is helpful to write the equation in the divided out form $y = 1 - \dfrac{7x - 5}{x^2 + 1}$.

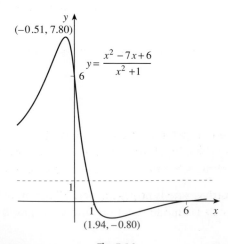

Fig. 5.14

Then you can see that $y \to 1$ as $x \to \infty$ and as $x \to -\infty$; when x is large and positive, $y < 1$, and when $|x|$ is large and x is negative, $y > 1$.

Differentiating, $\dfrac{dy}{dx} = \dfrac{7x^2 - 10x - 7}{(x^2 + 1)^2}$, so $\dfrac{dy}{dx} = 0$ when $x \approx 1.94$ and $x \approx -0.51$, with corresponding y-values -0.80 and 7.80. It is awkward to determine whether these are maxima or minima, but you can appeal to the continuity of the curve to complete the sketch, shown in Fig. 5.14.

Exercise 5B

1 Sketch the following graphs, giving the equations of any asymptotes and the coordinates of any maxima and minima.

(a) $y = \dfrac{1}{x(x-2)}$

(b) $y = \dfrac{x-1}{x(x-2)}$

(c) $y = \dfrac{(x-1)^2}{x(x-2)}$

(d) $y = x + \dfrac{1}{x-1}$

(e) $y = \dfrac{x^2}{(x+2)(x-2)}$

(f) $y = \dfrac{x}{(x+2)(x-2)}$

(g) $y = \dfrac{1}{x+2} + \dfrac{1}{x-2}$

(h) $y = \dfrac{1}{x^2 - 4}$

2 Sketch the following graphs, giving the equations of any asymptotes and the coordinates of any maxima and minima.

(a) $y = \dfrac{1}{x^2}$

(b) $y = \dfrac{x-1}{x^2}$

(c) $y = \dfrac{1}{(x-1)^2}$

(d) $y = \dfrac{x}{(x-1)^2}$

3 Sketch the following graphs, giving the equations of any asymptotes and the coordinates of any maxima and minima.

(a) $y = \dfrac{1}{x^2 + 1}$

(b) $y = \dfrac{x+1}{x^2 + 2x + 2}$

(c) $y = \dfrac{-x}{x^2 + 1}$

(d) $y = \dfrac{1+x}{x^2 + x + 1}$

4 For each of the following graphs, find the equations of any asymptotes, find the coordinates of the points where the graphs cross the coordinate axes, find the coordinates of any maxima and minima, and sketch the curve.

(a) $y = \dfrac{x^2 + 2}{x^2 + 2x + 3}$

(h) $y = \dfrac{x^2}{x^2 - 2x + 1}$

(c) $y = \dfrac{x^2 - 1}{x^2 - 2x + 1}$

(d) $y = \dfrac{x^2 - 1}{x^2 + 1}$

5 One of the asymptotes of the graph of $y = \dfrac{x-2}{x^2 + kx + 4}$ is $x = 4$. Find the value of k and give the equation of the other asymptote.

5.4 An algebraic technique

One piece of information you use in sketching graphs is the position of the maximum and minimum points. So far you have found these by differentiation, but for many rational functions there is another method which uses the theory of quadratic equations.

Look back at Fig. 5.5, which is reproduced on the next page as Fig. 5.15, and ask the question 'for what values of x does y take a particular value k?'

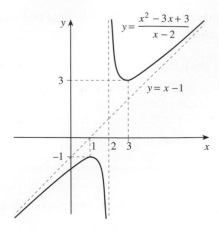

Fig. 5.15

You could solve this graphically by drawing the horizontal line $y = k$, and finding where it cuts the graph $y = \dfrac{x^2 - 3x + 3}{x - 2}$. You can see from the figure that if $k < -1$ or $k > 3$ there are two values of x, if $-1 < k < 3$ there are no values and if $k = -1$ or $k = 3$ there is just one value.

For a general value of y the values of x are given by the equation $y(x - 2) = x^2 - 3x + 3$, which can be written as a quadratic equation in x,

$$x^2 - (y + 3)x + (2y + 3) = 0.$$

How many values of x there are depends on the discriminant '$b^2 - 4ac$'. The discriminant in this case is $(y + 3)^2 - 4 \times 1 \times (2y + 3)$, which can be simplified as $y^2 - 2y - 3$, with factors $(y - 3)(y + 1)$.

If $y < -1$ or $y > 3$ this discriminant is positive, so there are two values of x. If $-1 < y < 3$ the discriminant is negative, so there are no values of x. This is just the result found above from Fig. 5.15.

When $y = -1$ the quadratic equation becomes $x^2 - 2x + 1 = 0$, which is $(x - 1)^2 = 0$, and when $y = 3$ the equation becomes $x^2 - 6x + 9 = 0$, which is $(x - 3)^2 = 0$. So the turning points are $(1, -1)$ and $(3, 3)$.

Example 5.4.1

Show that the graph $y = \dfrac{x - 1}{x^2 + 3}$ can only take values in the interval $-\frac{1}{2} \leqslant y \leqslant \frac{1}{6}$.

You can rewrite this equation in the form $y(x^2 + 3) = x - 1$ and then as a quadratic equation in x,

$$yx^2 - x + (3y + 1) = 0$$

The discriminant '$b^2 - 4ac$' for the quadratic expression $yx^2 - x + (3y + 1)$ is $1^2 - 4 \times y \times (3y + 1)$. For the equation $yx^2 - x + (3y + 1) = 0$ to have real roots, $1^2 - 4y(3y + 1) \geqslant 0$.

$$1 - 12y^2 - 4y \geqslant 0 \quad \Leftrightarrow \quad 12y^2 + 4y - 1 \leqslant 0$$
$$\Leftrightarrow \quad (6y - 1)(2y + 1) \leqslant 0$$
$$\Leftrightarrow \quad -\tfrac{1}{2} \leqslant y \leqslant \tfrac{1}{6}.$$

Therefore the only points on the graph of $y = \dfrac{x - 1}{x^2 + 3}$ are those for which $-\tfrac{1}{2} \leqslant y \leqslant \tfrac{1}{6}$.

You may wish to compare this method with that of C3 Example 10.2.2, which involves differentiating a quotient. The graph of $y = \dfrac{x - 1}{x^2 + 3}$ is shown in Fig. 5.16.

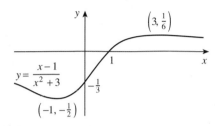

Fig. 5.16

Example 5.4.2

(a) Find the equations of the asymptotes of $y = \dfrac{2x^2 - 5x + 4}{x - 2}$.

(b) Find the values of y for which there are no points on the curve.

(a) The denominator is zero at $x = 2$, so $x = 2$ is a vertical asymptote. Writing $\dfrac{2x^2 - 5x + 4}{x - 2}$ in divided out form shows that $y = 2x - 1 + \dfrac{2}{x - 2}$. You can see that as $|x|$ gets large, the term $\dfrac{2}{x - 2}$ becomes very small, and the graph behaves like $y = 2x - 1$. The line $y = 2x - 1$ is an oblique asymptote.

(b) Writing $y = \dfrac{2x^2 - 5x + 4}{x - 2}$ in the form $y(x - 2) = 2x^2 - 5x + 4$ and rearranging it as a quadratic equation in x gives

$$2x^2 - (5 + y)x + (4 + 2y) = 0.$$

For a point (x, y) to exist on the graph of $y(x - 2) = 2x^2 - 5x + 4$, the discriminant must be non-negative, that is $(5 + y)^2 - 4 \times 2 \times (4 + 2y) \geqslant 0$.

$$(5 + y)^2 - 4 \times 2 \times (4 + 2y) \geqslant 0 \quad \Leftrightarrow \quad 25 + 10y + y^2 - 32 - 16y \geqslant 0$$
$$\Leftrightarrow \quad y^2 - 6y - 7 \geqslant 0$$
$$\Leftrightarrow \quad (y + 1)(y - 7) \geqslant 0$$
$$\Leftrightarrow \quad y \leqslant -1 \quad \text{or} \quad y \geqslant 7.$$

Therefore no part of the graph lies between $y = -1$ and $y = 7$.

Example 5.4.3

Show that the graph of $y = \dfrac{x^2 - x - 2}{(x-1)(x-3)}$ takes all possible values of y.

Rewriting the equation $y = \dfrac{x^2 - x - 2}{(x-1)(x-3)}$ as a quadratic equation in x gives

$y(x-1)(x-3) = x^2 - x - 2$, which can be rearranged as

$$(y-1)x^2 + (1-4y)x + (3y+2) = 0.$$

The discriminant of $(y-1)x^2 + (1-4y)x + (3y+2)$ is

$$(1-4y)^2 - 4 \times (y-1) \times (3y+2), \quad \text{which is} \quad 4y^2 - 4y + 9.$$

Notice that, by completing the square (see C1 Section 4.4),

$$4y^2 - 4y + 9 \equiv (2y-1)^2 + 8,$$

which is always positive.

Thus the equation $(y-1)x^2 + (1-4y)x + (3y+2) = 0$ has real roots whatever the value of y, so the graph takes all possible values of y.

This method, using the discriminant '$b^2 - 4ac$', works because the equation of the graph reduces to a quadratic equation in x.

Exercise 5C

Use the algebraic technique described in Section 5.4 for the questions in this exercise.

1 Prove that

(a) if $y = \dfrac{x^2 + x + 1}{x^2 + 1}$, then $\frac{1}{2} \leqslant y \leqslant \frac{3}{2}$,

(b) if $y = \dfrac{x^2 + 1}{x^2 + x + 1}$, then $\frac{2}{3} \leqslant y \leqslant 2$.

2 Prove that if $y = \dfrac{1 - 2x - x^2}{x^2}$, then $y \geqslant -2$.

3 Find any restrictions on the values that y can take for the following functions.

(a) $y = \dfrac{x+1}{(x-1)^2}$

(b) $y = \dfrac{x^2 - x}{2x - 1}$

(c) $y = \dfrac{8x - 3}{(2x-1)(2x+3)}$

4 Prove that if $y = \dfrac{x - k}{x^2 - 4x - k}$ can take all values as x varies, then $0 < k < 5$.

5 Find a condition on k so that $y = \dfrac{x - k}{x^2 - 4x + k}$ can take all values as x varies.

Miscellaneous exercise 5

1 Find the equations of the asymptotes of $y = x + 1 + \dfrac{1}{x+1}$.

2 Let $f(x) = \dfrac{1}{(x-2)(x+2)}$. For what values of x is $f(x)$ positive? Write down the equations of the asymptotes of $y = f(x)$.

3 Find the stationary values of the function $f(x) = \dfrac{x}{x^2 + 4}$, and write down the equations of any asymptotes. Sketch the graph of $y = f(x)$, showing the asymptotes and the stationary values.

4 Find any stationary values of the function $f(x) = \dfrac{x}{x^2 - 4}$, and write down the equations of the asymptotes. Sketch the graph of $y = f(x)$, showing the asymptotes and the stationary values.

5 Find the maximum and minimum values on the curve $y = \dfrac{x}{x^2 + 3x + 4}$, and sketch the curve.

6 Find a condition on p such that $y = \dfrac{x^2 + px}{x^2 + p}$ takes all values as x varies.

7 Find the equation of the oblique asymptote of the curve $y = \dfrac{x^2 + ax + b^2}{x + b}$, where $a \neq 2b$. What happens if $a = 2b$?

8 In each part of the question, suggest a possible equation for the graph which is sketched.

(a)
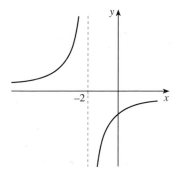

(b)
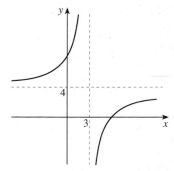

(c)
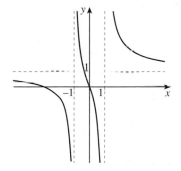

(d)
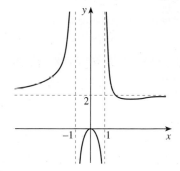

9 (a) Find the coordinates of the points at which the graph of $y = \dfrac{x^2 - 2}{(x - 2)^2}$ cuts the coordinate axes.

(b) Find the equations of both the asymptotes of the curve.

(c) Find the coordinates of the turning point on the graph.

(d) Sketch the graph. (OCR, adapted)

10 Sketch the graph of $y = \dfrac{x^2 + x + 1}{(x - 1)^2}$, and prove that, for all values of x, $y \geqslant \frac{1}{4}$.

(OCR, adapted)

11 The diagram shows a sketch of the curve with equation $y = \dfrac{3 + 6x}{(x - 1)^2}$.

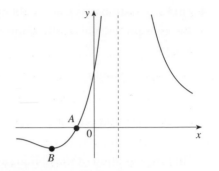

(a) Write down the coordinates of A, and state the equation of the vertical asymptote, shown as a broken line.

(b) Determine the coordinates of the minimum point B. Hence show that $\dfrac{3 + 6x}{(x - 1)^2} \geqslant -1$.

(OCR, adapted)

12 (a) Given that $k = \dfrac{(x + 2)^2}{x + 1}$, show that $x^2 + (4 - k)x + (4 - k) = 0$. Write down the condition for the roots of this quadratic equation to be real. Hence show that k cannot take values between 0 and 4.

(b) Find the coordinates of the turning points on the curve with equation $y = \dfrac{(x + 2)^2}{x + 1}$.

Sketch the curve, and mark clearly the positions of the turning points.   (OCR)

13 The curve C_1 has equation $y = \dfrac{x + a}{x - a}$, where a is a positive constant.

(a) Show that $\dfrac{dy}{dx} < 0$ at all points of C_1.

(b) Draw a sketch of C_1.

The curve C_2 has equation $y = \left(\dfrac{x + a}{x - a}\right)^2$.

(c) Show by differentiation that C_2 has exactly one stationary point and find the coordinates of this point.

(d) On a separate diagram draw a sketch of C_2.

(e) Show by means of a graphical argument that there are values of m, which need not be specified, such that the equation

$$m(x - a)^3 - (x + a)^2 = 0$$

has three distinct roots.   (OCR)

6 Polar coordinates

This chapter introduces a new kind of coordinate system, which is particularly suitable for curves which are drawn around one special point. When you have completed it, you should

- know how to plot points from their polar coordinates
- understand conventions which ensure that points have unique coordinates
- be able to draw graphs from their polar equations.
- be able to convert coordinates and equations from cartesian to polar form and vice versa
- be able to calculate areas of sectors and areas inside closed curves using integration
- understand that conventions may be breached if necessary to produce more complete graphs.

6.1 Definitions and conventions

There are two ways of pin-pointing a position on a map. You can give a map reference, or you can choose a well-known landmark and give the distance and bearing of the position from it.

In mathematics the equivalent of a map reference is the pair of cartesian coordinates (x, y). But it is sometimes better to give the position of a point in **polar coordinates** (r, θ), which correspond in mathematics to distance and bearing.

You have to begin by choosing an origin O (sometimes called the **pole**) and a line in a fixed direction, called the **initial line** (see Fig. 6.1).

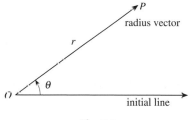

Fig. 6.1

The convention is to take this as the positive x-axis. The position of a point P is then defined by the distance $r = OP$, and the angle θ which the vector $\overrightarrow{OP}$ (sometimes called the **radius vector**) makes with the initial line. The convention is for this angle to be positive if the rotation from the initial line to the radius vector is anticlockwise, negative if the rotation is clockwise.

For example, to locate the point with polar coordinates $(4, \frac{3}{4}\pi)$, you begin at O, facing along the initial line, and rotate through an angle of $\frac{3}{4}\pi$ anticlockwise. You then move 4 units in the direction in which you are now facing. Clearly any pair of coordinates (r, θ) fixes the position of the corresponding point.

Unfortunately, the converse of this last statement is not true. That is, a particular point can have many polar coordinates. For example, the coordinates $(2, \frac{1}{2}\pi)$, $(2, \frac{5}{2}\pi)$, $(2, -\frac{3}{2}\pi)$, ... all define the same point. This is the point whose cartesian coordinates are $(0, 2)$.

This is sometimes inconvenient, and it can be avoided by restricting the angle θ so that it lies within an interval of width 2π. There are two obvious ways of doing this. You can require either that $0 \leqslant \theta < 2\pi$ or that $-\pi < \theta \leqslant \pi$. Which you choose is simply a convention; it will be useful to refer to these possibilities as the '2π-convention' and the 'π-convention' respectively.

With these conventions, any point other than O has a unique description (r, θ) in polar coordinates, with $r > 0$ and θ within an interval defined by the chosen convention.

For example, the point with cartesian coordinates $(0, -3)$ would have polar coordinates $(3, \frac{3}{2}\pi)$ using the 2π-convention, or $(3, -\frac{1}{2}\pi)$ using the π-convention.

The point O remains an exception. It has polar coordinates $(0, \theta)$ where θ can have any value. In practice this is not a problem, since polar coordinates are normally used for curves for which the origin is a special point.

6.2 Polar and cartesian coordinates

It is useful to be able to calculate the cartesian coordinates of a point from its polar coordinates, and vice versa. Suppose that a point P has cartesian coordinates (x, y) and polar coordinates (r, θ) (see Fig. 6.2).

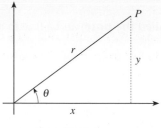

Fig. 6.2

The problem is to find expressions for x and y in terms of r and θ, and for r and θ in terms of x and y.

The definitions of cosine and sine given in C2 Sections 1.1 and 1.2 can be interpreted as showing that a point with polar coordinates $(1, \theta)$ has cartesian coordinates $(\cos\theta, \sin\theta)$. (At that stage in the course angles were in degrees, but the definitions apply equally with θ in radians.) If the associated Fig. 1.1 and Fig. 1.7 were enlarged by a scale factor of r, then it would follow that a point with polar coordinates (r, θ) has cartesian coordinates $(r\cos\theta, r\sin\theta)$.

The reverse process needs a little more care. Since the distance from $(0, 0)$ to (x, y) is $\sqrt{x^2 + y^2}$, and since by convention $r > 0$, it follows that $r = \sqrt{x^2 + y^2}$. Therefore, since $x = r\cos\theta$ and

$y = r \sin\theta$,

$$\cos\theta = \frac{x}{\sqrt{x^2+y^2}} \quad \text{and} \quad \sin\theta = \frac{y}{\sqrt{x^2+y^2}}.$$

These two equations together will give you in general a solution for θ in the interval $0 \le \theta < 2\pi$ or $-\pi < \theta \le \pi$.

> If the cartesian and polar coordinates of a point are (x, y) and (r, θ) respectively, then
>
> $$x = r\cos\theta, \quad y = r\sin\theta, \quad r = \sqrt{x^2+y^2},$$
>
> and (except at the origin)
> $$\cos\theta = \frac{x}{\sqrt{x^2+y^2}}, \quad \sin\theta = \frac{y}{\sqrt{x^2+y^2}}.$$

You do need both of the equations $\cos\theta = \dfrac{x}{\sqrt{x^2+y^2}}$ and $\sin\theta = \dfrac{y}{\sqrt{x^2+y^2}}$. Each one on its own has two solutions in the interval $0 \le \theta < 2\pi$ or $-\pi < \theta \le \pi$, but both together define the value of θ completely.

Example 6.2.1
Find the polar coordinates of the point with cartesian coordinates $(3, -4)$.

The formula for r gives $r = \sqrt{3^2 + (-4)^2} = \sqrt{25} = 5$, so that

$$\cos\theta = \tfrac{3}{5} = 0.6 \quad \text{and} \quad \sin\theta = -\tfrac{4}{5} = -0.8.$$

Now $\cos^{-1} 0.6 = 0.9273$ (to 4 decimal places), but $\sin 0.9273 = 0.8$, not -0.8 as required. The correct value of θ using the π-convention is -0.9273. The equivalent angle using the 2π-convention is $2\pi - 0.9273 = 5.3559$.

Some calculators have special keys for making these conversions, and it is worthwhile learning to use these. (They can also be used in mechanics for other vector quantities such as force and velocity, to find components and resultants.)

Exercise 6A

1 Using centimetre units, plot the points with the following polar coordinates.

(a) $(5, 0)$ (b) $(3, \pi)$ (c) $(4, 1)$

(d) $(6, \tfrac{3}{2}\pi)$ (e) $(4.5, -\tfrac{1}{3}\pi)$ (f) $(2, \tfrac{3}{4}\pi)$

2 Find the cartesian coordinates of the points whose polar coordinates are

(a) $(10, \tfrac{1}{2}\pi)$, (b) $(2, \tfrac{5}{6}\pi)$, (c) $(4, \tfrac{5}{4}\pi)$,

(d) $(6, -\tfrac{2}{3}\pi)$, (e) $(5, \pi)$, (f) $(3, 2)$.

3 Find the polar coordinates of the points with the following cartesian coordinates. Give your answers using (i) the 2π-convention, (ii) the π-convention.

(a) $(-3, 0)$ (b) $(12, 5)$ (c) $(2, -2)$

(d) $(0, -4)$ (e) $(-3, -4)$ (f) $(-1, \sqrt{3})$

4 Find the distance between the points whose polar coordinates are $(2, -\frac{4}{9}\pi)$ and $(3, \frac{8}{9}\pi)$.

5 Find in polar coordinates the mid-point of the line segment joining the points (r, α) and (r, β),

(a) if $0 < \beta - \alpha < \pi$,   (b) if $\pi < \beta - \alpha < 2\pi$.

6 A is the point $(10, \frac{1}{2}\pi)$ and P is the point $(4, \frac{1}{6}\pi)$. Q is the reflection of P in the line OA. Find the polar coordinates of Q.

7 C is the point $(2, \frac{1}{6}\pi)$ and $OCDE$ is a square. Find the polar coordinates of D and E.

8 L and M are the points with polar coordinates $(5, \frac{1}{3}\pi)$ and $(10, \frac{1}{3}\pi)$ respectively. LMN is an equilateral triangle. Find the polar coordinates of the two possible positions of N.

9 Prove that a necessary and sufficient condition for a point to be represented by the same number-pair (a, b) in both cartesian and polar coordinates is that it lies on the initial line.

6.3   Graphs with polar equations

A graph can be defined in polar coordinates, just as for cartesian coordinates, as the set of points whose coordinates satisfy an equation of the form $r = f(\theta)$.

You can use a graphic calculator or computer software to produce polar graphs, but first it is worthwhile drawing a few by hand. To do this it helps to use polar graph paper. Just as cartesian graph paper has printed lines with equations $x = $ constant (up the page) and $y = $ constant (across the page), so polar paper has lines radiating from O with equations $\theta = $ constant and circles centre O with equations $r = $ constant.

To begin, you need to draw up a table of values, plot the points and then join them.

Example 6.3.1
Draw the graph with equation $r = 2 + \cos\theta$ for $-\pi < \theta \leqslant \pi$.

The first step is to make a table of values of r for typical values of θ, as shown in Table 6.3.

θ	$-\frac{5}{6}\pi$	$-\frac{2}{3}\pi$	$-\frac{1}{2}\pi$	$-\frac{1}{3}\pi$	$-\frac{1}{6}\pi$	0
r	1.134	1.5	2	2.5	2.866	3

θ	$\frac{1}{6}\pi$	$\frac{1}{3}\pi$	$\frac{1}{2}\pi$	$\frac{2}{3}\pi$	$\frac{5}{6}\pi$	π
r	2.866	2.5	2	1.5	1.134	1

Table 6.3

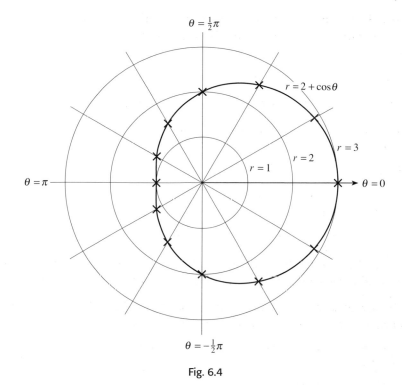

Fig. 6.4

Fig. 6.4 shows these points plotted on polar graph paper, and joined with a curve.

Fig. 6.4 also shows the equations of the circles, $r = $ constant, and the equations of some of the radii, which have the form $\theta = $ constant.

Exercise 6B

1 Draw up a table of values for $0 \leqslant \theta < 2\pi$ and plot the curves with equations
   (a) $r = 2\cos\theta$,
   (b) $r = 2\sin\theta$,
   (c) $r = 2\cos\left(\theta - \frac{1}{4}\pi\right)$.

2 Draw up a table of values for $-\pi < \theta \leqslant \pi$ and plot the curves with equations
   (a) $r = 2 - \sin\theta$,
   (b) $r = 2 - \sin 2\theta$,
   (c) $r = 2 - \sin 3\theta$.

3 Plot the curve $r = \theta$ for $0 \leqslant \theta < 2\pi$. What would happen if you continued to plot for values of θ which increased indefinitely?

6.4 The use of symmetry

The questions in Exercise 6B should have convinced you that you can save time when drawing curves in polar coordinates by using symmetry.

If you go back to the graph in Fig. 6.4 with the equation $r = 2 + \cos\theta$ for $-\pi < \theta \leqslant \pi$ you notice that the curve has symmetry about the initial line. That is, if a point on the curve has coordinates (r, θ), the point $(r, -\theta)$ also lies on the curve.

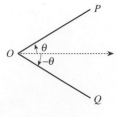

Fig. 6.5

Looking at it the other way round, suppose that the equation of the curve is $r = f(\theta)$ and that $f(\theta) \equiv f(-\theta)$ for all values of θ.

If you consider the point Q on the graph in the direction $-\theta$, the value of r is $f(-\theta)$. Since $f(-\theta) = f(\theta)$, this value of r is $f(\theta)$, the same as for the point P in the direction θ (see Fig. 6.5).

> If $f(\theta) \equiv f(-\theta)$ for all values of θ, the graph with polar equation $r = f(\theta)$ is symmetrical about the initial line $\theta = 0$.

Example 6.4.1
Show that the curve with equation $r = 1 - \cos\theta$ for $-\pi < \theta \leqslant \pi$ has symmetry about the initial line.

Let $f(\theta) = 1 - \cos\theta$.

Then

$$f(-\theta) \equiv 1 - \cos(-\theta)$$
$$\equiv 1 - \cos\theta$$
$$\equiv f(\theta),$$

so, from the result in the box above, the curve is symmetrical about the initial line.

The argument regarding symmetry about the line $\theta = 0$ can be generalised to provide a test for symmetry of any graph $r = f(\theta)$ about a line $\theta = \alpha$ (see Fig. 6.6).

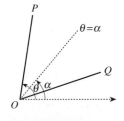

Fig. 6.6

Consider points P and Q on the graph which are at equal angles from the line $\theta = \alpha$. If P is in the direction θ, the radius vector $\overrightarrow{OP}$ makes an angle $\theta - \alpha$ with the line $\theta = \alpha$. So the direction of Q is $\alpha - (\theta - \alpha)$, which is $2\alpha - \theta$. So if $f(2\alpha - \theta) = f(\theta)$, then $OQ = OP$. It follows that, if this is true for all values of θ (that is, as an identity in θ), then the whole graph is symmetrical about the line $\theta = \alpha$.

> If $f(2\alpha - \theta) \equiv f(\theta)$ for all values of θ, the graph with polar equation $r = f(\theta)$ is symmetrical about the line $\theta = \alpha$.

Example 6.4.2
Draw the graph with equation $r = 2\sin 2\theta$ for $0 \leqslant \theta \leqslant \frac{1}{2}\pi$. Prove that it is symmetrical about the line $\theta = \frac{1}{4}\pi$.

In this example θ has been restricted to an interval over which $r \geqslant 0$. In this interval r increases from 0 to 2 and then decreases to 0.

Table 6.7 gives some values, and the plotted points are joined up in Fig. 6.8.

θ	0	$\frac{1}{12}\pi$	$\frac{1}{6}\pi$	$\frac{1}{4}\pi$	$\frac{1}{3}\pi$	$\frac{5}{12}\pi$	$\frac{1}{2}\pi$
r	0	1	1.732	2	1.732	1	0

Table 6.7

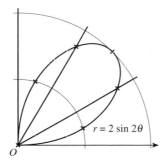

$r = 2\sin 2\theta$

Fig. 6.8

To establish the symmetry property, you need to show that $f(2 \times \frac{1}{4}\pi - \theta) \equiv f(\theta)$ with $f(\theta) = 2\sin 2\theta$, for all values of θ. Starting from the left side,

$$f\left(\tfrac{1}{2}\pi - \theta\right) \equiv 2\sin 2\left(\tfrac{1}{2}\pi - \theta\right)$$
$$\equiv 2\sin(\pi - 2\theta)$$
$$\equiv 2\sin 2\theta$$
$$\equiv f(\theta),$$

as required.

Exercise 6C

1 Show that the graph of $r = \sin\theta$ is symmetrical about the line $\theta = \frac{1}{2}\pi$. Sketch the graph of $r = \sin\theta$ for $0 \leqslant \theta < 2\pi$.

2 Generalise the result of Question 1 to show that any curve with an equation of the form $r = f(\sin\theta)$ is symmetrical about the line $\theta = \frac{1}{2}\pi$.

3 Prove that the graph of $r = \cos 2\theta$ has symmetry about both the lines $\theta = 0$ and $\theta = \frac{1}{2}\pi$. Is it also symmetrical about the line $\theta = \frac{1}{4}\pi$?

4 Investigate whether the curve $r = 2 + \cos 3\theta$, $-\pi < \theta \leqslant \pi$, has symmetry about the lines $\theta = \frac{1}{6}n\pi$ for $n = 0, 1, \ldots, 5$.

6.5   Maximum and minimum values of the radius vector

If you look back at Fig. 6.4 to the graph of $r = 2 + \cos\theta$ you will see that the graph lies wholly between the circles $r = 1$ and $r = 3$.

You could easily have predicted that from the equation $r = 2 + \cos\theta$, because $\cos\theta$ lies between -1 and 1.

Similarly you could predict that for the equation $r = \dfrac{3}{2 - \sin\theta}$ the graph lies between the circles $r = 1$ (when $\sin\theta = -1$) and $r = 3$ (when $\sin\theta = 1$).

In more complicated cases when the equation is $r = \mathrm{f}(\theta)$ you can differentiate $\mathrm{f}(\theta)$ to get information about the maximum and minimum values of r.

Example 6.5.1
For the graph with polar equation $r = 3 + 2\cos 3\theta$ with $-\pi < \theta \leqslant \pi$, find the greatest and least values of r, and the values of θ for which they occur.

Since $\cos 3\theta$ lies between -1 and 1, r lies between 1 and 5. The greatest value of r is 5, when $\theta = 0$ or $\theta = \pm\frac{2}{3}\pi$. The least value is 2, when $\theta = \pi$ or $\theta = \pm\frac{1}{3}\pi$.

Example 6.5.2
Find the maximum and minimum values of r for the curve with polar equation $r = 2 + \cos\theta + \cos 2\theta$ for $-\pi < \theta \leqslant \pi$.

There is no easy way to see which values of θ give maximum and minimum values for r, so begin by differentiating.

$$\frac{\mathrm{d}r}{\mathrm{d}\theta} = -\sin\theta - 2\sin 2\theta$$
$$= -\sin\theta - 4\sin\theta\cos\theta$$
$$= -\sin\theta(1 + 4\cos\theta).$$

$\dfrac{\mathrm{d}r}{\mathrm{d}\theta} = 0$ when $\sin\theta = 0$ and $\cos\theta = -0.25$, that is, when $\theta = 0, \pi$ and when $\cos\theta = -\frac{1}{4}$.

When $\theta = 0$, $r = 4$; when $\theta = \pi$, $r = 2$.

To find the value of $\cos 2\theta$ when $\cos\theta = -\frac{1}{4}$, recall that $\cos 2\theta = 2\cos^2\theta - 1$ giving $\cos 2\theta = 2 \times \left(\frac{1}{4}\right)^2 - 1 = -\frac{7}{8}$.

When $\cos\theta = -\frac{1}{4}$, $r = 2 + \left(-\frac{1}{4}\right) + \left(-\frac{7}{8}\right) = \frac{7}{8}$.

To find whether these are maximum or minimum values,

$$\frac{\mathrm{d}^2 r}{\mathrm{d}\theta^2} = -\cos\theta - 4\cos 2\theta.$$

When $\theta = 0$, $\dfrac{\mathrm{d}^2 r}{\mathrm{d}\theta^2} = -5$, so there is a maximum.

When $\theta = \pi$, $\dfrac{\mathrm{d}^2 r}{\mathrm{d}\theta^2} = -3$, also giving a maximum.

When $\cos\theta = -\frac{1}{4}$, $\cos 2\theta = -\frac{7}{8}$ (see above), so

$$\frac{\mathrm{d}^2 r}{\mathrm{d}\theta^2} = -\left(-\frac{1}{4}\right) - 4\left(-\frac{7}{8}\right) = \frac{15}{4},$$

which is positive, and so gives a minimum.

When $\theta = 0$ there is a maximum of 4; when $\theta = \pi$ there is a maximum of 2; and at the two points for which $\cos\theta = -\frac{1}{4}$ there are minima of $\frac{7}{8}$.

You can check the result using a graphic calculator.

6.6 The direction of the curve at the origin

In Example 6.4.2 the graph with equation $r = 2\sin 2\theta$ for $0 \leqslant \theta \leqslant \frac{1}{2}\pi$ was drawn. This graph is shown in Fig. 6.9.

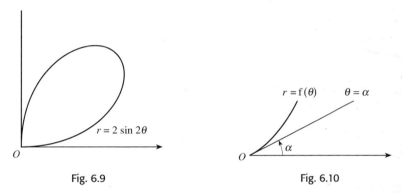

Fig. 6.9 Fig. 6.10

Notice that $r = 0$ when $\theta = 0$, but r is positive right down to $\theta = 0$; similarly, $r = 0$ when $\theta = \frac{1}{2}\pi$ but r is positive right up to $\theta = \frac{1}{2}\pi$. This can only happen (for a continuous function) if the lines $\theta = 0$ and $\theta = \frac{1}{2}\pi$ are tangents to the curve. This is an example of a general feature of polar graphs, illustrated in Fig. 6.10.

If $f(\alpha) = 0$ but $f(\theta) > 0$ in an interval $\alpha < \theta < \ldots$ or $\ldots < \theta < \alpha$, then the line $\theta = \alpha$ is a tangent to the graph of $r = f(\theta)$ at the origin (pole).

Example 6.6.1
For the graph with polar equation $r = 1 + \cos 3\theta$

(a) find the greatest and least values of r,

(b) find the equations of the tangents at the pole,

(c) show that all lines with equations $r = \frac{1}{3}k\pi$, where k is an integer, are lines of symmetry.

    (a) Since $\cos 3\theta$ lies between -1 and 1, r lies between 0 and 2. The greatest value of r is 2, when $\theta = 0$ or $\theta = \pm\frac{2}{3}\pi$ (using the π-convention). The least value is 0, when $\theta = \pi$ or $\theta = \pm\frac{1}{3}\pi$.

(b) Denoting $r = 1 + \cos 3\theta$ by $f(\theta)$, it is shown in part (a) that $f(\theta) = 0$ when $\theta = \pi$ or $\theta = \pm\frac{1}{3}\pi$, and that $f(\theta) > 0$ when $-\pi < \theta < -\frac{1}{3}\pi$, $-\frac{1}{3}\pi < \theta < \frac{1}{3}\pi$ or $\frac{1}{3}\pi < \theta < \pi$. It follows that the tangents at the pole are $\theta = -\frac{1}{3}\pi$, $\theta = \frac{1}{3}\pi$ and $\theta = \pi$.

(c) You have to prove that $f\left(\frac{2}{3}k\pi - \theta\right) \equiv f(\theta)$ for all values of θ. Starting from the left side,

$$f\left(\tfrac{2}{3}k\pi - \theta\right) \equiv 1 + \cos(2k\pi - 3\theta) \equiv 1 + \cos 3\theta \equiv f(\theta).$$

So all lines with equations $r = \frac{1}{3}k\pi$ are lines of symmetry.

Using the information in Example 6.6.1, try to sketch the graph for yourself.

Exercise 6D

1 Draw the curves with the following polar equations. Check your answers with a graphic calculator.

(a) $r = 3 + \sin\theta$

(b) $r = \cos^2\theta$

(c) $r = \dfrac{1}{2 + \cos\theta}$

(d) $r = \tan\theta$ for $0 < \theta < \frac{1}{2}\pi$

(e) $r = \sin\theta$ for $0 < \theta < \pi$

(f) $r = \sec\theta$ for $\frac{1}{2}\pi < \theta < \frac{1}{2}\pi$

(g) $r = 1 + \dfrac{\theta}{\pi}$ for $0 < \theta < 2\pi$

(h) $r = \cos\frac{1}{2}\theta$ for $-\pi < \theta < \pi$

2 For each of the following curves (i) draw a sketch, (ii) find the least and greatest values of r, (iii) state any tangents at the pole, (iv) identify (with proof) any lines of symmetry.

(a) $r = \theta^2$ for $-\pi < \theta < \pi$

(b) $r = 1 + \sin 2\theta$

(c) $r = \dfrac{1}{1 + 2\cos\theta}$ for $-\frac{2}{3}\pi < \theta < \frac{2}{3}\pi$

(d) $r = 1 - \sin^3\theta$

(e) $r = 2 + \sin\theta + \cos 2\theta$

(f) $r = 2 + \cos\theta - \cos^2\theta$

(g) $r = 5 - 3\cos\theta - 4\sin\theta$

(h) $r = 1 + \cos\theta\cos 2\theta$

6.7 Equations in polar and cartesian coordinates

The connections found in Section 6.2 between the cartesian and polar coordinates of points can also be used to convert equations of curves from cartesian to polar forms, and vice versa.

Example 6.7.1
Find the polar equations of

(a) $(x^2 + y^2)^2 = 4xy$ (b) the parabola $y = x^2$ (c) the line $x\cos\alpha + y\sin\alpha = p$, where $p > 0$.

(a) Writing $x = r\cos\theta$ and $y = r\sin\theta$,

$$((r\cos\theta)^2 + (r\sin\theta)^2)^2 = 4(r\cos\theta)(r\sin\theta),$$

which reduces to

$$r^4 = 4r^2\cos\theta\sin\theta.$$

If $r \neq 0$, then

$$r^2 = 2 \sin 2\theta.$$

The pole actually lies on the curve $r^2 = 2 \sin 2\theta$ as $r = 0$ when $\theta = 0$.

(b) The equation becomes $r \sin \theta = (r \cos \theta)^2$. If $r \neq 0$ and $\cos \theta \neq 0$,

$$r = \frac{\sin \theta}{\cos^2 \theta} = \sec \theta \tan \theta.$$

Although the value $r = 0$ was excluded in obtaining this equation, the origin does in fact appear if you substitute $\theta = 0$ or $\theta = \pi$ in the equation. Notice that these values of θ give the tangent at the origin to the parabola. There is, however, no point on the parabola corresponding to $\theta = \frac{1}{2}\pi$, where $\cos \theta = 0$.

(c) Writing $x = r \cos \theta$ and $y = r \sin \theta$, the equation becomes

$$r \cos \theta \cos \alpha + r \sin \theta \sin \alpha = p, \text{ that is } r \cos(\theta - \alpha) = p.$$

This polar equation is illustrated in Fig. 6.11.

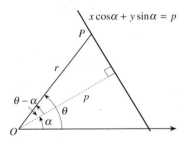

Fig. 6.11

Notice that the line has gradient $-\cot \alpha$, so that the perpendicular from O to the line has gradient $\tan \alpha$. This perpendicular therefore makes an angle α with the x-axis. Since $r = OP$, the length of the perpendicular is $r \cos(\theta - \alpha)$. This shows that the constant p in the equation is the length of the perpendicular from the origin to the line.

Example 6.7.2
Find the cartesian equations of the curves with polar equations

(a) $r = 2a \cos \theta$, for $-\frac{1}{2}\pi \leqslant \theta \leqslant \frac{1}{2}\pi$,   (b) $r^2 = a^2 \sin 2\theta$.

Both these equations contain a constant a which defines a scale to which the curve is drawn. In (a) the maximum value of r is $2a$, when $\theta = 0$; in (b) it is a, when $\theta = \frac{1}{4}\pi$ or $\theta = \frac{5}{4}\pi$.

(a) Since $\cos \theta = \dfrac{x}{r}$, the equation is $r^2 = 2ax$.

Writing r^2 as $x^2 + y^2$ leads to the cartesian equation

$$x^2 + y^2 = 2ax.$$

You should recognise this as the equation of a circle, $(x - a)^2 + y^2 = a^2$, with centre $(a, 0)$ and radius a. Figure 6.12 shows why the circle has the equation $r = 2a\cos\theta$, based on the property that the angle in a semicircle is a right angle.

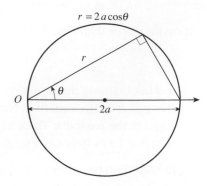

Fig. 6.12

(b) Since $2\sin\theta\cos\theta = 2\left(\dfrac{y}{r}\right)\left(\dfrac{x}{r}\right) = \dfrac{2xy}{r^2}$, you can write the equation as $r^4 = 2a^2 xy$ or

$$(x^2 + y^2)^2 = 2a^2 xy.$$

You can see from this equation that $xy \geqslant 0$, so that the graph lies entirely in the first and third quadrants. This fits with the polar equation, since (using the 2π-convention), $\sin 2\theta$ is positive only for $0 < \theta < \frac{1}{2}\pi$ or $\pi < \theta < \frac{3}{2}\pi$.

Exercise 6E

1 Find the cartesian equations of the curves with the following polar equations.

(a) $r = 2\sin\theta$ for $0 \leqslant \theta < \pi$

(b) $r = a\cos 2\theta$ for $-\frac{1}{4}\pi \leqslant \theta \leqslant \frac{1}{4}\pi$

(c) $r = a\operatorname{cosec}\theta$ for $0 < \theta < \pi$

(d) $r = \dfrac{4}{3 + \cos\theta}$

2 Find the polar equations of the curves with the following cartesian equations.

(a) $y = \dfrac{1}{x}$ for $x > 0$

(b) $x^2 + y^2 = 4$

(c) $(x - 1)^2 + (y - 1)^2 = 2$

(d) $\dfrac{1}{x} + \dfrac{1}{y} = \dfrac{1}{a}$, where $a > 0$, for $x > 0$, $y > 0$

6.8   Finding areas using polar coordinates

With cartesian graphs you know how to use integration to calculate areas and volumes of revolution contained between given values of x. A similar method can be used with polar graphs to find areas contained between given values of θ. That is, in Fig. 6.13, to find the area of the sector bounded by the graph $r = f(\theta)$ and the radii $\theta = \alpha$ and $\theta = \beta$.

The method is very similar to that for cartesian graphs.

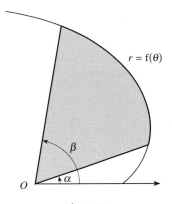

Fig. 6.13

If A denotes the area of the sector from $\theta = \alpha$ as far as any general value of θ, then A is a function of θ (see Fig. 6.14). If θ increases by $\delta\theta$, then r increases by δr and A increases by δA; and Fig. 6.15 shows that δA lies between the areas of two circular sectors with angle $\delta\theta$ and radii r and $r + \delta r$. So δA lies between $\frac{1}{2}r^2\delta\theta$ and $\frac{1}{2}(r + \delta r)^2\delta\theta$.

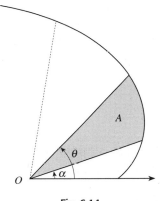

Fig. 6.14

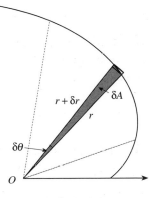

Fig. 6.15

That is, $\dfrac{\delta A}{\delta\theta}$ lies between $\frac{1}{2}r^2$ and $\frac{1}{2}(r + \delta r)^2$.

The next step is to consider the limit as $\delta\theta \to 0$. Then $\dfrac{\delta A}{\delta\theta}$ tends to $\dfrac{\mathrm{d}A}{\mathrm{d}\theta}$, and $\delta r \to 0$, so

$$\frac{\mathrm{d}A}{\mathrm{d}\theta} = \tfrac{1}{2}r^2.$$

You will recognise that this is the same kind of argument as was used for areas in C2 Sections 5.4 and for volumes in C3 Section 11.1. It follows that the area of the sector in Fig. 6.13 can be found as a definite integral:

> The area of the region bounded by the graph $r = f(\theta)$ and the radii $\theta = \alpha$ and $\theta = \beta$ is
>
> $$\int_{\alpha}^{\beta} \tfrac{1}{2}r^2 \, \mathrm{d}\theta = \int_{\alpha}^{\beta} \tfrac{1}{2}(f(\theta))^2 \, \mathrm{d}\theta.$$

Example 6.8.1

Fig. 6.16 shows the graph of $r = a\theta$, where a is a constant, for $0 < \theta < 2\pi$. Find the area of the shaded region.

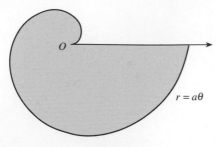

Fig. 6.16

If you imagine the radius OP rotating from $\theta = 0$ to $\theta = 2\pi$, it will sweep out the shaded region. So the area is

$$\int_0^{2\pi} \tfrac{1}{2}(a\theta)^2 \, d\theta = \int_0^{2\pi} \tfrac{1}{2}a^2\theta^2 \, d\theta$$

$$= \left[\tfrac{1}{6}a^2\theta^3\right]_0^{2\pi}$$

$$= \tfrac{1}{6}a^2(2\pi)^3 = \tfrac{4}{3}\pi^3 a^2.$$

Example 6.8.2

Find the area enclosed by the curve $r = 2 + \cos\theta$ (see Example 6.3.1).

This graph was drawn in Fig. 6.4 using the π-convention, and is repeated in Fig. 6.17.

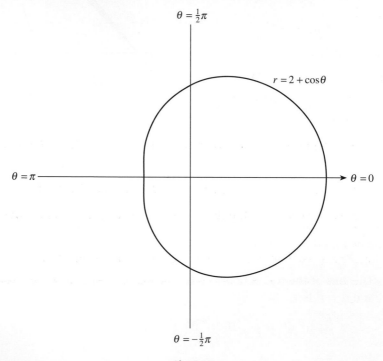

Fig. 6.17

The 'sector' beginning at $\theta = -\pi$ and ending at $\theta = \pi$ makes up the whole region inside the curve. So the area enclosed is

$$\int_{-\pi}^{\pi} \tfrac{1}{2}(2 + \cos\theta)^2 \, d\theta = \int_{-\pi}^{\pi} (2 + 2\cos\theta + \tfrac{1}{2}\cos^2\theta) \, d\theta$$

$$= \int_{-\pi}^{\pi} (2 + 2\cos\theta + \tfrac{1}{4}(1 + \cos 2\theta)) \, d\theta$$

$$= \left[\tfrac{9}{4}\theta + 2\sin\theta + \tfrac{1}{8}\sin 2\theta \right]_{-\pi}^{\pi}$$

$$= \tfrac{9}{4}(\pi - (-\pi))$$

$$= \tfrac{9}{2}\pi.$$

The equation $\dfrac{dA}{d\theta} = \tfrac{1}{2}r^2$ has important applications to the motion of planets and satellites. In about the year 1600 Kepler discovered from observations that the rate at which the radius from the sun to a planet sweeps out area is constant. That is, if O is the sun and r is the distance from the sun to the planet, then $\dfrac{dA}{dt} = \text{constant}$. Since $\dfrac{dA}{dt}$ can be written as $\dfrac{dA}{d\theta} \times \dfrac{d\theta}{dt}$, Kepler's law corresponds to the equation

$$\tfrac{1}{2}r^2 \dfrac{d\theta}{dt} = \text{constant}.$$

For example, when a comet comes close to the sun, the radius rotates very much more rapidly than it does when the comet is at a great distance.

Exercise 6F

1 Calculate the areas enclosed by the following curves and radii. Illustrate each calculation with a sketch.

(a) $r = c^\theta,\qquad \theta = 0, \theta = \pi$

(b) $r = \theta^2,\quad \theta = -\pi, \theta = \pi$

(c) $r = a + b\theta,\quad \theta = 0, \theta = 2\pi$

(d) $r = a\cos\theta,\quad \theta = -\tfrac{1}{4}\pi, \theta = \tfrac{1}{4}\pi$

(e) $r = a + b\sin\theta,\quad \theta = 0, \theta = \pi$

2 Find the area enclosed by the curve with equation $r^2 = a^2 \sin 2\theta$ for $0 \leqslant \theta \leqslant \tfrac{1}{2}\pi$. (See Example 6.7.2(b).)

3 Find the area of the loop of $r = 2\sin 2\theta$ for $0 \leqslant \theta \leqslant \tfrac{1}{2}\pi$. (See Fig. 6.8.)

4 Sketch the curve (a *cardioid*) with polar equation $r = a(1 + \cos\theta)$. Show that it encloses an area of $\tfrac{3}{2}\pi a^2$.

5 Find the area enclosed within the curve $r = a\cos\tfrac{1}{2}\theta$ for $-\pi < \theta \leqslant \pi$.

6.9*   Parabolas, polars and parameters

This section revises a number of topics in coordinate geometry, by applying a variety of methods to find some properties of parabolas. You may omit it if you wish.

Figure 6.18 shows the graph of

$$r = \frac{2a}{1 + \cos\theta} \text{ for } -\pi < \theta < \pi.$$

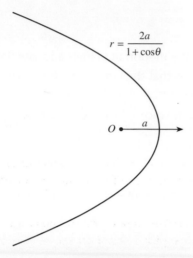

$$r = \frac{2a}{1 + \cos\theta}$$

O a

Fig. 6.18

Notice that θ cannot take the value π, since $1 + \cos\pi = 0$. Also, since $1 + \cos\theta$ decreases from 2 to 0 as θ increases from 0 to π, r increases from a without limit. The equation has the form $r = g(\cos\theta)$, and $\cos(-\theta) = \cos\theta$, so the graph is symmetrical about the initial line.

If you guessed that this graph is a parabola you would be right. Writing the equation as $r = 2a - r\cos\theta$, the cartesian equation is

$$\sqrt{x^2 + y^2} = 2a - x, \text{ or}$$
$$x^2 + y^2 = 4a^2 - 4ax + x^2, \text{ which is}$$
$$y^2 = 4a(a - x).$$

C4 Example 3.4.1 dealt with a parabola with parametric equations $x = at^2$, $y = 2at$ (Fig. 6.19). You can eliminate t by writing it as $\dfrac{y}{2a}$ and substituting:

$$x = a\left(\frac{y}{2a}\right)^2, \text{ that is } y^2 = 4ax.$$

How are the graphs of $y^2 = 4ax$ and $y^2 = 4a(a - x)$ related? If in the second equation you replace x by $-x$, it becomes $y^2 = 4a(x + a)$. If you then replace x by $(x - a)$, the equation becomes $y^2 = 4ax$. So these equations represent essentially the same curve; you get the first from the second by reflecting in the y-axis and then translating a distance a in the x-direction.

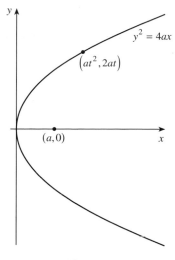

Fig. 6.19

The point which was the origin in the polar form has, as usual, a place of special importance for the curve. It is called the **focus** of the parabola. On the graph of $y^2 = 4ax$ this corresponds to the point $(a, 0)$.

Now that you know the equation of the parabola in cartesian, parametric and polar forms, you can use whichever is most convenient to find geometrical properties of the curve. Here are two properties which involve the focus.

Theorem   If F is the focus of a parabola, and PQ is any chord through F, then $\dfrac{1}{FP} + \dfrac{1}{FQ}$ is constant.

> **Proof**   Since this involves distances from the focus, it is best to use the polar equation. In Fig. 6.20, P corresponds to $\theta = \alpha$, where $0 < \alpha < \pi$, and Q to $\theta = \alpha - \pi$.

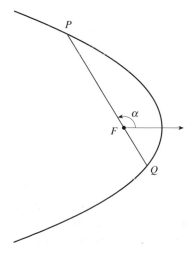

Fig. 6.20

Then since $r = \dfrac{2a}{1 + \cos\theta}$, $FP = \dfrac{2a}{1 + \cos\alpha}$ and $FQ = \dfrac{2a}{1 + \cos(\alpha - \pi)} = \dfrac{2a}{1 - \cos\alpha}$.

Therefore

$$\frac{1}{FP} + \frac{1}{FQ} = \frac{1}{2a}((1 + \cos\alpha) + (1 - \cos\alpha))$$

$$= \frac{1}{2a} \times 2 = \frac{1}{a}.$$

Theorem   Prove that, if a source of light is placed at the focus of a mirror in the shape of a parabola rotated about its axis of symmetry, all the light from the source will be reflected parallel to the axis.

Proof   The rule of reflection is that a ray and its reflection make the same angle with the tangent to the mirror (Fig. 6.21).

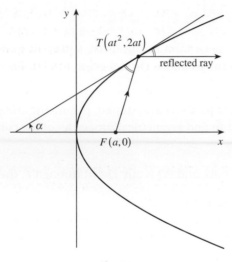

Fig. 6.21

You do not know how to find tangents in polar coordinates, so it is better to use parameters.

The gradient of the tangent at the point T, with coordinates $(at^2, 2at)$, is

$$\frac{\mathrm{d}y}{\mathrm{d}x} = \frac{\mathrm{d}y}{\mathrm{d}t} \bigg/ \frac{\mathrm{d}x}{\mathrm{d}t} = \frac{2a}{2at} = \frac{1}{t}.$$

If this tangent makes an angle α with the x-axis, then $\tan\alpha = \dfrac{1}{t}$.

If F is the focus $(a, 0)$, the line FT has gradient

$$\frac{2at - 0}{at^2 - a} = \frac{2t}{t^2 - 1}.$$

Dividing numerator and denominator by t^2, this can be written as

$$\frac{2/t}{1-1/t^2} = \frac{2\tan\alpha}{1-\tan^2\alpha} = \tan 2\alpha.$$

This shows that FT makes an angle 2α with the x-axis.

The ray FT therefore makes an angle $2\alpha - \alpha = \alpha$ with the tangent, so the ray is also reflected at an angle α. This means that the reflected ray is parallel to the x-axis.

6.10*   Breaching the conventions

You may omit this section if you wish.

The reason for introducing conventions restricting the values of r and θ is to ensure that each point (other than O) has unique polar coordinates. But when you draw polar graphs these conventions sometimes put up unnecessary barriers.

For example, if the function $f(\theta)$ has a period of 2π (such as $r = 2 + \cos\theta$, see Example 6.3.1) or a divisor of 2π (such as $r = \tan^2\theta$ with period π), then allowing θ to continue outside the interval defined by the convention will not produce any more points; the point (r, θ) will simply trace out the same graph again. But if $f(\theta)$ is not periodic, new points will continue to be added to the graph.

Example 6.10.1

Draw the graph of $r = \dfrac{\theta}{2\pi}$ for $\theta \geqslant 0$.

The graph starts at $(0,0)$, and after one rotation of the radius it reaches $(1, 2\pi)$. As θ continues to increase, the value of r is greater by 1 than it was the previous time that the radius vector pointed in the same direction.

The graph is shown in Fig. 6.22.

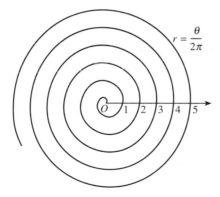

Fig. 6.22

It is called the *spiral of Archimedes*, because he wrote a book about its properties.

There are also some graphs which look incomplete unless r is allowed to take negative values. The interpretation is that, in plotting the point (r, θ), you face in the direction of the radius vector at an angle θ, but move backwards in that direction if r is negative. In Figs. 6.23 to 6.26 the graphs are shown with the portions for which $r < 0$ drawn dotted.

Example 6.10.2

Draw the graph of $r = 1 + 2\cos\theta$, using the π-convention.

Notice that $r = 0$ when $\cos\theta = -\frac{1}{2}$, that is when $\theta = -\frac{2}{3}\pi$ or $\frac{2}{3}\pi$. Between these values of θ, r is positive; but for $-\pi < \theta < -\frac{2}{3}\pi$ and $\frac{2}{3}\pi < \theta \leqslant \pi$, r is negative. When $\theta = \pi$, $r = -1$. The graph is shown in Fig. 6.23.

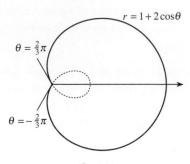

Fig. 6.23

Example 6.10.3

Draw the graphs, using the 2π-convention, of   (a) $r = \sin 4\theta$,   (b) $r = \sin 3\theta$.

The period of the function $\sin n\theta$ is $\dfrac{2\pi}{n}$, which is a divisor of 2π if n is an integer, so the graphs are certainly completed once $\theta = 2\pi$ is reached. Values of r are positive from 0 to $\dfrac{\pi}{n}$, negative from $\dfrac{\pi}{n}$ to $\dfrac{2\pi}{n}$, and so on alternately.

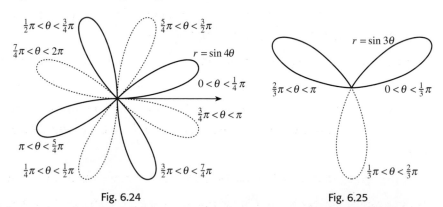

Fig. 6.24   Fig. 6.25

The graphs are shown in Figs. 6.24 and 6.25; an interesting difference is that (a) continues to produce new points up to $\theta = 2\pi$, but (b) is complete once you reach $\theta = \pi$ and then repeats the same points between π and 2π.

The next example is a graph which for completeness requires the conventions restricting both r and θ to be breached.

Example 6.10.4
Draw the graph of $r = \sin \frac{1}{2}\theta$.

This function has period 4π; r is positive for $0 < \theta < 2\pi$ and negative for $2\pi < \theta < 4\pi$.
The graph is shown in Fig. 6.26.

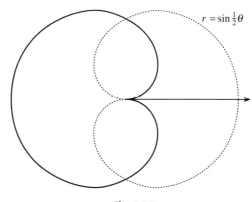

$r = \sin \frac{1}{2}\theta$

Fig. 6.26

Exercise 6G*

1 Sketch the graph of $r = e^{\theta}$ for $\theta \in \mathbb{R}$. Show that any portion of the curve defined by $\alpha \leqslant \theta \leqslant \alpha + \beta$ is an enlargement or contraction of the portion defined by $0 \leqslant \theta \leqslant \beta$.

2 Show that, as $\theta \to 0$, the graph of $r = \dfrac{2\pi}{\theta}$ approaches the line $y = 2\pi$. Draw a sketch to indicate the shape of the complete graph for $\theta > 0$.

3 Use a graphic calculator to show the complete graphs (with no restrictions on r or θ) of
(a) $r = \sin \frac{1}{3}\theta$,
(b) $r = \sin \frac{1}{4}\theta$,
(c) $r = \sin \frac{2}{3}\theta$,
(d) $r = \sin \frac{3}{4}\theta$.

4 Draw sketches to show the different possible shapes of graphs (*limaçons*) with equation $r = k + \cos \theta$ for $k \geqslant 0$. What area is represented by $\displaystyle\int_{-\pi}^{\pi} \frac{1}{2}(k + \cos \theta)^2 \, d\theta$ for various values of k?

5 Find the total area enclosed inside the graph of $r = \sin n\theta$, where $n \in \mathbb{N}$ and $n \geqslant 1$.

6 For the parabola in Section 6.9, show that $r + x = 2a$. Use this to show that, for any point P on the parabola in Fig. 6.20, the distance FP is equal to the perpendicular distance from P to a certain line. Describe the position of this line (the *directrix*) precisely.

7 Sketch the curves (*conchoids*) with polar equations $r = \sec\theta + k$, where r may take both positive and negative values, in the cases

   (a) $k = 0$,   (b) $k = 1$,   (c) $k = -1$,   (d) $k = -2$.

   Where appropriate, state the tangents at the pole.

   Show that one of the curves includes a loop, and find the area enclosed by it.

8 A 45° set square ABC has a right angle at B and $AB = BC = a$. Initially A is at the origin, B is at the point with cartesian coordinates $(a, 0)$ and C is at $(a, -a)$. The corner C moves up the line $x = a$ until it reaches $(a, 0)$, and the set square moves so that the edge AB always passes through the origin. Show that B describes a curve whose polar equation is
   $r = a(\sec\theta - \tan\theta)$ for $0 \leqslant \theta < \frac{1}{2}\pi$.

   Draw the whole of this curve (a *strophoid*) with the given equation for values of θ between 0 and 2π, allowing r to take both positive and negative values. Show that the curve includes a loop, and find the area enclosed by it.

9 Prove that, in Fig. 6.20, the area enclosed between the chord PQ and the parabola is $\frac{8}{3}a^2\operatorname{cosec}^3\alpha$.

Miscellaneous exercise 6

1 O is the pole, and A and B have polar coordinates $\left(8, -\frac{1}{12}\pi\right)$ and $\left(5, \frac{1}{4}\pi\right)$. Find

   (a) the distance AB,   (b) the area of the triangle OAB.

2 Sketch, on the same diagrams, the graphs of

   (a) $r = \cos 2\theta$ and $r = \sec 2\theta$,   (b) $r = 1 - 2\cos\theta$ and $r = \dfrac{1}{1 - 2\cos\theta}$.

   In each case, consider the values of θ between $-\pi$ and π for which $r > 0$.

3 Find the cartesian equations of the curves with polar equations

   (a) $r = \cos^3\theta$,   (b) $r = \sec^3\theta$.

4 Find the polar equation of the curve with cartesian equation $\dfrac{1}{x^2} + \dfrac{1}{y^2} = 1$. Use your answer to draw a sketch of the curve.

5 Sketch the curve with polar equation $r = \cos\theta(1 - \sin\theta)$ for $-\frac{1}{2}\pi \leqslant \theta \leqslant \frac{1}{2}\pi$. Find

   (a) the area enclosed by the curve,

   (b) the polar coordinates of the point of the curve furthest from the origin.

6 Draw on one diagram the curves G and H with polar equations $r = 2\cos\theta$ (Fig. 6.12) and $r = 1 + 2\cos\theta$ (Fig. 6.23).

   Let C be the point with polar coordinates $r = 1$, $\theta = 0$. Draw a line through C making an angle α with the initial line. Let this line meet the curve H at P, and let OP meet the curve G at Q. Denote the angle QCP by β. Identify two isosceles triangles in your figure, and deduce that $\alpha = 3\beta$.

   Show how this can be used to give a construction to trisect an angle. (For this reason the curve H is called a *trisectrix*.)

7 A curve C has cartesian equation $x^2 + y^2 = a(x - y)$. It is rotated about the origin through $45°$ anticlockwise to give a curve C'. Find the polar equation of C, and hence find the polar and cartesian equations of C'.

8 Find the polar equation of the curve H with cartesian equation $x^2 - y^2 = a^2$. Hence find the cartesian equation of the curve obtained by rotating H about the origin through an angle of $45°$ anticlockwise.

9 Sketch the curve E with cartesian equation $\dfrac{x^2}{25} + \dfrac{y^2}{9} = 1$. Write the equation of the curve E' obtained by translating E by -4 in the x-direction. Show that the polar equation of E' can be written as $r = \dfrac{9}{5 + 4\cos\theta}$.

For the curve E, F is the point $(4, 0)$ and PQ is a chord which passes through F. Prove that $\dfrac{1}{FP} + \dfrac{1}{FQ}$ is constant.

Deduce from the polar equation of E' that $r = \frac{4}{5}\left(\frac{9}{4} - x\right)$. Hence show that, if P is any point on the curve E, the distance of P from F is $\frac{4}{5}$ of its perpendicular distance from the line $x = 6\frac{1}{4}$.

10 Find the cartesian equation of the curve with polar equation $r = \cos^2\theta$. Hence show that the equation of the tangent to the curve at the point $\left(\frac{1}{2}, \frac{1}{4}\pi\right)$ is $r = \dfrac{1}{\sqrt{2}(3\sin\theta - \cos\theta)}$.

11* In suitable units the vertical cross-section through the axis of symmetry of an airship has polar equation $r = 2\cos\theta + \cos 3\theta$, where r may take both positive and negative values. Find the values of θ in the interval $0 \leqslant \theta \leqslant \pi$ for which r is zero, and show that the curve consists of three loops.

If the area of the top half of the large loop is given by $\displaystyle\int_0^\alpha f(\theta)\,d\theta$, write down the expression $f(\theta)$ and the value of α. Find the area of the large loop.   (OCR, adapted)

12* Sketch the curve (a *strophoid*) with equation $r = \dfrac{a\cos 2\theta}{\cos\theta}$, where r can take both positive and negative values. Show that the whole curve lies within the interval $-a \leqslant x \leqslant a$, and that for $-\frac{1}{4}\pi \leqslant \theta \leqslant \frac{1}{4}\pi$ the curve describes a loop. Calculate the area of the loop. (Compare with Exercise 6G Question 8.)

13* Plot the points on the curve with equation $r = \cos 2\theta + 2\cos\theta$ from $\theta = -\pi$ to $\theta = \pi$ at intervals of $\frac{1}{4}\pi$ allowing r to take both positive and negative values. Use these to draw a sketch of the complete curve.

There are four regions which are completely bounded by parts of the curve. Show that one of these has the points with cartesian coordinates $(1, 0)$, $(3, 0)$, $(1, 1)$ and $(1, -1)$ on its boundary. Find the area of this region.

14* Show that parametric equations for the curve $r = 1 + 2\cos\theta$ shown in Fig. 6.23 are

$$x = 1 + \cos\theta + \cos 2\theta, \quad y = \sin\theta + \sin 2\theta.$$

Find the minimum value of x, and the angle $\theta = \alpha$ between $\frac{1}{2}\pi$ and π for which x takes this value.

An apple-shaped surface is formed by rotating the outer loop of this curve about the initial line. Explain why the volume it encloses can be calculated as

$$\int_{\alpha}^{0} \pi y^2 \frac{\mathrm{d}x}{\mathrm{d}\theta}\, \mathrm{d}\theta - \int_{\alpha}^{\frac{2}{3}\pi} \pi y^2 \frac{\mathrm{d}x}{\mathrm{d}\theta}\, \mathrm{d}\theta,$$

and show that this is equal to $6\frac{3}{4}\pi$.

Revision exercise 1

1 Write down the first three non-zero terms of the Maclaurin series for $\cos 2x$, and hence find the first three terms of the Maclaurin series for $e^x \cos 2x$. (OCR)

2 The diagram shows the curve whose equation, in polar coordinates is $r = 1 + \sin\theta$ $(-\pi < \theta \leqslant \pi)$.

Find the exact value of the area of the shaded region between the curve and the lines $\theta = 0$ and $\theta = \pi$. (OCR)

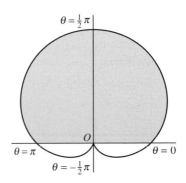

3 (a) Express $\dfrac{2(x-2)}{(x+2)(x^2+4)}$ in partial fractions.

 (b) Hence find the exact value of $\displaystyle\int_0^2 \dfrac{2(x-2)}{(x+2)(x^2+4)}\,\mathrm{d}x$. (OCR)

4 (a) Given that $y = \tanh^{-1}(\sin x)$, show that $\dfrac{\mathrm{d}y}{\mathrm{d}x} = \sec x$.

 (b) Use the method of integration by parts to show that
 $$\int_0^{\frac{1}{4}\pi} \sec^2 x \, \tanh^{-1}(\sin x)\,\mathrm{d}x = 1 - \sqrt{2} + \tfrac{1}{2}\ln(3 + 2\sqrt{2}).$$
 (OCR)

5 Find the equation of each asymptote of the curve $y = \dfrac{3x^2 - 2x + 4}{x^2 - x - 2}$. (OCR)

6 (a) Write down the first three terms of the Maclaurin series for e^{ax}, where a is a constant.

 (b) Hence, or otherwise, find the first three terms of the Maclaurin series for $(1 - bx)\,e^{ax}$, where a and b are constants.

 (c) It is given that the Maclaurin series for $(1 - bx)\,e^{ax}$ and e^{-2x^2} are identical, up to and including the terms in x^2. Find the possible values of a and b. (OCR)

7 The equation of a curve, in polar coordinates, is $r = 2\cos 2\theta$ $(-\pi < \theta \leqslant \pi)$.

 (a) Find the values of θ which give the directions of the tangents at the pole.

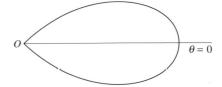

 One loop of the curve is shown in the diagram.

 (b) Find the exact value of the area of the region enclosed by the loop.

8 (a) Starting from the definition of $\cosh x$ in terms of e^x, show that $\cosh 2x = 2\cosh^2 x - 1$.

 (b) Solve the equation $\cosh 2x - 5\cosh x = 2$, giving each answer exactly, in terms of logarithms. (OCR)

9 It is given that $y = \sin^{-1}(ax)$, where a is a positive constant and $-\dfrac{1}{a} \leqslant x \leqslant \dfrac{1}{a}$.

   (a) Find $\dfrac{dx}{dy}$ in terms of y and a.

   (b) Hence find $\dfrac{dy}{dx}$ in terms of x and a.

   (c) Hence, or otherwise, find $\displaystyle\int \dfrac{1}{\sqrt{1 - 9x^2}}\, dx$.

   (d) Find the exact value of $\displaystyle\int_0^{\frac{1}{6}} \sqrt{1 - 9x^2}\, dx$.   (OCR)

10 (a) Find the Maclaurin series for $2\cos 3x$ and $\ln(1 - 3x)$, up to and including the terms in x^2.

    (b) Hence find the Maclaurin series for $\dfrac{2\cos 3x}{1 + \ln(1 - 3x)}$ up to and including the term in x^2.   (OCR)

11 The equation of a curve is $y = \dfrac{4x + 1}{2x^2 + 1}$.

    (a) Prove that $-1 \leqslant y \leqslant 2$.

    (b) Hence find the coordinates of the turning points on the curve, justifying which is a maximum and which is a minimum.

    (c) Find the exact area of the region bounded by the curve, the x- and y-axes and the line $x = 1$.   (OCR)

12 The diagram shows the curve $r = 1 + \sin 2\theta$, for $0 \leqslant \theta < 2\pi$.

    (a) Find the greatest value of r and the corresponding values of θ.

    (b) Explain why the line $\theta = \tfrac{3}{4}\pi$ is tangential to the curve at the pole.

    (c) Find the area enclosed by one loop of the curve.

    (d) Find the cartesian equation of the curve in the form $(x^2 + y^2)^m = (x + y)^n$.   (OCR)

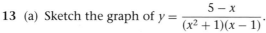

13 (a) Sketch the graph of $y = \dfrac{5 - x}{(x^2 + 1)(x - 1)}$.

    (b) Calculate the area bounded by the graph of $y = \dfrac{5 - x}{(x^2 + 1)(x - 1)}$, the line $x = 2$, the x-axis and the line $x = 3$, giving your answer in exact form.

14 Find, in terms of logarithms, the values of x for which $7\cosh x - \sinh x = 8$.   (OCR)

15 Find approximations to the value of $\displaystyle\int_0^{\frac{1}{6}\pi} \ln(1 + \sin x)\, dx$

    (a) by using the trapezium rule with 6 intervals,

    (b) by approximating to the integrand by its Maclaurin polynomial of degree 3.

    Give both of your answers to 4 significant figures.

16 (a) Find the derivative of $f(x) = \sin^{-1} \dfrac{x}{\sqrt{a^2 + x^2}}$ with respect to x, where a is a positive constant. Hence write $f(x)$ in a simpler form.

   (b) Find $\displaystyle\int_0^a f(x)\, dx$.

17 State the natural domain of the function defined by $f(x) = \cos^{-1} x + \tan^{-1} \sqrt{x}$. Find, correct to 4 significant figures, the maximum value of $f(x)$. Sketch the graph of $y = f(x)$.

18 Find numbers a, b, c and d such that the expansions of $(1 + ax^2)^b$ and $\dfrac{1 + cx^2}{1 + dx^2}$ agree with the expansion of $\cos x$ as far as the terms in x^4.

For these values of a, b, c and d, continue the expansions of the two expressions as far as the terms in x^6, and hence suggest which of them seems likely to provide the better approximation to the value of $\cos x$ for small values of x.

Verify your answer by comparing the values of the two expressions when $x = 0.1$ with the value of $\cos 0.1$.

19 (a) Prove that $\sinh^{-1} x = \ln(x + \sqrt{x^2 + 1})$.

   (b) Use the substitution $x = 3 + 3 \sinh u$ to show that
$$\int \sqrt{x^2 - 6x + 18}\, dx = \tfrac{9}{2} \int (1 + \cosh 2u)\, du.$$

   (c) Hence, find in logarithmic form, the value of $\displaystyle\int_3^7 \sqrt{x^2 - 6x + 18}\, dx$. 　　　(OCR)

20 Find the exact solutions of the equation $2 \cosh x + \sinh x = 2$. 　　　(OCR)

21 Differentiate
   (a) $\sin^{-1} \dfrac{x}{2}$, 　　　　　　　　　　　(b) $\cosh^{-1} \dfrac{2}{x}$,
   with respect to x, where $0 < x < 2$, simplifying your answers as much as possible.
   Find $\displaystyle\int \dfrac{2 + 3x}{x\sqrt{4 - x^2}}\, dx$. 　　　(MEI)

22 (a) Show that $\cosh^4 x = \tfrac{1}{8} \cosh 4x + \tfrac{1}{2} \cosh 2x + \tfrac{3}{8}$. Find the series expansion for $\cosh^4 x$, as far as the term in x^4.

   (b) Given that $\sinh \alpha = \tfrac{3}{4}$, show that $\sinh 2\alpha = \tfrac{15}{8}$ and find $\sinh 4\alpha$.

   (c) Show that $\displaystyle\int_0^3 (16 + u^2)^{\frac{3}{2}}\, du = \tfrac{735}{4} + 96 \ln 2$. 　　　(MEI)

23 (a) Show that $\displaystyle\int_3^5 \sqrt{x^2 - 9}\, dx = 10 - \tfrac{9}{2} \ln 3$.

   (b) Find the Maclaurin series for $\cosh^{-1} \left(\tfrac{5}{3} + x\right)$, as far as the term in x^2. 　　　(MEI)

24 Obtain, using successive differentiation, the first three non-zero terms of the Maclaurin series for $\sinh x$. By considering a suitable value of x, find the sum of the infinite series
$$\frac{1}{2} + \frac{9}{2 \times 4 \times 6} + \frac{9^2}{2 \times 4 \times 6 \times 8 \times 10} + \frac{9^3}{2 \times 4 \times 6 \times 8 \times 10 \times 12 \times 14} + \cdots. \qquad \text{(MEI)}$$

7 Series and integrals

This chapter shows that there are links between summing series and evaluating integrals. When you have completed it, you should

- be able to find estimates of areas under curves by summing series
- be able to use integrals to approximate to sums of series.

7.1 Approximating to integrals

In C2 Chapter 10 you saw how to find an approximation to an area, and hence an integral, using the trapezium rule; and in C3 Chapter 12 you saw how to find an approximation to an area or an integral using Simpson's rule.

One of the difficulties with these approximations is that it is often difficult to tell whether the approximation is above or below the true value of the area or the integral.

In simple situations you can see whether the trapezium rule approximation is too large or too small. If a graph is bending downwards over the whole interval from a to b, as in Fig. 7.1, then you can be certain that the trapezium rule will give you an underestimate of the true area. In Fig. 7.1 the amount of underestimate is represented by the area of the shaded region.

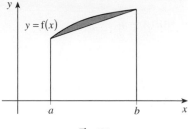

Fig. 7.1

If, on the other hand, a graph is bending upwards over the whole interval from a to b, as in Fig. 7.2, then you can be certain that the trapezium rule will give you an overestimate of the true area. In Fig. 7.2, where there are two trapezia, the amount of overestimate is represented by the area of the shaded region.

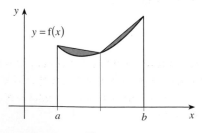

Fig. 7.2

However, if the graph sometimes bends upwards and sometimes downwards over the interval from a to b, you cannot be sure whether your approximation to the integral is an overestimate or an underestimate.

Moreover, in the situations shown in Fig. 7.1 and Fig. 7.2, all you can say is that the trapezium approximations are below and above the values of the respective integrals. It would be good to have some method of approximation which would guarantee that the actual value of the integral was sandwiched between two numbers. These two numbers are called **bounds:** the larger is an **upper bound** and the smaller is a **lower bound**.

This is one of the purposes of the rectangle approximation.

7.2 The rectangle approximation

The rectangle approximation relies on a very simple idea, illustrated in Fig. 7.3.

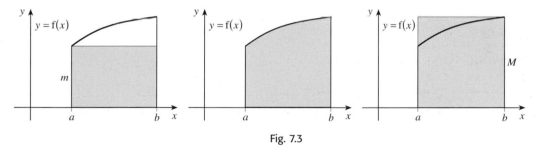

Fig. 7.3

From the left diagram in Fig. 7.3, if m is the least value of $f(x)$ in the interval $a \leqslant x \leqslant b$, then the area of the shaded rectangular region is

$$m(b - a).$$

In the middle diagram in Fig. 7.3 the area of the shaded region is

$$\int_a^b f(x)\,dx.$$

From the right diagram in Fig. 7.3, if M is the greatest value of $f(x)$ in the interval $a \leqslant x \leqslant b$, then the area of the shaded rectangular region is

$$M(b - a).$$

It follows, from looking at the areas of the shaded regions, that

$$m(b - a) \; < \; \int_a^b f(x)\,dx \; < \; M(b - a).$$

This inequality has the advantage that it is an exact statement, and there is no approximately equals sign which is hiding how accurate the approximation is. You also know that the difference between the upper and lower bounds is $M(b - a) - m(b - a) = (M - m)(b - a)$. So you can tell how accurate the upper and lower bounds are.

A double inequality of the type above will be called a *sandwich inequality*.

Example 7.2.1

(a) Use a diagram to show that $1 < \displaystyle\int_0^1 2^x \, dx < 2$.

(b) Derive the approximation $\frac{1}{2}(1 + \sqrt{2}) < \displaystyle\int_0^1 2^x \, dx < \frac{1}{2}(\sqrt{2} + 2)$.

(a) The first approximation comes from Fig. 7.4.

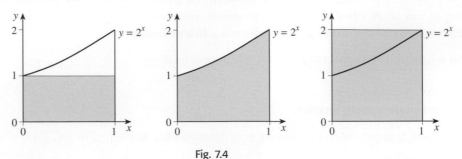

Fig. 7.4

(b) The second approximation comes from refining the first approximation by making two rectangles (see Fig. 7.5). The height of the curve at $x = \frac{1}{2}$ is $2^{\frac{1}{2}}$, which is $\sqrt{2}$.

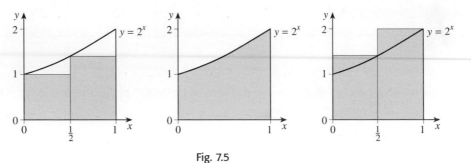

Fig. 7.5

The area of the left shaded region is $1 \times \frac{1}{2} + \sqrt{2} \times \frac{1}{2} = \frac{1}{2}(1 + \sqrt{2})$.

The area of the right shaded region is $\sqrt{2} \times \frac{1}{2} + 2 \times \frac{1}{2} = \frac{1}{2}(\sqrt{2} + 2)$.

So the sandwich inequality becomes

$$\frac{1}{2}(1 + \sqrt{2}) < \int_0^1 2^x \, dx < \frac{1}{2}(\sqrt{2} + 2).$$

Numerically,

$$1.207... < \int_0^1 2^x \, dx < 1.707... \, .$$

If you want to give the numbers in this inequality to 3 significant figures, and to be sure that your statement is correct, then you should round down the number on the left and round up the number on the right. That is,

$$1.20 < \int_0^1 2^x \, dx < 1.71.$$

If you divided the interval $0 \leqslant x \leqslant 1$ into ten sub-intervals each of width 0.1, you would get the sandwich inequality

$$0.1\,(2^0 + 2^{0.1} + \cdots + 2^{0.8} + 2^{0.9}) < \int_0^1 2^x \, dx < 0.1\,(2^{0.1} + 2^{0.2} + \cdots + 2^{0.9} + 2^1),$$

which becomes

$$1.39 < \int_0^1 2^x \, dx < 1.50.$$

You could rewrite the sandwich inequality

$$0.1\,(2^0 + 2^{0.1} + \cdots + 2^{0.8} + 2^{0.9}) < \int_0^1 2^x \, dx < 0.1\,(2^{0.1} + 2^{0.2} + \cdots + 2^{0.9} + 2^1),$$

using summation notation, as

$$0.1 \sum_{r=0}^{9} 2^{0.1r} < \int_0^1 2^x \, dx < 0.1 \sum_{r=1}^{10} 2^{0.1r}.$$

Example 7.2.2

(a) Use an area argument to show that $\int_3^4 \sqrt{1 + x^2} \, dx$ lies between $\sqrt{10}$ and $\sqrt{17}$.

(b) Refine the sandwich inequality $\sqrt{10} < \int_3^4 \sqrt{1 + x^2} \, dx < \sqrt{17}$ by sub-dividing the interval between 3 and 4 into 10 rectangles of width 0.1, and calculate numerical values for your sandwich inequality.

(c) Rewrite your inequality from part (b) using summation notation. How would it alter if you had 100 rectangles of width 0.01 instead of 10 rectangles of width 0.1?

(a) The lower bound of $\sqrt{1 + x^2}$ in $3 \leqslant x \leqslant 4$ is $\sqrt{1 + 3^2} = \sqrt{10}$, and the upper bound is $\sqrt{1 + 4^2} = \sqrt{17}$.

So

$$\sqrt{10} \times 1 < \int_3^4 \sqrt{1 + x^2} \, dx < \sqrt{17} \times 1,$$

which gives the required inequality.

(b)

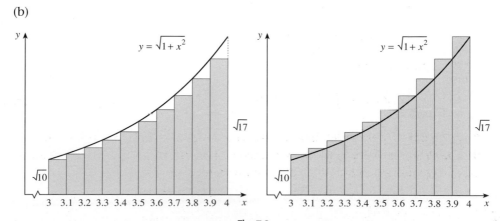

Fig. 7.6

Using Fig. 7.6,

$$\sqrt{1+3^2}\times 0.1 + \sqrt{1+3.1^2}\times 0.1 + \cdots + \sqrt{1+3.9^2}\times 0.1$$
$$< \int_3^4 \sqrt{1+x^2}\,dx$$
$$< \sqrt{1+3.1^2}\times 0.1 + \sqrt{1+3.2^2}\times 0.1 + \cdots + \sqrt{1+4.0^2}\times 0.1,$$

or

$$0.1\,(\sqrt{1+3^2} + \sqrt{1+3.1^2} + \cdots + \sqrt{1+3.9^2})$$
$$< \int_3^4 \sqrt{1+x^2}\,dx$$
$$< 0.1\,(\sqrt{1+3.1^2} + \sqrt{1+3.2^2} + \cdots + \sqrt{1+4.0^2}).$$

Using a calculator, this gives

$$3.592... < \int_3^4 \sqrt{1+x^2}\,dx < 3.688...$$

or

$$3.59 < \int_3^4 \sqrt{1+x^2}\,dx < 3.69,$$

where the left side has been rounded down and the right side has been rounded up.

(c) In summation notation this is

$$0.1\sum_{r=0}^{9}\sqrt{1+\left(3+\tfrac{1}{10}r\right)^2} < \int_3^4 \sqrt{1+x^2}\,dx < 0.1\sum_{r=1}^{10}\sqrt{1+\left(3+\tfrac{1}{10}r\right)^2}.$$

If there were 100 rectangles of width 0.01, the sandwich inequality would be

$$0.01\sum_{r=0}^{99}\sqrt{1+\left(3+\tfrac{1}{100}r\right)^2} < \int_3^4 \sqrt{1+x^2}\,dx < 0.01\sum_{r=1}^{100}\sqrt{1+\left(3+\tfrac{1}{100}r\right)^2}.$$

Exercise 7A

1 Find overestimates and underestimates of the areas under the following curves over the given intervals, by using rectangles with the stated widths. Compare your estimates with the exact values of the areas.

(a) $y = 2x + 3$, $0 \leqslant x \leqslant 1$; widths 0.5, 0.1

(b) $y = 3x^2$, $1 \leqslant x \leqslant 2$; widths 0.25, 0.1

(c) $y = \sqrt{x}$, $1 \leqslant x \leqslant 4$; widths 1, 0.5, 0.25

(d) $y = \sin^2 x$, $0 \leqslant x \leqslant \pi$; widths $\tfrac{1}{4}\pi$, $\tfrac{1}{6}\pi$

(e) $y = 4x - x^2$, $0 \leqslant x \leqslant 4$; widths 1, 0.1

2 Surfaces of revolution are formed by rotating the following curves over the given intervals about the axes specified. By using discs with the stated thicknesses, find overestimates and underestimates of the volumes enclosed. Compare your estimates with the exact values of the volumes. (Give your answers as multiples of π.)

(a) $y = 3x + 1$ over $0 \leqslant x \leqslant 2$ about the x-axis; thicknesses 0.4, 0.2, 0.1

(b) $y = \sqrt{x}$ over $1 \leqslant x \leqslant 2$ about the x-axis; thicknesses 0.5, 0.2, 0.1

(c) $y = x^2 - 1$ over $1 \leqslant x \leqslant 2$ about the y-axis; thicknesses 1, 0.5, 0.2

(d) $y = 1 + x^2$ over $-1 \leqslant x \leqslant 1$ about the x-axis; thicknesses 0.2, 0.1

(e) $y = x^4$ over $0 \leqslant x \leqslant 1$ about the y-axis; thicknesses 0.2, 0.1

3 (a) Show that

$$(1 + \ln 1) + (2 + \ln 2) + \cdots + (9 + \ln 9)$$
$$< \int_1^{10} (x + \ln x)\, dx \; < \; (2 + \ln 2) + (3 + \ln 3) + \cdots + (10 + \ln 10).$$

(b) Write this inequality in summation notation. Write down the difference between the overestimate and the underestimate.

(c) What would the difference between the overestimate and the underestimate become if on each side there were 90 rectangles, each of width 0.1, instead of 9 rectangles of width 1?

7.3 Finding bounds for sums of series

You know many ways of finding integrals, but have only met a few series which you can sum. However, by representing the sum of a series as the area of a set of rectangles, and comparing this with the area under a curve, you can sometimes find approximations to the sum.

Example 7.3.1
Find upper and lower bounds for $\sqrt{1} + \sqrt{2} + \sqrt{3} + \cdots + \sqrt{10}$.

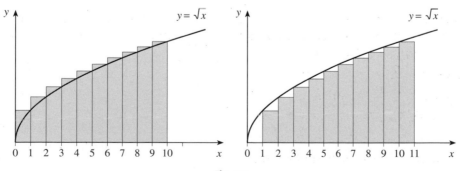

Fig. 7.7

In the left diagram of Fig. 7.7 the sum is represented as the area of a set of 10 rectangles, each having width 1 and with heights $\sqrt{1}, \sqrt{2}, \sqrt{3}, \ldots, \sqrt{10}$. These cover the interval $0 \leqslant x \leqslant 10$ of the x-axis.

The top right corners of these rectangles have coordinates $(1, \sqrt{1}), (2, \sqrt{2}), (3, \sqrt{3}), \ldots,$ $(10, \sqrt{10})$ all of which lie on the curve $y = \sqrt{x}$.

Clearly the sum of the areas of the rectangles is greater than the area under the curve, so that

$$\sum_{r=1}^{10} \sqrt{r} > \int_0^{10} \sqrt{x}\,dx$$

$$= \left[\tfrac{2}{3}x^{\frac{3}{2}}\right]_0^{10}$$

$$= \tfrac{2}{3} \times 10\sqrt{10} = \tfrac{20}{3}\sqrt{10},$$

giving

$$\tfrac{20}{3}\sqrt{10} < \sum_{r=1}^{10} \sqrt{r}.$$

This gives a lower bound for the sum.

To find an upper bound, push all the rectangles to the right by 1 unit, so that they cover the interval $1 \leqslant x \leqslant 11$. The right diagram of Fig. 7.7 shows that the top left corners of the rectangles now lie on $y = \sqrt{x}$, and it is easy to see that

$$\sum_{r=1}^{10} \sqrt{r} < \int_1^{11} \sqrt{x}\,dx$$

$$= \left[\tfrac{2}{3}x^{\frac{3}{2}}\right]_1^{11}$$

$$= \tfrac{2}{3}(11\sqrt{11} - 1) = \tfrac{22}{3}\sqrt{11} - \tfrac{2}{3},$$

giving

$$\sum_{r=1}^{10} \sqrt{r} < \tfrac{22}{3}\sqrt{11} - \tfrac{2}{3}.$$

So $$\tfrac{20}{3}\sqrt{10} < \sum_{r=1}^{10} \sqrt{r} < \tfrac{22}{3}\sqrt{11} - \tfrac{2}{3}.$$

There is nothing very magical about finishing with the number 10. It is no more difficult to think more generally.

Example 7.3.2
Find lower and upper bounds for the sum $\sqrt{1} + \sqrt{2} + \sqrt{3} + \cdots + \sqrt{n}$.

In the left diagram of Fig. 7.8 the sum is represented as the area of a set of n rectangles, each having width 1 and with heights $\sqrt{1}, \sqrt{2}, \sqrt{3}, \ldots, \sqrt{n}$. These cover the interval $0 \leqslant x \leqslant n$ of the x-axis.

The top right corners of these rectangles have coordinates $(1, \sqrt{1}), (2, \sqrt{2}), (3, \sqrt{3}), \ldots,$ $(n, \sqrt{n})$ all of which lie on the curve $y = \sqrt{x}$.

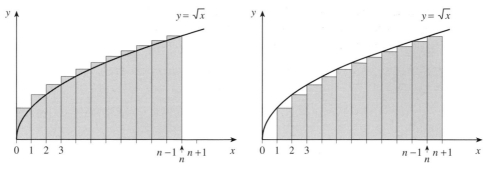

Fig. 7.8

Clearly the sum of the areas of the rectangles is greater than the area under the curve, so that

$$\sum_{r=1}^{n} \sqrt{r} > \int_{0}^{n} \sqrt{x}\,dx$$

$$= \left[\tfrac{2}{3}x^{\frac{3}{2}}\right]_{0}^{n}$$

$$= \tfrac{2}{3}n\sqrt{n},$$

giving

$$\tfrac{2}{3}n\sqrt{n} < \sum_{r=1}^{n} \sqrt{r}.$$

This gives a lower bound for the sum.

To find an upper bound, push all the rectangles to the right by 1 unit, so that they cover the interval $1 \le x \le n+1$. The right diagram of Fig. 7.8 shows that the top left corners of the rectangles now lie on $y = \sqrt{x}$, and it is easy to see that

$$\sum_{r=1}^{n} \sqrt{r} < \int_{1}^{n+1} \sqrt{x}\,dx$$

$$= \left[\tfrac{2}{3}x^{\frac{3}{2}}\right]_{1}^{n+1}$$

$$= \tfrac{2}{3}\left((n+1)\sqrt{n+1} - 1\right),$$

giving

$$\sum_{r=1}^{n} \sqrt{r} < \tfrac{2}{3}\left((n+1)\sqrt{n+1} - 1\right).$$

So $$\tfrac{2}{3}n\sqrt{n} < \sum_{r=1}^{n} \sqrt{r} < \tfrac{2}{3}\left((n+1)\sqrt{n+1} - 1\right).$$

This method gives remarkably good approximations. For example, if you put $n = 100$ in Example 7.3.2, you find that the sum of the square roots of the first 100 natural numbers lies between $\tfrac{2}{3} \times 100\sqrt{100} = 666.66...$ and $\tfrac{2}{3} \times (101\sqrt{101} - 1) = 676.02...$. The correct value of the sum is $671.46...$. Both bounds are within 1% of this.

Things are slightly different if the graph of the function is decreasing, as in the next example.

Example 7.3.3

Show that $\ln 101 < 1 + \dfrac{1}{2} + \dfrac{1}{3} + \cdots + \dfrac{1}{100} < 1 + \ln 100$.

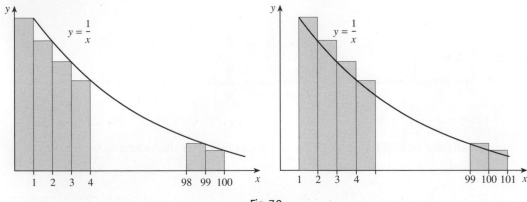

Fig. 7.9

The right diagram of Fig. 7.9 shows the sum $1 + \dfrac{1}{2} + \dfrac{1}{3} + \cdots + \dfrac{1}{100}$ represented as a set of 100 rectangles, each having width 1 and heights $1, \dfrac{1}{2}, \dfrac{1}{3}, \ldots, \dfrac{1}{100}$. These cover the interval $1 \leqslant x \leqslant 101$ of the x-axis. The top left corners of these rectangles have coordinates $(1, 1), \left(2, \dfrac{1}{2}\right), \left(3, \dfrac{1}{3}\right), \ldots, \left(100, \dfrac{1}{100}\right)$ all of which lie on the curve $y = \dfrac{1}{x}$. Clearly the sum of the areas of the rectangles is greater than the area under the curve, so that

$$1 + \frac{1}{2} + \frac{1}{3} + \cdots + \frac{1}{100} > \int_1^{101} \frac{1}{x}\,\mathrm{d}x$$
$$= \left[\ln x\right]_1^{101},$$
$$= \ln 101,$$

or $\qquad \ln 101 < 1 + \dfrac{1}{2} + \dfrac{1}{3} + \cdots + \dfrac{1}{100}.$

The left diagram shows all the shaded rectangles having moved to the left by 1 unit.

However, there is a problem, because you cannot have 0 as the lower limit of this integral which would then not exist. The solution is to ignore the first rectangle: the area under the curve between 1 and 100 is greater than the areas of the remainder of the rectangles, so

$$\frac{1}{2} + \frac{1}{3} + \cdots + \frac{1}{100} < \int_1^{100} \frac{1}{x}\,\mathrm{d}x = \left[\ln x\right]_1^{100} = \ln 100,$$

giving

$$\frac{1}{2} + \frac{1}{3} + \cdots + \frac{1}{100} < \ln 100.$$

Therefore, adding 1 (the area of the first rectangle) to both sides,

$$1 + \frac{1}{2} + \frac{1}{3} + \cdots + \frac{1}{100} < 1 + \ln 100.$$

So $\ln 101 < 1 + \frac{1}{2} + \frac{1}{3} + \cdots + \frac{1}{100} < 1 + \ln 100.$

Example 7.3.4

Find lower and upper bounds for $\displaystyle\sum_{r=m}^{n} \frac{1}{r^2}$, where $n > m > 1$.

Sketch for yourself the graph of $y = \frac{1}{x^2}$, and mark on it points with coordinates

$$\left(m, \frac{1}{m^2}\right), \left(m+1, \frac{1}{(m+1)^2}\right), \left(m+2, \frac{1}{(m+2)^2}\right), \ldots, \left(n, \frac{1}{n^2}\right).$$

Since $\frac{1}{x^2}$ is a decreasing function, you will get a lower bound by representing the sum by rectangles with these points at the top left corners, so that they cover the interval $m \leqslant x \leqslant n+1$.

The curve then lies inside the rectangles, so that

$$\sum_{r=m}^{n} \frac{1}{r^2} > \int_{m}^{n+1} \frac{1}{x^2}\,\mathrm{d}x = \left[-\frac{1}{x}\right]_{m}^{n+1} = \frac{1}{m} - \frac{1}{n+1},$$

which gives

$$\frac{1}{m} - \frac{1}{n+1} < \sum_{r=m}^{n} \frac{1}{r^2}.$$

To get an upper bound, push all the rectangles to the left by 1 unit.

They then cover the interval $m - 1 \leqslant x \leqslant n$, and have their top right corners on the curve, so that the curve lies above the rectangles.

Therefore

$$\sum_{r=m}^{n} \frac{1}{r^2} < \int_{m-1}^{n} \frac{1}{x^2}\,\mathrm{d}x = \left[-\frac{1}{x}\right]_{m-1}^{n} = \frac{1}{m-1} - \frac{1}{n}$$

giving

$$\sum_{r=m}^{n} \frac{1}{r^2} < \frac{1}{m-1} - \frac{1}{n}.$$

Combining these results, $\dfrac{n-m+1}{m(n+1)} < \displaystyle\sum_{r=m}^{n} \frac{1}{r^2} < \dfrac{n-m+1}{(m-1)n}.$

Before reading the next example try finding 100! on your calculator. If you are lucky you will get an answer, but it is more likely that your calculator will overflow and give you an error message. Here is a way that you can approximate to it.

Example 7.3.5

Find upper and lower bounds for $\ln 2 + \ln 3 + \ln 4 + \cdots + \ln 100$. Use your answer to find upper and lower bounds for 100!.

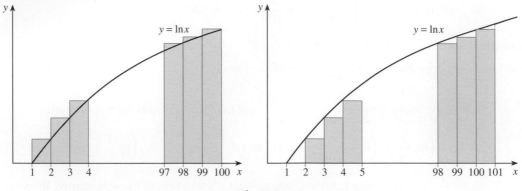

Fig. 7.10

In the left diagram of Fig. 7.10 you can see that

$$\ln 2 + \ln 3 + \ln 4 + \cdots + \ln 100 > \int_1^{100} \ln x \, dx$$

$$= \left[x \ln x - x \right]_1^{100} \quad \text{(see C4 Section 2.1)}$$

$$= (100 \ln 100 - 100) - (1 \ln 1 - 1)$$

$$= 100 \ln 100 - 99,$$

giving

$$100 \ln 100 - 99 < \ln 2 + \ln 3 + \ln 4 + \cdots + \ln 100.$$

In the right diagram of Fig. 7.10 you can see that

$$\ln 2 + \ln 3 + \ln 4 + \cdots + \ln 100 < \int_2^{101} \ln x \, dx$$

$$= \left[x \ln x - x \right]_2^{101}$$

$$= (101 \ln 101 - 101) - (2 \ln 2 - 2)$$

$$= 101 \ln 101 - 99 - 2 \ln 2,$$

giving

$$\ln 2 + \ln 3 + \ln 4 + \cdots + \ln 100 < 101 \ln 101 - 99 - 2 \ln 2.$$

This gives an upper bound for the sum.

So $100 \ln 100 - 99 < \ln 2 + \ln 3 + \ln 4 + \cdots + \ln 100 < 101 \ln 101 - 99 - 2 \ln 2.$

By calculating the left and right sides,

$$361.5\ldots < \ln 100! < 365.7\ldots,$$

which gives

$$e^{361.5...} < 100! < e^{365.7...}.$$

To write $e^{365.7...}$ in the form $b \times 10^d$, where $1 \leqslant b \leqslant 10$ and d is an integer, take logarithms to get

$$365.7... \log_{10} e = \log_{10} b + d,$$

where $0 \leqslant \log_{10} b < 1$ and d is an integer.

But $365.7... \log_{10} e = 158.839...$, so

$$d = 158 \quad \text{and} \quad \log_{10} b = 0.839...,$$

giving $b = 6.906...$.

Rounding up, $100! < 6.91 \times 10^{158}$.

Similarly for $e^{361.5...}$, which comes to $1.011... \times 10^{157}$, and on rounding down gives $1.01 \times 10^{157} < 100!$.

So $1.01 \times 10^{157} < 100! < 6.91 \times 10^{158}$.

Exercise 7B

1 Establish the following upper and lower bounds for the given sums.

(a) $4 - \ln 3 < \dfrac{2}{3} + \dfrac{3}{4} + \dfrac{4}{5} + \dfrac{5}{6} < 4 - \ln\left(\dfrac{7}{3}\right)$

(b) $2 - \dfrac{2}{\sqrt{5}} < \dfrac{1}{1\sqrt{1}} + \dfrac{1}{2\sqrt{2}} + \dfrac{1}{3\sqrt{3}} + \dfrac{1}{4\sqrt{4}} < 2$

(c) $20 - 2\sqrt{10} < \dfrac{1}{\sqrt{10}} + \dfrac{1}{\sqrt{11}} + \dfrac{1}{\sqrt{12}} + \cdots + \dfrac{1}{\sqrt{99}} < 2\sqrt{99} - 6$

2 Find upper and lower bounds for the following sums. Give your answers in decimal form to 4 significant figures, rounding upper bounds up and lower bounds down.

(a) $\sqrt[4]{100} + \sqrt[4]{101} + \sqrt[4]{102} + \cdots + \sqrt[4]{999}$

(b) $\dfrac{1}{101} + \dfrac{2}{102} + \dfrac{3}{103} + \cdots + \dfrac{99}{199}$

(c) $\displaystyle\sum_{r=1}^{89} \sin r°$

(d) $\displaystyle\sum_{r=1}^{100} \dfrac{1}{100^2 + r^2}$

3 If $n > m > 1$, find upper and lower bounds for

(a) $\displaystyle\sum_{r=m}^{n} \dfrac{1}{r^3}$

(b) $\displaystyle\sum_{r=m}^{n} \dfrac{r^2}{1 + 2r^3}$

(c) $\dfrac{n!}{m!}$

4 (a) By considering a suitable integral, show that $12 < \sqrt[3]{1} + \sqrt[3]{2} + \sqrt[3]{3} + \cdots + \sqrt[3]{8}$.

(b) Find an upper bound for $\displaystyle\sum_{r=1}^{8} \sqrt[3]{r}$.

(c) Use a similar method to find upper and lower bounds for $\displaystyle\sum_{r=101}^{200} \sqrt[3]{r}$.

5 (a) Draw a sketch of the curve $y = a^x$, where $a > 1$.

  (b) By writing a^x as $e^{x \ln a}$, show that $\dfrac{d}{dx} a^x = a^x \ln a$.

  (c) Use integrals to prove that

  $$\frac{a^n - 1}{a \ln a} < 1 + a + a^2 + \cdots + a^{n-1} < \frac{a^n - 1}{\ln a}.$$

  (d) Hence show that $\dfrac{a - 1}{a} < \ln a < a - 1$.

6 (a) Show that $\dfrac{d}{dx} \cosh^{-1}(2x + 1) = \dfrac{1}{\sqrt{x^2 + x}}$.

  (b) Prove that the improper integral $\displaystyle\int_0^n \frac{1}{\sqrt{x^2 + x}}\, dx$ exists.

  (c) Find an upper bound for the sum $\displaystyle\sum_{r=1}^n \frac{1}{\sqrt{r^2 + r}}$.

Miscellaneous exercise 7

1 By considering the areas of suitable rectangles, demonstrate that

$$\frac{1}{\sqrt{2}} + \frac{1}{\sqrt{5}} + \frac{1}{\sqrt{10}} < \int_0^3 \frac{1}{\sqrt{1 + x^2}}\, dx < 1 + \frac{1}{\sqrt{2}} + \frac{1}{\sqrt{5}}. \qquad \text{(OCR)}$$

2 Rectangles of equal width h are drawn under the graph of $y = 1 + x^2$ from $x = 0$ to $x = 3$. Illustrate this with a sketch. Show that the area of the fourth rectangle is $h + 9h^3$, and find (in terms of h) the total area of the first four rectangles.

  How many rectangles are there if $h = 0.1$? Show that the total area of the rectangles in this case is $3 + 0.1^3 \displaystyle\sum_{i=1}^{29} i^2$. Find the difference between the value of this sum and the exact area under the curve from $x = 0$ to $x = 3$ found by integration. (OCR)

3 Show that $\sqrt{10} + \sqrt{17} + \sqrt{26} < \displaystyle\int_3^6 \sqrt{1 + x^2}\, dx$, and find a similar upper bound for the integral.

4 Prove that $\ln(n^2 + 2n + 2) - \ln 2 < \displaystyle\sum_{r=1}^n \frac{2r}{1 + r^2} < 1 + \ln(1 + n^2) - \ln 2$.

5 (a) Show that, for $x > e$, $\dfrac{\ln x}{x}$ is a decreasing function of x.

  (b) Prove that $\dfrac{\ln 4}{4} + \dfrac{\ln 5}{5} + \cdots + \dfrac{\ln n}{n} < \tfrac{1}{2}((\ln n)^2 - (\ln 3)^2)$.

  (c) Find a similar lower bound for $\dfrac{\ln 4}{4} + \dfrac{\ln 5}{5} + \cdots + \dfrac{\ln n}{n}$.

6 Prove that $\displaystyle\sum_{r=1}^n \tanh r > \ln(\cosh n)$.

8 Approximations and errors

This chapter revisits the iterative method of solving equations described in C3 Chapter 8, and shows how to estimate the error in an approximate solution. When you have completed it, you should

- know the relation between the errors in successive terms of an iteration, and how it can be demonstrated algebraically and graphically
- be able to estimate how many iterations will be needed to find a root to given accuracy
- know how to use the relation between errors to take a short-cut to the value of the root
- understand the idea and the advantages of quadratic convergence.

8.1 Approximating to roots by iteration

If you need to solve an equation for which you do not know an exact method, it is necessary to use an approximate method.

You saw in C3 Chapter 8 that a powerful way of solving an equation $f(x) = 0$ is to rewrite it in the form $x = F(x)$, and then to approximate to a root by the terms of a sequence defined by the iteration $x_{r+1} = F(x_r)$ with a starting value close to the root.

Using this method in examples suggested some general results (see C3 Section 8.5).

- The sequence will converge to the root if the gradient of the graph of $y = F(x)$ at and around the root is not too large (roughly between -1 and 1).
- The smaller the modulus of the gradient, the fewer steps will be needed to reach the root to a given accuracy.
- If the gradient is negative the terms will be alternately above and below the root; if it is positive the terms will approach the root from one side.

You now know enough mathematical theory to be able to justify these observations.

The first step is to clarify what is meant by the error associated with an approximation. The aim is to get as close as possible to the root of the equation, which is an exact (but unknown) real number. The **error** is then defined by

> error = exact value − approximate value.

So, if a term x_n of a sequence is used to approximate to the root α of an equation, and the error is denoted by e_n, then

$$e_n = \alpha - x_n.$$

You may find that some books define the error the other way round, as (approximate value – exact value). The definition given here is the more usual one, but it does not matter which you use provided that you are consistent.

Example 8.1.1

Investigate approximations to the root of the equation $\sin x = x - 0.1$.

If you plot the graphs of $\sin x$ and $x - 0.1$, it is easy to see that there is only one root, which is about midway between 0.8 and 0.9. So try using the sequence $x_{r+1} = \sin x_r + 0.1$, with $x_0 = 0.85$, to approximate to the root.

If you go on long enough, you will find that the sequence converges on 0.853 75, which is the value of the root α correct to 5 decimal places.

Table 8.1 gives the terms of the sequence as far as $r = 10$, and also the errors $e_r = 0.853\ 75 - x_r$.

r	x_r	e_r	r	x_r	e_r
0	0.85	0.003 75	6	0.853 45	0.000 30
1	0.851 28	0.002 47	7	0.853 55	0.000 20
2	0.852 12	0.001 63	8	0.853 62	0.000 13
3	0.852 68	0.001 07	9	0.853 66	0.000 09
4	0.853 05	0.000 70	10	0.853 69	0.000 06
5	0.853 29	0.000 46			

Table 8.1

You can see that the errors are getting smaller all the time. If you examine them more closely, you will notice that they are reduced in about the same proportion at each step. This can be shown by working out $\dfrac{e_{r+1}}{e_r}$ for each pair of successive terms, as in Table 8.2.

r	0	1	2	3	4
$\dfrac{e_{r+1}}{e_r}$	0.659	0.660	0.656	0.654	0.657
r	5	6	7	8	9
$\dfrac{e_{r+1}}{e_r}$	0.652	0.667	0.650	0.692	0.667

Table 8.2

This table shows that at each step the error is reduced to about 0.66 of its previous value. To a good approximation, successive errors form a geometric sequence with common ratio 0.66.

Later values in Table 8.2 seem to vary more erratically because the numbers in Table 8.1 are given to only 5 decimal places. You can investigate this for yourself, using the value 0.853 750 16 for the root and keeping 8 decimal places in the table.

Example 8.1.2

Investigate the errors when the sequence $x_{r+1} = \sqrt[3]{1 - x_r}$ is used to find approximations to the root of $x^3 + x = 1$.

By trial you can find that $x^3 + x - 1$ has values -0.184 when $x = 0.6$ and 0.043 when $x = 0.7$. So, by the sign-change rule, the root of $x^3 + x = 1$ is between 0.6 and 0.7, but closer to 0.7. A suitable choice of starting value is $x_0 = 0.68$.

If you go on long enough, you find that the sequence converges on the value 0.682 33, to 5 decimal places. Table 8.3 gives the approximations produced by the sequence, the errors calculated as $e_r = 0.682\,33 - x_r$, and the ratios of successive errors $\dfrac{e_{r+1}}{e_r}$.

r	x_r	e_r	$\dfrac{e_{r+1}}{e_r}$	r	x_r	e_r	$\dfrac{e_{r+1}}{e_r}$
0	0.680 00	0.002 33	-0.712	6	0.682 01	0.000 32	-0.687
1	0.683 99	$-0.001\ 66$	-0.717	7	0.682 55	$-0.000\ 22$	-0.727
2	0.681 14	0.001 19	-0.714	8	0.682 17	0.000 16	-0.687
3	0.683 18	$-0.000\ 85$	-0.718	9	0.682 44	$-0.000\ 11$	-0.818
4	0.681 72	0.000 61	-0.721	10	0.682 24	0.000 09	
5	0.682 77	$-0.000\ 44$	-0.727				

Table 8.3

The approximations are alternately too small and too large, so that the errors are alternately positive and negative. You can see from the final column that the ratio of successive errors is more or less constant, with a value of about -0.72.

8.2 Theoretical analysis

To understand the property of errors illustrated by Examples 8.1.1 and 8.1.2, you can choose either an algebraic approach (as in this section) or a graphical equivalent (see Section 8.3).

The algebraic method uses a generalisation of the Maclaurin expansion

$$f(0) + \frac{f'(0)}{1!}x + \frac{f''(0)}{2!}x^2 + \dots$$

given in Section 3.3. This involves introducing a new function g such that

$$f(x) \equiv g(a + x)$$

where a is a constant. (For example, a could be $\frac{1}{2}\pi$, with $f(x) = \cos x$ and $g(x) = \sin x$.) This identity can be differentiated, using the chain rule on the right side, to give

$$f'(x) \equiv g'(a + x) \times 1 = g'(a + x),$$
$$f''(x) \equiv g''(a + x) \times 1 = g''(a + x), \quad \text{and so on.}$$

It follows, by putting $x = 0$, that $f(0) = g(a)$, $f'(0) = g'(a)$, $f''(0) = g''(a)$, and so on.

Now substitute these values in the Maclaurin expansion above. The result is the **Taylor expansion** for $g(a + x)$,

$$g(a) + \frac{g'(a)}{1!}x + \frac{g''(a)}{2!}x^2 + \cdots.$$

You can see that the Maclaurin expansion is just the Taylor expansion with $a = 0$. (It is now known that this result was used by James Gregory, who died in 1675, before either Brook Taylor, 1685–1731, or Colin Maclaurin, 1698–1746, was born.)

Taylor expansions are used in just the same way as Maclaurin expansions. An important application is to produce a sequence of polynomials

$$p_1(x) = g(a) + \frac{g'(a)}{1!}x, \qquad p_2(x) = g(a) + \frac{g'(a)}{1!}x + \frac{g''(a)}{2!}x^2, \qquad \text{and so on,}$$

which are approximately equal to $g(a + x)$ when x is small.

Example 8.2.1

Find a quadratic polynomial approximation to $\dfrac{1}{(2 + x)^3}$ when x is small.

You can already do this by writing the expression as $\frac{1}{8}\left(1 + \frac{1}{2}x\right)^{-3}$ and using the binomial expansion. Alternatively, think of it as $g(a + x)$, with $g(x) = x^{-3}$ and $a = 2$. Then $g'(x) = -3x^{-4}$ and $g''(x) = 12x^{-5}$, so that $g(2) = \frac{1}{8}$, $g'(2) = -\frac{3}{16}$ and $g''(2) = \frac{12}{32} = \frac{3}{8}$. This gives the Taylor quadratic polynomial approximation

$$\frac{1}{(2 + x)^3} \approx \frac{1}{8} + \left(-\frac{3}{16}\right)x + \frac{3}{16}x^2.$$

To apply Taylor expansions to the equation $x = F(x)$, notice that since $e_r = \alpha - x_r$ and $e_{r+1} = \alpha - x_{r+1}$, the iteration $x_{r+1} = F(x_r)$ can be written as

$$\alpha - e_{r+1} = F(\alpha - e_r).$$

Now the right side of this equation has the form $g(a + x)$, with F in place of g, α for a and $-e_r$ for x. Hopefully the error e_r is small, so the right side of this equation is approximately equal to

$$p_1(-e_r) = F(\alpha) + \frac{F'(\alpha)}{1!}(-e_r) = F(\alpha) - F'(\alpha)e_r.$$

The equation then becomes

$$\alpha - e_{r+1} \approx F(\alpha) - F'(\alpha)e_r.$$

But α is the exact root of $x = F(x)$, so that $\alpha = F(\alpha)$. The final form of the equation is then

$$e_{r+1} \approx F'(\alpha)e_r.$$

You can use this to check the numerical values for $\dfrac{e_{r+1}}{e_r}$ found in the examples.

Example 8.1.1 $F(x) = \sin x + 0.1$ and $\alpha \approx 0.853\,75$, so that $F'(x) = \cos x$,

$$F'(\alpha) \approx \cos 0.853\,75 \approx 0.657.$$

Example 8.1.2 $F(x) = \sqrt[3]{1-x} = (1-x)^{\frac{1}{3}}$ and $\alpha \approx 0.682\,33$, so that $F'(x) = \left(-\frac{1}{3}\right)(1-x)^{-\frac{2}{3}}$,

$$F'(\alpha) = \left(-\tfrac{1}{3}\right)(1 - 0.682\,33)^{-\frac{2}{3}} \approx -0.716.$$

The agreement with the ratios 0.66 and -0.72 found experimentally is very close.

The approximation

$$e_{r+1} \approx F'(\alpha)e_r$$

is the key which justifies all the general results listed at the beginning of Section 8.1.

The iterative method converges to the root α if the sequence of errors converges to zero. The error sequence is approximately geometric with common ratio $F'(\alpha)$, and this converges to zero if $F'(\alpha)$ lies between -1 and 1. The smaller the modulus of the gradient, $|F'(\alpha)|$, the more rapidly the error sequence converges to zero. Finally, if $F'(\alpha)$ is negative the signs of the errors are alternately $+$ and $-$, so that terms of the sequence x_r are alternately above and below α; if $F'(\alpha)$ is positive, all the errors have the same sign.

> If the iteration $x_{r+1} = F(x_r)$ is used to find approximations to a root α of the equation $x = F(x)$, the sequence of errors $e_r = \alpha - x_r$ is approximately geometric with common ratio $F'(\alpha)$, provided that $F'(\alpha) \neq 0$.

Example 8.2.2
The iteration $x_{r+1} = \cos x_r$, with $x_0 = 0.7$, is used to find approximations to the root of the equation $x = \cos x$. How many repetitions are needed to obtain an approximation within 10^{-6} of the root?

The starting value $x_0 = 0.7$ was obtained from the sign-change rule, by noting that $0.7 - \cos 0.7 = -0.064...$ and $0.8 - \cos 0.8 = 0.103...$. This shows that the root is between 0.7 and 0.8, and suggests that it is probably closer to 0.7 than to 0.8 so that $|e_0| < 0.05$. (You can check this by working out $0.75 - \cos 0.75$.)

Taking $F(x) = \cos x$, $F'(x) = -\sin x$. Since α is between 0.7 and 0.8, and $\sin 0.7 = 0.64...$ and $\sin 0.8 = 0.71...$, almost certainly $|F'(\alpha)| < 0.7$. In that case, $|e_r| < 0.05 \times (0.7)^r$. So to get within 10^{-6} of the root, choose r so that $0.05 \times (0.7)^r < 10^{-6}$, that is $(0.7)^r < 2 \times 10^{-5}$.

You can solve this by taking logarithms (either to base e or base 10):

$$r \log 0.7 < \log(2 \times 10^{-5}),$$

so that $r > \dfrac{\log(2 \times 10^{-5})}{\log 0.7} = 30.3...$

(with the inequality reversed because $\log 0.7$ is negative).

So 31 iterations should be enough to obtain the root to the required accuracy.

In fact, this calculation has been rather cautious in estimating the error e_0 and the value of $F'(\alpha)$. The iteration actually needs only 27 repetitions to get within 10^{-6} of the root 0.739 085 13. Since you do not know α before you start, you can only make rough estimates of e_0 and $F'(\alpha)$. But the method gives a good idea of how long it will take to achieve the desired accuracy.

8.3 Graphical representations

The results proved in the last section can also be demonstrated by graphical methods.

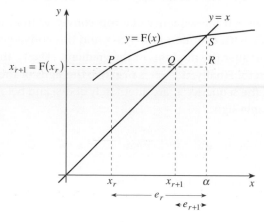

Fig. 8.4

Figure 8.4 shows the graphs of $y = F(x)$ and $y = x$, intersecting at a point S at which $x = \alpha$, where $F(\alpha) = \alpha$. P is the point on $y = F(x)$ for which $x = x_r$, so that $y = F(x_r) = x_{r+1}$. This relates an x-coordinate x_r to a y-coordinate x_{r+1}.

But to continue the sequence further you need to show x_{r+1} as an x-coordinate. The clue is to use the line $y = x$. Since Q lies on $y = x$ and has y-coordinate x_{r+1}, its x-coordinate is also x_{r+1}.

This construction now makes it possible to display the whole sequence as a set of points on the x-axis. This is shown in Fig. 8.5 for the case $0 < F'(\alpha) < 1$, and in Fig. 8.6 for the case $-1 < F'(\alpha) < 0$. These are called, for obvious reasons, a **staircase diagram** and a **cobweb diagram** respectively.

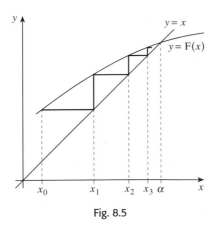

Fig. 8.5

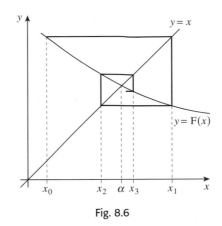

Fig. 8.6

You can see that, if $F'(\alpha)$ is positive, all the terms lie on the same side of the root; but if $F'(\alpha)$ is negative, they lie alternately above and below it.

Fig. 8.4 also shows the relation between the errors e_r and e_{r+1}. The length PR is equal to $\alpha - x_r$, which is the error e_r. Similarly QR is equal to e_{r+1}. But since the line QS has gradient 1, RS is also e_{r+1}. It follows that

$$\frac{e_{r+1}}{e_r} = \frac{RS}{PR},$$

which is the gradient of the chord PS. If the error e_r is small, this gradient is approximately equal to the gradient of the tangent to $F(x)$ at S. That is,

$$\frac{e_{r+1}}{e_r} \approx F'(\alpha).$$

Exercise 8A

1 For the sequence $x_{r+1} = 2\sin x_r$ with $x_0 = 1.9$, calculate x_1, x_2 and x_3 correct to 5 decimal places.

The equation $x = 2\sin x$ has a root $\alpha \approx 1.895\,49$, correct to 5 decimal places. If the terms of the sequence x_r are used to approximate to this root, calculate the errors e_0, e_1, e_2 and e_3, and the ratios $\dfrac{e_1}{e_0}$, $\dfrac{e_2}{e_1}$ and $\dfrac{e_3}{e_2}$. If $F(x) = 2\sin x$, compare these ratios with the value of $F'(\alpha)$.

2 For the sequence $x_{r+1} = \frac{1}{2}\cosh x_r$ with $x_0 = 0.6$, calculate the terms $x_1, x_2, \ldots$ correct to 5 decimal places until you reach two equal values. If these occur when $r = k$ and $k + 1$, state the value of k.

Taking this common value of x_k and x_{k+1} as an approximation to the root α of the equation $x = \frac{1}{2}\cosh x$, calculate the errors e_0, e_1, e_2, e_3 and e_4. Hence calculate the error ratio $\dfrac{e_{r+1}}{e_r}$ for $r = 0, 1, 2$ and 3.

If $F(x) = \frac{1}{2}\cosh x$, compare these ratios with the value of $F'(\alpha)$. Hence estimate the error in using x_{10} as an approximation to the root of the equation $x = \frac{1}{2}\cosh x$.

3 For the sequence $x_{r+1} = \sqrt[3]{17 - 2x_r}$ with $x_0 = 2.3$, calculate x_1, x_2, x_3 and x_4 correct to 5 decimal places. Show that, to this level of accuracy, x_5 and x_4 are the same.

Taking this common value as the root α of the equation $x^3 + 2x = 17$ correct to 5 decimal places, calculate the errors e_0, e_1, e_2 and e_3. Hence calculate the error ratio $\dfrac{e_{r+1}}{e_r}$ for $r = 0, 1$ and 2. If $F(x) = \sqrt[3]{17 - 2x}$, compare these error ratios with the value of $F'(\alpha)$.

4 Show that the equation $x^3 + 3x = 1$ has a root between 0.3 and 0.35. Why would you expect the iteration $x_{r+1} = \frac{1}{3}(1 - x_r^3)$ to give an efficient method of approximating to the root? Use this iteration with $x_0 = 0.32$ to find the root correct to 6 decimal places.

5 Show that the equation $x^5 + x = 10$ has a root between 1.5 and 1.6. Why would you expect the iteration $x_{r+1} = \sqrt[5]{10 - x_r}$ to give an efficient method of approximating to the root? Find the root correct to 5 decimal places.

6 Show that the quadratic equation $x^2 - 6x + 7 = 0$ has roots between 1.5 and 1.6, and between 4.4 and 4.5. The equation can be rearranged as $x = F(x)$, where $F(x)$ can take any of the forms $F_1(x) = \dfrac{x^2 + 7}{6}$, $F_2(x) = 6 - \dfrac{7}{x}$, $F_3(x) = \dfrac{7}{6 - x}$, $F_4(x) = \sqrt{6x - 7}$.

(a) Use graphs of $y = x$ and $y = F(x)$ to illustrate each of these.

(b) Explain why, for each $F(x)$, the sequence defined by $x_{r+1} = F(x_r)$ can be used to find approximations to one of the roots but not to the other. Identify in each case the root for which the process is effective.

(c) Use $F'(x)$ to decide which method gives the fastest convergence to each of the roots.

(d) Starting with $x_0 = 1.6$ or $x_0 = 4.4$ as appropriate, evaluate and record enough terms of each sequence to give the corresponding root correct to 5 decimal places.

(e) Use the fact that the exact roots are $3 \pm \sqrt{2}$ to evaluate the errors e_r for each iteration. Verify that these are approximately geometric sequences with common ratio approximately equal to the derivatives you calculated in part (c).

(f) For each sequence, estimate how many terms you must take in order to reduce the error to less than 10^{-8}.

7 Apply the ideas of Question 6 to the equation $x^2 + 4x - 13 = 0$ with roots close to -6.1 and 2.1, using $F_1(x) = \dfrac{13 - x^2}{4}$, $F_2(x) = \dfrac{13}{x} - 4$, $F_3(x) = \dfrac{13}{x + 4}$, $F_4(x) = \sqrt{13 - 4x}$ or $-\sqrt{13 - 4x}$.

Compare your conclusions with those in Question 6; identify any important differences.

8 The equation $x^3 - 9x - 2 = 0$ has roots close to -2.9, -0.2 and 3.1. Which of the arrangements $x = F(x)$, with $F_1(x) = \sqrt[3]{9x + 2}$, $F_2(x) = \dfrac{x^3 - 2}{9}$, $F_3(x) = \sqrt{9 + \dfrac{2}{x}}$ or $-\sqrt{9 + \dfrac{2}{x}}$, $F_4(x) = \dfrac{2}{x^2 - 9}$ gives the fastest convergence for the sequence $x_{r+1} = F(x_r)$ to each of the roots? Find approximations to these roots to 4 decimal places. Check your calculations by finding the sum and the product of your answers.

9 Repeat Question 8 for the equation $x^3 + 4x^2 - 4 = 0$ with roots close to -3.7, -1.2 and 0.9, using $F_1(x) = \sqrt[3]{4 - 4x^2}$, $F_2(x) = \dfrac{4}{x^2} - 4$, $F_3(x) = \dfrac{2}{\sqrt{x + 4}}$ or $-\dfrac{2}{\sqrt{x + 4}}$, $F_4(x) = \sqrt{1 - \frac{1}{4}x^3}$ or $-\sqrt{1 - \frac{1}{4}x^3}$.

10 Use the iteration method to find a root of each of the following equations with an error less than 10^{-5}. Before starting your calculation, estimate the number of terms you must take in order to achieve the required accuracy.

(a) $x^3 - 12x = 20$ (b) $x^3 - 3x^2 = 4$ (c) $x = \cos 2x$

(d) $x \cosh x = 1$ (e) $\cos x = \sinh x$ (f) $(x + 1)(x^2 + 1) = 10$

11 Draw diagrams similar to Figs. 8.5 and 8.6 to illustrate successive terms of the sequence defined by $x_{r+1} = F(x_r)$ if $x_0 > \alpha$ and

(a) $F'(\alpha) < -1$,   (b) $-1 < F'(\alpha) < 0$,   (c) $0 < F'(\alpha) < 1$,   (d) $F'(\alpha) > 1$.

12* Use Taylor expansions to find cubic polynomials which approximate to the following functions when x is small.

(a) $\tan\left(\tfrac{1}{4}\pi + x\right)$ (b) $\sqrt{9 + x}$ (c) $\sec\left(\tfrac{1}{3}\pi + x\right)$ (d) $\sin^{-1}\left(\tfrac{1}{2} + x\right)$

8.4* Jumping to a conclusion

This section describes a quick way of getting near the root of an equation by using a short cut. You may omit it if you wish.

The approximation $\dfrac{e_{r+1}}{e_r} \approx F'(\alpha)$ can be written as $\alpha - x_{r+1} \approx F'(\alpha)(\alpha - x_r)$.

When you do an iteration you find the values of x_r and x_{r+1}. If you could estimate the value of $F'(\alpha)$, you could use this approximation to find an estimate for α.

There are two possible ways of estimating $F'(\alpha)$. These work especially well if $F'(\alpha)$ is negative, as in Fig. 8.7.

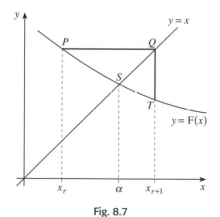

Fig. 8.7

One method is to note that the point P has coordinates $(x_r, F(x_r))$, that is (x_r, x_{r+1}), and similarly T has coordinates (x_{r+1}, x_{r+2}). You can see from the figure that the chord PT is very nearly parallel to the tangent to the curve at S. That is,

$$F'(\alpha) \approx \frac{F(x_{r+1}) - F(x_r)}{x_{r+1} - x_r} = \frac{x_{r+2} - x_{r+1}}{x_{r+1} - x_r}.$$

Alternatively, you can find $F'(x)$ and guess the value of x at which to evaluate it. If $F'(x)$ is not changing very quickly, it makes little difference if your guess is some distance away from α.

Example 8.4.1
Find an approximation to the root of $x(x+2)^2 = 1$.

A decimal search shows that the root is about 0.2. Take this as x_0.

Table 8.8 lists the first three terms of the iteration $x_{r+1} = \dfrac{1}{(2+x_r)^2}$.

r	0	1	2
x_r	0.2	0.206 61	0.205 38

Table 8.8

Since $F(x) = \dfrac{1}{(2+x)^2}$, $F'(x) = \dfrac{-2}{(2+x)^3}$. So $F'(\alpha) < 0$.

Taking $r = 0$, the approximation $\dfrac{x_{r+2} - x_{r+1}}{x_{r+1} - x_r}$ for $F'(\alpha)$ is

$$\frac{x_2 - x_1}{x_1 - x_0} = \frac{-0.001\ 23}{0.006\ 61} \approx -0.186.$$

Alternatively, since the approximations are in turn below and above the root, α lies between 0.205 38 and 0.206 61. Make a guess that α is about 0.206. Then

$$F'(\alpha) \approx F'(0.206) = \frac{-2}{2.206^3} \approx -0.186.$$

So the approximation $e_{r+1} \approx F'(\alpha)e_r$ with $r = 1$ gives

$$\alpha - 0.205\ 38 \approx -0.186(\alpha - 0.206\ 61),$$
$$\alpha \approx \frac{0.205\ 38 + 0.186 \times 0.206\ 61}{1 + 0.186} \approx 0.205\ 57.$$

You cannot be sure that this is correct to 5 decimal places. But you can now use this number as a new starting value for the iteration. In fact, the root of this equation is $0.205\ 569\ 4\ldots$, so the method takes you straight to the root to this degree of accuracy.

Exercise 8B*

1 For the following sequences $x_{r+1} = F(x_r)$ and initial values x_0, calculate x_1 and x_2, and then use the method of Section 8.4 to obtain a more accurate approximation to the root of the equation $x = F(x)$. Find to how many significant figures your answer is correct; if this is less than 5, repeat the process taking your approximation as the new value of x_0.

(a) $x_{r+1} = e^{-x_r^2}$, $x_0 = 0.65$ (b) $x_{r+1} = \cos x_r$, $x_0 = 0.74$

(c) $x_{r+1} = \sqrt{x_r + 3}$, $x_0 = 2.3$ (d) $x_{r+1} = \ln(x_r + 2)$, $x_0 = 1.2$

2 Show that the process described in Section 8.4 gives an improved approximation to α of

$$\frac{x_{r+2}x_r - x_{r+1}^2}{x_{r+2} + x_r - 2x_{r+1}}.$$ (This is known as *Aitken's δ^2 process*.)

8.5   The case $F'(\alpha) = 0$

The approximation $e_{r+1} \approx F'(\alpha)e_r$ is no use if $F'(\alpha) = 0$ since it then reduces to $e_{r+1} \approx 0$. This tells you that the error is small, but gives you no idea how small.

To see what happens in this case, go back to Section 8.2, where a first degree Taylor polynomial $p_1(x)$ was used as an approximation to $F(\alpha - e_r)$.

The argument begins as before, writing the iteration $x_{r+1} = F(x_r)$ as $\alpha - e_{r+1} = F(\alpha - e_r)$. But instead of approximating to $F(\alpha - e_r)$ by a first degree Taylor polynomial, use a second degree polynomial approximation,

$$F(\alpha - e_r) \approx F(\alpha) + \frac{F'(\alpha)}{1!}(-e_r) + \frac{F''(\alpha)}{2!}(-e_r)^2.$$

Since $F(\alpha) = \alpha$ and $F'(\alpha) = 0$, this reduces to

$$F(\alpha - e_r) \approx \alpha + \tfrac{1}{2}F''(\alpha)e_r^2.$$

The equation $\alpha - e_{r+1} = F(\alpha - e_r)$ therefore gives the approximation

$$\alpha - e_{r+1} \approx \alpha + \tfrac{1}{2}F''(\alpha)e_r^2.$$

So the approximate equation connecting successive errors is

$$e_{r+1} \approx -\tfrac{1}{2}F''(\alpha)e_r^2.$$

There are two things to notice about this result.

- Since the square of a small number is very small, the iterative sequence gets close to the limit α very quickly. A sequence for which the error at each stage is roughly proportional to the square of the error at the previous stage is said to have **quadratic convergence**.

- If $F''(\alpha)$ is positive, all the errors (except perhaps e_0) are negative; that is, all the terms of the iterative sequence (except perhaps the starting value) are greater than α. This is illustrated in Fig. 8.9, which starts like a cobweb but then becomes a staircase. If $F''(\alpha)$ is negative, all the errors (except perhaps e_0) are positive.

> If the iteration $x_{r+1} = F(x_r)$ is used to find approximations to a root α of the equation $x = F(x)$, and if $F'(\alpha) = 0$, the sequence has quadratic convergence to the root.

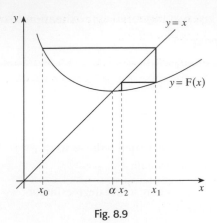

Fig. 8.9

Example 8.5.1
Show that the graph of $F(x) = x^3 - x^2 - x + 2$ has a minimum at $(1, 1)$.

An iteration is defined by

$$x_{r+1} = x_r^3 - x_r^2 - x_r + 2 \text{ with } x_0 = 0.8.$$

Show numerically that this sequence converges to 1, and calculate the errors e_r correct to 9 decimal places. Compare the actual errors with those predicted by the approximation $e_{r+1} \approx -\frac{1}{2}F''(1)e_r^2$.

Since $F'(x) = 3x^2 - 2x - 1$ and $F''(x) = 6x - 2$,

$$F'(1) = 0 \text{ and } F''(1) = 4 > 0.$$

So the graph of $F(x)$ has a minimum where $x = 1$. Also $F(1) = 1$. So there is a minimum at $(1, 1)$.

This shows that the graph of $F(x)$ in an interval around $(1, 1)$ has all the essential characteristics of Fig. 8.9, with $\alpha = 1$.

Table 8.10 lists the values of x_r and of $e_r = 1 - x_r$ to 9 decimal places until these become indistinguishable from 1 and 0. The final column shows the predicted values of e_{r+1} based on the approximation $e_{r+1} \approx -\frac{1}{2}F''(1)e_r^2$; since $F''(1) = 4$, this is

$$e_{r+1} = -2e_r^2.$$

r	x_r	e_r	predicted e_{r+1}
0	0.8	0.2	−0.08
1	1.072	−0.072	−0.010 368
2	1.010 741 248	−0.010 741 248	−0.000 230 749
3	1.000 231 988	−0.000 231 988	−0.000 000 108
4	1.000 000 108	−0.000 000 108	

Table 8.10

By following the broken lines linking the last two columns you can see how closely the predicted error values approximate to the actual errors.

In Example 8.5.1 the value of α, which is a root of the equation $x = F(x)$, is known. Example 8.5.2 uses quadratic convergence to solve an equation whose root is not known exactly.

Example 8.5.2

A sequence is defined by $x_{r+1} = \dfrac{2x_r^3 + 1}{3x_r^2 + 1}$ with $x_0 = 0.7$.

(a) Show numerically that the sequence converges.

(b) Show that the limit of the sequence is the root α of the equation $x^3 + x = 1$.

(c) Show numerically that the convergence appears to be quadratic.

(d) If $F(x) = \dfrac{2x^3 + 1}{3x^2 + 1}$, show that $F'(\alpha) = 0$.

(e) Show numerically that $\dfrac{e_1}{e_0^2}$ and $\dfrac{e_2}{e_1^2}$ are approximately equal to $-\frac{1}{2}F''(\alpha)$.

  (a) Successive terms of the sequence are, correct to 9 decimal places,

$$x_0 = 0.7, \quad x_1 = 0.682\ 591\ 093, \quad x_2 = 0.682\ 327\ 863,$$
$$x_3 = 0.682\ 327\ 803, \quad x_4 = 0.682\ 327\ 803, \ldots .$$

  Notice that, to this level of accuracy, x_3 and x_4 are the same. It is a reasonable guess that this is the limit of the sequence, correct to 9 decimal places.

  (b) Since the sequence converges, the limit is a root of the equation

$$x = \frac{2x^3 + 1}{3x^2 + 1}.$$

  This can be rearranged as

$$3x^3 + x = 2x^3 + 1, \qquad \text{that is} \qquad x^3 + x = 1.$$

  So $\alpha \approx 0.682\ 327\ 803$ is a root of the equation $x^3 + x = 1$. (In fact, it is easy to show that $x^3 + x$ is an increasing function, so α is the only root.)

  (c) The errors in the approximations x_0, x_1 and x_2 are

$$e_0 = \alpha - x_0 \approx -0.017\ 672\ 197 \approx -1.767 \times 10^{-2},$$
$$e_1 = \alpha - x_1 \approx -0.000\ 263\ 290 \approx -2.633 \times 10^{-4},$$
$$e_2 = \alpha - x_2 \approx -0.000\ 000\ 060 \approx -6.0 \times 10^{-8}.$$

  For convergence to be quadratic, the values of $\dfrac{e_1}{e_0^2}$ and $\dfrac{e_2}{e_1^2}$ should be approximately equal. so calculate $\dfrac{e_1}{e_0^2} \approx -0.843, \quad \dfrac{e_2}{e_1^2} \approx -0.865.$

  These ratios are close enough to suggest that convergence is quadratic.

(d) Using the quotient rule for differentiation,

$$F'(x) = \frac{6x^2(3x^2 + 1) - (2x^3 + 1)6x}{(3x^2 + 1)^2}$$

$$= \frac{6x^4 + 6x^2 - 6x}{(3x^2 + 1)^2}$$

$$= \frac{6x(x^3 + x - 1)}{(3x^2 + 1)^2}.$$

So $$F'(\alpha) = \frac{6\alpha(\alpha^3 + \alpha - 1)}{(3\alpha^2 + 1)^2}.$$

But α is a root of $x^3 + x = 1$, so $\alpha^3 + \alpha - 1 = 0$. Therefore $F'(\alpha) = 0$.

> This is the crucial theoretical point. It shows that the graph of $y = F(x)$ has $(\alpha, F(\alpha))$, which is (α, α), as a stationary point, as in Fig. 8.9. This is why the convergence is quadratic.

(e) After a rather heavy piece of algebra, the second derivative can be shown to be

$$F''(x) = \frac{-6(2x^3 - 9x^2 - 2x + 1)}{(3x^2 + 1)^3}.$$

This produces the value $F''(\alpha) \approx 1.708$, so that $-\frac{1}{2}F''(\alpha) \approx -0.854$. According to the theory, successive errors should be related by the approximate equation

$$e_{r+1} \approx -0.854e_r^2.$$

This is in line with the calculations in part (c).

It is interesting to compare this example with Example 8.1.2 in which the same cubic equation is solved. In the earlier example, with a first term accurate to 2 decimal places, the approximation is still only accurate to 3 decimal places after 10 iterations. But in this example, with a first term accurate to only 1 decimal place, the approximation is accurate to 9 decimal places after only 3 iterations. Such is the power of quadratic convergence!

But the problem is how to rearrange an equation so as to produce an iteration with quadratic convergence. One method of doing this is explained in the next chapter.

An iteration for calculating square roots provides an interesting example of quadratic convergence. To solve the equation $x^2 = N$, where $N > 0$, you might try writing it as $x = \dfrac{N}{x}$ and using the iteration $x_{r+1} = \dfrac{N}{x_r}$ with a suitable starting value. But this gets you nowhere.

> Find out how this iteration behaves if you take, say, $N = 5$ and $x_0 = 2$. If $F(x) = \dfrac{N}{x}$, what is $F'(\sqrt{N})$?

You can get round the problem by adding an extra term kx to both sides of the equation $x = \dfrac{N}{x}$ to get

$$kx + x = kx + \frac{N}{x}$$

which is

$$x = F(x), \qquad \text{with} \qquad F(x) = \frac{kx + \dfrac{N}{x}}{k + 1}.$$

(A similar method was used in C3 Example 8.5.2 to speed the convergence of an iteration.) If the constant k is chosen to make $F'(\sqrt{N}) = 0$, you can devise an iteration which converges quadratically.

So calculate

$$F'(x) = \frac{1}{k + 1}\left(k - \frac{N}{x^2}\right) \quad \text{which gives} \quad F'(\sqrt{N}) = \frac{1}{k + 1}\left(k - \frac{N}{(\sqrt{N})^2}\right) = \frac{k - 1}{k + 1}.$$

This will be 0 if $k = 1$. Therefore an iteration

$$x_{r+1} = F(x_r), \qquad \text{with} \qquad F(x) = \tfrac{1}{2}\left(x + \frac{N}{x}\right),$$

and a suitable value of x_0, converges quadratically to $\sqrt{N}$.

The relation between successive errors can be found algebraically:

$$e_{r+1} = \sqrt{N} - x_{r+1} = \sqrt{N} - \tfrac{1}{2}\left(x_r + \frac{N}{x_r}\right)$$

$$= -\frac{1}{2x_r}(x_r^2 - 2\sqrt{N} \times x_r + N) = -\frac{1}{2x_r}(x_r - \sqrt{N})^2 = -\frac{1}{2x_r}e_r^2.$$

Since the values of x_r are close to each other, this confirms that the convergence is quadratic.

Example 8.5.3
Find a fraction which approximates to $\sqrt{5}$ with an error of less than 10^{-6}.

Clearly $2 < \sqrt{5} < 2.5$. If you take a starting value greater than $\sqrt{5}$, all the terms of the iterative sequence $x_{r+1} = \tfrac{1}{2}\left(x_r + \dfrac{5}{x_r}\right)$ will be greater than $\sqrt{5}$. So take $x_0 = 2.5$. Then $2.5 > x_1 > x_2 > x_3 > \ldots > 2$ (see Fig. 8.9).

It follows that $\dfrac{1}{2x_r} < \dfrac{1}{4}$, so that $|e_{r+1}| < \tfrac{1}{4}|e_r|^2$. Since $|e_0| < \tfrac{1}{2}$,

$$|e_1| < \frac{1}{4} \times \left(\frac{1}{2}\right)^2 = \frac{1}{2^4},$$

$$|e_2| < \frac{1}{4} \times \left(\frac{1}{2^4}\right)^2 = \frac{1}{2^{10}},$$

$$|e_3| < \frac{1}{4} \times \left(\frac{1}{2^{10}}\right)^2 = \frac{1}{2^{22}}, \qquad \text{and so on.}$$

Since $2^{10} = 1024 > 10^3$, it follows that $2^{20} > 10^6$, and so $|e_3| < 10^{-6}$.

Now　$x_0 = \dfrac{5}{2}$,　$x_1 = \dfrac{1}{2}\left(\dfrac{5}{2} + \dfrac{5}{\frac{5}{2}}\right) = \dfrac{9}{4}$,　$x_2 = \dfrac{1}{2}\left(\dfrac{9}{4} + \dfrac{5}{\frac{9}{4}}\right) = \dfrac{161}{72}$,

$$x_3 = \dfrac{1}{2}\left(\dfrac{161}{72} + \dfrac{5}{\frac{161}{72}}\right) = \dfrac{51\,841}{23\,184}.$$

You can check with your calculator that $\dfrac{51\,841}{23\,184} \approx 2.236\,067\,978$ and $\sqrt{5} \approx 2.236\,067\,977$, so that the agreement is much better than the 10^{-6} required.

Exercise 8C

1 Show that the graph of $F(x) = x^3 - 2x^2 - 4x + 10$ has a minimum at $(2, 2)$.

An iteration is defined by $x_{r+1} = F(x_r)$ with $x_0 = 1.8$. Show numerically that the sequence converges to 2. Calculate the values of x_r and $e_r = 2 - x_r$ for $1 \leqslant r \leqslant 6$, correct to 9 decimal places. Compare the actual values of e_r with those predicted by the approximation $e_{r+1} \approx -\frac{1}{2}F''(2)e_r^2$.

2 Show that, for $x > 0$, $F(x) = x + \dfrac{4}{x^2} - 1$ produces a graph like Fig. 8.9, and find the value of α.

For the iteration defined by $x_{r+1} = F(x_r)$ with $x_0 = 2.2$, evaluate x_1, x_2, x_3 and x_4. Hence find the values of the errors e_r for $r = 1$, 2 and 3. Investigate how well the approximation $e_{r+1} \approx -\frac{1}{2}F''(\alpha)e_r^2$ predicts the successive values of e_r.

3 Show that the graph of $F(x) = \frac{3}{2} + x - \frac{1}{6}x^2$ has a maximum at $(3, 3)$.

An iteration is defined by $x_{r+1} = F(x_r)$ with $x_0 = 0$. Show by numerical calculation that the sequence converges to 3, and that in this case the errors $e_r = 3 - x_r$ are exactly equal to those predicted by the equation $e_{r+1} = -\frac{1}{2}F''(3)e_r^2$.

Prove this algebraically, by expressing $3 - x_{r+1}$ in terms of x_r.

4 Show that the cubic equation $x^3 - 3x + 1 = 0$ can be written in the form $x = F(x)$, where $F(x) = \dfrac{2x^3 - 1}{3(x^2 - 1)}$. Differentiate $F(x)$, and show that $F'(x) = 0$ when $x^3 - 3x + 1 = 0$. Illustrate these properties by plotting the graphs of $y = x$, $y = F(x)$ and $y = x^3 - 3x + 1$ on a calculator.

Demonstrate quadratic convergence to the roots of this cubic equation by calculating successive terms of the sequence defined by $x_{r+1} = F(x_r)$, using initial values $x_0 = 0.35$, 1.5 and -1.9, and then calculating the errors in successive terms of the sequence.

5 Repeat Question 4 for

(a) the equation $xe^{2x} = 1$, taking $F(x) = \dfrac{2x^2 + e^{-2x}}{2x + 1}$ and $x_0 = 0.4$;

(b) the equation $x = \cos x$, taking $F(x) = \dfrac{x \sin x + \cos x}{1 + \sin x}$ and $x_0 = 0.75$.

6 Show that, if $F(x) = \frac{1}{3}\left(2x + \frac{N}{x^2}\right)$, where $N > 0$, then $x = F(x)$ when $x = \sqrt[3]{N}$. Show also that
   $F'(x) = 0$ for this value of x. Use these results to find a sequence which has quadratic
   convergence to $\sqrt[3]{N}$, and apply this to calculate $\sqrt[3]{10}$ as accurately as you can.

7 Generalise Question 6 to find a sequence which has quadratic convergence to $\sqrt[m]{N}$, where
   m is a positive integer. Apply the process to the calculation of $x = \sqrt[5]{30}$.

Miscellaneous exercise 8

1 Explain the advantage of using an iteration $x_{r+1} = F(x_r)$ for which $F'(x)$ is small and negative
   over the interval between x_0 and x_1.

   Show that the equation $e^x = \cot x$ has a root between 0.5 and 0.55. Rewrite this equation as
   $x = F(x)$, where $F(x) = x + k(e^x - \cot x)$, and find a value of k for which $F'(x)$ is small and
   negative over the interval $0.5 < x < 0.55$. Use this to find the root correct to 5 decimal
   places.

2 Illustrate the iterative method by using it to solve the equations

   (a) $x = 3 + \frac{1}{4}x$,   (b) $x = 6 - \frac{1}{2}x$,

   taking an initial value $x_0 = 0$. For each iteration, calculate the errors e_0, e_1, e_2 and e_3, and
   suggest an expression for e_r.

   What happens if you try to apply the method to the equations

   (c) $x = \frac{5}{4}x - 1$,   (d) $x = 10 - \frac{3}{2}x$,   (e) $x = 8 - x$?

3 For each of the following equations, use graphs to decide the number of roots, and their
   approximate location. Then, by making a suitable rearrangement and using an iterative
   method, find the roots correct to 6 decimal places. (It was shown in C3 Section 8.5 that, if
   your first trial iteration $x_{r+1} = F(x_r)$ doesn't converge, then the iteration $x_{r+1} = F^{-1}(x_r)$
   usually does. Remember also that if you have a choice of possible rearrangements, the one
   with the smallest value of $F'(x)$ in the neighbourhood of the root will produce the iteration
   with the most rapid convergence.)

   (a) $x^2 - 3x - 7 = 0$ (b) $x^3 - 20x + 5 = 0$ (c) $x^4 - 4x^3 + 10 = 0$

   (d) $x^4 = e^x$ (e) $x^3 + 100\cos x = 0$ (f) $\sin x = \ln x$

4 (a) Show that the equation $4x = e^x$ has a solution, α, near to $x = 2$.

   (b) Show numerically that the iteration $x_{r+1} = \frac{1}{4}e^{x_r}$ fails to converge to α for starting values
      on each side of α. Show analytically that this iteration will not converge to α.

   (c) Show that, for any non-zero k, $x = k(\frac{1}{4}e^x) + (1 - k)x$ is a rearrangement of the original
      equation. Investigate numerically the convergence of the corresponding iterations in
      the two cases $k = 2$ and $k = -1$.

   (d) By considering the derivative of the right side of the equation in (c), show that the value
      of k which gives fastest convergence is about -0.9.   (MEI)

5 (a) Define two iterations by $x_{n+1} = (1 + ax_n^3)^{\frac{1}{4}}$ and $x_{n+1} = \left(\dfrac{x_n^4 - 1}{a}\right)^{\frac{1}{3}}$. Show that each, *if it converges*, does so to a root of the equation $x^4 - ax^3 - 1 = 0$.

(b)* Now take $a = 2$. Carry out whichever of these iterations you think suitable, starting from $x_0 = 2$, to calculate x_1, x_2, x_3, x_4. Use Aitken's acceleration method (that is, the method described in Section 8.4) on your values to find an improved estimate of the root near $x = 2$.

(c) Explain why, when a is very large, one root of the equation must be approximately a. State which of the above iterations is suitable to find this root, and prove your answer.   (OCR, adapted)

6 Show that the equation $\cos x = \sinh x$ (see Exercise 8A Question 10(e)) can be written in the form $x = F(x)$, where $F(x) = x + k(\cos x - \sinh x)$. Taking $x_0 = 0.7$, find a value of k for which $F'(x_0)$ is very small. Use this to solve the equation correct to 8 decimal places.

7 Use the method of Question 6 to find solutions to these equations to 8 decimal places.

(a) $x^2 + e^{-x} = 1$

(b) $x^2 = \sin x$

(c) $x = \frac{1}{10}e^x$ (two roots), taking $x_0 = 0.1$ and $x_0 = 3.6$

9 The Newton–Raphson method

This chapter is about the Newton–Raphson method, which is another way of finding roots of equations numerically. When you have completed it, you should

- know and be able to use the Newton–Raphson method
- understand the theory behind the method, and be able to demonstrate it graphically
- know how to estimate the error in answers obtained by using the method
- appreciate that the Newton–Raphson method can be developed into an iterative process with quadratic convergence to the root
- be able to choose an appropriate method for solving a given equation to a given degree of accuracy, taking into account the computing facilities available.

9.1 First principles

The Newton–Raphson method of solving equations was devised by Newton to tackle a problem about the position of a planet in its orbit at a given time. This required the solution of an equation of the form $x - k \sin x = nt$ (called *Kepler's equation*). Joseph Raphson (1648–1715), who was one of the first people to publicise Newton's work, included an example in his textbook applying the method to the solution of a polynomial equation.

Before describing the method in general, here are two examples.

Example 9.1.1
Find an approximation to the root of $x^3 + x = 1$.

> This is the equation solved by the iterative method in Example 8.1.2. It was shown there that a suitable choice of starting value is $x = 0.68$.
>
> If the exact root is α, the error in this first approximation is $\alpha - 0.68$. Denote this by e, so that $\alpha = 0.68 + e$.
>
> Now since α is the exact root, $\alpha^3 + \alpha = 1$. Substituting $0.68 + e$ for α gives $(0.68 + e)^3 + (0.68 + e) = 1$, which can be expanded as
>
> $$(0.68^3 + 3 \times 0.68^2 e + 3 \times 0.68 e^2 + e^3) + (0.68 + e) = 1.$$
>
> This can be simplified to
>
> $$2.3872e + 2.04e^2 + e^3 = 0.005\,568.$$
>
> This looks unpromising. The original equation was a cubic with simple coefficients. The new equation is still cubic, but with more unpleasant coefficients.

But the clue is to notice that e is a small number, so that the powers e^2 and e^3 are very small compared with e. This means that the second and third terms on the left are much smaller than the first, and little accuracy is lost by dropping them. It follows that, with reasonable accuracy,

$$2.3872e \approx 0.005\,568, \quad \text{which gives} \quad e \approx \frac{0.005\,568}{2.3872} \approx 0.002\,33.$$

You can see how good this approximation is by substituting this value for e in the cubic equation above. The three terms on the left are

$$2.3872 \times 0.002\,33 \approx 5.6 \times 10^{-3}, \quad 2.04 \times 0.002\,33^2 \approx 1.1 \times 10^{-5},$$

$$0.002\,33^3 \approx 1.3 \times 10^{-8}.$$

Clearly the first of these is so much greater than the others that the decision to drop the second and third terms is fully justified.

The error in the approximation 0.68 is about 0.002 33, so $\alpha \approx 0.682\,33$. This is correct to 5 decimal places, which shows how powerful the method can be.

Example 9.1.2
Find an approximation to the root of $\sin x = x - 0.1$.

This is the equation solved by the iterative method in Example 8.1.1. A suitable starting value was found to be 0.85, so write $\alpha = 0.85 + e$ where e is the error in this first approximation.

Since $\sin \alpha = \alpha - 0.1$, $\quad \sin(0.85 + e) = (0.85 + e) - 0.1$, so

$$\sin 0.85 \cos e + \cos 0.85 \sin e = 0.75 + e.$$

This cannot be solved exactly for e. But since e is small, $\cos e$ and $\sin e$ can be replaced by the first degree polynomial approximations derived from the Maclaurin expansions

$$\sin e = e - \frac{e^3}{3!} + \ldots \quad \text{and} \quad \cos e = 1 - \frac{e^2}{2!} + \ldots .$$

These approximations are $\sin e \approx e$ and $\cos e \approx 1$; substituting in the above equation, and giving numerical values for $\sin 0.85$ and $\cos 0.85$, yields

$$0.751\,280\,405 \times 1 + 0.659\,983\,145\,e \approx 0.75 + e,$$

so $e \approx \dfrac{0.001\,280\,405}{0.340\,016\,855} \approx 0.003\,77.$

The resulting approximation for α, $0.85 + 0.003\,77 = 0.853\,77$, is not quite as close as in Example 9.1.1; the correct value for α to 5 decimal places is 0.853 75. But the accuracy is still impressive, considering the small amount of work involved.

9.2   The general result

To apply the Newton–Raphson method, it is best to write the equation in the form $f(x) = 0$, where f is a known function. Suppose that, for a root α of the equation, a first approximation x_0 has been found (perhaps by using a graph or the sign-change rule). The aim is to find a better approximation.

If the error in the first approximation is e, then $e = \alpha - x_0$. So substitute $x_0 + e$ for α in the equation $f(\alpha) = 0$ to obtain an equation for e,

$$f(x_0 + e) = 0.$$

The next step is suggested by Example 9.1.2, where $\sin e$ and $\cos e$ were replaced by their first degree Taylor (or Maclaurin) polynomial approximations. In the general case, replace $f(x_0 + e)$ by its first degree Taylor approximation (see Section 8.2) to get

$$f(x_0) + \frac{f'(x_0)}{1!}e \approx 0, \quad \text{or more simply} \quad f(x_0) + f'(x_0)e \approx 0.$$

From this it follows that $e \approx -\dfrac{f(x_0)}{f'(x_0)}$, so $\alpha = x_0 + e \approx x_0 - \dfrac{f(x_0)}{f'(x_0)}$.

This is the basis of the **Newton–Raphson method**:

> If x_0 is an approximation to a root α of the equation $f(x) = 0$, then usually $x_0 - \dfrac{f(x_0)}{f'(x_0)}$ is a better approximation to α.

Example 9.2.1
Find an approximation to the positive root of the equation $x^2 = e^{-x}$.

Figure 9.1 shows the graphs of $y = x^2$ and $y = e^{-x}$.

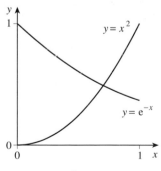

Fig. 9.1

The x-coordinate of their point of intersection is about 0.7, so take $x_0 = 0.7$.

Write the equation in the form $f(x) \equiv x^2 - e^{-x} = 0$, and differentiate to obtain $f'(x) = 2x + e^{-x}$. Then a better approximation to the root is

$$0.7 - \frac{f(0.7)}{f'(0.7)} \approx 0.7 - \frac{0.7^2 - e^{-0.7}}{2 \times 0.7 + e^{-0.7}}$$

$$\approx 0.7 - \left(\frac{-0.006\,585\,3}{1.8966} \right)$$

$$\approx 0.703\,47.$$

As a test for accuracy, you can calculate $f(0.703\,465) \approx -4.61 \times 10^{-6}$ and $f(0.703\,475) \approx 1.44 \times 10^{-5}$. So, by the sign-change rule, the approximation $0.703\,47$ gives the root correct to 5 decimal places.

Example 9.2.2

For the earth's motion round the sun the eccentricity is about $\frac{1}{60}$. One month after the time of closest approach, Kepler's equation is $x - \frac{1}{60} \sin x = \frac{1}{6}\pi$ (that is, $\frac{1}{12}$ of a revolution). Find x.

The term $\frac{1}{60} \sin x$ cannot be greater than $\frac{1}{60}$, so for a first approximation choose $x_0 = \frac{1}{6}\pi$.

Taking $f(x) = x - \frac{1}{60} \sin x - \frac{1}{6}\pi$, $f'(x) = 1 - \frac{1}{60} \cos x$,

so $f\left(\frac{1}{6}\pi\right) = \frac{1}{6}\pi - \frac{1}{60} \sin \frac{1}{6}\pi - \frac{1}{6}\pi$

$$= -\tfrac{1}{120},$$

and

$$f'\left(\tfrac{1}{6}\pi\right) = 1 - \tfrac{1}{60} \cos \tfrac{1}{6}\pi$$

$$= 1 - \tfrac{1}{120}\sqrt{3}.$$

A better approximation to the root is therefore

$$\tfrac{1}{6}\pi - \left(-\tfrac{1}{120} \Big/ \left(1 - \tfrac{1}{120}\sqrt{3}\right) \right) = \tfrac{1}{6}\pi + 0.008\,455.$$

In this application what is of most interest is the difference between x and $\frac{1}{6}\pi$, which measures the angular adjustment needed to allow for the earth's elliptic orbit. This difference is $0.008\,455$ radians, which corresponds in time to $\dfrac{0.008\,455}{2\pi}$ of a year, or about 0.49 days.

Example 9.2.3

Show that, for large values of x, the equation $x \tan x = 1$ has roots close to $x = n\pi$, where n is a positive integer. When n is large, find a better approximation to the root.

The equation $x \tan x = 1$ can be written as $\tan x = \dfrac{1}{x}$.

Fig. 9.2 shows that, when x is large, the graphs of $y = \tan x$ and $y = \dfrac{1}{x}$ intersect close to the points where $y = \tan x$ cuts the x-axis, that is $x = n\pi$.

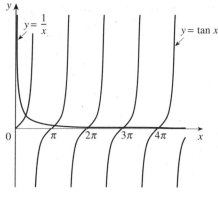

Fig. 9.2

There are a number of different ways of writing the equation to apply the Newton–Raphson method, for example

$$f(x) \equiv x \tan x - 1 = 0,$$

$$g(x) \equiv x \sin x - \cos x = 0,$$

$$h(x) \equiv \tan x - \frac{1}{x} = 0.$$

In this case, the first two give the same improved approximation, but the third gives a different answer. (There is no reason why the answers should always be the same; there are many approximations to an exact root.)

The product rule gives $f'(x) \equiv 1 \times \tan x + x \sec^2 x$, so that

$$f(n\pi) = n\pi \times 0 - 1 = -1, \quad f'(n\pi) = 0 + n\pi \times (\pm 1)^2 = n\pi.$$

The Newton–Raphson method gives a better approximation

$$x \approx n\pi - \frac{-1}{n\pi} = n\pi + \frac{1}{n\pi}.$$

9.3   A graphical representation

The Newton–Raphson method has a simple graphical interpretation.

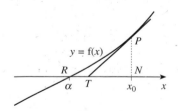

Fig. 9.3

Fig. 9.3 shows the graph of a function $f(x)$ in the neighbourhood of a root α of the equation $f(x) = 0$. The graph cuts the x-axis at R, and a point P on the graph close to R has x-coordinate x_0; N is the point $(x_0, 0)$. The tangent to the graph at P cuts the x-axis at T.

The expressions $f(x_0)$ and $f'(x_0)$ which appear in the Newton–Raphson formula are represented by NP and $\dfrac{NP}{TN}$ respectively, so

$$\frac{f(x_0)}{f'(x_0)} = \frac{NP}{NP/TN} = NP \times \frac{TN}{NP} = TN.$$

The x-coordinate of T is then $x_0 - TN = x_0 - \dfrac{f(x_0)}{f'(x_0)}.$

So the Newton–Raphson approximation states that T is closer to R than N is. This is obvious from Fig. 9.3, which shows the simplest case, in which $f(x_0)$ and $f'(x_0)$ are both positive, and the curve bends upwards so that $f''(x)$ is positive between α and x_0.

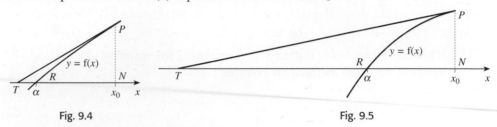

Fig. 9.4   Fig. 9.5

However, Figs. 9.4 and 9.5 show that you need to be cautious in using the method. In these figures $f(x_0)$ and $f'(x_0)$ are still positive, but the graph bends downwards, so $f''(x)$ is negative between α and x_0. The points T and N then lie on opposite sides of R.

In Fig. 9.4 $f'(x_0)$ is fairly large and the curve bends quite gently, so that $f''(x)$ is small.

It is still true that T is closer to R than N, so that $x_0 - \dfrac{f(x_0)}{f'(x_0)}$ is a better approximation to the root than x_0.

But in Fig. 9.5 $f'(x_0)$ is small and $f''(x)$ is large. You can see that in this case T is further from R than N, so that the method does not give a better approximation to the root. This is why the word 'usually' had to be used in the statement of the method in the last section.

Exercise 9A

1 In Fig. 9.3, write down the equation of the tangent at P. Use this to show that the x-coordinate of T is $x_0 - \dfrac{f(x_0)}{f'(x_0)}.$

2 Use the method in Section 9.1 to approximate to the roots of the following equations. Verify in each case that applying the general Newton–Raphson method in Section 9.2 leads to the same answer.

   (a) $x^4 + 3x^2 + 2x - 4 = 0$ close to 0.8

   (b) $x^3 + e^x - 2 = 0$ close to 0.6

   (c) $\cos x + x - 3 = 0$ close to 3.8

3 For the following functions $f(x)$ and initial values x_0 find the values of $f(x_0)$, $f'(x_0)$ and $f''(x_0)$. Use these to sketch the graph of $y = f(x)$ in the neighbourhood of $x = x_0$. Use the Newton–Raphson method to find a better approximation to a root of $f(x) = 0$ than x_0. Find whether your improved approximation is accurate to 4 decimal places.

(a) $2x \sin x - 3$, $x_0 = 2.5$ (b) $\ln x + e^{-x} - 1$, $x_0 = 2.5$

(c) $\sqrt{x} - \cos x$, $x_0 = 0.65$ (d) $(x^2 + 2)(x^3 + 3) - (x^4 + 4)$, $x_0 = -1.1$

4 Show that, for large values of x, the equation $x \sin x = 1$ has roots close to $x = n\pi$, where n is a positive integer. Find a better approximation to the root.

5 Show that each of the following equations has a root in the given interval. By choosing a suitable value of x_0 and using the Newton–Raphson method, find an approximation to the root, and determine to how many decimal places it is accurate. Then use the Newton–Raphson method again, taking the approximation you have found as the new value of x_0, to obtain a better approximation. Determine to how many decimal places this is accurate.

(a) $x^7 - 500 = 0$, $2.4 < x < 2.5$ (b) $x^2 - \cosh x = 0$, $1.6 < x < 1.7$

(c) $\sqrt{x} + \sqrt[3]{x} + \sqrt[4]{x} = 4$, $2.1 < x < 2.2$

6 Draw diagrams similar to Figs. 9.3 and 9.4 for all eight possible combinations of sign of $f(x_0)$, $f'(x_0)$ and $f''(x_0)$. For which of these combinations does T lie between R and N? (You will need these in Exercise 9B Question 6.)

9.4 Estimating accuracy

When you use any approximate method, an important question is always 'how accurate is the answer'? Of course, you can never answer this precisely; if you could, you could find the root exactly, so there would be no need to use an approximate method. But an approximate answer is of little use unless you have some idea of the order of magnitude of its accuracy.

A hint of how this question can be answered for the Newton–Raphson method was given in the paragraph in the grey box in Example 9.1.1, where the magnitudes of the dropped terms were compared with that of the term which was kept. A similar argument can be used in the general case.

The Newton–Raphson approximation was derived in Section 9.2 by using the first degree Taylor polynomial approximation for $f(x_0 + e)$, that is by dropping the terms involving e^2 and higher powers of e. When e is small, the term in e^2 will be the most significant of these; and this term can be retained by using the second degree Taylor polynomial. That is, the exact equation $f(x_0 + e) = 0$ is replaced by the approximation

$$f(x_0) + \frac{f'(x_0)}{1!}e + \frac{f''(x_0)}{2!}e^2 \approx 0;$$

or, more simply,

$$f(x_0) + f'(x_0)e + \tfrac{1}{2}f''(x_0)e^2 \approx 0.$$

Now, as before, take all the terms except the second to the other side of the equation, and divide by $f'(x_0)$:

$$e \approx -\frac{f(x_0)}{f'(x_0)} - \frac{f''(x_0)}{2f'(x_0)}e^2.$$

The first term on the right is the Newton–Raphson improvement, as before; the second term is small, since it has e^2 as a factor. So although you can't find it exactly, you can estimate it by replacing e in this term by its approximate value $-\frac{f(x_0)}{f'(x_0)}$. This gives

$$e \approx -\frac{f(x_0)}{f'(x_0)} - \frac{f''(x_0)}{2f'(x_0)}\left(-\frac{f(x_0)}{f'(x_0)}\right)^2 = -\frac{f(x_0)}{f'(x_0)} - \frac{(f(x_0))^2\,f''(x_0)}{2(f'(x_0))^3}.$$

> When, in the Newton–Raphson method, the first approximation x_0 is replaced by the improved approximation $x_0 - \dfrac{f(x_0)}{f'(x_0)}$, the error is given approximately by $-\dfrac{(f(x_0))^2\,f''(x_0)}{2(f'(x_0))^3}$.

Example 9.4.1

Estimate the error in the approximation to the root of $x^2 = e^{-x}$ found in Example 9.2.1.

The example used $f(x) = x^2 - e^{-x}$ with $x_0 = 0.7$, so that

$$f(x_0) = 0.7^2 - e^{-0.7} \approx -0.006\,585\,303\,8,$$

$$f'(x_0) = 2 \times 0.7 + e^{-0.7} \approx 1.896\,585\,304,$$

$$f''(x_0) = 2 - e^{-0.7} \approx 1.503\,414\,696.$$

Only the order of magnitude of the error is needed, so it is sufficient to retain 2 significant figures and to estimate the error as

$$-\frac{(-0.0066)^2 \times 1.5}{2 \times 1.9^3} \approx -4.8 \times 10^{-6}.$$

You might therefore expect the answer to be about 5 too large in the 6th decimal place. In fact, if the calculation in Example 9.2.1 had been carried to the 6th decimal place the answer would have been $0.703\,472$. The correct root to 6 decimal places is $0.703\,467$, which confirms this error estimate. The decision to give an answer to 5 decimal places in Example 9.2.1 was therefore well founded; the figure in the 5th place could be out by 1 at most, but the figure in the 6th place is unreliable.

You can see that the error estimate $-\dfrac{(f(x_0))^2\,f''(x_0)}{2(f'(x_0))^3}$ confirms the impression given by Figs. 9.4 and 9.5. For the method to work well the error has to be small. This happens if $|f(x_0)|$ and $|f''(x_0)|$ are both small and $|f'(x_0)|$ is large. But in Fig. 9.5 $|f''(x_0)|$ is large and $|f'(x_0)|$ is small, and this combination produces an unacceptably large error.

Notice also the contrast between Fig. 9.3 and Fig. 9.4, which differ in the sign of $f''(x_0)$. The error in Fig. 9.3 is negative, so that T is to the right of R; but in Fig. 9.4 the error is positive, with T to the left of R.

9.5   Newton–Raphson as an iteration

It can well happen that one application of the Newton–Raphson method is not good enough to produce the root of $f(x) = 0$ to the accuracy you want. In that case, you can use the first answer as a starting value for a second application.

Example 9.5.1
Find the smallest positive root of $x + \tan x = 2$ correct to 8 decimal places.

Writing $f(x) = x + \tan x - 2$, you find that $f(0.8) = -0.17\ldots$ and $f(0.9) = 0.16\ldots$, which suggests a root about 0.85.

So begin by taking $x_0 = 0.85$. Then a better approximation is $0.85 - \dfrac{f(0.85)}{f'(0.85)}$ where $f(x) = x + \tan x - 2$ and $f'(x) = 1 + \sec^2 x$. So calculate

$$x_0 = 0.85 - \frac{0.85 + \tan 0.85 - 2}{1 + \sec^2 0.85} = 0.853\,540\,045.$$

You have 9 decimal places here, but this answer may not give the root correct to 8 decimal places. So apply the method again, using $0.853\,540\,045$ in place of 0.85. This gives a second approximation $0.853\,530\,114$, which should be even closer to the root.

Is this close enough? To answer this, calculate a third approximation using $0.853\,530\,114$ as the input value. You will find that this gives you $0.853\,530\,114$ again, which suggests you are as close to the root as you are going to get.

With a suitable calculator, you can carry out these calculations very quickly. The method relies on the fact that the calculator uses ANS as a temporary memory.

Step 1   Enter the first approximation, in this case 0.85, into your calculator, and press ENTER. (On some calculators, this key is called EXE.)

Step 2   Enter ANS $- \dfrac{\text{ANS} + \tan \text{ANS} - 2}{1 + \sec^2 \text{ANS}}$.

Step 3   Press ENTER (EXE) for successive approximations to the solution.

The results suggest that, correct to 8 decimal places, the root is $0.853\,530\,11$.

To be quite sure, you can work out $f(x)$ with $x = 0.853\,530\,105$ and $x = 0.853\,530\,115$, and show that there is a change of sign in the interval. It turns out that the values are -2.95×10^{-8} and $+3.6 \times 10^{-9}$ respectively. From this you can say with certainty that the root is $0.853\,530\,11$ correct to 8 decimal places.

You will recognise this repeated application of the Newton–Raphson method as another example of iteration, defining a sequence by

$$x_{r+1} = x_r - \frac{f(x_r)}{f'(x_r)}$$

with a suitable value of x_0. Thus in Example 9.5.1,

$$x_0 = 0.85, \quad x_1 = 0.853\,540\,045, \quad x_2 = 0.853\,530\,114, \quad x_3 = 0.853\,530\,114$$

to 9 decimal places.

These calculations are represented graphically (though not to scale) in Fig. 9.6.

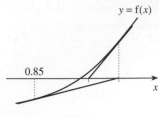

Fig. 9.6

The graph of f(x) has positive gradient and is bending upwards. Since f(0.85) < 0, the starting value is to the left of the root. However, the tangent at (0.85, f(0.85)) cuts the x-axis to the right of the root, so that subsequent approximations come in to the root from the right.

To see what is happening in closer detail, you can break down the calculation into its separate stages and set out the results as in Table 9.7. The first line gives the successive values of x_r calculated in Example 9.5.1. From the values of f(x_r), f'(x_r) and f''(x_r) calculated in the next three lines, you can calculate the 'correction' $-\dfrac{f(x_r)}{f'(x_r)}$ which takes you from x_r to x_{r+1}, and also the error estimate $-\dfrac{(f(x_r))^2\,f''(x_r)}{2(f'(x_r))^3}$ which gives you an idea how good an approximation x_{r+1} will be.

x	0.85	0.853 540 045	0.853 530 114
f(x)	−0.011 667 286	0.000 032 916	0
f'(x)	3.295 801 366	3.314 445 903	
f''(x)	5.226 771 596	5.306 991 455	
$-\dfrac{f(x)}{f'(x)}$	0.003 540 045	−0.000 009 931	
Error estimate	−9.9 × 10^{-6}	−7.9 × 10^{-11}	

Table 9.7

Although the first approximation was quite close to the root, you can see that the error after the first application of the Newton–Raphson formula was about 1 in the 5th decimal place. This is because the root is in a region where the curve is bending quite fast, as is shown by the large value of f''(x). To get accuracy to 8 decimal places, a second round of the Newton–Raphson method is used, starting at 0.853 540 045, the answer from the first application.

Table 9.7 shows that the error after the second round is about 8 in the 11th decimal place, so you can be confident that the root is 0.853 530 11 correct to 8 decimal places.

Example 9.5.2

(a) Prove that the equation $x^5 + x^3 - 50 = 0$ has only one real root, and that this lies between 2 and 3.

(b) Use a Newton–Raphson iteration to find this root correct to 8 decimal places.

(c) Show numerically that the sequence of approximations converges to the root quadratically.

(a) Denoting $x^5 + x^3 - 50$ by $f(x)$, the derivative $f'(x) = 5x^4 + 3x^2$. This is positive for all values of x except $x = 0$, where $f'(x) = 0$. So $f(x)$ is an increasing function, and its graph can only cut the y-axis in one point.

Since $f(2) = 32 + 8 - 50 = -10$, and $f(3) = 243 + 27 - 50 = 220$, the values of the function change sign between 2 and 3. So the root lies between 2 and 3.

(b) Successive terms of the iteration are obtained from the equation

$$x_{r+1} = x_r - \frac{f(x_r)}{f'(x_r)}$$
$$= x_r - \frac{x_r^5 + x_r^3 - 50}{5x_r^4 + 3x_r^2}.$$

The numerical calculations in part (a) suggest that the root is close to 2, so take $x_0 = 2$.

This gives

$$x_1 = 2.108\,695\,652, \quad x_2 = 2.099\,158\,015, \quad x_3 = 2.099\,075\,828,$$
$$x_4 = 2.099\,075\,822, \quad x_5 = 2.099\,075\,822, \quad \dots .$$

The values of x_4 and x_5 are the same to 9 decimal places, so you can be almost certain that the root of $f(x) = 0$ is $2.099\,075\,82$ correct to 8 decimal places.

If you want to be 100% sure, you could work out

$$f(2.099\,075\,815) = -7.37 \times 10^{-7} \quad \text{and} \quad f(2.099\,075\,825) = 3.66 \times 10^{-7}$$

and note the sign change; or you could calculate the error estimate as

$$-\frac{(f(x_5))^2\, f''(x_5)}{2(f'(x_5))^3} \approx -9 \times 10^{-20},$$

which is so small as to remove any doubt.

(c) The errors in the terms of the sequence, calculated as $e_r = x_5 - x_r$, are

$$e_0 = 0.099\,075\,822, \quad e_1 = -0.009\,619\,830,$$
$$e_2 = -0.000\,082\,193, \quad e_3 = -0.000\,000\,006.$$

To show the convergence is quadratic, calculate the ratios

$$\frac{e_1}{e_0^2} \approx -0.980, \quad \frac{e_2}{e_1^2} \approx -0.888, \quad \frac{e_3}{e_2^2} \approx -0.888.$$

These are sufficiently close to justify the conclusion.

9.6 Why Newton–Raphson converges so quickly

What is impressive about the Newton–Raphson method is that it gives a very accurate approximation very quickly. Whereas the iterations in Chapter 8 might require 20 or 30 steps to get to an accuracy of 5 decimal places, a Newton–Raphson iteration will often get there after one or two steps. The reason for this is that Newton–Raphson iteration is an example of quadratic convergence, described in Section 8.5. This is proved in the following theorem.

Theorem   The Newton–Raphson iteration

$$x_{r+1} = F(x_r), \quad \text{where} \quad F(x) \equiv x - \frac{f(x)}{f'(x)},$$

converging to a root α of $f(x) = 0$, has quadratic convergence.

> **Proof**   Notice first that $F(\alpha) = \alpha - \frac{f(\alpha)}{f'(\alpha)} = \alpha$, since $f(\alpha) = 0$. That is,
>
> $$x = x - \frac{f(x)}{f'(x)}$$
>
> can be thought of as a rearrangement of $f(x) = 0$ in the form $x = F(x)$.
>
> Also, writing $F(x)$ in the form $x - f(x) \times \dfrac{1}{f'(x)}$ and using the product rule of differentiation gives
>
> $$F'(x) = 1 - f'(x) \times \frac{1}{f'(x)} - f(x) \times \left(-\frac{1}{(f'(x))^2} \right) f''(x)$$
>
> $$= \frac{f(x)\, f''(x)}{(f'(x))^2}.$$
>
> Therefore $F'(\alpha) = \dfrac{f(\alpha)\, f''(\alpha)}{(f'(\alpha))^2} = 0$, since $f(\alpha) = 0$. This is the condition given in Section 8.5 for the iteration $x_{r+1} = F(x_r)$ to converge quadratically to α.

This is illustrated well by Example 9.5.1. The error in the original starting value was about 3.5×10^{-3}. The errors after the next two steps are about -10^{-5} and -8×10^{-11}. So $e_1 \approx -0.8e_0^2$, and $e_2 \approx -0.8e_1^2$.

Exercise 9B

1 Use the Newton–Raphson method for each of the following equations, with the given initial value x_0, to find a better approximation, and estimate the error. Hence give the root to as many decimal places as the method justifies.

   (a) $x^3 - 3x^2 - 2 = 0$, $x_0 = 3.2$

   (b) $\sqrt{x - 1} - \dfrac{5}{x^2} = 0$, $x_0 = 2.1$

   (c) $x + e^x - 6 = 0$, $x_0 = 1.5$

   (d) $x \ln x = 5$, $x_0 = 3.8$

2 Iterate the Newton–Raphson method for each of the following equations, with the given initial value x_0, to find the root as accurately as your calculator permits.

   (a) $x^2 - \cos x = 0$, $x_0 = 0.8$ (b) $\sinh x - \sqrt{4 - x^2} = 0$, $x_0 = 1.2$ (c) $e^{-x} = \sin x$, $x_0 = 0.6$

3 Analyse the iterative solutions to the equations in Question 2 by means of a table similar to Table 9.7.

4 Choose an initial value and use the Newton–Raphson method for as many iterations as you need to find approximations to the roots of the following equations correct to 8 decimal places.

   (a) $2x^5 + x - 1 = 0$ (b) $x^3 e^x = 1$ (c) $x + \sin x = 1$ (d) $x \sinh x = \cosh x$

5 If a chain of length $2l$ is stretched between two points at the same level a distance $2a$ apart, then it will sag by an amount $\dfrac{\cosh \lambda a - 1}{\lambda}$, where λ is a solution of $\lambda l = \sinh a\lambda$. Find the sag, correct to 3 significant figures, if a chain of length 21 metres is stretched between two points 20 metres apart.

6* With the notation of the Theorem in Section 9.6, show that $F''(\alpha) = \dfrac{f''(\alpha)}{f'(\alpha)}$. Hence use the result in Section 8.5 to show that successive errors in a Newton–Raphson iteration are related by the approximation $e_{r+1} \approx -\dfrac{f''(\alpha)}{2f'(\alpha)} e_r^2$. Demonstrate this numerically by evaluating successive error estimates in a Newton–Raphson iteration to the root of the equation $\tan x - x - 1 = 0$ with $x_0 = 1.1$.

What is the significance of the minus sign in this relation, and in the formula for the Newton–Raphson error estimate? Use the graphs which you drew in Exercise 9A Question 6 to demonstrate the necessity for these minus signs.

7* Use the Newton–Raphson method to obtain an iteration which converges to $\sqrt[m]{N}$, where N is a positive number and m is a positive integer. (See Exercise 8C Question 7.) Show that successive errors in the iteration are related approximately by $e_{r+1} \approx -\dfrac{m-1}{2\sqrt[m]{N}} e_r^2$. (Use the result in Question 6.)

If x_0 is taken as the integer next above $\sqrt[m]{N}$, and if this is appreciably larger than $\frac{1}{2}(m-1)$, then show that the error should be less than 10^{-D} after k iterations, where k is the integer next above $\dfrac{1}{\log 2} \log \left(1 + \dfrac{D}{\log(2x_0/(m-1))} \right)$ and log denotes the logarithm to base 10.

9.7 Which is the best method?

You now know several methods of finding roots of equations: the sign-change rule and a variety of forms of iterative sequence $x_{r+1} = F(x_r)$, including the Newton–Raphson method. How do you decide which to use for any particular equation?

A lot depends on the accuracy to which you want the answer, and on the computing facilities you are using. For example, the sign-change rule is a very useful way of deciding where to start an iteration, but if you are working with a simple calculator it becomes very laborious if you want an accurate answer (see C3 Section 8.2). However, if you are using a graphic calculator, then being able to zoom in to a root by using smaller and smaller windows makes it possible to get an answer to several decimal places very quickly.

With simple iteration you often need 20 or 30 steps to reach the accuracy you need, but for some equations each step is very easy. For example, to find the root of $x = \cos x$ (see Example 8.2.2) you simply keep pressing the COS key until the number in the display settles down to a constant value. Even more complicated iterations can often be made into simple programs which you can set up with a computer (perhaps on a spreadsheet) or a programmable calculator.

The question then arises whether it is worthwhile doing a calculation like that in Example 8.2.2 to estimate how many steps will be needed, or whether it is better just to run the program (say 10 steps at a time) and stop when it appears to have converged sufficiently.

Other possibilities are to modify an iteration to speed up convergence (as in C3 Example 8.5.2), or to use Newton–Raphson. Each step of the iteration will then be more complicated, but you need far fewer steps. You also have the possibility of doing the first few steps of a simple iteration and then jumping to a more accurate answer by the method described in Section 8.4. You have to balance the reduction in computing time against the time it takes to do the extra algebra.

There is no one answer to the question in the heading of this section. Which method is best varies according to circumstances.

Exercise 9C

The equations in Exercise 9C allow you to investigate for yourself the relative merits of different methods for finding a root of an equation. For each equation restrict yourself to a particular calculator or computer facility, and then try a variety of methods to decide which is best at getting the answer to a given degree of accuracy.

1 $x^4 + 2x^3 + 3x^2 + 4x = 5$

2 $(x + 1)(x^3 + 3) = x^2 + 2$

3 $\sqrt{x + 1} + \sqrt{x + 2} + \sqrt{x + 3} = 10$

4 $e^x + x^2 = 100$

5 $x \cosh x = 2$

6 $\sin x = \ln x$

> Make up some more for yourself!

Miscellaneous exercise 9

1 Let $f(x) = (x - 3)(x^2 + 1) - 10$. Show that the equation $f(x) = 0$ has a root between $x = 3$ and $x = 4$. Find an approximate solution of $f(x) = 0$ by applying the Newton–Raphson process twice, starting with $x = 4$.   (OCR)

2 Use the Newton–Raphson method with an initial value $x = 0.75$ to find, correct to 3 decimal places, the positive root of the equation $x = \cos x$.   (OCR)

3 Use the Newton–Raphson method to find, correct to 3 decimal places, the root of $x^5 - 5x = 21$ which is nearly equal to 2.   (OCR)

4 Use the Newton–Raphson approximation, with initial approximation 3, to find, correct to 3 decimal places, the only real root of the equation $x \ln x = 4$.   (OCR)

5 Use the Newton–Raphson method to find, correct to 3 decimal places, the root of the equation $x^3 - 10x = 25$ which is close to 4. (OCR)

6 Find, correct to 5 decimal places, the coordinates of the points of intersection of

   (a) $y = \operatorname{sech} x$ and $y = \dfrac{1}{1 + x^2}$,

   (b) $y = \cos x$ and $y = 1 - \frac{1}{2}x$,

   (c) $y = x^3$ and the circle with centre $(1, 1)$ and radius 2.

7 Sketch the graph of $y = x \operatorname{sech} x$. Find the coordinates of the stationary points.

8* (a) Show on a sketch graph that, when $|a|$ is small, the equation $\sin x = ax$ has a root near to π. Use one step of the Newton–Raphson method to obtain an approximation to the root. Show that your answer is approximately $\pi(1 - a)$.

   (b) Find similar approximations to the roots nearest $2n\pi$ and $(2n + 1)\pi$ of the equation $\sin x = \dfrac{b}{x}$ when $|b|$ is small. Give your solutions in the form $2n\pi(1 + pb)$ and $(2n + 1)\pi(1 - qb)$, where p and q are constants to be determined. (OCR)

9 (a) Sketch the curve with equation $y = \tan x - 2x$ for $0 < x < \frac{1}{2}\pi$ to show that the equation $\tan x - 2x = 0$ has a solution, α, in that interval.

   (b) Obtain the Newton–Raphson iterative formula for the equation $\tan x - 2x = 0$.

   (c) Consider the Newton–Raphson iteration with the two starting values $x_0 = 0.9$ and $x_0 = 1.1$. Show that the iteration converges with one of these starting values but not with the other.

   (d) There is a value k such that if $k < x_0 < \frac{1}{2}\pi$ the Newton–Raphson iteration with starting value x_0 will converge to α. Show the value k on your sketch; show also the tangent to the curve at $x = k$.

   (e) If the starting value x_0 is less than k, the Newton–Raphson iteration may not converge to α. Describe two of the distinct cases which can arise. (MEI)

10* Sketch the graph of $y = \dfrac{\cos x}{\cosh x}$ and find the least number k such that $\cos x + k \cosh x \geqslant 0$ for all real values of x.

11* The quadratic equation $3z^2 - 2z + 1 = 0$ has a root close to $0.3 + 0.5\,i$. Assuming that the Newton–Raphson method can be extended to equations with complex unknowns, and that the rules for differentiation are the same as for real functions, find a closer approximation to the root. Illustrate with an Argand diagram the relation between the initial approximation, the closer approximation and the exact root $\frac{1}{3}(1 + \sqrt{2}i)$.

12* Use the Newton–Raphson method to find, to 3 decimal places, a closer approximation to the root of $z^3 - 4z + 5 = 0$ near to $1.2 + 0.7\,i$.

10 Integration using trigonometric functions

This chapter assembles all the important results about differentiation and integration which involve trigonometric functions. When you have completed it, you should

- know the key derivatives and integrals, and how to obtain others from them
- be familiar with a variety of methods of finding trigonometric integrals
- be able to select and use appropriate trigonometric or hyperbolic substitutions for evaluating integrals.

Before reading the chapter you will find it helpful to review some derivatives of trigonometric functions by working through Exercise 10A. Questions 1(a), (b), (e), (g) and (h) are especially important and are worth remembering.

Exercise 10A

1 Taking the derivatives of $\sin x$ and $\cos x$ as the starting point, prove the following results. In parts (e) to (i), give a reason for the inequality conditions.

(a) $\dfrac{\mathbf{d}}{\mathbf{dx}} \tan x = \sec^2 x$

(b) $\dfrac{\mathbf{d}}{\mathbf{dx}} \sec x = \sec x \tan x$

(c) $\dfrac{\mathrm{d}}{\mathrm{dx}} \cot x = -\operatorname{cosec}^2 x$

(d) $\dfrac{\mathrm{d}}{\mathrm{dx}} \operatorname{cosec} x = -\operatorname{cosec} x \cot x$

(e) If $0 < x < \pi$, $\dfrac{\mathbf{d}}{\mathbf{dx}} \ln(\sin x) = \cot x$

(f) If $-\frac{1}{2}\pi < x < \frac{1}{2}\pi$, $\dfrac{\mathrm{d}}{\mathrm{dx}} \ln(\cos x) = -\tan x$

(g) If $-\frac{1}{2}\pi < x < \frac{1}{2}\pi$, $\dfrac{\mathbf{d}}{\mathbf{dx}} \ln(\sec x) = \tan x$

(h) If $-\frac{1}{2}\pi < x < \frac{1}{2}\pi$, $\dfrac{\mathbf{d}}{\mathbf{dx}} \ln(\sec x + \tan x) = \sec x$

(i) If $0 < x < \pi$, $\dfrac{\mathrm{d}}{\mathrm{dx}} \ln\left(\tan \frac{1}{2}x\right) = \operatorname{cosec} x$

2 Rewrite the results in Question 1 in the form of indefinite integrals. For parts (e) to (i), give alternative indefinite integrals for other intervals of values of x.

3 Show that $\dfrac{\mathrm{d}}{\mathrm{dx}}(\sin^2 x) = \dfrac{\mathrm{d}}{\mathrm{dx}}(-\cos^2 x) = \dfrac{\mathrm{d}}{\mathrm{dx}}(-\frac{1}{2}\cos 2x)$. What is the connection between $\sin^2 x$, $-\cos^2 x$ and $-\frac{1}{2}\cos 2x$?

10.1   Methods of integrating trigonometric functions

The derivatives of $\sin x$ and $\cos x$, together with rules such as the chain rule and the product rule, are enough to enable you to differentiate almost any expression involving trigonometric functions. But integration is less predictable.

Even such a simple integral as $\int \sqrt{\sin x}\, dx$ is impossible to find. It is not just that you don't yet know enough to be able to work it out. There is in fact no function f(x) involving the functions with which you are familiar (powers, logarithm, exponential, and so on) such that

$$f'(x) = \sqrt{\sin x}.$$

It is not easy to tell by inspection whether it is going to be possible to integrate a particular function or not. There are, however, a few general procedures, and with experience you should recognise which (if any) are likely to work in a particular case.

This section revises some of the methods which you have already met in earlier parts of the course. Its purpose is to help you to decide which method is likely to be most effective when you meet a trigonometrical integral in the course of some application.

(i) Using trigonometric identities

Identities, such as Pythagoras' identities and the addition formulae, can often be used to convert a trigonometric integrand into a form whose integral you already know. Some of the most useful ones were listed in C4 Section 1.6, but here are some more examples.

Example 10.1.1

Find $\int \tan^2 x\, dx$.

One of the trigonometric forms of Pythagoras' theorem is $1 + \tan^2 x = \sec^2 x$, and you know the integral of $\sec^2 x$ (see Exercise 10A Question 1(a)). So

$$\int \tan^2 x\, dx = \int (\sec^2 x - 1)\, dx$$
$$= \tan x - x + k.$$

Example 10.1.2

Evaluate $\int_0^{\frac{1}{2}\pi} \sqrt{1 + \sin 2x}\, dx$.

There is no obvious identity to apply here, but there are two possible lines of attack.

Method 1   Although there is no standard identity of the form $1 + \sin 2x \equiv \dots$, you have met the identity $1 + \cos 2x \equiv 2\cos^2 x$. So is there a way of turning $\sin 2x$ into a cosine?

An obvious answer is to use the symmetry property $\sin 2x \equiv \cos\left(\frac{1}{2}\pi - 2x\right)$. Then

$$1 + \sin 2x \equiv 1 + \cos\left(\tfrac{1}{2}\pi - 2x\right) \equiv 1 + \cos 2\left(\tfrac{1}{4}\pi - x\right) \equiv 2\cos^2\left(\tfrac{1}{4}\pi - x\right).$$

So

$$\int_0^{\frac{1}{2}\pi} \sqrt{1 + \sin 2x}\, dx = \int_0^{\frac{1}{2}\pi} \sqrt{2\cos^2\left(\tfrac{1}{4}\pi - x\right)}\, dx$$

$$= \int_0^{\frac{1}{2}\pi} \sqrt{2}\cos\left(\tfrac{1}{4}\pi - x\right) dx$$

$$= \left[-\sqrt{2}\sin\left(\tfrac{1}{4}\pi - x\right)\right]_0^{\frac{1}{2}\pi}$$

$$= -\sqrt{2}\sin\left(-\tfrac{1}{4}\pi\right) + \sqrt{2}\sin\left(\tfrac{1}{4}\pi\right)$$

$$= -\sqrt{2} \times \left(-\frac{1}{\sqrt{2}}\right) + \sqrt{2} \times \frac{1}{\sqrt{2}}$$

$$= 1 + 1 = 2.$$

Method 2   You might be tempted to begin by replacing $\sin 2x$ by $2\sin x \cos x$, but $\sqrt{1 + 2\sin x \cos x}$ doesn't immediately look very promising. However, you could think of $2\sin x \cos x$ as the middle term when you expand $(\sin x + \cos x)^2$; and then you would probably realise that the other two terms would be $\sin^2 x$ and $\cos^2 x$, and that $\sin^2 x + \cos^2 x \equiv 1$. So

$$1 + 2\sin x \cos x \equiv (\sin^2 x + \cos^2 x) + 2\sin x \cos x \equiv (\sin x + \cos x)^2.$$

Then

$$\int_0^{\frac{1}{2}\pi} \sqrt{1 + \sin 2x}\, dx = \int_0^{\frac{1}{2}\pi} \sqrt{(\sin x + \cos x)^2}\, dx$$

$$= \int_0^{\frac{1}{2}\pi} (\sin x + \cos x)\, dx$$

$$= \left[-\cos x + \sin x\right]_0^{\frac{1}{2}\pi}$$

$$= (-0 + 1) - (-1 + 0) = 2.$$

Notice that with both methods you have to take the square root of a squared expression. When this occurs, it is important to check that the expression given for the square root is positive over the whole interval of integration.

(ii) Using integration by substitution

If the integrand can be put into a form such as $f(\sin x) \cos x$, $f(\cos x) \sin x$ or $f(\tan x) \sec^2 x$, then you can transform the integral by using a substitution such as $u = \sin x$, $u = \cos x$ or $u = \tan x$.

Example 10.1.3

Find (a) $\displaystyle\int \frac{\cos x}{(1 + \sin x)^2}\, dx$,   (b) $\displaystyle\int \cos^4 x \sin^3 x\, dx$,   (c) $\displaystyle\int \sec^4 x\, dx$.

(a) If $u = \sin x$, then $\dfrac{du}{dx} = \cos x$, so

$$\int \frac{\cos x}{(1 + \sin x)^2}\, dx = \int \frac{1}{(1 + \sin x)^2} \times \frac{du}{dx}\, dx = \int \frac{1}{(1 + u)^2}\, du$$

$$= -\frac{1}{1 + u} + k = -\frac{1}{1 + \sin x} + k.$$

(b) In the form given the integrand is not in either of the forms $f(\sin x) \cos x$ or $f(\cos x) \sin x$. But you can write it as

$$\cos^4 x \sin^2 x \sin x \equiv \cos^4 x(1 - \cos^2 x) \sin x.$$

Then, if $u = \cos x$, $\dfrac{du}{dx} = -\sin x$, so

$$\int \cos^4 x \sin^3 x \, dx = \int \cos^4 x(1 - \cos^2 x) \times \left(-\frac{du}{dx}\right) dx$$

$$= \int -u^4 (1 - u^2) \, du$$

$$= \tfrac{1}{7}u^7 - \tfrac{1}{5}u^5 + k = \tfrac{1}{7}\cos^7 x - \tfrac{1}{5}\cos^5 x + k.$$

(c) Write $\sec^4 x$ as $\sec^2 x \sec^2 x \equiv (1 + \tan^2 x) \sec^2 x$. Then the substitution $u = \tan x$ gives

$$\int \sec^4 x \, dx = \int (1 + \tan^2 x) \times \frac{du}{dx} \, dx = \int (1 + u^2) \, du$$

$$= u + \tfrac{1}{3}u^3 + k = \tan x + \tfrac{1}{3}\tan^3 x + k.$$

With practice you may find that in simple examples you can do the substitution in your head and write the answer down in a single step.

Example 10.1.4

Evaluate $\displaystyle\int_0^{\frac{1}{6}\pi} \cos^5 3x \, dx$.

By now, when you have a simple integral such as $\displaystyle\int \cos 3x \, dx$ to find, you probably write it as $\tfrac{1}{3} \sin 3x + k$ almost instinctively. But with a more complicated integral such as $\displaystyle\int \cos^5 3x \, dx$ you may still find it safer to begin by replacing the $3x$ by a single letter u, using the substitution $x = \tfrac{1}{3}u$. Then $\dfrac{dx}{du} = \tfrac{1}{3}$, and the limits of integration 0 and $\tfrac{1}{6}\pi$ for x become 0 and $\tfrac{1}{2}\pi$ for u. So

$$\int_0^{\frac{1}{6}\pi} \cos^5 3x \, dx = \int_0^{\frac{1}{2}\pi} \cos^5 u \times \tfrac{1}{3} \, du$$

$$= \tfrac{1}{3} \int_0^{\frac{1}{2}\pi} \cos^5 u \, du.$$

It is not immediately obvious that the integrand $\cos^5 u$ is of the form $f(\sin u) \cos u$. But notice that you can use the identity $\cos^2 u + \sin^2 u \equiv 1$ to write any even power of $\cos u$ as a polynomial in $\sin u$. Thus

$$\cos^4 u \equiv (1 - \sin^2 u)^2 \equiv 1 - 2\sin^2 u + \sin^4 u,$$

so $\cos^5 u \equiv (1 - 2\sin^2 u + \sin^4 u) \cos u.$

It follows that a substitution $s = \sin u$, with $\dfrac{ds}{du} = \cos u$, transforms the integral

$$\int_0^{\frac{1}{2}\pi} \cos^5 u \, du \text{ to } \int_0^{\frac{1}{2}\pi} (1 - 2s^2 + s^4) \times \dfrac{ds}{du} \, du, \text{ which is}$$

$$\int_0^1 (1 - 2s^2 + s^4) \, ds = \left[s - \tfrac{2}{3}s^3 + \tfrac{1}{5}s^5 \right]_0^1$$
$$= (1 - \tfrac{2}{3} + \tfrac{1}{5}) - 0$$
$$= \tfrac{8}{15}.$$

So $\displaystyle\int_0^{\frac{1}{6}\pi} \cos^5 3x \, dx = \tfrac{1}{3} \int_0^{\frac{1}{2}\pi} \cos^5 u \, du = \tfrac{1}{3} \times \tfrac{8}{15} = \tfrac{8}{45}.$

In an example like this you could shorten the working by making a single substitution $s = \sin 3x$ instead of the two substitutions $u = 3x$ and $s = \sin u$. This would be quicker, but there is more risk of making a mistake. The choice is up to you, but remember that the most important thing is to get the answer right.

(iii) Using integration by parts

Integration by parts is the standard method if the integrand is the product of a trigonometric function and some other function such as a polynomial or an exponential. You can also use it sometimes for products of two trigonometric functions.

Example 10.1.5

Find (a) $\displaystyle\int x \sec^2 x \, dx$,   (b) $\displaystyle\int \cos x \ln(\cos x) \, dx$,   with $-\tfrac{1}{2}\pi < x < \tfrac{1}{2}\pi$,   (c) $\displaystyle\int e^{2x} \sin x \, dx$.

(a) Express the integrand as $u\dfrac{dv}{dx}$, where $u = x$ and $\dfrac{dv}{dx} = \sec^2 x$, so that $v = \tan x$. Then

$$\int x \sec^2 x \, dx = x \tan x - \int 1 \times \tan x \, dx = x \tan x - \ln |\sec x| + k,$$

using the result in Exercise 10A Question 1(g).

(b) You don't know how to integrate $\ln(\cos x)$, so take $u = \ln(\cos x)$, $\dfrac{dv}{dx} = \cos x$, that is $v = \sin x$. Then, if $-\tfrac{1}{2}\pi < x < \tfrac{1}{2}\pi$,

$$\int \cos x \ln(\cos x) \, dx = \int \ln(\cos x) \cos x \, dx$$
$$= \ln(\cos x) \sin x - \int \dfrac{1}{\cos x} \times (-\sin x) \times \sin x \, dx$$
$$= \ln(\cos x) \sin x + \int \dfrac{1 - \cos^2 x}{\cos x} \, dx$$
$$= \ln(\cos x) \sin x + \int (\sec x - \cos x) \, dx$$
$$= \ln(\cos x) \sin x + \ln(\sec x + \tan x) - \sin x + k.$$

(c) Take $u = e^{2x}$, $\dfrac{dv}{dx} = \sin x$, so that $v = -\cos x$:

$$\int e^{2x} \sin x \, dx = -e^{2x} \cos x + \int 2e^{2x} \cos x \, dx$$

But $\int e^{2x} \cos x \, dx$ is no easier to find than $\int e^{2x} \sin x \, dx$!

However, if you use the same method again, taking $u = 2e^{2x}$, $\dfrac{dv}{dx} = \cos x$,

$$\int 2e^{2x} \cos x \, dx = 2e^{2x} \sin x - \int 4e^{2x} \sin x \, dx.$$

Putting the two equations together,

$$\int e^{2x} \sin x \, dx = -e^{2x} \cos x + 2e^{2x} \sin x - 4\int e^{2x} \sin x \, dx,$$

so $5 \int e^{2x} \sin x \, dx = -e^{2x} \cos x + 2e^{2x} \sin x,$

$$\int e^{2x} \sin x \, dx = \tfrac{1}{5}e^{2x}(2\sin x - \cos x) + k.$$

In part (c) the arbitrary constant seems to be rather an afterthought! When you integrate by parts it is usually only necessary to include a constant when you carry out the final integration; but in this example you never actually do the final integration. But you mustn't forget the constant.

You should not think of the three methods described in this section as mutually exclusive. There are some trigonometric integrals which can be found by more than one method. As a final example, here is an integral which can be found using either an identity, a substitution or integration by parts.

Example 10.1.6

Find $\int \sin 3x \cos x \, dx$.

Method 1 (using an identity)   The product $\sin 3x \cos x$ appears in each of the identities

$$\sin(3x + x) \equiv \sin 3x \cos x + \cos 3x \sin x$$

and $\sin(3x - x) \equiv \sin 3x \cos x - \cos 3x \sin x.$

Adding these gives

$$\sin 4x + \sin 2x \equiv 2 \sin 3x \cos x.$$

So $\int \sin 3x \cos x \, dx = \int \tfrac{1}{2}(\sin 4x + \sin 2x) \, dx$

$$= -\tfrac{1}{8} \cos 4x - \tfrac{1}{4} \cos 2x + k.$$

Method 2 (using a substitution)   By writing $\sin 3x$ as $\sin(2x + x)$ it can be expressed purely in terms of $\sin x$:

$$\sin 3x \equiv (2 \sin x \cos x) \cos x + (\cos^2 x - \sin^2 x) \sin x$$
$$\equiv \sin x(2 \cos^2 x + \cos^2 x - \sin^2 x)$$
$$\equiv \sin x(3(1 - \sin^2 x) - \sin^2 x)$$
$$\equiv 3 \sin x - 4 \sin^3 x.$$

So $\displaystyle\int \sin 3x \cos x \, dx = \int (3 \sin x - 4 \sin^3 x) \cos x \, dx.$

The integrand now has the form $f(\sin x) \cos x$, so the substitution $u = \sin x$, with $\dfrac{du}{dx} = \cos x$, converts the integral to

$$\int (3u - 4u^3) \, du = \tfrac{3}{2}u^2 - u^4 + k$$
$$= \tfrac{3}{2} \sin^2 x - \sin^4 x + k.$$

Method 3 (using integration by parts)   Taking $u = \sin 3x$ and $\dfrac{dv}{dx} = \cos x$, so that $v = \sin x$, in the usual equation for integration by parts gives

$$\int \sin 3x \cos x \, dx = \sin 3x \sin x - \int 3 \cos 3x \sin x \, dx$$
$$= \sin 3x \sin x - 3 \int \cos 3x \sin x \, dx.$$

This doesn't look very promising; it is as difficult to integrate $\cos 3x \sin x$ as $\sin 3x \cos x$. But if you integrate by parts a second time, taking $u = \cos 3x$ and $\dfrac{dv}{dx} = \sin x$, so that $v = - \cos x$, you get

$$\int \cos 3x \sin x \, dx = \cos 3x \times (- \cos x) - \int (-3 \sin 3x) \times (- \cos x) \, dx$$
$$= - \cos 3x \cos x - 3 \int \sin 3x \cos x \, dx$$

This brings you back to the original integral! So substituting the second integral into the first equation,

$$\int \sin 3x \cos x \, dx = \sin 3x \sin x - 3 \left(-\cos 3x \cos x - 3 \int \sin 3x \cos x \, dx \right)$$
$$= \sin 3x \sin x + 3 \cos 3x \cos x + 9 \int \sin 3x \cos x \, dx.$$

That is,

$$\int \sin 3x \cos x \, dx = -\tfrac{1}{9}(\sin 3x \sin x + 3 \cos 3x \cos x) + k.$$

With Method 3 you get the same problem with the arbitrary constant as in Example 10.1.5(c), for the same reason.

You will see that in this example the three methods appear to give three different answers. As a check, use a graphic calculator to display the graphs of the three functions, and see how they are related. Then see if you can justify your conclusion algebraically.

10.2   A useful substitution

If $t = \tan \frac{1}{2}x$, the double angle formula gives

$$\tan x = \tan 2(\tfrac{1}{2}x) = \frac{2\tan\frac{1}{2}x}{1 - \tan^2\frac{1}{2}x} = \frac{2t}{1 - t^2}.$$

You can then use Pythagoras' identity to obtain

$$\sec^2 x = 1 + \tan^2 x = 1 + \frac{4t^2}{(1 - t^2)^2} = \frac{(1 - t^2)^2 + 4t^2}{(1 - t^2)^2}$$

$$= \frac{1 - 2t^2 + t^4 + 4t^2}{(1 - t^2)^2} = \frac{1 + 2t^2 + t^4}{(1 - t^2)^2} = \frac{(1 + t^2)^2}{(1 - t^2)^2}.$$

Remarkably this is an exact square, so that you can take square roots to obtain

$$\sec x = \pm\frac{1 + t^2}{1 - t^2}.$$

To settle the question of the sign, note that if $-\frac{1}{2}\pi < x < \frac{1}{2}\pi$, $\sec x > 0$ and $t^2 < 1$. If $-\pi < x < -\frac{1}{2}\pi$ or $\frac{1}{2}\pi < x < \pi$, $\sec x < 0$ and $t^2 > 1$. (Outside the range $-\pi < x < \pi$, both $\sec x$ and $\tan \frac{1}{2}x$ repeat with period 2π.) Since $1 + t^2$ is always positive, the ambiguous sign is always +, so that

$$\sec x = \frac{1 + t^2}{1 - t^2} \quad \text{(except when } x = -\tfrac{1}{2}\pi \text{ or } \tfrac{1}{2}\pi, \text{ where neither side is defined).}$$

You can now express other trigonometric functions in terms of t:

$$\cos x = \frac{1}{\sec x} = \frac{1 - t^2}{1 + t^2},$$

$$\sin x = \tan x \times \cos x = \frac{2t}{1 - t^2} \times \frac{1 - t^2}{1 + t^2} = \frac{2t}{1 + t^2}.$$

There are no exceptions to these; they hold also when $x = \pm\frac{1}{2}\pi$.

Also $\dfrac{dt}{dx} = \frac{1}{2}\sec^2\frac{1}{2}x = \frac{1}{2}(1 + t^2)$, so $\dfrac{dx}{dt} = \dfrac{1}{\dfrac{dt}{dx}} = \dfrac{2}{1 + t^2}$.

If $t = \tan\frac{1}{2}x$,

$$\sin x = \frac{2t}{1 + t^2}, \quad \cos x = \frac{1 - t^2}{1 + t^2} \quad \text{and} \quad \frac{dx}{dt} = \frac{2}{1 + t^2}.$$

This means that you can use the substitution $t = \tan \frac{1}{2}x$ to convert integrals involving trigonometric functions of x into integrals involving algebraic functions of t.

Example 10.2.1

Find $\int \operatorname{cosec} x\, dx$.

$$\int \frac{1}{\sin x}\, dx = \int \frac{1+t^2}{2t} \times \frac{2}{1+t^2}\, dt = \int \frac{1}{t}\, dt = \ln|t| + k = \ln|\tan \tfrac{1}{2}x| + k.$$

Example 10.2.2

Evaluate $\displaystyle\int_0^{\frac{1}{3}\pi} \frac{1}{4 + 5\cos x}\, dx$.

When $x = \frac{1}{3}\pi$, $t = \tan \frac{1}{6}\pi = \dfrac{1}{\sqrt{3}}$, so

$$\int_0^{\frac{1}{3}\pi} \frac{1}{4 + 5\cos x}\, dx = \int_0^{\frac{1}{\sqrt{3}}} \frac{1}{4 + 5\left(\dfrac{1-t^2}{1+t^2}\right)} \times \frac{2}{1+t^2}\, dt$$

$$= \int_0^{\frac{1}{\sqrt{3}}} \frac{2}{4(1+t^2) + 5(1-t^2)}\, dt = \int_0^{\frac{1}{\sqrt{3}}} \frac{2}{9 - t^2}\, dt.$$

You can evaluate this integral by using partial fractions:

$$\int_0^{\frac{1}{\sqrt{3}}} \frac{2}{9-t^2}\, dt = \int_0^{\frac{1}{\sqrt{3}}} \frac{1}{3}\left(\frac{1}{3+t} + \frac{1}{3-t}\right) dt$$

$$= \left[\tfrac{1}{3}(\ln(3+t) - \ln(3-t))\right]_0^{\frac{1}{\sqrt{3}}}$$

$$= \tfrac{1}{3}\left(\ln\left(\left(3 + \frac{1}{\sqrt{3}}\right)\middle/\left(3 - \frac{1}{\sqrt{3}}\right)\right) - \ln\left(\tfrac{3}{3}\right)\right)$$

$$= \tfrac{1}{3}\ln\left(\frac{3\sqrt{3}+1}{3\sqrt{3}-1}\right).$$

Example 10.2.3

Find $\displaystyle\int \frac{1}{3 + 2\cos 2\theta + \sin 2\theta}\, d\theta$.

This is an integral similar to Example 10.2.2 but with 2θ in place of x. So instead of substituting t for $\tan \frac{1}{2}x$ you might substitute $t = \tan\theta$. This would give

$$\tan 2\theta = \frac{2t}{1-t^2}, \quad \cos 2\theta = \frac{1-t^2}{1-t^2}, \quad \sin 2\theta = \frac{2t}{1+t^2}$$

as before, but now $\dfrac{dt}{d\theta} = \sec^2\theta$, so $\dfrac{d\theta}{dt} = \dfrac{1}{\sec^2\theta} = \dfrac{1}{1+t^2}$. So

$$\int \frac{1}{3 + 2\cos 2\theta + \sin 2\theta}\, d\theta = \int \frac{1}{3 + 2\dfrac{1-t^2}{1+t^2} + \dfrac{2t}{1+t^2}} \times \frac{1}{1+t^2}\, dt$$

$$= \int \frac{1}{3(1+t^2) + 2(1-t^2) + 2t}\, dt$$

$$= \int \frac{1}{t^2 + 2t + 5}\, dt.$$

This integral can be found by writing the denominator as $(t+1)^2 + 4$ and making the substitution $u = t + 1$. Then

$$\int \frac{1}{(t+1)^2 + 4}\, dt = \int \frac{1}{u^2 + 4}\, du$$
$$= \tfrac{1}{2} \tan^{-1} \tfrac{1}{2} u + k$$
$$= \tfrac{1}{2} \tan^{-1} \tfrac{1}{2}(t+1) + k.$$

So $\displaystyle\int \frac{1}{3 + 2\cos 2\theta + \sin 2\theta}\, d\theta = \tfrac{1}{2} \tan^{-1}\left(\tfrac{1}{2}(\tan\theta + 1)\right) + k.$

The substitution $t = \tan \tfrac{1}{2}x$ is also sometimes useful in solving trigonometric equations.

Example 10.2.4
Find the solutions of $4\sin x + 3\cos x + 2 = 0$ in the interval $-\pi < x < \pi$.

The substitution $t = \tan \tfrac{1}{2}x$ converts the equation to

$$4 \times \frac{2t}{1 + t^2} + 3 \times \frac{1 - t^2}{1 + t^2} + 2 = 0,$$
$$8t + 3(1 - t^2) + 2(1 + t^2) = 0,$$
$$t^2 - 8t - 5 = 0,$$

with solution $t = 4 \pm \sqrt{21}$. This gives $\tfrac{1}{2}x = -0.5275...$ or $1.4548...$, so $x = -1.06$ or 2.91, correct to 3 significant figures.

But beware! There are some questions for which this method gives you only part of the solution. See Exercise 10B Question 10.

***

Exercise 10B

1 Use suitable identities to find the following integrals.

(a) $\displaystyle\int \cot^2 x \, dx$ 　　　　(b) $\displaystyle\int \tan^3 x \, dx$ 　　　　(c) $\displaystyle\int \tan^4 x \, dx$

2 Use substitutions to find the following integrals.

(a) $\displaystyle\int \cos x \sqrt{\sin x}\, dx$ 　　(b) $\displaystyle\int \cos^3 x \sin^2 x \, dx$ 　　(c) $\displaystyle\int \sin^5 x \, dx$

(d) $\displaystyle\int \frac{\cos^3 \theta}{\sin^2 \theta}\, d\theta$ 　　(e) $\displaystyle\int \frac{\cos\theta + \sin\theta}{\cos\theta - \sin\theta}\, d\theta$ 　　(f) $\displaystyle\int \frac{\sec^2 t}{1 + \tan t}\, dt$

3 Write in their simplest forms $(\sec\theta + \tan\theta)(\sec\theta - \tan\theta)$, $(1 - \sin\theta)(1 + \sin\theta)$ and $(\cos\theta + \sin\theta)^2$. Use your answers to find the following integrals.

(a) $\displaystyle\int \frac{1}{(\sec\theta + \tan\theta)^2}\, d\theta$ 　　(b) $\displaystyle\int \frac{1}{1 - \sin\theta}\, d\theta$ 　　(c) $\displaystyle\int (1 + \sin 2\theta)^{\frac{3}{2}}\, d\theta$

4 Use integration by parts to find the following integrals.

(a) $\displaystyle\int x \operatorname{cosec}^2 x \, dx$ 　　(b) $\displaystyle\int \sin x \, \ln(\sin x)\, dx$ for $0 < x < \pi$

(c) $\displaystyle\int \sec^2 x \, \ln(\sec x)\, dx$ for $0 < x < \tfrac{1}{2}\pi$

5 Use integration by parts to find the following integrals.

(a) $\displaystyle\int e^{\theta}\cos\theta\,d\theta$ (b) $\displaystyle\int e^{\theta}\sin 2\theta\,d\theta$ (c) $\displaystyle\int e^{\theta\cos\alpha}\cos(\theta\sin\alpha)\,d\theta$

6 If $\displaystyle f(x) = \int\frac{\cos x}{\cos x + \sin x}\,dx$ and $\displaystyle g(x) = \int\frac{\sin x}{\cos x + \sin x}\,dx$, find $f(x) + g(x)$ and $f(x) - g(x)$,
and hence find $f(x)$ and $g(x)$. Use your answers to find the values of

(a) $\displaystyle\int_{0}^{\frac{1}{2}\pi}\frac{1}{1 + \tan x}\,dx$,   (b) $\displaystyle\int_{0}^{\frac{1}{4}\pi}\frac{1 - \tan x}{1 + \tan x}\,dx$.

7 If $\tan\frac{1}{2}x = 0.5$, find the values of $\sin x$ and $\cos x$.

8 If $\sin x = 0.6$, find the possible values of $\tan\frac{1}{2}x$.

9 Use the substitution $t = \tan\frac{1}{2}x$ to find the solutions of the following equations in the
interval $-\pi < x < \pi$, correct to 4 decimal places.

(a) $7\sin x + \cos x = 5$ (b) $4\sin x - 7\cos x = 1$ (c) $8\cos x - \sin x = 4$

10 Use each of the three methods (a), (b) and (c) to find the roots between $0°$ and $360°$ of the
equation $5\sin x - 3\cos x = 3$.

(a) Express the left side in the form $R\sin(x - \alpha)$.

(b) Take the term $3\cos x$ to the right side of the equation and use double angle formulae to
express both sides as functions of $\frac{1}{2}x$.

(c) Express $\sin x$ and $\cos x$ in terms of $t = \tan\frac{1}{2}x$, and solve an algebraic equation for t.

Why does the answer given by (c) differ from those given by (a) and (b)?

11 Use the substitution $t = \tan\frac{1}{2}x$ to find the following integrals.

(a) $\displaystyle\int\frac{5}{3\sin x + 4\cos x}\,dx$ (b) $\displaystyle\int\sec x\,dx$ (c) $\displaystyle\int\frac{1}{7\cos x - \sin x + 5}\,dx$

12 Find the following integrals.

(a) $\displaystyle\int x\cot^2 x\,dx$ (b) $\displaystyle\int\frac{1}{\sec t - 1}\,dt$ (c) $\displaystyle\int\frac{\cot\theta}{1 - \sin\theta}\,d\theta$

(d) $\displaystyle\int\cos x\ln(\sin x)\,dx$ (e) $\displaystyle\int\frac{\sin\theta}{\cos\theta - \sin\theta}\,d\theta$ (f) $\displaystyle\int\cot^4 x\,dx$

(g) $\displaystyle\int\frac{\sin t}{1 + \cos t}\,dt$ (h) $\displaystyle\int\frac{1}{12\sin\theta - 5\cos\theta}\,d\theta$ (i) $\displaystyle\int\tan u\ln(\sec u)\,du$

(j) $\displaystyle\int\frac{1}{1 + \cot x}\,dx$

13 One of the three integrals (a), (b) and (c) can be found exactly, but the others can't. Find
the one which comes out exactly, and investigate the difficulties which arise when you try
to find the others.

(a) $\displaystyle\int x\tan x\,dx$ (b) $\displaystyle\int x\tan^2 x\,dx$ (c) $\displaystyle\int x^2\tan x\,dx$

10.3   Trigonometric and hyperbolic substitutions

In Chapters 1 and 4 the rules for differentiating inverse functions were reversed to obtain the integrals

$$\int \frac{1}{a^2 + x^2}\, dx = \frac{1}{a}\tan^{-1}\frac{x}{a} + k, \qquad \int \frac{1}{\sqrt{a^2 - x^2}}\, dx = \sin^{-1}\frac{x}{a} + k,$$

$$\int \frac{1}{\sqrt{x^2 - a^2}}\, dx = \cosh^{-1}\frac{x}{a} + k, \qquad \int \frac{1}{\sqrt{a^2 + x^2}}\, dx = \sinh^{-1}\frac{x}{a} + k,$$

where a is a positive constant. But these could also have been found using integration by substitution. For example, the substitution $x = a\sinh u$, with $\dfrac{dx}{du} = a\cosh u$, converts $\displaystyle\int \frac{1}{\sqrt{a^2 + x^2}}\, dx$ to

$$\int \frac{1}{\sqrt{a^2 + a^2 \sinh^2 u}} \times a\cosh u\, du = \int \frac{a\cosh u}{\sqrt{a^2(1 + \sinh^2 u)}}\, du$$

$$= \int \frac{a\cosh u}{a\cosh u}\, du$$

$$= \int 1\, du$$

$$= u + k.$$

Since $\dfrac{x}{a} = \sinh u$, it follows that $u = \sinh^{-1}\dfrac{x}{a}$, so

$$\int \frac{1}{\sqrt{a^2 + x^2}}\, dx = \sinh^{-1}\frac{x}{a} + k.$$

The other integrals can be found in the same way, using the substitutions $x = a\tan u$, $x = a\sin u$ and $x = a\cosh u$.

> Throughout this section it will be assumed that the variables x and u are positive. Then all the square roots will also be positive. If you have to find an integral of this kind over an interval of negative values of x, it is best to begin by substituting $x = -y$, so that y is positive.

Although in these examples the substitutions are merely another way of proving results you know already, they can also often be used to find other integrals involving powers of $a^2 - x^2$, $a^2 + x^2$ or $x^2 - a^2$. The substitutions depend for their success on using one of the Pythagoras-type identities

$$\cos^2 u + \sin^2 u \equiv 1, \qquad 1 + \tan^2 u \equiv \sec^2 u,$$
$$\cosh^2 u - \sinh^2 u \equiv 1, \qquad 1 - \tanh^2 u \equiv \operatorname{sech}^2 u.$$

> There are similar identities connecting $\operatorname{cosec} u$ and $\cot u$, $\operatorname{cosech} u$ and $\coth u$. There is no advantage in using these for the original substitution, but they may be needed at a later stage when you substitute back to get the final answer in terms of x rather than u.

It is clear from the form of these identities that

- for integrals involving $a^2 + x^2$ you could use $x = a \tan u$ or $x = a \sinh u$
- for integrals involving $a^2 - x^2$ you could use $x = a \sin u$ or $x = a \tanh u$
- for integrals involving $x^2 - a^2$ you could use $x = a \cosh u$ or $x = a \sec u$.

For $a^2 - x^2$ you could also use $x = a \cos u$ or $x = a \operatorname{sech} u$, but these are better avoided, because over the relevant domain with $u > 0$ these are decreasing functions, and this introduces complications with minus signs.

Example 10.3.1

Find $\displaystyle\int \frac{1}{(x^2 - 9)^{\frac{3}{2}}} \, dx$.

> **Method 1**   The substitution $x = 3 \cosh u$ converts the integral to
>
> $$\int \frac{1}{(9 \cosh^2 u - 9)^{\frac{3}{2}}} \times \sinh u \, du = \int \frac{3 \sinh u}{(9 \sinh^2 u)^{\frac{3}{2}}} \times du$$
>
> $$= \int \frac{3 \sinh u}{27 \sinh^3 u} \, du$$
>
> $$= \tfrac{1}{9} \int \operatorname{cosech}^2 u \, du.$$
>
> Exercise 4C Question 5(c) found the result $\dfrac{d}{dx} \coth x = -\operatorname{cosech}^2 x$, so
>
> $$\tfrac{1}{9} \int \operatorname{cosech}^2 u \, du = -\tfrac{1}{9} \coth u + k.$$
>
> To complete the solution you have to express $\coth u$ in terms of x, where $\cosh u = \tfrac{1}{3} x$. To do this, use
>
> $$\sinh u = \sqrt{\cosh^2 u - 1} = \sqrt{\tfrac{1}{9} x^2 - 1}.$$
>
> So $\coth u = \dfrac{\cosh u}{\sinh u}$
>
> $$= \frac{\tfrac{1}{3} x}{\sqrt{\tfrac{1}{9} x^2 - 1}}$$
>
> $$= \frac{x}{\sqrt{9 \left(\tfrac{1}{9} x^2 - 1 \right)}}$$
>
> $$= \frac{x}{\sqrt{x^2 - 9}},$$
>
> and $\displaystyle\int \frac{1}{(x^2 - 9)^{\frac{3}{2}}} \, dx = -\tfrac{1}{9} \frac{x}{\sqrt{x^2 - 9}} + k.$
>
> **Method 2**   The substitution $x = 3 \sec u$ converts the integral to
>
> $$\int \frac{1}{(9 \sec^2 u - 9)^{\frac{3}{2}}} \times 3 \sec u \tan u \, du = \int \frac{3 \sec u \tan u}{(9 \tan^2 u)^{\frac{3}{2}}} \, du$$
>
> $$= \int \frac{3 \sec u \tan u}{27 \tan^3 u} \, du$$
>
> $$= \tfrac{1}{9} \int \frac{\sec u}{\tan^2 u} \, du.$$

Now

$$\frac{\sec u}{\tan^2 u} = \frac{1}{\cos u} \div \frac{\sin^2 u}{\cos^2 u}$$

$$= \frac{1}{\cos u} \times \frac{\cos^2 u}{\sin^2 u}$$

$$= \frac{1}{\sin u} \times \frac{\cos u}{\sin u}$$

$$= \operatorname{cosec} u \cot u.$$

Exercise 10A Question 1(d) shows that $\dfrac{d}{dx}\operatorname{cosec} x = -\operatorname{cosec} x \cot x$, so

$$\tfrac{1}{9} \int \frac{\sec u}{\tan^2 u}\, du = \tfrac{1}{9}\int -\operatorname{cosec} u \cot u\, du$$

$$= -\tfrac{1}{9}\operatorname{cosec} u + k.$$

To complete the solution you have to express $\operatorname{cosec} u$ in terms of x, where $\sec u = \tfrac{1}{3}x$. To do this, use

$$\tan u = \sqrt{\sec^2 u - 1} = \sqrt{\tfrac{1}{9}x^2 - 1}.$$

So $\qquad \operatorname{cosec} u = \dfrac{\sec u}{\tan u}$

$$= \frac{\tfrac{1}{3}x}{\sqrt{\tfrac{1}{9}x^2 - 1}}$$

$$= \frac{x}{\sqrt{9\left(\tfrac{1}{9}x^2 - 1\right)}}$$

$$= \frac{x}{\sqrt{x^2 - 9}},$$

and $\displaystyle\int \frac{1}{(x^2 - 9)^{\frac{3}{2}}}\, dx = -\tfrac{1}{9}\frac{x}{\sqrt{x^2 - 9}} + k.$

In this example both substitutions work equally well. You can use whichever you prefer, and the work involved is very similar. But sometimes one substitution gives you an easier integral to find than the alternative.

Example 10.3.2

Find $\displaystyle\int \sqrt{4 + x^2}\, dx$.

Method 1 In C4 Section 2.2 the integral $\displaystyle\int \sqrt{4 - x^2}\, dx$ was found by using the substitution $x = 2\sin u$. This suggests that the substitution $x = 2\sinh u$ could be used to find $\displaystyle\int \sqrt{4 + x^2}\, dx$.

The substitution $x = 2\sinh u$ converts $4 + x^2$ to $4 + 4\sinh^2 u = 4\cosh^2 u$, so that $\sqrt{4 + x^2} = 2\cosh u$ (since $\cosh u > 0$). Also $\dfrac{dx}{du} = 2\cosh u$. Therefore

$$\int \sqrt{4 + x^2}\, dx = \int 2\cosh u \times 2\cosh u\, du = \int 4\cosh^2 u\, du.$$

This can be integrated by using the $\cosh 2A$ formula (with u for A) in its backwards form $2\cosh^2 u = \cosh 2u + 1$, so

$$\int 4\cosh^2 u\, du = \int 2(\cosh 2u + 1)\, du = \sinh 2u + 2u + k.$$

To express this in terms of x, notice first that $\sinh 2u = 2\sinh u \cosh u$. Now $2\sinh u = x$, and $\cosh u = \sqrt{1 + \sinh^2 u} = \sqrt{1 + \left(\tfrac{1}{2}x\right)^2} = \tfrac{1}{2}\sqrt{4 + x^2}$.

Therefore $\sinh 2u = \tfrac{1}{2}x\sqrt{4 + x^2}$. Also $\sinh u = \tfrac{1}{2}x$, so that $u = \sinh^{-1}\tfrac{1}{2}x$. Putting all this together,

$$\int \sqrt{4 + x^2}\, dx = \tfrac{1}{2}x\sqrt{4 + x^2} + 2\sinh^{-1}\tfrac{1}{2}x + k.$$

Method 2 If you start with the substitution $x = 2\tan z$, the integral becomes

$$\int \sqrt{4 + 4\tan^2 z} \times 2\sec^2 z\, dz = \int \sqrt{4\sec^2 z} \times 2\sec^2 z\, dz$$

$$= \int 4\sec^3 z\, dz.$$

(You will soon see why the letter z has been used instead of u.)

Now $\displaystyle\int \sec^3 z\, dz$ is not too easy to find, but you can write it as $\displaystyle\int \sec z \times \sec^2 z\, dz$ and integrate by parts, writing $u = \sec z$ and $\dfrac{dv}{dz} = \sec^2 z$, so that $v = \tan z$. Then

$$\int \sec^3 z\, dz = \sec z \tan z - \int (\sec z \tan z) \times \tan z\, dz$$

$$= \sec z \tan z - \int \sec z \tan^2 z\, dz.$$

The new integral, $\displaystyle\int \sec z \tan^2 z\, dz$, is no easier to find than $\displaystyle\int \sec^3 z\, dz$, but by replacing $\tan^2 z$ by $\sec^2 z - 1$ you can write

$$\int \sec^3 z\, dz = \sec z \tan z - \int \sec z\, (\sec^2 z - 1)\, dz$$

$$= \sec z \tan z - \int \sec^3 z\, dz + \int \sec z\, dz,$$

so that

$$2\int \sec^3 z\, dz = \sec z \tan z + \int \sec z\, dz.$$

Now you found in Exercise 10A Question 1(h) that $\dfrac{d}{dx}\ln(\sec x + \tan x) = \sec x$, so

$$\int \sec z\, dz = \ln(\sec z + \tan z) + k.$$

Therefore

$$2\int \sec^3 z \, dz = \sec z \tan z + \ln(\sec z + \tan z) + k$$

$$= \tan z\sqrt{1 + \tan^2 z} + \ln\left(\sqrt{1 + \tan^2 z} + \tan z\right) + k.$$

The point of replacing $\sec z$ by $\sqrt{1 + \tan^2 z}$ in the last line is so that you can use the equation $x = 2\tan z$ to rewrite the equation in terms of x.

$$\int \sqrt{4 + x^2} \, dx = \int 4\sec^3 z \, dz$$

$$= 2\left(\tfrac{1}{2}x\sqrt{1 + \left(\tfrac{1}{2}x\right)^2} + \ln\left(\tfrac{1}{2}x + \sqrt{1 + \left(\tfrac{1}{2}x\right)^2}\right) + k\right)$$

$$= \tfrac{1}{2}x\sqrt{4 + x^2} + 2\ln\left(\tfrac{1}{2}x + \sqrt{1 + \left(\tfrac{1}{2}x\right)^2}\right) + k' \quad \text{where } k' = 2k.$$

You will recognise $\ln\left(\tfrac{1}{2}x + \sqrt{1 + \left(\tfrac{1}{2}x\right)^2}\right)$ as the logarithmic form of $\sinh^{-1}\tfrac{1}{2}x$, so the integral can be written as

$$\int \sqrt{4 + x^2} \, dx = \tfrac{1}{2}x\sqrt{4 + x^2} + 2\sinh^{-1}\tfrac{1}{2}x + k'.$$

In Example 10.3.2 either substitution will work, but you will probably think that the first method is easier than the second.

If the integrand itself contains a trigonometric or hyperbolic expression, this will determine the choice of substitution.

Example 10.3.3

Find $\displaystyle\int \frac{\sin^{-1} x}{\sqrt{1 - x^2}} \, dx$.

With $\sin^{-1} x$ in the numerator, it is obviously better to substitute $x = \sin u$ than the alternative $x = \tanh u$. Then $\sin^{-1} x = u$, so the integral becomes

$$\int \frac{u}{\sqrt{1 - \sin^2 u}} \times \cos u \, du = \int \frac{u \cos u}{\cos u} \, du$$

$$= \int u \, du$$

$$= \tfrac{1}{2}u^2 + k.$$

Therefore

$$\int \frac{\sin^{-1} x}{\sqrt{1 - x^2}} \, dx = \tfrac{1}{2}(\sin^{-1} x)^2 + k.$$

A minor complication occurs if the coefficient of x^2 is a constant other that 1, but this is easily disposed of, as shown in the next example.

Example 10.3.4

Find $\displaystyle\int_0^1 (4 - 3x^2)^{-\frac{5}{2}}\, dx$.

To make use of the identity $1 - \sin^2 u \equiv \cos^2 u$, you need to replace $3x^2$ by $4\sin^2 u$, so substitute $x = \dfrac{2}{\sqrt{3}} \sin u$. Thus, when $x = 1$, $\sin u = \dfrac{\sqrt{3}}{2}$, so $u = \frac{1}{3}\pi$.

$$\int_0^1 (4 - 3x^2)^{-\frac{5}{2}}\, dx = \int_0^{\frac{1}{3}\pi} (4 - 4\sin^2 u)^{-\frac{5}{2}} \times \frac{2}{\sqrt{3}} \cos u\, du$$

$$= \int_0^{\frac{1}{3}\pi} \frac{\dfrac{2}{\sqrt{3}} \cos u}{32 \cos^5 u}$$

$$= \frac{1}{16\sqrt{3}} \int_0^{\frac{1}{3}\pi} \sec^4 u\, du.$$

To integrate $\sec^4 u$, write it as $(1 + \tan^2 u)\sec^2 u$, so that

$$\int_0^{\frac{1}{3}\pi} \sec^4 u\, du = \int_0^{\frac{1}{3}\pi} (1 + \tan^2 u)\sec^2 u\, du$$

$$= \left[\tan u + \tfrac{1}{3}\tan^3 u \right]_0^{\frac{1}{3}\pi}$$

$$= \sqrt{3} + \tfrac{1}{3} \times 3\sqrt{3}$$

$$= 2\sqrt{3}.$$

Therefore

$$\int_0^1 (4 - 3x^2)^{-\frac{5}{2}}\, dx = \frac{1}{16\sqrt{3}} \times 2\sqrt{3}$$

$$= \tfrac{1}{8}.$$

Example 10.3.5

Find $\displaystyle\int \sqrt{\dfrac{x}{1 - x}}\, dx$.

To take advantage of one of Pythagoras' identities for this integral you can substitute $x = \sin^2 u$. This converts the integral to

$$\int \sqrt{\frac{\sin^2 u}{\cos^2 u}} \times 2 \sin u \cos u\, du = \int \frac{\sin u}{\cos u} \times 2 \sin u \cos u\, du$$

$$= \int 2 \sin^2 u\, du = \int (1 - \cos 2u)\, du$$

$$= u - \tfrac{1}{2}\sin 2u + k = u - \sin u \cos u + k.$$

In terms of x, this is

$$\int \sqrt{\frac{x}{1 - x}}\, dx = \sin^{-1}\sqrt{x} - \sqrt{x}\sqrt{1 - x} + k = \sin^{-1}\sqrt{x} - \sqrt{x(1 - x)} + k.$$

Exercise 10C

1 Use trigonometric substitutions to evaluate the following definite integrals.

(a) $\int_0^1 \dfrac{x^2}{\sqrt{4-x^2}}\,dx$

(b) $\int_0^1 \dfrac{\tan^{-1} x}{(1+x^2)^{\frac{3}{2}}}\,dx$

(c) $\int_1^3 \dfrac{x^2}{(x^2+3)^2}\,dx$

(d) $\int_{2\sqrt{2}}^4 \dfrac{1}{x\sqrt{x^2-4}}\,dx$

2 Write down the values of the following integrals. Investigate how you could get the same answers by using a trigonometric substitution.

(a) $\int \dfrac{1}{\sqrt{1+x^2}}\,dx$

(b) $\int \dfrac{1}{\sqrt{x^2-9}}\,dx$

(c) $\int \dfrac{1}{\sqrt{1+9x^2}}\,dx$

3 Find the values of $\int_0^{\frac{3}{4}} (1+x^2)^n \sinh^{-1} x\,dx$ when

(a) $n=-\frac{1}{2}$,

(b) $n=-\frac{3}{2}$,

(c) $n=0$,

(d) $n=\frac{1}{2}$.

4 Find the following integrals, given that $x>0$. Check your answers by differentiation.

(a) $\int \dfrac{1}{x^2\sqrt{x^2-25}}\,dx$

(b) $\int \sqrt{4x^2-1}\,dx$

(c) $\int \dfrac{x^2}{4x^2+25}\,dx$

(d) $\int x^2\sqrt{1+x^2}\,dx$

(e) $\int \dfrac{\sqrt{9+x^2}}{x^2}\,dx$

(f) $\int \sqrt{\dfrac{x}{1+x}}\,dx$

(g) $\int \sqrt{\dfrac{x}{x-1}}\,dx$

Miscellaneous exercise 10

1 By using the substitution $u=\sin x$, find $\int \sin^3 x \sin 2x\,dx$, giving your answer in terms of x. (OCR)

2 A region R in the first quadrant is bounded by the curve $y=\tan x$, the x-axis and the line $x=\frac{1}{4}\pi$. Show that the exact value of the volume of the solid formed when R is rotated completely about the x-axis is $\pi - \frac{1}{4}\pi^2$. (OCR)

3 Find the exact value of $\int_0^3 \sqrt{x(4-x)}\,dx$, using the substitution $x=4\sin^2 u$. (OCR)

4 Find $\int \cos x\sqrt{1-\cos x}\,dx$, using the substitution $u=\cos \frac{1}{2}x$. (OCR)

5 Find the exact value of $\int_0^{\frac{1}{4}\pi} \dfrac{\sin 2x}{3-\cos 2x}\,dx$. (OCR)

6 If $x=5\sin\theta -3$, show that $16-6x-x^2=25\cos^2\theta$. Hence find $\int \dfrac{1}{\sqrt{16-6x-x^2}}\,dx$. (OCR)

7 Using the substitution $x = 3 + \tan\theta$, find $\displaystyle\int \frac{1}{x^2 - 6x + 10}\,dx$.   (OCR)

8 Use the expressions for $\sin x$ and $\cos x$ in terms of $\tan\frac{1}{2}x$ to find three different sets of Pythagorean triples. (A Pythagorean triple is a set of natural numbers a, b, c such that $a^2 + b^2 = c^2$.)

9 Find the cartesian equation of the curve for which parametric equations are $x = 8\operatorname{cosec} u$, $y = 6\cot u$ for $-\pi < u < \pi$, $u \neq 0$. By writing $t = \tan\frac{1}{2}u$, find an alternative pair of parametric equations for the curve. Use these to make a sketch of the curve.

   Find the equation of the tangent to the curve at the point where $t = p$. Hence find the point on the curve at which the tangent passes through $(4, -3)$.

10 Find the solution of the differential equation $\dfrac{dy}{dx} = \dfrac{8x\cos^2 x}{y}$ which satisfies $y = \sqrt{3}$ when $x = 0$.   (MEI)

11 The variables x and y are related by the differential equation $\dfrac{dy}{dx} = \sin x\,\sin 2y$
    $(0 < y < \frac{1}{2}\pi)$, and $y = \frac{1}{4}\pi$ when $x = 0$. Show that, when $x = \pi$, $y = \tan^{-1}e^4$.   (OCR)

12 For $x > 0$ and $0 < y < \frac{1}{2}\pi$, the variables y and x are connected by the differential equation $\dfrac{dy}{dx} = \dfrac{\ln x}{\cot y}$, and $y = \frac{1}{6}\pi$ when $x = e$. Find the value of y when $x = 1$, giving your answer correct to three significant figures. Use the differential equation to show that this value of y is a stationary value, and determine its nature.   (MEI)

13 Use substitutions to evaluate the following definite integrals.

   (a) $\displaystyle\int_0^1 \frac{1}{1 + x^2}\,dx$ (b) $\displaystyle\int_1^2 \frac{1}{\sqrt{4 - x^2}}\,dx$ (c) $\displaystyle\int_1^3 \frac{1}{x^2 + 3}\,dx$

   (d) $\displaystyle\int_0^\infty \frac{1}{9x^2 + 16}\,dx$ (e) $\displaystyle\int_0^1 (1 - x^2)^{\frac{3}{2}}\,dx$ (f) $\displaystyle\int_2^\infty (x^2 - 1)^{-\frac{3}{2}}\,dx$

   (g) $\displaystyle\int_2^4 \frac{1}{\sqrt{x^2 - 4}}\,dx$ (h) $\displaystyle\int_2^4 \frac{1}{x\sqrt{x^2 - 4}}\,dx$ (i) $\displaystyle\int_0^1 \frac{1}{1 + \sqrt{1 - x^2}}\,dx$

   (j) $\displaystyle\int_1^{\sqrt{2}} \frac{1}{1 + \sqrt{x^2 - 1}}\,dx$

14 Use a substitution to find an exact expression for the area under the graph of $y = \sec^{-1} x$ from $x = 1$ to $x = 2$.

15 The region bounded by the axes and the graph of $y = \cos^{-1} x$ is rotated about the x-axis to form a solid of revolution. Find its volume.

16 Show that $\displaystyle\int_0^{\sqrt{3}} \sin^{-1}\frac{1}{2}x\,dx = \frac{\pi}{\sqrt{3}} - 1$.   (MEI)

17* (a) Show that $\cos x - \sin x = \sqrt{2}\cos\left(x + \frac{1}{4}\pi\right)$ and hence integrate $\displaystyle\int_0^X \frac{dx}{\cos x - \sin x}$, where $0 < X < \frac{1}{4}\pi$. By letting $X \to \frac{1}{4}\pi$ in your answer find if $\displaystyle\int_0^{\frac{1}{4}\pi} \frac{dx}{\cos x - \sin x}$ exists.

(b) Evaluate $\displaystyle\int_0^X \frac{dx}{(\cos x - \sin x)^2}$, $\quad 0 < X < \frac{1}{4}\pi$.

(c) The graph of $\cos x - \sin x$ cuts the axes at $P(0, 1)$ and $Q(\frac{1}{4}\pi, 0)$. By considering the chord PQ and the tangent at P, show that $1 - \dfrac{4x}{\pi} < \cos x - \sin x < 1 - x$ for $0 < x < \frac{1}{4}\pi$. Hence find numbers A, B such that $A < \displaystyle\int_0^{\frac{1}{4}\pi} \frac{dx}{\sqrt{\cos x - \sin x}} < B$, and deduce that the integral exists.

(OCR)

11 Reduction formulae

This chapter deals with a particular type of integral in which an expression in the integrand is raised to a power n. When you have completed it, you should

- be able to find reduction formulae for such integrals

- know various ways in which the integrand can be manipulated so as to get the integral into the form required.

11.1 Straightforward examples

Example 11.1.1

Find (a) $\displaystyle\int_1^e x^3 \ln x \, dx$, (b) $\displaystyle\int_1^e x(\ln x)^3 \, dx$.

Both these integrals can be found using integration by parts. It is easier to differentiate $\ln x$ and $(\ln x)^3$ than to integrate them, so in the standard formula it is best to take the factor involving $\ln x$ as u and the other factor as $\dfrac{dv}{dx}$.

(a) If $\dfrac{dv}{dx} = x^3$, then $v = \tfrac{1}{4}x^4$, so

$$\int_1^e x^3 \ln x \, dx = \int_1^e \ln x \times x^3 \, dx$$
$$= \left[\ln x \times \left(\tfrac{1}{4}x^4\right)\right]_1^e - \int_1^e \frac{1}{x} \times \tfrac{1}{4}x^4 \, dx$$
$$= \left(1 \times \left(\tfrac{1}{4}e^4\right) - 0 \times \tfrac{1}{4}\right) - \int_1^e \tfrac{1}{4}x^3 \, dx$$
$$= \tfrac{1}{4}e^4 - \left[\tfrac{1}{16}x^4\right]_1^e$$
$$= \tfrac{1}{4}e^4 - \left(\tfrac{1}{16}e^4 - \tfrac{1}{16}\right)$$
$$= \tfrac{1}{16}(3e^4 + 1).$$

(b) If $u = (\ln x)^3$ and $\dfrac{dv}{dx} = x$, then $\dfrac{du}{dx} = 3(\ln x)^2 \times \dfrac{1}{x}$ and $v = \tfrac{1}{2}x^2$, so

$$\int_1^e x(\ln x)^3 \, dx = \int_1^e (\ln x)^3 \times x \, dx$$
$$= \left[(\ln x)^3 \times \left(\tfrac{1}{2}x^2\right)\right]_1^e - \int_1^e 3(\ln x)^2 \times \frac{1}{x} \times \tfrac{1}{2}x^2 \, dx$$
$$= \left(1^3 \times \left(\tfrac{1}{2}e^2\right) - 0 \times \tfrac{1}{2}\right) - \tfrac{3}{2}\int_1^e (\ln x)^2 \times x \, dx$$
$$= \tfrac{1}{2}e^2 - \tfrac{3}{2}\int_1^e (\ln x)^2 \times x \, dx.$$

Now there is a problem: the last integral is very much like the one you started with! But at least the power of $\ln x$ is 1 less than it was, so it might be worth trying integration by parts again, this time with $u = (\ln x)^2$.

$$\int_1^e (\ln x)^2 \times x \, dx = \left[(\ln x)^2 \times \left(\tfrac{1}{2} x^2 \right) \right]_1^e - \int_1^e 2 \ln x \times \frac{1}{x} \times \tfrac{1}{2} x^2 \, dx$$

$$= \tfrac{1}{2} e^2 - \int_1^e \ln x \times x \, dx.$$

Again the power of $\ln x$ has been reduced by 1. Try once more, with $u = \ln x$.

$$\int_1^e x \ln x \, dx = \int_1^e \ln x \times x \, dx$$

$$= \left[\ln x \times \left(\tfrac{1}{2} x^2 \right) \right]_1^e - \int_1^e \frac{1}{x} \times \tfrac{1}{2} x^2 \, dx$$

$$= \tfrac{1}{2} e^2 - \tfrac{1}{2} \int_1^e x \, dx$$

$$= \tfrac{1}{2} e^2 - \tfrac{1}{2} \left[\tfrac{1}{2} x^2 \right]_1^e$$

$$= \tfrac{1}{2} e^2 - \tfrac{1}{4} (e^2 - 1)$$

$$= \tfrac{1}{4} (e^2 + 1).$$

Now you are home. You can substitute this answer into the previous integral to get

$$\int_1^e (\ln x)^2 \times x \, dx = \tfrac{1}{2} e^2 - \tfrac{1}{4} (e^2 + 1)$$

$$= \tfrac{1}{4} (e^2 - 1).$$

Then, substituting this in the first integral,

$$\int_1^e x (\ln x)^3 \, dx = \tfrac{1}{2} e^2 - \tfrac{3}{2} \times \tfrac{1}{4} (e^2 - 1)$$

$$= \tfrac{1}{8} (e^2 + 3).$$

So $\int_1^e x (\ln x)^3 \, dx = \tfrac{1}{8} (e^2 + 3).$

In this example, part (a) is quite straightforward but part (b) involves working down a chain of integrations in which the power of $\ln x$ goes down by 1 at each step. What you are in effect doing is to repeat the same process a number of times. It would be simpler to introduce more general notation so that all the steps are covered by the same equation.

So instead of three integrations in which the power of $\ln x$ is 3, 2 and 1 in turn, write this power as n. Then

$$\int_1^e x (\ln x)^n \, dx = \int_1^e (\ln x)^n \times x \, dx$$

$$= \left[(\ln x)^n \times \tfrac{1}{2} x^2 \right] - \int_1^e n (\ln x)^{n-1} \times \frac{1}{x} \times \tfrac{1}{2} x^2 \, dx$$

$$= \tfrac{1}{2} e^2 - \tfrac{1}{2} n \int_1^e x (\ln x)^{n-1} \, dx.$$

What you are dealing with here is a sequence of integrals, and it is convenient to use standard sequence notation to show this. So denote the integral by I_n, so that

$$I_n = \int_1^e x (\ln x)^n \, dx.$$

The equation connecting successive integrals in the sequence can then be written as

$$I_n = \tfrac{1}{2}e^2 - \tfrac{1}{2}nI_{n-1}.$$

An equation like this is called a **reduction formula**, because the power of $\ln x$ is reduced at each step.

You can think of this formula as an inductive definition of the sequence. To complete the definition you need to know the value of I_n for some particular value of n. In this example it is easy to find

$$I_0 = \int_1^e (\ln x)^0 \times x \, dx$$

$$= \int_1^e x \, dx$$

$$= \left[\tfrac{1}{2}x^2\right]_1^e$$

$$= \tfrac{1}{2}(e^2 - 1).$$

From this you can use the reduction formula with n equal to 1, 2, 3, ... in turn to find

$$I_1 = \tfrac{1}{2}e^2 - \tfrac{1}{2}I_0 = \tfrac{1}{2}e^2 - \tfrac{1}{4}(e^2 - 1) = \tfrac{1}{4}(e^2 + 1),$$
$$I_2 = \tfrac{1}{2}e^2 - \tfrac{2}{2}I_1 = \tfrac{1}{2}e^2 - \tfrac{1}{4}(e^2 + 1) = \tfrac{1}{4}(e^2 - 1),$$
$$I_3 = \tfrac{1}{2}e^2 - \tfrac{3}{2}I_2 = \tfrac{1}{2}e^2 - \tfrac{3}{8}(e^2 - 1) = \tfrac{1}{8}(e^2 + 3),$$

and so on.

It is important to ask for what values of n the reduction formula is valid. Since the calculation involves a term with a factor 0^n, it can only work if $n > 0$. There is nothing in the working to require that n is an integer; but since the only value of n for which you can work out I_n independently is $n = 0$, the reduction formula is only useful if n is a positive integer. (Notice that if $0 < n < 1$ the integrand in I_{n-1} tends to infinity as $x \to 1$; but that does not prevent the integral from having a finite value.)

Example 11.1.2

Use a reduction formula to find $\int x^4 e^{3x} \, dx$.

The aim of the reduction formula is to lower the power of x in the integrand until the integral becomes $\int e^{3x} \, dx$, which you know how to integrate. So begin by defining

$$I_n = \int x^n e^{3x} \, dx,$$

and integrate by parts. Since you want to reduce n, take u to be x^n and let $\dfrac{dv}{dx} = e^{3x}$. Then

$$I_n = x^n \times \tfrac{1}{3}e^{3x} - \int nx^{n-1} \times \tfrac{1}{3}e^{3x} \, dx$$

$$= \tfrac{1}{3}x^n e^{3x} - \tfrac{1}{3}n \int x^{n-1} e^{3x} \, dx$$

$$= \tfrac{1}{3}(x^n e^{3x} - nI_{n-1}).$$

Also

$$I_0 = \int e^{3x}\,dx$$
$$= \tfrac{1}{3}e^{3x} + k.$$

So, putting $n = 1, 2, 3, 4$ in turn,

$$I_1 = \tfrac{1}{3}(xe^{3x} - I_0), \qquad I_2 = \tfrac{1}{3}(x^2 e^{3x} - 2I_1),$$
$$I_3 = \tfrac{1}{3}(x^3 e^{3x} - 3I_2), \qquad I_4 = \tfrac{1}{3}(x^4 e^{3x} - 4I_3).$$

These equations give

$$I_4 = \tfrac{1}{81}(27x^4 - 36x^3 + 36x^2 - 24x + 8)e^{3x} + \tfrac{8}{27}k.$$

There is no point in leaving the arbitrary constant in the form $\tfrac{8}{27}k$. Write this as k', and then

$$I_4 = \tfrac{1}{81}(27x^4 - 36x^3 + 36x^2 - 24x + 8)e^{3x} + k'.$$

The algebra is quite involved, so it is worth checking the answer by differentiation.

Integration by parts is the commonest way of getting reduction formulae, but it is not the only method. The next example makes use of a trigonometric identity.

Example 11.1.3

Find $\int \tan^n x\,dx$, where n is a positive integer.

You can reduce the index n in this integral by writing $\tan^n x$ as $\tan^{n-2} x \tan^2 x$, and using the identity $\tan^2 x \equiv \sec^2 x - 1$.

$$\int \tan^n x\,dx = \int \tan^{n-2} x(\sec^2 x - 1)\,dx = \int \tan^{n-2} x \sec^2 x\,dx - \int \tan^{n-2} x\,dx.$$

Now since $\dfrac{d}{dx}\tan x = \sec^2 x$, the first integral can be written down directly (or if you prefer by using the substitution $t = \tan x$). Writing $\int \tan^n x\,dx$ as I_n,

$$I_n = \frac{1}{n-1}\tan^{n-1} x - I_{n-2}.$$

In this reduction formula the index n goes down by 2, to $n - 2$ rather than $n - 1$. If you apply it repeatedly, you will eventually get down to I_0 if n is even, or to I_1 if n is odd. These can both be found:

$$I_0 = \int \tan^0 x\,dx = \int 1\,dx = x + k,$$
$$I_1 = \int \tan x\,dx = \ln|\sec x| + k.$$

From this you can find in succession

$$I_2 = \tan x - I_0 = \tan x - x - k,$$
$$I_3 = \tfrac{1}{2}\tan^2 x - I_1 = \tfrac{1}{2}\tan^2 x - \ln|\sec x| - k,$$
$$I_4 = \tfrac{1}{3}\tan^3 x - I_2 = \tfrac{1}{3}\tan^3 x - \tan x + x + k,$$
$$I_5 = \tfrac{1}{4}\tan^4 x - I_3 = \tfrac{1}{4}\tan^4 x - \tfrac{1}{2}\tan^2 x + \ln|\sec x| + k,$$

and so on.

Exercise 11A

1 Use the reduction formula in Section 11.1 for $\displaystyle\int_1^e x(\ln x)^n\,dx$ to evaluate $\displaystyle\int_1^e x(\ln x)^5\,dx$.

2 Find a reduction formula for $I_n = \displaystyle\int x^n e^{\frac{1}{2}x}\,dx$, and use it to find $I_n = \displaystyle\int x^3 e^{\frac{1}{2}x}\,dx$. Check your answer by differentiation.

3 If $I_n = \displaystyle\int x^2(\ln x)^n\,dx$, obtain the reduction formula $I_n = \tfrac{1}{3}x^3(\ln x)^n - \tfrac{1}{3}nI_{n-1}$. Hence find $I_3 = \displaystyle\int x^2(\ln x)^3\,dx$. Check your answer by differentiation.

4 If I_n denotes $\displaystyle\int \tanh^n x\,dx$, prove that $I_n = I_{n-2} - \dfrac{1}{n-1}\tanh^{n-1}x$ (unless $n=1$). Hence find

(a) $\displaystyle\int \tanh^5 x\,dx$,   (b) $\displaystyle\int \tanh^6 x\,dx$.

5 If I_n denotes $\displaystyle\int_{\frac{1}{4}\pi}^{\frac{1}{2}\pi} \cot^n\theta\,d\theta$, find and use a reduction formula to obtain expressions for

(a) I_7,   (b) I_8.

Give a reason why $I_8 < I_7$, and verify numerically that your answers to (a) and (b) satisfy this inequality.

6 If I_n denotes $\displaystyle\int_1^e (\ln x)^n\,dx$, prove that $I_n = e - nI_{n-1}$. (Hint: write $(\ln x)^n$ as $(\ln x)^n \times 1$, and integrate by parts.)

Hence find $\displaystyle\int_1^e (\ln x)^4\,dx$.

7 Find and use a reduction formula to evaluate $\displaystyle\int_0^1 (1-x)^5 e^x\,dx$.

By considering the function $f(x) = (1-x)^5 e^x$ over the interval $0 < x < 1$, prove that the value of this integral lies between 0 and 1. Hence show that $e \approx 2.72$.

8 If C_n denotes $\displaystyle\int_0^\pi x^n \cos x\,dx$, and S_n denotes $\displaystyle\int_0^\pi x^n \sin x\,dx$, find expressions for C_n and S_n in terms of S_{n-1} and C_{n-1} and state the values of n for which these are valid.

Hence find $\displaystyle\int_0^\pi x^5 \sin x\,dx$.

9 If I_n denotes $I_n = \displaystyle\int_0^1 x^n e^{-x} \, dx$, show that, if $n > 0$, $I_n = -\dfrac{1}{e} + nI_{n-1}$. Hence use

mathematical induction to prove that $I_n = n! \left(1 - \dfrac{1}{e} \left(1 + \dfrac{1}{1!} + \dfrac{1}{2!} + \cdots + \dfrac{1}{n!}\right)\right)$.

10 If C_n denotes $\displaystyle\int_0^1 x^n \cosh x \, dx$ and S_n denotes $\displaystyle\int_0^1 x^n \sinh x \, dx$, prove that $C_n = \sinh 1 - nS_{n-1}$,

and find a similar expression for S_n in terms of C_{n-1}. Hence evaluate $\displaystyle\int_0^1 x^5 \sinh x \, dx$ correct to 4 decimal places.

11 With the notation of Question 10, prove that, if $n \in \mathbb{N}$ and $n \geqslant 1$,

$$\frac{C_{2n}}{(2n)!} = \frac{\sinh 1}{(2n)!} - \frac{\cosh 1}{(2n-1)!} + \frac{C_{2n-2}}{(2n-2)!}.$$

Hence prove by mathematical induction that

$$\frac{C_n}{(2n)!} = \sinh 1 \left(1 + \frac{1}{2!} + \frac{1}{4!} + \cdots + \frac{1}{(2n)!}\right) - \cosh 1 \left(\frac{1}{1!} + \frac{1}{3!} + \cdots + \frac{1}{(2n-1)!}\right).$$

11.2 Algebraic and trigonometric techniques

Often an application of integration by parts is not enough by itself, but a reduction formula can be found by using an algebraic or trigonometric identity.

Example 11.2.1

If I_n denotes $\displaystyle\int_0^1 (1 + x^2)^n \, dx$, find a reduction formula connecting I_n with I_{n-1}.

It is not obvious that integration by parts can be applied to this integral, but writing the integrand as $(1 + x^2)^n \times 1$, and taking $u = (1 + x^2)^n$ and $\dfrac{dv}{dx} = 1$, gives

$$\int_0^1 (1 + x^2)^n \, dx = \left[(1 + x^2)^n \times x\right]_0^1 - \int_0^1 n(1 + x^2)^{n-1} \times 2x \times x \, dx$$

$$= 2^n - 2n \int_0^1 x^2 (1 + x^2)^{n-1} \, dx.$$

Unfortunately the integral on the right side is not I_{n-1}, so this equation doesn't immediately produce the required reduction formula.

You can get round this problem by writing the extra factor x^2 in the integral as $(1 + x^2) - 1$, so that the integrand becomes

$$((1 + x^2) - 1)(1 + x^2)^{n-1}, \quad \text{which is} \quad (1 + x^2)^n - (1 + x^2)^{n-1}.$$

The equation then becomes

$$\int_0^1 (1 + x^2)^n \, dx = 2^n - 2n \int_0^1 ((1 + x^2)^n - (1 + x^2)^{n-1}) \, dx$$

$$= 2^n - 2n \int_0^1 (1 + x^2)^n \, dx + 2n \int_0^1 (1 + x^2)^{n-1} \, dx.$$

That is,

$$I_n = 2^n - 2nI_n + 2nI_{n-1},$$

which can be rearranged as

$$(2n+1)I_n = 2^n + 2nI_{n-1}.$$

This is a reduction formula of the required form.

Example 11.2.2

Find $\displaystyle\int_0^\pi \sin^n x \,dx$, where n is a positive integer greater than 1.

The clue here is to begin by writing $\sin^n x$ as $\sin^{n-1} x \sin x$. Then $\dfrac{dv}{dx} = \sin x$, so that $v = -\cos x$.

$$\int_0^\pi \sin^n x \,dx = \left[\sin^{n-1} x \times (-\cos x)\right]_0^\pi - \int_0^\pi (n-1)\sin^{n-2} x \cos x \times (-\cos x)\,dx.$$

Since $n > 1$, $\sin^{n-1} \pi$ and $\sin^{n-1} 0$ are both 0, so that

$$\int_0^\pi \sin^n x \,dx = (n-1)\int_0^\pi \sin^{n-2} x \cos^2 x \,dx.$$

This is not yet in the form you want, but you can write $\cos^2 x$ as $1 - \sin^2 x$ to get

$$\int_0^\pi \sin^n x \,dx = (n-1)\int_0^\pi \sin^{n-2} x(1 - \sin^2 x)\,dx.$$

Therefore, denoting $\displaystyle\int_0^\pi \sin^n x \,dx$ by I_n,

$$I_n = (n-1)(I_{n-2} - I_n),$$

which you can rearrange to give

$$nI_n = (n-1)I_{n-2}.$$

Using this repeatedly, with $n - 2$, $n - 4$, ... in place of n,

$$I_n = \frac{n-1}{n}I_{n-2}$$

$$= \frac{n-1}{n} \times \frac{n-3}{n-2}I_{n-4}$$

$$= \frac{n-1}{n} \times \frac{n-3}{n-2} \times \frac{n-5}{n-4}I_{n-6}$$

$$= \ldots.$$

Since this formula reduces the index by 2 each time, repeated application will reduce it to 0 if n is even and to 1 if n is odd. It is easy to evaluate

$$I_0 = \int_0^\pi \sin^0 x \,dx$$

$$= \int_0^\pi 1\,dx$$

$$= [x]_0^\pi$$

$$= \pi,$$

and

$$I_1 = \int_0^{\pi} \sin^1 x \, dx$$

$$= \int_0^{\pi} \sin x \, dx$$

$$= [-\cos x]_0^{\pi}$$

$$= 1 - (-1)$$

$$= 2.$$

Therefore, if n is even,

$$I_n = \frac{n-1}{n} \times \frac{n-3}{n-2} \times \frac{n-5}{n-4} \times \cdots \times \frac{1}{2} I_0$$

$$= \frac{(n-1)(n-3)(n-5)\ldots 1}{n(n-2)(n-4)\ldots 2} \pi,$$

and if n is odd,

$$I_n = \frac{n-1}{n} \times \frac{n-3}{n-2} \times \frac{n-5}{n-4} \times \cdots \times \frac{2}{3} I_1$$

$$= \frac{(n-1)(n-3)(n-5)\ldots 2}{n(n-2)(n-4)\ldots 3} \times 2.$$

Example 11.2.3

Find a reduction formula for $I_n = \int \frac{x^n}{\sqrt{1+x}} \, dx$.

Integrating by parts with $u = x^n$ and $\frac{dv}{dx} = \frac{1}{\sqrt{1+x}}$, so that $v = 2\sqrt{1+x}$,

$$I_n = 2x^n\sqrt{1+x} - \int 2nx^{n-1}\sqrt{1+x} \, dx$$

$$= 2x^n\sqrt{1+x} - 2n\int x^{n-1}\sqrt{1+x} \, dx.$$

The problem now is that, to express the integral on the right side in terms of I_{n-1}, you want the square root as the denominator of a fraction. You can do this by writing $\sqrt{1+x}$ as $\frac{1+x}{\sqrt{1+x}}$, so that

$$x^{n-1}\sqrt{1+x} \equiv x^{n-1}\frac{1+x}{\sqrt{1+x}}$$

$$\equiv x^{n-1}\left(\frac{1}{\sqrt{1+x}} + \frac{x}{\sqrt{1+x}}\right)$$

$$\equiv \frac{x^{n-1}}{\sqrt{1+x}} + \frac{x^n}{\sqrt{1+x}}.$$

The equation then becomes

$$I_n = 2x^n\sqrt{1+x} - 2n(I_{n-1} + I_n),$$

so that

$$(2n+1)I_n = 2x^n\sqrt{1+x} - 2nI_{n-1}.$$

There are no general rules to guide you to the algebraic identity which will convert an integral into a form which leads to a reduction formula. In Example 11.2.1 replacing x^2 by $(1 + x^2) - 1$ was effective; in Example 11.2.3 the clue was to write $\sqrt{1 + x}$ as $\dfrac{1 + x}{\sqrt{1 + x}}$. These are typical of the procedures used, but they are not the only possibilities. Choosing one which will work is a skill which comes more easily with practice.

Exercise 11B

1 If I_n denotes $\displaystyle\int_0^1 \frac{x^n}{\sqrt{1 + 3x}}\, dx$, show that $3(2n + 1)I_n = 4 - 2nI_{n-1}$ for $n > 0$. Use this to evaluate $\displaystyle\int_0^1 \frac{x^3}{\sqrt{1 + 3x}}\, dx$.

2 Find and use reduction formulae to evaluate (a) $\displaystyle\int_0^{\frac{1}{3}\pi} \cos^6 u\, du$,   (b) $\displaystyle\int_0^{\ln 2} \sinh^4 u\, du$. Check your answer to part (b) by expressing $\sinh u$ in exponential form before integrating.

3 This question is about the integral $I_n = \displaystyle\int_0^1 (1 + x^2)^n\, dx$ in Example 11.2.1.

   (a) Verify that the method used to obtain the reduction formula is valid for all real values of n.

   (b) What form does the reduction formula $(2n + 1)I_n = 2^n + 2nI_{n-1}$ take when $n = 0$? Check that this is correct by an independent method.

   (c) Use the substitution $x = \tan u$ to evaluate $\displaystyle\int_0^1 (1 + x^2)^{-\frac{3}{2}}\, dx$. Show that this is consistent with the value given by the reduction formula with $n = -\frac{1}{2}$.

   (d) Use the reduction formula to find

   (i) $\displaystyle\int_0^1 (1 + x^2)^3\, dx$,   (ii) $\displaystyle\int_0^1 (1 + x^2)^{\frac{3}{2}}\, dx$,   (iii) $\displaystyle\int_0^1 \frac{1}{(1 + x^2)^3}\, dx$.

4 This question is about the integral $I_n = \displaystyle\int \frac{x^n}{\sqrt{1 + x}}\, dx$ in Example 11.2.3.

   (a) Use the substitution $x = \sinh^2 u$ to show that $I_{\frac{1}{2}} = \sqrt{x(1 + x)} - \sinh^{-1}\sqrt{x} + k$.

   (b) Use the reduction formula $(2n + 1)I_n = 2x^n\sqrt{1 + x} - 2nI_{n-1}$ to find $I_{\frac{5}{2}}$.

5 Find and use a reduction formula to evaluate (a) $\displaystyle\int_0^1 \frac{1}{(4 - x^2)^3}\, dx$,   (b) $\displaystyle\int_0^1 \frac{1}{(4 - x^2)^{\frac{7}{2}}}\, dx$.

6 If I_n denotes $\displaystyle\int_0^\infty \frac{1}{(1 + x^2)^n}\, dx$, prove that $2nI_{n+1} = (2n - 1)I_n$, and state the values of n for which this reduction formula is valid. Hence find a formula for I_n if

   (a) n is a positive integer,   (b) $n = m + \frac{1}{2}$ where m is a positive integer.

7 If I_n denotes $\displaystyle\int_0^{\frac{1}{2}\pi} e^x \cos^n x\, dx$, show that $(n^2 + 1)I_n = n(n - 1)I_{n-2} - 1$, and state the values of n for which the reduction formula is valid. Find I_0 and I_1, and deduce I_2 and I_3.

8 Find $\displaystyle\int_0^5 \frac{x^3}{\sqrt{4 + x}}\, dx$, (a) using a reduction formula,   (b) using the substitution $4 + x = u$.

9 Let I_n denote the indefinite integral $\displaystyle\int \sec^n x \,dx$. By writing $\sec^n x$ as $\sec^{n-2} x \sec^2 x$ prove that

$(n-1)I_n = \sec^{n-2} x \tan x + (n-2)I_{n-2}$. Hence find $\displaystyle\int \sec^3 x \,dx$, $\displaystyle\int \sec^4 x \,dx$ and $\displaystyle\int \sec^5 x \,dx$.

Verify your answers by differentiation.

Miscellaneous exercise 11

1 It is given that $I_n = \displaystyle\int_0^1 x^n e^x \,dx \ (n \geqslant 0)$. Show that $I_n = e - nI_{n-1} (n \geqslant 1)$. Hence show that

$I_3 = 6 - 2e$. (OCR)

2 It is given that $I_n = \displaystyle\int_0^{\frac{1}{2}\pi} x^n \sin x \,dx$.

(a) Show that, for $n \geqslant 2$, $I_n = n\left(\frac{1}{2}\pi\right)^{n-1} - n(n-1)I_{n-2}$.

(b) Evaluate I_3, giving your answer in terms of π. (OCR)

3 Given that $I_n = \displaystyle\int_0^{\frac{1}{2}\pi} \sin^n x \,dx$, where n is a non-negative integer, show that

$(n+2)I_{n+2} = (n+1)I_n$. Hence find the exact values of I_4 and I_5. (OCR)

4 Let $I_n = \displaystyle\int \cosh^n x \,dx$. Show that $nI_n = \sinh x \cosh^{n-1} x + (n-1)I_{n-2}$. Hence show that

$\displaystyle\int_0^{\ln 2} \cosh^4 x \,dx = \frac{3}{8}\left(\frac{245}{128} + \ln 2\right)$. (OCR)

5 Define I_n by $I_n = \displaystyle\int_0^1 \frac{x^n}{\sqrt{1+x^2}} \,dx$, $n \geqslant 0$. Evaluate I_0 and I_1; give your answers to 4 significant figures.

Establish the reduction formula $I_n = \dfrac{\sqrt{2} - (n-1)I_{n-2}}{n}$ for suitable values of n, which you should state. Hence calculate I_5 and I_6 to 3 significant figures.

Prove, by setting up a suitable inequality for the integrand, that $I_n \to 0$ as $n \to \infty$. (OCR)

6 (a) Show that $\dfrac{d}{dx}(\cos 2x \sin^{n-1} 2x) = 2(n-1)\sin^{n-2} 2x - 2n\sin^n 2x$.

(b) It is given that $I_n = \displaystyle\int_{-\frac{1}{2}\pi}^{\frac{1}{2}\pi} \sin^n 2x \,dx \ (n \geqslant 0)$.

Use the result in (a) to show that $I_n = \left(\dfrac{n-1}{n}\right)I_{n-2} \ (n \geqslant 2)$. Hence find I_8, leaving your answer in the form $k\pi$, where k is a fraction in its lowest terms. (OCR)

7 Define $I_n = \displaystyle\int_1^e x^k(\ln x)^n \,dx$, where k is any constant number other than -1 and n is a positive integer or zero. Show that, for $n \geqslant 1$, $(k+1)I_n = e^{k+1} - nI_{n-1}$.

Hence find $\displaystyle\int_1^e \frac{(\ln x)^2}{\sqrt{x}} \,dx$.

What is the value of I_n when $k = -1$?

8 If I_n denotes $\displaystyle\int_0^\infty t^n e^{-at}\,dt$, where a is a positive constant, prove that $aI_n = nI_{n-1}$ provided that $n > 0$. Use the method of mathematical induction to deduce that, if n is a positive integer, $I_n = \dfrac{n!}{a^{n+1}}$. (Use a generalisation of the results in C3 Miscellaneous exercise 10 Question 10.)

9 Let I_n denote $\displaystyle\int_{-\infty}^\infty x^n \phi(x)\,dx$, where $\phi(x)$ is the normal probability function given by

$\phi(x) = \dfrac{1}{\sqrt{2\pi}}e^{-\frac{1}{2}x^2}$. By splitting up the integrand as the product of x^{n-1} and $x\phi(x)$, establish the reduction formula $I_n = (n-1)I_{n-2}$ provided that $n > 1$.

Given that $I_0 = 1$, find an expression for I_n for any positive integer n.

10 If I_n denotes $\displaystyle\int_0^1 \dfrac{e^x}{(1+x)^n}\,dx$, show that $nI_{n+1} = 1 - \left(\frac{1}{2}\right)^n e + I_n$, and state the values of n for which this is valid. If n is a positive integer, what is the disadvantage of trying to use this reduction formula to find I_n?

11 If $I_{m,n}$ denotes $\displaystyle\int_0^{\frac{1}{2}\pi} \sin^m\theta\cos^n\theta\,d\theta$, prove that $I_{m,n} = \dfrac{n-1}{m+n}I_{m,n-2}$. By using a suitable substitution, show also that $I_{m,n} = I_{n,m}$, and deduce that $I_{m,n} = \dfrac{m-1}{m+n}I_{m-2,n}$. Find

(a) $\displaystyle\int_0^{\frac{1}{2}\pi} \sin^8\theta\cos^9\theta\,d\theta$, (b) $\displaystyle\int_0^{\frac{1}{2}\pi} \sin^9\theta\cos^{10}\theta\,d\theta$, (c) $\displaystyle\int_0^{\frac{1}{2}\pi} \sin^8\theta\cos^{10}\theta\,d\theta$.

12 If $I_{m,n}$ denotes $\displaystyle\int_0^\infty \dfrac{x^m}{(x^2+a^2)^n}\,dx$, find a relation between $I_{m,n}$ and $I_{m-2,n-1}$, and state the values of m and n for which this is valid. Hence evaluate

(a) $\displaystyle\int_0^\infty \left(\dfrac{x}{x^2+a^2}\right)^7\,dx$, (b) $\displaystyle\int_0^\infty \dfrac{x^4}{(x^2+a^2)^{\frac{7}{2}}}\,dx$.

13 If I_n denotes $\dfrac{1}{n!}\displaystyle\int_0^x t^n e^{-t}\,dt$, find a relation connecting I_n and I_{n-1}. Deduce that the value of e^x exceeds its Maclaurin polynomial of degree n by $\dfrac{e^x}{n!}\displaystyle\int_0^x t^n e^{-t}\,dt$.

12 The graph of $y^2 = f(x)$

This chapter is about the relationship between the graphs of $y = f(x)$ and $y^2 = f(x)$. When you have completed it, you should

- know how to sketch the graph of $y^2 = f(x)$ given the graph of $y = f(x)$
- know that the graph of $y^2 = f(x)$ is symmetrical about the x-axis
- know that if the graphs of $y = f(x)$ and $y^2 = f(x)$ intersect they do so when $y = 0$ or $y = 1$
- know the gradients of both graphs are zero for the same values of x provided $y \neq 0$
- know how to predict the gradient of $y^2 = f(x)$ as it crosses the x-axis.

12.1 Graphs involving square roots

Suppose that you know the shape of the graph of $y = f(x)$. What can you deduce about the graph $y^2 = f(x)$?

You can get the graph of $y^2 = f(x)$ quickly on your graphic calculator by recognising that if $y^2 = f(x)$, then $y = \pm\sqrt{f(x)}$, so the graph of $y^2 = f(x)$ consists of the two graphs $y = \sqrt{f(x)}$ and $y = -\sqrt{f(x)}$. One of these lies wholly above or on the x-axis, and the other below or on it. You can therefore draw the graph of $y^2 = f(x)$ by drawing $y = \sqrt{f(x)}$ and then combining it with its reflection in the x-axis to produce a symmetrical graph.

Example 12.1.1
(a) Sketch the curves $y = x$ and $y^2 = x$.

(b) Use your calculator to sketch, on the same set of axes, the graphs of $y = x(4 - x)$ and $y^2 = x(4 - x)$.

What features do these graphs have in common?

The sketches are shown in Figs. 12.1 and 12.2. The solid graphs are the graphs of $y^2 = x$ and $y^2 = x(4 - x)$.

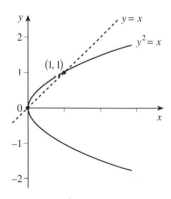

Fig. 12.1

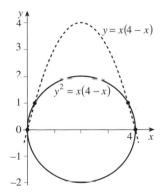

Fig. 12.2

In each case, the solid graph exists only when the dashed graph is above or on the x-axis. The solid graph and the dashed graph meet where $y = 0$ and where $y = 1$.

The graph of $y^2 = x(4 - x)$ looks like a circle. If you write its equation in the form $x^2 - 4x + y^2 = 0$, or $(x - 2)^2 + y^2 = 4$, the work of C1 Chapter 13 tells you that it is a circle with centre $(2, 0)$ and radius 2.

Both of the properties mentioned in Example 12.1.1 above are general properties, and do not rely on the specific curves being drawn.

- If the value of f(x) is negative in any interval on the x-axis, then, since $y^2 \geqslant 0$, the graph of $y^2 = f(x)$ does not exist in that interval.

- If the graphs of $y^2 = f(x)$ and $y = f(x)$ intersect they do so where $y^2 = y$, that is where $y = 0$ or $y = 1$. The graphs do not intersect anywhere else.

It is also worth noting that if $f(x) > 1$, then $f(x) > \sqrt{f(x)}$, and if $0 < f(x) < 1$, then $\sqrt{f(x)} > f(x)$. This means that, apart from points where $f(x) = 0$, the part of the graph of $y^2 = f(x)$ for which y is positive is always closer to the line $y = 1$ than the graph of $y = f(x)$. You can see this in Figs. 12.1 and 12.2.

12.2   Properties of gradient

In this section, the letter y always refers to the y in the equation $y^2 = f(x)$, except when $y = f(x)$ is mentioned explicitly.

If you look again at Figs. 12.1 and 12.2, you will see that when f(x) is increasing, $y = \sqrt{f(x)}$ is also increasing; similarly, they decrease together. If they have stationary points, they have them at the same values of x.

Increasing and decreasing functions

You can see that a function and its square root increase and decrease together by differentiating $y^2 = f(x)$ implicitly. You then find

$$2y\frac{dy}{dx} = f'(x).$$

Consider now the points on $y^2 = f(x)$ for which y is positive, as opposed to the points for which y is zero. Then $\frac{dy}{dx}$ and f'(x) have the same sign. Therefore, when $f'(x) > 0$, $\frac{dy}{dx} > 0$; similarly, when $f'(x) < 0$, $\frac{dy}{dx} < 0$.

Stationary values

From the equation $2y\frac{dy}{dx} = f'(x)$, it follows that, if $y \neq 0$ when $f'(x) = 0$, then $\frac{dy}{dx} = 0$.

The condition $y \neq 0$ is important: if $y = 0$ the result could be false. For example, draw the graphs of $y = x^2$ and $y^2 = x^2$ on your calculator. When $y = 0$, one of the graphs has a minimum; the other has $\dfrac{dy}{dx} = \pm 1$.

The gradient when $y = 0$

The gradient at points on the x-axis, where $f(x) = 0$, needs more detailed investigation.

In the equation $2y\dfrac{dy}{dx} = f'(x)$, if $y = 0$ then $\dfrac{dy}{dx}$ is undefined. But Figs. 12.1 and 12.2 show that it is possible for the graph of $y^2 = f(x)$ to have a tangent parallel to the y-axis. You know from C4 Section 8.2 that this occurs when $\dfrac{dx}{dy} = 0$.

To find $\dfrac{dx}{dy}$, differentiate the equation $y^2 = f(x)$ with respect to y. Then

$$2y = f'(x)\dfrac{dx}{dy}.$$

You can see from this that, if $f'(x) \neq 0$, then

$$y = 0 \quad \Rightarrow \quad \dfrac{dx}{dy} = 0,$$

so that the tangent is parallel to the y-axis. This is illustrated in Fig. 12.3.

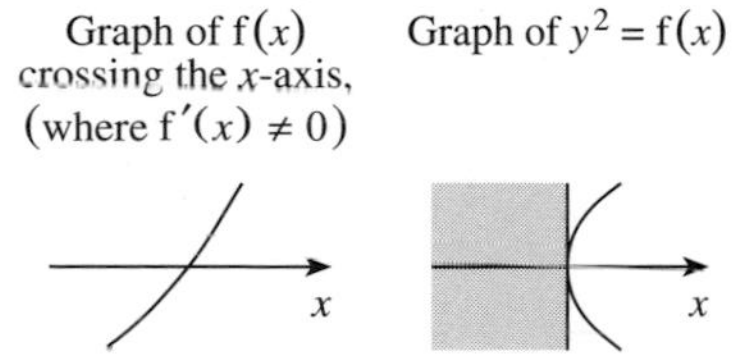

Graph of $f(x)$ crossing the x-axis, (where $f'(x) \neq 0$)   Graph of $y^2 = f(x)$

Fig. 12.3

The shaded part of the graph indicates that this is a 'forbidden region'.

But if $f'(x) = 0$ when $y = 0$, the equations $2y\dfrac{dy}{dx} = f'(x)$ and $2y = f'(x)\dfrac{dx}{dy}$ become

$$2 \times 0 \times \dfrac{dy}{dx} = 0 \quad \text{and} \quad 2 \times 0 = 0 \times \dfrac{dx}{dy}.$$

Neither equation tells you anything about the gradient of $y^2 = f(x)$. Fig. 12.4 shows that there are many cases. There is no general rule, and you must consider each function on its merits.

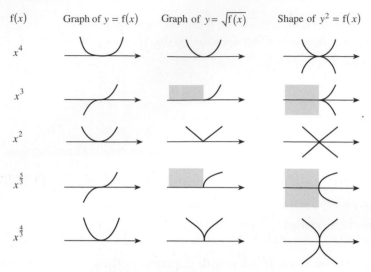

$f(x)$	Graph of $y = f(x)$	Graph of $y = \sqrt{f(x)}$	Shape of $y^2 = f(x)$
x^4			
x^3			
x^2			
$x^{\frac{5}{3}}$			
$x^{\frac{4}{3}}$			

Fig. 12.4

Here are properties which should enable you to sketch the graph of $y^2 = f(x)$ given the graph of $y = f(x)$.

If $f(x) < 0$, the graph of $y^2 = f(x)$ does not exist.

The graphs of $y = f(x)$ and $y^2 = f(x)$ intersect where $y = 0$ or $y = 1$.

Provided that $y > 0$, the gradients of $y = f(x)$ and $y = \sqrt{f(x)}$ have the same sign, and have stationary values at the same values of x.

At points where $f(x) = 0$, provided that $f'(x) \neq 0$, the graph of $y^2 = f(x)$ crosses the x-axis in the direction parallel to the y-axis.

The graph of $y^2 = f(x)$ is symmetrical about the x-axis.

Example 12.2.1

Fig. 12.5 shows a sketch of the graph of $y = f(x)$, for some function $f(x)$. On the same axes sketch the graph of $y^2 = f(x)$.

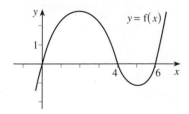

Fig. 12.5

The method used is to draw $y = \sqrt{f(x)}$, and then to reflect the result in the x-axis. Each step of the text is illustrated in Fig. 12.6.

Shade in the 'no-go regions' where $f(x) < 0$.

Draw the line $y = 1$ and mark the points where the
graph of $y = f(x)$ meets the lines $y = 0$ (the x-axis),
and $y = 1$. The graph of $y = \sqrt{f(x)}$ must pass through
these points.

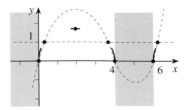

Fig. 12.6

Remember that the graph of $y = \sqrt{f(x)}$ is always
closer to the line $y = 1$ than the graph of $y = f(x)$
(except when $f(x) = 0$).

Identify the point on $y = f(x)$ for which $y > 0$ and $f'(x) = 0$. Mark the corresponding
point on $y = \sqrt{f(x)}$ which also has a gradient of zero.

At the points where the graph of $y = f(x)$ crosses the
x-axis, the graph of $y^2 = f(x)$ has a vertical tangent.
Note that the gradient of $y = f(x)$ is not zero at these
points.

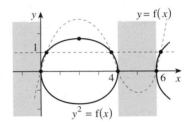

Fig. 12.7

You can now join the points and pieces to obtain a
line for which y is positive.

Now recall that the graph of $y^2 = f(x)$ is symmetrical
about the x-axis and complete the curve which is
the solid curve in Fig. 12.7.

With practice this process is quite quick.

Example 12.2.2
Draw the graph of $y = x(x - 2)$; deduce from it the shape of the graph of $y^2 = x(x - 2)$.

Fig. 12.8 shows the graph of $y = x(x - 2)$, which is the parabola drawn with a dashed
line.

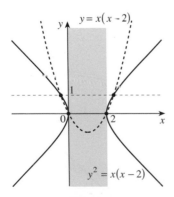

Fig. 12.8

The solid line is the graph of $y^2 = x(x - 2)$. It exists only when $y = x(x - 2)$ is positive.

The graphs of $y = x(x - 2)$ and $y^2 = x(x - 2)$ meet when $y = 0$ and $y = 1$.

The graph of $y^2 = x(x - 2)$ has vertical tangents when $y = 0$, and is symmetrical about
the x-axis.

Example 12.2.3

Fig. 12.9 shows the graph of $y = \dfrac{(x+1)(x-2)}{(x-1)(x-3)}$, which was discussed in Example 5.2.1.

Use the graph to draw a sketch of $y^2 = \dfrac{(x+1)(x-2)}{(x-1)(x-3)}$.

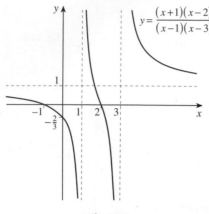

Fig. 12.9

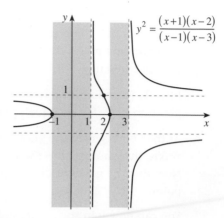

Fig. 12.10

From Fig. 12.9, $\dfrac{(x+1)(x-2)}{(x-1)(x-3)} \geqslant 0$ only in the intervals $x \leqslant -1$, $1 < x \leqslant 2$ and $x > 3$.

Therefore the graph of $y^2 = \dfrac{(x+1)(x-2)}{(x-1)(x-3)}$ exists only for these intervals.

The graphs of $y = \dfrac{(x+1)(x-2)}{(x-1)(x-3)}$ and $y^2 = \dfrac{(x+1)(x-2)}{(x-1)(x-3)}$ intersect when $y = 0$ and when $y = 1$, that is at $(-1, 0)$, $\left(1\frac{2}{3}, 1\right)$ and $(2, 0)$.

The tangents to $y = \dfrac{(x+1)(x-2)}{(x-1)(x-3)}$ at $(-1, 0)$ and $(2, 0)$ are not horizontal, so, from the result in the blue box (page 200), the graph of $y^2 = \dfrac{(x+1)(x-2)}{(x-1)(x-3)}$ has vertical tangents at these points.

The next example shows the kinds of things that can happen when you start with a graph which has a discontinuity in its gradient.

Example 12.2.4

Sketch the graphs of $y = 1 - |x|$ and $y^2 = 1 - |x|$.

The graph of $y = 1 - |x|$ is shown in Fig. 12.11. You can see that the 'no-go regions' for $y^2 = 1 - |x|$ are $x < -1$ and $x > 1$.

The graph of $y = 1 - |x|$ crosses the x-axis at $45°$, so the tangents to the graph at these points on $y^2 = 1 - |x|$ are both parallel to the y-axis.

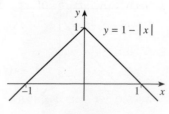

Fig. 12.11

The only points on the graph of $y^2 = 1 - |x|$ which you need to treat with suspicion are the sharp corners at the point $(0, \pm1)$. What is the gradient there?

To answer this question, it is helpful to say that the graph of $y^2 = 1 - |x|$ is the same as

$$y^2 = \begin{cases} 1 - x & \text{for } x \geqslant 0, \\ 1 + x & \text{for } x < 0. \end{cases}$$

Now consider $y^2 = 1 - x$ for $x > 0$. Differentiating $y^2 = 1 - x$ implicitly,

$$2y\frac{dy}{dx} = -1,$$

so when y is close to 1, $\dfrac{dy}{dx}$ is close to $-\frac{1}{2}$.

Similar considerations show that when $x < 0$, and y is close to 1, $\dfrac{dy}{dx}$ is close to $\frac{1}{2}$.

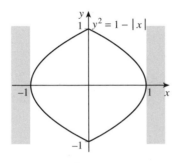

Fig. 12.12

The graph is shown in Fig. 12.12. There is a maximum at $(0, 1)$ and a minimum at $(0, -1)$.

Note that $(0, 1)$ and $(0, -1)$ are not stationary points, because there is no tangent at these points.

Exercise 12

1 Sketch the graphs of
   (a) $y^2 = 3x - 6$,   (b) $y^2 = 2x + 9$,   (c) $y^2 = 5 - x$,   (d) $y^2 = \frac{1}{2}x + 2 = 0$

2 Sketch the graphs of
   (a) $y^2 = x(x - 9)$,   (b) $y^2 = x^2 - 9$,   (c) $y^2 = 9 - x^2$,   (d) $y^2 = x(9 - x)$.

3 Sketch the graphs of
   (a) $y^2 = x^2 + 2$,   (b) $y^2 = (x - 2)^2 + 1$,   (c) $y^2 = x^2 + 2x + 9$,   (d) $y^2 = (x + 1)^2$.

4 (a) Sketch the graph of $y = x^3 + 8$ and hence sketch the graph of $y^2 = x^3 + 8$.
   (b) Sketch the graph of $y = x^3 - 1$ and hence sketch the graph of $y^2 = x^3 - 1$.

5 Sketch graphs of the following, paying particular attention to the form of the graph near the point $(3, 0)$.

   (a) $y^2 = (x - 1)(x - 3)$ (b) $y^2 = (x - 1)(x - 3)^2$

   (c) $y^2 = (x - 1)(x - 3)^3$ (d) $y^2 = (x - 1)(x - 3)^4$

6 Determine the coordinates of the stationary points on the curve $y = x^2(6 - x)$. Sketch the graph of $y = x^2(6 - x)$.

   Also sketch the graph of $y^2 = x^2(6 - x)$; state the coordinates of the points where the tangent is parallel to the x-axis, and find the gradient of the curve at the origin.

7 Sketch the graph of $y^2 = (11 + x)(9 - x)$. Show that this is the equation of a circle and determine its radius and centre.

8 In the following equations, a and b are positive constants. Which of the following could be the equation of the curve shown?

   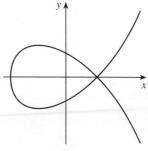

   (a) $y^2 = (x + a)(x - b)$ (b) $y^2 = (x + a)^2(x - b)$

   (c) $y^2 = (x + a)(x - b)^3$ (d) $y^2 = (x + a)^3(x - b)$

   (e) $y^2 = (x + a)(x - b)^2$ (f) $y^2 = (x + a)(x - b)^4$

9 In the following equations, p and q are positive constants. Which of the following could be the equation of the curve shown?

   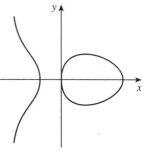

   (a) $y^2 = x(x + p)(x - q)$ (b) $y^2 = (x + p)(x - q)$

   (c) $y^2 = x(p + x)(q - x)$ (d) $y^2 = x^2(x + p)(x - q)^2$

   (e) $y^2 = x(x + p)^2(x - q)$ (f) $y^2 = x^3(p + x)(q - x)$

10 Find the coordinates of the points of intersection of the curves $y = x^2 - 6x + 9$ and $y^2 = x^2 - 6x + 9$ and illustrate with sketch graphs.

11 Sketch the graphs of $y = \sin x$, $y = \cos x$ and $y = \tan x$ for $0 \leqslant x \leqslant 4\pi$. Hence sketch the graphs of $y^2 = \sin x$, $y^2 = \cos x$ and $y^2 = \tan x$ for $0 \leqslant x \leqslant 4\pi$.

12 Sketch the graphs of

   (a) $y^2 = e^x$,   (b) $y^2 = e^x - 1$,   (c) $y^2 = 4e^{-3x}$,   (d) $y^2 = e^{2x} - e^2$.

13 The diagram shows the graph $y = f(x)$, which has a minimum point at $(-3, 1)$ and a maximum point at $(2, 5)$. Copy the diagram and, on the same axes, draw the graph of $y^2 = f(x)$ showing how the two graphs are related. State the coordinates of the points of $y^2 = f(x)$ at which the tangent is parallel to the x-axis.

   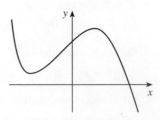

14   Sketch the graph of $y = 9 - 4x^2$ and hence sketch the graph of $y^2 = 9 - 4x^2$. (This is the equation of an ellipse; its equation is more usually written as $4x^2 + y^2 = 9$.)

15   Sketch the graph of the ellipse $4x^2 - 12x + y^2 = 7$.

16   Sketch on the same diagram the graphs of $y^2 = x^2 + 1$ and $y^2 = x^2$. (The first graph is a rectangular hyperbola and the second graph shows its asymptotes.)

17   Show that the asymptotes of the curve $y = \dfrac{x^2}{x + 3}$ are $x = -3$ and $y = x - 3$.

   (a) Sketch the graph of $y = \dfrac{x^2}{x + 3}$.

   (b) Sketch the curve $y^2 = \dfrac{x^2}{x + 3}$, paying particular attention to the shape of the curve at the origin.

18   Sketch in separate diagrams the graphs of

   (a) $y^2 = x - 2$,   (b) $y^2 = (x - 2)^2$,   (c) $y^2 = (x - 2)^3$,   (d) $y^2 = (x - 2)^4$.

Miscellaneous exercise 12

1   Sketch in separate diagrams the curves with equations

   (a) $y = x(1 - x^2)$,   (b) $y^2 = x(1 - x^2)$.   (OCR)

2   A sketch of the graph of $y = f(x)$ is shown in the diagram. On separate diagrams, sketch the graphs of

   (a) $y^2 = f(x)$,   (b) $y = \sqrt{f(x)}$.   (OCR)

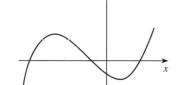

3   On separate diagrams sketch the graphs of

   (a) $y = x^2(x + b)$,   (b) $y^2 = x^2(x + b)$.

   where b is a positive constant. You should indicate clearly the slope of each curve near points where $y = 0$.   (OCR)

4   Sketch on separate diagrams the curves whose equations are

   (a) $y = \dfrac{x}{1 + x}$,   (b) $y^2 = \dfrac{x}{1 + x}$.   (OCR)

5   The graph of $y = f(x)$ has asymptotes $x = 0$, $x = a$ and $y = 0$ and is shown in the figure. Sketch the graphs of

   (a) $y = |f(x)|$,   (b) $y^2 = f(x)$.   (OCR)

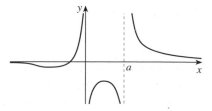

6   Sketch the graph of $y^2 = \dfrac{x + a}{x + b}$, where a and b are positive constants such that $b > a$.   (OCR)

7 Sketch on separate diagrams the curves with equations

(a) $y = \dfrac{1}{x^2 - a^2}$,

(b) $y = \left| \dfrac{1}{x^2 - a^2} \right|$,

(c) $y^2 = \dfrac{1}{x^2 - a^2}$,

where a is a positive constant. You should state, in each case, the equation of any asymptote(s) and the coordinates of any stationary points.   (OCR)

8 The equation of a curve is $y^2 = \dfrac{x}{1 + x^2}$. Show that the y-axis is a tangent to the curve at the origin and find the coordinates of all the turning points on the curve. Sketch the curve.   (OCR)

9 The sketches show the graphs of $y^2 = f(x)$ and $y = |f(x)|$ for a certain function f.

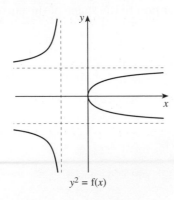

$y^2 = f(x)$

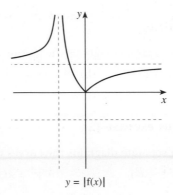

$y = |f(x)|$

(a) Sketch the graph of $y = f(x)$.

(b) Sketch the graph of $y = f(|x|)$.   (OCR)

10 The notation $[x]$ means the greatest integer whose value is not greater than x. (So, for example, $[3.7] = 3$, $[2.0] = 2$ and $[-1.85] = -2$.) Sketch the graphs of

(a) $y = [x]$,

(b) $y^2 = [x]$,

(c) $y = x - [x]$,

(d) $y^2 = x - [x]$.

11 Sketch the graphs of

(a) $y = \sqrt{\sin x}$

(b) $y = \sqrt{1 + \cos x}$

(c) $y = \sqrt{1 - \cos x}$

Revision exercise 2

1 By means of the substitution $t = \tan \frac{1}{2}x$, find $\int_0^{\frac{2}{3}\pi} \dfrac{1}{1 + \sin x}\, dx$, giving your answer in the form $a - \sqrt{b}$, where a and b are integers. (OCR)

2 The equation $x \cosh x - 2 \sinh x = 0$ has one positive root, α.

   (a) Show that α lies between 1.8 and 2.

   (b) Taking $x_1 = 2$ as a first approximation to α, use the Newton–Raphson method to find a second approximation. (OCR)

3 (a) By considering $\int_k^{k+1} \dfrac{1}{x}\, dx$ geometrically, show that, for $k > 0$, $\dfrac{1}{k+1} < \int_k^{k+1} \dfrac{1}{x}\, dx < \dfrac{1}{k}$.

   (b) Hence prove that $\ln(1 + N) < \displaystyle\sum_{r=1}^{N} \dfrac{1}{r} < 1 + \ln N$, where N is a positive integer. (OCR)

4 Find, in terms of logarithms, the exact values of x for which $7 \sinh x + 20 \cosh x = 24$. (OCR)

5 (a) Given that $I_n = \displaystyle\int_0^1 x^n \sqrt{1 - x}\, dx$, prove that, for $n \geqslant 1$, $(2n+3)I_n = 2nI_{n-1}$.

   (b) Hence find the exact value of I_2. (OCR)

6 The sketch shows the curve $y = F(x)$ and the line $y = x$. The equation $x = F(x)$ has a root α and $-1 < F'(x) < 0$ near $x = \alpha$.

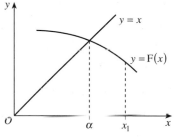

   (a) Starting with a copy of the sketch, draw a cobweb diagram to show why an iteration of the form $x_{n+1} = F(x_n)$ with starting value $x_1(>\alpha)$, will give successive approximations which are closer to α. Show x_2 and x_3 on your diagram.

   (b) The equation $x^3 + 2x - 40 = 0$ has a root near $x = 3$. This equation can be written in the form

   (i) $x = \frac{1}{2}(40 - x^3)$,   (ii) $x = (40 - 2x)^{\frac{1}{3}}$.

   State, giving a reason, whether each of (i) and (ii) is suitable for the use of the iterative method described in part (a). (OCR)

7 It is given that $I_n = \displaystyle\int_0^1 x^n e^x\, dx$.

   (a) Show that $I_n = e - nI_{n-1}$ for $n \geqslant 1$.

   (b) Find the exact value of $I_n = \displaystyle\int_0^1 x^4 e^x\, dx$. (OCR)

8 A curve has equation $y = \dfrac{4x(5-x)}{x+4}$.

(a) Find $\dfrac{dy}{dx}$. Hence find the coordinates of the two stationary points.

(b) Write down the equation of the asymptote parallel to the y-axis. Express the equation of the curve in divided out form, and hence find the equation of the oblique asymptote.

(c) Sketch the curve.

(d) On a separate diagram, sketch the curve with equation $y^2 = \dfrac{4x(5-x)}{x+4}$. Give the coordinates of the four points on this curve where the tangent is parallel to the x-axis, and the two points where the tangent is parallel to the y-axis.   (MEI, adapted)

9 (a) The diagram shows the curve $y = f(x)$ cutting the x-axis at P where $x = \alpha$. The tangent to $y = f(x)$ at the point A where $x = x_1$ cuts the x-axis at the point B where $x = x_2$. Show that $x_2 = x_1 - \dfrac{f(x_1)}{f'(x_1)}$.

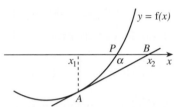

(b) Sketch a diagram showing a case where $f(x)$ and x_1 are such that $|x_2 - \alpha| > |x_1 - \alpha|$.

(c) The line $y = 4x$ intersects the curve $y = 3 + 2\cos x$ at the point Q. Taking $\frac{1}{3}\pi$ as a first approximation to the value of x at Q, use the Newton–Raphson method to find a second approximation, giving your answer correct to 2 decimal places.   (OCR)

10 The diagram shows the graph of a function $y = f(x)$.

Show on a sketch, the graph of

(a) $y = |f(x)|$,

(b) $y^2 = f(x)$,

(c) $y = \sqrt{f(x)}$.

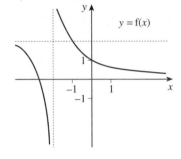

11 Find

(a) $\displaystyle\int_{\frac{1}{4}\pi}^{\frac{1}{3}\pi} \cot^4 x \, dx$,

(b) $\displaystyle\int_{0}^{\frac{1}{2}\pi} \dfrac{\cos x}{\sqrt{1+\sin x}} \, dx$,

(c) $\displaystyle\int_{0}^{\frac{1}{4}x} x \tan^2 x \, dx$,

(d) $\displaystyle\int_{0}^{\frac{1}{2}\pi} e^{3x} \cos 4x \, dx$.

12 The equation $x^3 + 3x^2 - 1 = 0$ has a root between 0 and 1. Use the Newton–Raphson method, with initial approximation 0.5, to find this root correct to 2 decimal places. Give a clear reason why it would be impossible to use the Newton–Raphson method with initial approximation 0.   (OCR)

13 Show that $\dfrac{d}{dx}(x^{n-1}\sqrt{16-x^2}) = \dfrac{16(n-1)x^{n-2}}{\sqrt{16-x^2}} - \dfrac{nx^n}{\sqrt{16-x^2}}$. Deduce, or prove otherwise,

that if $I_n = \displaystyle\int_{0}^{2} \dfrac{x^n}{\sqrt{16-x^2}} \, dx$, then, for $n \geqslant 2$, $nI_n = 16(n-1)I_{n-2} - 2^n\sqrt{3}$.

Hence find the exact value of I_2.   (OCR)

14 (a) One step of the Newton–Raphson method for solving the equation $f(x) = 0$ can be expressed as $x_2 = x_1 - \dfrac{f(x_1)}{f'(x_1)}$. Draw a sketch to illustrate the method.

   (b) Suppose that x_0 is near to x_1. Write down an approximation to $f'(x_1)$ based on x_0 and x_1. Substitute this approximation into the equation in part (a) to obtain the result
$$x_2 \approx \frac{f(x_0)x_1 - f(x_1)x_0}{f(x_0) - f(x_1)}.$$

   (c) Let $f(x) = x - \cos x$. Show that the equation has a root in the interval $(0.5, 1)$. Use the iteration $x_{n+2} = \dfrac{f(x_n)x_{n+1} - f(x_{n+1})x_n}{f(x_n) - f(x_{n+1})}$ to solve the equation, correct to 6 significant figures, taking $x_0 = 0.5$ and $x_1 = 1.0$.

   (d) By considering the errors in x_2, x_3 and x_4 show that the convergence of this iteration appears to be better than first order.

   (e) Give one advantage and one disadvantage of using the iteration in part (c) rather than the Newton–Raphson method.   (MEI)

15 Given that $I_n = \displaystyle\int_0^1 x^n \cos \pi x \, dx$, for $n \geqslant 0$, show that $\pi^2 I_n + n(n-1)I_{n-2} + n = 0$.

   Hence show that $\displaystyle\int_0^1 x^4 \cos \pi x \, dx = \dfrac{4(6 - \pi^2)}{\pi^4}$.   (OCR)

16 (a) Draw a diagram to show that $\displaystyle\sum_{r=m+1}^{n} \frac{1}{r^3} < \int_m^n \frac{1}{x^3}\, dx$, and write down a similar integral I such that $\displaystyle\sum_{r=m+1}^{n} \frac{1}{r^3} > I$.

   (b) Given that $\displaystyle\sum_{r=1}^{25} \frac{1}{r^3} = 1.20129$, correct to 5 decimal places, and that the series $\displaystyle\sum_{r=1}^{\infty} \frac{1}{r^3}$ is convergent, show that $1.2020 < \displaystyle\sum_{r=1}^{\infty} \frac{1}{r^3} < 1.2021$.   (MEI, adapted)

17 (a) Show that the equation $9e^{-x} = x^2$, $x > 0$, has a solution, α, near to $x = 1.5$.

   (b) Show that two possible rearrangements of the equation are $x = 3e^{-\frac{1}{2}x}$ and $x = \ln\left(\dfrac{9}{x^2}\right)$.

   (c) Each of these rearrangements is used iteratively with starting value $x = 1.5$ in order to find the solution, α. Show, numerically or otherwise, that one iteration converges and the other diverges.

   (d) An iteration which diverges can sometimes be used to obtain a solution as follows.

      Use x_0 to find x_1 from the iterative formula.

      Let $x_2 = \frac{1}{2}(x_0 + x_1)$.

      Use x_2 to find x_3 from the iterative formula.

      Let $x_4 = \frac{1}{2}(x_2 + x_3)$, etc.

      Use this method on the diverging iteration in part (c) to discover whether it produces the required solution, α, in this case.   (MEI)

18 (a) Sketch the curve with equation $y = \dfrac{x}{x - 1}$, giving the equations of all its asymptotes.

   (b) Sketch the curve with equation $y = \sqrt{\dfrac{x}{x - 1}}$.

19 The equation $x^2 + x = e^{-x}$ is given to have only one root, X, with $0.44 < X < 0.45$.

(a) Show that the iteration $x_{n+1} = \dfrac{e^{-x_n}}{x_n + 1}$ (when started in the given interval) converges to X. Use the value of $F'(x)$ for a suitable function F to estimate the number of steps needed to reduce the initial error by a factor of 10^{-2}.

(b)* Calculate x_1, x_2, x_3 from the iteration in (a) when $x_0 = 0.45$. Use the method of Section 8.4 on x_1, x_2, x_3 to find an approximation to X.

(c) Show that both the iterations $x_{n+1} = e^{-x_n} - x_n^2$ and $x_{n+1} = -1 + \dfrac{e^{-x_n}}{x_n}$ can be derived from the original equation, and that both diverge.

(d) A combined iteration is $x_{n+1} = \frac{3}{2}\left(e^{-x_n} - x_n^2\right) - \frac{1}{2}\left(-1 + \dfrac{e^{-x_n}}{x_n}\right)$. Show that this iteration converges rapidly (near $x_0 = 0.45$) to X. Calculate two steps of this iteration with $x_0 = 0.45$. (OCR)

20 Let $I_n = \displaystyle\int_0^1 \cosh^n x \, dx$. By considering $\dfrac{d}{dx}(\sinh x \cosh^{n-1} x)$, or otherwise, show that

$$nI_n = ab^{n-1} + (n-1)I_{n-2}, \text{ where } a = \sinh 1 \text{ and } b = \cosh 1.$$

Show that $I_4 = \frac{1}{8}(2ab^3 + 3ab + 3)$. (OCR)

Practice examination 1 for FP2

Time 1 hour 30 minutes

Answer all the questions.

You are permitted to use a graphic calculator in this paper.

1 The diagram shows a sketch of the graph of $y = f(x)$, where $f(x) = \dfrac{a + bx}{c + dx}$ for some constants a, b, c, d. The curve meets the axes at the points $(-1, 0)$ and $(0, 1)$, and the line $x = 1$ is an asymptote to the curve.

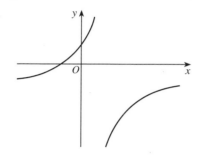

   (i) Find $f(x)$, and state the equation of the horizontal asymptote to the curve.   [5]

   (ii) Sketch the graph of $y^2 = f(x)$.   [2]

2 Let $f(x) = \sin\left(x + \tfrac{1}{4}\pi\right)$.

   (i) Find the Maclaurin series for $f(x)$, up to and including the term in x^4.   [4]

   (ii) Calculate the error that results when these terms of this Maclaurin series are used to estimate the value of $\sin \tfrac{1}{2}\pi$.   [3]

3 The polar equation of a curve is $r \cos \tfrac{1}{2}\theta = a$, for $-\pi < \theta < \pi$, where a is a positive constant.

   (i) Show that $r \sin \theta$ may be expressed as $2a \sin \tfrac{1}{2}\theta$, and deduce that, as $\theta \to \pm\pi$, the curve approaches the lines with cartesian equations $y = \pm 2a$.   [4]

   (ii) Sketch the curve.   [2]

   (iii) Calculate the area of the sector of the curve between $\theta = \pm\tfrac{1}{2}\pi$.   [4]

4   (i) Starting from the definition of sinh in terms of exponentials, prove that

$$\sinh^{-1} x = \ln(x + \sqrt{x^2 + 1}).$$
     [4]

   (ii) Hence prove that $\dfrac{d}{dx}(\sinh^{-1} x) = \dfrac{1}{\sqrt{x^2 + 1}}$.   [3]

   (iii) By using a binomial expansion and then integrating, deduce that, for small values of x, $\sinh^{-1} x \approx x - \tfrac{1}{6}x^3 + \tfrac{3}{40}x^5$.   [4]

5   (i) Express $\dfrac{5x^2}{(x^2 - 4)(x^2 + 1)}$ in partial fractions.   [6]

   (ii) Hence find the exact value of $\displaystyle\int_0^1 \dfrac{5x^2}{(x^2 - 4)(x^2 + 1)}\,\mathrm{d}x$.   [5]

6 The equation $x = \ln(x + 2)$ has a positive root α which is a little greater than 1. The iteration $x_{n+1} = \ln(x_n + 2)$, with $x_1 = 1$, is used to calculate an approximation to α.

   (i) Draw a diagram to illustrate the convergence of the iteration towards α.   [3]

   The approximations $x_1, x_2, x_3, \ldots$ to α have errors $e_1, e_2, e_3, \ldots$ respectively. Successive (small) errors are such that $e_{n+1} \approx k e_n$, where $k = 0.3$ correct to 1 significant figure.

   (ii) Show how this value of k is obtained from the form of the equation and the approximate value of α.   [2]

   You are given that $\alpha < 1.2$, so that e_1 is less than 0.2.

   (iii) Use this information, together with the approximate value of k, to estimate the number of iterations required to give an approximation to α with an error less than 10^{-5}.   [3]

   (iv) Carry out the number of iterations found in part (iii), and verify by identifying an appropriate sign change that α is in fact within 10^{-5} of the approximation calculated.   [4]

7   (i) Show that $\tanh\left(\frac{1}{2}\ln 3\right) = \frac{1}{2}$.   [3]

   Let $I_n = \displaystyle\int_0^{\frac{1}{2}\ln 3} \tanh^n \theta \, \mathrm{d}\theta$.

   (ii) By writing $\tanh^n \theta$ as $\tanh^{n-2} \theta \, (1 - \operatorname{sech}^2 \theta)$, show that, for $n \geqslant 2$,

   $$I_n = I_{n-2} - \frac{1}{(n-1)\,2^{n-1}}.$$ [3]

   (iii) Deduce that $I_{2N} = \frac{1}{2}\ln 3 - \displaystyle\sum_{r=1}^{N} \frac{1}{(2r-1)\,2^{2r-1}}$.   [3]

   (iv) By considering I_n as representing the area under a curve and using a single rectangle as an approximation to this area, show that $I_n < \left(\frac{1}{2}\right)^{n+1} \ln 3$, for $n > 0$.   [3]

   (v) Use parts (iii) and (iv) to deduce the sum to infinity of the series

   $$\frac{1}{1 \times 2} + \frac{1}{3 \times 2^3} + \frac{1}{5 \times 2^5} + \ldots\,.$$ [2]

Practice examination 2 for FP2

Time 1 hour 30 minutes

Answer all the questions.

You are permitted to use a graphic calculator in this paper.

1 (i) Starting from the definition of tanh in terms of exponentials, prove that
$$\tanh^{-1} x = \tfrac{1}{2} \ln \left(\frac{1+x}{1-x} \right).$$
[3]

   (ii) Use the Maclaurin series for $\ln(1+x)$ to deduce that $\tanh^{-1} x = x + \tfrac{1}{3}x^3 + \tfrac{1}{5}x^5 + \ldots$. [3]

2 Use the substitution $t = \tan \tfrac{1}{2}x$ to find $\displaystyle \int_0^{\frac{1}{2}\pi} \frac{1}{1 + \sin x}\, \mathrm{d}x.$ [6]

3 The diagram shows the curve $y = \dfrac{1}{x^2}$ together with rectangles of unit width above the curve.

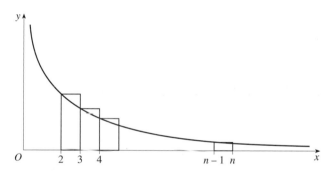

   (i) By considering appropriate areas, show that $\displaystyle \sum_{r=2}^{n-1} \frac{1}{r^2} > \frac{1}{2} - \frac{1}{n}.$ [3]

   (ii) By considering rectangles under the curve, show that $\displaystyle \sum_{r=3}^{n} \frac{1}{r^2} < \frac{1}{2} - \frac{1}{n}.$ [1]

   (iii) Deduce that $\displaystyle \sum_{r=1}^{\infty} \frac{1}{r^2}$ lies between $\tfrac{3}{2}$ and $\tfrac{7}{4}$. [3]

4 (i) Use formulae for $\sinh 2x$ and $\cosh 2x$ in terms of $\sinh x$ and $\cosh x$ to show that
$$\tanh 2x = \frac{2 \tanh x}{1 + \tanh^2 x}.$$
[3]

   (ii) The equation $\tanh 2x = k \tanh x$, where k is a positive constant, is satisfied by a non-zero value of x. Show that $1 < k < 2$. [5]

5 The equation of a curve, in polar coordinates, is $r = a(\sin\theta + \cos\theta)$, where a is a positive constant.

(i) Find the area of the region bounded by the lines $\theta = 0$, $\theta = \frac{1}{2}\pi$ and the part of the curve for which $0 \leqslant \theta \leqslant \frac{1}{2}\pi$. [4]

(ii) Express the equation of the curve in cartesian coordinates, and hence show that the curve is a circle. [3]

(iii) Sketch the curve, and state a set of values of θ corresponding to the complete circle. [3]

6   (i) Use integration by parts to show that

$$\int (1 - x^2)^n \, dx = x(1 - x^2)^n + 2n \int x^2 (1 - x^2)^{n-1} \, dx,$$

where n is a positive integer. [2]

The definite integral $\int_0^1 (1 - x^2)^n \, dx$ is denoted by I_n.

(ii) Show that $I_n = \dfrac{2n}{2n+1} I_{n-1}$. [3]

(iii) Write down the value of I_0, and prove by induction that $I_n = \dfrac{4^n (n!)^2}{(2n+1)!}$. [4]

7 The equation of a curve is $y = \dfrac{x^2}{x - a}$, where a is a positive constant.

(i) Find the equations of the asymptotes of the curve. [3]

(ii) Show that there are no points of the curve for which $0 < y < 4a$. [4]

(iii) Find the coordinates of the stationary points of the curve. [4]

(iv) Sketch the curve. [2]

8   (i) By writing $\dfrac{u^2}{1 + u^2}$ as $1 - \dfrac{1}{1 + u^2}$, show that the value of x for which $\displaystyle\int_0^x \dfrac{u^2}{1 + u^2} \, du = 1$ satisfies the equation $x = 1 + \tan^{-1} x$. [2]

(ii) The root α of the equation $x = 1 + \tan^{-1} x$ is approximately equal to 2. Find an approximate relationship between small errors in successive approximations to α when the iteration $x_{n+1} = 1 + \tan^{-1} x_n$ is used. [3]

(iii) Use the Newton–Raphson method, applied to the equation $x - \tan^{-1} x - 1 = 0$, with 2 as the first approximation, to find the next two approximations. [4]

(iv) For the application of the Newton–Raphson method in part (iii), the first approximation, 2, is less than α, but the next two approximations (and all further approximations) are greater than α. Illustrate this behaviour by means of a sketch of the graph of $y = x - \tan^{-1} x - 1$ in the neighbourhood of α, showing how the first three approximations are related geometrically. [4]

Module FP3
Further Pure 3

1 First order differential equations

This chapter describes methods of solving more complicated differential equations than those met in C4. When you have completed it, you should

- be able to solve linear first order equations by using an integrating factor
- be able to use a given substitution to solve other first order equations.

1.1 Solution using the product rule

In C4 Chapter 7 you solved differential equations like $\dfrac{dy}{dx} = \cos x$ and $\dfrac{dy}{dx} = y^2$ (so $\dfrac{dx}{dy} = \dfrac{1}{y^2}$).

C4 Chapter 8 introduced more general equations like $\dfrac{dy}{dx} = y^2 \cos x$, where the variables are said to be 'separable'.

An equation like this can be written as

$$\frac{1}{y^2}\frac{dy}{dx} = \cos x,$$

where the left side is the derivative with respect to x of a function of y alone, and the right side is the derivative of a function of x. Thus

$$\frac{1}{y^2}\frac{dy}{dx} = \frac{d}{dx}\left(-\frac{1}{y}\right) \quad \text{and} \quad \cos x = \frac{d}{dx}(\sin x),$$

so the solution is

$$-\frac{1}{y} = \sin x + k.$$

Using this method you can solve any equation of the form $\dfrac{dy}{dx} = \dfrac{f(x)}{g(y)}$ so long as you can do the actual integration.

All these equations are examples of **first order equations**, because they involve only the first derivative $\dfrac{dy}{dx}$. But not all first order equations can be separated in this way. For example, if you have the equation

$$3x^2 y + x^3 \frac{dy}{dx} = x^4$$

to solve, no amount of algebraic manoeuvre will enable you to get $\dfrac{dy}{dx}$ into the form $\dfrac{f(x)}{g(y)}$.

In fact, this equation is easy to solve, because you should recognise the left side as the derivative of the product of two functions. Thus

$$3x^2 y + x^3 \frac{dy}{dx} \quad \text{is} \quad \frac{d}{dx}(x^3) \times y + x^3 \frac{dy}{dx},$$

which is $\dfrac{d}{dx}(x^3 y)$, so the equation can be written as

$$\frac{\mathrm{d}}{\mathrm{d}x}(x^3 y) = x^4.$$

The solution is

$$x^3 y = \tfrac{1}{5}x^5 + k,$$

or more conveniently

$$y = \tfrac{1}{5}x^2 + \frac{k}{x^3}.$$

The trouble is that it is most unlikely that you will be asked to solve

$$3x^2 y + x^3 \frac{\mathrm{d}y}{\mathrm{d}x} = x^4,$$

because all the terms of this equation have a common factor x^2. It is more likely that the equation will be presented as

$$3y + x\frac{\mathrm{d}y}{\mathrm{d}x} = x^2,$$

and then the left side is not the derivative of a product. How could you tell that the key to solving this equation is to multiply each term by x^2? Read on!

1.2   Integrating factors

The first part of this chapter is concerned with the general problem of solving differential equations of the form

$$\frac{\mathrm{d}y}{\mathrm{d}x}\mathrm{f}(x) + y\mathrm{g}(x) = \mathrm{h}(x),$$

where f, g and h are given functions. A differential equation like this is said to be **linear**, because $\frac{\mathrm{d}y}{\mathrm{d}x}$ and y appear only to the first degree; the equation has no terms involving $\left(\frac{\mathrm{d}y}{\mathrm{d}x}\right)^m$ or y^m with $m \neq 1$, nor are there any products like $y\frac{\mathrm{d}y}{\mathrm{d}x}$.

It isn't necessary to write this equation with three given functions, because you can divide through by $\mathrm{f}(x)$ to get

$$\frac{\mathrm{d}y}{\mathrm{d}x} + y\frac{\mathrm{g}(x)}{\mathrm{f}(x)} = \frac{\mathrm{h}(x)}{\mathrm{f}(x)}$$

and then express $\dfrac{\mathrm{g}(x)}{\mathrm{f}(x)}$ as a single function $\mathrm{p}(x)$, and $\dfrac{\mathrm{h}(x)}{\mathrm{f}(x)}$ as $\mathrm{q}(x)$.

> The **standard form** of a first order linear differential equation is
>
> $$\frac{\mathrm{d}y}{\mathrm{d}x} + y\mathrm{p}(x) = \mathrm{q}(x),$$
>
> where $\mathrm{p}(x)$ and $\mathrm{q}(x)$ are given functions of x.

For example, the standard form of the equation discussed in Section 1.1 would be

$$\frac{dy}{dx} + y \times \frac{3}{x} = x.$$

You already know that this can be integrated by multiplying by x^3, which makes the left side $\frac{dy}{dx} \times x^3 + y \times 3x^2 = \frac{d}{dx}(yx^3)$. The question is, how can you find this multiplying factor x^3 from the knowledge that $p(x) = \frac{3}{x}$?

The answer comes in two steps. First, notice that

$$\int \frac{3}{x} \, dx = 3 \ln x + k = \ln x^3 + k.$$

So you could say that the 'simplest' integral of $\frac{3}{x}$ is $\ln x^3$.

The second step is to get from $\ln x^3$ to the multiplying factor x^3, and to do this you simply have to take the exponential, since $e^{\ln x^3} = x^3$.

This works as a general rule. The multiplier x^3 is an example of an **integrating factor**. It is a function that you can use to convert a first order differential equation in standard form into a form which can be integrated.

> To find an integrating factor for the differential equation
>
> $$\frac{dy}{dx} + y\,p(x) = q(x)$$
>
> first find the simplest integral of $p(x)$, and call it $I(x)$; then $e^{I(x)}$ is an integrating factor.

Example 1.2.1

Find the general solution of the differential equation $\frac{dy}{dx} - \frac{y}{x} = x$.

This is already in standard form, with $p(x) = -\frac{1}{x}$. So find the simplest integral of $-\frac{1}{x}$, which is $-\ln x$, or $\ln \frac{1}{x}$. An integrating factor is therefore $e^{\ln \frac{1}{x}}$, which is simply $\frac{1}{x}$.

Multiplying the differential equation by $\frac{1}{x}$ gives

$$\frac{dy}{dx} \times \frac{1}{x} + y \times \left(\frac{1}{x^2} \right) = 1.$$

The left side of this is $\frac{d}{dx}\left(y \times \frac{1}{x} \right)$, so the equation can be written as

$$\frac{d}{dx}\left(y \times \frac{1}{x} \right) = 1.$$

This can be integrated as

$$y \times \frac{1}{x} = x + k,$$

or more conveniently

$$y = x^2 + kx.$$

In an example like this, since the process is quite complicated, it is a good idea to check the answer by direct substitution. If $y = x^2 + kx$, then $\frac{dy}{dx} = 2x + k$ and $\frac{y}{x} = x + k$, so $\frac{dy}{dx} - \frac{y}{x} = (2x + k) - (x + k) = x$, as required.

When you solve a first order differential equation, the general solution involves an arbitrary constant k. For each value of k the equation represents a curve, called a **solution curve**. In Example 1.2.1 all the solution curves are parabolas through the origin, including $y = x^2$ when $k = 0$. Fig. 1.1 shows a selection of these curves for various values of k.

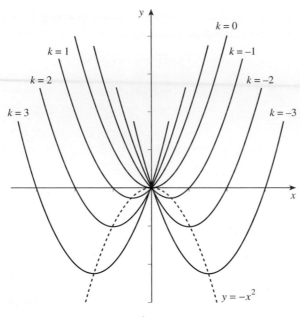

Fig. 1.1

It is interesting to notice that the minimum points on all the solution curves lie on the curve $y = -x^2$, shown dotted in Fig. 1.1. You can see the reason for this by going back to the differential equation and putting $\frac{dy}{dx} = 0$. This gives $-\frac{y}{x} = x$, which is $y = -x^2$.

The next example requires you to find the particular solution curve which passes through a given point.

Example 1.2.2

Find the curve through (0, 1) whose equation satisfies the differential equation $\frac{dy}{dx} + y = e^x$.

For this differential equation p(x) is simply 1, and the simplest integral of this is x. So an integrating factor is e^x.

Multiplying the equation by e^x gives

$$\frac{dy}{dx} \times e^x + y \times e^x = e^{2x}.$$

The left side is $\frac{d}{dx}(ye^x)$, so the equation can be written as $\frac{d}{dx}(ye^x) = e^{2x}$, and then integrated to give

$$ye^x = \tfrac{1}{2}e^{2x} + k.$$

The question asks for the solution for which $y = 1$ when $x = 0$, so substitute these values to obtain $1 = \tfrac{1}{2} + k$, giving $k = \tfrac{1}{2}$. The solution is therefore

$$ye^x = \tfrac{1}{2}e^{2x} + \tfrac{1}{2},$$

which is best written as

$$y = \tfrac{1}{2}e^x + \tfrac{1}{2}e^{-x}.$$

If you have already studied FP2 Chapter 4, you will recognise this equation as $y = \cosh x$.

Fig. 1.2 shows a number of solution curves for the differential equation, with the curve through (0, 1) emphasised as a heavier line. In this case not all the curves have stationary points; for those which do, these points lie on $y = e^x$ (shown dotted in Fig. 1.2), which you get by putting $\frac{dy}{dx} = 0$ in the differential equation.

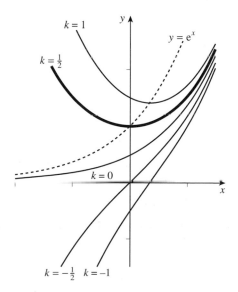

Fig. 1.2

It is important to remember that, to use the integrating factor rule, you have to begin with the differential equation in standard form. But it is always worth checking first that the equation isn't already in a form which can be integrated directly, as was the case with the example in Section 1.1. This is the point of the first step in the following algorithm.

> To find the general solution of the differential equation
> $\frac{dy}{dx} f(x) + y\, g(x) = h(x)$ using an integrating factor:
>
> **Step 1**   If $g(x) = f'(x)$, write the equation as $\frac{d}{dx}(y\, f(x)) = h(x)$ and go to Step 6.
>
> **Step 2**   Divide the equation by $f(x)$ to obtain the standard form
> $\frac{dy}{dx} + y\, p(x) = q(x)$.
>
> **Step 3**   Find the simplest integral of $p(x)$; denote it by $I(x)$.
>
> **Step 4**   Write $u(x) = e^{I(x)}$, and simplify this if possible. This is the integrating factor.
>
> **Step 5**   Multiply the equation (in its form after Step 2) by $u(x)$, and write the equation as $\frac{d}{dx}(y\, u(x)) = q(x)\, u(x)$.
>
> **Step 6**   Integrate the equation with respect to x, including an arbitrary constant.
>
> **Step 7**   Put the solution into the form $y = \ldots$ by dividing by the function which multiplies y (that is $u(x)$ or $f(x)$).

Example 1.2.3

Find the general solution of $\frac{dy}{dx} \cos x + y \sin x = \tan x$.

Step 1 $f'(x)$ is $\frac{d}{dx}(\cos x) = -\sin x$, which does not equal $g(x) = \sin x$.

Step 2   Divide by $\cos x$ to obtain $\frac{dy}{dx} + y \tan x = \tan x \sec x$.

Step 3 $p(x) = \tan x;$ $\int \tan x \, dx = \ln \sec x + k$, so take $I(x) = \ln \sec x$.

Step 4   The integrating factor is $u(x) = e^{\ln \sec x} = \sec x$.

Step 5   Multiply by $\sec x$: $\frac{dy}{dx} \sec x + y \sec x \tan x = \tan x \sec^2 x$, which is

$\frac{d}{dx}(y \sec x) = \tan x \sec^2 x.$

Step 6   Integrating, $y \sec x = \frac{1}{2} \tan^2 x + k$.

Step 7   Dividing by $\sec x$, $y = \dfrac{\sin^2 x}{2 \cos x} + k \cos x.$

This is a perfectly acceptable answer to the question. However, it is worth noticing that it can be written as

$$y = \frac{1 - \cos^2 x}{2 \cos x} + k \cos x,$$

which is

$$y = \tfrac{1}{2}(\sec x - \cos x) + k \cos x = \tfrac{1}{2} \sec x + \left(k - \tfrac{1}{2}\right) \cos x.$$

Since k is an arbitrary constant, $k - \tfrac{1}{2}$ can be replaced by a single arbitrary constant c, giving the simplest form of the solution as

$$y = \tfrac{1}{2} \sec x + c \cos x.$$

After such a complicated calculation it is worth checking the answer to make sure you have not made a mistake. If $y = \tfrac{1}{2} \sec x + c \cos x$, then $\dfrac{dy}{dx} = \tfrac{1}{2} \sec x \tan x - c \sin x$, so that the left side of the original equation is

$$\left(\tfrac{1}{2} \sec x \tan x - c \sin x\right) \cos x + \left(\tfrac{1}{2} \sec x + c \cos x\right) \sin x$$
$$= \tfrac{1}{2} \tan x - c \sin x \cos x + \tfrac{1}{2} \tan x + c \cos x \sin x$$
$$= \tan x, \quad \text{as required.}$$

One small point to notice at Step 3 is that strictly the integral of $\tan x$ is $\ln | \sec x |$; that is, it is $\ln \sec x$ or $\ln(-\sec x)$ depending on whether $\sec x$ is positive or negative. If you use the minus sign, then at Step 4 you get $u(x) = -\sec x$ rather than $\sec x$. But this is not important, since it clearly makes no difference at Step 5 whether you multiply the equation by $\sec x$ or $-\sec x$.

1.3* Why the method works

You may omit this section if you wish.

It is quite easy to see why the rule for finding the integrating factor works. Since $I(x)$ is an integral of $p(x)$, it follows that $p(x) = I'(x)$. The left side of the differential equation, in standard form, is therefore

$$\frac{dy}{dx} + y I'(x).$$

After multiplying by $e^{I(x)}$, this becomes

$$\frac{dy}{dx} e^{I(x)} + y e^{I(x)} I'(x).$$

Now if $u(x) = e^{I(x)}$, then differentiation by the chain rule gives $u'(x) = e^{I(x)} \times I'(x)$. So

$$\frac{dy}{dx} e^{I(x)} + y e^{I(x)} I'(x) = \frac{dy}{dx} u(x) + y u'(x), \text{ which is } \frac{d}{dx}(y u(x)).$$

You may also question why the algorithm in Section 1.2 specifies that you should choose $I(x)$ to be the *simplest* integral of $p(x)$. The answer is that you needn't. But if you chose some other integral of $p(x)$, this would have the form $I(x) + c$, for some constant c. The integrating factor would then be $e^{I(x)+c}$, which is $e^{I(x)} \times e^c$. So the only effect of taking one of the other integrals of p(x) for I(x) is to multiply the equation through by an additional numerical constant e^c, which is pointless.

Exercise 1A

1 Find general solutions of the following differential equations.

(a) $y + x\dfrac{dy}{dx} = x^2$

(b) $x\cos t + \dfrac{dx}{dt}\sin t = 1$

(c) $\dfrac{1}{x}\dfrac{dy}{dx} - \dfrac{1}{x^2}y = \dfrac{1}{x^3}$

(d) $e^{x^2}\dfrac{du}{dx} + 2xe^{x^2}u = 2$

2 Find the equation of the solution curve through the given point for each of the following differential equations.

(a) $2xy + x^2\dfrac{dy}{dx} = 1$ through $(1, 0)$

(b) $2y\sin x\cos x + \dfrac{dy}{dx}\sin^2 x = \cos x$ through $\left(\tfrac{1}{2}\pi, 1\right)$

(c) $\dfrac{y}{\sqrt{x}} + 2\sqrt{x}\dfrac{dy}{dx} = x$ through $(1, 1)$

3 Use integrating factors to find the general solutions of the following differential equations. Check your answers by substituting back into the original equations.

(a) $\dfrac{du}{dx} + \dfrac{2u}{x} = 1$

(b) $\dfrac{dy}{dx} - y\tan x = 2\sin x$

(c) $\dfrac{dx}{dt} - 4x = e^{2t}$

(d) $\dfrac{dy}{dx} - \dfrac{3y}{x} = x$

(e) $\dfrac{dy}{dt} + y\tan t = \cos t$

(f) $\dfrac{dy}{dx}\sin x + y\sec x = \cos^2 x$

4 For the following differential equations, find the equations of the solution curves which pass through the given points. Illustrate your answers with sketch graphs.

(a) $\dfrac{dy}{dx} + 3y = 9x$ through $(0, -2)$, $(0, -1)$, $(0, 0)$, $(0, 1)$, $(0, 2)$

(b) $x\dfrac{dy}{dx} + 2y = x^2$, for $x > 0$, through $(1, 0)$, $(1, 1)$, $(1, 2)$, $(2, 0)$, $(2, 1)$, $(2, 2)$

(c) $y\sin x + \dfrac{dy}{dx}\cos x = 2\tan x$, for $-\tfrac{1}{2}\pi < x < \tfrac{1}{2}\pi$, through $(0, -2)$, $(0, -1)$, $(0, 0)$, $(0, 1)$, $(0, 2)$

(d) $x\dfrac{dy}{dx} = 3y + 2x$, for $x \neq 0$, through $(-1, -1)$, $(-1, 0)$, $(-1, 1)$, $(1, -1)$, $(1, 0)$, $(1, 1)$

5 A curve passing through the point $(1, 1)$ has the property that, at each point P of the curve, the gradient of the curve is 1 less than the gradient of OP. Find the equation of the curve, and illustrate your answer with a graph.

6 A sack containing a liquid chemical is placed in a tank. The chemical seeps out of the sack at a rate of $0.1x$ litres per hour, where x is the number of litres of the chemical remaining in the sack after t hours. The chemical in the tank evaporates at a rate $0.2y$ litres per hour, where y is the number of litres of the chemical in the tank after t hours. If the sack originally contained 50 litres of the chemical, find differential equations for x and for y, and solve them. Find the greatest amount of chemical in the tank, and when this occurs.

7 A will-o'-the-wisp is oscillating in a straight line so that its displacement from the origin at time t is $a + b\sin ct$, where a, b and c are positive constants. It is chased by a kitten which moves so that its velocity at any time is equal to cy, where y is the displacement of the will-o'-the-wisp from the kitten. If x denotes the displacement of the kitten from the origin at time t, find a differential equation connecting x and t. Show that, after some time, x is approximately equal to $a + \dfrac{1}{\sqrt{2}}b\sin(ct - \tfrac{1}{4}\pi)$. Draw graphs to illustrate the positions of the kitten and the will-o'-the-wisp during the chase.

8 A rope hangs over a rough circular peg of radius r. It is just about to slip with a vertical length p on one side and a vertical length q on the other, where $q > p$. It can be shown that, if the coefficient of friction is 1, the quantity $u = \dfrac{T}{\gamma g}$ satisfies the differential equation $\dfrac{du}{d\theta} - u = r(\cos\theta - \sin\theta)$. ($\gamma$ is the mass of the rope per unit length, g is the acceleration due to gravity, θ is the angle that the radius to a point on the peg makes with the vertical and T is the tension in the rope at that point.) Given that $u = p$ when $\theta = -\tfrac{1}{2}\pi$, and $u = q$ when $\theta = \tfrac{1}{2}\pi$, prove that $q = pe^{\pi} + r(1 + e^{\pi})$.

9 Find the general solution of the differential equation $x\dfrac{dy}{dx} = 2(y - x)$ for $x \neq 0$. Investigate the regions in which the gradient of the solution curve is positive, and those in which it is negative,

   (a) from the equation of the solution,

   (b) from the differential equation.

   Illustrate your answers with sketches of some solution curves.

10 Find the general solution of the differential equation $x\dfrac{dy}{dx} + y = \dfrac{1}{x^2}$ for $x > 0$. Use the differential equation to show that the stationary points on the solution curves all lie on $y = \dfrac{1}{x^2}$, and verify this from your equation for the general solution. Draw graphs to illustrate this property.

   By differentiating the differential equation, show that $\dfrac{d^2y}{dx^2} = \dfrac{2}{x^2}\left(y - \dfrac{2}{x^2}\right)$. Hence identify the regions in which the solution curves bend upwards, and those in which they bend downwards. Check your answer from your graphs.

1.4 Transforming equations by substitution

You have now met most of the common types of first order differential equation, but occasionally more complicated equations turn up. You can sometimes solve these by substituting a new variable for y, so as to reduce the equation to one of the types which you can already solve. Here are five examples which illustrate some of the possibilities; these are all standard types, and the substitution is given in the question or explained in the solution.

Not all first order differential equations can be solved in this way, and there is no general rule for finding a substitution which will work.

Example 1.4.1

Use the substitution $2x + y = z$ to find the solution of the differential equation
$\dfrac{dy}{dx} = \dfrac{2x + y - 2}{2x + y + 1}$ for which $y = 1$ when $x = 0$.

Before starting to answer this question, it is worth checking for yourself that there is no direct way of solving the equation by any of the methods you know already, such as separation of variables or as a linear differential equation.

Since y is a function of x, and $z = 2x + y$, z is also a function of x. So it can be differentiated with respect to x, to give

$$\frac{dz}{dx} = 2 + \frac{dy}{dx}.$$

The differential equation connecting x with y can then be replaced by one connecting x with z, as

$$\frac{dz}{dx} - 2 = \frac{z - 2}{z + 1}.$$

This can be written more simply as

$$\begin{aligned}
\frac{dz}{dx} &= 2 + \frac{z - 2}{z + 1} \\
&= \frac{2(z + 1) + z - 2}{z + 1} \\
&= \frac{3z}{z + 1}.
\end{aligned}$$

You will recognize this as an equation of the form $\dfrac{dz}{dx} = f(z)$. So you can solve it by writing $\dfrac{dz}{dx}$ as $1 \div \dfrac{dx}{dz}$, so that the equation takes the form

$$\frac{dx}{dz} = \frac{z + 1}{3z}.$$

Then, integrating with respect to z,

$$\begin{aligned}
x &= \int \frac{z + 1}{3z}\, dz \\
&= \tfrac{1}{3} \int \left(1 + \frac{1}{z}\right) dz \\
&= \tfrac{1}{3}(z + \ln z) + k.
\end{aligned}$$

If you wanted the general solution of the differential equation, you would now substitute back $z = 2x + y$ and simplify the result. But in this example it is given that $y = 1$ when $x = 0$, so that $z = 2 \times 0 + 1 = 1$ when $x = 0$. The constant k can therefore be found from the equation

$$0 = \tfrac{1}{3}(1 + \ln 1) + k,$$

which gives $k = -\tfrac{1}{3}$.

The required solution is therefore

$$x = \tfrac{1}{3}((2x + y) + \ln(2x + y)) - \tfrac{1}{3},$$

which can be simplified as

$$x - y + 1 = \ln(2x + y).$$

This is as far as it is useful to go. The equation expresses the relation between x and y implicitly, but it is not possible to write y explicitly as a function of x, or x as a function of y.

Example 1.4.2

Use the substitution $y = \dfrac{1}{z}$ to solve the differential equation $\dfrac{dy}{dx} - \dfrac{y}{x} = 2y^2$.

Notice that the given differential equation is not linear, because it includes a term containing y^2. The effect of the substitution is to convert it into a linear equation for z in terms of x.

If $y = \dfrac{1}{z}, \dfrac{dy}{dx} = -\dfrac{1}{z^2}\dfrac{dz}{dx}.$

If you substitute these expressions for y and $\dfrac{dy}{dx}$ in the differential equation, you get

$$-\frac{1}{z^2}\frac{dz}{dx} - \frac{1}{xz} = \frac{2}{z^2},$$

which you can rearrange as

$$\frac{dz}{dx} + \frac{z}{x} = -2$$

This is a linear first order equation for z as a function of x. You can easily check that the integrating factor is x, and that

$$x\frac{dz}{dx} + z = -2x$$

can be written as

$$\frac{d}{dx}(xz) = -2x.$$

Integration gives $xz = k - x^2$, so

$$z = \frac{k - x^2}{x} \text{ and } y = \frac{1}{z} = \frac{x}{k - x^2}.$$

The solution of the given differential equation is $y = \dfrac{x}{k - x^2}$, where k is an arbitrary constant.

Example 1.4.3

A curve passes through $(1, 0)$ and, at each point P, the direction of the tangent makes an angle of $\frac{1}{4}\pi$ with the direction OP, as shown in Fig. 1.3. Find the equation of the curve.

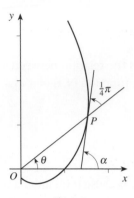

Fig. 1.3

If OP makes an angle θ with the x-axis, and the tangent makes an angle α with the x-axis, then $\alpha = \frac{1}{4}\pi + \theta$, so that

$$\frac{dy}{dx} = \tan\alpha = \tan\left(\tfrac{1}{4}\pi + \theta\right)$$

$$= \frac{\tan\frac{1}{4}\pi + \tan\theta}{1 - \tan\frac{1}{4}\pi \tan\theta} = \frac{1 + \dfrac{y}{x}}{1 - \dfrac{y}{x}} = \frac{x + y}{x - y}.$$

There is a standard method for solving equations for which $\dfrac{dy}{dx}$ can be expressed in terms of $\dfrac{y}{x}$. The clue is to introduce a new variable $u = \dfrac{y}{x}$, so that $y = xu$. Then, by the product rule, $\dfrac{dy}{dx} = u + x\dfrac{du}{dx}$. You can then substitute for y and $\dfrac{dy}{dx}$ in the differential equation to get

$$u + x\frac{du}{dx} = \frac{1 + u}{1 - u},$$

so

$$x\frac{du}{dx} = \frac{1 + u}{1 - u} - u = \frac{1 + u - u(1 - u)}{1 - u} = \frac{1 + u^2}{1 - u}.$$

You can rearrange this as $\dfrac{1 - u}{1 + u^2}\dfrac{du}{dx} = \dfrac{1}{x}$, which is an equation with separable variables.

Now
$$\int \frac{1 - u}{1 + u^2}\,du = \int \left(\frac{1}{1 + u^2} - \frac{u}{1 + u^2}\right) du$$
$$= \tan^{-1} u - \tfrac{1}{2}\ln(1 + u^2) + k.$$

The equation can therefore be integrated with respect to x as

$$\tan^{-1} u - \tfrac{1}{2}\ln(1 + u^2) + k = \ln|x|.$$

To find k note that the curve passes through $(1, 0)$, so that $u = \frac{0}{1} = 0$ when $x = 1$. So

$$\tan^{-1} 0 - \tfrac{1}{2}\ln(1 + 0^2) + k = \ln|1|, \text{ giving } k = 0.$$

Finally, substitute back u as $u = \dfrac{y}{x}$, which gives the solution

$$\tan^{-1}\frac{y}{x} = \tfrac{1}{2}\ln\left(1 + \frac{y^2}{x^2}\right) + \ln|x|.$$

This can be simplified by writing $|x|$ as $\sqrt{x^2}$ and combining the logarithms,

$$\tan^{-1}\frac{y}{x} = \ln\left(\sqrt{\left(1 + \frac{y^2}{x^2}\right)} \times \sqrt{x^2}\right)$$

$$= \ln\sqrt{\left(1 + \frac{y^2}{x^2}\right) \times x^2} = \ln\sqrt{x^2 + y^2}.$$

If you have read FP2 Chapter 6 you will recognise that this equation would look far less formidable if it were written in polar coordinates. If you replace $\tan^{-1}\dfrac{y}{x}$ by θ, and $\sqrt{x^2 + y^2}$ by r, it becomes

$$\theta = \ln r, \quad \text{or} \quad r = e^{\theta}.$$

The curve is called an *equiangular spiral*, because the tangent always makes the same angle with the radius.

Example 1.4.4*

Find the general solution of the differential equation $x^4\dfrac{dy}{dx} = x^2y^2 + 2xy + x^2 + 1$.

If you compare the form of this equation with the general linear equation at the beginning of Section 1.2, you will see that, in addition to terms of the form $\dfrac{dy}{dx}f(x)$, $yg(x)$ and $h(x)$, there is also a term of the form $y^2k(x)$. Equations of this kind are called *Riccati equations*, after the Venetian mathematician who published a paper about them in 1724.

There is no general method for finding solutions of Riccati equations. But they have the surprising property that, if you can find one solution $y = F(x)$, then the general solution can be found by making a substitution $y = F(x) + u$, where u is a function of x. This gives a differential equation for u, and one of two things may happen.

- The equation may be one of the types which you already know how to solve (which is what happens in this example).
- The equation may be similar to Example 1.4.2, and can be solved by making a further substitution $u = \dfrac{1}{z}$, where z is a function of x.

So begin by trying to guess a solution. Since all the functions of x which appear in the equation are powers of x, it is possible that it might be satisfied by a function such as $y = ax^m$ for some numbers a and m. If this is so, then the identity

$$x^4(amx^{m-1}) \equiv x^2(ax^m)^2 + 2x(ax^m) + x^2 + 1$$

would have to hold for all values of x. This can be written as

$$amx^{m+3} \equiv a^2x^{2m+2} + 2ax^{m+1} + x^2 + x^0.$$

It is not hard to see that, since there must be other terms to balance the terms x^2 and x^0, this can happen only if $m+3=2$ and $m+1=0$, so that $m=-1$. The identity then becomes

$$-ax^2 \equiv a^2 + 2a + x^2 + 1, \quad \text{or} \quad (a+1)x^2 + (a+1)^2 \equiv 0.$$

Both coefficients are 0 if $a=-1$, so the equation is satisfied by $y=-\dfrac{1}{x}$.

To find the general solution, take $F(x) = -\dfrac{1}{x}$, and make the substitution $y=-\dfrac{1}{x}+u$. Then

$$\frac{dy}{dx} = \frac{1}{x^2} + \frac{du}{dx}.$$

So the differential equation becomes

$$x^4\left(\frac{1}{x^2} + \frac{du}{dx}\right) = x^2\left(-\frac{1}{x}+u\right)^2 + 2x\left(-\frac{1}{x}+u\right) + x^2 + 1.$$

This can be simplified to give

$$x^2\frac{du}{dx} = u^2,$$

which is a differential equation with separable variables. Writing it as

$$\frac{1}{u^2}\frac{du}{dx} = \frac{1}{x^2},$$

the integral is

$$-\frac{1}{u} = -\frac{1}{x} + k,$$

that is

$$u = \frac{x}{1-kx}.$$

So the general solution of the differential equation for y is

$$y = -\frac{1}{x} + \frac{x}{1-kx},$$

where k is an arbitrary constant.

You sometimes need to use a substitution to solve a differential equation which arises in mechanics. In the next example solving the differential equation is only part of the problem; once you have the equation it must be interpreted in physical terms.

Example 1.4.5*
An object slides down a track whose shape is part of a circle of radius r, as shown in Fig. 1.4. Its velocity at the top of the track is u. The velocity v when the radius makes an angle θ with the vertical satisfies the differential equation

$$2v\frac{dv}{d\theta} - v^2 = gr(2\sin\theta - \cos\theta).$$

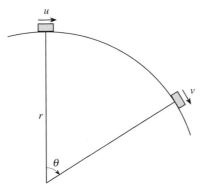

Fig. 1.4

(This is the equation you get when the coefficient of friction is $\frac{1}{2}$; g is the constant acceleration of gravity.)

Investigate the subsequent motion.

> This is not a linear equation, since it contains terms in v^2 and a product $2v\dfrac{\mathrm{d}v}{\mathrm{d}\theta}$. But you should recognise that $2v\dfrac{\mathrm{d}v}{\mathrm{d}\theta}$ is $\dfrac{\mathrm{d}}{\mathrm{d}\theta}(v^2)$. So if w is written in place of v^2, the equation becomes
>
> $$\frac{\mathrm{d}w}{\mathrm{d}\theta} - w = gr(2\sin\theta - \cos\theta),$$
>
> which is linear.
>
> The integrating factor is $\mathrm{e}^{\mathrm{I}(\theta)}$, where $\mathrm{I}(\theta)$ is the simplest integral of -1 with respect to θ, so that $\mathrm{I}(\theta) = -\theta$. After multiplication by the integrating factor $\mathrm{e}^{-\theta}$, the equation becomes
>
> $$\frac{\mathrm{d}}{\mathrm{d}\theta}(w\mathrm{e}^{-\theta}) = gr\mathrm{e}^{-\theta}(2\sin\theta - \cos\theta).$$
>
> You could integrate $\mathrm{e}^{-\theta}\sin\theta$ and $\mathrm{e}^{\theta}\cos\theta$ by two applications of integration by parts (see FP2 Example 10.1.5(c), where such a method was used). It turned out in that example that the result is a combination of functions of the same kind, so you would expect that
>
> $$\int \mathrm{e}^{-\theta}(2\sin\theta - \cos\theta)\,\mathrm{d}\theta = \mathrm{e}^{-\theta}(a\sin\theta + b\cos\theta).$$
>
> The quickest way to find the numbers a and b is to differentiate:
>
> $$\mathrm{e}^{-\theta}(2\sin\theta - \cos\theta) = -\mathrm{e}^{-\theta}(a\sin\theta + b\cos\theta) + \mathrm{e}^{-\theta}(a\cos\theta - b\sin\theta).$$
>
> The coefficients of $\mathrm{e}^{-\theta}\sin\theta$ and $\mathrm{e}^{-\theta}\cos\theta$ must agree, so that
>
> $$2 = -a - b \quad \text{and} \quad -1 = -b + a,$$
>
> giving
>
> $$a = -\tfrac{3}{2},\ b = -\tfrac{1}{2}.$$

The solution of the differential equation is therefore

$$we^{-\theta} = gre^{-\theta}\left(-\tfrac{3}{2}\sin\theta - \tfrac{1}{2}\cos\theta\right) + k,$$

where k is chosen so that w (that is v^2) is equal to u^2 when $\theta = 0$:

$$u^2 = -\tfrac{1}{2}gr + k, \quad \text{or} \quad k = u^2 + \tfrac{1}{2}gr.$$

Substituting back w as v^2, and rearranging,

$$v^2 = \tfrac{1}{2}gre^{\theta}\left(\frac{2u^2}{gr} - (e^{-\theta}(3\sin\theta + \cos\theta) - 1)\right).$$

This completes the solution of the differential equation. You now need to interpret it in terms of the problem to which it refers.

You might well ask what is the use of this solution. There is no great merit in knowing the speed of the object at any point along the track. What is of interest is the general form of the solution, which can be written as

$$v = Ce^{\frac{1}{2}\theta}\sqrt{A - f(\theta)},$$

where $C = \sqrt{\tfrac{1}{2}gr}$, $A = \dfrac{2u^2}{gr}$ and $f(\theta) = e^{-\theta}(3\sin\theta + \cos\theta) - 1$.

Figure 1.5 shows the graph of $f(\theta)$.

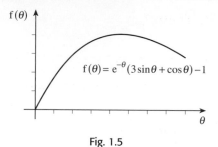

Fig. 1.5

You will see that $f(0) = 0$, and you can easily check for yourself that the maximum value occurs when $\tan\theta = \tfrac{1}{2}$, and that the maximum value is about 0.4. Thus there are two possibilities.

If $A < 0.4$, v will become zero for some value of θ less than $\tan^{-1}\tfrac{1}{2}$, after which the differential equation no longer applies. If $A > 0.4$, the expression $A - f(\theta)$ first decreases but, after $\theta = \tan^{-1}\tfrac{1}{2}$, it starts to increase. Since the other factor $e^{\frac{1}{2}\theta}$ is also increasing, v itself increases.

So, if $\dfrac{2u^2}{gr} < 0.4$, that is $u < \sqrt{0.2gr}$, the object will be brought to rest by the friction from the track at some point before $\theta = \tan^{-1}\tfrac{1}{2}$. If $u > \sqrt{0.2gr}$, it will slow down at first but will then pick up speed as gravity overcomes the force of friction.

Exercise 1B

1 Use the substitution $y = xu$ to find the general solution of the differential equation

$$(x + y)\frac{dy}{dx} = y.$$

2 Find the general solution of the differential equation $\dfrac{dy}{dx} = \dfrac{x^2 + y^2}{2xy}$ by using the substitutions

(a) $y = xu$,   (b) $y = \sqrt{v}$.

3 Find the general solution of the differential equation $x\dfrac{dy}{dx} + 2xy^2 = y$ by using the substitution $y = \dfrac{1}{u}$. Check your answer in the original equation.

4 Find the solution of the differential equation $\dfrac{dy}{dx} + \dfrac{y}{x} = \sqrt{\dfrac{y}{x}}$ for $x > 1$, given that $y = 0$ when $x = 1$, by using the substitution $y = u^2$.

5 Find the value of q such that the substitution $y = u^q$ converts the differential equation $x\dfrac{dy}{dx} + 2y = x^2 y^3$ into a linear differential equation connecting u and x. Hence find the general solution of the original equation.

6 Use the method of Question 5 to find the solution curve of the differential equation $x\dfrac{dy}{dx} - y = \dfrac{x}{y^2}$ which passes through the point $(2, 5)$.

7 Show that the differential equation $\dfrac{dy}{dx} + y = x^m y^n$, where m is a positive integer, can be solved by using the substitution $y = u^q$ where $q = -\dfrac{1}{n-1}$. Hence find the general solutions of the differential equations

(a) $\dfrac{dy}{dx} + y = x^2 y^3$,   (b) $\dfrac{dy}{dx} + y = x\sqrt{y}$.

8 A curve C has the property that, at any point P on the curve, the angle which the tangent makes with the x-axis is twice the angle which OP makes with the x-axis. Show that C satisfies the differential equation $\dfrac{dy}{dx} = \dfrac{2xy}{x^2 - y^2}$. Use the method of Example 1.4.3 to solve this equation. Identify the solution geometrically, and use a geometrical argument to show that the curve you have identified has the property described.

9 Show that one solution of $\dfrac{dy}{dx} = 1 - 2x(x - y)^2$ is $y = x$. Use the substitution $y = x + \dfrac{1}{u}$ to find the general solution.

10 The differential equation $\dfrac{dy}{dx} = 4x^2 y - y^2 + 4x(1 - x^3)$ has a solution of the form $y = ax^m$. Find the values of m and a, and then use the method of Example 1.4.4 to find the general solution. Draw graphs to illustrate the family of solution curves.

Miscellaneous exercise 1

1 Find the general solution of the differential equation $\dfrac{ds}{dt} - 3s = te^{3t}$, giving s in terms
of t. (OCR)

2 Find the general solution of the differential equation $x\dfrac{dy}{dx} + 4y = x$, giving y explicitly in
terms of x. Find also the particular solution for which $y = 1$ when $x = 1$. (OCR)

3 Find the general solution of the differential equation $\dfrac{dy}{dx} - 3x^2 y = xe^{x^3}$, giving y explicitly
in terms of x. Find also the particular solution for which $y = 1$ when $x = 0$. (OCR)

4 Find y in terms of x, given that $\dfrac{dy}{dx} + 2xy = 10e^{-x^2}$ and that $y = 20$ when $x = 0$. (OCR)

5 Find the general solution of the differential equation $\dfrac{dy}{dx} + y\cot x = x$. Find also the
particular solution for which $y = 0$ when $x = \frac{1}{2}\pi$. (OCR)

6 The general solution of the differential equation $x\dfrac{dy}{dx} + (x+1)y = 1$ is represented by a
family of curves. Find the general solution of the differential equation, and find the
equation of the particular curve which passes through the point $(1, 2)$. (OCR)

7 Given that $-1 < x < 1$, find the general solution of the differential equation
$(1 - x^2)\dfrac{dy}{dx} - xy + 1 = 0$. Find the particular solution for which $y = \frac{1}{2}\pi$ when $x = 0$. (OCR)

8 The differential equation $\dfrac{dy}{dx} + \dfrac{y}{x\ln x} = \dfrac{1}{x}$, with $y = 1$ when $x = e$, is to be solved using an
integrating factor. Find the integrating factor, and solve the differential equation. Sketch
the solution curve for $x > 1$. (MEI)

9 Use the substitution $z = x + y$ to find the general solution of the differential equation
$\dfrac{dy}{dx} = \cos(x + y)$.

10 Show that the differential equation $\dfrac{dy}{dx} = \dfrac{x^2 - y^2}{y}$ can be transformed into a linear
differential equation by means of the substitution $y = \sqrt{z}$. Hence find the general solution
of the differential equation.

11 By using the substitution $y = xu$, find the equation of the curve which passes through
$(1, 0)$ and satisfies the differential equation $\dfrac{dy}{dx} = \dfrac{2x}{x + y}$.

12 This question is about the differential equation $\dfrac{dy}{dx} = y^2 + y\cot x$.
   (a) Show that the equation is satisfied by $y = \tan x$ and by $y = \tan\frac{1}{2}x$.
   (b) Find the general solution by substituting
      (i) $y = \dfrac{1}{z}$,   (ii) $y = u\tan x$,
      where z and u are functions of x. Show that the solutions obtained by both methods
      can be expressed by the same equation.
   (c) Find the values of the arbitrary constant in your solution which give the two particular
      solutions in part (a).

13 The gradient at any point $P(x, y)$ of a curve is proportional to the sum of the coordinates of P. The curve passes through the point $(1, -2)$ and its gradient at $(1, -2)$ is -4. Find the equation of the curve. Show that the line $y = -x - \frac{1}{4}$ is an asymptote to the curve.   (OCR)

14 Water starts pouring into an empty open tank whose capacity is 1000 litres, and t seconds later the volume, V litres, of water in the tank is such that $\frac{dV}{dt} + \frac{1}{20}V = \frac{1}{4}t + 1$. Find V in terms of t, and hence show that, for large values of t, $V \approx 5t - 80$. Hence determine, to the nearest second, the value of t when the tank begins to overflow.   (OCR)

15 A car moves from rest along a straight road. After t seconds the velocity is v metres per second. The motion is modelled by $\frac{dv}{dt} + \alpha v = e^{\beta t}$, where α and β are positive constants. Find v in terms of α, β and t and show that, as long as the above model applies, the car does not come to rest.   (OCR)

16 (a) Find by trial a particular solution of the differential equation $\frac{dy}{dx} + y = x^2$ of form $y = ax^2 + bx + c$.

(b) Find the equation of the solution curve which passes through $(0, A)$.

(c) Explain why, if a solution curve has a stationary point, that point lies on $y = x^2$.

(d) Show that, if there is a point on a solution curve at which $\frac{d^2y}{dx^2} = 0$, that point lies on $y = x^2 - 2x$.

(e) Plot the graphs of $y = x^2$ and $y = x^2 - 2x$ for $-3 \leqslant x \leqslant 4$. On the same diagram, sketch the solution curve which passes through $(0, 2)$. Sketch also the solution curve which passes through $(0, 1)$, indicating clearly how it satisfies the properties established in parts (c) and (d).   (OCR, adapted)

17 Consider solutions to the differential equation $\frac{dy}{dx} + y = x$.

(a) If a solution curve has a stationary point show that the point lies on the line $y = x$.

(b) Explain why any solution curve that meets the line $y = x + 1$ cuts the line at right angles.

(c) The general solution of the differential equation has the form $y = Ae^{-x} + P(x)$, where $P(x)$ is a polynomial. Find $P(x)$.

(d) On a single diagram sketch the graphs $y = P(x)$, $y = x$, $y = x + 1$, and the solution curves through $(0, 1)$ and $(0, 0)$.

(e) Show that the solution curve through $(0, -2)$ has no stationary point, and sketch this curve.   (OCR)

18 Find the general solution of the differential equation $x\frac{dy}{dx} + 2y = \sqrt{1 + x^2}$. Find the particular solution which satisfies the condition that $y = 1$ when $x = 1$. How does y behave when x becomes very small?

Use the first three non-zero terms in the expansion of $(1 + x^2)^{\frac{3}{2}}$ to write down the power series expansion of the general solution y for small values of x up to and including the term in x^2. Hence find the particular solution of the differential equation which crosses the x-axis from the region $x > 0$ into the region $x < 0$. Is it possible to obtain other solutions of the differential equation in the region $x < 0$? Explain your answer.   (MEI)

19* Use the substitutions $Y = y^3$, $X = x^2$ to reduce the equation $3y^2 x^3 \frac{dy}{dx} + 2nx^2 y^3 = 2 \sin x^2$
to the linear equation $\frac{dY}{dX} + \frac{n}{X} Y = \frac{1}{X^2} \sin X$. Integrate this equation in the case $n = 4$. In
this case, given that Y is a solution which tends to a limit as X tends to 0, use the
Maclaurin expansions for $\sin X$ and $\cos X$ to find this limit.   (OCR)

20 The differential equation $\frac{dy}{dx} \sin x - y \cos x = e^{-kx} \sin^2 x$ $(k \geqslant 0)$ is to be solved, where k is a
constant.

(a) In the case $k > 0$, show that the general solution is $y = \left(A - \frac{1}{k} e^{-kx} \right) \sin x$, where A is
an arbitrary constant.

(b) Find the particular solution in the cases

(i) $\frac{dy}{dx} = \frac{1}{k}$ when $x = 0$,   (ii) $\frac{dy}{dx} = -\frac{1}{k}$ when $x = 0$.

Describe the differences in the behaviour of the two solutions for large positive values
of x.

(c) In the case $k = 0$, find the general solution of the equation. Describe its behaviour for
large positive values of x.   (MEI)

21 (a) A long pendulum swinging for a considerable length of time can be used to
demonstrate the rotation of the earth. In these circumstances the appropriate
equation is assumed to be $\frac{d^2\theta}{dt^2} + k \left(\frac{d\theta}{dt} \right)^2 = -G \sin\theta$, where k and G are constants
and θ is the pendulum's displacement from the downward vertical. Use the
transformations $\omega = \frac{d\theta}{dt}$, $\frac{d^2\theta}{dt^2} = \omega \frac{d\omega}{d\theta}$, $\omega^2 = E$ to reduce the equation to the linear
form $\frac{dE}{d\theta} + 2kE = -2G \sin\theta$. Solve this equation to find E in terms of θ.

(b) Successive positions of rest are $\theta = -\alpha$ and $\theta = \beta$, where $\alpha > \beta > 0$. Find an equation
relating α and β.   (OCR)

22 This question is about the solutions of the differential equation $y \frac{dy}{dx} = 3y - 2x$.

(a) Show that there are two (straight line) solutions of the form $y = kx$. Give the two
corresponding values of k.

(b) If $u = \frac{y}{x}$, find $\frac{dy}{dx}$ in terms of x, u and $\frac{du}{dx}$. Use your answer to show that u satisfies the
differential equation $-xu \frac{du}{dx} = u^2 - 3u + 2$.

(c) Use partial fractions to show that the general solution of the original differential
equation is given by $(y - 2x)^2 = a(y - x)$ where a is a constant.

(d) Find the equation of the solution curve through the point $(0, y_0)$ where $y_0 \neq 0$. Show
that all the solution curves with $y_0 > 0$ lie in a certain half-plane.

(e) Show that when a solution curve crosses the line $y = mx$ it does so with gradient $3 - \frac{2}{m}$
and use this to sketch, for $x \geqslant 0$, the solution curve through the point $(0, -1)$.   (OCR)

23 (a) Verify that $y = \dfrac{1}{x^3}$ is a solution of the differential equation $\dfrac{dy}{dx} = \dfrac{y}{x} - x^2 y^2 - \dfrac{3}{x^4}$. Find another solution of the form $y = \dfrac{\lambda}{x^3}$ where λ is a constant.

(b) Show that the substitution $y = \dfrac{1}{x^3} + \dfrac{1}{z}$ reduces the original equation to the linear differential equation $\dfrac{dz}{dx} - \dfrac{z}{x} = x^2$. Solve this equation, and hence find the general solution of the original equation.

(c) Show how the two particular solutions of part (a) arise from your general solution in part (b).

(d) For which solutions of the original equation is it possible for y to be defined for all $x > 0$? (OCR)

24* A function $y = f(x)$ satisfies the differential equation $\dfrac{dy}{dx} + 2xy = 1$, and $y = 1$ when $x = 0$.

Explain why it is not possible to find an algebraic expression for $f(x)$.

Use the differential equation to show that $f''(x) = -2f(x) - 2x f'(x)$, and differentiate this to find a similar equation for $f'''(x)$.

Use these results to find a Maclaurin polynomial of degree 3 which approximates to $f(x)$ when x is small.

Check your answer by taking the solution process as far as you can, and then using Maclaurin approximations for e^{x^2} and e^{-x^2}.

2 Lines and planes

This chapter is about using vectors to work with lines and planes in three-dimensional space. When you have completed it, you should

- understand the significance of all the symbols in the equation of a line in the form

$$\frac{x - a}{p} = \frac{y - b}{q} = \frac{z - c}{r}$$

- be able to use the equation of a plane in any of the forms $\mathbf{r} = \mathbf{a} + s\mathbf{b} + t\mathbf{c}$, $(\mathbf{r} - \mathbf{a}) \cdot \mathbf{n} = 0$ or $ax + by + cz = d$
- be able to solve problems involving lines and planes in three dimensions.

2.1 Straight lines

You know that the cartesian equation of a straight line in two dimensions has the form $ax + by = c$. In C4 Sections 4.6 and 4.7, you saw that if O is the origin, and if a line is drawn through the point A with position vector $\mathbf{a}$ in the direction of the vector $\mathbf{p}$, the position vector of any point R on the line is given by

$$\mathbf{r} = \mathbf{a} + t\mathbf{p}$$

where t is a parameter. This is illustrated in Fig. 2.1.

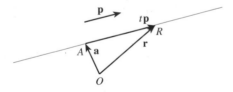

Fig. 2.1

You can think of the equation as saying 'To carry out the translation from O to R, start at O, get onto the line at A and then go in the direction of the vector $\mathbf{p}$ until you reach R' (having travelled t times the length of $\mathbf{p}$).

In the next section you will meet the cartesian equation of the line in three dimensions, but the vector form is more concise and is the one you should use if you have a choice.

> Points of a line through A in the direction of $\mathbf{p}$ have position vectors
> $\mathbf{r} = \mathbf{a} + t\mathbf{p}$, where t is a variable scalar. This is called the **vector equation** of the line.

To find the equation of the line joining two points A and B with position vectors $\mathbf{a}$ and $\mathbf{b}$, shown in Fig. 2.2, first find the direction of the line, which is given by the vector

$$\mathbf{p} = \overrightarrow{AB} = \mathbf{b} - \mathbf{a}.$$

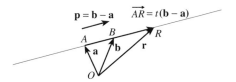

Fig. 2.2

You can then use this vector $\mathbf{p}$ in the equation $\mathbf{r} = \mathbf{a} + t\mathbf{p}$.

Example 2.1.1

Determine whether the points with coordinates $(5, 1, -6)$ and $(-7, 5, 9)$ lie on the line joining $A(1, 2, -1)$ to $B(-3, 3, 4)$.

Using the alphabet convention, C4 Section 4.4, in which O is the origin, $\mathbf{a}$ is the position vector of A, and so on, a vector in the direction of the line is

$$\overrightarrow{AB} = \mathbf{b} - \mathbf{a} = \begin{pmatrix} -3 \\ 3 \\ 4 \end{pmatrix} - \begin{pmatrix} 1 \\ 2 \\ -1 \end{pmatrix} = \begin{pmatrix} -4 \\ 1 \\ 5 \end{pmatrix}.$$

The equation of line AB is $\mathbf{r} = \begin{pmatrix} 1 \\ 2 \\ -1 \end{pmatrix} + t \begin{pmatrix} -4 \\ 1 \\ 5 \end{pmatrix}$, or $\begin{pmatrix} x \\ y \\ z \end{pmatrix} = \begin{pmatrix} 1 \\ 2 \\ -1 \end{pmatrix} + t \begin{pmatrix} -4 \\ 1 \\ 5 \end{pmatrix}.$

To find whether $(5, 1, -6)$ lies on this line, substitute $x = 5$, $y = 1$ and $z = -6$ to get the vector equation

$$\begin{pmatrix} 5 \\ 1 \\ -6 \end{pmatrix} = \begin{pmatrix} 1 \\ 2 \\ 1 \end{pmatrix} + t \begin{pmatrix} -4 \\ 1 \\ 5 \end{pmatrix}, \quad \text{or} \quad \begin{pmatrix} 4 \\ -1 \\ -5 \end{pmatrix} = t \begin{pmatrix} -4 \\ 1 \\ 5 \end{pmatrix}.$$

This vector equation is consistent with solution $t = -1$, so $(5, 1, -6)$ lies on AB.

To find whether $(-7, 5, 9)$ lies on AB, try to solve the vector equation

$$\begin{pmatrix} -7 \\ 5 \\ 9 \end{pmatrix} = \begin{pmatrix} 1 \\ 2 \\ -1 \end{pmatrix} + t \begin{pmatrix} -4 \\ 1 \\ 5 \end{pmatrix}, \quad \text{or} \quad \begin{pmatrix} -8 \\ 3 \\ 10 \end{pmatrix} = t \begin{pmatrix} -4 \\ 1 \\ 5 \end{pmatrix}.$$

You can see quickly that this vector equation is inconsistent: the first and third components give $t = 2$, while the second component gives $t = 3$. There is no value of t which satisfies all the equations, so $(-7, 5, 9)$ does not lie on AB.

Example 2.1.2

Prove that the straight line with equation $\mathbf{r} = \begin{pmatrix} 1 \\ 2 \\ -3 \end{pmatrix} + t \begin{pmatrix} 2 \\ -1 \\ 4 \end{pmatrix}$ meets the line joining

(2, 4, 4) to (3, 3, 5), and find the cosine of the angle between the lines.

The line joining (2, 4, 4) and (3, 3, 5) has direction $\begin{pmatrix} 3 \\ 3 \\ 5 \end{pmatrix} - \begin{pmatrix} 2 \\ 4 \\ 4 \end{pmatrix} = \begin{pmatrix} 1 \\ -1 \\ 1 \end{pmatrix}$ and so has

equation $\mathbf{r} = \begin{pmatrix} 2 \\ 4 \\ 4 \end{pmatrix} + s \begin{pmatrix} 1 \\ -1 \\ 1 \end{pmatrix}$.

To prove that the lines intersect, you have to show that there is a point on one line which is the same as a point on the other. Suppose that the lines meet when the parameter of the first line is t and the parameter of the second line is s. Then

$$\begin{pmatrix} 1 \\ 2 \\ -3 \end{pmatrix} + t \begin{pmatrix} 2 \\ -1 \\ 4 \end{pmatrix} = \begin{pmatrix} 2 \\ 4 \\ 4 \end{pmatrix} + s \begin{pmatrix} 1 \\ -1 \\ 1 \end{pmatrix}; \quad \text{that is,} \quad \left.\begin{array}{r} 2t - s = 1 \\ -t + s = 2 \\ 4t - s = 7 \end{array}\right\}.$$

These equations are consistent, with solution $t = 3$ and $s = 5$. Hence the lines intersect. (The point of intersection is $(7, -1, 9)$.)

The angle between the lines is the angle between their direction vectors. Calling this angle θ and using the dot product (see C4 Section 9.2),

$$\begin{pmatrix} 2 \\ -1 \\ 4 \end{pmatrix} \cdot \begin{pmatrix} 1 \\ -1 \\ 1 \end{pmatrix} = \left| \begin{pmatrix} 2 \\ -1 \\ 4 \end{pmatrix} \right| \left| \begin{pmatrix} 1 \\ -1 \\ 1 \end{pmatrix} \right| \cos\theta, \quad \text{giving} \quad \cos\theta = \frac{7}{\sqrt{21}\sqrt{3}} = \frac{\sqrt{7}}{3}.$$

2.2 Cartesian equations of a straight line

You can find the cartesian equations of a straight line by eliminating the parameter t.

For example, for the equation $\mathbf{r} = \begin{pmatrix} 1 \\ 2 \\ -3 \end{pmatrix} + t \begin{pmatrix} 2 \\ -1 \\ 4 \end{pmatrix}$ in Example 2.1.2, writing $\mathbf{r} = \begin{pmatrix} x \\ y \\ z \end{pmatrix}$ puts

the equation in the form

$$\begin{pmatrix} x \\ y \\ z \end{pmatrix} = \begin{pmatrix} 1 \\ 2 \\ -3 \end{pmatrix} + t \begin{pmatrix} 2 \\ -1 \\ 4 \end{pmatrix}, \text{ which you can rewrite as } \begin{pmatrix} x-1 \\ y-2 \\ z+3 \end{pmatrix} = t \begin{pmatrix} 2 \\ -1 \\ 4 \end{pmatrix}.$$

You can now split this vector equation into three simultaneous equations

$$x - 1 = 2t, \quad y - 2 = -t, \quad z + 3 = 4t, \quad \text{which give} \quad \frac{x-1}{2} = \frac{y-2}{-1} = \frac{z+3}{4} = t.$$

The equations $\dfrac{x-1}{2} = \dfrac{y-2}{-1} = \dfrac{z+3}{4}$, which do not involve t, are the **cartesian equations** for the line.

In general:

> Cartesian equations of the line through (a, b, c) with direction $\begin{pmatrix} l \\ m \\ n \end{pmatrix}$ are
>
> $$\frac{x-a}{l} = \frac{y-b}{m} = \frac{z-c}{n}.$$

There are two observations to make about these equations.

- There are two equations, not a single equation. You will see later that an equation of the form $ax + by + cz = d$, which you might have expected to be the equation of a line in three dimensions, is actually the equation of a plane.

- The equations of some particularly simple lines, that is those with l or m or $n = 0$, cannot be put in this form. For example, the x-axis is a line through the origin $(0, 0, 0)$ in the direction $\begin{pmatrix} 1 \\ 0 \\ 0 \end{pmatrix}$. To use the result in the shaded box you would have to write it as $\frac{x}{1} = \frac{y}{0} = \frac{z}{0}$, but you shouldn't because division by zero is impossible. (In this case, correct cartesian equations are $y = 0, z = 0$.) In practical problems you would try to organise your coordinate system so that your lines are parallel to the axes, so this could be quite a common occurrence.

You can avoid the cartesian form by turning it immediately into the vector form. For example, by putting each part of the equation equal to t, the cartesian equations

$$\frac{x-a}{l} = \frac{y-b}{m} = \frac{z-c}{n} \quad \text{become} \quad x = a + lt, \quad y = b + mt, \quad z = c + nt,$$

which are equivalent to the vector equation $\mathbf{r} = \begin{pmatrix} a \\ b \\ c \end{pmatrix} + t \begin{pmatrix} l \\ m \\ n \end{pmatrix}.$

Example 2.2.1

Change the cartesian equations $x = 2y = 3z + 1$ and $1 - x = \dfrac{3 - 2y}{4} = z$ of straight lines into vector equations.

As a first step put each of these equations equal to t, which will be the parameter.

The first set is

$$x = 2y = 3z + 1 = t,$$

which you can rearrange as the three equations

$$\left. \begin{array}{r} x = t \\ 2y = t \\ 3z + 1 = t \end{array} \right\}.$$

Solving these for x, y and z gives

$$\left. \begin{array}{l} x = t \\ y = \tfrac{1}{2}t \\ z = \tfrac{1}{3}t - \tfrac{1}{3} \end{array} \right\}, \quad \text{which is the same as} \quad \left. \begin{array}{l} x = \phantom{-\tfrac{1}{3} + {}} t \\ y = \phantom{-\tfrac{1}{3} + {}} \tfrac{1}{2}t \\ z = -\tfrac{1}{3} + \tfrac{1}{3}t \end{array} \right\}.$$

These three equations are then equivalent to

$$\begin{pmatrix} x \\ y \\ z \end{pmatrix} = \begin{pmatrix} 0 \\ 0 \\ -\tfrac{1}{3} \end{pmatrix} + t \begin{pmatrix} 1 \\ \tfrac{1}{2} \\ \tfrac{1}{3} \end{pmatrix}, \quad \text{which is the same as} \quad \mathbf{r} = \begin{pmatrix} 0 \\ 0 \\ -\tfrac{1}{3} \end{pmatrix} + t \begin{pmatrix} 1 \\ \tfrac{1}{2} \\ \tfrac{1}{3} \end{pmatrix}.$$

A similar process for the second set of equations gives

$$\left. \begin{array}{r} 1 - x = t \\ 3 - 2y = 4t \\ z = t \end{array} \right\} \quad \text{or} \quad \left. \begin{array}{l} x = 1 - t \\ y = \tfrac{3}{2} - 2t \\ z = \phantom{1 - {}} t \end{array} \right\},$$

which is equivalent to $\begin{pmatrix} x \\ y \\ z \end{pmatrix} = \begin{pmatrix} 1 \\ \tfrac{3}{2} \\ 0 \end{pmatrix} + t \begin{pmatrix} -1 \\ -2 \\ 1 \end{pmatrix}$ or $\mathbf{r} = \begin{pmatrix} 1 \\ \tfrac{3}{2} \\ 0 \end{pmatrix} + t \begin{pmatrix} -1 \\ -2 \\ 1 \end{pmatrix}.$

Example 2.2.2

Given that $(p, q, 2)$ lies on the line $\dfrac{x - 3}{2} = \dfrac{y + 1}{4} = \dfrac{z - 5}{3}$, find p and q.

In this case the vector form of the straight line has no advantage.

Substituting $(p, q, 2)$ into the equation $\dfrac{x - 3}{2} = \dfrac{y + 1}{4} = \dfrac{z - 5}{3}$ gives

$$\frac{p - 3}{2} = \frac{q + 1}{4} = \frac{2 - 5}{3},$$

which quickly results in $p = 1$, $q = -5$.

Example 2.2.3

Find the cartesian equations of the line l joining $(-1, 4, 1)$ to $(3, 6, 2)$, and find whether this line intersects the line m with cartesian equation $\dfrac{x - 1}{1} = \dfrac{y - 1}{2} = \dfrac{z - 1}{-2}$.

The direction vector of the line l is $\begin{pmatrix} 3 \\ 6 \\ 2 \end{pmatrix} - \begin{pmatrix} -1 \\ 4 \\ 1 \end{pmatrix} = \begin{pmatrix} 4 \\ 2 \\ 1 \end{pmatrix}.$

The cartesian equations of l are then $\dfrac{x + 1}{4} = \dfrac{y - 4}{2} = \dfrac{z - 1}{1}.$

To find whether l intersects m, use the vector form and replace the cartesian equations of l and m by

$$\mathbf{r} = -\mathbf{i} + 4\mathbf{j} + \mathbf{k} + t(4\mathbf{i} + 2\mathbf{j} + \mathbf{k}) \quad \text{and} \quad \mathbf{r} = \mathbf{i} + \mathbf{j} + \mathbf{k} + t(\mathbf{i} + 2\mathbf{j} - 2\mathbf{k}).$$

Suppose that l and m meet where their parameters are r and s.

Then

$$-\mathbf{i} + 4\mathbf{j} + \mathbf{k} + r(4\mathbf{i} + 2\mathbf{j} + \mathbf{k}) = \mathbf{i} + \mathbf{j} + \mathbf{k} + s(\mathbf{i} + 2\mathbf{j} - 2\mathbf{k}).$$

Equating the coefficients of $\mathbf{i}, \mathbf{j}$ and $\mathbf{k}$ gives the equations

$$
\left.\begin{aligned}
-1 + 4r &= 1 + s \\
4 + 2r &= 1 + 2s \\
1 + r &= 1 - 2s
\end{aligned}\right\}
\Leftrightarrow
\left.\begin{aligned}
4r - s &= 2 \\
2r - 2s &= -3 \\
r + 2s &= 0
\end{aligned}\right\}
\quad \text{(tidying the equations)}
$$

$$
\Leftrightarrow
\left.\begin{aligned}
r + 2s &= 0 \\
2r - 2s &= -3 \\
4r - s &= 2
\end{aligned}\right\}
\quad
\begin{aligned}
r_1' &= r_3 \\
\\
r_3' &= r_1
\end{aligned}
$$

$$
\Leftrightarrow
\left.\begin{aligned}
r + 2s &= 0 \\
- 6s &= -3 \\
- 9s &= 2
\end{aligned}\right\}
\quad
\begin{aligned}
\\
r_2' &= r_2 - 2r_1. \\
r_3' &= r_3 - 4r_1
\end{aligned}
$$

The last two equations show that the set of equations is inconsistent, so the two lines do not intersect.

Example 2.2.4
(a) Find the coordinates of N, the foot of the perpendicular from the point $P(1, 0, 4)$ to the line l with vector equation $\mathbf{r} = \begin{pmatrix} 1 \\ 4 \\ -1 \end{pmatrix} + t \begin{pmatrix} 3 \\ -1 \\ 2 \end{pmatrix}$.

(b) Find the perpendicular distance from P to l.

(c) Find the coordinates of the reflection E of P in l.

   (a) The strategy for finding N will be to find the direction vector of a line from P to any point on l, say T, and then to choose the parameter corresponding to T so that the line is perpendicular to l. See Fig. 2.3.

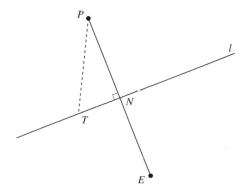

Fig. 2.3

Let T be any point on l with parameter t. Its position vector is

$$\mathbf{r} = \begin{pmatrix} 1 \\ 4 \\ -1 \end{pmatrix} + t \begin{pmatrix} 3 \\ -1 \\ 2 \end{pmatrix}.$$

Then a vector in the direction PT is

$$\left(\begin{pmatrix} 1 \\ 4 \\ -1 \end{pmatrix} + t\begin{pmatrix} 3 \\ -1 \\ 2 \end{pmatrix}\right) - \begin{pmatrix} 1 \\ 0 \\ 4 \end{pmatrix} = \begin{pmatrix} 0 \\ 4 \\ -5 \end{pmatrix} + t\begin{pmatrix} 3 \\ -1 \\ 2 \end{pmatrix}.$$

If this is perpendicular to l, then it is perpendicular to the direction vector of l,

namely, $\begin{pmatrix} 3 \\ -1 \\ 2 \end{pmatrix}$.

So $\left(\begin{pmatrix} 0 \\ 4 \\ -5 \end{pmatrix} + t\begin{pmatrix} 3 \\ -1 \\ 2 \end{pmatrix}\right) \cdot \begin{pmatrix} 3 \\ -1 \\ 2 \end{pmatrix} = 0.$

Therefore

$$(0 + 3t) \times 3 + (4 - t) \times (-1) + (-5 + 2t) \times 2 = 0,$$

giving $t = 1$.

The position vector of N is therefore $\begin{pmatrix} 1 \\ 4 \\ -1 \end{pmatrix} + 1 \times \begin{pmatrix} 3 \\ -1 \\ 2 \end{pmatrix} = \begin{pmatrix} 4 \\ 3 \\ 1 \end{pmatrix}$, so its

coordinates are $(4, 3, 1)$.

(b) The length of the perpendicular is the modulus of $\overrightarrow{PN}$.

$$\overrightarrow{PN} = \begin{pmatrix} 4 \\ 3 \\ 1 \end{pmatrix} - \begin{pmatrix} 1 \\ 0 \\ 4 \end{pmatrix} = \begin{pmatrix} 3 \\ 3 \\ -3 \end{pmatrix},$$

so

$$|\overrightarrow{PN}| = \sqrt{\begin{pmatrix} 3 \\ 3 \\ -3 \end{pmatrix} \cdot \begin{pmatrix} 3 \\ 3 \\ -3 \end{pmatrix}} = \sqrt{3^2 + 3^2 + (-3)^2} = \sqrt{27} = 3\sqrt{3}.$$

The length of the perpendicular is $3\sqrt{3}$.

(c) As $\overrightarrow{PE} = 2\overrightarrow{PN} = 2\begin{pmatrix} 3 \\ 3 \\ -3 \end{pmatrix} = \begin{pmatrix} 6 \\ 6 \\ 6 \end{pmatrix}$, E has position vector

$$\begin{pmatrix} 1 \\ 0 \\ 4 \end{pmatrix} + \begin{pmatrix} 6 \\ 6 \\ -6 \end{pmatrix} = \begin{pmatrix} 7 \\ 6 \\ -2 \end{pmatrix}.$$

So E has coordinates $(7, 6, -2)$.

Exercise 2A

1 Write down vector equations for the following straight lines which pass through the given points and lie in the given directions.

(a) $(1, 2, 3)$, $\begin{pmatrix} 0 \\ 1 \\ 2 \end{pmatrix}$ (b) $(0, 0, 0)$, $\begin{pmatrix} 0 \\ 0 \\ 1 \end{pmatrix}$ (c) $(2, -1, 1)$, $\begin{pmatrix} 3 \\ -1 \\ 1 \end{pmatrix}$ (d) $(3, 0, 2)$, $\begin{pmatrix} 4 \\ -2 \\ 3 \end{pmatrix}$

2 Find vector equations for the lines joining the following pairs of points.

(a) $(2, -1, 2)$, $(3, -1, 4)$ (b) $(1, 2, 2)$, $(2, -2, 2)$ (c) $(3, 1, 4)$, $(-1, 2, 3)$

3 Which of these equations of straight lines represent the same straight line as each other?

(a) $\mathbf{r} = \begin{pmatrix} 1 \\ 4 \\ 2 \end{pmatrix} + t\begin{pmatrix} 2 \\ -1 \\ 2 \end{pmatrix}$ (b) $\mathbf{r} = \begin{pmatrix} 3 \\ 3 \\ 4 \end{pmatrix} + t\begin{pmatrix} 2 \\ -1 \\ 2 \end{pmatrix}$

(c) $\mathbf{r} = 5\mathbf{i} + 2\mathbf{j} + 6\mathbf{k} + t(-2\mathbf{i} + \mathbf{j} - 2\mathbf{k})$ (d) $\mathbf{r} = \mathbf{i} + 4\mathbf{j} + 2\mathbf{k} + t(-2\mathbf{i} + \mathbf{j} - 2\mathbf{k})$

(e) $\mathbf{r} = -\mathbf{i} + 5\mathbf{j} + t(2\mathbf{i} - \mathbf{j} + 2\mathbf{k})$ (f) $\mathbf{r} = -\mathbf{i} + 5\mathbf{j} + t(-2\mathbf{i} + \mathbf{j} - 2\mathbf{k})$

4 Find whether or not the point $(-3, 1, 5)$ lies on the following lines.

(a) $\mathbf{r} = \begin{pmatrix} 1 \\ 3 \\ 1 \end{pmatrix} + t\begin{pmatrix} -2 \\ -1 \\ 2 \end{pmatrix}$ (b) $\mathbf{r} = \begin{pmatrix} 0 \\ 1 \\ 2 \end{pmatrix} + t\begin{pmatrix} 1 \\ 0 \\ 3 \end{pmatrix}$ (c) $\mathbf{r} = \begin{pmatrix} 1 \\ -2 \\ 4 \end{pmatrix} + t\begin{pmatrix} -4 \\ -3 \\ -1 \end{pmatrix}$

5 Determine whether the following sets of points lie on a straight line.

(a) $(1, 2, -1)$, $(2, 4, -3)$, $(4, 8, -7)$ (b) $(5, 2, -3)$, $(-1, 6, -11)$, $(3, -2, 4)$

6 Find the point of intersection, if any, of the following pairs of lines.

(a) $\mathbf{r} = \begin{pmatrix} 1 \\ 3 \\ 1 \end{pmatrix} + s\begin{pmatrix} -2 \\ -1 \\ 2 \end{pmatrix}$, $\mathbf{r} = \begin{pmatrix} 0 \\ -2 \\ 8 \end{pmatrix} + t\begin{pmatrix} 1 \\ -1 \\ 1 \end{pmatrix}$

(b) $\mathbf{r} = \begin{pmatrix} 1 \\ -1 \\ 2 \end{pmatrix} + s\begin{pmatrix} -1 \\ 2 \\ -1 \end{pmatrix}$, $\mathbf{r} = \begin{pmatrix} 1 \\ 3 \\ -1 \end{pmatrix} + t\begin{pmatrix} 2 \\ -8 \\ 5 \end{pmatrix}$

7 Find, where possible, the cartesian equations of the following lines.

(a) $\mathbf{r} = \begin{pmatrix} 2 \\ -4 \\ 1 \end{pmatrix} + t\begin{pmatrix} 1 \\ -1 \\ 2 \end{pmatrix}$ (b) $\mathbf{r} = \begin{pmatrix} 1 \\ 5 \\ 0 \end{pmatrix} + t\begin{pmatrix} 0 \\ 1 \\ -2 \end{pmatrix}$ (c) $\mathbf{r} = \begin{pmatrix} 0 \\ 0 \\ 1 \end{pmatrix} + t\begin{pmatrix} 1 \\ 3 \\ 2 \end{pmatrix}$

8 Find the point of intersection, if any, of each of the following pairs of lines.

(a) $\dfrac{x - 1}{3} = \dfrac{y - 2}{-1} = \dfrac{z + 1}{2}$ and $\dfrac{x - 3}{4} = \dfrac{y - 2}{-2} = \dfrac{z}{3}$

(b) $\dfrac{x - 2}{4} = y = \dfrac{1 - z}{2}$ and $\dfrac{x - 1}{3} = \dfrac{y - 4}{3} = z - 1$

(c) $\dfrac{1 - x}{2} = y + 1 = 2 - z$ and $\dfrac{x}{3} = y - 1 = \dfrac{z - 2}{3}$

9 Find the cosine of the acute angle between the lines with equations

$$\frac{x+3}{2} = \frac{y-4}{-2} = \frac{z-1}{-1} \quad \text{and} \quad \mathbf{r} = 3\mathbf{i} - 2\mathbf{j} + 4\mathbf{k} + t(-2\mathbf{i} + 3\mathbf{j} + 6\mathbf{k}).$$

10 P is the point $(3, 2, 1)$. Find the coordinates of the point N on the line
$$\frac{x+2}{3} = y - 1 = \frac{z-2}{2}$$ such that PN is perpendicular to the line.

11 Find the reflection of the point $(6, -4, 11)$ in the line $\mathbf{r} = \begin{pmatrix} 4 \\ -2 \\ 3 \end{pmatrix} + t\begin{pmatrix} 1 \\ 2 \\ -2 \end{pmatrix}$.

2.3 The vector equation of a plane

Suppose that you wish to replace a tile on a roof, and that you need to have some way of specifying that tile among the other tiles on the roof. You could do it by thinking in terms of the vectors $\mathbf{p}$ and $\mathbf{q}$ along the slanting edge and the horizontal edge of the roof respectively.

For instance, the tile shown in Fig. 2.4 might be the tile with vector $\frac{1}{2}\mathbf{p} + \frac{2}{3}\mathbf{q}$ relative to the point A.

However, if you wish to take the origin O at the base of the vertical from the ground to A the position vector of the tile relative to O would be $\mathbf{a} + \frac{1}{2}\mathbf{p} + \frac{2}{3}\mathbf{q}$.

You probably agree that you could specify the position of any tile on the roof by choosing the coefficients of $\mathbf{p}$ and $\mathbf{q}$ suitably.

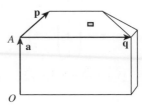

Fig. 2.4

You can generalise this thinking to define a plane.

Let O be the origin, and let A be a point with position vector $\mathbf{a}$. Let $\mathbf{p}$ and $\mathbf{q}$ be any two non-zero vectors which are not in the same or opposite directions. Then the locus of points R such that $\mathbf{r} = \mathbf{a} + s\mathbf{p} + t\mathbf{q}$, where s and t are parameters which can take any real value, is called the **plane** through A defined by $\mathbf{p}$ and $\mathbf{q}$.

Fig. 2.5 shows the plane through A in the direction defined by $\mathbf{p}$ and $\mathbf{q}$, and the point R for which $\mathbf{r} = \mathbf{a} + 2\mathbf{p} + \frac{1}{2}\mathbf{q}$, that is with parameters $s = 2$ and $t = \frac{1}{2}$.

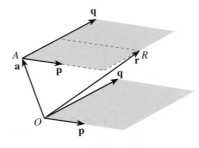

Fig. 2.5

The role of the vector $\mathbf{a}$ in this equation is quite different from the role of the vectors $\mathbf{p}$ and $\mathbf{q}$. The vector $\mathbf{a}$ is the position vector of a point on the plane; $\mathbf{p}$ and $\mathbf{q}$ are vectors which are parallel to two vectors in the plane.

> Compare this equation with the vector equation $\mathbf{r} = \mathbf{a} + t\mathbf{p}$ of a line; $\mathbf{a}$ is the position vector of a point on the line, and $\mathbf{p}$ is a vector in the direction of the line.

Notice also the important condition that $\mathbf{p}$ and $\mathbf{q}$ are non-zero vectors which are not in the same or opposite directions. If either of them was the zero vector the plane would degenerate to a line; if they were in the same or opposite directions they would not enable you to reach every point of the plane. Vectors which are in the same or opposite directions are called **parallel**. Thus for the equation $\mathbf{r} = \mathbf{a} + s\mathbf{p} + t\mathbf{q}$ to represent a plane, $\mathbf{p}$ and $\mathbf{q}$ must be non-zero, non-parallel vectors.

> Points of a plane through A with position vector $\mathbf{a}$ defined by the non-zero, non-parallel vectors $\mathbf{p}$ and $\mathbf{q}$ have position vectors $\mathbf{r} = \mathbf{a} + s\mathbf{p} + t\mathbf{q}$, where s and t are variable scalars. This is called the **vector equation of the plane**.

Example 2.3.1

Find a vector equation of the plane through the points $A(1, 1, 1)$, $B(1, -3, 2)$ and $C(1, 0, 1)$.

Two vectors whose directions are parallel to the plane are

$$\overrightarrow{AB} = \begin{pmatrix} 1 \\ -3 \\ 2 \end{pmatrix} - \begin{pmatrix} 1 \\ 1 \\ 1 \end{pmatrix} = \begin{pmatrix} 0 \\ -4 \\ 1 \end{pmatrix} \text{ and } \overrightarrow{AC} = \begin{pmatrix} 1 \\ 0 \\ 1 \end{pmatrix} - \begin{pmatrix} 1 \\ 1 \\ 1 \end{pmatrix} = \begin{pmatrix} 0 \\ -1 \\ 0 \end{pmatrix}.$$

Thus a vector equation of the plane is $\mathbf{r} = \begin{pmatrix} 1 \\ 1 \\ 1 \end{pmatrix} + s\begin{pmatrix} 0 \\ -4 \\ 1 \end{pmatrix} + t\begin{pmatrix} 0 \\ -1 \\ 0 \end{pmatrix}.$

Example 2.3.2

Find the point P where the line $\mathbf{r} = \begin{pmatrix} 2 \\ -1 \\ 2 \end{pmatrix} + k\begin{pmatrix} 4 \\ -6 \\ 1 \end{pmatrix}$ meets the plane

$$\mathbf{r} = \begin{pmatrix} 1 \\ 0 \\ -1 \end{pmatrix} + s\begin{pmatrix} 0 \\ 1 \\ 1 \end{pmatrix} + t\begin{pmatrix} 1 \\ -1 \\ 0 \end{pmatrix}.$$

Let the parameter of P on the line be k, and the parameters of P on the plane be s and t. Then

$$\begin{pmatrix} 2 \\ -1 \\ 2 \end{pmatrix} + k\begin{pmatrix} 4 \\ -6 \\ 1 \end{pmatrix} = \begin{pmatrix} 1 \\ 0 \\ -1 \end{pmatrix} + s\begin{pmatrix} 0 \\ 1 \\ 1 \end{pmatrix} + t\begin{pmatrix} 1 \\ -1 \\ 0 \end{pmatrix}, \text{ that is } \left. \begin{array}{rr} 4k \quad -t = -1 \\ -6k - s + t = \ 1 \\ k - s \ \ = -3 \end{array} \right\}.$$

Solving these equations by the usual method gives $k = -1$, $s = 2$ and $t = -3$.

As $k = -1$, the point of intersection has position vector

$$\begin{pmatrix} 2 \\ -1 \\ 2 \end{pmatrix} + (-1)\begin{pmatrix} 4 \\ -6 \\ 1 \end{pmatrix} = \begin{pmatrix} -2 \\ 5 \\ 1 \end{pmatrix}.$$

Its coordinates are therefore $(-2, 5, 1)$.

Checking by using the values of s and t shows that the point of intersection P has

position vector $\begin{pmatrix} 1 \\ 0 \\ -1 \end{pmatrix} + 2 \begin{pmatrix} 0 \\ 1 \\ 1 \end{pmatrix} + (-3) \begin{pmatrix} 1 \\ -1 \\ 0 \end{pmatrix} = \begin{pmatrix} -2 \\ 5 \\ 1 \end{pmatrix}$, as expected.

Example 2.3.3

Eliminate the parameters s and t to find a cartesian equation of the plane

$$\mathbf{r} = \begin{pmatrix} 1 \\ 2 \\ 3 \end{pmatrix} + s \begin{pmatrix} 1 \\ -1 \\ -1 \end{pmatrix} + t \begin{pmatrix} 2 \\ -1 \\ 1 \end{pmatrix}.$$

Writing this equation as $\begin{pmatrix} x \\ y \\ z \end{pmatrix} = \begin{pmatrix} 1 \\ 2 \\ 3 \end{pmatrix} + s \begin{pmatrix} 1 \\ -1 \\ -1 \end{pmatrix} + t \begin{pmatrix} 2 \\ -1 \\ 1 \end{pmatrix}$ and equating

components gives

$$x - 1 = s + 2t, \quad y - 2 = -s - t, \quad z - 3 = -s + t.$$

Adding the first two equations gives $x + y - 3 = t$, and adding the first and third equations gives $x + z - 4 = 3t$, so $3(x + y - 3) = x + z - 4$, giving $2x + 3y - z = 5$.

This suggests that planes may have linear cartesian equations.

It isn't always as easy as this to eliminate the parameters. You will see in Section 2.5 a method for finding the equation of a plane which is often quicker.

2.4 The cartesian equation of a line in two dimensions

In two dimensions, you can describe the direction of a line by a single number, its gradient. (The only exception is a line parallel to the y-axis.) Things are not so simple for a plane in three dimensions. You can't describe the direction of a line by a single number. But even in two dimensions it is simpler to describe the direction of a line by a vector rather than a gradient, as the following example shows. The second method suggests an approach which you can extend to three dimensions.

Example 2.4.1

Find the equation of the line through $(1, 2)$ perpendicular to the non-zero vector $\begin{pmatrix} l \\ m \end{pmatrix}$.

Method 1   The gradient of the given vector is $\dfrac{m}{l}$, so the required line has gradient $-\dfrac{l}{m}$. Its equation is therefore

$$y - 2 = -\frac{l}{m}(x - 1),$$

which simplifies directly to $lx + my = l + 2m$.

This method breaks down if either l or m is zero. The line in the direction of the vector $\begin{pmatrix} l \\ m \end{pmatrix}$ has gradient $\frac{m}{l}$, provided that $l \neq 0$ as in Fig. 2.6.

If $l = 0$, then the vector $\begin{pmatrix} l \\ m \end{pmatrix}$ is parallel to the y-axis. (Recall

that $\begin{pmatrix} l \\ m \end{pmatrix}$ is not the zero vector.) The line perpendicular to it is parallel to the x-axis, and is therefore $y = 2$. This is the same as $lx + my = l + 2m$ when $l = 0$.

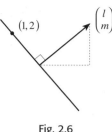

Fig. 2.6

The case when $m = 0$ is similar. The equation is still $lx + my = l + 2m$, so the required perpendicular is $lx + my = l + 2m$ in all cases.

Look at the left side of this equation. The line perpendicular to the vector $\begin{pmatrix} l \\ m \end{pmatrix}$ has an equation of the form $lx + my = k$ where k is a constant. This suggests Method 2.

Method 2   Let $\mathbf{n} = \begin{pmatrix} l \\ m \end{pmatrix}$ be the perpendicular to the line, and $\mathbf{a}$ be the position vector of $(1, 2)$. Let $\mathbf{r}$ be the position vector of any other point on the line. See Fig. 2.7.

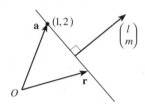

Fig. 2.7

Then $\mathbf{r} - \mathbf{a}$ is a vector in the direction of the line, and is therefore perpendicular to $\mathbf{n}$. (Recall that in general $\mathbf{p} \cdot \mathbf{q} = |\mathbf{p}||\mathbf{q}| \cos \theta$ where θ is the angle between $\mathbf{p}$ and $\mathbf{q}$. If $\mathbf{p}$ and $\mathbf{q}$ are perpendicular, so that $\cos \theta = 0$, then $\mathbf{p} \cdot \mathbf{q} = 0$.)

Therefore $(\mathbf{r} - \mathbf{a}) \cdot \mathbf{n} = 0$, or $\mathbf{r} \cdot \mathbf{n} = \mathbf{a} \cdot \mathbf{n}$.

If $\mathbf{n} = \begin{pmatrix} l \\ m \end{pmatrix}$, $\mathbf{r} = \begin{pmatrix} x \\ y \end{pmatrix}$ and $\mathbf{a} = \begin{pmatrix} 1 \\ 2 \end{pmatrix}$, then the equation $\mathbf{r} \cdot \mathbf{n} = \mathbf{a} \cdot \mathbf{n}$ becomes

$$\begin{pmatrix} x \\ y \end{pmatrix} \cdot \begin{pmatrix} l \\ m \end{pmatrix} = \begin{pmatrix} 1 \\ 2 \end{pmatrix} \cdot \begin{pmatrix} l \\ m \end{pmatrix},$$

that is

$$lx + my = l + 2m,$$

Method 2 shows what is generally the best way to find the cartesian equation of a plane.

2.5   The cartesian equation of a plane

Let $\mathbf{n}$ be a vector perpendicular to a plane, called the **normal** to the plane, and let $\mathbf{a}$ be the position vector of a point on the plane. Let $\mathbf{r}$ be the position vector of any other point on the plane, as in Fig. 2.8.

Then $\mathbf{r} - \mathbf{a}$ is a vector parallel to the plane, and is therefore perpendicular to $\mathbf{n}$. Therefore $(\mathbf{r} - \mathbf{a}) \cdot \mathbf{n} = 0$, or $\mathbf{r} \cdot \mathbf{n} = \mathbf{a} \cdot \mathbf{n}$.

This equation, $\mathbf{r} \cdot \mathbf{n} = \mathbf{a} \cdot \mathbf{n}$, is another form of the equation of a plane.

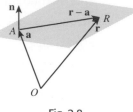

Fig. 2.8

If you write $\mathbf{r} = \begin{pmatrix} x \\ y \\ z \end{pmatrix}$ and $\mathbf{n} = \begin{pmatrix} p \\ q \\ r \end{pmatrix}$, then the equation $\mathbf{r} \cdot \mathbf{n} = \mathbf{a} \cdot \mathbf{n}$ becomes

$$px + qy + rz = \mathbf{a} \cdot \mathbf{n}.$$

This is the cartesian form of the equation of a plane. Notice that the right side is a constant, and the coefficients on the left side are the components of the normal vector. Thus, you can write down the equation of the plane directly if you know a vector normal to it and you know a point on it.

The equation of a plane can take three forms.

> Points of a plane through A defined by the non-zero, non-parallel vectors $\mathbf{p}$ and $\mathbf{q}$ have position vectors $\mathbf{r} = \mathbf{a} + s\mathbf{p} + t\mathbf{q}$, where s and t are variable scalars. This is called the **vector equation** of the plane.
>
> Points of a plane through A and perpendicular to the normal vector $\mathbf{n}$ have position vectors $\mathbf{r}$ which satisfy $\mathbf{r} \cdot \mathbf{n} = \mathbf{a} \cdot \mathbf{n}$. This is called the **normal equation** of the plane.
>
> Points of a plane through A and perpendicular to the normal vector
> $\mathbf{n} = \begin{pmatrix} p \\ q \\ r \end{pmatrix}$ have coordinates (x, y, z) which satisfy $px + qy + rz = k$ where
> k is a constant determined by the coordinates of A. This is called the **cartesian equation** of the plane.

Here are some examples which show the techniques you can use for solving problems.

Finding the cartesian equation of a plane

Example 2.5.1

Find the cartesian equation of the plane through the point $(1, 2, 3)$ with normal $\begin{pmatrix} 4 \\ 5 \\ 6 \end{pmatrix}$.

Method 1   The equation is $4x + 5y + 6z = k$, where k is a constant.

The constant has to be chosen so that the plane passes through $(1, 2, 3)$.

It is therefore $4x + 5y + 6z = 4 \times 1 + 5 \times 2 + 6 \times 3 = 32$, so the equation is $4x + 5y + 6z = 32$.

Method 2   Using the equation $\mathbf{r} \cdot \mathbf{n} = \mathbf{a} \cdot \mathbf{n}$ gives $\begin{pmatrix} x \\ y \\ z \end{pmatrix} \cdot \begin{pmatrix} 4 \\ 5 \\ 6 \end{pmatrix} = \begin{pmatrix} 1 \\ 2 \\ 3 \end{pmatrix} \cdot \begin{pmatrix} 4 \\ 5 \\ 6 \end{pmatrix}$.

This is $4x + 5y + 6z = 4 \times 1 + 5 \times 2 + 6 \times 3 = 32$, which is $4x + 5y + 6z = 32$.

Finding where a line meets a plane

Example 2.5.2

Find the coordinates of the point of intersection of the following lines with the plane $3x + 2y + 4z = 11$.

(a) $\mathbf{r} = \begin{pmatrix} 1 \\ 0 \\ 1 \end{pmatrix} + t \begin{pmatrix} 2 \\ 1 \\ -3 \end{pmatrix}$ (b) $\mathbf{r} = \begin{pmatrix} 1 \\ 0 \\ 1 \end{pmatrix} + t \begin{pmatrix} 2 \\ 1 \\ -2 \end{pmatrix}$ (c) $\mathbf{r} = \begin{pmatrix} 1 \\ 0 \\ 2 \end{pmatrix} + t \begin{pmatrix} 2 \\ 1 \\ -2 \end{pmatrix}$

All these examples start in the same way.

(a) Rewriting the line in the form $\begin{pmatrix} x \\ y \\ z \end{pmatrix} = \begin{pmatrix} 1 \\ 0 \\ 1 \end{pmatrix} + t \begin{pmatrix} 2 \\ 1 \\ -3 \end{pmatrix}$ and taking components

yields the equations $x = 1 + 2t$, $y = 0 + t$ and $z = 1 - 3t$. Substituting these into the equation of the plane gives

$$3(1 + 2t) + 2t + 4(1 - 3t) = 11, \quad \text{which gives} \quad t = -1.$$

So the line meets the plane at the point with parameter -1, namely $(-1, -1, 4)$.

(b) Rewriting the line in the form $\begin{pmatrix} x \\ y \\ z \end{pmatrix} = \begin{pmatrix} 1 \\ 0 \\ 1 \end{pmatrix} + t \begin{pmatrix} 2 \\ 1 \\ -2 \end{pmatrix}$ and taking components

yields the equations $x = 1 + 2t$, $y = 0 + t$ and $z = 1 - 2t$. Substituting these into the equation of the plane gives

$$3(1 + 2t) + 2t + 4(1 - 2t) = 11, \quad \text{which gives} \quad 7 + 0t = 11 \quad \text{or} \quad 0 = 4.$$

In this case the equations are inconsistent, so there is no solution. The line therefore does not meet the plane, so it is parallel to the plane.

(c) Rewriting the line in the form $\begin{pmatrix} x \\ y \\ z \end{pmatrix} = \begin{pmatrix} 1 \\ 0 \\ 2 \end{pmatrix} + t \begin{pmatrix} 2 \\ 1 \\ -2 \end{pmatrix}$ and taking components

yields the equations $x = 1 + 2t$, $y = t$ and $z = 2 - 2t$. Substituting these into the equation of the plane gives

$$3(1 + 2t) + 2t + 4(2 - 2t) = 11, \quad \text{which gives} \quad 11 + 0t = 11 \quad \text{or} \quad 0 = 0.$$

In this case the equations are consistent, and are satisfied by all values of t. So all

the points which satisfy the equation $\mathbf{r} = \begin{pmatrix} 1 \\ 0 \\ 2 \end{pmatrix} + t \begin{pmatrix} 2 \\ 1 \\ -2 \end{pmatrix}$ also satisfy

$3x + 2y + 4z = 11$. The line therefore lies in the plane.

Finding the perpendicular distance from a point to a plane

Examples 2.5.3 and 2.5.4 show rather similar problems tackled by very different methods. Example 2.5.3 shows how to find the length of a perpendicular from a point to a plane, and Example 2.5.4 finds both the foot of the perpendicular from the point to the plane, and the length of the perpendicular.

Example 2.5.3

Find the perpendicular distance of the point $P(4, 5, 6)$ from the plane $x + 2y - 2z = 9$.

Figure 2.9 shows P and the plane with the normal $\mathbf{n}$ given

by $\begin{pmatrix} 1 \\ 2 \\ -2 \end{pmatrix}$. Notice that you could use any multiple of $\begin{pmatrix} 1 \\ 2 \\ -2 \end{pmatrix}$.

M is the foot of the perpendicular from P, T is any point in the plane, and $\mathbf{p}$ is the vector PT. The perpendicular distance is then $PM = PT \cos \theta$, which you can find from the scalar product $\mathbf{n} \cdot \mathbf{p} = |\mathbf{n}||\mathbf{p}| \cos \theta$ by dividing by $|\mathbf{n}|$, which in this case is $\sqrt{1^2 + 2^2 + (-2)^2} = 3$.

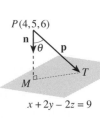

$P(4,5,6)$

$x + 2y - 2z = 9$

Fig. 2.9

A simple way to find the coordinates of a point T lying in the plane is to put $y = z = 0$, giving $x = 9$, so T is $(9, 0, 0)$.

Then $\overrightarrow{PT} = \begin{pmatrix} 9 \\ 0 \\ 0 \end{pmatrix} - \begin{pmatrix} 4 \\ 5 \\ 6 \end{pmatrix} = \begin{pmatrix} 5 \\ -5 \\ -6 \end{pmatrix}$, so $\mathbf{p} = \begin{pmatrix} 5 \\ -5 \\ -6 \end{pmatrix}$.

Finally,

$$PM = \frac{\mathbf{n} \cdot \mathbf{p}}{|\mathbf{n}|} = \frac{\begin{pmatrix} 1 \\ 2 \\ -2 \end{pmatrix} \cdot \begin{pmatrix} 5 \\ -5 \\ -6 \end{pmatrix}}{3}$$
$$= \tfrac{1}{3}(1 \times 5 + 2 \times (-5) + (-2) \times (-6))$$
$$= \tfrac{1}{3}(5 - 10 + 12)$$
$$= \tfrac{7}{3}.$$

The length of the perpendicular is $\tfrac{7}{3}$.

In this example we were lucky, because $\mathbf{n}$ was in the correct direction. If $\mathbf{n}$ had been chosen in the other direction, then $\mathbf{n} \cdot \mathbf{p}$ would have turned out negative, and you would have to take the modulus. Example 2.5.5 shows this.

This result turns out to be extremely easy to generalise. See Exercise 2B Question 12.

Example 2.5.4

(a) Find the coordinates of the foot of the perpendicular from the point (4, 5, 6) to the plane $x + 2y - 2z = 9$.

(b) Find the length of this perpendicular.

(a) The normal to the plane $x + 2y - 2z = 9$ has direction $\begin{pmatrix} 1 \\ 2 \\ -2 \end{pmatrix}$, and so the line

through (4, 5, 6) perpendicular to the plane has equation $\mathbf{r} = \begin{pmatrix} 4 \\ 5 \\ 6 \end{pmatrix} + t \begin{pmatrix} 1 \\ 2 \\ -2 \end{pmatrix}$.

This meets the plane $x + 2y - 2z = 9$ where $(4 + t) + 2(5 + 2t) - 2(6 - 2t) = 9$, that is where $9t = 7$, or $t = \frac{7}{9}$.

The position vector of the point of intersection is $\begin{pmatrix} 4 \\ 5 \\ 6 \end{pmatrix} + \frac{7}{9} \begin{pmatrix} 1 \\ 2 \\ -2 \end{pmatrix} = \begin{pmatrix} \frac{43}{9} \\ \frac{59}{9} \\ \frac{40}{9} \end{pmatrix}$. The

coordinates of the foot of the perpendicular are $\left(\frac{43}{9}, \frac{59}{9}, \frac{40}{9} \right)$.

(b) You could find the distance of this point from (4, 5, 6) by using the distance formula, but there is a quicker way.

The length of the vector from (4, 5, 6) to the plane is $\frac{7}{9}$ of the length of the vector

$\begin{pmatrix} 1 \\ 2 \\ -2 \end{pmatrix}$, which is $\sqrt{1^2 + 2^2 + (-2)^2} = 3$. So the perpendicular distance is $\frac{7}{9} \times 3 = \frac{7}{3}$.

Finding the angle between a line and a plane

Example 2.5.5

Find the acute angle between the line $\dfrac{x - 1}{2} = \dfrac{y - 3}{4} = \dfrac{z - 5}{1}$ and the plane $x - y + z = 0$.

As shown in Fig. 2.10, take $\mathbf{n}$ to be a vector normal to the plane, and $\mathbf{p}$ a vector along the line. You can find the angle θ from the dot product $\mathbf{n} \cdot \mathbf{p}$, and the angle between the line and the plane is then $\frac{1}{2}\pi - \theta$.

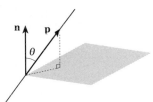

Fig. 2.10

Writing $\dfrac{x - 1}{2} = \dfrac{y - 3}{4} = \dfrac{z - 5}{1} = t$ shows that the line

has direction vector $\begin{pmatrix} 2 \\ 4 \\ 1 \end{pmatrix}$. The normal to the plane

is $\begin{pmatrix} 1 \\ -1 \\ 1 \end{pmatrix}$. So the angle θ between $\mathbf{n}$ and $\mathbf{p}$ is given by

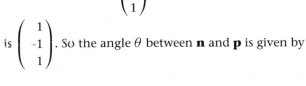

Then, $\cos\theta = \dfrac{-1}{\sqrt{21}\sqrt{3}} = -\dfrac{1}{3\sqrt{7}}$.

There is a problem. Since $\cos\theta$ is negative, the angle θ is obtuse, so Fig. 2.10 can't be a good representation of the situation. The relation between $\mathbf{p}$ and $\mathbf{n}$ is correctly shown in Fig. 2.11.

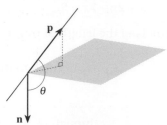

Fig. 2.11

The required angle is $\theta - \tfrac{1}{2}\pi$, which is

$$\cos^{-1}\left(-\dfrac{1}{3\sqrt{7}}\right) - \tfrac{1}{2}\pi = \left(\pi - \cos^{-1}\dfrac{1}{3\sqrt{7}}\right) - \tfrac{1}{2}\pi$$

$$= \tfrac{1}{2}\pi - \cos^{-1}\dfrac{1}{3\sqrt{7}}$$

$$= \sin^{-1}\dfrac{1}{3\sqrt{7}}.$$

Finding the cartesian equation of a plane through three points

Example 2.5.6

Find the cartesian equation of the plane through $A(1, 2, 1)$, $B(2, -1, -4)$ and $C(1, 0, -1)$.

You can tackle this problem in several ways. You could say that the equation is of the form $ax + by + cz = d$, substitute the coordinates of the points and solve the resulting equations for a, b, c and d.

You could say that $\overrightarrow{AB} = \begin{pmatrix} 2 \\ -1 \\ -4 \end{pmatrix} - \begin{pmatrix} 1 \\ 2 \\ 1 \end{pmatrix} = \begin{pmatrix} 1 \\ -3 \\ -5 \end{pmatrix}$ and $\overrightarrow{AC} = \begin{pmatrix} 1 \\ 0 \\ -1 \end{pmatrix} - \begin{pmatrix} 1 \\ 2 \\ 1 \end{pmatrix} = \begin{pmatrix} 0 \\ -2 \\ -2 \end{pmatrix}$

lie in the plane, so the vector equation of the plane is $\mathbf{r} = \begin{pmatrix} 1 \\ 2 \\ 1 \end{pmatrix} + s\begin{pmatrix} 1 \\ -3 \\ -5 \end{pmatrix} + t\begin{pmatrix} 0 \\ -2 \\ -2 \end{pmatrix}$.

You could then eliminate the parameters s and t to find the cartesian equation.

Here is a third method which involves finding the normal to the plane.

Let $\begin{pmatrix} p \\ q \\ r \end{pmatrix}$ be normal to the plane. As $\begin{pmatrix} 1 \\ -3 \\ -5 \end{pmatrix}$ and $\begin{pmatrix} 0 \\ -2 \\ -2 \end{pmatrix}$ are vectors parallel to the

plane, they are perpendicular to the normal, so both products $\begin{pmatrix} 1 \\ -3 \\ -5 \end{pmatrix} \cdot \begin{pmatrix} p \\ q \\ r \end{pmatrix}$ and

$\begin{pmatrix} 0 \\ -2 \\ -2 \end{pmatrix} \cdot \begin{pmatrix} p \\ q \\ r \end{pmatrix}$ are zero.

Therefore $\left.\begin{array}{r} p - 3q - 5r = 0 \\ -2q - 2r = 0 \end{array}\right\}$, or $\left.\begin{array}{r} p - 3q - 5r = 0 \\ q + r = 0 \end{array}\right\}$. Using the method of
FP1 Chapter 1 put $r = t$, then $q = -t$ and, substituting in the first equation, $p = 2t$.

Thus $\begin{pmatrix} p \\ q \\ r \end{pmatrix} = \begin{pmatrix} 2t \\ -t \\ t \end{pmatrix} = t \begin{pmatrix} 2 \\ -1 \\ 1 \end{pmatrix}$ is normal to the plane for all t, except $t = 0$. Since

you need only one normal, put $t = 1$, giving $\begin{pmatrix} 2 \\ -1 \\ 1 \end{pmatrix}$ as the normal to the plane.

Therefore the equation is $2x - y + z = k$, and since $(1, 2, 1)$ lies on the plane, the
equation is $2x - y + z = 2 \times 1 - 1 \times 2 + 1 \times 1 = 1$, or $2x - y + z = 1$.

It is good practice to verify that the other points also lie on this plane.

Note that another, more efficient, method is given in Chapter 4.

Finding the angle between two planes

Example 2.5.7
A pyramid of height 3 units stands symmetrically on a rectangular base $ABCD$ with
$AB = 2$ units and $BC = 4$ units. Find the angle between two adjacent slanting faces.

You could solve this problem by trigonometrical methods, but it is useful to see
how you can use vector methods. The strategy is to find the angle between the
planes by finding the angle between the normals to the planes.

Let V be the vertex. Take the origin at the centre of the base, and the x- and y-axes
parallel to CB and AB, as in Fig. 2.12.

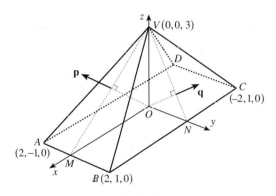

Fig. 2.12

Then the coordinates of A, B, C and V are respectively $(2, -1, 0)$, $(2, 1, 0)$, $(-2, 1, 0)$
and $(0, 0, 3)$.

The normal vector **p** to the face VAB is in the direction of the perpendicular from O to VM, where M is the mid-point of AB with coordinates $(2, 0, 0)$. By symmetry, **p** has no y-component, and it is perpendicular to $\overrightarrow{MV} = \begin{pmatrix} 0 \\ 0 \\ 3 \end{pmatrix} - \begin{pmatrix} 2 \\ 0 \\ 0 \end{pmatrix} = \begin{pmatrix} -2 \\ 0 \\ 3 \end{pmatrix}$, so **p** can be taken as $\begin{pmatrix} 3 \\ 0 \\ 2 \end{pmatrix}$.

Similarly the normal vector **q** to the face VBC has no x-component and is perpendicular to $\overrightarrow{NV} = \begin{pmatrix} 0 \\ -1 \\ 3 \end{pmatrix}$, so take $\mathbf{q} = \begin{pmatrix} 0 \\ 3 \\ 1 \end{pmatrix}$.

Let the angle between **p** and **q** be θ. Then

$$\left| \begin{pmatrix} 3 \\ 0 \\ 2 \end{pmatrix} \right| \left| \begin{pmatrix} 0 \\ 3 \\ 1 \end{pmatrix} \right| \cos\theta = \begin{pmatrix} 3 \\ 0 \\ 2 \end{pmatrix} \cdot \begin{pmatrix} 0 \\ 3 \\ 1 \end{pmatrix}$$

so $\quad \cos\theta = \dfrac{2}{\sqrt{13}\sqrt{10}} = \dfrac{2}{\sqrt{130}} \quad$ and $\quad \theta \approx 79.9°$.

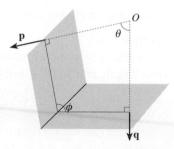

Figure 2.13 illustrates the relation between the angle θ between **p** and **q**, and the angle ϕ between the faces of the pyramid, as viewed from inside the pyramid. This shows that $\phi = 180° - \theta \approx 100.1°$.

The faces of the pyramid are therefore at $100.1°$ to each other.

Fig. 2.13

2.6   Interpreting simultaneous equations geometrically

In FP1 Chapter 1 you saw how to solve simultaneous equations with three unknowns. The first case was in FP1 Example 1.4.1, where the equation $x + 2y + 3z = 6$ had the solution, expressed in vector form,

$$\begin{pmatrix} x \\ y \\ z \end{pmatrix} = \begin{pmatrix} 6 - 2s - 3t \\ s \\ t \end{pmatrix} = \begin{pmatrix} 6 \\ 0 \\ 0 \end{pmatrix} + s \begin{pmatrix} -2 \\ 1 \\ 0 \end{pmatrix} + t \begin{pmatrix} -3 \\ 0 \\ 1 \end{pmatrix}.$$

You are now in a position to interpret $x + 2y + 3z = 6$ as the cartesian equation of a plane, and the solution of the equation as the vector form of the equation of a plane.

Two planes meet in a line   In FP1 Example 1.4.2, the vector form of the solution of the equations $\left. \begin{array}{l} x + 2y + 3z = 6 \\ 2x + 3y + z = 7 \end{array} \right\}$ was $\begin{pmatrix} x \\ y \\ z \end{pmatrix} = \begin{pmatrix} -4 + 7t \\ 5 - 5t \\ t \end{pmatrix} = \begin{pmatrix} -4 \\ 5 \\ 0 \end{pmatrix} + t \begin{pmatrix} -7 \\ -5 \\ 1 \end{pmatrix}.$

Thus two planes whose cartesian equations are given generally meet in the line whose vector equation is the solution to the equations.

Note that the planes could be parallel.

Three planes meet in a point   In FP1 Example 1.2.3, the equations

$$\left.\begin{array}{r} 2x + y - z = 2 \\ x - 2y + 3z = 7 \\ 3x + 5y - z = 0 \end{array}\right\}$$

had the solution $x = 2$, $y = -1$, $z = 1$. This corresponds to the general situation where the three planes meet in a point.

Three planes form a prism   However, in FP1 Example 1.4.3, the equations

$$\left.\begin{array}{r} x - y + z = 2 \\ 2x + 3y - z = 4 \\ 3x + 7y - 3z = 5 \end{array}\right\}$$

were inconsistent, and there was no solution. This corresponds to the case where the three planes whose cartesian equations are given form a **prism**, as shown in Fig. 2.14.

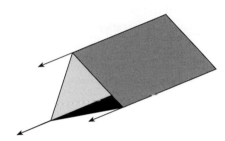

Fig. 2.14

You can check that the planes corresponding to the first two equations meet in the line

$$\begin{pmatrix} x \\ y \\ z \end{pmatrix} = \begin{pmatrix} 2 \\ 0 \\ 0 \end{pmatrix} + t \begin{pmatrix} -2 \\ 3 \\ 5 \end{pmatrix}.$$

The planes corresponding to the first and third equations and those corresponding to the second and third equations meet in the lines

$$\begin{pmatrix} x \\ y \\ z \end{pmatrix} = \begin{pmatrix} 1.5 \\ 0.5 \\ 1 \end{pmatrix} + t \begin{pmatrix} -2 \\ 3 \\ 5 \end{pmatrix} \quad \text{and} \quad \begin{pmatrix} x \\ y \\ z \end{pmatrix} = \begin{pmatrix} 1 \\ 2 \\ 4 \end{pmatrix} + t \begin{pmatrix} -2 \\ 3 \\ 5 \end{pmatrix}.$$

You can see that the three lines are parallel, all having the direction $\begin{pmatrix} -2 \\ 3 \\ 5 \end{pmatrix}$.

Three planes form a sheaf   The equations in FP1 Example 1.4.4,

$$\left.\begin{array}{c} x - y + z = 2 \\ 2x + 3y - z = 4 \\ 3x + 7y - 3z = 6 \end{array}\right\}, \quad \text{had the solution} \quad \begin{pmatrix} x \\ y \\ z \end{pmatrix} = \begin{pmatrix} 2 \\ 0 \\ 0 \end{pmatrix} + t \begin{pmatrix} -2 \\ 3 \\ 5 \end{pmatrix}.$$

This corresponds to the case where the three planes with the given equations meet in a line, forming a **sheaf**, as in Fig. 2.15.

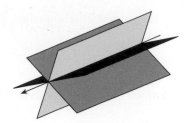

Fig. 2.15

There are other cases of inconsistency, such as when two of the planes are parallel and the third is not parallel to them, and also when all three planes are parallel. These cases are left for you to interpret, and to draw your own pictures.

Exercise 2B

1 For each part, find the vector equation of the plane through the given points. Keep your answers for use in Question 10.

(a) $(1, 0, 0)$, $(0, 0, 0)$, $(0, 1, 0)$

(b) $(1, -1, 0)$, $(0, 1, -1)$, $(-1, 0, 1)$

(c) $(1, 2, 3)$, $(2, -1, 2)$, $(3, 1, -1)$

(d) $(4, -1, 2)$, $(0, 0, 3)$, $(-1, 2, 0)$

2 Express the following lines, which are given in cartesian form, in vector form.

(a) $\dfrac{x-1}{2} = \dfrac{y+3}{4} = z$

(b) $\dfrac{2x-1}{-2} = \dfrac{3y}{7} = 5z$

(c) $2x = 3y = 4z$

3 Where possible, express the following lines, which are given in vector form, in cartesian form.

(a) $\mathbf{r} = \mathbf{i} - 2\mathbf{k} + t(\mathbf{i} - 2\mathbf{j} - \mathbf{k})$

(b) $\mathbf{r} = 3\mathbf{j} + t(\mathbf{i} - \mathbf{k})$

(c) $\mathbf{r} = \mathbf{k} + t(2\mathbf{i} + 3\mathbf{k})$

4 For each part, find the coordinates of the point where the given line meets the given plane.

(a) $\mathbf{r} = \begin{pmatrix} -2 \\ 7 \\ 0 \end{pmatrix} + r \begin{pmatrix} -1 \\ 1 \\ 1 \end{pmatrix}$, $\quad \mathbf{r} = \begin{pmatrix} 1 \\ 2 \\ -1 \end{pmatrix} + s \begin{pmatrix} 1 \\ 0 \\ 2 \end{pmatrix} + t \begin{pmatrix} 1 \\ 2 \\ 0 \end{pmatrix}$

(b) $\mathbf{r} = \begin{pmatrix} -1 \\ -7 \\ 8 \end{pmatrix} + r \begin{pmatrix} 4 \\ 2 \\ -2 \end{pmatrix}$, $\quad \mathbf{r} = \begin{pmatrix} 4 \\ 1 \\ -1 \end{pmatrix} + s \begin{pmatrix} 2 \\ -1 \\ 3 \end{pmatrix} + t \begin{pmatrix} -1 \\ 0 \\ 1 \end{pmatrix}$

(c) $\mathbf{r} = \begin{pmatrix} 5 \\ -8 \\ -5 \end{pmatrix} + r \begin{pmatrix} 1 \\ 2 \\ -1 \end{pmatrix}$, $\quad \mathbf{r} = \begin{pmatrix} 1 \\ 0 \\ -3 \end{pmatrix} + s \begin{pmatrix} -1 \\ 1 \\ 0 \end{pmatrix} + t \begin{pmatrix} 0 \\ 1 \\ -1 \end{pmatrix}$

5 Find the coordinates of the point where the line through the origin and $(1, 1, 1)$ meets the plane through the points $(-1, 1, -2)$, $(1, 5, -5)$ and $(0, 2, -3)$.

6 Find the cartesian equation of the plane through $(1, 1, 1)$ normal to the vector $\begin{pmatrix} 5 \\ -8 \\ 4 \end{pmatrix}$.

7 Find the cartesian equation of the plane through $(2, -1, 1)$ normal to the vector $2\mathbf{i} - \mathbf{j} - \mathbf{k}$.

8 Find a vector perpendicular to both $\mathbf{i} + 2\mathbf{j} - \mathbf{k}$ and $3\mathbf{i} - \mathbf{j} + \mathbf{k}$. Hence find the cartesian equation of the plane parallel to both $\mathbf{i} + 2\mathbf{j} - \mathbf{k}$ and $3\mathbf{i} - \mathbf{j} + \mathbf{k}$ and which passes through the point $(2, 0, -3)$.

9 Find the cartesian equation of the plane with vector equation

$$\mathbf{r} = \begin{pmatrix} 1 \\ -1 \\ -3 \end{pmatrix} + s \begin{pmatrix} -1 \\ 1 \\ 0 \end{pmatrix} + t \begin{pmatrix} 0 \\ 1 \\ -1 \end{pmatrix}.$$

10 Find the cartesian equations of the planes in Question 1.

11 Find the coordinates of two points A and B on the plane $2x + 3y + 4z = 4$. Verify that the vector $\overrightarrow{AB}$ is perpendicular to the normal to the plane.

12 Use the method of Example 2.5.3 to show that the length of the perpendicular from the point (X, Y, Z) to the plane $ax + by + cz = d$ is $\left| \dfrac{aX + bY + cZ - d}{\sqrt{a^2 + b^2 + c^2}} \right|$.

   (a) Use this to verify the result in Example 2.5.3.

   (b) Find the distance of $(6, 2, 4)$ from $3x + 12y - 4z = 13$.

13 Find the coordinates of the foot of the perpendicular from the point $(2, -3, 6)$ to the plane $2x - 3y + 6z = 0$. Hence find the perpendicular distance of the point from the plane.

14 Find the perpendicular distance of the point $(3, 1, -2)$ from the plane $2x + y - 2z = 8$.

15 Verify that the line with equation $\mathbf{r} = 2\mathbf{i} + 4\mathbf{j} + \mathbf{k} + t(-4\mathbf{i} + 4\mathbf{j} + 5\mathbf{k})$ lies wholly in the plane with equation $3x - 2y + 4z = 2$.

16 Find the equation of the plane through $(1, 2, -1)$ parallel to the plane $5x + y + 7z = 20$.

17 Find the equation of the line through $(4, 2, -1)$ perpendicular to the plane $3x + 4y - z = 1$.

18 A cave has a planar roof passing through the points $(0, 0, -19)$, $(5, 0, -20)$ and $(0, 5, -22)$. A tunnel is being bored through the rock from the point $(0, 3, 4)$ in the direction $-\mathbf{i} + 2\mathbf{j} - 20\mathbf{k}$. Find in degrees, correct to the nearest degree, the angle between the tunnel and the cave roof.

Miscellaneous exercise 2

1 Prove that the lines with equations $\dfrac{x-2}{3} = \dfrac{-2-y}{3} = z+2$ and $-x = y = -z$ intersect, and find the coordinates of their point of intersection.

2 Find whether the point $(0, 3, 4)$ lies on the line which passes through $(2, 1, -3)$ and $(1, 2, 6)$.

3 Find the acute angle between the lines with equations $\mathbf{r} = \begin{pmatrix} 4 \\ 1 \\ 3 \end{pmatrix} + s \begin{pmatrix} 1 \\ 1 \\ 1 \end{pmatrix}$ and

$\mathbf{r} = \begin{pmatrix} 2 \\ 2 \\ 7 \end{pmatrix} + t \begin{pmatrix} 1 \\ -1 \\ -2 \end{pmatrix}$.

4 Find the cartesian equation of the plane through $(1, 3, -7)$, $(2, -5, -3)$ and $(-5, 7, 2)$.

5 Two planes with equations $\mathbf{r} \cdot \begin{pmatrix} 3 \\ 1 \\ 1 \end{pmatrix} = 2$ and $\mathbf{r} \cdot \begin{pmatrix} 2 \\ 5 \\ -1 \end{pmatrix} = 15$ intersect in the line L.

   (a) Find a direction for the line L.

   (b) Show that the point $(1, 2, -3)$ lies in both planes, and write down a vector equation for the line L.   (OCR)

6 Two planes, $\varPi_1$ and $\varPi_2$, are defined by the equations $x + 2y + z = 4$ and $2x - 3y = 6$ respectively.

   (a) Find the acute angle between $\varPi_1$ and $\varPi_2$.

   (b) The planes $\varPi_1$ and $\varPi_2$ intersect in the line l. Find a vector equation of l.

7 Determine the value of the constant k for which the system of equations

$$\left. \begin{array}{rcrcrcr} 2x & - & y & - & z & = & 3 \\ -4x & + & 7y & + & 3z & = & -5 \\ kx & + & y & - & z & = & 5 \end{array} \right\}$$

   does not have a unique solution. For this value of k, determine the complete solution to this system. Interpret this solution geometrically.   (OCR)

8 The straight line L_1 with vector equation $\mathbf{r} = \mathbf{a} + l\mathbf{b}$ cuts the plane $2x - 3y + z = 6$ at right angles, at the point $(5, 1, -1)$.

   (a) Explain why suitable choices for $\mathbf{a}$ and $\mathbf{b}$ would be $\mathbf{a} = 5\mathbf{i} + \mathbf{j} - \mathbf{k}$ and $\mathbf{b} = 2\mathbf{i} - 3\mathbf{j} + \mathbf{k}$.

   Another straight line, L_2, has vector equation $\mathbf{r} = s(\mathbf{i} + 3\mathbf{j} + 2\mathbf{k})$.

   (b) (i) Find the angle between the directions of L_1 and L_2, giving your answer to the nearest degree.

   (ii) Verify that L_2 cuts the plane $2x - 3y + z = 6$ at the point $(-1.2, -3.6, -2.4)$.

   (iii) Prove that L_1 and L_2 do not meet.   (OCR)

9 The line l_1 passes through the point P with position vector $2\mathbf{i} + \mathbf{j} - \mathbf{k}$ and has direction vector $\mathbf{i} - \mathbf{j}$. The line l_2 passes through the point Q with position vector $5\mathbf{i} - 2\mathbf{j} - \mathbf{k}$ and has direction vector $\mathbf{j} + 2\mathbf{k}$.

(a) Write down equations for l_1 and l_2 in the form $\mathbf{r} = \mathbf{a} + t\mathbf{b}$.

(b) Show that Q lies on l_1.

(c) Find either the acute angle or the obtuse angle between l_1 and l_2.

(d) Show that the vector $\mathbf{n} = 2\mathbf{i} + 2\mathbf{j} - \mathbf{k}$ is perpendicular to both l_1 and l_2.

(e) Find the cartesian equation for the plane containing l_1 and l_2. (OCR)

10 The line l has equation $\mathbf{r} = 2\mathbf{i} + 5\mathbf{j} - 3\mathbf{k} + \lambda(5\mathbf{i} - 2\mathbf{j} - 4\mathbf{k})$ and the plane Π has equation $\mathbf{r} \cdot (5\mathbf{i} + \mathbf{j} + 2\mathbf{k}) + 6 = 0$. Find

(a) the angle between l and Π, correct to the nearest degree.

(b) the position vector of the point of intersection of l and Π.

(c) the exact value of the perpendicular distance from the point with position vector $2\mathbf{i} + 5\mathbf{j} - 3\mathbf{k}$ to Π. (OCR)

11 The line l has equation $\mathbf{r} = \mathbf{i} + \mathbf{k} + t(\mathbf{i} + 2\mathbf{j})$ and the plane P has equation $x + y - z = 6$.

(a) Find the coordinates of the point of intersection of l and P.

(b) The perpendicular from $(1, 0, 1)$ meets P at A. Show that the coordinates of A are $(3, 2, -1)$.

(c) Write down the coordinates of the reflection of the point $(1, 0, 1)$ in P.

(d) Find the equation of the reflection of the line l in P. (OCR)

12 Find the value of a for which the simultaneous equations

$$3x + 2y - z = 10,$$
$$5x - y - 4z = 17,$$
$$x + 5y + az = b,$$

do not have a unique solution for x, y and z.

Show that, for this value of a, the equations are inconsistent unless $b = 3$.

For the case where the equations represent three planes having a common line of intersection, L, find equations for L giving your answer in the form

$$\frac{x - p}{l} = \frac{y - q}{m} = \frac{z - r}{n}.$$ (OCR)

3 Linear differential equations

This chapter shows how to solve linear differential equations of first and second order, concentrating on those with constant coefficients. When you have completed it, you should

- recognise linear first and second order differential equations
- know that the solution is of the form particular integral plus complementary function
- know how to find the complementary function for an equation with constant coefficients when the auxiliary equation has real roots, which may be repeated
- know how to find particular integrals by trial with undetermined coefficients.

3.1 Second order differential equations

All the differential equations you have met so far involved only $\frac{dy}{dx}$, x and y. But mathematical models for many practical situations are expressed by differential equations which also bring in $\frac{d^2y}{dx^2}$. These are called **second order** differential equations.

Example 3.1.1

At the start of one year the population of rabbits on an island is 5000, and is increasing at a rate of 300 per month. The variation in the rate of increase (or decrease) depends on the current population, according to the law $\frac{d^2P}{dt^2} = 50 - 0.01P$. Verify that this situation is described by the equation $P = 5000 + 3000 \sin 0.1t$, where t is the time in months after the start of the year, and interpret this equation.

From the given equation for P,

$$\frac{dP}{dt} = 300 \cos 0.1t \quad \text{and} \quad \frac{d^2P}{dt^2} = -30 \sin 0.1t.$$

There are three things to check.

- When $t = 0$, $P = 5000$. That is, the population is 5000 at the start of the year.
- When $t = 0$, $\frac{dP}{dt} = 300$. That is, the population is increasing at a rate of 300 per month at the start of the year.
- For general t, the expression for $\frac{d^2P}{dt^2}$ can be written as

$$\frac{d^2P}{dt^2} = -0.01 \times 3000 \sin 0.1t = -0.01(P - 5000) = 50 - 0.01P.$$

That is, P satisfies the given second order differential equation.

The equation shows that, over a period of several years, the population varies from a maximum of 8000 rabbits to a minimum of 2000. The complete cycle takes place over a period of $\frac{2\pi}{0.1}$ months, that is about $5\frac{1}{4}$ years.

Notice that in this example there are two initial conditions to check: the values of P and of $\dfrac{dP}{dt}$ when $t = 0$. This is typical of second order differential equations. The general solution usually contains two arbitrary constants, so two conditions are needed to find them.

The next example illustrates how an equation with two arbitrary constants can be associated with a second order differential equation.

Example 3.1.2

Find a differential equation satisfied by $y = Ax^2 + B\sqrt{x}$ for all values of A and B.

Method 1 To get a differential equation which doesn't involve A or B, you need to eliminate the two constants. This requires three equations, of which one is given. You can get two more by finding $\dfrac{dy}{dx}$ and $\dfrac{d^2y}{dx^2}$.

If $\qquad y = Ax^2 + Bx^{\frac{1}{2}},$

then $\qquad \dfrac{dy}{dx} = 2Ax + \tfrac{1}{2}Bx^{-\frac{1}{2}}$

and $\qquad \dfrac{d^2y}{dx^2} = 2A - \tfrac{1}{4}Bx^{-\frac{3}{2}}.$

A and B can be eliminated by using a method similar to that for solving linear equations. Begin by eliminating B by combining the first and second equations, and the second and third equations.

$$y - 2x\dfrac{dy}{dx} = A(x^2 - 4x^2) + B(x^{\frac{1}{2}} - x^{\frac{1}{2}}) = -3Ax^2,$$

$$\dfrac{dy}{dx} + 2x\dfrac{d^2y}{dx^2} = A(2x + 4x) + B(\tfrac{1}{2}x^{-\frac{1}{2}} - \tfrac{1}{2}x^{-\frac{1}{2}}) = 6Ax.$$

You can now eliminate A between these two equations.

$$2\left(y - 2x\dfrac{dy}{dx}\right) + x\left(\dfrac{dy}{dx} + 2x\dfrac{d^2y}{dx^2}\right) = A(-6x^2 + 6x^2) = 0.$$

This can be rearranged to give the differential equation

$$2x^2\dfrac{d^2y}{dx^2} - 3x\dfrac{dy}{dx} + 2y = 0.$$

Method 2 With this method the elimination is simpler, but the differentiation is more complicated.

If you rewrite an equation so that one of the terms is simply a constant, then this will disappear when you differentiate. So begin by writing

$$y = Ax^2 + Bx^{\frac{1}{2}} \quad \text{as} \quad x^{-\frac{1}{2}}y = Ax^{\frac{3}{2}} + B.$$

Then differentiate (using the product rule for the term on the left) to get

$$-\tfrac{1}{2}x^{-\frac{3}{2}}y + x^{-\frac{1}{2}}\dfrac{dy}{dx} = \tfrac{3}{2}Ax^{\frac{1}{2}}.$$

The constant B has disappeared.

Now divide this equation by $x^{\frac{1}{2}}$, to give

$$-\tfrac{1}{2}x^{-2}y + x^{-1}\frac{dy}{dx} = \tfrac{3}{2}A.$$

When you differentiate this, you get

$$\left(x^{-3}y - \tfrac{1}{2}x^{-2}\frac{dy}{dx}\right) + \left(-x^{-2}\frac{dy}{dx} + x^{-1}\frac{d^2y}{dx^2}\right) = 0.$$

Now the constant A has also disappeared.

Finally, multiplying by $2x^3$ and rearranging,

$$2x^2\frac{d^2y}{dx^2} - 3x\frac{dy}{dx} + 2y = 0.$$

But of course, this example is the reverse of the problem that you usually want to solve, which is how to get from the differential equation $2x^2\dfrac{d^2y}{dx^2} - 3x\dfrac{dy}{dx} + 2y = 0$ to the equation $y = Ax^2 + B\sqrt{x}$ with two arbitrary constants. The rest of this chapter shows how to do this for a particular kind of second order differential equation.

3.2   Linear differential equations

The first order differential equations described as 'linear' in Chapter 1 are those in which $\dfrac{dy}{dx}$ and y appear only to the first degree. After dividing through by the coefficient of $\dfrac{dy}{dx}$, they can be described by the general form

$$\frac{dy}{dx} + y\,p(x) = q(x).$$

The notion of linearity extends to differential equations of second order, and the general form is then

$$\frac{d^2y}{dx^2} + \frac{dy}{dx}p(x) + y\,r(x) = q(x).$$

A typical first order linear equation is that in Example 1.2.3, where it was shown that the general solution of

$$\frac{dy}{dx}\cos x + y\sin x = \tan x$$

is $y = \tfrac{1}{2}\sec x + C\cos x$, where C is an arbitrary constant.

> It will be convenient in this chapter and in Chapter 8 to use capital letters to denote arbitrary constants, and lower-case letters for other constants.

You will see that the solution is the sum of two parts: one is a specific function and the other contains a multiplicative arbitrary constant. It is interesting to investigate what happens when you substitute each of these parts into the left side of the equation.

If $y = \frac{1}{2}\sec x$, then

$$\frac{dy}{dx}\cos x + y\sin x = \left(\frac{1}{2}\sec x\tan x\right)\cos x + \left(\frac{1}{2}\sec x\right)\sin x$$

$$= \frac{1}{2}\tan x + \frac{1}{2}\tan x = \tan x.$$

If $y = C\cos x$, then

$$\frac{dy}{dx}\cos x + y\sin x = (-C\sin x)\cos x + (C\cos x)\sin x = 0.$$

That is, $y = \frac{1}{2}\sec x$ is a solution of the given differential equation

$$\frac{dy}{dx}\cos x + y\sin x = \tan x;$$

and $y = C\cos x$ is a solution (in fact, the general solution) of the equation

$$\frac{dy}{dx}\cos x + y\sin x = 0.$$

Much the same occurs with second order linear equations.

Example 3.1.1 is typical. The differential equation can be written as

$$\frac{d^2 P}{dt^2} + 0.01P = 50.$$

This is clearly linear, and you can check for yourself that

$$P = 5000 + A\sin 0.1t + B\cos 0.1t$$

is a solution for any values of the constants A and B. If you substitute the separate parts $P = 5000$ and $P = A\sin 0.1t + B\cos 0.1t$ in the expression $\frac{d^2 P}{dt^2} + 0.01P$ on the left side of the equation, you get the answers 50 for the first and 0 for the second. These are examples of a general rule.

> The general solution of a linear differential equation is the sum of two parts: a **particular integral**, which is a solution of the differential equation, and a **complementary function**, which is the general solution of the equation with 0 in place of the terms which are independent of y.

The word 'complementary' means 'completing'. The complementary function is what you have to add to the particular integral to complete the solution of the differential equation.

For the first order equation $\frac{dy}{dx} + y\,p(x) = q(x)$, if $F(x)$ is a particular integral, and $G(x)$ is any solution of the equation with 0 on the right side, then

$$F'(x) + F(x)\,p(x) = q(x) \quad\text{and}\quad G'(x) + G(x)\,p(x) = 0.$$

Since $\dfrac{d}{dx}(F(x)+G(x)) = F'(x)+G'(x)$ it follows that

$$y = F(x)+G(x) \quad \Leftrightarrow \quad \frac{dy}{dx}+p(x)\,y = (F'(x)+G'(x))+(F(x)+G(x))\,p(x)$$

$$= (F'(x)+F(x)\,p(x)) + \cdot(G'(x)+G(x)\,p(x))$$

$$= q(x)+0 = q(x).$$

So a particular integral added to any solution in the complementary function satisfies the original equation. And by a similar argument, if y is any solution of the given equation, then $y - p(x)$ belongs to the complementary function.

Exactly the same argument applies to second order linear equations.

The importance of this result is that, for linear equations, you can split the problem of solution into two parts: finding the complementary function and finding a particular integral. The rest of this chapter deals with these in turn.

Exercise 3A

1   For the following differential equations, state whether they are of first or second order, and whether they are linear or non‑linear.

(a) $\dfrac{dy}{dx} = \dfrac{1}{x}+\dfrac{1}{y}$

(b) $\dfrac{d^2 x}{dt^2}+x = \sin 2t$

(c) $x^2\dfrac{d^2 y}{dx^2} - e^x\dfrac{dy}{dx} = y$

(d) $\dfrac{du}{dt} = tu+t^2$

(e) $x\dfrac{d^2 x}{dt^2} = t\dfrac{dx}{dt}$

(f) $xy^2\dfrac{dy}{dx} = 1+y$

2   For the following equations, find differential equations which they satisfy for all values of the arbitrary constants A and B.

(a) $y = Ax^2 + e^x$

(b) $Ax + By = 1$

(c) $x = A\sin 2t + B\cos 2t$

(d) $y = Ax + \dfrac{B}{x}$

3   For the following equations and differential equations, verify that the equation satisfies the differential equation for all values of the arbitrary constants A and B.

(a) $y = A\sqrt{x}$; $2x\dfrac{dy}{dx} = y$

(b) $y = A\sqrt{x}+2x$; $2x\dfrac{dy}{dx} = y+2x$

(c) $y = Ae^t + Be^{-t}$; $\dfrac{d^2 y}{dt^2} - y = 0$

(d) $y = Ae^t + (t+B)e^{-t}$; $\dfrac{d^2 y}{dt^2} - y = -2e^{-t}$

4   A truck is towing a trailer. The coupling connecting them can be modelled as a stiff spring. Both the truck and trailer are initially stationary. The truck starts to move at a constant speed of 4 metres per second, and pulls the trailer along behind it. If the trailer has moved x metres in t seconds, its motion is described by the differential equation

$$\frac{d^2 x}{dt^2} + 0.04x = 0.16t.$$

Verify that the differential equations and the initial conditions are all satisfied by the equation $x = 4(t - 5\sin 0.2t)$.

5 Solve the following differential equations, and identify a particular integral and the complementary function.

(a) $\dfrac{dx}{dt} = \cos t$

(b) $\dfrac{d^2 y}{dx^2} = \dfrac{1}{x^2}$

(c) $\dfrac{dy}{dx} \sin x + y \cos x = 1$

(d) $\dfrac{dy}{dx} \sin x - y \cos x = 1$

(e) $\dfrac{d}{dx}\left(x \dfrac{dy}{dx}\right) = 1$

(f) $x^2 \dfrac{d^2 y}{dx^2} + 2x \dfrac{dy}{dx} = \dfrac{1}{x^2}$

6 For these differential equations find the complementary function, guess and verify a particular integral, and hence write down the general solution.

(a) $\dfrac{dy}{dx} - 3y = 2e^x$

(b) $\dfrac{dy}{dx} + \dfrac{y}{x} = 4x^2$

(c) $\dfrac{d^2 y}{dx^2} + \dfrac{dy}{dx} = 2e^{-2x}$

7 A stone falls vertically into a lake and sinks to the bottom. It enters the water at a speed of 3 metres per second, and t seconds later its depth is z metres. The fall of the stone is modelled by the differential equation

$$\frac{d^2 z}{dt^2} + 2\frac{dz}{dt} = 10.$$

Show that this differential equation is satisfied by an equation of the form $z = 5t + A + Be^{-2t}$. Find the values of A and B which give the correct values for the depth z and the speed $\dfrac{dz}{dt}$ at time $t = 0$. Draw sketch graphs to show how the depth and speed vary with time as the stone sinks.

3.3 Finding complementary functions: constant coefficients

Many linear differential equations which occur in practice have the form

$$a\frac{dy}{dx} + by = q(x) \quad \text{or} \quad a\frac{d^2 y}{dx^2} + b\frac{dy}{dx} + cy = q(x)$$

where the coefficients a, b and c are constants. For these, the complementary functions, which satisfy

$$a\frac{dy}{dx} + by = 0 \quad \text{or} \quad a\frac{d^2 y}{dx^2} + b\frac{dy}{dx} + cy = 0,$$

are specially easy to find.

You already know the solution of the first order equation. This is the equation for exponential growth which was solved in C4 Section 7.3. Recasting this in x, y notation, you can obtain the solution of $\dfrac{dy}{dx} = \lambda y$ as $y = Ce^{\lambda x}$, where C is an arbitrary constant. In this case $\lambda = -\dfrac{b}{a}$, or $a\lambda + b = 0$. So the result can be written as:

The complementary function for the differential equation

$$a\frac{dy}{dx} + by = q(x)$$

is $y = Ce^{\lambda x}$, where λ is the root of the equation $a\lambda + b = 0$.

Introducing the equation $a\lambda + b = 0$, which is called the **auxiliary equation**, may seem an unnecessary complication. It is, however, the key which opens the door to the solution of the second order equation. For this the auxiliary equation is the quadratic equation

$$a\lambda^2 + b\lambda + c = 0.$$

Before tackling the general theory, it is useful to look at a numerical example.

Example 3.3.1

(a) Investigate whether there are any numbers C and λ such that $y = Ce^{\lambda x}$ satisfies the differential equation $\dfrac{d^2 y}{dx^2} - 5\dfrac{dy}{dx} + 6y = 0$.

(b) Find a more general solution of the equation.

(a) If $y = Ce^{\lambda x}$, then $\dfrac{dy}{dx} = C\lambda e^{\lambda x}$ and $\dfrac{d^2 y}{dx^2} = C\lambda^2 e^{\lambda x}$. So if y satisfies the differential equation, then

$$C\lambda^2 e^{\lambda x} - 5C\lambda e^{\lambda x} + 6Ce^{\lambda x} = 0 \qquad \text{for all values of } x.$$

This can be written as

$$Ce^{\lambda x}(\lambda^2 - 5\lambda + 6) = 0, \qquad \text{so} \quad Ce^{\lambda x}(\lambda - 2)(\lambda - 3) = 0.$$

Now $e^{\lambda x}$ cannot be zero, and $C = 0$ gives you a correct but uninteresting solution. The useful solutions are given by $\lambda = 2$ and $\lambda = 3$.

What has been shown so far is that, if $\lambda = 2$ or $\lambda = 3$, then $y = Ce^{\lambda x}$ satisfies the differential equation whatever the value of C.

So two solutions of the differential equation are $y = Ae^{2x}$ and $y = Be^{3x}$, where A and B are arbitrary constants.

(b) To find a more general solution, you want a function of which Ae^{2x} and Be^{3x} are special cases. An obvious possibility is $y = Ae^{2x} + Be^{3x}$. For this function

$$\frac{dy}{dx} = 2Ae^{2x} + 3Be^{3x} \quad \text{and} \quad \frac{d^2 y}{dx^2} = 4Ae^{2x} + 9Be^{3x}.$$

So $\dfrac{d^2 y}{dx^2} - 5\dfrac{dy}{dx} + 6y = (4Ae^{2x} + 9Be^{3x}) - 5(2Ae^{2x} + 3Be^{3x}) + 6(Ae^{2x} + Be^{3x})$

$$= (4 - 10 + 6)Ae^{2x} + (9 - 15 + 6)Be^{3x}$$

$$= 0.$$

So a more general solution of the equation is indeed $y = Ae^{2x} + Be^{3x}$.

The example suggests a more general result:

If the auxiliary equation $a\lambda^2 + b\lambda + c = 0$ for the differential equation $a\dfrac{d^2 y}{dx^2} + b\dfrac{dy}{dx} + cy = q(x)$ has distinct roots α and β, the complementary function is $y = Ae^{\alpha x} + Be^{\beta x}$.

Notice that this says more than part (b) of Example 3.3.1. There it was shown that
$y = Ae^{2x} + Be^{3x}$ is a solution of $\dfrac{d^2y}{dx^2} - 5\dfrac{dy}{dx} + 6y = 0$. What the blue box asserts is that all the solutions are of this form. The proof which follows establishes the result by deduction rather than verifying an inspired guess.

If the auxiliary equation has two roots α and β, you know from FP1 Section 8.1 that
$\alpha + \beta = -\dfrac{b}{a}$ and $\alpha\beta = \dfrac{c}{a}$. The complementary function is the most general function satisfying

$$\frac{d^2y}{dx^2} - (\alpha + \beta)\frac{dy}{dx} + \alpha\beta y = 0.$$

This can be rearranged as $\dfrac{d^2y}{dx^2} - \beta\dfrac{dy}{dx} = \alpha\left(\dfrac{dy}{dx} - \beta y\right)$, or

$$\frac{d}{dx}\left(\frac{dy}{dx} - \beta y\right) = \alpha\left(\frac{dy}{dx} - \beta y\right).$$

If you write u in place of $\dfrac{dy}{dx} - \beta y$, this becomes

$$\frac{du}{dx} = \alpha u,$$

which you know how to solve.

So $u = Ce^{\alpha x}$, that is $\dfrac{dy}{dx} - \beta y = Ce^{\alpha x}$.

This is a first order linear equation, which you could solve using an integrating factor $e^{-\beta x}$. But you can use a neat trick to avoid this. Go back to the original equation and swap α and β, writing the equation for the complementary function as

$$\frac{d}{dx}\left(\frac{dy}{dx} - \alpha y\right) = \beta\left(\frac{dy}{dx} - \alpha y\right).$$

Then by exactly the same argument as before, with α and β interchanged,

$$\frac{dy}{dx} - \alpha y = De^{\beta x}.$$

Now subtract this equation from $\dfrac{dy}{dx} - \beta y = Ce^{\alpha x}$, found above. You then get the solution

$$(\alpha - \beta)y = Ce^{\alpha x} - De^{\beta x}.$$

You can simplify the constants by writing $\dfrac{C}{\alpha - \beta} = A$ and $\dfrac{-D}{\alpha - \beta} = B$. This completes the proof, that the most general solution of the equation $\dfrac{d^2y}{dx^2} + a\dfrac{dy}{dx} + by = 0$ is $y = Ae^{\alpha x} + Be^{\beta x}$.

The equations in this chapter all have real roots α and β. You will meet equations with complex roots in Chapter 8.

Example 3.3.2

Find the complementary function for the differential equation $\dfrac{d^2y}{dx^2} + 6\dfrac{dy}{dx} + 5y = 2x$.

Begin by writing the auxiliary equation $\lambda^2 + 6\lambda + 5 = 0$, which factorises as $(\lambda + 1)(\lambda + 5) = 0$. The roots α and β are -1 and -5. The complementary function is therefore $Ae^{-x} + Be^{-5x}$.

You can check this by substituting this expression for y in the left side of the differential equation, showing that it boils down to 0.

Example 3.3.3

Find the solution of $\dfrac{d^2y}{dt^2} + \dfrac{dy}{dt} - 6y = 0$ for which $y = 7$ when $t = 0$ and y remains finite as $t \to \infty$.

> Linear differential equations often have time, represented by t, as the independent variable. You need to be able to solve them using any notation which is appropriate.

The auxiliary equation is $\lambda^2 + \lambda - 6 = 0$, with roots -3 and 2. The solution of the differential equation therefore has the form

$$y = Ae^{-3t} + Be^{2t}.$$

For y to remain finite as $t \to \infty$, the coefficient B must be 0, so that $y = Ae^{-3t}$. When $t = 0$, $y = Ae^0 = A$, so that $A = 7$. The solution is therefore $y = 7e^{-3t}$.

This method of finding the complementary function only works if the auxiliary equation has distinct roots α and β. If it has a repeated root α, you can carry the previous argument as far as the solution $u = Ce^{\alpha x}$, which in this case leads to

$$\frac{dy}{dx} - \alpha y = Ce^{\alpha x}.$$

But you can't now get a second equation by swapping α and β.

Fortunately this first order linear equation is very easy to solve. Multiplying by the integrating factor, which is $e^{-\alpha x}$, gives

$$\frac{dy}{dx}e^{-\alpha x} - y(\alpha e^{-\alpha x}) = C \quad \text{or} \quad \frac{d}{dx}(ye^{-\alpha x}) = C.$$

Integrating this gives $ye^{-\alpha x} = Cx + D$, that is $y = (Cx + D)e^{\alpha x}$.

> If the auxiliary equation for the differential equation
> $$a\frac{d^2y}{dx^2} + b\frac{dy}{dx} + cy = q(x) \text{ has a repeated root } \alpha, \text{ the complementary}$$
> function is $(Cx + D)e^{\alpha x}$.

Example 3.3.4

Find the complementary function for the differential equation $\dfrac{d^2y}{dt^2} - 6\dfrac{dy}{dt} + 9y = e^{3x}$.

The auxiliary equation $\lambda^2 - 6\lambda + 9 = 0$, or $(\lambda - 3)^2 = 0$, has a repeated root $\lambda = 3$. The complementary function is therefore $y = (Cx + D)e^{3x}$.

You can check this by differentiating and substituting y, $\dfrac{dy}{dx}$ and $\dfrac{d^2y}{dx^2}$ in the left side of the differential equation. If $y = (Cx + D)e^{3x}$, then

$$\frac{dy}{dx} = Ce^{3x} + (Cx + D) \times 3e^{3x} = (3Cx + C + 3D)e^{3x},$$

and $$\frac{d^2y}{dx^2} = 3Ce^{3x} + (3Cx + C + 3D) \times 3e^{3x} = (9Cx + 6C + 9D)e^{3x}.$$

So $$\frac{d^2y}{dt^2} - 6\frac{dy}{dt} + 9y = ((9Cx + 6C + 9D) - 6(3Cx + C + 3D) + 9(Cx + D))e^{3x}$$

$$= ((9C - 18C + 9C)x + (6C - 6C) + (9D - 18D + 9D))e^{3x}$$

$$= 0, \quad \text{as required.}$$

3.4* Complementary functions; the general case

The method of solving first order equations using an integrating factor described in Chapter 1 can't be extended to general second order equations $\dfrac{d^2y}{dx^2} + \dfrac{dy}{dx}p(x) + yr(x) = q(x)$, in which the coefficients are functions rather than constants.

There is no such simple method of finding the complementary function for a second order equation. But it is still true that:

> The complementary function for a second order linear differential equation has the form $AG_1(x) + BG_2(x)$, where G_1 and G_2 are two independent functions and A and B are arbitrary constants.

The word 'independent' means that one function is not a constant multiple of the other.

Example 3.4.1

Show that $G_1(x) = x$ and $G_2(x) = e^x$ belong to the complementary function of the differential equation $(1 - x)\dfrac{d^2y}{dx^2} + x\dfrac{dy}{dx} - y = (1 - x)^2$. State the complete complementary function.

Substituting $G_1(x)$ and $G_2(x)$ for y in the left side of the equation gives

$$(1 - x)0 + x \times 1 - x \quad \text{and} \quad (1 - x)e^x + xe^x - e^x,$$

both of which reduce to 0.

The complementary function is therefore $Ax + Be^x$.

Exercise 3B

1 Find general solutions of the following linear differential equations.

(a) $\dfrac{d^2y}{dx^2} - 4\dfrac{dy}{dx} + 3y = 0$ (b) $\dfrac{d^2y}{dx^2} + 3\dfrac{dy}{dx} - 4y = 0$ (c) $\dfrac{d^2x}{dt^2} + 7\dfrac{dx}{dt} + 12x = 0$

(d) $\dfrac{d^2x}{dt^2} + 12\dfrac{dx}{dt} + 36x = 0$ (e) $\dfrac{d^2u}{dx^2} + 6\dfrac{du}{dx} = 0$ (f) $4\dfrac{d^2y}{dt^2} - 4\dfrac{dy}{dt} + y = 0$

2 For each of the following differential equations find the solution which satisfies the given conditions, and sketch its graph.

(a) $\dfrac{d^2y}{dx^2} + 3\dfrac{dy}{dx} + 2y = 0$; $y = 1$ and $\dfrac{dy}{dx} = 0$ when $x = 0$

(b) $\dfrac{d^2u}{dt^2} + 5\dfrac{du}{dt} - 6u = 0$; $u = 2$ when $t = 0$, and u remains finite as $t \to \infty$

(c) $\dfrac{d^2x}{dt^2} - 9x = 0$; $x = 0$ and $\dfrac{dx}{dt} = 3$ when $t = 0$

(d) $\dfrac{d^2z}{dy^2} - 2\dfrac{dz}{dy} = 0$; $z = 1$ when $y = 0$, and $z = 0$ when $y = 1$

(e) $\dfrac{d^2z}{dt^2} + 6\dfrac{dz}{dt} + 9z = 0$; $z = 1$ and $\dfrac{dz}{dt} = -4$ when $t = 0$

(f) $\dfrac{d^2y}{dx^2} - 6\dfrac{dy}{dx} + 8y = 0$; $y = 1$ and $\dfrac{dy}{dx} = 1$ when $x = 0$

3 Find complementary functions for the following differential equations.

(a) $\dfrac{dy}{dx} + 2y = 10e^{3x}$ (b) $\dfrac{dy}{dx} - 3y = 6$

(c) $\dfrac{d^2y}{dx^2} + 5\dfrac{dy}{dx} + 4y = 8x - 6$ (d) $3\dfrac{d^2u}{dt^2} + 4\dfrac{du}{dt} + u = e^{-2t}$

(e) $\dfrac{d^2x}{dt^2} + \dfrac{dx}{dt} = e^{-t}$ (f) $\dfrac{d^2v}{dx^2} - 4\dfrac{dv}{dx} + 4v = 8x + 4$

3.5 Finding particular integrals

To complete the solution of a linear differential equation you have to find a particular integral; that is, any one function that satisfies the equation. This section suggests ways of doing this.

When you differentiate a polynomial you get another polynomial. When you differentiate an exponential e^{ax} you get a similar exponential. When you differentiate a mixture of sines and cosines you get a mixture of sines and cosines. These facts are often the key to finding a particular integral.

In solving linear equations your aim is to find a function $y = F(x)$ which, when differentiated once or twice and mixed with the coefficients, produces the given function $q(x)$ on the right. It is likely that, if $q(x)$ is a polynomial, the function $F(x)$ will be a polynomial; and similarly for exponentials and mixtures of sines and cosines.

So to find a particular integral, try a function similar to the q(x) you are aiming at, but with undetermined coefficients. When you substitute this in the left side, you will (if you have made a good choice) get some equations to solve for the coefficients.

The method is best understood from some examples.

Example 3.5.1

Solve the differential equation $\dfrac{dy}{dx} + 4y = \sin 2x$.

You might think first of trying $y = a \sin 2x$. But if you differentiate this to find $\dfrac{dy}{dx}$ you get a term involving $\cos 2x$. So try $y = a \sin 2x + b \cos 2x$, and hope that the cosine terms go out, so that you are left with just a $\sin 2x$ term.

Notice that capital letters have not been used for the coefficients. These are not arbitrary constants, although for the time being they are unknown.

If $y = a \sin 2x + b \cos 2x$, the left side of the differential equation is

$$(2a \cos 2x - 2b \sin 2x) + 4(a \sin 2x + b \cos 2x)$$
$$= (4a - 2b) \sin 2x + (2a + 4b) \cos 2x.$$

For the cosines to go out, you need $2a + 4b = 0$, or $a = -2b$. The expression in the line above then reduces to

$$(4(-2b) - 2b) \sin 2x = -10b \sin 2x.$$

The goal is to get $\sin 2x$ on the right, so choose $b = -0.1$. This gives $a = -2 \times (-0.1) = 0.2$.

So a particular integral is $0.2 \sin 2x - 0.1 \cos 2x$.

You have to add to this the complementary function, which is Ce^{-4x}.

The general solution of the differential equation is therefore

$$y = 0.2 \sin 2x - 0.1 \cos 2x + Ce^{-4x}.$$

Example 3.5.2

Solve the differential equation $\dfrac{d^2y}{dx^2} + 6\dfrac{dy}{dx} + 5y = 2x$, given that $y = 0$ and $\dfrac{dy}{dx} = 0$ when $x = 0$.

The right side is a polynomial of degree 1, so try to find a solution of the form $y = ax + b$. This gives $\dfrac{dy}{dx} = a$ and $\dfrac{d^2y}{dx^2} = 0$. The left side of the differential equation is then $0 + 6a + 5(ax + b)$, or $5ax + (6a + 5b)$.

The aim is to find a and b so that this is $2x$. Equating coefficients, $5a = 2$ and $6a + 5b = 0$. Therefore $a = 0.4$ and $b = -0.48$.

It was shown in Example 3.3.2 that the complementary function is $Ae^{-x} + Be^{-5x}$. The general solution is therefore

$$y = 0.4x - 0.48 + Ae^{-x} + Be^{-5x}.$$

It remains to use the initial conditions to find A and B. Since $\dfrac{dy}{dx}$ is involved, begin by differentiating to get

$$\frac{dy}{dx} = 0.4 - Ae^{-x} - 5Be^{-5x}.$$

The conditions $y = 0$ and $\dfrac{dy}{dx} = 0$ when $x = 0$ give two equations for A and B,

$$0 = -0.48 + A + B \quad \text{and} \quad 0 = 0.4 - A - 5B.$$

These have solutions $A = 0.5$ and $B = -0.02$.

The solution satisfying the given initial conditions is therefore

$$y = 0.4x - 0.48 + 0.5\,e^{-x} - 0.02\,e^{-5x}.$$

Example 3.5.3

Find the general solution of the differential equation $\dfrac{d^2 y}{dx^2} - 6\dfrac{dy}{dx} + 9y = e^{3x}$.

It was shown in Example 3.3.4 that the complementary function is $(Cx + D)e^{3x}$.

The usual procedure suggests trying a particular integral of the form ae^{3x}. But that will not work in this case: since ae^{3x} is part of the complementary function, substituting $y = ae^{3x}$ in the left side produces 0 on the right side.

There is a general rule which often works in such cases:

> If the usual trial integral $y = F(x)$ does not work because it is part of the complementary function, try $y = x F(x)$ instead.

In this example a trial integral $y = axe^{3x}$ will not work either, because that too is part of the complementary function. So try $y = ax^2 e^{3x}$. Then

$$\frac{dy}{dx} = a(2x)e^{3x} + ax^2(3e^{3x}) = a(2x + 3x^2)e^{3x},$$

$$\frac{d^2 y}{dx^2} = a(2 + 6x)e^{3x} + a(2x + 3x^2)(3e^{3x}) = a(2 + 12x + 9x^2)e^{3x}.$$

Substituting these in the left side of the equation gives

$$\frac{d^2 y}{dx^2} - 6\frac{dy}{dx} + 9y = a(2 + 12x + 9x^2)e^{3x} - 6a(2x + 3x^2)e^{3x} + 9ax^2 e^{3x}$$

$$= a(2 + (12 - 6 \times 2)x + (9 - 6 \times 3 + 9)x^2)e^{3x} = 2ae^{3x}.$$

To get e^{3x} on the right side you have to make $2a = 1$, so $a = \frac{1}{2}$, and the general solution is $y = \frac{1}{2}x^2 e^{3x} + (Cx + D)e^{3x}$, or $y = \left(\frac{1}{2}x^2 + Cx + D\right)e^{3x}$.

Exercise 3C

1 Find particular integrals for the following differential equations. (See Exercise 3B Question 3.)

(a) $\dfrac{dy}{dx} + 2y = 10e^{3x}$

(b) $\dfrac{dy}{dx} - 3y = 6$

(c) $\dfrac{d^2y}{dx^2} + 5\dfrac{dy}{dx} + 4y = 8x - 6$

(d) $3\dfrac{d^2u}{dt^2} + 4\dfrac{du}{dt} + u = e^{-2t}$

(e) $\dfrac{d^2x}{dt^2} + \dfrac{dx}{dt} = e^{-t}$

(f) $\dfrac{d^2v}{dx^2} - 4\dfrac{dv}{dx} + 4v = 8x + 4$

2 Find the general solution of each of the following differential equations.

(a) $\dfrac{d^2y}{dx^2} - 4y = 12x$

(b) $2\dfrac{d^2x}{dt^2} + 3\dfrac{dx}{dt} + x = 6e^t$

(c) $2\dfrac{d^2x}{dt^2} + 3\dfrac{dx}{dt} + x = 6e^{-t}$

(d) $\dfrac{d^2z}{dx^2} + 3\dfrac{dz}{dx} = 6$

(e) $\dfrac{d^2x}{dt^2} - x = 4\cos t$

(f) $\dfrac{d^2y}{dx^2} - 2\dfrac{dy}{dx} + y = e^x$

3 For the following differential equations find solutions which satisfy the given conditions.

(a) $\dfrac{d^2y}{dx^2} - 4\dfrac{dy}{dx} + 3y = 6$; $y = 2$ and $\dfrac{dy}{dx} = -2$ when $x = 0$

(b) $2\dfrac{d^2x}{dt^2} + 5\dfrac{dx}{dt} + 2x = 5\sin t$; $x = 2$ and $\dfrac{dx}{dt} = -3$ when $t = 0$

(c) $\dfrac{d^2y}{dx^2} + \dfrac{dy}{dx} = 2y - 3e^x$; $y = 2$ when $x = 0$, and $y = 0$ when $x = 2$

(d) $\dfrac{d^2y}{dt^2} + 2\dfrac{dy}{dt} - 3y = 10\sin t$; $y = 0$ when $t = 0$, and y remains finite as $t \to \infty$

(e) $\dfrac{d^2u}{dx^2} + 2\dfrac{du}{dx} + u = e^{-x}$; $u = 1$ when $x = 0$, and $\dfrac{du}{dx} = 0$ when $x = 2$

(f)* $\dfrac{d^2y}{dx^2} - y = \cosh x$; $y = 0$ and $\dfrac{dy}{dx} = 0$ when $x = 0$

4* Verify that $y = x$ and $y = \dfrac{1}{x}$ satisfy the differential equation $x^2\dfrac{d^2y}{dx^2} + x\dfrac{dy}{dx} - y = 0$.

Write down the general solution of $x^2\dfrac{d^2y}{dx^2} + x\dfrac{dy}{dx} - y = 1$.

5* Show that the differential equation $2x^2\dfrac{d^2y}{dx^2} - x\dfrac{dy}{dx} + y = 0$ has two independent solutions of the form $y = x^k$. Hence find the general solution of $2x^2\dfrac{d^2y}{dx^2} - x\dfrac{dy}{dx} + y = 10x^3$.

Miscellaneous exercise 3

When the independent variable is time, denoted by t, a commonly used convention is to abbreviate the symbols $\dfrac{dx}{dt}$ to $\dot{x}$ and $\dfrac{d^2x}{dt^2}$ to $\ddot{x}$ (and similarly with letters other than x). To give you practice with this convention, it is used in Questions 5, 8, 9 and 10 of this exercise.

1 Find the general solution of the differential equation $\dfrac{d^2y}{dx^2} - 3\dfrac{dy}{dx} - 4y = 50\sin 2x$. Given that $y = 0$ when $x = 0$, and that y remains finite as $x \to \infty$, find y in terms of x.   (OCR)

2 Find differential equations for which the following are general solutions.

   (a) $y = Ae^x + Be^{-2x} + 3\sin x$ (b) $y = x^2 + Ae^x + Be^{3x}$

   (c) $y = (x + A)e^{2x} + Be^{-2x}$ (d) $y = 2x + A + Be^{-x}$

   (e) $y = (x^2 + Ax + B)e^x$ (f)* $y = (x^2 + A)\cosh 3x + B\sinh 3x$

3 (a) Find the general solution of the differential equation $\dfrac{d^2y}{dx^2} + 3\dfrac{dy}{dx} + 2y = 2x + 1$.

   (b) Find the particular solution for which $y = -1$ and $\dfrac{dy}{dx} = 0$ when $x = 0$. For this

   solution, show that $\dfrac{dy}{dx} = 0$ when $2u^2 - u - 1 = 0$, where $u = e^{-x}$. Deduce that $\dfrac{dy}{dx} = 0$ only when $x = 0$.

   Find the value of x for which $\dfrac{d^2y}{dx^2} = 0$. Hence show that $\dfrac{dy}{dx} \leqslant \tfrac{9}{8}$ for all values of x, and sketch the graph of y against x.   (MEI)

4 Find and sketch the curves which satisfy the given differential equations and pass through the given points.

   (a) $\dfrac{d^2y}{dx^2} - \dfrac{dy}{dx} - 2y = 3e^{-x}$, through $(0, 1)$ and $(1, 0)$

   (b) $\dfrac{d^2y}{dx^2} - 2\dfrac{dy}{dx} + y = 2e^x$, through $(-1, 0)$ and $(1, 0)$

   (c)* $\dfrac{d^2y}{dx^2} - y = 2\sinh x$, through $(-1, 0)$ and $(0, 1)$

5 Solve the following differential equations with the given initial conditions.

   (a) $\ddot{x} - x = 5t$; $x = -1$ and $\dot{x} = 0$ when $t = 0$

   (b) $\ddot{x} - 4x = 10\cos t$; $x = 0$ and $\dot{x} = 0$ when $t = 0$

   (c) $\ddot{x} - 4x = 8e^{2t}$; $x = 0$ and $\dot{x} = 6$ when $t = 0$

6* Solve the differential equation $x^2\dfrac{d^2y}{dx^2} - 3x\dfrac{dy}{dx} + 3y = -2x^2$, given that the solution for y is a polynomial in x.

7* Find an integrating factor u(x) such that u(x)$\left(\dfrac{d^2y}{dx^2} + \dfrac{2}{x}\dfrac{dy}{dx}\right)$ can be written in the form

$\dfrac{d}{dx}\left(u(x)\dfrac{dy}{dx}\right)$. Hence find the general solution of the differential equation $\dfrac{d^2y}{dx^2} + \dfrac{2}{x}\dfrac{dy}{dx} = x$.

Identify the complementary function and the particular integral in your solution, and check these by direct substitution in the left side of the differential equation.

8 Investigate the nature of the solutions of the following differential equations for $t > 0$, with the given initial conditions. Give particular attention to the following questions, and illustrate your answers with sketch graphs.

- Does x tend to ∞, $-\infty$ or a finite limit as $t \to \infty$?
- Do x, $\dot{x}$ ever take the value 0?

(a) $\ddot{x} + 6\dot{x} + 5x = 0$; $x = 1$ and $\dot{x} = 1$ when $t = 0$

(b) $\ddot{x} - 6\dot{x} + 8x = 0$; $x = 1$ and $\dot{x} = 3$ when $t = 0$

(c) $\ddot{x} - 4\dot{x} + 4x = 0$; $x = 1$ and $\dot{x} = 1$ when $t = 0$

(d) $\ddot{x} - 3\dot{x} - 4x = 0$; $x = 1$ and $\dot{x} = -2$ when $t = 0$

(e) $\ddot{x} + 10\dot{x} + 25x = 0$; $x = 1$ and $\dot{x} = 2$ when $t = 0$

9* Investigate the solution of the differential equation $\ddot{x} - 2\alpha\,\dot{x} + \alpha^2 x = 0$ (where $\alpha \neq 0$) for $t \geqslant 0$, if initially $x = 1$ and $\dot{x} = c$ when $t = 0$. Find the conditions for

(a) x to remain finite, to tend to ∞, or to tend to $-\infty$, as $t \to \infty$;

(b) x to be zero for some $t > 0$;   (c) $\dot{x}$ to be zero for some $t > 0$.

Consider the possible orders of the numbers 0, α and c, and illustrate your conclusions with sketch graphs. Check your answers by reference to Question 6 (c) and (e).

10* Investigate the solution of the differential equation $\ddot{x} - (\alpha + \beta)\dot{x} + \alpha\beta x = 0$ (where $\alpha > \beta$) for $t \geqslant 0$, if initially $x = 1$ and $\dot{x} = c$ when $t = 0$. Find the conditions for

(a) x to remain finite, to tend to ∞, or to tend to $-\infty$, as $t \to \infty$;

(b) x to be zero for some $t > 0$;   (c) $\dot{x}$ to be zero for some $t > 0$.

Check your answers by reference to Question 6 (a), (b) and (d).

11* A closed electric circuit is activated by an electromotive force $E = V_0 \sin nt$, where t is time and V_0, n are constants. If the capacitance, inductance and resistance in the circuit (all positive and constant) are denoted by C, L and R respectively, the current I in the circuit at time t satisfies the differential equation

$$L\frac{d^2 I}{dt^2} + R\frac{dI}{dt} + \frac{1}{C}I = \frac{dE}{dt}.$$

Describe the variation of I with t in a circuit for which $CR^2 > 4L$, and show that after some time it settles down to a regular oscillation given by $I = a \sin nt + b \cos nt$, where a and b are constants.

Show that this can be written in the form $I = K \sin(nt + \alpha)$, where K and α are constants. Find an expression for K in terms of V_0, C, L, R and n.

4 The vector product

This chapter introduces the vector product of two vectors in three dimensions. When you have completed it, you should be able to

- find the vector product $\mathbf{p} \times \mathbf{q}$ of two vectors $\mathbf{p}$ and $\mathbf{q}$
- solve a variety of problems involving lines and planes in three dimensions.

4.1 The vector product

In C4 Chapter 9, you met the scalar product, or dot product, of two vectors, by which you combine two vectors and get a result which is a scalar. The vector product $\mathbf{p} \times \mathbf{q}$ of two vectors $\mathbf{p}$ and $\mathbf{q}$, sometimes for obvious reasons called the cross product, is a different kind of product. The result $\mathbf{p} \times \mathbf{q}$ is a vector.

The vector $\mathbf{p} \times \mathbf{q}$ has magnitude $|\mathbf{p}||\mathbf{q}| \sin \theta$, where θ is the angle between $\mathbf{p}$ and $\mathbf{q}$ and $0 \leqslant \theta \leqslant \pi$. The direction of $\mathbf{p} \times \mathbf{q}$ is perpendicular to both $\mathbf{p}$ and $\mathbf{q}$ such that if you point the first finger of your right hand in the $\mathbf{p}$ direction and the middle finger in the $\mathbf{q}$ direction, your thumb will point in the direction $\mathbf{p} \times \mathbf{q}$.

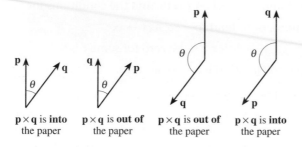

Fig. 4.1

Figure 4.1 shows four pairs of vectors $\mathbf{p}$ and $\mathbf{q}$ in the plane of the paper, and indicates the direction of the vector product $\mathbf{p} \times \mathbf{q}$, which is either into or out of the paper, in each case.

It is worth thinking through the actions with your fingers and thumb and making sure you agree with these directions in Fig. 4.1.

The direction of the resulting vector will be denoted by the unit vector $\hat{\mathbf{n}}$. Thus

$$\mathbf{p} \times \mathbf{q} = |\mathbf{p}||\mathbf{q}| \sin \theta \, \hat{\mathbf{n}}.$$

The method of getting the unit vector $\hat{\mathbf{n}}$ is called the **right-handed rule**.

> The **vector product**, or **cross product**, of two vectors **p** and **q** is given by
> $$\mathbf{p} \times \mathbf{q} = |\mathbf{p}||\mathbf{q}| \sin\theta \, \hat{\mathbf{n}}$$
> where $\hat{\mathbf{n}}$ is a unit vector perpendicular to both **p** and **q** in the right-handed sense.

The definition of the vector product is essentially three-dimensional. The vector product is not defined for vectors which have only two components.

Just as for the dot product, there are a number of rules for manipulating the vector product.

Example 4.1.1
Find the vector products   (a) $\mathbf{i} \times \mathbf{j}$,   (b) $\mathbf{k} \times \mathbf{k}$,   (c) $\mathbf{j} \times \mathbf{i}$.

Figure 4.2 shows the vectors **i**, **j** and **k**.

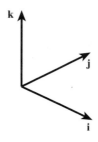

Fig. 4.2

(a) The magnitude of $\mathbf{i} \times \mathbf{j}$ is $1 \times 1 \times \sin\frac{1}{2}\pi = 1$, and its direction is **k**. A vector of length 1 in the direction of **k** is **k** itself. Therefore $\mathbf{i} \times \mathbf{j} = \mathbf{k}$.

(b) The magnitude of $\mathbf{k} \times \mathbf{k}$ is $1 \times 1 \times \sin 0 = 0$, so $\mathbf{k} \times \mathbf{k} = \mathbf{0}$.

(c) The magnitude of $\mathbf{j} \times \mathbf{i}$ is $1 \times 1 \times \sin\frac{1}{2}\pi = 1$, and its direction is $-\mathbf{k}$. A vector of length 1 in the direction of $-\mathbf{k}$ is $-\mathbf{k}$ itself. Therefore $\mathbf{j} \times \mathbf{i} = -\mathbf{k}$.

The answers to parts (a) and (c) in the example are a special case of $\mathbf{p} \times \mathbf{q} = -\mathbf{q} \times \mathbf{p}$. If you look again at Fig. 4.1, you will see that using the right-handed rule on **q** and **p** is the reverse of using it on **p** and **q**. Thus the directions of $\mathbf{q} \times \mathbf{p}$ and $\mathbf{p} \times \mathbf{q}$ are directly opposite each other, but the magnitudes are the same. Therefore $\mathbf{p} \times \mathbf{q} = -\mathbf{q} \times \mathbf{p}$.

If s is a scalar, then $s(\mathbf{p} \times \mathbf{q}) = (s\mathbf{p}) \times \mathbf{q}$. The proof, like the corresponding proof for dot products, depends on whether s is positive or negative. You are asked to prove this in Exercise 4A Question 5.

Notice that, assuming that $s(\mathbf{p} \times \mathbf{q}) = (s\mathbf{p}) \times \mathbf{q}$,

$$\mathbf{p} \times (s\mathbf{q}) = -((s\mathbf{q}) \times \mathbf{p}) = -(s(\mathbf{q} \times \mathbf{p})) = -s(\mathbf{q} \times \mathbf{p}) = -s(-(\mathbf{p} \times \mathbf{q})) = s(\mathbf{p} \times \mathbf{q}),$$

so $\mathbf{p} \times (s\mathbf{q}) = s(\mathbf{p} \times \mathbf{q})$, as you would expect.

Summarising these results:

> For vectors $\mathbf{p}$ and $\mathbf{q}$, and a scalar s:
>
> $\mathbf{p} \times \mathbf{q} = -\mathbf{q} \times \mathbf{p};$
>
> $s(\mathbf{p} \times \mathbf{q}) = (s\mathbf{p}) \times \mathbf{q} = \mathbf{p} \times (s\mathbf{q}).$

4.2*   The distributive rule

The distributive rule, which is essential for manipulating vector products, states that:

> For vectors $\mathbf{p}$, $\mathbf{q}$ and $\mathbf{r}$
>
> $(\mathbf{p} + \mathbf{q}) \times \mathbf{r} = \mathbf{p} \times \mathbf{r} + \mathbf{q} \times \mathbf{r}.$

The proof of the distributive rule is difficult. You should omit it on a first reading.

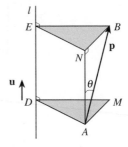

The proof used is similar to the proof, in C4 Section 9.3, of the distributive rule for dot products. The result will first be proved for the case when $\mathbf{r}$ is a unit vector $\mathbf{u}$, drawn vertically.

In Fig. 4.3, $\mathbf{u}$ is a unit vector in the direction of the vertical line l, and $\mathbf{p} = \overrightarrow{AB}$. The shaded triangles ADM and BEN represent horizontal planes through A and B, cutting the line l at D and E. AN is parallel to l, so AN is perpendicular to NB.

Fig. 4.3

Then the magnitude of $\mathbf{p} \times \mathbf{u}$ is

$$1 \times |\mathbf{p}| \sin \theta = AB \sin \theta = NB.$$

The vector $\mathbf{p} \times \mathbf{u}$, which is perpendicular to both $\mathbf{u}$ and $\mathbf{p}$, is in the horizontal plane and perpendicular to NB.

Similarly, in Fig. 4.4, $\mathbf{q} = \overrightarrow{BC}$ and the triangles CFK and CKL lie in the horizontal plane through C which cuts l at F.

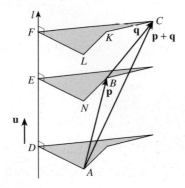

Fig. 4.4

The vector $\mathbf{q} \times \mathbf{u}$ has magnitude KC and is a horizontal vector perpendicular to KC.

And the vector $\mathbf{p} + \mathbf{q}$ is represented by $\overrightarrow{AC}$, so $(\mathbf{p} + \mathbf{q}) \times \mathbf{u}$ has magnitude LC, and direction perpendicular to LC.

Now notice that, in Fig. 4.4, since the shaded parts of the horizontal planes are congruent, the magnitude and direction of NB are equal to those of LK.

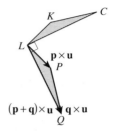

Fig. 4.5 shows a plan view of the triangle LKC, and a copy of triangle LKC rotated through a right angle to get triangle LPQ. Then

$$\mathbf{p} \times \mathbf{u} = \overrightarrow{LP}, \quad \mathbf{q} \times \mathbf{u} = \overrightarrow{PQ}, \quad (\mathbf{p} + \mathbf{q}) \times \mathbf{u} = \overrightarrow{LQ}.$$

Since $\overrightarrow{LP} + \overrightarrow{PQ} = \overrightarrow{LQ}$, it follows that

$$\mathbf{p} \times \mathbf{u} + \mathbf{q} \times \mathbf{u} = (\mathbf{p} + \mathbf{q}) \times \mathbf{u}.$$

Fig. 4.5

It only remains to show from $\mathbf{p} \times \mathbf{u} + \mathbf{q} \times \mathbf{u} = (\mathbf{p} + \mathbf{q}) \times \mathbf{u}$ that $\mathbf{p} \times \mathbf{r} + \mathbf{q} \times \mathbf{r} = (\mathbf{p} + \mathbf{q}) \times \mathbf{r}$. As $\mathbf{u}$ is a unit vector in the direction of $\mathbf{r}$, $\mathbf{r} = s\mathbf{u}$ where s is a positive constant.

$$\begin{aligned}
(\mathbf{p} + \mathbf{q}) \times \mathbf{r} &= (\mathbf{p} + \mathbf{q}) \times (s\mathbf{u}) \\
&= s((\mathbf{p} + \mathbf{q}) \times \mathbf{u}) \\
&= s(\mathbf{p} \times \mathbf{u} + \mathbf{q} \times \mathbf{u}) \\
&= s(\mathbf{p} \times \mathbf{u}) + s(\mathbf{q} \times \mathbf{u}) \\
&= \mathbf{p} \times (s\mathbf{u}) + \mathbf{q} \times (s\mathbf{u}) \\
&= \mathbf{p} \times \mathbf{r} + \mathbf{q} \times \mathbf{r}.
\end{aligned}$$

When you have understood the proof for this case, you will then be able to modify the proof for the case when $\mathbf{r}$ is not vertical by re-drawing Fig. 4.3. In the modification of the proof you will need to replace the term 'vertical' by 'in the direction of l', and the term 'horizontal plane' by 'plane perpendicular to l'.

4.3 Vector products and components

The distributive rule, $(\mathbf{p} + \mathbf{q}) \times \mathbf{r} = \mathbf{p} \times \mathbf{r} + \mathbf{q} \times \mathbf{r}$, enables you to establish results about the vector product in component form.

Example 4.1.1 showed the results of some simple calculations involving vector products. Here is a summary of those and similar calculations.

For the basic unit vectors, $\mathbf{i}$, $\mathbf{j}$ and $\mathbf{k}$,

$$\mathbf{i} \times \mathbf{i} = \mathbf{0}, \qquad \mathbf{i} \times \mathbf{j} = \mathbf{k}, \qquad \mathbf{i} \times \mathbf{k} = -\mathbf{j},$$

$$\mathbf{j} \times \mathbf{i} = -\mathbf{k}, \qquad \mathbf{j} \times \mathbf{j} = \mathbf{0}, \qquad \mathbf{j} \times \mathbf{k} = \mathbf{i},$$

$$\mathbf{k} \times \mathbf{i} = \mathbf{j}, \qquad \mathbf{k} \times \mathbf{j} = -\mathbf{i}, \qquad \mathbf{k} \times \mathbf{k} = \mathbf{0}.$$

It follows that, if vectors $\mathbf{p}$ and $\mathbf{q}$ are written in component form as $\mathbf{p} = p_1\mathbf{i} + p_2\mathbf{j} + p_3\mathbf{k}$ and $\mathbf{q} = q_1\mathbf{i} + q_2\mathbf{j} + q_3\mathbf{k}$, then

$$
\begin{aligned}
\mathbf{p} \times \mathbf{q} &= (p_1\mathbf{i} + p_2\mathbf{j} + p_3\mathbf{k}) \times (q_1\mathbf{i} + q_2\mathbf{j} + q_3\mathbf{k}) \\
&= p_1q_1\mathbf{i} \times \mathbf{i} + p_2q_1\mathbf{j} \times \mathbf{i} + p_3q_1\mathbf{k} \times \mathbf{i} + p_1q_2\mathbf{i} \times \mathbf{j} + p_2q_2\mathbf{j} \times \mathbf{j} \\
&\quad + p_3q_2\mathbf{k} \times \mathbf{j} + p_1q_3\mathbf{i} \times \mathbf{k} + p_2q_3\mathbf{j} \times \mathbf{k} + p_3q_3\mathbf{k} \times \mathbf{k} \\
&= p_1q_1\mathbf{0} + p_2q_1(-\mathbf{k}) + p_3q_1\mathbf{j} + p_1q_2\mathbf{k} + p_2q_2\mathbf{0} \\
&\quad + p_3q_2(-\mathbf{i}) + p_1q_3(-\mathbf{j}) + p_2q_3\mathbf{i} + p_3q_3\mathbf{0} \\
&= (p_2q_3 - p_3q_2)\mathbf{i} + (p_3q_1 - p_1q_3)\mathbf{j} + (p_1q_2 - p_2q_1)\mathbf{k}.
\end{aligned}
$$

In component form:

> The vector product of $\mathbf{p} = \begin{pmatrix} p_1 \\ p_2 \\ p_3 \end{pmatrix}$ and $\mathbf{q} = \begin{pmatrix} q_1 \\ q_2 \\ q_3 \end{pmatrix}$ is
>
> $$\begin{pmatrix} p_1 \\ p_2 \\ p_3 \end{pmatrix} \times \begin{pmatrix} q_1 \\ q_2 \\ q_3 \end{pmatrix} = \begin{pmatrix} p_2q_3 - p_3q_2 \\ p_3q_1 - p_1q_3 \\ p_1q_2 - p_2q_1 \end{pmatrix}.$$

This result is useful for finding a vector perpendicular to two other vectors, and hence for finding a normal to a plane when you know two vectors which lie in the plane.

Some people like to remember the expression for a vector product in the determinant form $\begin{pmatrix} p_1 \\ p_2 \\ p_3 \end{pmatrix} \times \begin{pmatrix} q_1 \\ q_2 \\ q_3 \end{pmatrix} = \det \begin{pmatrix} \mathbf{i} & p_1 & q_1 \\ \mathbf{j} & p_2 & q_2 \\ \mathbf{k} & p_3 & q_3 \end{pmatrix}.$

Example 4.3.1

Find the vector product $\begin{pmatrix} 1 \\ -3 \\ -5 \end{pmatrix} \times \begin{pmatrix} 0 \\ -1 \\ -2 \end{pmatrix}$.

From the formula, $\begin{pmatrix} 1 \\ -3 \\ -5 \end{pmatrix} \times \begin{pmatrix} 0 \\ -1 \\ -2 \end{pmatrix} = \begin{pmatrix} (-3) \times (-2) - (-5) \times (-1) \\ (-5) \times 0 - 1 \times (-2) \\ 1 \times (-1) - (-3) \times 0 \end{pmatrix} = \begin{pmatrix} 1 \\ 2 \\ -1 \end{pmatrix}.$

> It is very easy to check whether you have the vector product correct, because you can mentally find the dot product of your answer with each of the original vectors. If both the dot products are zero, your vector product has a good chance of being correct.

The remainder of the chapter shows you the kinds of methods you can use to solve problems about lines and planes. Although the techniques you need to solve these problems are relatively few, they can be applied in many different ways.

Example 4.3.2

Find the area of the triangle ABC with vertices $A(1, 2, 3)$, $B(4, 6, 2)$ and $C(6, 8, 10)$.

Since the area of the triangle ABC is given by $\frac{1}{2} AB \times AC \times \sin\theta$, where θ = angle BAC, the vector product is useful for finding it, as the area is half the magnitude of $\vec{AB} \times \vec{AC}$.

$$\vec{AB} = \begin{pmatrix} 4 \\ 6 \\ 2 \end{pmatrix} - \begin{pmatrix} 1 \\ 2 \\ 3 \end{pmatrix} = \begin{pmatrix} 3 \\ 4 \\ -1 \end{pmatrix} \quad \text{and} \quad \vec{AC} = \begin{pmatrix} 6 \\ 8 \\ 10 \end{pmatrix} - \begin{pmatrix} 1 \\ 2 \\ 3 \end{pmatrix} = \begin{pmatrix} 5 \\ 6 \\ 7 \end{pmatrix}, \text{ so}$$

$$\vec{AB} \times \vec{AC} = \begin{pmatrix} 3 \\ 4 \\ -1 \end{pmatrix} \times \begin{pmatrix} 5 \\ 6 \\ 7 \end{pmatrix} = \begin{pmatrix} 28 - (-6) \\ -5 - 21 \\ 18 - 20 \end{pmatrix} = \begin{pmatrix} 34 \\ -26 \\ -2 \end{pmatrix}.$$

The area of the triangle is therefore

$$\frac{1}{2}\sqrt{34^2 + (-26)^2 + (-2)^2} = \frac{1}{2} \times 2\sqrt{17^2 + 13^2 + 1^2} = \sqrt{459} = 3\sqrt{51}.$$

The area of the triangle is $3\sqrt{51}$.

Exercise 4A

1 Use the definition of the vector product to calculate the following.

(a) $\mathbf{i} \times \mathbf{k}$ (b) $\mathbf{j} \times \mathbf{j}$ (c) $\mathbf{i} \times \mathbf{j}$

(d) $\mathbf{i} \times \mathbf{i}$ (e) $\mathbf{k} \times \mathbf{j}$ (f) $\mathbf{j} \times \mathbf{k}$

(g) $\mathbf{i} \times (\mathbf{k} \times \mathbf{j})$ (h) $\mathbf{i} \cdot (\mathbf{k} \times \mathbf{j})$ (i) $\mathbf{i} \times (\mathbf{j} \times \mathbf{i})$

2 Use the component formula to calculate the following vector products. Check your answers by ensuring that the dot product of your answer with each of the given vectors is zero.

(a) $\begin{pmatrix} 1 \\ 2 \\ 3 \end{pmatrix} \times \begin{pmatrix} -2 \\ 3 \\ -2 \end{pmatrix}$ (b) $\begin{pmatrix} -2 \\ 3 \\ -1 \end{pmatrix} \times \begin{pmatrix} 1 \\ -5 \\ 0 \end{pmatrix}$ (c) $\begin{pmatrix} 4 \\ -5 \\ 7 \end{pmatrix} \times \begin{pmatrix} 2 \\ -3 \\ 6 \end{pmatrix}$

(d) $\begin{pmatrix} 5 \\ -1 \\ 2 \end{pmatrix} \times \begin{pmatrix} 4 \\ 0 \\ 0 \end{pmatrix}$ (e) $\begin{pmatrix} 1 \\ 0 \\ 0 \end{pmatrix} \times \begin{pmatrix} 0 \\ 1 \\ 0 \end{pmatrix}$ (f) $\begin{pmatrix} 1 \\ 0 \\ 2 \end{pmatrix} \times \begin{pmatrix} 0 \\ 1 \\ 2 \end{pmatrix}$

3 Calculate the following vector products.

(a) $(2\mathbf{i} - \mathbf{j} - \mathbf{k}) \times (\mathbf{j} + \mathbf{k})$ (b) $(\mathbf{i} - \mathbf{j}) \times (\mathbf{j} - \mathbf{k})$

(c) $(\mathbf{i} + 3\mathbf{j} - 2\mathbf{k}) \times (2\mathbf{i} - 3\mathbf{j} + 6\mathbf{k})$ (d) $(\mathbf{i} + 2\mathbf{j} - 2\mathbf{k}) \times (-2\mathbf{i} - \mathbf{j} + 2\mathbf{k})$

(e) $(3\mathbf{i} + 5\mathbf{j} - 4\mathbf{k}) \times \mathbf{i}$ (f) $(6\mathbf{i} + 2\mathbf{j} - 3\mathbf{k}) \times (2\mathbf{i} - 3\mathbf{j} + 6\mathbf{k})$

4 Calculate the area of the triangle with vertices $(-3, 1, 3)$, $(2, 2, 2)$ and $(5, 4, 3)$.

5 Prove that $s(\mathbf{p} \times \mathbf{q}) = (s\mathbf{p}) \times \mathbf{q}$ for any vectors $\mathbf{p}$ and $\mathbf{q}$ and for any scalar s, which could be positive or negative.

4.4 Equations of planes and lines

In this section, the vector product is applied to finding the equations of planes, and to determining the lines of intersection of pairs of planes.

Example 4.4.1 shows a different way of working Example 2.5.6.

Example 4.4.1
Find the cartesian equation of the plane through $A(1, 2, 1)$, $B(2, -1, -4)$ and $C(1, 0, -1)$.

The vectors $\overrightarrow{AB} = \begin{pmatrix} 2 \\ -1 \\ -4 \end{pmatrix} - \begin{pmatrix} 1 \\ 2 \\ 1 \end{pmatrix} = \begin{pmatrix} 1 \\ -3 \\ -5 \end{pmatrix}$ and $\overrightarrow{AC} = \begin{pmatrix} 1 \\ 0 \\ -1 \end{pmatrix} - \begin{pmatrix} 1 \\ 2 \\ 1 \end{pmatrix} = \begin{pmatrix} 0 \\ -2 \\ -2 \end{pmatrix}$ are

parallel to the plane, so the normal to the plane is in the direction

$$\begin{pmatrix} 1 \\ -3 \\ -5 \end{pmatrix} \times \begin{pmatrix} 0 \\ -2 \\ -2 \end{pmatrix} = \begin{pmatrix} 6 - 10 \\ 0 - (-2) \\ -2 - 0 \end{pmatrix} = \begin{pmatrix} -4 \\ 2 \\ -2 \end{pmatrix}.$$

Therefore the equation of the plane is $-4x + 2y - 2z = k$.

Since $(1, 2, 1)$ lies on the plane, the equation is

$$-4x + 2y - 2z = -4 \times 1 + 2 \times 2 - 2 \times 1$$
$$= -2$$

or

$$2x - y + z = 1.$$

Example 4.4.2
Find a vector equation of the line of intersection of the planes $x - y + 2z = 5$ and $3x + 2y + z = 5$.

To find the line of intersection of the planes you need to find the position vector of a point on the line of intersection, and the direction of the line.

To find a point on the line, put $z = 0$ and then solve $x - y = 5$ and $3x + 2y = 5$, to get $y = -2$ and $x = 3$. The point $(3, -2, 0)$ therefore lies on the line.

To find the direction of the line, note that as it lies in both planes it must be perpendicular to the normals of both planes. Thus its direction is

$$\begin{pmatrix} 1 \\ -1 \\ 2 \end{pmatrix} \times \begin{pmatrix} 3 \\ 2 \\ 1 \end{pmatrix} = \begin{pmatrix} -1 - 4 \\ 6 - 1 \\ 2 - (-3) \end{pmatrix} = \begin{pmatrix} -5 \\ 5 \\ 5 \end{pmatrix}.$$

Therefore, dividing by the factor 5 for simplicity, the direction of the line is $\begin{pmatrix} -1 \\ 1 \\ 1 \end{pmatrix}$, so

the vector equation of the line is $\mathbf{r} = \begin{pmatrix} 3 \\ -2 \\ 0 \end{pmatrix} + t \begin{pmatrix} -1 \\ 1 \\ 1 \end{pmatrix}$.

It does not matter which point on the line you take. If you had put $y = 0$, and then found $z = 2$ and $x = 1$, you would have obtained a different vector equation for the same line. In fact, sometimes there may not be a point for which $z = 0$ on the line; in that case put $y = 0$, and if this doesn't work put $x = 0$. One of them must work!

Example 4.4.3

Find the cartesian equation of the plane containing the point $(2, 1, 4)$ and the straight line with cartesian equations $\dfrac{x - 1}{3} = \dfrac{y + 2}{5} = z - 1$.

Fig. 4.6 shows a diagram of this situation.

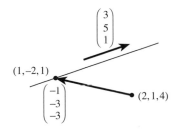

Fig. 4.6

Writing the straight line in the form $\dfrac{x - 1}{3} = \dfrac{y + 2}{5} = z - 1 = t$, you find that

$\begin{pmatrix} x \\ y \\ z \end{pmatrix} = \begin{pmatrix} 1 \\ -2 \\ 1 \end{pmatrix} + t \begin{pmatrix} 3 \\ 5 \\ 1 \end{pmatrix}$, so $(1, -2, 1)$ lies on the line and the line's direction is $\begin{pmatrix} 3 \\ 5 \\ 1 \end{pmatrix}$.

To find the normal to the plane, you need two vectors in the plane before you can use the vector product. Two such vectors are the direction vector of the line, $\begin{pmatrix} 3 \\ 5 \\ 1 \end{pmatrix}$, and

the vector from $(2, 1, 4)$ to $(1, -2, 1)$, that is $\begin{pmatrix} 1 \\ -2 \\ 1 \end{pmatrix} - \begin{pmatrix} 2 \\ 1 \\ 4 \end{pmatrix} = \begin{pmatrix} -1 \\ -3 \\ -3 \end{pmatrix}$.

The normal to the plane is

$$\begin{pmatrix} 3 \\ 5 \\ 1 \end{pmatrix} \times \begin{pmatrix} -1 \\ -3 \\ -3 \end{pmatrix} = \begin{pmatrix} -15 - (-3) \\ -1 - (-9) \\ -9 - (-5) \end{pmatrix} = \begin{pmatrix} -12 \\ 8 \\ -4 \end{pmatrix}.$$

Thus, dividing by -4, the vector $\begin{pmatrix} 3 \\ -2 \\ 1 \end{pmatrix}$ is normal to the plane.

The equation of the plane is $3x - 2y + z = k$, and since $(1, -2, 1)$ lies in the plane, $3x - 2y + z = 3 + 4 + 1 = 8$.

The equation of the required plane is $3x - 2y + z = 8$.

Exercise 4B

1 Find the equation of the plane containing the lines $\mathbf{r} = s\begin{pmatrix} 1 \\ 2 \\ 3 \end{pmatrix}$ and $\mathbf{r} = t\begin{pmatrix} 4 \\ 5 \\ 6 \end{pmatrix}$.

2 Find the direction of the normal to the plane with vector equation

$$\mathbf{r} = 2\mathbf{i} - 3\mathbf{j} - \mathbf{k} + s(\mathbf{i} - 2\mathbf{j} - 4\mathbf{k}) + t(3\mathbf{j} + 2\mathbf{k})$$

and hence write down the cartesian equation of the plane.

3 For each part, find the cartesian equation of the plane through the given points.
   (a) $(1, 0, 3), (2, -4, 3), (4, -1, 2)$ (b) $(2, -1, -1), (-5, 3, 2), (4, -1, -3)$
   (c) $(-3, 1, 3), (2, 2, 2), (5, 4, 3)$ (d) $(1, 2, 3), (5, 6, 8), (0, 1, 2)$

4 Find whether or not the four points $(1, 5, 4), (2, 0, 3), (3, -5, 0)$ and $(0, 10, 6)$ lie in a plane.

5 Find a cartesian equation of the line of intersection of the planes $x + 3y - 6z = 2$ and $2x + 7y - 3z = 7$.

6 Find the vector equation of the line through $(4, 2, -3)$ and parallel to the line of intersection of the planes $3x - 2y = 6$ and $4x + 2z = 7$.

7 Find the equation of the plane through $(3, -2, 4)$ and $(2, -1, 3)$ which is parallel to the line joining $(1, 1, 1)$ to $(2, 3, 5)$.

8 Show that the lines $\mathbf{r} = 3\mathbf{i} + 2\mathbf{j} + \mathbf{k} + t(-\mathbf{i} + 2\mathbf{j} + \mathbf{k})$ and $\mathbf{r} = 3\mathbf{i} + 9\mathbf{j} + 2\mathbf{k} + t(2\mathbf{i} + 3\mathbf{j} - \mathbf{k})$ are coplanar, and find the cartesian equation of the plane which contains them. (Lines that are **coplanar** lie in the same plane.)

9 Find the equation of the plane which passes through the point $(1, 2, 3)$ and contains the line of intersection of the planes $2x - y + z = 4$ and $x + y + z = 4$.

4.5 Other techniques

The methods and techniques which have now been established can be used to solve a number of problems in three dimensions. Here are some examples.

The distance of a point from a line

Example 4.5.1

Find the perpendicular distance from the point $P(2, 1, 4)$ to the straight line with cartesian equations $\dfrac{x-1}{3} = \dfrac{y+2}{5} = z - 1$.

You saw one way of finding the perpendicular distance from a point to a line in Example 2.2.4. This method uses the vector product. Figure 4.7 shows the situation.

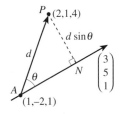

Fig. 4.7

The line can be written in vector form $\begin{pmatrix} x \\ y \\ z \end{pmatrix} = \begin{pmatrix} 1 \\ -2 \\ 1 \end{pmatrix} + t \begin{pmatrix} 3 \\ 5 \\ 1 \end{pmatrix}$, so its direction is

$\begin{pmatrix} 3 \\ 5 \\ 1 \end{pmatrix}$ and $(1, -2, 1)$ is a point on it. Call this point A, and let N be the point where the perpendicular from P meets the line.

If AP has length d, and the angle between AP and the given line is θ, the perpendicular distance PN is $d \sin \theta$.

The factor $\sin \theta$ suggests a vector product. In fact, $d \sin \theta |\mathbf{n}|$ is the magnitude of the vector product $\overrightarrow{AB} \times \mathbf{n}$, where $\mathbf{n}$ is a vector in the direction of the line.

$$\overrightarrow{AP} = \begin{pmatrix} 2 \\ 1 \\ 4 \end{pmatrix} - \begin{pmatrix} 1 \\ -2 \\ 1 \end{pmatrix} = \begin{pmatrix} 1 \\ 3 \\ 3 \end{pmatrix} \quad \text{and} \quad \mathbf{n} = \begin{pmatrix} 3 \\ 5 \\ 1 \end{pmatrix},$$

so $\dfrac{\overrightarrow{AP} \times \mathbf{n}}{|\mathbf{n}|} = \begin{pmatrix} 1 \\ 3 \\ 3 \end{pmatrix} \times \dfrac{1}{\sqrt{35}} \begin{pmatrix} 3 \\ 5 \\ 1 \end{pmatrix} = \dfrac{1}{\sqrt{35}} \begin{pmatrix} -12 \\ 8 \\ -4 \end{pmatrix} = \dfrac{4}{\sqrt{35}} \begin{pmatrix} -3 \\ 2 \\ -1 \end{pmatrix}.$

Finally, $\left| \dfrac{4}{\sqrt{35}} \begin{pmatrix} -3 \\ 2 \\ -1 \end{pmatrix} \right| = \dfrac{4}{\sqrt{35}} \times \sqrt{9 + 4 + 1} = \dfrac{4\sqrt{14}}{\sqrt{35}} = \dfrac{4\sqrt{2}}{\sqrt{5}}.$

The perpendicular distance from P to the line is $\dfrac{4\sqrt{2}}{\sqrt{5}}$.

In general you get the following result.

> The perpendicular distance from the point $\mathbf{p}$ to the line $\mathbf{r} = \mathbf{a} + t\mathbf{b}$ is given by
>
> $$\frac{1}{|\mathbf{b}|}|(\mathbf{p} - \mathbf{a}) \times \mathbf{b}|.$$

The shortest distance between two lines

If you have two lines which do not intersect it is useful to think in terms of a rectangular room. Imagine that one of the lines is the edge of the ceiling and the other is a diagonal of the floor. The left side of Fig. 4.8 shows this.

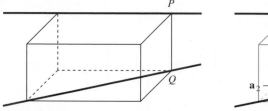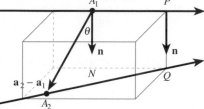

Fig. 4.8

With this construction it is clear that the line PQ, the vertical in the corner of the room, is perpendicular to both the line in the ceiling and the line in the floor. PQ is the shortest distance between the two lines.

The right side of Fig. 4.8 shows the same two lines with the room framework coloured blue. Let the equation of the line in the ceiling be $\mathbf{r} = \mathbf{a}_1 + s\mathbf{b}_1$ and the equation of the floor diagonal be $\mathbf{r} = \mathbf{a}_2 + t\mathbf{b}_2$, where $\mathbf{a}_1$ and $\mathbf{a}_2$ are the position vectors of any points on the lines, and $\mathbf{b}_1$ and $\mathbf{b}_2$ are the direction vectors of the lines.

Drop the perpendicular from A_1 to the floor, meeting the floor at N. Then $A_1 N = PQ$.

The direction vector of PQ and $A_1 N$ is $\mathbf{b}_1 \times \mathbf{b}_2$ (it is perpendicular to both lines). Let $\mathbf{n} = \mathbf{b}_1 \times \mathbf{b}_2$.

Finally, let θ be the angle between $A_1 A_2$ and $A_1 N$.

Then the length PQ is given by

$$PQ = A_1 N$$
$$= A_1 A_2 \cos\theta$$
$$= |\mathbf{a}_2 - \mathbf{a}_1| \cos\theta$$
$$= \frac{|(\mathbf{a}_2 - \mathbf{a}_1) \cdot \mathbf{n}|}{|\mathbf{n}|}.$$

If two lines l_1 and l_2 are given by $\mathbf{r} = \mathbf{a}_1 + t\mathbf{b}_1$ and $\mathbf{r} = \mathbf{a}_2 + t\mathbf{b}_2$ respectively, the shortest distance d between l_1 and l_2 is given by

$$d = \frac{|(\mathbf{a}_2 - \mathbf{a}_1) \cdot \mathbf{n}|}{|\mathbf{n}|} \quad \text{where } \mathbf{n} = \mathbf{b}_1 \times \mathbf{b}_2.$$

Example 4.5.2

Find the shortest distance between the two lines l_1 and l_2 given by the vector equations

$$\mathbf{r} = \begin{pmatrix} 1 \\ 2 \\ 3 \end{pmatrix} + t\begin{pmatrix} -2 \\ 1 \\ -5 \end{pmatrix} \text{ and } \mathbf{r} = \begin{pmatrix} 3 \\ -4 \\ -1 \end{pmatrix} + t\begin{pmatrix} 1 \\ 1 \\ 1 \end{pmatrix} \text{ respectively.}$$

Since the direction vectors of the lines are $\begin{pmatrix} -2 \\ 1 \\ -5 \end{pmatrix}$ and $\begin{pmatrix} 1 \\ 1 \\ 1 \end{pmatrix}$, a line perpendicular to both of them has direction

$$\begin{pmatrix} -2 \\ 1 \\ -5 \end{pmatrix} \times \begin{pmatrix} 1 \\ 1 \\ 1 \end{pmatrix} = \begin{pmatrix} 1 - (-5) \\ (-5) - (-2) \\ -2 - 1 \end{pmatrix} = \begin{pmatrix} 6 \\ -3 \\ -3 \end{pmatrix}.$$

Let $\mathbf{n} = \begin{pmatrix} 6 \\ -3 \\ -3 \end{pmatrix}$, so

$$|\mathbf{n}| = \sqrt{6^2 + (-3)^2 + (-3)^2} = \sqrt{54}.$$

With the notation in the box, $\mathbf{a}_1 = \begin{pmatrix} 1 \\ 2 \\ 3 \end{pmatrix}$ and $\mathbf{a}_2 = \begin{pmatrix} 3 \\ -4 \\ -1 \end{pmatrix}$, so

$$\mathbf{a}_2 - \mathbf{a}_1 = \begin{pmatrix} 3 \\ -4 \\ -1 \end{pmatrix} - \begin{pmatrix} 1 \\ 2 \\ 3 \end{pmatrix} = \begin{pmatrix} 2 \\ -6 \\ -4 \end{pmatrix}.$$

Then the shortest distance is

$$\frac{|\overrightarrow{A_1 A_2} \cdot \mathbf{n}|}{|\mathbf{n}|} = \frac{|(\mathbf{a}_2 - \mathbf{a}_1) \cdot \mathbf{n}|}{|\mathbf{n}|}$$

$$= \frac{\left| \begin{pmatrix} 2 \\ -6 \\ -4 \end{pmatrix} \cdot \begin{pmatrix} 6 \\ -3 \\ -3 \end{pmatrix} \right|}{\sqrt{54}}$$

$$= \frac{1}{\sqrt{54}} |12 + 18 + 12|$$

$$= \frac{42}{\sqrt{54}} = \frac{14}{\sqrt{6}}.$$

Example 4.5.3 following is not about a specific technique.

Example 4.5.3

(a) Find the cartesian equation of the plane Π which passes through the point P with coordinates $(3, 2, 0)$ and which is perpendicular to the planes with equations $x + y = 3$ and $y - z = 2$.

(b) Let l be the line in Π which passes through P and which is perpendicular to OP, where O is the origin. Find the vector equation of l.

(a) If Π is perpendicular to the planes $x + y = 3$ and $y - z = 2$, the normal to Π is perpendicular to the normals to the planes, which are $\begin{pmatrix} 1 \\ 1 \\ 0 \end{pmatrix}$ and $\begin{pmatrix} 0 \\ 1 \\ -1 \end{pmatrix}$.

A vector perpendicular to $\begin{pmatrix} 1 \\ 1 \\ 0 \end{pmatrix}$ and $\begin{pmatrix} 0 \\ 1 \\ -1 \end{pmatrix}$ is $\begin{pmatrix} 1 \\ 1 \\ 0 \end{pmatrix} \times \begin{pmatrix} 0 \\ 1 \\ -1 \end{pmatrix} = \begin{pmatrix} -1 \\ 1 \\ 1 \end{pmatrix}$.

So the required plane is

$$-x + y + z = -3 + 2 + 0 = -1,$$

or $x - y - z = 1.$

(b) The direction of OP is $\overrightarrow{OP} = \begin{pmatrix} 3 \\ 2 \\ 0 \end{pmatrix} - \begin{pmatrix} 0 \\ 0 \\ 0 \end{pmatrix} = \begin{pmatrix} 3 \\ 2 \\ 0 \end{pmatrix}$.

As l is perpendicular to $\overrightarrow{OP}$ and to the normal to Π it is in the direction

$\begin{pmatrix} 3 \\ 2 \\ 0 \end{pmatrix} \times \begin{pmatrix} -1 \\ 1 \\ 1 \end{pmatrix} = \begin{pmatrix} 2 \\ -3 \\ 5 \end{pmatrix}$. Its vector equation is $\mathbf{r} = \begin{pmatrix} 3 \\ 2 \\ 0 \end{pmatrix} + t \begin{pmatrix} 2 \\ -3 \\ 5 \end{pmatrix}$.

Exercise 4C

1 (a) Find in vector form, the equations of the lines with cartesian equations

$$x - 1 = \frac{y + 2}{2} = \frac{z}{-1} \quad \text{and} \quad \frac{x - 4}{2} = \frac{y + 4}{3} = \frac{z + 4}{-1}.$$

(b) Find a vector $\mathbf{n}$ in the direction of the common perpendicular to the lines in part (a).

(c) Explain why, for some fixed value of α, the equation

$$\mathbf{r} = \mathbf{i} - 2\mathbf{j} + \alpha(\mathbf{i} + 2\mathbf{j} - \mathbf{k}) + s(\mathbf{i} - \mathbf{j} - \mathbf{k}),$$

where s is a parameter, represents the common perpendicular to the two lines.

(d) Find α and s, and find where the common perpendicular meets the line with equation $\frac{x - 4}{2} = \frac{y + 4}{3} = \frac{z + 4}{-1}$.

(e) Hence find the length of the common perpendicular. Check your answer using the result in the blue box preceding Example 4.5.2.

2 Find the vector equation of the common perpendicular to the lines with cartesian equations $x = y = z$ and $\dfrac{x}{-2} = y - 1 = \dfrac{z - 12}{-4}$.

3 (a) Find the equation of the plane which contains the origin and the straight line l with cartesian equation $x - 1 = y - 1 = z - 2$.

   (b) Find a vector in the direction of the perpendicular from the origin to l.

   (c) Find the coordinates of the foot of the perpendicular from the origin to l.

4 Find the distance of the point $(1, 1, 4)$ from the line $\mathbf{r} = \mathbf{i} - 2\mathbf{j} + \mathbf{k} + t(-2\mathbf{i} + \mathbf{j} + 2\mathbf{k})$.

5 The planes Π_1 and Π_2 have equations $x - y = 3$ and $x + z = 0$ respectively.

   (a) Find a vector equation for the line of intersection of the planes Π_1 and Π_2.

   (b) Find a vector equation for the perpendicular from the origin to the line of intersection of the planes Π_1 and Π_2.

6* Note that the formula in the box preceding Example 4.5.2 for the distance between two straight lines does not hold if the lines are parallel.

   What goes wrong in the argument used in the derivation of the formula in the case when the lines are parallel?

Miscellaneous exercise 4

1 Find the following cross products.

   (a) $\begin{pmatrix} 8 \\ -3 \\ 1 \end{pmatrix} \times \begin{pmatrix} 7 \\ -2 \\ 0 \end{pmatrix}$ (b) $\begin{pmatrix} 4 \\ -1 \\ -3 \end{pmatrix} \times \begin{pmatrix} 3 \\ 5 \\ 1 \end{pmatrix}$ (c) $\begin{pmatrix} 2 \\ 0 \\ 1 \end{pmatrix} \times \begin{pmatrix} 1 \\ 0 \\ 2 \end{pmatrix}$

2 Find the following cross products.

   (a) $(3\mathbf{i} - 2\mathbf{k}) \times 2\mathbf{k}$ (b) $5\mathbf{k} \times (\mathbf{i} + 2\mathbf{j} - 3\mathbf{k})$ (c) $(2\mathbf{i} + \mathbf{j}) \times (2\mathbf{i} + \mathbf{j})$

3 Find the equation of the plane through $(1, 2, -4)$ perpendicular to the line joining $(3, 1, -1)$ to $(1, 4, 7)$.

4 Prove that the planes $2x - 3y + z = 4$, $x + 4y - z = 7$ and $3x - 10y + 3z = 1$ meet in a line.

5 Find the equation of the plane which passes through the point $(3, -4, 1)$ and which is parallel to the plane containing the point $(1, 2, -1)$ and the line $x = y = z$.

6 The planes Π_1 and Π_2 have equations $\mathbf{r} \cdot (\mathbf{i} - 2\mathbf{j} + 2\mathbf{k}) = 1$ and $\mathbf{r} \cdot (2\mathbf{i} + 2\mathbf{j} - \mathbf{k}) = 3$ respectively. Find

   (a) the acute angle between Π_1 and Π_2, correct to the nearest degree,

   (b) the equation of the line of intersection of Π_1 and Π_2, in the form $\mathbf{r} = \mathbf{a} + t\mathbf{b}$.   (OCR)

7 The lines l_1 and l_2 have equations $\mathbf{r} = (5\mathbf{i} + \mathbf{j} + 5\mathbf{k}) + \lambda(\mathbf{i} - \mathbf{j} - 2\mathbf{k})$ and
$\mathbf{r} = (\mathbf{i} + 11\mathbf{j} + 2\mathbf{k}) + \lambda(-4\mathbf{i} - 14\mathbf{j} + 2\mathbf{k})$.

(a) Find the exact value of the shortest distance between l_1 and l_2.

(b) Find an equation for the plane containing l_1 and parallel to l_2 in the form
$ax + by + cz = d$. (OCR)

8 The line L has equation $\mathbf{r} = (3\mathbf{i} + 4\mathbf{j} - 3\mathbf{k}) + t(2\mathbf{i} - \mathbf{j} - 2\mathbf{k})$ and the point P has position
vector $4\mathbf{j} + 3\mathbf{k}$. Find an equation of the plane which contains both L and P, giving your
answer in the form $ax + by + cz = d$. (OCR)

9 Two skew lines, l_1 and l_2, have equations $\mathbf{r} = \mathbf{i} - \mathbf{j} + 4\mathbf{k} + s(3\mathbf{j} + \mathbf{k})$ and
$\mathbf{r} = 2\mathbf{i} + 3\mathbf{j} + t(-2\mathbf{i} + \mathbf{k})$ respectively. Find

(a) a vector perpendicular to both l_1 and l_2,

(b) the shortest distance between l_1 and l_2. (OCR)

10 Find the length of the common perpendicular between the lines $x = y - 1 = 2z - 1$ and
$2x = -y = 3z$.

11 The position vectors $\mathbf{a}$, $\mathbf{b}$ and $\mathbf{c}$ of A, B and C relative to an origin O are
$\begin{pmatrix} 4 \\ 3 \\ -3 \end{pmatrix}$, $\begin{pmatrix} 2 \\ 0 \\ 2 \end{pmatrix}$ and $\begin{pmatrix} 5 \\ 1 \\ -1 \end{pmatrix}$ respectively.

(a) Write down the vectors $\mathbf{c} - \mathbf{a}$ and $\mathbf{b} - \mathbf{a}$.

(b) Use a vector method to calculate the area of the triangle ABC. (OCR)

12 Let l_1 denote the line passing through the points $A(2, -1, 1)$ and $B(0, 5, -7)$, and l_2 denote
the line passing through the points $C(1, -1, 1)$ and $D(1, -4, 5)$.

(a) Write down a vector equation of the line l_1 and a vector equation of the line l_2.

(b) Show that the lines l_1 and l_2 intersect, and determine the point of intersection.

(c) Calculate the acute angle between the lines l_1 and l_2.

(d) Determine a vector perpendicular to both lines l_1 and l_2 and hence show that the
cartesian equation of the plane containing l_1 and l_2 is $4y + 3z = -1$.

13 The position vectors $\mathbf{a}$, $\mathbf{b}$ and $\mathbf{c}$ of three points A, B and C are $\begin{pmatrix} 2 \\ -1 \\ 4 \end{pmatrix}$, $\begin{pmatrix} 1 \\ 1 \\ 3 \end{pmatrix}$ and $\begin{pmatrix} 3 \\ -2 \\ 1 \end{pmatrix}$
respectively.

(a) Determine $(\mathbf{a} - \mathbf{b}) \times (\mathbf{c} - \mathbf{b})$.

(b) Hence, or otherwise,

(i) find a vector equation for the plane through A, B and C giving your answer in the
form $\mathbf{r} \cdot \mathbf{n} = d$;

(ii) find, in surd form, an expression for the area of the triangle ABC. (OCR)

14 Two lines have vector equations $\mathbf{r} = \begin{pmatrix} 12 \\ 0 \\ 2 \end{pmatrix} + \lambda \begin{pmatrix} 14 \\ 4 \\ -5 \end{pmatrix}$ and $\mathbf{r} = \begin{pmatrix} -1 \\ 1 \\ 6 \end{pmatrix} + \mu \begin{pmatrix} -1 \\ 1 \\ 1 \end{pmatrix}$.

(a) Determine a unit vector, $\mathbf{u}$, which is perpendicular to both lines.

(b) Find the shortest distance between the two lines. (OCR)

15 The line l_1 passes through the point A, whose position vector is $\mathbf{i} - \mathbf{j} - 5\mathbf{k}$, and is parallel to the vector $\mathbf{i} - \mathbf{j} - 4\mathbf{k}$. The line l_2 passes through the point B, whose position vector is $2\mathbf{i} - 9\mathbf{j} - 14\mathbf{k}$, and is parallel to the vector $2\mathbf{i} + 5\mathbf{j} + 6\mathbf{k}$. The point P on l_1 and the point Q on l_2 are such that PQ is perpendicular to both l_1 and l_2.

(a) Find the length of PQ.

(b) Find a vector perpendicular to the plane Π which contains PQ and l_2.

(c) Find the perpendicular distance from A to Π. (OCR)

16 The points A and B have position vectors $\mathbf{a} = \begin{pmatrix} -1 \\ 4 \\ 7 \end{pmatrix}$ and $\mathbf{b} = \begin{pmatrix} 8 \\ -7 \\ 4 \end{pmatrix}$ respectively. The line l_1 has vector equation $\mathbf{r} = \begin{pmatrix} -1 \\ 4 \\ 7 \end{pmatrix} + \lambda \begin{pmatrix} -1 \\ 4 \\ 3 \end{pmatrix}$ where λ is a scalar parameter, while the line l_2 passes through B and is parallel to the vector $\begin{pmatrix} 1 \\ 4 \\ -1 \end{pmatrix}$.

(a) Write down the vector $\mathbf{b} - \mathbf{a}$.

(b) Write down a vector equation for the line l_2.

(c) Determine the unit vector $\hat{\mathbf{n}}$, where $\hat{\mathbf{n}}$ is perpendicular to both the lines l_1 and l_2.

(d) Find the shortest distance between l_1 and l_2. (OCR)

17 The coordinates of four points are $A(2, -9, -5)$, $B(5, -4, -4)$, $C(8, 15, 4)$ and $D(7, 18, 6)$.

(a) Calculate the vector product $\overrightarrow{AB} \times \overrightarrow{CD}$.

(b) Show that the lines AB and CD intersect, and find the coordinates of the point of intersection.

(c) Find, in the form $ax + by + cz + d = 0$, the equation of the plane Π which contains the four points A, B, C and D.

(d) Find the equation of the plane which contains the line AB and is perpendicular to the plane Π. (MEI)

18* Find a formula in terms of the vectors $\mathbf{a}$, $\mathbf{b}$, $\mathbf{c}$ and $\mathbf{d}$ for the shortest distance between the lines $\mathbf{r} = \mathbf{a} + t\mathbf{b}$ and $\mathbf{r} = \mathbf{c} + t\mathbf{d}$.

5 Complex numbers in polar form

New insights about complex numbers come by expressing them in terms of modulus and argument. When you have completed this chapter, you should

- know how to express a complex number in polar form
- be able to multiply and divide complex numbers in polar form
- know how to represent multiplication and division geometrically
- be able to solve geometrical problems involving angles using complex numbers
- be able to write square roots in polar form
- know that complex numbers can be written as exponentials.

Section 5.4 uses the Maclaurin series for e^x, $\sin x$ and $\cos x$ which are explained in FP2 Chapter 3.

5.1 Modulus and argument

FP1 Chapter 9 introduced two quantities associated with a complex number $z = x + y\mathrm{i}$.

- The modulus, $|z|$, is defined as $\sqrt{x^2 + y^2}$. Important properties of the modulus are that $|z| \geqslant 0$ and that $|z|^2 = zz^*$.

- The argument, $\arg z$, is defined as the angle θ in the interval $-\pi < \theta \leqslant \pi$ such that

$$\cos\theta = \frac{x}{|z|} \quad \text{and} \quad \sin\theta = \frac{y}{|z|}.$$

The argument is not defined if $z = 0$.

If z is represented in an Argand diagram by a point Z, as in Fig. 5.1, then $|z|$ is the distance OZ, and $\arg z$ is the angle which the displacement $\overrightarrow{OZ}$ makes with the real axis.

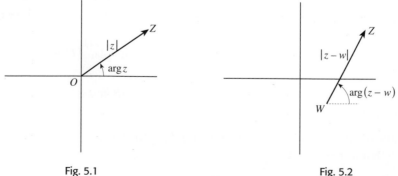

Fig. 5.1   Fig. 5.2

More generally, if two complex numbers z and w are represented in an Argand diagram by points W and Z, as in Fig. 5.2, then $|z - w|$ is the distance WZ, and $\arg(z - w)$ is the angle which the displacement $\overrightarrow{WZ}$ makes with the direction of the real axis.

In Fig. 5.1, if you know the values of $|z|$ and $\arg z$, then you can locate the point Z by starting at O and moving a distance $|z|$ along a line whose direction makes an angle $\arg z$ with the real axis. So knowing both $|z|$ and $\arg z$ is sufficient to determine the complex number z.

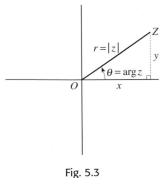

Fig. 5.3

It is usual to use the letter r to stand for $|z|$, and θ for $\arg z$, as in Fig. 5.3. If $r \neq 0$, the equations

$$\cos\theta = \frac{x}{|z|} = \frac{x}{r} \quad \text{and} \quad \sin\theta = \frac{y}{|z|} = \frac{y}{r}$$

can be rearranged as

$$x = r\cos\theta \quad \text{and} \quad y = r\sin\theta.$$

It follows that

$$z = x + y\mathrm{i} = r\cos\theta + r\sin\theta\,\mathrm{i} = r(\cos\theta + \mathrm{i}\sin\theta).$$

This is called the polar form of the complex number z. (It is better to write the second term in the bracket as $\mathrm{i}\sin\theta$ rather than as $\sin\theta\,\mathrm{i}$, which might be confused with $\sin(\theta\mathrm{i})$.)

> The complex number $z(\neq 0)$ can be written in **polar form** as
> $z = r(\cos\theta + \mathrm{i}\sin\theta)$, where $r = |z| > 0$ is the modulus and
> $\theta = \arg z$, with $-\pi < \theta \leq \pi$, is the argument.

Polar form is also called **modulus–argument form**.

You can use either geometric or algebraic methods to find the polar form of a complex number. These are shown in the next two examples.

Example 5.1.1
Use an Argand diagram to express in polar form

(a) $1 + \mathrm{i}$,   (b) $-3\mathrm{i}$,   (c) -2.

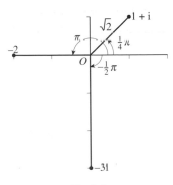

Figure 5.4 is an Argand diagram showing the three numbers. It is easy to write down the moduli and arguments from the figure, with the conditions $|z| \geq 0$ and $-\pi < \arg z \leq \pi$.

(a) $1 + \mathrm{i} = \sqrt{2}\left(\cos\tfrac{1}{4}\pi + \mathrm{i}\sin\tfrac{1}{4}\pi\right)$.

(b) $-3\mathrm{i} = 3\left(\cos\left(-\tfrac{1}{2}\pi\right) + \mathrm{i}\sin\left(-\tfrac{1}{2}\pi\right)\right)$.

(c) $-2 = 2(\cos\pi + \mathrm{i}\sin\pi)$.

Fig. 5.4

Example 5.1.2
Express $z = \pi - e\mathrm{i}$ in modulus–argument form, giving the modulus correct to 3 significant figures and the argument correct to 3 decimal places.

Method 1   Begin by calculating $|z| = \sqrt{\pi^2 + e^2} = 4.154....$ Put this into the calculator memory for use in calculating the argument.

If $\arg z = \theta$, then

$$\cos\theta = \frac{\pi}{4.154...} = 0.7562... \quad \text{and} \quad \sin\theta = \frac{-e}{4.154...} = -0.6543....$$

The roots of $\cos\theta = 0.7562...$ in the interval $-\pi < \theta \leqslant \pi$ are $0.7132...$ and $-0.7132....$

The roots of $\sin\theta = -0.6543...$ in the interval $-\pi < \theta \leqslant \pi$ are $-0.7132...$ and $-(\pi - 0.7132...) = -2.4283....$

Since θ has to satisfy both equations, $\arg z$ is the common root, which is $-0.7132....$ So in modulus–argument form, to the specified accuracy,

$$\pi - ei = 4.15(\cos(-0.713) + i\sin(-0.713))$$

Method 2   If your calculator has a cartesian–polar conversion key, input the cartesian coordinates $x = \pi$, $y = -e$ and read off the modulus and argument $4.154...$ and $-0.7132....$ Check that $-0.7132...$ lies between $-\pi$ and π, so that the calculator gives the argument within the required interval. Then, to the specified accuracy,

$$\pi - ei = 4.15(\cos(-0.713) + i\sin(-0.713)).$$

If you have read FP2 Chapter 6, you will recognise the modulus and argument of z as the polar coordinates (r, θ) of the point Z in Fig. 5.3. This is why the modulus–argument form of a complex number is called the 'polar form'.

There is, though, an important difference. In polar coordinates two conventions about the angle θ are often used, either that $0 \leqslant \theta < 2\pi$ or that $-\pi < \theta \leqslant \pi$. Also, it was pointed out in FP2 Section 6.10 that it is convenient sometimes to allow r to take negative values, or for θ to take values in an interval of extent greater than 2π. In the complex number application, $|z|$ can never be negative, and $\arg z$ must always be taken in the interval from $-\pi$ up to and including π.

Exercise 5A

1 Show these numbers on an Argand diagram, and write them in the form $a + bi$. Where appropriate leave surds in your answers, or give answers correct to 2 decimal places.

(a) $2\left(\cos\frac{1}{3}\pi + i\sin\frac{1}{3}\pi\right)$ (b) $10\left(\cos\frac{3}{4}\pi + i\sin\frac{3}{4}\pi\right)$ (c) $5\left(\cos\left(-\frac{1}{2}\pi\right) + i\sin\left(-\frac{1}{2}\pi\right)\right)$

(d) $3(\cos\pi + i\sin\pi)$ (e) $10(\cos 2 + i\sin 2)$ (f) $\cos(-3) + i\sin(-3)$

2 Write these complex numbers in polar form. Where appropriate express the argument as a rational multiple of π, otherwise give the modulus and argument correct to 2 decimal places.

(a) 5 (b) $2i$ (c) -10 (d) $-i$

(e) $\sqrt{3} + i$ (f) $1 - \sqrt{3}i$ (g) $-2 + 2i$ (h) $-\sqrt{2} - \sqrt{2}i$

(i) $12 + 5i$ (j) $4 - 3i$ (k) $-1 + 2i$ (l) $-2 - 3i$

5.2   Multiplication and division

If s and t are complex numbers, the sum $s + t$ can be shown geometrically by the parallelogram rule in an Argand diagram (see FP1 Section 7.7). But you do not yet have a geometric way of representing multiplication. The key to this is to express s and t in polar form.

Suppose that s has modulus p and argument α, and t has modulus q and argument β.

Then

$$st = p(\cos\alpha + i\sin\alpha) \times q(\cos\beta + i\sin\beta)$$
$$= pq(\cos\alpha\cos\beta + i\sin\alpha\cos\beta + i\cos\alpha\sin\beta + i^2\sin\alpha\sin\beta)$$
$$= pq((\cos\alpha\cos\beta - \sin\alpha\sin\beta) + i(\sin\alpha\cos\beta + \cos\alpha\sin\beta)).$$

You will recognise the expressions inside the brackets as the expanded forms for $\cos(\alpha + \beta)$ and $\sin(\alpha + \beta)$. Therefore

$$st = pq(\cos(\alpha + \beta) + i\sin(\alpha + \beta)).$$

So pq (which is positive, since $p > 0$ and $q > 0$) is the modulus of st. It may also be true that $\alpha + \beta$ is the argument of st; but if addition takes $\alpha + \beta$ outside the interval $-\pi < \theta \le \pi$, then you must adjust $\alpha + \beta$ by adding or subtracting 2π to bring it inside the interval.

This shows that the modulus of the product st is found by multiplying the moduli of s and t, and the argument of the product is found by adding the arguments of s and t, with a possible adjustment by adding or subtracting 2π.

Example 5.2.1

If $s = 1 + 2i$ and $t = 2 + 3i$,

(a) calculate st;

(b) find the modulus and argument of s, t and st;

(c) verify that $|s| \times |t| = |st|$ and $\arg s + \arg t = \arg(st)$.

(a) $st = (1 + 2i)(2 + 3i)$

$\qquad = 2 + 3i + 4i + 6i^2$

$\qquad = 2 + 3i + 4i - 6$

$\qquad = -4 + 7i.$

(b) $|s| = \sqrt{1^2 + 2^2} = \sqrt{5}$, $|t| = \sqrt{2^2 + 3^2} = \sqrt{13}$ and $|st| = \sqrt{(-4)^2 + 7^2} = \sqrt{65}$.

If $\arg s = \theta$, $\arg t = \phi$ and $\arg(st) = \psi$,

$$\cos\theta = \frac{1}{\sqrt{5}} \text{ and } \sin\theta = \frac{2}{\sqrt{5}}, \text{ so } \arg s = 1.107\ldots;$$

$$\cos\phi = \frac{2}{\sqrt{13}} \text{ and } \sin\phi = \frac{3}{\sqrt{13}}, \text{ so } \arg t = 0.982\ldots;$$

$$\cos\psi = \frac{-4}{\sqrt{65}} \text{ and } \sin\psi = \frac{7}{\sqrt{65}}, \text{ so } \arg(st) = 2.089\ldots.$$

(c) $|s| \times |t| = \sqrt{5} \times \sqrt{13} = \sqrt{5 \times 13} = \sqrt{65} = |st|,$

$\qquad$ and $\arg s + \arg t = 1.107\ldots + 0.982\ldots = 2.089\ldots.$

Since complex numbers are multiplied by multiplying the moduli and adding the arguments, you would expect them to be divided by dividing the moduli and subtracting the arguments.

To show this, define s and t as before and let $w = \dfrac{s}{t}$. Then $wt = s$, so by the multiplication rule

$$|w| \times |t| = |s| \quad \text{and} \quad \arg w + \arg t = \arg s,$$

possibly adjusted by adding or subtracting 2π.

So $|w| = \dfrac{|s|}{|t|}$ and $\arg w = \arg s - \arg t,$

possibly adjusted by adding or subtracting 2π.

> The rules for multiplication and division in modulus–argument form are
>
> $$|st| = |s||t|, \quad \arg(st) = \arg s + \arg t + k(2\pi),$$
>
> $$\left|\frac{s}{t}\right| = \frac{|s|}{|t|}, \quad \arg\left(\frac{s}{t}\right) = \arg s - \arg t + k(2\pi),$$
>
> where in each case the number $k\,(= -1, 0 \text{ or } 1)$ is chosen to ensure that the argument lies in the interval $-\pi < \theta \leqslant \pi$.

Example 5.2.2
Show $s = -\sqrt{3} + i$ and $t = \sqrt{2} + \sqrt{2}\,i$ as points in an Argand diagram. Find st and $\dfrac{s}{t}$ in polar form, and put them into the diagram.

You will recognise in Fig. 5.5 triangles with angles of $\tfrac{1}{6}\pi$ and $\tfrac{1}{4}\pi$, so that

Fig. 5.5

 s has modulus $p = 2$ and argument $\alpha = \tfrac{5}{6}\pi$,

 t has modulus $q = 2$ and argument $\beta = \tfrac{1}{4}\pi$.

It follows that st has modulus $pq = 2 \times 2 = 4$. Since $\alpha + \beta = \tfrac{5}{6}\pi + \tfrac{1}{4}\pi = \tfrac{13}{12}\pi$, which is greater than π, the argument of st must be adjusted to $\tfrac{13}{12}\pi - 2\pi = -\tfrac{11}{12}\pi$.

Also $\dfrac{s}{t}$ has modulus $\dfrac{p}{q} = \dfrac{2}{2} = 1$. Its argument is $\alpha - \beta = \tfrac{5}{6}\pi - \tfrac{1}{4}\pi = \tfrac{7}{12}\pi$; this is between $-\pi$ and π, so no adjustment is necessary.

Therefore

$$st = 4\left(\cos\left(-\tfrac{11}{12}\pi\right) + i\sin\left(-\tfrac{11}{12}\pi\right)\right) \quad \text{and} \quad \frac{s}{t} = \cos\tfrac{7}{12}\pi + i\sin\tfrac{7}{12}\pi.$$

The corresponding points are shown on an Argand diagram in Fig. 5.6.

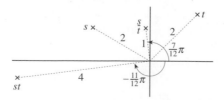

Fig. 5.6

Example 5.2.3

If z is a complex number, prove that

(a) zz^* has argument 0,   (b) $\dfrac{z}{z^*}$ has modulus 1.

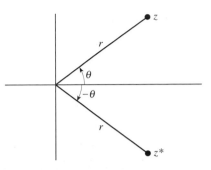

Fig. 5.7

In an Argand diagram z and z^* are represented by points symmetrically placed with respect to the real axis. If z has modulus r and argument θ, z^* has modulus r and argument $-\theta$. See Fig. 5.7.

Using the rules for the argument of st and the modulus of $\dfrac{s}{t}$,

(a) zz^* has argument $\theta + (-\theta) = 0$,

(b) $\dfrac{z}{z^*}$ has modulus $\dfrac{r}{r} = 1$.

Exercise 5B

1 If $s = 2\left(\cos \frac{1}{3}\pi + i\sin \frac{1}{3}\pi\right)$, $t = \cos \frac{1}{4}\pi + i\sin \frac{1}{4}\pi$ and $u = 4\left(\cos\left(-\frac{5}{6}\pi\right) + i\sin\left(-\frac{5}{6}\pi\right)\right)$, write the following in polar form.

(a) st (b) $\dfrac{s}{t}$ (c) $\dfrac{t}{s}$ (d) su

(e) $\dfrac{u}{s}$ (f) $\dfrac{t}{u}$ (g) s^2 (h) u^2

(i) $st^2 u$ (j) $\dfrac{2s}{tu}$ (k) s^* (l) st^*

(m) ts^* (n) $\dfrac{u^*}{t^2}$ (o) $\dfrac{1}{t}$ (p) $\dfrac{2}{s}$

(q) $\dfrac{4i}{u^*}$ (r) $\dfrac{s^3}{u}$

2 If $s = 3\left(\cos \frac{1}{5}\pi + i\sin \frac{1}{5}\pi\right)$ and if $s^2 t = 18\left(\cos\left(-\frac{4}{5}\pi\right) + i\sin\left(-\frac{4}{5}\pi\right)\right)$, express t in polar form.

3 If $s = \cos \frac{2}{3}\pi + i\sin \frac{2}{3}\pi$ and $t = \cos \frac{1}{4}\pi + i\sin \frac{1}{4}\pi$, show in an Argand diagram

(a) s,   (b) st,   (c) st^2,

(d) st^3,   (e) $\dfrac{s}{t}$,   (f) $\dfrac{s}{t^2}$.

4 Repeat Question 3 with $s = 4\left(\cos \frac{2}{3}\pi + i\sin \frac{2}{3}\pi\right)$ and $t = 2\left(\cos \frac{1}{4}\pi + i\sin \frac{1}{4}\pi\right)$.

5 Give the argument of the following complex numbers.

(a) $\cos \frac{4}{3}\pi + i\sin \frac{4}{3}\pi$ (b) $\cos 2 - i\sin 2$ (c) $\sin \frac{1}{6}\pi + i\cos \frac{1}{6}\pi$

(d) $1 + i\tan \frac{1}{3}\pi$ (e) $1 + i\tan \frac{2}{3}\pi$ (f) $-\cos \frac{1}{5}\pi + i\sin \frac{1}{5}\pi$

(g) $\sin \frac{4}{7}\pi - i\cos \frac{4}{7}\pi$ (h) $i + \tan \frac{2}{7}\pi$ (i) $1 - i\cot \frac{1}{8}\pi$

6 Give the answers to the following questions in polar form.

(a) If $s = \cos\theta + i\sin\theta$, express s^* in terms of θ.

(b) If $s = \cos\theta + i\sin\theta$, express $\dfrac{1}{s}$ in terms of θ.

(c) If $t = r(\cos\theta + i\sin\theta)$, express t^* in terms of r and θ.

(d) If $t = r(\cos\theta + i\sin\theta)$, express $\dfrac{1}{t}$ in terms of r and θ.

7 Write $1 + \sqrt{3}\,i$ and $1 - i$ in polar form. Hence express $\dfrac{(1+\sqrt{3}\,i)^4}{(1-i)^6}$ in the form $a + b\,i$.

8 By converting into and out of polar form, evaluate the following with the aid of a calculator. Use the binomial theorem to check your answers.

(a) $(1 + 2\,i)^3$ (b) $(3i - 2)^5$ (c) $(3 - i)^{-4}$

9 Show in an Argand diagram the points representing the complex numbers i, $-i$ and $\sqrt{3}$. Hence write down the values of

(a) $\arg(\sqrt{3} - i)$,   (b) $\arg(\sqrt{3} + i)$,   (c) $\arg\dfrac{\sqrt{3}+i}{\sqrt{3}-i}$,   (d) $\arg\dfrac{2i}{\sqrt{3}+i}$.

5.3 Square roots of complex numbers

FP1 Section 7.8 gave a method of finding square roots of complex numbers in the form $a + b\,i$. You can also use a method based on polar form.

A special case of the rule for multiplying two complex numbers is that, if $s = p(\cos\alpha + i\sin\alpha)$, then $s^2 = p^2(\cos 2\alpha + i\sin 2\alpha)$. That is, to square a complex number, you square the modulus and double the argument (adjusting by 2π if necessary).

It follows that, to find a square root, you take the square root of the modulus and halve the argument. That is,

$$\sqrt{s} = \sqrt{p}\left(\cos\tfrac{1}{2}\alpha + i\sin\tfrac{1}{2}\alpha\right).$$

This is illustrated on an Argand diagram in Fig. 5.8.

The equation gives only one of the two square roots. Since the two square roots of s are of the form $\pm\sqrt{s}$, they are symmetrically placed around the origin in the Argand diagram. So the other root also has modulus $\sqrt{p}$, and has argument $\tfrac{1}{2}\alpha \pm \pi$, where the $+$ or $-$ sign is chosen so that the argument is between $-\pi$ and π.

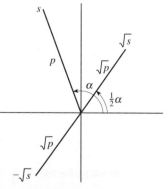

Fig. 5.8

> The square roots of a complex number s have modulus $\sqrt{|s|}$ and arguments $\tfrac{1}{2}\arg s$ and $\tfrac{1}{2}\arg s \pm \pi$, where the sign is $+$ if $\arg s < 0$ and $-$ if $\arg s \geqslant 0$.

Example 5.3.1

Find the square roots of   (a) $8\,\mathrm{i}$,   (b) $3 - 4\,\mathrm{i}$ (see FP1 Example 7.8.1).

(a) $8\,\mathrm{i}$ has modulus 8 and argument $\frac{1}{2}\pi$. So its square roots have modulus $\sqrt{8} = 2\sqrt{2}$ and arguments $\frac{1}{4}\pi$ and $\frac{1}{4}\pi - \pi = -\frac{3}{4}\pi$. In cartesian form, these are

$$2\sqrt{2}\left(\frac{1}{\sqrt{2}} + \frac{1}{\sqrt{2}}\mathrm{i}\right) \quad\text{and}\quad 2\sqrt{2}\left(-\frac{1}{\sqrt{2}} - \frac{1}{\sqrt{2}}\mathrm{i}\right),$$

that is $2 + 2\,\mathrm{i}$ and $-2 - 2\,\mathrm{i}$.

(b) $3 - 4\,\mathrm{i}$ has modulus $\sqrt{3^2 + (-4)^2} = 5$ and argument $-\tan^{-1}\frac{4}{3} = -0.927\,295\,2\ldots$. The square roots therefore have modulus $\sqrt{5}$ and arguments $-0.463\,647\,6\ldots$ and $-0.463\,647\,6\ldots + \pi$. In cartesian form, these are $2 - \mathrm{i}$ and $-2 + \mathrm{i}$.

5.4 The exponential form

The rule that, when you multiply two numbers, you add the arguments may have reminded you of a similar rule for logarithms, that $\log mn = \log m + \log n$. There is a reason for this; the arguments of complex numbers and logarithms can both be thought of as indices.

Even more extraordinary, the link between the two comes from Maclaurin series.

> Maclaurin series are explained in FP2 Chapter 3, where it is shown that many functions can be expressed as infinite series. For example, the binomial series (see C4 Chapter 5) is the Maclaurin series for functions of the form $(1 + x)^n$. If you have not already done the FP2 course, you may want to look at Sections 3.1 to 3.3, and to work Exercise 3B Question 1 before reading on.

The series used in this section are

$$e^x = 1 + \frac{x}{1!} + \frac{x^2}{2!} + \frac{x^3}{3!} + \frac{x^4}{4!} + \ldots,$$

$$\cos x = 1 - \frac{x^2}{2!} + \frac{x^4}{4!} - \frac{x^6}{6!} + \ldots,$$

$$\sin x = x - \frac{x^3}{3!} + \frac{x^5}{5!} - \frac{x^7}{7!} + \ldots.$$

These series look quite similar to each other. Can you find the connection between them?

It is convenient to replace x by θ, and to write

$$\cos\theta = 1 - \frac{\theta^2}{2!} + \frac{\theta^4}{4!} - \frac{\theta^6}{6!} + \ldots \quad\text{and}\quad \sin\theta = \theta - \frac{\theta^3}{3!} + \frac{\theta^5}{5!} - \frac{\theta^7}{7!} + \ldots$$

These can be put together to give a series for $\cos\theta + \mathrm{i}\sin\theta$:

$$\cos\theta + \mathrm{i}\sin\theta = \left(1 - \frac{\theta^2}{2!} + \frac{\theta^4}{4!} - \ldots\right) + \mathrm{i}\left(\theta - \frac{\theta^3}{3!} + \frac{\theta^5}{5!} - \ldots\right)$$

$$= 1 + \frac{\theta\,\mathrm{i}}{1!} - \frac{\theta^2}{2!} - \frac{\theta^3\,\mathrm{i}}{3!} + \frac{\theta^4}{4!} + \frac{\theta^5\,\mathrm{i}}{5!} - \ldots.$$

Now since $i^2 = -1$, you can write $-\theta^2$ as $(\theta\, i)^2$. Similarly, $-\theta^3\, i = (\theta\, i)^3$, $\theta^4 = (\theta\, i)^4$, and so on. So

$$\cos\theta + i\sin\theta = 1 + \frac{\theta\, i}{1!} + \frac{(\theta\, i)^2}{2!} + \frac{(\theta\, i)^3}{3!} + \frac{(\theta\, i)^4}{4!} + \frac{(\theta\, i)^5}{5!} + \ldots.$$

You will recognise the right side of this equation as the expansion

$$e^x = 1 + \frac{x}{1!} + \frac{x^2}{2!} + \frac{x^3}{3!} + \ldots$$

with $\theta\, i$ in place of x. So this suggests that

$$\cos\theta + i\sin\theta \text{ can be written as } e^{\theta\, i}.$$

Is this a 'proof'? Not strictly, since e^x has so far only been defined when x is real. But notice that, if $e^{\theta\, i}$ is written as $\cos\theta + i\sin\theta$, then

$$e^{\alpha\, i} \times e^{\beta\, i} = (\cos\alpha + i\sin\alpha)(\cos\beta + i\sin\beta)$$
$$= \cos(\alpha + \beta) + i\sin(\alpha + \beta)$$
$$= e^{(\alpha+\beta)\, i} = e^{\alpha\, i + \beta\, i},$$

which is the usual multiplication rule for indices. This suggests that it would be a good idea to *define* $e^{\theta\, i}$ as $\cos\theta + i\sin\theta$. Then many of the properties of the exponential function that you know already, such as the multiplication rule and the Maclaurin expansion, would still hold.

Most people who use complex numbers in practice use the compact notation $e^{\theta\, i}$ in preference to the rather clumsy form $\cos\theta + i\sin\theta$ that you have used so far in this chapter.

> If θ is a real number, $e^{\theta\, i}$ is defined as $e^{\theta\, i} = \cos\theta + i\sin\theta$.
> The polar form of a complex number, $z = r(\cos\theta + i\sin\theta)$, can be written as $z = re^{\theta\, i}$, where $r > 0$ and $-\pi < \theta \leqslant \pi$.

Example 5.4.1
Express $1 + \sqrt{3}\, i$ in polar form as $re^{\theta\, i}$.

Fig. 5.9 represents $1 + \sqrt{3}\, i$ as a point in an Argand diagram. Since

$$r = \sqrt{1 + (\sqrt{3})^2} = 2 \quad \text{and} \quad \theta = \tan^{-1}\sqrt{3} = \tfrac{1}{3}\pi,$$
$$1 + \sqrt{3}\, i = 2e^{\frac{1}{3}\pi\, i}.$$

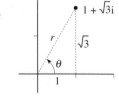

Fig. 5.9

A special case of the definition of $e^{\theta\, i}$, with $\theta = \pi$, gives

$$e^{\pi\, i} = \cos\pi + i\sin\pi = -1 + 0i = -1.$$

Rearranged, this produces an amusing equation connecting $0, 1, \pi$, e and i, arguably the five most important numbers in mathematics:

$$e^{\pi\, i} + 1 = 0.$$

You now have a definition of e^z when z is either a real number x or an imaginary number yi. It is natural to ask whether the process could be extended to produce a definition of e^z when z is any complex number $x + y$i.

The obvious way of doing this is to define e^{x+yi} as $e^x \times e^{yi}$. And since y is real, e^{yi} is $\cos y + i \sin y$.

> If $z = x + y$i , the **exponential function** e^z is defined by
>
> $$e^z = e^x(\cos y + i \sin y).$$

Example 5.4.2
In an Argand diagram, describe the relationship between the points A, B, C representing

(a) e^{1+2i},   (b) e^{-1+2i},   (c) e^{1-2i}.

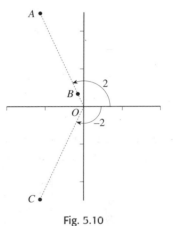

(a) $e^{1+2i} = e^1 (\cos 2 + i \sin 2) = e(\cos 2 + i \sin 2)$,
    which has modulus e and argument 2.

(b) $e^{-1+2i} = e^{-1} (\cos 2 + i \sin 2) = \dfrac{1}{e}(\cos 2 + i \sin 2)$,

    which has modulus $\dfrac{1}{e}$ and argument 2.

(c) $e^{1-2i} = e^1(\cos(-2) + i \sin(-2)) = e(\cos 2 - i \sin 2)$,
    which has modulus e and argument -2.

In the Argand diagram (Fig. 5.10) the points A and B have the same argument, so B lies on the line OA.

The points A and C have the same modulus, but their arguments have opposite signs. They are therefore reflections of each other in the real axis. That is, e^{1+2i} and e^{1-2i} are conjugate complex numbers.

Fig. 5.10

The calculations in Example 5.4.2 illustrate a general property, that e^{x+yi} has modulus e^x. If $-\pi < y \leqslant \pi$, e^{x+yi} has argument y; but if y is outside this interval, you must add or subtract a suitable multiple of 2π to find the number which lies within this interval.

> If $z = x + y$i, $|e^z| = e^x$ and $\arg e^z = y + k(2\pi)$, where k is chosen so that $-\pi < \arg e^z \leqslant \pi$.

Example 5.4.3*
What can you say about z if $e^z = 2i$?

If $z = x + y$i,

$$e^x(\cos y + i \sin y) = 2i.$$

Equating the real and imaginary parts on the two sides,

$$e^x \cos y = 0 \quad \text{and} \quad e^x \sin y = 2.$$

Since x is real, $e^x > 0$. The equations then show that

$$\cos y = 0 \quad \text{and} \quad \sin y > 0.$$

So y takes one of the values $\ldots, -\frac{7}{2}\pi, -\frac{3}{2}\pi, \frac{1}{2}\pi, \frac{5}{2}\pi, \ldots$; you can write this more concisely as

$$y = \tfrac{1}{2}\pi + 2n\pi, \text{ where } n \in \mathbb{Z}.$$

In each of these cases $\sin y = 1$, so the second of the equations above gives $e^x = 2$. Therefore $x = \ln 2$.

So if $e^z = 2i$, z can be any one of the numbers $\ln 2 + \left(2n + \frac{1}{2}\right)\pi i$, where n is an integer. Some of these are shown on an Argand diagram in Fig. 5.11.

Fig. 5.11

Exercise 5C

1 Use the modulus–argument method to find the square roots of the following complex numbers.

(a) $4\left(\cos \frac{2}{5}\pi + i \sin \frac{2}{5}\pi\right)$ (b) $9\left(\cos \frac{4}{7}\pi - i \sin \frac{4}{7}\pi\right)$ (c) $-2i$

(d) $20i - 21$ (e) $1 + i$ (f) $5 - 12i$

2 Find

(a) the square roots of $8\sqrt{3}i - 8$,   (b) the fourth roots of $8\sqrt{3}i - 8$.

3 Express the following numbers in the form $re^{\theta i}$, where $r > 0$ and $-\pi < \theta \leqslant \pi$.

(a) i   (b) -3

(c) $-4i$ (d) $1 + i$

(e) $-\sqrt{3} - i$ (f) $1 + i \tan \phi$ (where $-\frac{1}{2}\pi < \phi < \frac{1}{2}\pi$)

4 In an Argand diagram, plot the complex numbers

(a) $e^{\pi i}$,   (b) $e^{\frac{1}{2}\pi i}$,   (c) $2e^{-i}$,   (d) e^{4i},

(e) e^{1+i},   (f) e^{-1+i},   (g) e^{1-i}.

5 Find the square roots of

(a) $e^{\frac{2}{3}\pi i}$,   (b) e^{1+2i}.

6 If y is real, simplify $\dfrac{e^{yi} - e^{-yi}}{e^{yi} + e^{-yi}}$.

7 Use the definition of e^z to prove that, if $s = a + bi$, then

(a) $(e^s)^2 = e^{2s}$,   (b) $(e^s)^3 = e^{3s}$,   (c) $(e^s)^{-1} = e^{-s}$.

8 Use the definition of e^z to prove that, if $s = a + bi$ and $t = c + di$, then $e^s \times e^t = e^{s+t}$.

9 Use the definition of e^z to prove that, if $s = a + b\,i$, then $\dfrac{d}{dx}e^{sx} = se^{sx}$.

10 If $z = \cos\theta + i\sin\theta$, find the modulus and argument of e^z in terms of θ.

11 Express the following numbers in the form e^z, giving the value of z to 3 decimal places.

(a) $2 + i$ (b) $1 - 4\,i$ (c) $-3 - i$

Explain why the answers are not unique.

12 Prove that, if z is a complex number, then $e^z + e^{z^*}$ and $e^z \times e^{z^*}$ are both real. What can you say about $e^z - e^{z^*}$ and $e^z \div e^{z^*}$?

5.5 Complex numbers and vectors

You will by now have noticed that there are close similarities between complex numbers and vectors. Here are some examples.

Complex numbers may be represented either by points in an Argand diagram or by translations. The number z is represented in the Argand diagram by the point Z to which the origin is moved by the translation (Fig. 5.12).

Vectors may correspond either to points (position vectors) or to translations (displacement vectors). The position vector $\mathbf{a}$ of a point A is the displacement vector which translates the origin to A (Fig. 5.13).

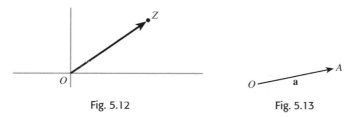

Fig. 5.12   Fig. 5.13

(Note the use of the 'alphabet convention'; the same letter is used for the complex number and the point, and for the point and its position vector. This will be used throughout this section.)

The translation which takes W to Z represents the complex number $z - w$ (Fig. 5.14).

The displacement vector of the translation which takes A to B is $\mathbf{b} - \mathbf{a}$ (Fig. 5.15).

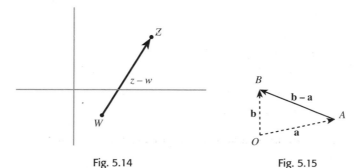

Fig. 5.14   Fig. 5.15

If $z = w + s$, then $OWZS$ is a parallelogram (Fig. 5.16).

If $\mathbf{c} = \mathbf{a} + \mathbf{b}$, then $OACB$ is a parallelogram (Fig. 5.17).

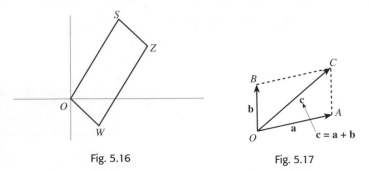

Fig. 5.16   Fig. 5.17

If $z = cw$, where c is a positive real number, then Z is c times as far from O as W, in the same direction (Fig. 5.18).

If $\mathbf{b} = c\mathbf{a}$, where c is a positive real number, then B is c times as far from O as A, in the same direction (Fig. 5.19).

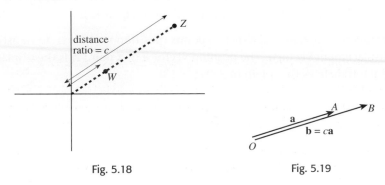

Fig. 5.18   Fig. 5.19

But there are also some ways in which complex numbers and vectors differ. For example, vectors can be used in any number of dimensions, but the representation of complex numbers is restricted to two dimensions.

Even comparing complex numbers with two-dimensional vectors, multiplication is quite different in the two systems. You know two ways of multiplying vectors, but neither of these corresponds to the rule for multiplying complex numbers.

> The scalar product $\mathbf{a} \cdot \mathbf{b}$ of two vectors is always a real number, but the product of two complex numbers is usually a complex number.

> The vector product $\mathbf{a} \times \mathbf{b}$ is a vector perpendicular to both $\mathbf{a}$ and $\mathbf{b}$. This only has meaning when vectors are used in three dimensions, but the geometry of complex numbers is two-dimensional.

So long as you are concerned only with addition, subtraction and multiplication by a real number, there is an exact parallel between complex numbers and two-dimensional vectors. If you want to use these algebraic operations to solve a problem in geometry, you can do it either with complex numbers or with vectors, whichever you prefer. But complex numbers and vectors are used in quite different ways when they are combined by multiplication.

The next section shows how both addition and multiplication of complex numbers can be represented together in a single geometric system.

5.6 Spiral enlargement

Suppose that a number $t = q(\cos \beta + i \sin \beta)$ is represented by a translation $\overrightarrow{AT}$ (see Fig. 5.20).

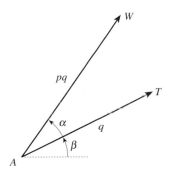

Fig. 5.20

How would you represent the number $w = st$, where $s = p(\cos \alpha + i \sin \alpha)$?

Since multiplication by s multiplies the modulus by p, and increases the angle with the real axis by α, w could be represented by a translation $\overrightarrow{AW}$ whose length is p times the length of $\overrightarrow{AC}$ and whose direction makes an angle α with the direction of $\overrightarrow{AT}$ in the anticlockwise sense.

A transformation of a plane which multiplies lengths of translations by a scale factor of p and rotates them through an angle α is called a **spiral enlargement**.

> If complex numbers are represented by translations of a plane, multiplication by a complex number s has the effect of a spiral enlargement of scale factor $|s|$ and angle $\arg s$.

Example 5.6.1
The complex number $z = 1 + 2i$ is represented by the translation $\overrightarrow{AT}$.
(a) Describe the translation $\overrightarrow{AB}$ represented by $2iz$.
(b) A translation $\overrightarrow{AC}$ is obtained from $\overrightarrow{AT}$ by a clockwise rotation through $\frac{1}{6}\pi$ combined with an enlargement of scale factor 2. What complex number is represented by $\overrightarrow{AC}$?

(a) The complex number $2i$ has modulus 2 and argument $\frac{1}{2}\pi$. So $2iz$ represents a translation obtained from $\overrightarrow{AT}$ by doubling its length and rotating it through an angle of $\frac{1}{2}\pi$ anticlockwise.

This is shown in Fig. 5.21. Since $2\,i(1+2\,i) = -4 + 2\,i$, $\overrightarrow{AB}$ is a translation of -4 units in the direction of the real axis and 2 units in the direction of the imaginary axis.

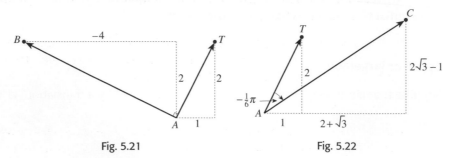

Fig. 5.21   Fig. 5.22

(b) The complex number with modulus 2 and argument $-\frac{1}{6}\pi$ is

$$2\left(\cos\left(-\tfrac{1}{6}\pi\right) + i\sin\left(-\tfrac{1}{6}\pi\right)\right) = 2\left(\tfrac{1}{2}\sqrt{3} - \tfrac{1}{2}i\right) = \sqrt{3} - i.$$

So the complex number represented by $\overrightarrow{AC}$ is

$$(\sqrt{3} - i)(1 + 2i) = \sqrt{3} - i + 2\sqrt{3}\,i + 2 = (2 + \sqrt{3}) + (2\sqrt{3} - 1)i.$$

This is shown in Fig. 5.22.

Example 5.6.2

In an Argand diagram the points A and B represent the complex numbers $1 - 2i$ and $3 - i$. An isosceles triangle ABC has a right angle at B, as shown in Fig. 5.23. Find the number represented by the point C.

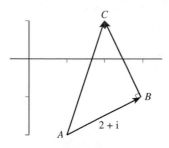

Fig. 5.23

The translation $\overrightarrow{AB}$ represents the complex number $(3 - i) - (1 - 2i)$, which is $2 + i$.

Method 1   The translation $\overrightarrow{AC}$ is obtained from $\overrightarrow{AB}$ by a spiral enlargement of angle $\frac{1}{4}\pi$ anticlockwise and scale factor $\sqrt{2}$. This is effected by multiplying $2 + i$ by

$$\sqrt{2}\left(\cos\tfrac{1}{4}\pi + i\sin\tfrac{1}{4}\pi\right) = \sqrt{2}\left(\frac{1}{\sqrt{2}} + \frac{1}{\sqrt{2}}i\right) = 1 + i,$$

which gives

$$(1 + i)(2 + i) = 1 + 3i.$$

In the Argand diagram the point A represents the complex number $1 - 2i$. The point C reached from this by a translation of $1 + 3i$ is $(1 - 2i) + (1 + 3i)$, which is $2 + i$.

Method 2   Instead of getting to C by a translation $\overrightarrow{AC}$ from A, you could get there by a translation $\overrightarrow{BC}$ from B.

The translation $\overrightarrow{BC}$ has the same magnitude as $\overrightarrow{AB}$ in a direction perpendicular to $\overrightarrow{AB}$. The spiral enlargement which changes $\overrightarrow{AB}$ to $\overrightarrow{BC}$ is therefore effected by multiplying $2 + i$ by $1\left(\cos \frac{1}{2}\pi + i \sin \frac{1}{2}\pi\right)$, which is i, giving

$$i(2 + i) = -1 + 2i.$$

In the Argand diagram B represents the complex number $3 - i$. The point C reached from this by a translation of $-1 + 2i$ is $(3 - i) + (-1 + 2i)$, which is $2 + i$.

Notice how, in these examples, complex numbers can correspond to points in an Argand diagram, or to translations, or to spiral enlargements. You are already familiar with this when the numbers are real; real numbers can be used to describe the position of a point on a number line, or a translation up or down the line, or the scale factor of an enlargement. Complex numbers make it possible to do the same thing in a plane.

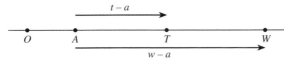

Fig. 5.24

Suppose that on the real number line in Fig. 5.24 you have two points A and T, with coordinates a and t, and that you want the coordinate of a point W such that the translation $\overrightarrow{AW}$ is s times the translation $\overrightarrow{AT}$. Then the translations $\overrightarrow{AT}$ and $\overrightarrow{AW}$ would correspond to the numbers $t - a$ and $w - a$, giving the equation

$$w - a = s(t - a).$$

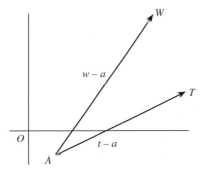

Fig. 5.25

Now suppose that, in Fig. 5.25 (which is derived from Fig. 5.20) the points A, T and W represent complex numbers a, t and w in an Argand diagram. Then if the translation $\overrightarrow{AW}$ is obtained from $\overrightarrow{AT}$ by a spiral enlargement described by the complex number s, you can write in just the same way

$$w - a = s(t - a),$$

and $w = a + s(t - a).$

Example 5.6.3

The points A and B in an Argand diagram correspond to complex numbers a and b. Find the complex numbers which correspond to the two possible positions of C such that ABC is an equilateral triangle.

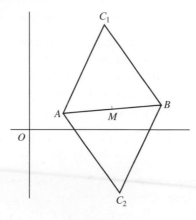

Fig. 5.26

Method 1   In Fig. 5.26 the two possible positions of C are denoted by C_1 and C_2. The spiral enlargements which change $\overrightarrow{AB}$ into $\overrightarrow{AC_1}$ and $\overrightarrow{AC_2}$ have modulus 1 and arguments $+\frac{1}{3}\pi$ and $-\frac{1}{3}\pi$ respectively. They are therefore

$$\cos \tfrac{1}{3}\pi + i \sin \tfrac{1}{3}\pi = \tfrac{1}{2} + \tfrac{1}{2}\sqrt{3}\,i$$

and $\cos\left(-\tfrac{1}{3}\pi\right) + i \sin\left(-\tfrac{1}{3}\pi\right) = \tfrac{1}{2} - \tfrac{1}{2}\sqrt{3}\,i.$

So C_1 and C_2 correspond to the complex numbers

$$c_1 = a + \left(\tfrac{1}{2} + \tfrac{1}{2}\sqrt{3}\,i\right)(b-a) = \left(\tfrac{1}{2} - \tfrac{1}{2}\sqrt{3}\,i\right)a + \left(\tfrac{1}{2} + \tfrac{1}{2}\sqrt{3}\,i\right)b$$

and $c_2 = a + \left(\tfrac{1}{2} - \tfrac{1}{2}\sqrt{3}\,i\right)(b-a) = \left(\tfrac{1}{2} + \tfrac{1}{2}\sqrt{3}\,i\right)a + \left(\tfrac{1}{2} - \tfrac{1}{2}\sqrt{3}\,i\right)b.$

Method 2   You could also reach C_1 and C_2 by starting at M, the mid-point of AB, which corresponds to the complex number $\frac{1}{2}(a+b)$. From there the translations $\overrightarrow{MC_1}$ and $\overrightarrow{MC_2}$ are perpendicular to $\overrightarrow{AB}$ and $\frac{1}{2}\sqrt{3}$ times as large. So the complex numbers corresponding to C_1 and C_2 can be found as

$$\tfrac{1}{2}(a+b) \pm \tfrac{1}{2}\sqrt{3}\,i(b-a).$$

Now take the point A in Fig. 5.25 to be the origin. Then Fig. 5.27 shows the points T and W in the Argand diagram, representing numbers t and w, where $w = st$ and s describes the spiral enlargement which converts the translation $\overrightarrow{OT}$ to $\overrightarrow{OW}$.

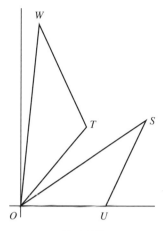

Fig. 5.27

But s, as a complex number, can also be represented by a point S in the Argand diagram. Where is it?

To answer this question, note that s can be written as $s \times 1$, and that the number 1 is represented by the point U on the real axis 1 unit from O. That is, the spiral enlargement which converts $\overrightarrow{OT}$ to $\overrightarrow{OW}$ also converts $\overrightarrow{OU}$ to $\overrightarrow{OS}$. This means that OTW and OUS are similar triangles.

> In an Argand diagram, the triangles formed by the points
> representing $0, t, st$ and $0, 1, s$ are similar.

Example 5.6.4*
ABC is a triangle. Fig. 5.28 shows three similar triangles BUC, CVA and AWB drawn external to ABC. Prove that the centroids of the triangles ABC and UVW coincide.

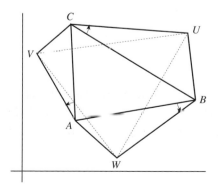

Fig. 5.28

The centroid of a triangle, the point where the medians intersect, was defined in C4 Example 4.5.2. There it was given as the point with position vector $\frac{1}{3}(\mathbf{a}+\mathbf{b}+\mathbf{c})$, where $\mathbf{a}$, $\mathbf{b}$ and $\mathbf{c}$ are the position vectors of the vertices of the triangle. But since complex numbers under addition behave exactly like two-dimensional vectors, the result carries straight over to an Argand diagram. If A, B and C correspond to complex numbers a, b and c then the centroid of the triangle corresponds to $\frac{1}{3}(a+b+c)$. Try writing out the proof for yourself using complex numbers instead of position vectors.

What is new in the Argand diagram is that you now have a way of dealing with the similar triangles. Suppose that multiplication by a number s gives the spiral enlargement that transforms $\overrightarrow{CB}$ into $\overrightarrow{CU}$. Then the same spiral enlargement transforms $\overrightarrow{AC}$ into $\overrightarrow{AV}$, and $\overrightarrow{BA}$ into $\overrightarrow{BW}$. So, if U, V and W correspond to complex numbers u, v and w, you can write

$$u - c = s(b - c), \quad v - a = s(c - a) \quad \text{and} \quad w - b = s(a - b).$$

If you add these three equations, you get

$$(u - c) + (v - a) + (w - b) = s((b - c) + (c - a) + (a - b)) = 0,$$

so

$$u + v + w = a + b + c.$$

Therefore $\frac{1}{3}(u + v + w) = \frac{1}{3}(a + b + c)$. That is, ABC and UVW have the same centroid.

Exercise 5D

1　A is the point in an Argand diagram representing $1 + 3\,\mathrm{i}$. Find the complex numbers represented by the two points B such that $OB = \sqrt{2} \times OA$ and angle $AOB = \frac{1}{4}\pi$.

2　A is the point in an Argand diagram representing $3 - 2\,\mathrm{i}$. Find the complex numbers represented by the two points B such that $OB = 2OA$ and angle $AOB = \frac{1}{3}\pi$.

3　Points A and B represent $1 + \mathrm{i}$ and $2 - \mathrm{i}$ in an Argand diagram. C is a point such that $AC = 2AB$ and angle $BAC = \frac{1}{2}\pi$. Find two possibilities for the complex number represented by C.

4　The figure shows an Argand diagram in which A and T are the points $1 + \mathrm{i}$ and $4 - \mathrm{i}$. W is a point such that $AW = 2AT$ and angle $TAW = \frac{1}{3}\pi$. Find the number represented by W.

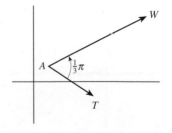

5　With the data of Example 5.2.1 (that is, $s = 1 + 2\mathrm{i}$ and $t = 2 + 3\mathrm{i}$) plot on an accurate Argand diagram the points U, S, T and W representing 1, s, t and st. Verify from your diagram that the triangles OTW and OUS are similar.

6 A point S represents the complex number s in an Argand diagram. Draw diagrams to show how to construct the points which represent

   (a) s^2,   (b) s^3,   (c) $\dfrac{1}{s}$.

7 Points S and T represent the complex numbers s and t in an Argand diagram. Draw a diagram to show how to construct the point which represents $\dfrac{s}{t}$.

8 A snail starts at the origin of an Argand diagram and walks along the real axis for an hour, covering a distance of 8 metres. At the end of each hour it changes its direction by $\frac{1}{2}\pi$ anticlockwise; and in each hour it walks half as far as it did in the previous hour. Find where it is

   (a) after 2 hours,   (b) after 4 hours,   (c) after 8 hours,   (d) eventually.

9 Repeat Question 8 if the change of direction is through $\frac{1}{4}\pi$ and it walks $\dfrac{1}{\sqrt{2}}$ times as far as in the previous hour.

10 Points A, B and C are represented in an Argand diagram by complex numbers a, b and c. If C is the reflection of A in the line OB, prove that $\dfrac{c}{b} = \left(\dfrac{a}{b}\right)^*$. Use this to calculate c if $a = 1 + i$ and $b = 1 + 2i$.

   Check your answer by showing that

   (a) the mid-point of AC lies on OB,

   (b) the translation $\overrightarrow{AC}$ is perpendicular to $\overrightarrow{OB}$.

11 Points A, B and C represent i, $3 - i$ and $4 + 2i$ in an Argand diagram. D is the reflection of C in the line AB. Find the complex number which is represented by D.

12 A and B are points in an Argand diagram representing the complex numbers 1 and i. P is a point on the circle having AB as a diameter. If P represents the complex number z, find the value of $\arg \dfrac{z - 1}{z - i}$ if P is in

   (a) the first quadrant,   (b) the second quadrant,   (c) the fourth quadrant.

13 Identify the set of points in an Argand diagram for which $\arg \dfrac{z - 3}{z - 4i} = \frac{1}{2}\pi$.

14 If A and B represent complex numbers a and b in an Argand diagram, identify the set of points for which $\arg \dfrac{z - a}{z - b} = \pi$.

15 Identify the set of points in an Argand diagram for which $\arg \dfrac{z - i}{z + i} = \frac{1}{4}\pi$.

Miscellaneous exercise 5

1 Given that $z = \tan \alpha + i$, where $0 < \alpha < \frac{1}{2}\pi$, and $w = 4\left(\cos \frac{1}{10}\pi + i \sin \frac{1}{10}\pi\right)$, find in their simplest forms

    (a) $|z|$,   (b) $|zw|$,   (c) $\arg z$,   (d) $\arg \dfrac{z}{w}$.   (OCR)

2 Given that $(5 + 12i)z = 63 + 16i$, find $|z|$ and $\arg z$, giving this answer in radians correct to 3 significant figures. Given also that $w = 3\left(\cos \frac{1}{3}\pi + i \sin \frac{1}{3}\pi\right)$, find

    (a) $\left|\dfrac{z}{w}\right|$,   (b) $\arg(zw)$.   (OCR)

3 Find the modulus and argument of $1 + i \tan \theta$ in the cases

    (a) $0 < \theta < \frac{1}{2}\pi$,   (b) $\frac{1}{2}\pi < \theta < \pi$,   (c) $\pi < \theta < \frac{3}{2}\pi$,   (d) $\frac{3}{2}\pi < \theta < 2\pi$.

4 If $z = \cos 2\theta + i \sin 2\theta$, find the modulus and argument of $1 - z$ in the cases

    (a) $0 < \theta < \frac{1}{2}\pi$,   (b) $-\frac{1}{2}\pi < \theta < 0$.

    Illustrate your answer using an Argand diagram.

5 If $a = 2$, $b = \sqrt{3} + i$ and $c = \sqrt{2} + \sqrt{2}\,i$, use an Argand diagram to express $b - a$, $c - b$ and $c - a$ exactly in the form $r e^{\theta i}$.

6 Show that $e^{2\alpha i} + e^{2\beta i}$ can be written as $e^{(\alpha + \beta)i}\left(e^{(\alpha - \beta)i} + e^{-(\alpha - \beta)i}\right)$.

    By showing that the expression in brackets is equal to $2\cos(\alpha - \beta)$, and equating real parts, obtain the identity $\cos 2\alpha + \cos 2\beta = 2\cos(\alpha + \beta)\cos(\alpha - \beta)$.

    Use a similar method to find comparable expressions for $\sin 2\alpha + \sin 2\beta$ and $\cos 2\alpha - \cos 2\beta$.

7 A point Z in an Argand diagram represents $z = e^{\theta i}$, where $0 < \theta < \pi$.

    (a) By writing $z + 1$ as $e^{\frac{1}{2}\theta i}\left(e^{\frac{1}{2}\theta i} + e^{-\frac{1}{2}\theta i}\right)$, find the modulus and argument of $z + 1$.

    (b) Use a similar method to find the modulus and argument of $z - 1$.

    (c) Find the argument of $\dfrac{z - 1}{z + 1}$.

    Interpret your answers geometrically, and investigate how they should be modified if $-\pi < \theta < 0$.

8 In an Argand diagram U and V represent the numbers 1 and -1, and Z represents a variable number z with positive imaginary part. If angle UZW has a constant value α (where $0 < \alpha < \pi$), show that $\dfrac{z - 1}{z + 1} = \lambda e^{\alpha i}$, where λ is a real number. Deduce that

$$\frac{z - 1}{z + 1}e^{-\alpha i} = \frac{z^* - 1}{z^* + 1}e^{\alpha i}.$$

    By rearranging this as $(zz^* - 1)(e^{\alpha i} - e^{-\alpha i}) = (z - z^*)(e^{\alpha i} + e^{-\alpha i})$, and expressing this in cartesian coordinates, show that Z lies on a circle with centre $(0, \cot \alpha)$ through U and V.

9 Points S and T in an Argand diagram represent numbers s and t.

    (a) If OS is perpendicular to OT, show that $s = \lambda i t$, where λ is a real number.

    (b) Write an expression for s^* in terms of λ, i and t, and hence show that $s^*t + st^* = 0$.

    (c) If $s = a + bi$ and $t = c + di$, express the condition in part (b) in terms of a, b, c and d.

    (d) Obtain the condition in part (c) by using the scalar product of vectors $\mathbf{s} = a\mathbf{i} + b\mathbf{j}$ and $\mathbf{t} = c\mathbf{i} + d\mathbf{j}$.

10 A and B are two points on a computer screen. A program produces a trace on the screen to execute the following algorithm.

    Step 1 Start at any point P on the screen.

    Step 2 From the current position describe a quarter circle anticlockwise about A.

    Step 3 From the current position describe a quarter circle anticlockwise about B.

    Step 4 Repeat Step 2.

    Step 5 Repeat Step 3, and stop.

Take A, B and P as points representing complex numbers a, b and p in an Argand diagram, and the new positions after each of steps 2 to 5 as representing q, r, s and t.

Explain why $q = a + i(p - a)$, and write similar equations for r, s and t. Deduce that the trace ends where it began.

11 A, B, C and D are four points on a computer screen. A program selects a point P on the screen at random and then produces a trace by rotating successively through a right angle about A, B, C and D. Show that, if the trace ends where it began, the line segments AC and BD are equal in length and perpendicular to each other.

12 ABC is a triangle such that the order A, B, C takes you anticlockwise round the triangle. Squares $ACPQ$, $BCRS$ are drawn outside the triangle ABC. If A, B and C represent complex numbers a, b and c in an Argand diagram, find the complex numbers represented by Q, S and the mid-point M of QS. Show that the position of M doesn't depend on the position of C, and find how it is related to the points A and B.

13 Points in an Argand diagram representing the complex numbers $-2i, 4, 2 + 4i$ and $2i$ form a convex quadrilateral. Squares are drawn outside the quadrilateral on each of the four sides. Find the numbers represented by the centres P, Q, R and S of the four squares. Hence prove that

    (a) $PR = QS$,   (b) PR is perpendicular to QS.

Show that the same conclusion follows for any four points forming a convex quadrilateral.

14 In an Argand diagram points A, B, C, U, V and W represent complex numbers a, b, c, u, v and w. If the triangles ABC and UVW are directly similar, explain why $\dfrac{c-a}{b-a} = \dfrac{w-u}{v-u}$, and show that this can be written as $aw + bu + cv = av + bw + cu$.
('Directly similar' means that, if you go round the triangles in the order A, B, C and U, V, W, then you go round both triangles in the same sense.) Prove that the converse result is also true. Hence show that a necessary and sufficient condition for a triangle to be equilateral is that $a^2 + b^2 + c^2 = bc + ca + ab$.

15 The fixed points A and B represent the complex numbers a and b in an Argand diagram with origin O.

(a) The variable point P represents the complex number z, and λ is a real variable. Describe the locus of P in relation to A and B in the following cases, illustrating your loci in separate diagrams.

(i) $z - a = \lambda b$ (ii) $z - a = \lambda(z - b)$ (iii) $z - a = i\lambda(z - b)$

(b) By writing $a = |a|\,e^{i\alpha}$ and $b = |b|\,e^{i\beta}$, show that $|\operatorname{Im}(ab^*)| = 2\Delta$, where Δ is the area of triangle OAB.

Revision exercise 3

1. Find the vector product of the vectors $2\mathbf{i} + 3\mathbf{j} - 6\mathbf{k}$ and $-3\mathbf{i} + 6\mathbf{j} + 2\mathbf{k}$.

2. The position vectors of the points A, B and C are $3\mathbf{i} - \mathbf{j} + 7\mathbf{k}$, $2\mathbf{i} + 6\mathbf{j} - 5\mathbf{k}$ and $4\mathbf{i} - \mathbf{j} + 2\mathbf{k}$ respectively.

   (a) Find the area of the triangle ABC.

   (b) Find the equation of the plane ABC in the form $\mathbf{r} \cdot \mathbf{n} = p$, where $\mathbf{n}$ is a unit vector.

3. Find the perpendicular distance between the lines with equations
   $\mathbf{r} = 2\mathbf{i} - 3\mathbf{j} + 13\mathbf{k} + \lambda\,(\mathbf{i} - 2\mathbf{j} + 4\mathbf{k})$ and $\mathbf{r} = 3\mathbf{i} + 5\mathbf{j} - 7\mathbf{k} + \mu\,(2\mathbf{i} - \mathbf{j} + 3\mathbf{k})$, where λ and μ
   are real parameters.

4. Find the equation of the curve C which passes through the origin and satisfies the
   differential equation $\dfrac{\mathrm{d}y}{\mathrm{d}x} + 2xy = x^3$.

5. Find (i) the complementary function and (ii) a particular integral of each of the following
   differential equations.

   (a) $\dfrac{\mathrm{d}^2 y}{\mathrm{d}x^2} - 3\dfrac{\mathrm{d}y}{\mathrm{d}x} + 2y = 2x^2 - 10x + 8$
   (b) $\dfrac{\mathrm{d}^2 y}{\mathrm{d}x^2} - \dfrac{\mathrm{d}y}{\mathrm{d}x} = 2e^{2x}$

   (c) $\dfrac{\mathrm{d}^2 y}{\mathrm{d}x^2} - 5\dfrac{\mathrm{d}y}{\mathrm{d}x} + 4y = 20\sin 2x - 10\cos 2x$

6. If $z = \cos\theta + i\sin\theta$, where $-\pi < \theta \leq \pi$, find the modulus and argument of (a) z^2 and
   (b) $1 + z^2$, distinguishing the cases

   (i) $\theta = 0$,
   (ii) $\theta = \frac{1}{2}\pi$,
   (iii) $\theta = \pi$,
   (iv) $\theta = -\frac{1}{2}\pi$,

   (v) $0 < \theta < \frac{1}{2}\pi$,
   (vi) $\frac{1}{2}\pi < \theta < \pi$,
   (vii) $-\frac{1}{2}\pi < \theta < 0$,
   (viii) $-\pi < \theta < -\frac{1}{2}\pi$.

7. Find the solution of the differential equation $\dfrac{\mathrm{d}y}{\mathrm{d}x} - 3y = 8e^{-x}$ which approaches 0 as $x \to \infty$.

8. Show that $y = Ax e^x + B e^x$ is a complementary function for the differential equation
   $\dfrac{\mathrm{d}^2 y}{\mathrm{d}x^2} - 2\dfrac{\mathrm{d}y}{\mathrm{d}x} + y = x^2 - 2x - 2$ and find a particular integral.

9. The lines l_1 and l_2 intersect at the point C with position vector $\mathbf{i} + 5\mathbf{j} + 11\mathbf{k}$. The equations
   of l_1 and l_2 are $\mathbf{r} = \mathbf{i} + 5\mathbf{j} + 11\mathbf{k} + \lambda\,(3\mathbf{i} + 2\mathbf{j} - 2\mathbf{k})$ and $\mathbf{r} = \mathbf{i} + 5\mathbf{j} + 11\mathbf{k} + \mu\,(8\mathbf{i} + 11\mathbf{j} + 6\mathbf{k})$,
   where λ and μ are real parameters. Find, in the form $ax + by + cz = d$, an equation of the
   plane Π which contains l_1 and l_2.

   The point A has position vector $4\mathbf{i} - \mathbf{j} + 5\mathbf{k}$ and the line through A perpendicular to Π
   meets Π at B. Find

   (a) the length of AB,

   (b) the perpendicular distance of B from l_1, giving your answer correct to 3 significant
   figures.

10 A, B and C are points in an Argand diagram representing the complex numbers $-1 + 0\,\mathrm{i}$, $1 + 0\,\mathrm{i}$ and $0 + \mathrm{i}$ respectively, and P is the point representing the complex number z. The displacements $\overrightarrow{AB}$ and $\overrightarrow{BP}$ make angles α and β with the x-axis, and the angle $APB = \frac{1}{4}\pi$.

   (a) Show that $\arg(z - 1) - \arg(z + 1) = \frac{1}{4}\pi$.

   (b) Show that $\dfrac{z + 1}{z^* + 1} = \cos 2\alpha + \mathrm{i} \sin 2\alpha$ and write down a similar expression for $\dfrac{z - 1}{z^* - 1}$.

   (c) Show that $\dfrac{(z - 1)(z^* + 1)}{(z^* - 1)(z + 1)} = \mathrm{i}$ and deduce that $zz^* + \mathrm{i}(z - z^*) = 1$.

   (d) Show that the equation in part (c) can be written as $(z - \mathrm{i})(z^* + \mathrm{i}) = 2$ and deduce that $|z - \mathrm{i}| = 2$.

   (e) State in words what geometrical property is established by combining the results of parts (a) to (d).

11 This question is about the differential equation $x^2 \dfrac{\mathrm{d}y}{\mathrm{d}x} = 2xy - y^2$.

   (a) Show that there are two solutions of the form $y = ax + b$, where a and b are constants.

   (b) This is a Riccati equation, which can be solved by using the substitution $y = \mathrm{F}(x) + z$, where $y = \mathrm{F}(x)$ is a known solution and z is a function of x. By taking $y = \mathrm{F}(x)$ to be the solution in part (a) for which $a \neq 0$, use this substitution to find the general solution of the differential equation.

   (c) The differential equation can also be solved using the substitution $y = \dfrac{1}{w}$, where w is a function of x. Show that this converts the equation into a first order linear differential equation, and complete the solution by using the standard algorithm. Do your solutions to parts (b) and (c) agree with each other?

   (d) By writing the solution in the form $y = x + \dfrac{1}{c} + \dfrac{1}{c\,(cx - 1)}$, sketch a few typical solution curves, giving particular attention to any asymptotes, stationary points and the form near $x = 0$.

   (e) Explain why any stationary points of a solution curve must lie on one or other of the lines $y = 0$ and $y = 2x$. Does your answer to part (d) bear this out?

   (f) By differentiating the differential equation, show that on any solution curve $\dfrac{\mathrm{d}^2 y}{\mathrm{d}x^2} = \dfrac{2y\,(x - y)^2}{x^4}$. What does this tell you about the direction of bending of the solution curves?

12 With respect to an origin O, the point A has position vector $30\mathbf{i} - 3\mathbf{j} - 5\mathbf{k}$. The line l passes through O and is parallel to the vector $4\mathbf{i} - 5\mathbf{j} - 3\mathbf{k}$. The point B on l is such that AB is perpendicular to l. In either order,

   (a) find the length of AB,   (b) find the position vector of B.

   The plane Π passes through A and is parallel to both l and the vector $-2\mathbf{i} + 2\mathbf{j} + \mathbf{k}$. The point Q on AB is such that $AQ = \frac{1}{4}QB$. Find, correct to 2 decimal places, the perpendicular distance from Q to Π.   (OCR)

13 The plane π has equation $\mathbf{r} \cdot (2\mathbf{i} - 3\mathbf{j} + 6\mathbf{k}) = 0$, and P and Q are the points with position vectors $7\mathbf{i} + 6\mathbf{j} + 5\mathbf{k}$ and $\mathbf{i} + 3\mathbf{j} - \mathbf{k}$ respectively. Find the position vector of the point in which the line passing through P and Q meets the plane π.

Find, in the form $ax + by + cz = d$, the equation of the plane which contains the line PQ and which is perpendicular to π.

14 The plane Π has equation $\mathbf{r} = 6\mathbf{i} + 2\mathbf{j} + \mathbf{k} + \theta(3\mathbf{i} + \mathbf{j}) + \phi\,(\mathbf{j} - 2\mathbf{k})$.

The line l_1, which does not lie in Π, has equation $\mathbf{r} = 2\mathbf{i} + \mathbf{j} - 3\mathbf{k} + \lambda\,(3\mathbf{i} - \mathbf{j} + 4\mathbf{k})$.

The line l_2 has equation $\mathbf{r} = 2\mathbf{i} + \mathbf{j} - 3\mathbf{k} + \mu\,(\mathbf{i} + 3\mathbf{j} - 2\mathbf{k})$.

(a) Show that l_1 is parallel to Π.

(b) Find the position vector of the point in which l_2 meets Π.

(c) Find the perpendicular distance from the point with position vector
$4\mathbf{i} - 5\mathbf{j} + 7\mathbf{k}$ to l_1.   (OCR)

6 De Moivre's theorem

This chapter presents a theorem about nth powers of complex numbers, which can also be used to find nth roots. When you have completed it, you should

- know the statement and the proof of de Moivre's theorem
- know the nth roots of unity and their representation in an Argand diagram
- know algebraic properties of the nth roots of unity, and be able to use them in algebraic and geometric applications
- know how to find the nth roots of any complex number.

This chapter contains references to polar coordinates (see FP2 Sections 6.1–3 and 6.7),

6.1 Powers of complex numbers

The rules for multiplying and dividing complex numbers are especially simple if the numbers are written in polar form (sometimes called modulus–argument form), as $r(\cos\theta + i\sin\theta)$; see Chapter 5. This is because of the rule

$$(\cos\alpha + i\sin\alpha)(\cos\beta + i\sin\beta) = \cos(\alpha + \beta) + i\sin(\alpha + \beta).$$

This rule can also be written in its exponential version as

$$e^{\alpha i}e^{\beta i} = e^{(\alpha+\beta)i}.$$

When the indices are more complicated algebraic expressions, it is helpful to use the alternative notation $\exp(z)$ in place of e^z. The rule then takes the form

$$\exp(\alpha i)\exp(\beta i) = \exp((\alpha + \beta)i).$$

> The advantage of using the exp notation is mainly felt in printed mathematics. If index notation is used with something like $\left(\dfrac{\alpha}{n} + \dfrac{2r\pi}{n}\right)i$ in the index, the expression looks very top-heavy, and the type is so small that it is difficult to read. When you are writing mathematics for yourself, these considerations are not so important. In this chapter exp has often been used from the start, so that you can get used to it with simple examples.

Putting both α and β equal to ϕ leads to the double angle formula

$$(\exp(\phi i))^2 = \exp(\phi i)\exp(\phi i) = \exp((\phi + \phi)i) = \exp(2\phi i).$$

Then putting $\alpha = 2\phi$ and $\beta = \phi$ gives

$$(\exp(\phi i))^3 = (\exp(\phi i))^2 \exp(\phi i) = \exp(2\phi i)\exp(\phi i) = \exp(3\phi i)$$

and so on. These results suggest a general rule.

De Moivre's theorem   For $n \in \mathbb{Z}$, $(\exp(\phi i))^n = \exp(n\phi i)$.

Proof   It is convenient to begin by clearing some special cases out of the way.

The result is trivial for $n = 1$, since both sides are $\exp(\phi i)$.

If $n = 0$, the left side is $(\exp(\phi i))^0 = 1$ and the right side is $\exp(0) = 1$.

If $n = -1$, the left side is $(\exp(\phi i))^{-1} = \dfrac{1}{\exp(\phi i)}$ and the right side is $\exp(-\phi i)$. Since, by the multiplication rule, $\exp(\phi i)\exp(-\phi i) = \exp((\phi - \phi)i) = \exp(0) = 1$, it follows that $(\exp(\phi i))^{-1} = \dfrac{1}{\exp(\phi i)} = \exp(-\phi i)$.

For positive values of n, you can use mathematical induction. The basis case, for $n = 1$, has already been noted. The inductive step is that, if $(\exp(\phi i))^k = \exp(k\phi i)$, then

$$
\begin{aligned}
(\exp(\phi i))^{k+1} &= (\exp(\phi i))^k \exp(\phi i) \\
&= \exp(k\phi i)\exp(\phi i) \\
&= \exp((k\phi + \phi)i) \\
&= \exp((k + 1)\phi i).
\end{aligned}
$$

This establishes the theorem for all positive integers n.

If n is a negative integer, write n as $-m$. Then

$$
\begin{aligned}
(\exp(\phi i))^n &= (\exp(\phi i))^{-m} \\
&= \frac{1}{(\exp(\phi i))^m} \\
&= \frac{1}{\exp(m\phi i)} \quad \text{(using the theorem for positive integral index } m) \\
&= \exp(-m\phi i) \qquad \text{(since } \exp(m\phi i)\exp(-m\phi i) = \exp(0) = 1) \\
&= \exp(n\phi i).
\end{aligned}
$$

This completes the proof for all $n \in \mathbb{Z}$.

You will need to recognise this result in all three notations.

> **De Moivre's theorem**, for $n \in \mathbb{Z}$.
> Trigonometric version: $(\cos\phi + i\sin\phi)^n = \cos n\phi + i\sin n\phi$.
> Exponential version: $(e^{\phi i})^n = e^{n\phi i}$,   or $(\exp(\phi i))^n = \exp(n\phi i)$.

De Moivre was born in France, but emigrated to England as a young man in 1688 to escape religious persecution. Although he certainly knew the theorem named after him, it was first published in its trigonometrical form by Euler in 1748.

322 Further Pure 3

Example 6.1.1

Evaluate (a) $\left(\frac{1}{2}\sqrt{3}+\frac{1}{2}i\right)^{18}$, (b) $(1+i)^{-10}$, (c) $(0.8+0.6i)^{15}$.

(a) Since $\frac{1}{2}\sqrt{3}=\cos\frac{1}{6}\pi$ and $\frac{1}{2}=\sin\frac{1}{6}\pi$, the number $\frac{1}{2}\sqrt{3}+\frac{1}{2}i$ can be written in polar form as $e^{\frac{1}{6}\pi i}$. Therefore, by de Moivre's theorem,

$$\left(\tfrac{1}{2}\sqrt{3}+\tfrac{1}{2}i\right)^{18} = \left(e^{\frac{1}{6}\pi i}\right)^{18}$$
$$= e^{18\times\frac{1}{6}\pi i}$$
$$= e^{3\pi i}$$
$$= -1.$$

(b) $1+i$ has modulus $\sqrt{2}$ and argument $\frac{1}{4}\pi$, so $1+i=\sqrt{2}e^{\frac{1}{4}\pi i}$. Therefore

$$(1+i)^{-10} = (\sqrt{2})^{-10}\left(e^{\frac{1}{4}\pi i}\right)^{-10}$$
$$= 2^{-5}e^{-10\times\frac{1}{4}\pi i}$$
$$= \tfrac{1}{32}e^{-\frac{5}{2}\pi i}$$
$$= \tfrac{1}{32}\times(-i)$$
$$= -\tfrac{1}{32}i.$$

(c) $0.8+0.6i$ has modulus 1 and argument $0.6435\ldots$. Therefore

$$(0.8+0.6i)^{15} = (e^{0.6435\ldots i})^{15}$$
$$= e^{15\times0.6435\ldots i}$$
$$= e^{9.6525\ldots i}$$
$$= -0.974-0.226i, \text{ correct to 3 significant figures.}$$

De Moivre's theorem has a delightful representation in an Argand diagram. As $z=\cos\phi+i\sin\phi$ has modulus 1, all the powers of z also have modulus 1. This means that all integral powers of z correspond to points on the unit circle. The theorem shows that these points are equally spaced round the circle, as shown in Fig. 6.1.

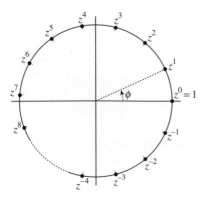

Fig. 6.1

Example 6.1.2

Show in an Argand diagram the points corresponding to z^n, $n \in \mathbb{Z}$, where

(a) $z = 0.9e^i$,   (b) $z = 1 + i$.

In each case find the polar equation of a curve which passes through all the points.

Polar equations are explained in FP2 Section 6.3.

(a) If $z = 0.9e^i$, then $z^n = 0.9^n e^{ni}$ is represented on an Argand diagram by a point with polar coordinates $r = 0.9^n$, $\theta = n$. As n increases, values of r decrease in geometric progression, and values of θ increase in arithmetic progression with common difference 1 radian.

The points all lie on the curve with equation $r = 0.9^\theta$ (see Fig. 6.2).

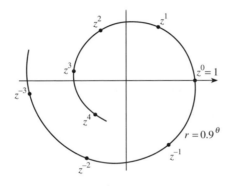

Fig. 6.2

Since $0.9 = e^{\ln 0.9}$, $r = 0.9^\theta$ can be written as $r = e^{\theta \ln 0.9} \approx e^{-0.105\theta}$.

(b) The number $1 + i$ has modulus $\sqrt{2}$ and argument $\frac{1}{4}\pi$, so $z = 2^{\frac{1}{2}} \exp\left(\frac{1}{4}\pi i\right)$ and $z^n = 2^{\frac{1}{2}n} \exp\left(n\left(\frac{1}{4}\pi i\right)\right)$.

Thus $r = 2^{\frac{1}{2}n}$ and $\theta = \frac{1}{4}n\pi$.

As n increases, values of r increase geometrically with common ratio $\sqrt{2}$, and values of θ increase arithmetically with common difference $\frac{1}{4}\pi$.

Since $n = \dfrac{4\theta}{\pi}$, the points all lie on the curve with equation $r = 2^{2\theta/\pi}$, or

$$r = \exp\left(\frac{2\theta \ln 2}{\pi}\right) \approx e^{0.441\theta} \text{ (see Fig. 6.3)}.$$

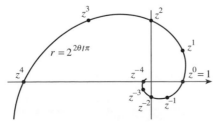

Fig. 6.3

The curves in both parts (a) and (b) are examples of *equiangular spirals* (see the grey box following Example 1.4.3).

6.2   The *n*th roots of unity

Fig. 6.1 can only show a small number of points z^r, where $z = e^{\phi i}$. If you go on plotting these points on an Argand diagram, there are two possibilities. Either you get a new point each time (so that eventually the points are densely packed round the circumference of the unit circle), or they start to repeat. Since the angle increases by the same amount each time, as soon as you get one repetition all subsequent points will also be repetitions.

One of the points is of course $z^0 = 1$, and in fact the first repetition with a positive index is always $z^n = 1$, for some index n. To prove this, you need only note that if the first repetition were $z^n = z^m$, with $n > m \geqslant 1$, then you could divide by z to get $z^{n-1} = z^{m-1}$ with $n - 1 > m - 1 \geqslant 0$, which contradicts the claim that $z^n = z^m$ is the first repetition. So m must be 0, which means that $z^n = 1$ is the first repetition.

It then follows that there are just n different values of z^r, and that these are $1, z, z^2, z^3, \ldots,$ z^{n-1}. The points representing these on an Argand diagram are vertices of a regular polygon.

The vertex of the polygon nearest to 1 (anticlockwise) has argument $\dfrac{2\pi}{n}$. If ω denotes $\exp\left(\dfrac{2\pi}{n}\, i\right)$, then the remaining vertices in order round the polygon are $\omega^2, \omega^3, \ldots, \omega^{n-1}$. This is shown in Fig. 6.4, drawn for the case $n = 9$.

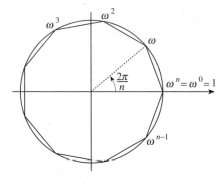

Fig. 6.4

An important result is that each of these numbers raised to the nth power equals 1. This is because, for any $r \in \mathbb{Z}$,

$$(\omega^r)^n = \omega^{rn} = (\omega^n)^r = 1^r = 1.$$

You can also see this geometrically. If you go round a regular n-gon jumping r points at each step, then after n steps you will have made r complete revolutions ending up at 1.

The complex numbers $1, \omega, \omega^2, \omega^3, \ldots, \omega^{n-1}$ are therefore all nth roots of 1. They are usually known by the slightly quaint name of the nth roots of unity.

> The **nth roots of unity** are $1, \omega, \omega^2, \omega^3, \ldots, \omega^{n-1}$, where
> $$\omega = \exp\left(\frac{2\pi}{n}\,\mathrm{i}\right); \text{ that is, } \exp\left(\frac{2r\pi}{n}\,\mathrm{i}\right) \text{ for } 0 \leqslant r \leqslant n-1.$$

You can also derive the second equation in the blue box algebraically. If $z = k\mathrm{e}^{\theta\,\mathrm{i}}$, where $k > 0$, then $z^n = k^n\mathrm{e}^{n\theta\,\mathrm{i}}$. For this to equal $1 = 1\mathrm{e}^{0\mathrm{i}}$, k^n must equal 1 and $n\theta$ must differ from 0 by a multiple of 2π. That is, $k = 1$ and $\theta = \dfrac{2r\pi}{n}$, where $r \in \mathbb{Z}$.

Notice that this holds for any integer r. The restriction $0 \leqslant r \leqslant n-1$ in the definition above ensures that the n values of z are all different; but you can achieve this equally well by letting r take any n consecutive integral values. The integers from 0 to $n-1$ are not always the most convenient, as the next example shows.

Example 6.2.1
Pair off the non-real nth roots of unity as conjugate complex numbers

(a) when $n = 5$,   (b) when $n = 6$.

    The roots are shown in Argand diagrams in Figs. 6.5 and 6.6.

(a) The points are at the vertices of a regular pentagon, with radii separated by angles of $\frac{2}{5}\pi$. Apart from 0, the arguments of the roots are $\frac{2}{5}\pi, \frac{4}{5}\pi, -\frac{4}{5}\pi, -\frac{2}{5}\pi$. Thus the non-real roots are $\exp\left(\frac{2}{5}r\pi\,\mathrm{i}\right)$ for $r = \pm 1$ and ± 2.

(b) The points are at the vertices of a regular hexagon, with radii separated by angles of $\frac{2}{6}\pi = \frac{1}{3}\pi$. There are two real roots, 1 and -1, and the arguments of the other roots are $\frac{1}{3}\pi, \frac{2}{3}\pi, -\frac{2}{3}\pi, -\frac{1}{3}\pi$. Thus the non-real roots are $\exp\left(\frac{1}{3}r\pi\,\mathrm{i}\right)$ for $r = \pm 1$ and ± 2.

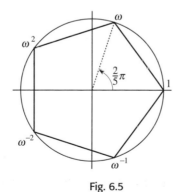

Fig. 6.5

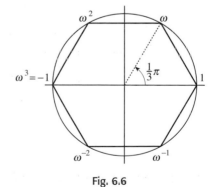

Fig. 6.6

You should check the generalisation of this example for yourself.

> For any natural number $n \geqslant 3$, the nth roots of unity are
> $$1 \text{ and } \exp\left(\frac{2r\pi}{n}\,\mathrm{i}\right) \text{ for } r = \pm 1, \pm 2, \ldots, \pm\tfrac{1}{2}(n-1) \text{ if } n \text{ is odd;}$$
> $$1, -1 \text{ and } \exp\left(\frac{2r\pi}{n}\,\mathrm{i}\right) \text{ for } r = \pm 1, \pm 2, \ldots, \pm\left(\tfrac{1}{2}n-1\right) \text{ if } n \text{ is even.}$$

Exercise 6A

1   Use de Moivre's theorem to express the following in the form $a + b$i. Give the answers exactly where possible, otherwise give them to 3 significant figures.

(a) $(1 - \mathrm{i})^8$

(b) $(1 - \sqrt{3}\,\mathrm{i})^{-9}$

(c) $\left(\exp\frac{1}{4}\pi\mathrm{i}\right)^9$

(d) $\left(\cos\frac{3}{5}\pi + \mathrm{i}\sin\frac{3}{5}\pi\right)^{15}$

(e) $\left(\sin\frac{1}{7}\pi + \mathrm{i}\cos\frac{1}{7}\pi\right)^{-35}$

(f) $(8 - 6\,\mathrm{i})^{30}$

(g) $(0.6 + 0.7\,\mathrm{i})^{-8}$

(h) $\left(\dfrac{7 + 4\,\mathrm{i}}{8 + \mathrm{i}}\right)^{10}$

2   Show in an Argand diagram the points corresponding to z^r, $r \in \mathbb{Z}$, for the following values of z. State for each the smallest positive value of r (if any) for which z^r is real, and whether z^r is positive or negative for this value of r.

(a) i

(b) e^{i}

(c) $\exp\frac{4}{5}\pi\mathrm{i}$

(d) $\cos\frac{1}{3}\pi + \mathrm{i}\sin\frac{1}{3}\pi$

(e) $\sqrt{3} + \mathrm{i}$

(f) $2 - \mathrm{i}$

(g) $\dfrac{1}{1 + \mathrm{i}}$

(h) $\dfrac{3 + 4\,\mathrm{i}}{5}$

3   (a) Write down, in an exact form, all the 8th roots of 1 in the form $a + b$i.

(b) Write down in the form $a + b$i, to 3 decimal places, all the 7th roots of 1.

4   Find the nth roots of -1 for

(a) $n = 2$,

(b) $n = 3$,

(c) $n = 4$,

(d) $n = 5$,

(e) $n = 6$,

and arrange the complex roots in conjugate pairs. Suggest and prove a generalisation of your results for any positive integer n.

6.3   Applications in algebra and geometry

The cube roots of unity, 1, ω and ω^2 where $\omega = \exp\frac{2}{3}\pi\mathrm{i}$, are the roots of the equation

$$z^3 - 1 = 0.$$

Now you know from FP1 Section 8.3 that the sum of the roots of the cubic equation $az^3 + bz^2 + cz + d = 0$ is $-\dfrac{b}{a}$. In this case $a = 1$ and $b = 0$, so

$$1 + \omega + \omega^2 = 0.$$

This important relation has many applications.

Example 6.3.1

Multiply out the product $(a + b\omega + c\omega^2)(a + b\omega^2 + c\omega)$, where $\omega = \exp\frac{2}{3}\pi\mathrm{i}$.

> The product has nine terms. Those involving a^2, b^2 and c^2 are $aa = a^2$, $(b\omega)(b\omega^2) = b^2\omega^3 = b^2$ and $(c\omega^2)(c\omega) = c^2\omega^3 = c^2$, since $\omega^3 = 1$. The terms involving bc are
>
> $$(b\omega)(c\omega) + (c\omega^2)(b\omega^2) = bc(\omega^2 + \omega^4) = bc(\omega^2 + \omega) = bc(-1) = -bc.$$

This simplification uses $\omega^4 = (\omega^3)\omega = \omega$ and $1 + \omega + \omega^2 = 0$.

Similarly, the terms involving ca and ab are

$$a(c\omega) + (c\omega^2)a = ca(\omega + \omega^2) = ca(-1) = -ca,$$

and $$a(b\omega^2) + (b\omega)a = ab(\omega^2 + \omega) = ab(-1) = -ab.$$

This gives for the complete product

$$(a + b\omega + c\omega^2)(a + b\omega^2 + c\omega) \equiv a^2 + b^2 + c^2 - bc - ca - ab.$$

Example 6.3.2

A triangle is formed by points representing complex numbers a, b and c in an Argand diagram. Find the condition for the triangle to be equilateral.

There are two cases. Going round the triangle anticlockwise, the points A, B, C corresponding to a, b, c may occur in the order ABC (Fig. 6.7) or ACB (Fig. 6.8).

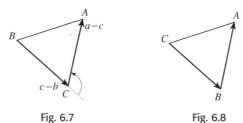

Fig. 6.7   Fig. 6.8

In Fig. 6.7 the displacement $\overrightarrow{BC}$ is transformed into $\overrightarrow{CA}$ by a rotation through $+\frac{2}{3}\pi$. In complex number arithmetic this is equivalent to obtaining $a - c$ by multiplying $c - b$ by a number with modulus 1 and argument $\frac{2}{3}\pi$, that is by the cube root of unity ω.

So $a - c = (c - b)\omega$,   that is $a + b\omega - c(1 + \omega) = 0$,

or $a + b\omega + c\omega^2 = 0$ (since $1 + \omega + \omega^2 = 0$).

You can get the equivalent condition for Fig. 6.8 by interchanging b and c in this condition, which gives

$$a + c\omega + b\omega^2 = 0,   \text{that is}   a + b\omega^2 + c\omega = 0.$$

For one or the other of these conditions to be true, it is necessary and sufficient that

$$(a + b\omega + c\omega^2)(a + b\omega^2 + c\omega) = 0.$$

Using the result of Example 6.3.1, you can write this rule as

$$a^2 + b^2 + c^2 - bc - ca - ab = 0.$$

Example 6.3.3

Find the condition for the roots of the equation $z^3 + pz^2 + qz + r = 0$ to represent the vertices of an equilateral triangle in an Argand diagram.

Since $(a + b + c)^2 = a^2 + b^2 + c^2 + 2bc + 2ca + 2ab$, the condition at the end of Example 6.3.2 can be written as

$$(a + b + c)^2 = 3bc + 3ca + 3ab.$$

You know from FP1 Section 8.3 that $a + b + c = -p$ and $bc + ca + ab = q$. The condition is therefore

$$(-p)^2 = 3q, \quad \text{that is} \quad p^2 = 3q.$$

The equation $1 + \omega + \omega^2 = 0$ connecting the cube roots of unity can be generalised to give a similar equation for the nth roots. You can prove this either by extending the condition for the sum of the roots to be zero to the nth degree equation $z^n - 1 = 0$, or by using the formula for the sum of a geometric progression. If $\omega = \exp\left(\dfrac{2\pi}{n} i\right)$, then

$$1 + \omega + \omega^2 + \cdots + \omega^{n-1} = \frac{1 - \omega^n}{1 - \omega} = 0, \quad \text{since } \omega^n = 1.$$

> For $n \in \mathbb{N}$, $n > 1$, the sum of the nth roots of unity,
> $1 + \omega + \omega^2 + \cdots + \omega^{n-1}$, is equal to zero.

Exercise 6B

1 If $\omega = e^{\frac{2}{3}\pi i}$, simplify the following (expressing your answer in terms of ω where appropriate).

(a) ω^5 (b) ω^{-3} (c) $1 + \omega^2$ (d) $\omega + \dfrac{1}{\omega}$

(e) $(1 - \omega)^2$ (f) $(1 - \omega)(1 - \omega^2)$ (g) $\dfrac{1}{(1 + \omega)^2}$ (h) $\dfrac{1 + \omega}{1 + \omega^2}$

2 If $\omega = e^{\frac{2}{5}\pi i}$, simplify the following.

(a) ω^5 (b) ω^{-4}

(c) $(1 + \omega)(1 + \omega^2)$ (d) $(1 - \omega)(1 - \omega^2)(1 - \omega^3)(1 - \omega^4)$

3 If $\omega = e^{\frac{2}{9}\pi i}$, show that $(1 + \omega)(1 + \omega^2)(1 + \omega^4) = -\omega^8$.

4 If $\omega = e^{\frac{2}{3}\pi i}$, and if $x + y + z = a$, $x + \omega y + \omega^2 z = b$ and $x + \omega^2 y + \omega z = c$, express $a + b + c$, $a + \omega^2 b + \omega c$ and $a + \omega b + \omega^2 c$ in terms of x, y and z.

Hence solve for x, y and z the simultaneous equations

$$\left.\begin{array}{r} x + y + z = 1 \\ x + \omega y + \omega^2 z = 2 \\ x + \omega^2 y + \omega z = 3 \end{array}\right\},$$

giving your answers in the form $p + q\omega$ where p and q are real numbers.

5 Multiply out the products

   (a) $(a + b\omega)(a + b\omega^2)$ where $\omega = \exp(\tfrac{2}{3}\pi\,i)$,

   (b) $(a + b\omega)(a + b\omega^2)(a + b\omega^3)(a + b\omega^4)$ where $\omega = \exp(\tfrac{2}{5}\pi\,i)$.

6* If $\alpha = \exp(\tfrac{2}{5}\pi\,i)$, $\beta = \exp(\tfrac{4}{5}\pi\,i)$, $\gamma = \exp(\tfrac{6}{5}\pi\,i)$ and $\delta = \exp(\tfrac{8}{5}\pi\,i)$, express β, γ and δ as powers of α.

If

$$p = a + b\alpha + c\alpha^2 + d\alpha^3 + e\alpha^4,$$
$$q = a + b\beta + c\beta^2 + d\beta^3 + e\beta^4,$$
$$r = a + b\gamma + c\gamma^2 + d\gamma^3 + e\gamma^4,$$
$$s = a + b\delta + c\delta^2 + d\delta^3 + e\delta^4$$

and the product $pqrs$ is multiplied out, find the coefficients of

  (a) a^4,   (b) a^3b,   (c) a^2b^2,   (d) a^2bc,   (e) $abcd$.

7 A triangle ABC is drawn in an Argand diagram, with its vertices labelled anticlockwise round the triangle. Equilateral triangles BCX, CAY, ABZ are drawn outside the triangle. Show that $x = -b\omega^2 - c\omega$, where $\omega = \exp(\tfrac{2}{3}\pi\,i)$, and write down similar expressions for y and z. Hence find complex numbers representing the displacements $\overrightarrow{XA}$, $\overrightarrow{YB}$ and $\overrightarrow{ZC}$. Show that these displacements are equal in magnitude, and that they make angles of $\tfrac{2}{3}\pi$ with each other. (It can also be proved that the lines XA, YB and ZC meet at a single point, but this is not easy to prove using complex numbers.)

8 With the notation of Question 7, let P, Q and R be the centres of the three equilateral triangles. Prove that the triangle PQR is equilateral.

6.4   An application to factors

Writing the roots as conjugate complex pairs, as in Section 6.2, is useful when you want to combine complex factors in pairs to produce factors with real coefficients. The key identity for this purpose is

$$(z - e^{\theta i})(z - e^{-\theta i}) \equiv z^2 - (e^{\theta i} + e^{-\theta i})z + 1 \equiv z^2 - 2z\cos\theta + 1,$$

using the fact that

$$e^{\theta i} + e^{-\theta i} \equiv (\cos\theta + i\sin\theta) + (\cos\theta - i\sin\theta) = 2\cos\theta.$$

You know from the factor theorem that, if $z_1, z_2, \ldots, z_n$ are the nth roots of unity, then

$$z^n - 1 \equiv (z - z_1)(z - z_2)\ldots(z - z_n).$$

So, from the pairing of these roots and the results in the blue box at the end of Section 6.2:

> If n is odd, the factors of $z^n - 1$ are $z - 1$ and $z^2 - 2z\cos\left(\dfrac{2r\pi}{n}\right) + 1$ for $r = 1,\ 2,\ \ldots,\ \frac{1}{2}(n-1)$.
>
> If n is even, the factors of $z^n - 1$ are $z - 1$, $z + 1$ and $z^2 - 2z\cos\left(\dfrac{2r\pi}{n}\right) + 1$ for $r = 1,\ 2,\ \ldots,\ \left(\frac{1}{2}n - 1\right)$.

For example, from Example 6.2.1, you can deduce that

$$z^5 - 1 \equiv (z-1)\left(z^2 - 2z\cos\tfrac{2}{5}\pi + 1\right)\left(z^2 - 2z\cos\tfrac{4}{5}\pi + 1\right)$$
$$\equiv (z-1)\left(z^2 - 2z\cos\tfrac{2}{5}\pi + 1\right)\left(z^2 + 2z\cos\tfrac{1}{5}\pi + 1\right),$$

since $\cos\frac{4}{5}\pi = \cos\left(\pi - \frac{4}{5}\pi\right) = -\cos\frac{1}{5}\pi$; and that

$$z^6 - 1 \equiv (z-1)(z+1)\left(z^2 - 2z\cos\tfrac{1}{3}\pi + 1\right)\left(z^2 - 2z\cos\tfrac{2}{3}\pi + 1\right)$$
$$\equiv (z-1)(z+1)\left(z^2 - z + 1\right)\left(z^2 + z + 1\right),$$

since $\cos\left(\frac{1}{3}\pi\right) = \frac{1}{2}$ and $\cos\left(\frac{2}{3}\pi\right) = -\frac{1}{2}$.

6.5 The nth roots of a general complex number

Example 6.5.1
Find the fifth roots of i, and illustrate them on an Argand diagram.

Since $i^2 = -1$, $i^4 = (-1)^2 = 1$, so $i^5 = i$. One fifth root of i is therefore i itself.

If z is any fifth root of i, then $z^5 = i$. Since $i^5 = i$, this equation can be written as $z^5 = i^5$, so $\left(\dfrac{z}{i}\right)^5 = \dfrac{z^5}{i^5} = 1$. This means that $\dfrac{z}{i}$ must be one of the fifth roots of unity. If these are denoted by 1, ω, ω^2, ω^3 and ω^4, where $\omega = \exp\left(\frac{2}{5}\pi\,i\right)$, then z is equal to i, $i\omega$, $i\omega^2$, $i\omega^3$ or $i\omega^4$.

Now i has argument $\frac{1}{2}\pi$, and multiplying by ω rotates this about the origin through $\frac{2}{5}\pi$. So i, $i\omega$, $i\omega^2$, ... have arguments $\frac{1}{2}\pi$, $\frac{1}{2}\pi + \frac{2}{5}\pi$, $\frac{1}{2}\pi + \frac{4}{5}\pi$, ..., adjusted by 2π where necessary. The fifth roots of i are therefore $\exp\left(\frac{1}{2}\pi\,i\right)$, $\exp\left(\frac{9}{10}\pi\,i\right)$, $\exp\left(-\frac{7}{10}\pi\,i\right)$, $\exp\left(-\frac{3}{10}\pi\,i\right)$ and $\exp\left(\frac{1}{10}\pi\right)$.

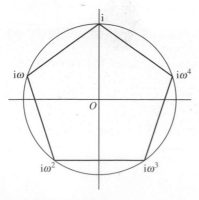

Fig. 6.9

These roots are shown in an Argand diagram in Fig. 6.9 as points on the unit circle at the vertices of a regular pentagon. Notice that, unlike the fifth roots of unity in Example 6.2.1, these roots don't split into conjugate pairs.

The results of Example 6.5.1 can be generalised. Whenever you find the nth roots of any complex number, you always get points in an Argand diagram at the vertices of a regular polygon with its centre at the origin.

The algebraic argument used in Section 6.2 to find the nth roots of unity can be extended to find the nth roots of any complex number, written in modulus–argument form as $a\mathrm{e}^{\alpha\,\mathrm{i}}$, where $a > 0$. If $z = k\mathrm{e}^{\theta\,\mathrm{i}}$ is an nth root, with $k > 0$, then you want to determine k and θ so that

$$k^n \mathrm{e}^{n\theta\,\mathrm{i}} = a\mathrm{e}^{\alpha\,\mathrm{i}}.$$

For this to be true, k^n must equal a, and $n\theta$ must differ from α by a multiple of 2π. That is, $k = \sqrt[n]{a}$ and $n\theta = \alpha + 2r\pi$, which gives

$$\theta = \frac{\alpha}{n} + \frac{2r\pi}{n}.$$

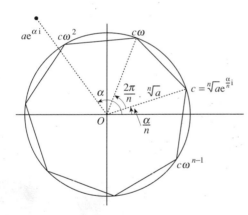

Fig. 6.10

Fig. 6.10 shows these nth roots in an Argand diagram. They all lie on a circle with centre O and radius $\sqrt[n]{a}$, at angles which go up in steps of $\dfrac{2\pi}{n}$ as r increases through $\mathbb{Z}$. You therefore get different roots for any n consecutive integral values of r, such as $0 \le r \le n - 1$, and they then start to repeat. The corresponding points are at the vertices of a regular n-gon, and can be written in the form $c\omega^r$, where c denotes the root $\sqrt[n]{a}\exp\left(\dfrac{\alpha}{n}\,\mathrm{i}\right)$.

The nth roots of the complex number $a\mathrm{e}^{\alpha\,\mathrm{i}}$ are

$$\sqrt[n]{a}\exp\left(\left(\frac{\alpha}{n} + \frac{2r\pi}{n}\right)\mathrm{i}\right) = \sqrt[n]{a}\exp\left(\frac{\alpha}{n}\,\mathrm{i}\right)\omega^r$$

for $r \in \mathbb{Z}$, $0 \le r \le n - 1$, where $\omega = \exp\left(\dfrac{2\pi}{n}\,\mathrm{i}\right)$.

Example 6.5.2

Find the cube roots of $12\sqrt{3} - 36i$, and show these in an Argand diagram.

The number $12\sqrt{3} - 36i$ has modulus $12\sqrt{3+9} = 24\sqrt{3}$, and argument α such that

$$\cos\alpha = \frac{12\sqrt{3}}{24\sqrt{3}} = \tfrac{1}{2} \quad \text{and} \quad \sin\alpha = \frac{-36}{24\sqrt{3}} = -\tfrac{1}{2}\sqrt{3},$$

so that $\alpha = -\tfrac{1}{3}\pi$. You therefore want to find numbers $ke^{\theta i}$ such that

$$(ke^{\theta i})^3 = 24\sqrt{3}e^{-\frac{1}{3}\pi i},$$

that is

$$k^3 e^{3\theta i} = 24\sqrt{3}e^{-\frac{1}{3}\pi i}.$$

Therefore

$$k^3 = 24\sqrt{3} = 8 \times 3\sqrt{3}$$

and $\quad 3\theta = -\tfrac{1}{3}\pi + 2r\pi$ for some integer r.

Since k is a real positive number, $k = 2\sqrt{3}$; and you can get values of θ in the interval $-\pi < \theta \leqslant \pi$ by taking r to be -1, 0 or 1. This gives

$$\theta = -\tfrac{7}{9}\pi, \quad \theta = -\tfrac{1}{9}\pi \text{ or } \theta = \tfrac{5}{9}\pi.$$

The cube roots of $12\sqrt{3} - 36i$ are therefore $2\sqrt{3}e^{-\frac{7}{9}\pi i}$, $2\sqrt{3}e^{-\frac{1}{9}\pi i}$ and $2\sqrt{3}e^{\frac{5}{9}\pi i}$.

Figure 6.11 shows these roots on an Argand diagram. The points lie on a circle centre O with radius $2\sqrt{3}$, at the vertices of an equilateral triangle.

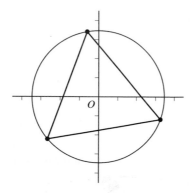

Fig. 6.11

Example 6.5.3

Write $z^8 + z^4 + 1$ as the product of 4 quadratic factors with real coefficients.

The method is to solve the equation $z^8 + z^4 + 1 = 0$ and then to find real quadratic factors by combining conjugate pairs of roots.

A simple way to begin is to notice that, since $\cos \frac{2}{3}\pi = -\frac{1}{2}$, $z^8 + z^4 + 1$ can be written as $(z^4)^2 - 2z^4 \cos \frac{2}{3}\pi + 1$. It can therefore be split into factors as

$$\left(z^4 - e^{\frac{2}{3}\pi i}\right)\left(z^4 - e^{-\frac{2}{3}\pi i}\right).$$

So the roots of $z^8 + z^4 + 1 = 0$ are a combination of the roots of

$$z^4 = e^{\frac{2}{3}\pi i} \quad \text{with those of} \quad z^4 = e^{-\frac{2}{3}\pi i}.$$

Using the result in the blue box with $a = 1$, $\alpha = \frac{2}{3}\pi$ and $n = 4$ the first equation has roots $\exp\left(\left(\frac{1}{6}\pi + \dfrac{2r\pi}{4}\right)i\right)$ for $r = 0, 1, 2$ and 3; that is,

$$e^{\frac{1}{6}\pi i}, \quad e^{\frac{2}{3}\pi i}, \quad e^{\frac{7}{6}\pi i} \quad \text{and} \quad e^{\frac{5}{3}\pi i}.$$

These are the numbers represented by the points marked with solid dots in Fig. 6.12.

Similarly, taking $\alpha = -\frac{2}{3}\pi$, the roots of the second equation have the form $\exp\left(\left(-\frac{1}{6}\pi + \dfrac{2s\pi}{4}\right)i\right)$. But, to show the conjugate pairs, take the values of s to be 0, -1, -2 and -3. This gives the roots as

$$e^{-\frac{1}{6}\pi i}, \quad e^{-\frac{2}{3}\pi i}, \quad e^{-\frac{7}{6}\pi i} \quad \text{and} \quad e^{-\frac{5}{3}\pi i}.$$

These are represented by the points marked with open dots in Fig. 6.12.

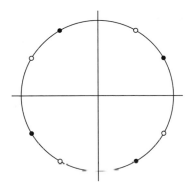

Fig. 6.12

You then get 4 pairs of factors of $z^8 + z^4 + 1$:

$$\left(z - e^{\frac{1}{6}\pi i}\right)\left(z - e^{-\frac{1}{6}\pi i}\right) = z^2 - 2z\cos\frac{1}{6}\pi + 1 = z^2 - \sqrt{3}z + 1,$$
$$\left(z - e^{\frac{2}{3}\pi i}\right)\left(z - e^{-\frac{2}{3}\pi i}\right) = z^2 - 2z\cos\frac{2}{3}\pi + 1 = z^2 + z + 1,$$
$$\left(z - e^{\frac{7}{6}\pi i}\right)\left(z - e^{-\frac{7}{6}\pi i}\right) = z^2 - 2z\cos\frac{7}{6}\pi + 1 = z^2 + \sqrt{3}z + 1.$$
$$\left(z - e^{\frac{5}{3}\pi i}\right)\left(z - e^{-\frac{5}{3}\pi i}\right) = z^2 - 2z\cos\frac{5}{3}\pi + 1 = z^2 - z + 1.$$

That is,

$$z^8 + z^4 + 1 = (z^2 - \sqrt{3}z + 1)(z^2 + z + 1)(z^2 + \sqrt{3}z + 1)(z^2 - z + 1).$$

Exercise 6C

1 Find exact expressions for

   (a) the cube roots of i,

   (b) the fourth roots of $-8(1 + \sqrt{3}\,i)$,

   (c) the sixth roots of -64.

   Use the binomial theorem to check your answers.

2 Find, correct to 3 decimal places,

   (a) the fourth roots of $-i$,

   (b) the fifth roots of $4(1 + i)$,

   (c) the cube roots of $35 + 120i$.

3 Express the following polynomials as the product of real factors. Check your answers by multiplying out the factors.

   (a) $z^4 + 1$ (b) $z^8 - 16$ (c) $z^4 + z^2 + 1$ (d) $z^6 - z^3 + 1$

4 For the following values of z, p and q, write down all the values of (i) $\left(z^{\frac{1}{q}}\right)^p$ and (ii) $\left(z^p\right)^{\frac{1}{q}}$.
   Give your answers in the form $e^{\theta i}$, where $-\pi < \theta \leqslant \pi$, and illustrate them on an Argand diagram. What general result is suggested by your answers?

   (a) $z = e^{\pi i}$, $p = 5$, $q = 3$ (b) $z = e^{\frac{1}{4}\pi i}$, $p = 4$, $q = 2$

   (c) $z = e^{\frac{1}{2}\pi i}$, $p = 6$, $q = 4$ (d) $z = e^{\frac{3}{4}\pi i}$, $p = 3$, $q = 6$

5* An equilateral triangle ABC has vertices at the points 1, ω, ω^2 in an Argand diagram, where $\omega = \exp\frac{2}{3}\pi i$, and P is the point $\frac{1}{2}(1 + i)$. Use the identity $z^3 - 1 \equiv (z - 1)(z - \omega)(z - \omega^2)$ to show that the product of the distances PA, PB and PC is $\frac{1}{4}\sqrt{26}$.

6* A regular pentagon $ABCDE$ has its vertices on a circle with radius r and centre O. A point P is at a distance d from O, and angle $AOP = \theta$. Prove that the product of the distances PA, PB, PC, PD and PE is $\sqrt{d^{10} - 2d^5 r^5 \cos 5\theta + r^{10}}$.

7* The vertices of an n-gon $P_0 P_1 P_2 \ldots P_{n-1}$ lie on a circle of unit radius, and Q is the mid-point of the arc $P_0 P_1$. Find the products of the distances

   (a) QP_0, QP_1, QP_2, ..., QP_{n-1},   (b) $P_0 P_1$, $P_0 P_2$, $P_0 P_3$, ..., $P_0 P_{n-1}$.

Miscellaneous exercise 6

1 Write $z_1 = 1 + i$ and $z_2 = 2(-1 + i)$ in polar form. Show that $z_1^3 = z_2$.

   Find the two other cube roots of z_2 in polar form, and sketch the three cube roots in an Argand diagram.

   Write down the cube roots of $z_3 = 2(-1 - i)$ in polar form.   (OCR)

2 Write the complex number $8i$ in the form $re^{\theta i}$ (where $r > 0$ and $-\pi < \theta \leqslant \pi$).

   Find the three cube roots of $8i$, giving your answers in the form $a + bi$. Illustrate these cube roots on an Argand diagram.

   Hence solve the equation $(iz - 2\sqrt{3})^3 = 8i$, giving your answers in the form $a + bi$.   (MEI)

3 If $\omega = \cos\theta + \mathrm{i}\sin\theta$, show that $\dfrac{1+\omega}{1-\omega} = \mathrm{i}\cot\frac{1}{2}\theta$.

Write down the roots of $z^n = -1$, where n is a positive integer. Hence, by writing z as $\dfrac{x-1}{x+1}$, prove that the roots of $(x-1)^n = -(x+1)^n$ are $\mathrm{i}\cot\dfrac{(2r+1)\pi}{2n}$ for $r = 0, 1, 2, \ldots, n-1$.

(OCR)

4 Find all the fourth roots of -4, giving your answers in the form $p + q\,\mathrm{i}$, where p and q are real. Hence solve the equation $(z-1)^4 = -4(z+1)^4$, giving your answers in the form $x + y\,\mathrm{i}$ where x and y are real.

(OCR)

5 Solve the equation $z^5 + 32 = 0$, giving the roots in the form $r\mathrm{e}^{\alpha\mathrm{i}}$ (where $r > 0$ and $-\pi < \alpha \leqslant \pi$). Illustrate the roots on an Argand diagram.

If $\left(\dfrac{1-2w}{w}\right)^5 + 32 = 0$, show that w has the form $\frac{1}{4}(1 - \mathrm{i}\tan\beta)$, and state the four possible values of β in the interval $-\pi < \beta \leqslant \pi$. On a separate Argand diagram, illustrate the four possible values of w.

(MEI)

6 In Example 6.3.3 show that, if $p^2 = 3q$, the cubic equation can be written in the form $\left(z + \frac{1}{3}p\right)^3 = s$. Use this to prove by another method that the points in an Argand diagram representing the roots form an equilateral triangle.

7 A triangle ABC is drawn in an Argand diagram, with its vertices labelled clockwise round the triangle. Starting at any point P in the plane, rotate anticlockwise through angles of $\frac{2}{3}\pi$ about A, B and C in succession to arrive at points Q, R and S. Show that S and P coincide if and only if the triangle ABC is equilateral.

8 ABC is a triangle in an Argand diagram. Starting at any point P in the plane, rotate through angles of $\frac{1}{3}\pi$ about A, B, C, A, B and C in succession to arrive at points Q, R, S, T, U and V. Show that V is the same point as P.

Investigate similar results for

(a) a quadrilateral $ABCD$,   (b) a pentagon $ABCDE$.

9 If $\omega = \mathrm{e}^{\frac{2}{3}\pi\mathrm{i}}$, find the determinant and the inverse of the matrix $\begin{pmatrix} 1 & 1 & 1 \\ 1 & \omega^2 & \omega \\ 1 & \omega & \omega^2 \end{pmatrix}$.

10 Show that, if $\omega = \mathrm{e}^{\frac{2}{3}\pi\mathrm{i}}$, the matrix $\begin{pmatrix} 1 & \omega & \omega^2 \\ \omega^2 & 1 & \omega \\ \omega & \omega^2 & 1 \end{pmatrix}$ is singular.

Find equations which must connect a, b and c if the simultaneous equations

$$\left. \begin{array}{r} x + \omega y + \omega^2 z = a \\ \omega^2 x + y + \omega z = b \\ \omega x + \omega^2 y + z = c \end{array} \right\}$$

are to have solutions for x, y and z.

7 Further trigonometry

This chapter shows how some trigonometric results can be developed by using de Moivre's theorem. When you have completed it, you should

- be able to express trigonometric functions of multiples of an angle in terms of functions of the angle itself
- be able to use these relations to investigate the roots of polynomial equations
- be able to express powers of sines and cosines of an angle in terms of trigonometric functions of multiples of the angle
- know that some power series can be extended to complex variables
- be able to use sums of power series to find sums of trigonometric series.

7.1 Real and imaginary parts

If $z = x + y\mathrm{i}$ is a complex number, then x and y are respectively the real and imaginary parts of z. You are familiar with the notation

$$\mathrm{Re}\,(z) = x \quad \text{and} \quad \mathrm{Im}(z) = y.$$

Applying this to de Moivre's theorem, $(\cos\theta + \mathrm{i}\sin\theta)^n = \cos n\theta + \mathrm{i}\sin n\theta$, gives

$$\mathrm{Re}\,((\cos\theta + \mathrm{i}\sin\theta)^n) = \cos n\theta \quad \text{and} \quad \mathrm{Im}((\cos\theta + \mathrm{i}\sin\theta)^n) = \sin n\theta.$$

To simplify the look of the algebra, it will be convenient in this chapter to abbreviate $\cos\theta$, $\sin\theta$ and $\tan\theta$ to c, s and t. Then

$$\cos n\theta = \mathrm{Re}\,((c + s\,\mathrm{i})^n) \quad \text{and} \quad \sin n\theta = \mathrm{Im}((c + s\,\mathrm{i})^n).$$

You can easily verify for yourself the following properties of the functions Re and Im.

> The real and imaginary parts of z are denoted by $\mathrm{Re}(z)$ and $\mathrm{Im}(z)$.
>
> For complex numbers z and w, and a real number a,
>
> $$\mathrm{Re}(az) = a\mathrm{Re}(z), \qquad\qquad \mathrm{Im}(az) = a\mathrm{Im}(z),$$
> $$\mathrm{Re}(z + w) = \mathrm{Re}(z) + \mathrm{Re}(w), \quad \mathrm{Im}(z + w) = \mathrm{Im}(z) + \mathrm{Im}(w),$$
> $$z + z^* = 2\mathrm{Re}(z), \qquad\qquad z - z^* = 2\mathrm{Im}(z)\,\mathrm{i}.$$

7.2 Multiple angle formulae

When you first met the double angle formulae, they were obtained as a special case of the addition formulae, writing $B = A$ in the formula for $\sin(A + B)$ to get $\sin 2A$. It is easy to extend this to $\sin 3A = \sin(A + 2A)$ and $\sin 4A = \sin 2(2A)$, but the method gets laborious if you try to use it to find $\sin nA$ for a large value of n, where $n \in \mathbb{N}$.

It is much easier to use the expressions in the last section for $\cos n\theta$ and $\sin n\theta$ as the real and imaginary parts of $(c + s\,i)^n$, which can be expanded by the binomial theorem as

$$(c + s\,i)^n = c^n + \binom{n}{1} c^{n-1} (s\,i) + \binom{n}{2} c^{n-2} (s\,i)^2 + \binom{n}{3} c^{n-3} (s\,i)^3 + \cdots$$

$$+ \binom{n}{n-1} c(s\,i)^{n-1} + (s\,i)^n.$$

Since the successive powers of i are $i^2 = -1$, $i^3 = -i$, $i^4 = 1$, and they then repeat indefinitely following the pattern $i, -1, -i, 1$, the terms of the binomial expansion are real and imaginary in turn. It follows that

$$\cos n\theta = \mathrm{Re}((c + s\,i)^n) = c^n - \binom{n}{2} c^{n-2} s^2 + \binom{n}{4} c^{n-4} s^4 - \cdots,$$

and $$\sin n\theta = \mathrm{Im}((c + s\,i)^n) = \binom{n}{1} c^{n-1} s - \binom{n}{3} c^{n-3} s^3 + \binom{n}{5} c^{n-5} s^5 - \cdots.$$

The dots at the end of these expansions indicate that they continue for as long as the powers of c are non-negative and the powers of s are less than or equal to n. The precise expression for the last term depends on whether n is odd or even, and its sign depends on the remainder when n is divided by 4.

Example 7.2.1

Find expressions in terms of powers of $\cos\theta$ and/or $\sin\theta$ for

(a) $\cos 5\theta$,   (b) $\sin 7\theta$,   (c) $\sin 8\theta$.

(a) $\cos 5\theta = \mathrm{Re}((c + s\,i)^5) = c^5 - \binom{5}{2} c^3 s^2 + \binom{5}{4} c s^4$

$$= c^5 - 10 c^3 s^2 + 5 c s^4.$$

You could leave the answer in this form, but it is often more useful to give it in terms of c alone, using Pythagoras' identity to write s^2 as $1 - c^2$. Then $s^4 = (1 - c^2)^2$, so

$$\cos 5\theta = c^5 - 10 c^3 (1 - c^2) + 5 c (1 - c^2)^2$$
$$= c^5 - 10 c^3 (1 - c^2) + 5 c (1 - 2 c^2 + c^4)$$
$$= c^5 - 10 c^3 + 10 c^5 + 5 c - 10 c^3 + 5 c^5$$
$$= (1 + 10 + 5) c^5 + (-10 - 10) c^3 + 5 c$$
$$= 16 \cos^5\theta - 20 \cos^3\theta + 5 \cos\theta,$$

replacing the abbreviation c by $\cos\theta$.

(b) $\sin 7\theta = \mathrm{Im}((c + si)^n) = \binom{7}{1} c^6 s - \binom{7}{3} c^4 s^3 + \binom{7}{5} c^2 s^5 - \binom{7}{7} s^7$

$$= 7 c^6 s - 35 c^4 s^3 + 21 c^2 s^5 - s^7.$$

Since c appears only to even powers, you can replace c^2 by $1 - s^2$ to obtain an expansion involving only s.

That is,

$$\sin 7\theta = 7(1-s^2)^3 s - 35(1-s^2)^2 s^3 + 21(1-s^2)s^5 - s^7$$
$$= 7s - 21s^3 + 21s^5 - 7s^7$$
$$- 35s^3 + 70\,s^5 - 35\,s^7$$
$$+ 21s^5 - 21\,s^7$$
$$- s^7$$
$$= 7\sin\theta - 56\sin^3\theta + 112\sin^5\theta - 64\sin^7\theta.$$

It is easy to make a mistake in working through this algebra, so it is a good idea to check the coefficients by taking a particular value for θ. For example, putting $\theta = \frac{1}{2}\pi$ gives $\sin\frac{7}{2}\pi = -1$ on the left, and $7 - 56 + 112 - 64 = -1$ on the right.

(c) $\sin 8\theta = \binom{8}{1}c^7 s - \binom{8}{3}c^5 s^3 + \binom{8}{5}c^3 s^5 - \binom{8}{7}cs^7$

$$= 8c^7 s - 56c^5 s^3 + 56c^3 s^5 - 8cs^7.$$

You can't write this as a polynomial in either c or s alone, because both c and s appear to odd powers. But it is possible to keep just a single factor of c or s and to express the remaining factor entirely in terms of the other. Thus

$$\sin 8\theta = 8cs(c^6 - 7c^4 s^2 + 7c^2 s^4 - s^6)$$
$$= 8cs((1-s^2)^3 - 7(1-s^2)^2 s^2 + 7(1-s^2)s^4 - s^6)$$
$$= 8cs(1 - 3s^2 + 3s^4 - s^6$$
$$- 7s^2 + 14s^4 - 7s^6$$
$$+ 7s^4 - 7s^6$$
$$- s^6)$$
$$= 8\cos\theta\sin\theta(1 - 10\sin^2\theta + 24\sin^4\theta - 16\sin^6\theta).$$

In this case values of θ such as 0, $\frac{1}{2}\pi$ or π are of no use as a check on the coefficients, since both sides are obviously zero. But you could use $\frac{1}{4}\pi$, for which $\sin\theta = \cos\theta = \frac{1}{\sqrt{2}}$, so that the left side is 0 and the right side is

$$8 \times \tfrac{1}{2}\left(1 - \tfrac{10}{2} + \tfrac{24}{4} - \tfrac{16}{8}\right) = 4(1 - 5 + 6 - 2) = 0.$$

Example 7.2.2
Find expressions in terms of $\tan\theta$ for (a) $\tan 5\theta$, (b) $\tan 6\theta$.

(a) You can express $\tan 5\theta$ in terms of c and s by using

$$\tan 5\theta = \frac{\sin 5\theta}{\cos 5\theta} = \frac{5c^4 s - 10c^2 s^3 + s^5}{c^5 - 10c^3 s^2 + 5cs^4}.$$

The method is now to divide both the top and bottom lines of this fraction by c^5.

Then $\dfrac{c^4 s}{c^5} = \dfrac{s}{c} = t,\quad \dfrac{c^3 s^2}{c^5} = \dfrac{s^2}{c^2} = t^2$, and so on.

So $\tan 5\theta = \dfrac{5t - 10t^3 + t^5}{1 - 10t^2 + 5t^4}$, where $t = \tan\theta$.

(b) The same method gives

$$\tan 6\theta = \frac{\sin 6\theta}{\cos 6\theta} = \frac{6c^5 s - 20c^3 s^3 + 6cs^5}{c^6 - 15c^4 s^2 + 15c^2 s^4 - s^6}$$

$$= \frac{6t - 20t^3 + 6t^5}{1 - 15t^2 + 15t^4 - t^6} \quad \text{(dividing both top and bottom by } c^6 \text{)}.$$

It is easy to generalise Example 7.2.2 to give a formula for $\tan n\theta$ for any $n \in \mathbb{N}$, as

$$\tan n\theta = \frac{nt - \binom{n}{3} t^3 + \cdots}{1 - \binom{n}{2} t^2 + \cdots}.$$

Notice that the highest power of $\tan\theta$ is in the numerator when n is odd, and in the denominator when n is even.

7.3 Application to polynomial equations

The expansions found in the last section can be used to express the roots of some polynomial equations in trigonometric form.

Example 7.3.1
Write each of the following equations as polynomial equations in $c = \cos\theta$, and solve them.
(a) $\cos 5\theta = 0$ (b) $\cos 5\theta = 1$

Use your answers to find expressions for $\cos\frac{1}{10}\pi$, $\cos\frac{3}{10}\pi$, $\cos\frac{1}{5}\pi$ and $\cos\frac{2}{5}\pi$. ·

(a) Using $\cos 5\theta = 16c^5 - 20c^3 + 5c$ from Example 7.2.1(a),

$$\cos 5\theta = 0 \quad \Leftrightarrow \quad 16c^5 - 20c^3 + 5c = 0.$$

Now $\cos 5\theta$ is equal to 0 if 5θ is an odd multiple of $\frac{1}{2}\pi$, so that $\theta = \frac{1}{10}\pi, \frac{3}{10}\pi, \frac{5}{10}\pi$ and so on. Since $\cos\theta$ is a decreasing function over the interval $0 \leqslant \theta \leqslant \pi$, you get different values for $c = \cos\theta$ by taking $\theta = \frac{1}{10}r\pi$ for $r = 1, 3, 5, 7$ and 9. As expected, the quintic polynomial equation $16c^5 - 20c^3 + 5c = 0$ has five roots.

Now the root $c = 0$ corresponds to $r = 5$, since $\cos\frac{5}{10}\pi = \cos\frac{1}{2}\pi = 0$. It follows that $\cos\frac{1}{10}\pi$, $\cos\frac{3}{10}\pi$, $\cos\frac{7}{10}\pi$ and $\cos\frac{9}{10}\pi$ are the roots of $16c^4 - 20c^2 + 5 = 0$.

Notice that

$$\cos\tfrac{7}{10}\pi = \cos\left(\pi - \tfrac{3}{10}\pi\right) = -\cos\tfrac{3}{10}\pi \quad \text{and} \quad \cos\tfrac{9}{10}\pi = \cos\left(\pi - \tfrac{1}{10}\pi\right) = -\cos\tfrac{1}{10}\pi.$$

The roots can therefore be written as $\pm\cos\frac{1}{10}\pi$ and $\pm\cos\frac{3}{10}\pi$.

Now the equation for $16c^4 - 20c^2 + 5 = 0$ is a quadratic in c^2, with roots

$$c^2 = \frac{20 \pm \sqrt{80}}{32} = \frac{5 \pm \sqrt{5}}{8}.$$

Since $\cos \frac{1}{10}\pi > \cos \frac{3}{10}\pi > 0$, it follows that

$$\cos \tfrac{1}{10}\pi = \sqrt{\frac{5+\sqrt{5}}{8}} \quad \text{and} \quad \cos \tfrac{3}{10}\pi = \sqrt{\frac{5-\sqrt{5}}{8}}.$$

(b) Beginning as in part (a),

$$\cos 5\theta = 1 \quad \Leftrightarrow \quad 16c^5 - 20c^3 + 5c - 1 = 0.$$

For $\cos 5\theta$ to equal 1, 5θ must be a multiple of 2π, so that $\theta = \frac{2}{5}r\pi$ for $r \in \mathbb{Z}$. This gives $c = \cos 0 = 1, c = \cos \frac{2}{5}\pi, c = \cos \frac{4}{5}\pi$, but no more, since $\cos \frac{6}{5}\pi = \cos\left(2\pi - \frac{4}{5}\pi\right) = \cos \frac{4}{5}\pi$, and similarly $\cos \frac{8}{5}\pi = \cos \frac{2}{5}\pi$, after which $\frac{10}{5}\pi = 2\pi$ begins a repetition of the cycle.

You can easily check that $c = 1$ is a root of the polynomial equation, so that a factor $c - 1$ can be separated out, giving

$$(c - 1)(16c^4 + 16c^3 - 4c^2 - 4c + 1) = 0.$$

This leaves the equation

$$16c^4 + 16c^3 - 4c^2 - 4c + 1 = 0$$

with the other two roots, $\cos \frac{2}{5}\pi$ and $\cos \frac{4}{5}\pi$.

Clearly there is something odd here! You would expect a quartic equation to have four roots, not two. So it seems that the two roots might be repeated roots, in which case the quartic polynomial would be the square of a quadratic, $Pc^2 + Qc + R$ for some constants P, Q and R.

To investigate this, note that

$$(Pc^2 + Qc + R)^2 \equiv P^2c^4 + 2PQc^3 + (Q^2 + 2PR)c^2 + 2QRc + R^2.$$

So if the hunch is correct, it should be possible to find P, Q and R so that

$$P^2 = 16, \quad 2PQ = 16, \quad Q^2 + 2PR = -4, \quad 2QR = -4 \quad \text{and} \quad R^2 = 1.$$

Working from left to right, you can easily find that the first three equations are satisfied by $P = 4$, $Q = 2$ and $R = -1$, and that these values also fit the last two equations. So

$$16c^4 + 16c^3 - 4c^2 - 4c + 1 \equiv (4c^2 + 2c - 1)^2.$$

It is now easy to complete the analysis. The quadratic equation

$$4c^2 + 2c - 1 = 0$$

has roots $\dfrac{-2 \pm \sqrt{20}}{8}$, or $\dfrac{-1 \pm \sqrt{5}}{4}$, and these are the values of $\cos \frac{2}{5}\pi$ and $\cos \frac{4}{5}\pi$. By considering the signs, it follows that

$$\cos \tfrac{2}{5}\pi = \frac{\sqrt{5}-1}{4} \quad \text{and} \quad \cos \tfrac{4}{5}\pi = -\frac{\sqrt{5}+1}{4}.$$

Finally, note that $\cos \frac{1}{5}\pi = \cos\left(\pi - \frac{4}{5}\pi\right) = -\cos \frac{4}{5}\pi$, so $\cos \frac{1}{5}\pi = \dfrac{\sqrt{5}+1}{4}$.

Example 7.3.2

Use the expansion of $\tan n\theta$ for some value of n to find $\tan \frac{1}{12}\pi$.

Since $3 \times \frac{1}{12}\pi = \frac{1}{4}\pi$, and $\tan \frac{1}{4}\pi = 1$, $\frac{1}{12}\pi$ is one of the roots of $\tan 3\theta = 1$. Writing $\tan 3\theta$ in terms of $t = \tan\theta$, this equation is

$$\frac{3t - t^3}{1 - 3t^2} = 1,$$

which can be rearranged as $t^3 - 3t^2 - 3t + 1 = 0$.

To find all the roots of this cubic equation, you need three roots of $\tan 3\theta = 1$ which give different values of $t = \tan\theta$. These can be taken as $3\theta = \frac{1}{4}\pi, \frac{5}{4}\pi$ and $\frac{9}{4}\pi$, so that $\theta = \frac{1}{12}\pi, \frac{5}{12}\pi$ and $\frac{9}{12}\pi = \frac{3}{4}\pi$.

Now $\tan \frac{3}{4}\pi = -1$, so one factor of the cubic must be $t + 1$. The equation is then

$$(t + 1)(t^2 - 4t + 1) = 0,$$

so $\tan \frac{1}{12}\pi$ and $\tan \frac{5}{12}\pi$ are the roots of $t^2 - 4t + 1 = 0$.

Since $\tan \frac{1}{12}\pi < \tan \frac{5}{12}\pi$, $\tan \frac{1}{12}\pi$ is the smaller root, $t = 2 - \sqrt{3}$.

Example 7.3.3

(a) Find an equation which is satisfied by $\sin \frac{1}{7}r\pi$, where r is any integer. Hence find an equation whose roots are $\sin^2 \frac{1}{7}\pi$, $\sin^2 \frac{2}{7}\pi$ and $\sin^2 \frac{3}{7}\pi$.

(b) Deduce the values of
(i) $\sin^2 \frac{1}{7}\pi + \sin^2 \frac{2}{7}\pi + \sin^2 \frac{3}{7}\pi$,   (ii) $\sin \frac{1}{7}\pi \sin \frac{2}{7}\pi \sin \frac{3}{7}\pi$,
(iii) $\operatorname{cosec}^2 \frac{1}{7}\pi + \operatorname{cosec}^2 \frac{2}{7}\pi + \operatorname{cosec}^2 \frac{3}{7}\pi$.

(a) If $\theta = \frac{1}{7}r\pi$, then $7\theta = r\pi$, so that $\sin 7\theta = 0$. It was shown in Example 7.2.1(b) that, if $s = \sin\theta$, then

$$\sin 7\theta = 7s - 56s^3 + 112s^5 - 64s^7.$$

So an equation satisfied by $\sin \frac{1}{7}r\pi$ is

$$7s - 56s^3 + 112s^5 - 64s^7 = 0.$$

Now although there are infinitely many values of $\frac{1}{7}r\pi$, there are only 7 different values of $\sin \frac{1}{7}r\pi$, which can be taken to be $\sin\left(-\frac{3}{7}\pi\right)$, $\sin\left(-\frac{2}{7}\pi\right)$, $\sin\left(-\frac{1}{7}\pi\right)$, $\sin 0$, $\sin \frac{1}{7}\pi$, $\sin \frac{2}{7}\pi$ and $\sin \frac{3}{7}\pi$. Taking out the factor s, corresponding to the root $s = 0$, the equation satisfied by $\pm \sin \frac{1}{7}\pi$, $\pm \sin \frac{2}{7}\pi$ and $\pm \sin \frac{3}{7}\pi$ is

$$7 - 56s^2 + 112s^4 - 64s^6 = 0.$$

To find the equation satisfied by $\sin^2 \frac{1}{7}\pi$, $\sin^2 \frac{2}{7}\pi$ and $\sin^2 \frac{3}{7}\pi$ you can use the method of substitution described in FP1 Chapter 8. If u is any one of these numbers, then $\pm\sqrt{u}$ is one of the six roots of the equation

$$7 - 56s^2 + 112s^4 - 64s^6 = 0,$$

so u satisfies the equation

$$7 - 56(\pm\sqrt{u})^2 + 112(\pm\sqrt{u})^4 - 64(\pm\sqrt{u})^6 = 0.$$

That is

$$7 - 56u + 112u^2 - 64u^3 = 0,$$

or

$$64u^3 - 112u^2 + 56u - 7 = 0.$$

(b) (i) The sum of the roots of the cubic equation for u is $-\frac{-112}{64} = \frac{7}{4}$, so

$$\sin^2 \tfrac{1}{7}\pi + \sin^2 \tfrac{2}{7}\pi + \sin^2 \tfrac{3}{7}\pi = \tfrac{7}{4}.$$

(ii) The product of the roots of the equation for u is $-\frac{-7}{64} = \frac{7}{64}$, so

$$\sin^2 \tfrac{1}{7}\pi \sin^2 \tfrac{2}{7}\pi \sin^2 \tfrac{3}{7}\pi = \tfrac{7}{64}.$$

Since $\frac{1}{7}\pi$, $\frac{2}{7}\pi$ and $\frac{3}{7}\pi$ are all between 0 and $\frac{1}{2}\pi$, their sines are all positive, so their product is positive. That is,

$$\sin \tfrac{1}{7}\pi \sin \tfrac{2}{7}\pi \sin \tfrac{3}{7}\pi = \sqrt{\tfrac{7}{64}} = \tfrac{1}{8}\sqrt{7}.$$

(iii) You can find the equation whose roots are $\operatorname{cosec}^2 \frac{1}{7}\pi$, $\operatorname{cosec}^2 \frac{2}{7}\pi$ and $\operatorname{cosec}^2 \frac{3}{7}\pi$ by using the substitution method again. If v is any one of these numbers, then $\dfrac{1}{v}$ is one of the roots of the equation for u, so

$$64\left(\frac{1}{v}\right)^3 - 112\left(\frac{1}{v}\right)^2 + 56\left(\frac{1}{v}\right) - 7 = 0.$$

That is,

$$7v^3 - 56v^2 + 112v - 64 = 0.$$

The sum of the roots of this equation is $-\frac{-56}{7} = 8$. So

$$\operatorname{cosec}^2 \tfrac{1}{7}\pi + \operatorname{cosec}^2 \tfrac{2}{7}\pi + \operatorname{cosec}^2 \tfrac{3}{7}\pi = 8.$$

There are no simple expressions in surd form for the sines of multiples of $\frac{1}{7}\pi$, so the simplicity of these answers is rather surprising. Try checking them with a calculator.

The next example uses angles in degrees rather than radians. Obviously the addition formulae are valid whichever unit is used, but you have to be careful to restrict the use of degrees to this part of the discussion. When you refer to the argument of a complex number, or use the exponential notation $e^{\theta i}$, it is essential to use radian notation.

Example 7.3.4

Use a substitution $x = k \cos\theta$, where θ is measured in degrees, for some number k, to solve the cubic equation $x^3 - 3x - 1 = 0$.

This equation was solved by numerical methods in C3 Example 8.5.1. With the methods of this chapter you can find exact expressions for the roots.

The expansion of $\cos 3\theta$ is

$$c^3 - 3cs^2 = c^3 - 3c(1 - c^2) = 4c^3 - 3c,$$

so $\cos 3\theta = 4\cos^3\theta - 3\cos\theta.$

The aim is to find a value of k so that, with the given substitution,

$$x^3 - 3x = (k\cos\theta)^3 - 3k\cos\theta = k^3\cos^3\theta - 3k\cos\theta$$

is a multiple of $\cos 3\theta$. This requires $\dfrac{k^3}{4} = \dfrac{3k}{3}$, or $k^2 - 4$ (since $k = 0$ is unhelpful).

Take the root $k = 2$. Then substituting $x = 2\cos\theta$, the equation $x^3 - 3x = 1$ becomes

$$8\cos^3\theta - 6\cos\theta = 1,$$

which is

$$2\cos 3\theta = 1, \quad \text{or} \quad \cos 3\theta = \tfrac{1}{2}.$$

You want three roots of this equation which give different values for $\cos\theta$. Taking $3\theta = 60°$, $420°$ and $780°$ gives $\theta = 20°$, $140°$ and $260°$, so $x = 2\cos 20° \approx 1.879$, $x = 2\cos 140° \approx -1.532$ and $x = 2\cos 260° \approx -0.347$, correct to 3 decimal places.

This example leads to a method of solving many cubic equations of the form $x^3 + ax^2 + bx + c = 0$. First, you can make the substitution $x = y - \tfrac{1}{3}a$, to get a cubic equation for y for which the coefficient of y^2 is 0. Then you can complete the solution by using the method of Example 7.3.4. (See also Example 7.7.1.)

You might wonder whether there are also methods of solving equations of higher degree. The answer is 'yes' for quartic equations, but that is as far as you can go. It was proved by the Norwegian mathematician Niels Abel (1802 1829), using ideas from groups, that there is no general method of solving polynomial equations of degree higher than 4.

However, some special equations of higher degree can be solved by methods like the one in Example 7.3.4. One example of a solvable quintic equation is the subject of Exercise 7A Question 13.

Exercise 7A

1 Find expressions for the following in terms of $c = \cos\theta$ and $s = \sin\theta$. Check your answers by substituting a suitable value for θ in the original expression and in the answer.

   (a) $\sin 3\theta$ (b) $\sin 5\theta$ (c) $\cos 6\theta$

   (d) $\sin 6\theta$ (e) $\cos 9\theta$ (f) $\sin 9\theta$

2 Find expressions for the following in terms of $t = \tan\theta$.

   (a) $\tan 4\theta$ (b) $\tan 7\theta$ (c) $\tan 8\theta$

3 Write the equation $\cos 4\theta = -\frac{1}{2}$ as a polynomial equation in $c = \cos\theta$. Factorise this equation, and match its roots with those of the original equation.

4 Write the equation $\sin 6\theta = 0$ as an equation in $c = \cos\theta$ and $s = \sin\theta$. Factorise this equation, and match its roots with those of the original equation.

5 Use the expansion of $\sin 8\theta$ found in Example 7.2.1(c) to find an equation whose roots are $\pm\sin\frac{1}{8}\pi, \pm\sin\frac{3}{8}\pi$. Hence find an expression for $\sin\frac{1}{8}\pi$ in surd form.

6 Show that $\tan\frac{1}{16}\pi$ is a root of the equation $t^4 + 4t^3 - 6t^2 - 4t + 1 = 0$. What are the other roots? Show that the equation can be expressed in the form $u^2 + 4u - 4 = 0$, where $u = t - t^{-1}$. Hence find the value of $\tan\frac{1}{16}\pi$.

7 Show that $\tan 9°$ is the smallest positive root of the equation $t^4 - 4t^3 - 14t^2 - 4t + 1 = 0$. Writing $t + t^{-1} = u$, obtain the equation $u^2 - 4u - 16 = 0$. Hence show that $\tan 9° = 1 + \sqrt{5} - \sqrt{5 + 2\sqrt{5}}$.

8 Prove that three roots of $\cos 5\theta + \cos 4\theta = 0$ are $\frac{1}{9}\pi, \frac{5}{9}\pi$ and $\frac{7}{9}\pi$. Hence, if α, β and γ denote $\cos\frac{1}{9}\pi$, $\cos\frac{5}{9}\pi$ and $\cos\frac{7}{9}\pi$, find the values of $\alpha + \beta + \gamma$, $\beta\gamma + \gamma\alpha + \alpha\beta$ and $\alpha\beta\gamma$.

9 Write $\sin 5\theta = \frac{1}{2}$ as a polynomial equation in $s = \sin\theta$. Find five different roots of this equation in trigonometric form, and hence find one simple factor of the polynomial. Deduce that $x^4 + x^3 - 4x^2 - 4x + 1 = 0$ has roots $2\sin\frac{1}{30}r\pi$ for $r = 1, 13, -7$ and -11.

10 Write the equation $\cos 3\theta = -\frac{1}{2}$ as a polynomial equation in $c = \cos\theta$. Show that the roots can be written as $\cos\alpha$, $\cos\beta$ and $\cos\gamma$, where α, β and γ are all between 0 and π. Use your equation to show that $\cos\frac{2}{9}\pi + \cos\frac{4}{9}\pi = \cos\frac{1}{9}\pi$, and to find the value of $\cos\frac{1}{9}\pi \cos\frac{2}{9}\pi \cos\frac{4}{9}\pi$.

11 Show that the values of θ which satisfy the equation $\tan 4\theta + \tan 3\theta = 0$ are of the form $\frac{1}{7}r\pi$, where r is an integer. Write this as a polynomial equation in $t = \tan\theta$, and state the roots of this equation.

   By removing the factor t and substituting $u = t^2$, find the cubic equation whose roots are $\tan^2\frac{1}{7}\pi$, $\tan^2\frac{2}{7}\pi$ and $\tan^2\frac{3}{7}\pi$. Hence find the values of

   (a) $\tan^2\frac{1}{7}\pi + \tan^2\frac{2}{7}\pi + \tan^2\frac{3}{7}\pi$,   (b) $\tan\frac{1}{7}\pi \tan\frac{2}{7}\pi \tan\frac{3}{7}\pi$.

   Use a calculator to check your answers to (a) and (b).

12 (a) Show that the substitution $x = \frac{2}{\sqrt{3}} \cos\theta$ converts the equation $x^3 - x = 0.1$ into an equation of the form $\cos 3\theta = a$. Use this substitution to solve the equation for x, giving answers correct to 3 decimal places.

   (b) Find a number k for which the substitution $x = k \cos\theta$ converts the equation $x^3 - 6x = 1$ into an equation of the form $\cos 3\theta = a$. Use this substitution to solve the equation for x.

13 Show that if $x = k \cos\theta$, for a suitable value of k, the equation $x^5 - 5x^3 + 5x + 1 = 0$ can be written in the form $\cos 5\theta = a$. Hence find the five roots of the polynomial equation, correct to 3 decimal places.

14 Show that if $c = \cos\theta$ and $s = \sin\theta$, then

$$(c + s\,i)^n + (c - s\,i)^n = 2\cos n\theta \quad \text{and} \quad (c + s\,i)^n - (c - s\,i)^n = 2i \sin n\theta.$$

Use these to obtain the expressions for $\cos n\theta$ and $\sin n\theta$ in Section 7.2.

7.4 The formulae in reverse

The multiple angle formulae give $\cos n\theta$ or $\sin n\theta$ in terms of powers of $\cos\theta$ or $\sin\theta$. But sometimes it is useful to reverse the process to express powers of $\cos\theta$ or $\sin\theta$ in terms of functions of multiple angles.

You can do this by combining binomial expansions and de Moivre's theorem. The key is to notice that, if z denotes $z = \cos\theta + i\sin\theta$, then $\frac{1}{z}$ is $\cos\theta - i\sin\theta$, so

$$2\cos\theta = z + \frac{1}{z} \quad \text{and} \quad 2i\sin\theta = z - \frac{1}{z}.$$

Also, by de Moivre's theorem, $z^s = \cos s\theta + i\sin s\theta$ and $\frac{1}{z^s} = \cos s\theta - i\sin s\theta$. Therefore:

> If $z = e^{\theta i} = \cos\theta + i\sin\theta$ and $s \in \mathbb{N}$,
> $$2\cos s\theta = z^s + \frac{1}{z^s} \quad \text{and} \quad 2i\sin s\theta = z^s - \frac{1}{z^s}.$$

Example 7.4.1

Find expressions in terms of multiple angles for   (a) $\cos^5\theta$,   (b) $\sin^6\theta$.

(a) If $z = \cos\theta + i\sin\theta$,

$$(2\cos\theta)^5 = \left(z + \frac{1}{z}\right)^5 = z^5 + 5z^4 \times \frac{1}{z} + 10z^3 \times \frac{1}{z^2} + 10z^2 \times \frac{1}{z^3} + 5z \times \frac{1}{z^4} + \frac{1}{z^5}$$

$$= z^5 + 5z^3 + 10z + \frac{10}{z} + \frac{5}{z^3} + \frac{1}{z^5},$$

which can be rearranged as

$$\left(z^5 + \frac{1}{z^5}\right) + 5\left(z^3 + \frac{1}{z^3}\right) + 10\left(z + \frac{1}{z}\right).$$

So, using the result in the blue box with $s = 5$, 3 and 1,

$$32 \cos^5 \theta = 2 \cos 5\theta + 5(2 \cos 3\theta) + 10(2 \cos \theta).$$

That is, $\cos^5 \theta = \frac{1}{16}(\cos 5\theta + 5 \cos 3\theta + 10 \cos \theta).$

(b) $(2\mathrm{i} \sin \theta)^6 = \left(z - \dfrac{1}{z} \right)^6$

$$= z^6 - 6z^5 \times \frac{1}{z} + 15z^4 \times \frac{1}{z^2} - 20z^3 \times \frac{1}{z^3} + 15z^2 \times \frac{1}{z^4} - 6z \times \frac{1}{z^5} + \frac{1}{z^6}$$

$$= z^6 - 6z^4 + 15z^2 - 20 + \frac{15}{z^2} - \frac{6}{z^4} + \frac{1}{z^6}$$

$$= \left(z^6 + \frac{1}{z^6} \right) - 6\left(z^4 + \frac{1}{z^4} \right) + 15\left(z^2 + \frac{1}{z^2} \right) - 20,$$

so $-64 \sin^6 \theta = 2 \cos 6\theta - 6(2 \cos 4\theta) + 15(2 \cos 2\theta) - 20.$
That is, $\sin^6 \theta = -\frac{1}{32}(\cos 6\theta - 6 \cos 4\theta + 15 \cos 2\theta - 10).$

Be careful in calculating the constant term! The coefficients inside the bracket are
$\binom{6}{0}, -\binom{6}{1}, \binom{6}{2}$, but $-\frac{1}{2}\binom{6}{3}$.

The method is especially useful for finding integrals of powers of sines and cosines.

Example 7.4.2
Find $\displaystyle\int \sin^5 \theta \, \mathrm{d}\theta$.

As $(2\mathrm{i} \sin \theta)^5 = \left(z - \dfrac{1}{z} \right)^5 = z^5 - 5z^3 + 10z - \dfrac{10}{z} + \dfrac{5}{z^3} - \dfrac{1}{z^5}$

$$= \left(z^5 - \frac{1}{z^5} \right) - 5\left(z^3 - \frac{1}{z^3} \right) + 10\left(z - \frac{1}{z} \right),$$

$$32\mathrm{i} \sin^5 \theta = 2\mathrm{i} \sin 5\theta - 5(2\mathrm{i} \sin 3\theta) + 10(2\mathrm{i} \sin \theta).$$

Therefore

$$\sin^5 \theta = \frac{1}{16}(\sin 5\theta - 5 \sin 3\theta + 10 \sin \theta).$$

So $\displaystyle\int \sin^5 \theta \, \mathrm{d}\theta = \frac{1}{16}\left(-\frac{1}{5} \cos 5\theta + \frac{5}{3} \cos 3\theta - 10 \cos \theta \right) + k$

$$= -\frac{1}{80} \cos 5\theta + \frac{5}{48} \cos 3\theta - \frac{5}{8} \cos \theta + k.$$

Exercise 7B

1 Express these powers in terms of sines and/or cosines of multiples of θ. Check your answers by substituting a suitable value for θ in the original expression and in the answer.

(a) $\cos^3 \theta$ (b) $\sin^4 \theta$ (c) $\cos^6 \theta$

(d) $\sin^7 \theta$ (e) $\sin^3 \theta \cos^2 \theta$ (f) $\sin^4 \theta \cos^3 \theta$

2 Find the following indefinite integrals in terms of sines and/or cosines of multiples of θ.

(a) $\displaystyle\int \cos^4 \theta \, d\theta$ (b) $\displaystyle\int \sin^3 \theta \, d\theta$ (c) $\displaystyle\int \sin^2 \theta \cos^3 \theta \, d\theta$

3 Evaluate

(a) $\displaystyle\int_0^{\frac{1}{4}\pi} \sin^4 \theta \, d\theta$,   (b) $\displaystyle\int_0^{\frac{1}{2}\pi} \cos^8 \theta \, d\theta$,   (c) $\displaystyle\int_{-\frac{1}{2}\pi}^{\frac{1}{2}\pi} \sin^4 \theta \cos^2 \theta \, d\theta$.

4 If $n \in \mathbb{N}$, prove that $\displaystyle\int_0^{\frac{1}{2}\pi} \cos^{2n} \theta \, d\theta = \frac{\pi}{2^{2n+1}} \binom{2n}{n}$.

7.5 Power series with a complex variable

You have met many series of the form

$$u_0 + u_1 x + u_2 x^2 + u_3 x^3 + \dots$$

where the coefficients $u_0, u_1, u_2, u_3, \dots$ form a sequence of real numbers and x is a real variable. These are examples of **power series**, because each term contains a power of x.

Some of these power series have a finite number of terms, ending with $u_n x^n$, so that the series is a polynomial. Examples are binomial expansions for $(1 + x)^n$ when $n \in \mathbb{N}$ and finite geometric progressions. Other series continue indefinitely, and for certain values of x (the interval of validity) they converge to a limit. Examples of these are binomial expansions when n is not a positive integer, infinite geometric series and Maclaurin series for functions such as e^x, $\sin x$ and $\ln(1 + x)$.

> Maclaurin series are explained in FP2 Sections 3.1 to 3.3.

What happens if the real variable x is replaced by a complex variable z (the coefficients remaining real)? For finite series it clearly makes no difference, since the laws of complex algebra are the same as those of real algebra (except for inequalities). But infinite series need to be looked at more carefully.

Infinite geometric series

Infinite geometric series are easy to deal with, because you know the formula

$$a + az + az^2 + \dots + az^{n-1} = \frac{a(1 - z^n)}{1 - z} \qquad \text{where } a \neq 0 \text{ and } z \neq 1,$$

which can be proved for complex z in the same way as it was for real r in C2 Section 6.2. The condition for this sum to converge to a limit as $n \to \infty$ is that z^n must tend to 0.

The behaviour of z^n as n varies was described in Section 6.1, and is illustrated in Figs. 6.1, 6.2 and 6.3. When $|z| = 1$ the points representing z^n are equally stepped round the unit circle, and so never converge to a limit. (The value $z = 1$ is excluded, because the formula for the sum of a geometric series then doesn't hold.) When $|z| > 1$ the sequence of points spirals out without limit, but when $|z| < 1$ it spirals inwards, and can be brought as close to 0 as you like by taking n large enough.

So the only difference between the real and the complex case is that the interval of validity (real numbers between -1 and 1) is replaced by a **region of validity** (complex numbers with modulus less than 1).

> The infinite geometric series $\sum_{s=0}^{\infty} az^s$ converges to $\dfrac{a}{1-z}$ if $|z| < 1$.

This result can be shown geometrically by a diagram like Fig. 7.1, which is drawn for the values $a = 1$ and $z = \frac{1}{2}(1 + i)$. Starting from the origin, displacements $\overrightarrow{OP_0}, \overrightarrow{P_0P_1}, \overrightarrow{P_1P_2}, \ldots$ represent the terms $a, az, az^2, \ldots$ of the series.

The displacement $\overrightarrow{OP_n}$ then represents the finite sum $\sum_{s=0}^{n} az^s$. You can see the points P_n getting ever closer to a limiting point L, which represents $\dfrac{a}{1-z}$ in the Argand diagram.

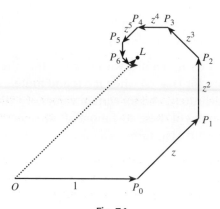

Fig. 7.1

For the particular values used in Fig. 7.1, each displacement is obtained from its predecessor by a spiral enlargement: scalar multiplication by $|z| = \dfrac{1}{\sqrt{2}}$ combined with a rotation of $\arg z = \frac{1}{4}\pi$. The limit is

$$\frac{1}{1 - \frac{1}{2}(1 + i)} = \frac{2}{1 - i} = \frac{2(1 + i)}{(1 - i)(1 + i)} = \frac{2(1 + i)}{2} = 1 + i.$$

Binomial expansions

The infinite geometric series is a special case of the binomial expansion $(1 - z)^n$ when $n = -1$. Infinite binomial expansions when n is a negative integer can all be used in the complex form $(1 + z)^n$, within a region of validity $|z| < 1$. The proof is more difficult than for the geometric series, however, and won't be attempted here.

The extension to non-integral values of n is more complicated. For example, if $n = \frac{1}{5}$, the series is still convergent for $|z| < 1$, but you have to decide which of the five complex fifth roots of $1 + z$ is the limit.

The exponential series*

The Maclaurin series for e^x (see FP2 Section 3.3) can be generalised directly for a complex variable, as

$$e^z = 1 + \frac{z}{1!} + \frac{z^2}{2!} + \frac{z^3}{3!} + \cdots,$$

and this is valid for all values of z. The proof is too difficult to give here, but a geometrical illustration is very convincing.

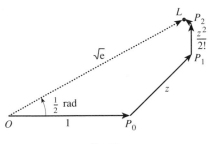

Fig. 7.2

Figure 7.2 shows the series for $z = \frac{1}{2}(1 + i)$, converging to the limit $e^{\frac{1}{2}} e^{\frac{1}{2}i}$ with modulus $\sqrt{e}$ and argument $\frac{1}{2}$ (see Section 5.4).

The definitions of the trigonometric functions $\sin x$ and $\cos x$ have not yet been extended to complex domains. When this is done it can be shown that the series expansions for these functions remain valid when the variable is complex.

However, since the exponential function is not one–one (because $\exp z_1 = \exp z_2$ if z_1 and z_2 differ by a multiple of $2\pi i$), there are additional difficulties in extending the definition of natural logarithm, and therefore in generalising the $\ln(1 + x)$ series for a complex variable.

7.6 Trigonometric series

If in a power series you put $z = e^{\theta i} = \cos \theta + i \sin \theta$, you get

$$u_0 + u_1 e^{\theta i} + u_2 (e^{\theta i})^2 + u_3 (e^{\theta i})^3 + \cdots = u_0 + u_1 e^{\theta i} + u_2 e^{2\theta i} + u_3 e^{3\theta i} + \cdots.$$

If the coefficients are real, each term $u_s e^{s\theta i}$ has real part $u_s \cos s\theta$ and imaginary part $u_s \sin s\theta$. So if S denotes the sum of the power series,

$$\text{Re}(S) = u_0 + u_1 \cos \theta + u_2 \cos 2\theta + u_3 \cos 3\theta + \cdots$$
$$\text{and} \quad \text{Im}(S) = \quad u_1 \sin \theta + u_2 \sin 2\theta + u_3 \sin 3\theta + \cdots.$$

Series like this are called **trigonometric series**.

You can sometimes reverse this process, and find an expression for the sum of a trigonometric series as the real or imaginary part of the sum of a power series.

Example 7.6.1

Find expressions for the sums of the series

(a) $1 + \frac{1}{2}\cos\theta + \frac{1}{4}\cos 2\theta + \frac{1}{8}\cos 3\theta + \cdots,$

(b) $\binom{n}{1}\sin\theta + \binom{n}{2}\sin 2\theta + \binom{n}{3}\sin 3\theta + \cdots + \sin n\theta,$ where $n \in \mathbb{N}$,

(c)* $1 + \dfrac{\cos\theta}{1!} + \dfrac{\cos 2\theta}{2!} + \dfrac{\cos 3\theta}{3!} + \cdots.$

(a) This is the real part of the infinite geometric series

$$1 + \tfrac{1}{2}e^{\theta i} + \tfrac{1}{4}e^{2\theta i} + \tfrac{1}{8}e^{3\theta i} + \cdots = 1 + \tfrac{1}{2}e^{\theta i} + \tfrac{1}{4}(e^{\theta i})^2 + \tfrac{1}{8}(e^{\theta i})^3 + \cdots$$

with common ratio $z = \frac{1}{2}e^{\theta i}$. Since $|z| = \frac{1}{2} < 1$, this series is convergent, with

limit $\dfrac{1}{1 - \frac{1}{2}e^{\theta i}}$.

To find the real part, you have to convert this fraction into the form $a + b$i. You can do this by multiplying top and bottom by the conjugate of the denominator, which is $1 - \frac{1}{2}e^{-\theta i}$. The denominator then becomes

$$\left(1 - \tfrac{1}{2}e^{\theta i}\right)\left(1 - \tfrac{1}{2}e^{-\theta i}\right) = 1 - \tfrac{1}{2}(e^{\theta i} + e^{-\theta i}) + \tfrac{1}{4}(e^{\theta i}e^{-\theta i})$$

$$= 1 - \tfrac{1}{2}(2\cos\theta) + \tfrac{1}{4} = \tfrac{5}{4} - \cos\theta.$$

The real part of the numerator $1 - \frac{1}{2}e^{-\theta i}$ is $1 - \frac{1}{2}\cos\theta$. The sum of the trigonometric series is therefore

$$\frac{1 - \frac{1}{2}\cos\theta}{\frac{5}{4} - \cos\theta} = \frac{2(2 - \cos\theta)}{5 - 4\cos\theta}.$$

(b) You can write the series as the imaginary part of the finite binomial expansion

$$1 + \binom{n}{1}e^{\theta i} + \binom{n}{2}e^{2\theta i} + \cdots + e^{n\theta i} = 1 + \binom{n}{1}e^{\theta i} + \binom{n}{2}(e^{\theta i})^2 + \cdots + (e^{\theta i})^n$$

$$= (1 + e^{\theta i})^n.$$

The simplest way of separating this into real and imaginary parts is to write $1 + e^{\theta i}$ as

$$\left(e^{-\frac{1}{2}\theta i} + e^{\frac{1}{2}\theta i}\right)e^{\frac{1}{2}\theta i} = 2\cos\tfrac{1}{2}\theta\, e^{\frac{1}{2}\theta i}.$$

So $(1 + e^{\theta i})^n = 2^n \cos^n \frac{1}{2}\theta\, e^{\frac{1}{2}n\theta i}$, whose imaginary part is $2^n \cos^n \frac{1}{2}\theta \sin \frac{1}{2}n\theta$.

(c) The series is the real part of

$$1 + \frac{e^{\theta i}}{1!} + \frac{e^{2\theta i}}{2!} + \frac{e^{3\theta i}}{3!} + \cdots = 1 + \frac{e^{\theta i}}{1!} + \frac{(e^{\theta i})^2}{2!} + \frac{(e^{\theta i})^3}{3!} + \cdots$$

$$= \exp(e^{\theta i}), \quad \text{or} \quad \exp(\cos\theta + i\sin\theta).$$

Now the real part of $\exp(a + b$i$)$, or $e^a\, e^{b$i$}$, is $e^a \cos b$, so the real part of $\exp(\cos\theta + i\sin\theta)$ is

$$e^{\cos\theta}\cos(\sin\theta).$$

Exercise 7C

1 Show that

   (a) $1 + 4\cos 2\theta + 6\cos 4\theta + 4\cos 6\theta + \cos 8\theta = 16\cos 4\theta \cos^4 \theta$,

   (b) $1 + \cos 2\theta + \cos 4\theta + \cos 6\theta + \cos 8\theta = \dfrac{\cos 4\theta \sin 5\theta}{\sin \theta}$ provided that $\theta \neq n\pi$, $n \in \mathbb{Z}$.

2 Show that the sum $e^{\theta i} - e^{3\theta i} + e^{5\theta i} - \cdots - e^{19\theta i}$ can be expressed in the form $\dfrac{1 - e^{200 i}}{2\cos \theta}$

   provided that θ is not an odd multiple of $\frac{1}{2}\pi$. Hence find expressions for the sums

   $\sin \theta - \sin 3\theta + \sin 5\theta - \cdots - \sin 19\theta$ and $\cos \theta - \cos 3\theta + \cos 5\theta - \cdots - \cos 19\theta$.

3 Show that $\dfrac{e^{n\theta i} - 1}{e^{\theta i} - 1} = \dfrac{\sin \frac{1}{2}n\theta}{\sin \frac{1}{2}\theta} e^{\frac{1}{2}(n-1)\theta i}$, provided that θ is not a multiple of 2π.

   Use this to find an expression for the sum

   $$\cos \alpha + \cos(\alpha + \theta) + \cos(\alpha + 2\theta) + \cdots + \cos(\alpha + (n-1)\theta).$$

   Show that this sum is 0 if θ is a multiple of $\dfrac{2\pi}{n}$ but not of 2π. Give a geometrical explanation for this.

4 Sum the following trigonometric series.

   (a) $\sin \theta - \frac{1}{3}\sin 2\theta + \frac{1}{9}\sin 3\theta - \frac{1}{27}\sin 4\theta + \ldots$.

   (b)* $\dfrac{\sin \theta}{1!} - \dfrac{\sin 2\theta}{2!} + \dfrac{\sin 3\theta}{3!} - \dfrac{\sin 4\theta}{4!} + \ldots$.

   (c) $1 - \dbinom{n}{1}\cos \theta \cos \theta + \dbinom{n}{2}\cos^2 \theta \cos 2\theta - \dbinom{n}{3}\cos^3 \theta \cos 3\theta + \cdots$

   $+ (-1)^n \cos^n \theta \cos n\theta$,

   distinguishing the cases $n = 4k$, $n = 4k+1$, $n = 4k+2$ and $n = 4k+3$, where $k \in \mathbb{N}$.

5 Find the sums of the following series when $z = 0.2 + 0.6\,\mathrm{i}$. Give your answers correct to 2 decimal places, and illustrate them with a diagram.

   (a) $1 + 2z + 3z^2 + 4z^3 + \ldots$

   (b)* $1 + \dfrac{z}{1!} + \dfrac{z^2}{2!} + \dfrac{z^3}{3!} + \ldots$

   (c) $1 + 5z + 10z^2 + 10z^3 + 5z^4 + z^5$

   (d) $1 + z + z^2 + z^3 + z^4 + z^5$

6* Overestimates and underestimates are made of the area under the graph $y = \cos x$ over the interval $0 \leqslant x \leqslant \beta$, where $\beta \leqslant \frac{1}{2}\pi$, using n rectangles of equal width. By summing suitable trigonometric series, find formulae for these estimates in terms of n and β, and investigate their limits as $n \to \infty$.

7.7* Some hyperbolic analogies

This is an optional section, for those who have already used hyperbolic functions in the FP2 course. You may omit it if you wish.

Is there a result equivalent to de Moivre's theorem for hyperbolic functions?

The theorem can be written in exponential notation, if n is a positive integer, as

$$(e^{\theta i})^n = e^{n\theta i} \quad \text{and} \quad (e^{-\theta i})^n = e^{-n\theta i}.$$

But if applied with a real rather than an imaginary index, this is simply the rule

$$(e^u)^n = e^{nu} \quad \text{and} \quad (e^{-u})^n = e^{-nu}.$$

> The letter θ is commonly used as the variable for trigonometric functions because it is often thought of as an angle. With hyperbolic functions there is no suggestion that angles are involved, so a different letter is more appropriate.

Now the hyperbolic functions

$$\cosh u = \tfrac{1}{2}(e^u + e^{-u}) \quad \text{and} \quad \sinh u = \tfrac{1}{2}(e^u - e^{-u})$$

were defined to satisfy the equations

$$\cosh u + \sinh u = e^u \quad \text{and} \quad \cosh u - \sinh u = e^{-u}.$$

And if u is replaced by nu, the equations become

$$\cosh nu + \sinh nu = e^{nu} \quad \text{and} \quad \cosh nu - \sinh nu = e^{-nu}.$$

So the exponential equations $(e^u)^n = e^{nu}$ and $(e^{-u})^n = e^{-nu}$ can be written

$$(\cosh u + \sinh u)^n = \cosh nu + \sinh nu$$

and

$$(\cosh u - \sinh u)^n = \cosh nu - \sinh nu.$$

Compare these equations with de Moivre's theorem in trigonometric notation,

$$(\cos\theta + i\sin\theta)^n = \cos n\theta + i\sin n\theta \quad \text{and} \quad (\cos\theta - i\sin\theta)^n = \cos n\theta - i\sin n\theta.$$

It looks from this as if trigonometric applications of de Moivre's theorem could be adapted to give hyperbolic results by replacing

$$\cos\theta + i\sin\theta \quad \text{by} \quad \cosh u + \sinh u,$$

and

$$\cos\theta - i\sin\theta \quad \text{by} \quad \cosh u - \sinh u.$$

Analogues of the multiple angle formulae

Expressions for $\cos n\theta$ and $\sin n\theta$ were found in Section 7.2 by equating real and imaginary parts in the trigonometric form of de Moivre's theorem. Now the real and imaginary parts of a complex number z are given by

$$2\mathrm{Re}(z) = z + z^* \quad \text{and} \quad 2\,i\,\mathrm{Im}(z) = z - z^*.$$

If $z = \cos\theta + i\sin\theta$, then $z^* = \cos\theta - i\sin\theta$, and

$$z^n = \cos n\theta + i\sin n\theta \quad \text{and} \quad (z^n)^* = (z^*)^n = \cos n\theta - i\sin n\theta.$$

So

$$2\cos n\theta = z^n + (z^n)^*$$
$$= (\cos\theta + i\sin\theta)^n + (\cos\theta - i\sin\theta)^n$$

and

$$2i\sin n\theta = z^n - (z^n)^*$$
$$= (\cos\theta + i\sin\theta)^n - (\cos\theta - i\sin\theta)^n.$$

For example, with $n = 5$, writing c for $\cos\theta$ and s for $\sin\theta$,

$$2\cos 5\theta = (c + si)^5 + (c - si)^5 \quad \text{and} \quad 2i\sin 5\theta = (c + si)^5 - (c - si)^5.$$

These lead to the expansions

$$\cos 5\theta = c^5 - 10c^3s^2 + 5cs^4 \quad \text{and} \quad \sin 5\theta = 5c^4s - 10c^2s^3 + s^5.$$

Replacing $\cos\theta + i\sin\theta$ by $\cosh u + \sinh u$, and $\cos\theta - i\sin\theta$ by $\cosh u - \sinh u$, you get the equivalent equations for hyperbolic functions,

$$2\cosh nu = (\cosh u + \sinh u)^n + (\cosh u - \sinh u)^n$$

and

$$2\sinh nu = (\cosh u + \sinh u)^n - (\cosh u - \sinh u)^n.$$

With $n = 5$, writing C for $\cosh u$ and S for $\sinh u$,

$$2\cosh 5u = (C + S)^5 + (C - S)^5 \quad \text{and} \quad 2\sinh 5u = (C + S)^5 - (C - S)^5,$$

giving

$$\cosh 5u = C^5 + 10C^3S^2 + 5CS^4 \quad \text{and} \quad \sinh 5u = 5C^4S + 10C^2S^3 + S^5.$$

You will see that the only difference between these and the corresponding trigonometric formulae is that all the signs are $+$, rather than alternately $+$ and $-$.

When the expressions are adapted to produce expansions entirely in terms of c or s, C or S, the situation is rather different. For the trigonometric examples, writing s^2 as $1 - c^2$, or c^2 as $1 - s^2$,

$$\cos 5\theta = c^5 - 10c^3(1 - c^2) + 5c(1 - c^2)^2$$
$$= 16c^5 - 20c^3 + 5c$$

and

$$\sin 5\theta = 5(1 - s^2)^2s - 10(1 - s^2)s^3 + s^5$$
$$= 16s^5 - 20s^3 + 5s.$$

But for the hyperbolic examples, writing S^2 as $C^2 - 1$, or C^2 as $S^2 + 1$,

$$\cosh 5u = C^5 + 10C^3(C^2 - 1) + 5C(C^2 - 1)^2$$
$$= 16C^5 - 20C^3 + 5C$$

and

$$\sinh 5u = 5(S^2 + 1)^2 S + 10(S^2 + 1)S^3 + S^5$$
$$= 16S^5 + 20S^3 + 5S.$$

So the expansion for $\cosh 5u$ has exactly the same form as that for $\cos 5\theta$. However, in the expansion for $\sinh 5u$ the coefficients are numerically the same as those for $\sin 5\theta$ but all the signs are $+$. This is true for all values of n, not just for $n = 5$.

Solving cubic equations

The method used in Example 7.3.4 for solving the cubic equation $x^3 - 3x - 1 = 0$ using a substitution $x = k \cos \theta$, θ in degrees, only works for equations with 3 real roots (of which one can be a repeated root). For equations with only one real root you can use a hyperbolic substitution instead.

Example 7.7.1
Solve the equations　(a) $x^3 - 3x - 5 = 0$,　(b) $x^3 + 3x = 7$.

(a) If you try substituting $x = 2\cos\theta$, θ in degrees, as in Example 7.3.4, the equation becomes

$$8\cos^3\theta - 6\cos\theta - 5 = 0,$$

which is $\cos 3\theta = \frac{5}{2}$. This obviously has no roots, since $\frac{5}{2} > 1$.

But the corresponding hyperbolic substitution $x = 2\cosh u$ leads to the equation

$$8\cosh^3 u - 6\cosh u - 5 = 0,$$

which is $\cosh 3u = \frac{5}{2}$. This has a root

$$u = \tfrac{1}{3}\cosh^{-1} 2.5$$
$$= \tfrac{1}{3} \times 1.566...$$
$$= 0.522...,$$

giving

$$x = 2\cosh 0.522...$$
$$= 2.279, \text{ correct to 3 decimal places.}$$

Because cosh is an even function, the equation $\cosh 3u = \frac{5}{2}$ has another root $u = -\tfrac{1}{3}\cosh^{-1} 2.5$, but this gives the same value for x. The cubic equation for x has only one root; it is the equation solved approximately by decimal search in C3 Section 8.2.

(b) This equation can't be solved by substituting $x = 2\cos\theta$ or $x = 2\cosh u$, because the coefficient of x is positive. But the expansion of $\sinh 3u$ is $4\sinh^3 u + 3\sinh u$, and a substitution $x = 2\sinh u$ converts the equation to

$$8\sinh^3 u + 6\sinh u = 7,$$

which is

$$\sinh 3u = \tfrac{7}{2}.$$

This has a root

$$u = \tfrac{1}{3}\sinh^{-1} 3.5$$
$$= 0.655...,$$

giving

$$x = 2\sinh 0.655...$$
$$= 1.406, \text{ correct to 3 significant figures.}$$

In this way you can solve any cubic equation of the form $x^3 + px + q = 0$, using one of the substitutions $x = k\cos\theta$, $x = k\cosh u$ or $x = k\sinh u$ for a suitable value of k.

The formulae in reverse

It is easy to find formulae, similar to the trigonometric formulae, for powers of $\cosh u$ or $\sinh u$ direct from the definitions

$$\cosh u = \tfrac{1}{2}(e^u + e^{-u}) \quad \text{and} \quad \sinh u = \tfrac{1}{2}(e^u - e^{-u});$$

that is,

$$\cosh u = \tfrac{1}{2}\left(z + \frac{1}{z}\right) \quad \text{and} \quad \sinh u = \tfrac{1}{2}\left(z - \frac{1}{z}\right), \quad \text{where} \quad z = e^u.$$

When you pair terms of the binomial expansions such as

$$z^3 + \frac{1}{z^3} \quad \text{or} \quad z^3 - \frac{1}{z^3},$$

these can be replaced by

$$e^{3u} + e^{-3u} = 2\cosh 3u \quad \text{or} \quad e^{3u} - e^{-3u} = 2\sinh 3u.$$

Example 7.7.2

Express $\sinh^6 u$ as the sum of terms of the form $a_r \cosh ru$.

The working is very similar to that of Example 7.4.1(b). Writing $z = e^u$,

$$(2\sinh u)^6 = \left(z - \frac{1}{z}\right)^6$$
$$= \left(z^6 + \frac{1}{z^6}\right) - 6\left(z^4 + \frac{1}{z^4}\right) + 15\left(z^2 + \frac{1}{z^2}\right) - 20.$$

So

$$64 \sinh^6 u = 2 \cosh 6u - 12 \cosh 4u + 30 \cosh 2u - 20,$$

giving

$$\sinh^6 u = \tfrac{1}{32}(\cosh 6u - 6 \cosh 4u + 15 \cosh 2u - 10).$$

Exercise 7D*

1 Write the following in terms of $\cosh u$ and/or $\sinh u$.

(a) $\cosh 3u$ (b) $\sinh 3u$ (c) $\cosh 5u$ (d) $\sinh 7u$ (e) $\sinh 8u$

2 Solve the following equations, giving roots correct to 3 decimal places.

(a) $x^3 - 6x = 8$ (b) $x^3 - 9x = 15$ (c) $x^3 + 6x = 5$

(d) $x^3 - 12x + 20 = 0$ (e) $x^3 - 12x + 5 = 0$

3 Express x in terms of u such that $2 \cosh su$ can be written as $x^s + \dfrac{1}{x^s}$. Use this to express the following powers in terms of hyperbolic functions of multiples of u. (Compare Exercise 7B Question 1.)

(a) $\cosh^3 u$ (b) $\sinh^4 u$ (c) $\cosh^6 u$

(d) $\sinh^7 u$ (e) $\sinh^3 u \cosh^2 u$ (f) $\sinh^4 u \cosh^3 u$

4 Find the following indefinite integrals, expressing your answers in terms of hyperbolic functions. (Compare Exercise 7B Question 2.)

(a) $\displaystyle\int \cosh^4 u \, du$ (b) $\displaystyle\int \sinh^3 u \, du$ (c) $\displaystyle\int \sinh^2 u \cosh^3 u \, du$

5 Sum the series $\sinh u - \tfrac{1}{3} \sinh 2u + \tfrac{1}{9} \sinh 3u - \tfrac{1}{27} \sinh 4u + \ldots$, and state the values of u for which your answer is valid. (Compare Exercise 7C Question 4(a).)

6 Sum the series

$$1 - \binom{n}{1} \cosh u \cosh u + \binom{n}{2} \cosh^2 u \cosh 2u - \cdots + (-1)^n \cosh^n u \cosh nu,$$

distinguishing the cases when n is even and n is odd. (Compare Exercise 7C Question 4(c).)

Miscellaneous exercise 7

1 Use de Moivre's theorem to show that $\sin 5\theta = 16 \sin^5 \theta - 20 \sin^3 \theta + 5 \sin \theta$. Hence show that $\sin \tfrac{1}{30}\pi$ is a root of the equation $32x^5 - 40x^3 + 10x - 1 = 0$.   (OCR)

2 Prove that the only real solutions of the equation $\sin 5\theta = 5 \sin \theta$ are given by $\theta = n\pi$, where n is an integer.   (OCR)

3 By considering the equation $\tan 5\theta = 0$, show that the exact value of the smaller positive root of the equation $t^4 - 10t^2 + 5 = 0$ is $\tan \tfrac{1}{5}\pi$.   (OCR)

4 Use de Moivre's theorem to show that $\cos 6\theta = 32\cos^6\theta - 48\cos^4\theta + 18\cos^2\theta - 1$. Deduce that, for all θ, $0 \leqslant \cos^6\theta - \frac{3}{2}\cos^4\theta + \frac{9}{16}\cos^2\theta \leqslant \frac{1}{16}$. (OCR)

5 Use the results of Example 7.3.1 to give exact expressions of the coordinates of the vertices of a regular pentagon with its centre at the origin and one vertex at the point $(0, 1)$. (See Fig. 6.9 in Example 6.5.1.) Check your answers by showing that all the sides are of equal length.

6* Write the equation $\sin 7\theta = -1$ as an equation in $s = \sin\theta$, and state its roots. Hence show that $\sin\frac{1}{14}\pi - \sin\frac{3}{14}\pi + \sin\frac{5}{14}\pi = \frac{1}{2}$.

7 Show that, if $\cos 4\theta = \cos 3\theta$, then θ is $\frac{2}{7}r\pi$ for some $r \in \mathbb{Z}$. Hence find a cubic equation whose roots are $\cos\frac{2}{7}\pi$, $\cos\frac{4}{7}$ and $\cos\frac{6}{7}\pi$. Use a numerical method to calculate the positive root of this equation correct to 6 decimal places. Then use the sum and the product of the roots to calculate the other two roots to the same degree of accuracy.

8 Expand $\left(z - \dfrac{1}{z}\right)^4 \left(z + \dfrac{1}{z}\right)^2$, and hence find the constants p, q, r and s such that $\sin^4\theta\cos^2\theta = p + q\cos 2\theta + r\cos 4\theta + s\cos 6\theta$.

Using a suitable substitution, show that $\displaystyle\int_1^2 x^4\sqrt{4-x^2}\,dx = \frac{4}{3}\pi + \sqrt{3}$. (MEI)

9* Sketch the curve whose polar equation is $r = a\cos^3\theta$, and calculate the area of the region enclosed by it. (See FP2, Sections 6.3 and 6.8.)

10 Find the volume of revolution formed by rotating the region under the graph $y = \sin^4 x$ for $0 \leqslant x \leqslant \pi$ about the x-axis.

11 Sum the geometric series $z + z^2 + z^3 + \cdots + z^8$, $z \neq 1$.

Show that if $z = e^{\theta i}$ then $1 - z^8 = -2ie^{4\theta i}\sin 4\theta$. Write down a similar expression for $1 - z$.

Hence find $\displaystyle\sum_{r=1}^{8}\cos r\theta$. (OCR)

12 Infinite series C and S are defined as follows:

$$C = \frac{\cos\theta}{2} - \frac{\cos 2\theta}{4} + \frac{\cos 3\theta}{8} - \frac{\cos 4\theta}{16} + \cdots, \qquad S = \frac{\sin\theta}{2} - \frac{\sin 2\theta}{4} + \frac{\sin 3\theta}{8} - \frac{\sin 4\theta}{16} + \cdots.$$

Show that $C + Si = \dfrac{2e^{\theta i} + 1}{5 + 4\cos\theta}$. Hence find expressions for C and S in terms of $\cos\theta$ and $\sin\theta$. (MEI)

13* Show that the quartic equation $x^4 - 8x^2 + 4 = 0$ may be written in the form $(f(x))^2 - (g(x))^2 = 0$, where $f(x) = x^2 - 2$ and $g(x)$ is suitably chosen. Use this to find the roots of the quartic equation in the form $\pm(c \pm d\sqrt{3})$, where c and d are integers.

Prove that $\cos 4\theta = 8\cos^4\theta - 8\cos^2\theta + 1$, and use this to show that, if x is replaced by $k\cos\theta$ with k suitably chosen, the quartic equation may be expressed in the form $\cos 4\theta = \frac{1}{2}$.

Obtain the roots of the quartic equation in the form $k\cos\theta_i$. Hence express $\cos 15°$ in surd form. (OCR)

14* Write down the expansions of $\exp z$, $\exp \omega z$ and $\exp \omega^2 z$ as power series, where $\omega = \exp \frac{2}{3}\pi i$. Hence find the sum of the series $1 + \dfrac{z^3}{3!} + \dfrac{z^6}{6!} + \dfrac{z^9}{9!} + \ldots$, and deduce the sum of the trigonometric series $1 + \dfrac{\cos 3\theta}{3!} + \dfrac{\cos 6\theta}{6!} + \dfrac{\cos 9\theta}{9!} + \ldots$.

15* Prove that, if $n \in \mathbb{N}$, $\displaystyle\sum_{s=0}^{\infty} \frac{1}{(sn)!} = \frac{1}{n} \sum_{r=0}^{n-1} \exp\left(\cos \frac{2r\pi}{n}\right) \cos\left(\sin \frac{2r\pi}{n}\right)$.

Verify this numerically in the cases $n = 4$, $n = 5$ and $n = 6$.

16 The triangular numbers t_s, where $s \in \mathbb{N}$, are defined recursively by $t_1 = 1$ and $t_{s+1} = t_s + (s+1)$. Use the expansion of $(1-z)^{-3}$ to find the value of $\displaystyle\sum_{s=1}^{\infty} \left(\tfrac{1}{2}\right)^s t_s \cos \tfrac{1}{3}s\pi$.

8 Calculus with complex numbers

The word 'calculus' covers the techniques of differentiation and integration and their applications. Using complex functions can simplify some of these applications, and bring an unexpected unity to the subject. When you have completed the chapter, you should

- understand the extension of the rule for differentiating e^{cx} when c is a complex number
- be able to find complementary functions for linear differential equations when the auxiliary equation has complex roots
- know how to use complex numbers to integrate functions involving products of exponential and trigonometric functions
- know how to use complex numbers to find particular integrals for linear differential equations with a trigonometrical function on the right side.

The most important part of this chapter is in Sections 8.1 and 8.2, which fill a gap left in Chapter 3: how to find a complementary function when the roots of the auxiliary equation are not real. The remaining sections deal with two types of problem which you already know how to solve by other methods; however, the answer can often be found more neatly by treating a trigonometric function as the real or imaginary part of a complex exponential. You may omit these sections if you wish.

8.1 The exponential function

In Section 5.4 it was suggested that, for the complex number $z = x + yi$, the exponential function should be defined as

$$e^z = e^x(\cos y + i \sin y).$$

This was justified first from the form of the Maclaurin expansion for e^{yi}, but it can then be shown that other familiar properties of the exponential function follow from this definition. One of these is the rule for differentiating e^{cx} when c is a complex number.

You know that, if c is real, then $\dfrac{d}{dx}e^{cx} = ce^{cx}$. Does this remain true when c is complex?

Begin by considering the case when c is a pure imaginary number $c = bi$, where b is real. Then, if x is real, $e^{bix} = e^{(bx)i} = \cos bx + i \sin bx$.

You can differentiate this to give

$$\frac{d}{dx}e^{bix} = -b \sin bx + bi \cos bx$$
$$= bi(\cos bx + i \sin bx) = bie^{bix}.$$

So the rule still works if c is a pure imaginary number.

More generally, if $c = a + bi$, then you can differentiate e^{cx} using the product rule as

$$\frac{d}{dx}e^{cx} = \frac{d}{dx}(e^{ax} \times e^{bix}) = \frac{d}{dx}(e^{ax}) \times e^{bix} + e^{ax} \times \frac{d}{dx}(e^{bix})$$

$$= ae^{ax} \times e^{bix} + e^{ax} \times bie^{bix}$$

$$= (a + bi)e^{ax+bix} = ce^{cx}.$$

Again, this rule is restricted to a real variable x. You do not yet have a definition of differentiation with respect to a complex variable z.

> If c is complex and x is real, then
>
> $$\frac{d}{dx}e^{cx} = ce^{cx}.$$

You can use this generalisation as the basis of various applications.

8.2 Complementary functions

When you try to find the complementary function for a second order differential equation with constant coefficients, $a\frac{d^2y}{dx^2} + b\frac{dy}{dx} + cy = q(x)$, the first step is to find the roots of the auxiliary equation $a\lambda^2 + b\lambda + c = 0$. For all the examples in Chapter 3 these roots were real (distinct or repeated). But in many situations to which these differential equations apply the auxiliary equations have complex roots.

The method of solution is the same, but an extra step is needed at the end to convert the answer into a real form.

Example 8.2.1

Solve the differential equation $\frac{d^2y}{dx^2} - 6\frac{dy}{dx} + 13y = 0$, given that $y = 1$ and $\frac{dy}{dx} = 1$ when $x = 0$.

The auxiliary equation is

$$\lambda^2 - 6\lambda + 13 = 0,$$

whose roots are $3 \pm 2i$ So the general solution of the differential equation is

$$y = Ae^{(3+2i)x} + B^{(3-2i)x},$$

where A and B are arbitrary constants.

You now have to use the initial conditions to find the values of A and B. There are two possible ways of proceeding.

Method 1   With this method you continue to work with complex numbers as long as you can.

Begin by differentiating to find

$$\frac{dy}{dx} = A(3 + 2i)e^{(3+2i)x} + B(3 - 2i)e^{(3-2i)x}.$$

Substituting the given values of y and $\dfrac{dy}{dx}$ when $x = 0$,

$$1 = Ae^0 + Be^0 = A + B$$

and

$$1 = A(3 + 2i)e^0 + B(3 - 2i)e^0$$
$$= (3 + 2i)A + (3 - 2i)B.$$

So A and B must be chosen to satisfy the simultaneous equations

$$\left. \begin{array}{r} A + \quad\quad B = 1 \\ (3 + 2i)A + (3 - 2i)B = 1 \end{array} \right\}.$$

The second equation can be written as

$$3(A + B) + 2i(A - B) = 1.$$

Since $A + B = 1$, this gives

$$3 + 2i(A - B) = 1,$$

so $\quad\quad A - B = \dfrac{-2}{2i} = i.$

Combining this with $A + B = 1$ produces the solution $A = \frac{1}{2}(1 + i)$, $B = \frac{1}{2}(1 - i)$.

The solution of the differential equation is therefore

$$y = \tfrac{1}{2}(1 + i)e^{(3+2i)x} + \tfrac{1}{2}(1 - i)e^{(3-2i)x}$$
$$= \tfrac{1}{2}(1 + i)e^{3x}(\cos 2x + i\sin 2x) + \tfrac{1}{2}(1 - i)e^{3x}(\cos(-2x) + i\sin(-2x))$$
$$= \tfrac{1}{2}e^{3x}((1 + i)\cos 2x + (i - 1)\sin 2x + (1 - i)\cos 2x - (i + 1)\sin 2x)$$
$$= \tfrac{1}{2}e^{3x}(2\cos 2x - 2\sin 2x)$$
$$= e^{3x}(\cos 2x - \sin 2x).$$

Method 2 With this method you solve the problem in terms of real coefficients.

Begin by writing the general solution as

$$y = Ae^{3x}(\cos 2x + i\sin 2x) + Be^{3x}(\cos 2x - i\sin 2x)$$
$$= e^{3x}((A + B)\cos 2x + (A - B)i\sin 2x).$$

It is now simpler to replace the constants $A + B$ and $(A - B)i$ by single constants C and D, so that

$$y = e^{3x}(C\cos 2x + D\sin 2x).$$

Students sometimes think that D must be an imaginary number, but this is not so. In any problem with real initial conditions, C and D will be real. It is the original constants A and B which are complex; since their sum is real and their difference is imaginary, A and B are conjugate complex numbers.

Now use the initial conditions to find C and D. Differentiating,

$$\frac{dy}{dx} = 3e^{3x}(C\cos 2x + D\sin 2x) + e^{3x}(-2C\sin 2x + 2D\cos 2x).$$

Since $y = 1$ and $\dfrac{dy}{dx} = 1$ when $x = 0$,

$$1 = C \text{ and } 1 = 3C + 2D.$$

These equations give $C = 1$ and $D = -1$, so the solution is

$$y = e^{3x}(\cos 2x - \sin 2x).$$

Example 8.2.2

Find the complementary function for the differential equation
$$\frac{d^2x}{dt^2} + 2\frac{dx}{dt} + 5x = e^{-2t}(2\cos t + \sin t).$$

The auxiliary equation $\lambda^2 + 2\lambda + 5 = 0$ has roots $-1 \pm 2\,\mathrm{i}$, so the complementary function is $Ae^{(-1+2\mathrm{i})t} + Be^{(-1-2\mathrm{i})t}$.

This can be written as

$$Ae^{-t}(\cos 2t + \mathrm{i}\sin 2t) + Be^{-t}(\cos(-2t) + \mathrm{i}\sin(-2t))$$
$$= e^{-t}(A\cos 2t + A\,\mathrm{i}\sin 2t + B\cos 2t - B\,\mathrm{i}\sin 2t)$$
$$= e^{-t}((A + B)\cos 2t + (A - B)\,\mathrm{i}\sin 2t).$$

It is simpler to replace the constants $A + B$ and $(A - B)\,\mathrm{i}$ by single constants C and D, giving the complementary function in the final form

$$e^{-t}(C\cos 2t + D\sin 2t).$$

Another way of writing the complementary function in this example is
$Re^{-t}\cos(2t - \alpha)$, where $R = \sqrt{C^2 + D^2}$ and $\cos\alpha = \dfrac{C}{R}$, $\sin\alpha = \dfrac{D}{R}$.

Exercise 8A

1 Find the complementary function for the following differential equations.

(a) $\dfrac{d^2y}{dx^2} + 4\dfrac{dy}{dx} + 40y = x$ (b) $\dfrac{d^2y}{dx^2} + 4\dfrac{dy}{dx} = 10$ (c) $\dfrac{d^2y}{dx^2} + 4y = \sin x$

(d) $\dfrac{d^2y}{dx^2} + 6\dfrac{dy}{dx} - 40y = x$ (e) $\dfrac{d^2x}{dt^2} - 4\dfrac{dx}{dt} + 5x = e^t$ (f) $\dfrac{d^2x}{dt^2} + 4\dfrac{dx}{dt} - 5x = e^{-t}$

2 Find general solutions of the following differential equations.

(a) $\dfrac{d^2y}{dx^2} + 4\dfrac{dy}{dx} + 5y = 0$ (b) $\dfrac{d^2y}{dx^2} - 6\dfrac{dy}{dx} + 25y = 0$

(c) $\dfrac{d^2x}{dt^2} + 9x = 4e^{-t}$ (d) $\dfrac{d^2u}{dt^2} + 2\dfrac{du}{dt} + 2u = t$

3 For each differential equation find the solution which satisfies the given conditions.

(a) $\dfrac{d^2y}{dx^2} - 4\dfrac{dy}{dx} + 8y = 0$; $y = 1$ and $\dfrac{dy}{dx} = 2$ when $x = 0$

(b) $\dfrac{d^2x}{dt^2} + 4\dfrac{dx}{dt} + 13x = 0$; $x = 1$ and $\dfrac{dx}{dt} = 4$ when $t = 0$

(c) $\dfrac{d^2u}{dt^2} + 2\dfrac{du}{dt} + 2u = 2t^2$; $u = 0$ and $\dfrac{du}{dt} = 0$ when $t = 0$

(d) $\dfrac{d^2x}{dt^2} + 2\dfrac{dx}{dt} + 10x = 9e^{-t}$; $x = 1$ and $\dfrac{dx}{dt} = 2$ when $t = 0$

8.3   Integration

Integrals involving expressions such as $e^{ax}\cos bx$ are tiresome to find by usual methods. Integration by parts must be applied twice to get the answer. The following example shows how such integrals can be found more easily using complex numbers.

Example 8.3.1

Find $\displaystyle\int e^x \cos 3x\,dx$.

The integrand is the real part of $e^x(\cos 3x + i \sin 3x)$, which is $e^x e^{3ix}$, or $e^{(1+3i)x}$. Since differentiation of e^{cx} with c complex follows the usual rule, so does the corresponding integration. Thus

$$\int e^{(1+3i)x}\,dx = \frac{1}{1+3i}e^{(1+3i)x} + k.$$

You can simplify this by writing $\dfrac{1}{1+3i}$ as $\dfrac{1}{1+3i} \times \dfrac{1-3i}{1-3i} = \dfrac{1-3i}{10}$. Therefore

$$\frac{1}{1+3i}e^{(1+3i)x} = \tfrac{1}{10}e^x(1-3i)(\cos 3x + i\sin 3x).$$

The required integral is the real part of $\displaystyle\int e^{(1+3i)x}\,dx$:

$$\int e^x \cos 3x\,dx = \tfrac{1}{10}e^x(\cos 3x + 3\sin 3x) + k.$$

8.4   Finding particular integrals

A similar method can be used to find particular integrals for some linear differential equations with constant coefficients. If the right side of the equation is a cosine or a sine, it is often easiest to treat it as the real or imaginary part of an exponential function with a complex power. The first example shows an alternative way of solving the first order equation in Example 3.5.1.

Example 8.4.1

Find a particular integral for $\dfrac{dy}{dx} + 4y = \sin 2x$.

The right side is the imaginary part of e^{2ix}. So consider first the differential equation

$$\frac{dz}{dx} + 4z = e^{2ix}.$$

Since the right side is an exponential, look for a trial solution of the form $z = ae^{2ix}$. Since $\dfrac{dz}{dx} = 2a\,ie^{2ix}$, this will work if

$$2a\,ie^{2ix} + 4a\,e^{2ix} \equiv e^{2ix}.$$

So choose a so that $(2i + 4)a = 1$, that is

$$a = \frac{1}{2(2 + i)} = \frac{2 - i}{2(2 + i)(2 - i)} = \tfrac{1}{10}(2 - i).$$

This gives a particular integral for z,

$$z = \tfrac{1}{10}(2 - i)e^{2ix} = \tfrac{1}{10}(2 - i)(\cos 2x + i\sin 2x).$$

A particular integral for y is the imaginary part of z, which is

$$\tfrac{1}{10}(2\sin 2x - \cos 2x).$$

Example 8.4.2*

Find a particular integral for $\dfrac{d^2x}{dt^2} + 2\dfrac{dx}{dt} + 5x = e^{-2t}(2\cos t + \sin t)$.

This is the differential equation whose complementary function was found in Example 8.2.2 to be

$$x = e^{-t}(C\cos 2t + D\sin 2t).$$

Expressions like the bracket on the right side of the original equation arise when you find the real part of a product such as $(a + bi)(\cos t + i\sin t)$. To get $2\cos t + \sin t$, you need to take $a = 2$ and $-b = 1$. So, writing $\cos t + i\sin t$ as e^{it}, the right side of the differential equation is the real part of $e^{-2t} \times (2 - i)e^{it}$, which can be written as $(2 - i)e^{(-2+i)t}$.

Begin by considering the differential equation

$$\frac{d^2z}{dt^2} + 2\frac{dz}{dt} + 5z = (2 - i)e^{(-2+i)t},$$

and try a solution $z = ae^{(-2+i)t}$.

Then $\quad \dfrac{dz}{dt} = a(-2 + i)e^{(-2+i)t} \quad$ and $\quad \dfrac{d^2z}{dt^2} = a(-2 + i)^2e^{(-2+i)t} = a(3 - 4i)e^{(-2+i)t}.$

This makes the left side of the equation

$$ae^{(-2+i)t}((3 - 4i) + 2(-2 + i) + 5) = a(4 - 2i)e^{(-2+i)t},$$

which has to be identically equal to the right side $(2 - i)e^{(-2+i)t}$.

So the required value of a is $\dfrac{2-i}{4-2i} = \dfrac{1}{2}$.

This gives a particular integral $z = \frac{1}{2}e^{(-2+i)t} = \frac{1}{2}e^{-2t}(\cos t + i\sin t)$.

From this you can deduce that a particular integral of the original differential equation is $x = \frac{1}{2}e^{-2t}\cos t$. The reasoning is as follows.

Write z as $x + yi$. The differential equation for z becomes

$$\frac{d^2x}{dt^2} + \frac{d^2y}{dt^2}i + 2\left(\frac{dx}{dt} + \frac{dy}{dt}i\right) + 5(x + yi) = (2-i)e^{-2t}(\cos t + i\sin t).$$

Equating the real parts shows that the equation

$$\frac{d^2x}{dt^2} + 2\frac{dx}{dt} + 5x = e^{-2t}(2\cos t + \sin t)$$

has a particular integral $x = \frac{1}{2}e^{-2t}\cos t$.

Combining this result with the complementary function $x = e^{-t}(C\cos 2t + D\sin 2t)$ from Example 8.2.2 gives the complete solution of the differential equation:

$$x = \tfrac{1}{2}e^{-2t}\cos t + e^{-t}(C\cos 2t + D\sin 2t).$$

Example 8.4.3

Solve the differential equation $\dfrac{d^2x}{dt^2} + p^2x = 2p\sin pt$.

The auxiliary equation is $\lambda^2 + p^2 = 0$, with roots $\pm pi$, so the complementary function is $Ae^{pit} + Be^{-pit}$, which is $A(\cos pt + i\sin pt) + B(\cos pt - i\sin pt)$, or $C\cos pt + D\sin pt$.

The right side is the imaginary part of $2p\,e^{pit}$. But the particular integral can't be of this form, since e^{pit} is part of the complementary function. So follow the general rule suggested in Section 3.5: for the equation $\dfrac{d^2z}{dt^2} + p^2z = 2p\,e^{pit}$, take a trial solution $z = at\,e^{pit}$. This gives

$$\frac{dz}{dt} = ae^{pit} + at(p\,ie^{pit}) = ae^{pit} + atp\,ie^{pit},$$

$$\frac{d^2z}{dt^2} = ap\,ie^{pit} + ap\,ie^{pit} + at(pi)^2e^{pit} = 2ap\,ie^{pit} - atp^2e^{pit},$$

giving the left side $\dfrac{d^2z}{dt^2} + p^2z = 2ap\,ie^{pit}$.

This has to equal $2p\,e^{pit}$, so take $ai - 1$, giving $a = \dfrac{1}{i} = -i$.

The particular integral is then $z = -it(\cos pt + i\sin pt)$. For the given equation the imaginary part is required, which is $x = -t\cos pt$.

The complete solution is therefore

$$x = -t\cos pt + C\cos pt + D\sin pt.$$

Exercise 8B

1 Use complex numbers to find the following indefinite integrals.

(a) $\displaystyle\int e^{2x}\cos x\,dx$ (b) $\displaystyle\int e^{x}\sin 4x\,dx$ (c) $\displaystyle\int e^{-x}\cos 2x\,dx$

(d) $\displaystyle\int e^{-4x}\sin 3x\,dx$ (e) $\displaystyle\int xe^{2x}\cos 3x\,dx$ (f) $\displaystyle\int e^{-x}(2\cos 3x+\sin 3x)\,dx$

2 Find particular integrals for the following differential equations.

(a) $\dfrac{dy}{dt}+2y=5\cos t$

(b) $\dfrac{dy}{dt}-y=e^{t}\cos 2t$

(c) $\dfrac{d^{2}x}{dt^{2}}+4\dfrac{dx}{dt}-3x=\sin 2t$

(d) $\dfrac{d^{2}u}{dt^{2}}+\dfrac{du}{dt}-2u=\cos t$

(e) $\dfrac{d^{2}u}{dx^{2}}-2\dfrac{du}{dx}-3u=\sin x+3\cos x$

(f)* $\dfrac{d^{2}y}{dx^{2}}-6\dfrac{dy}{dx}+9y=e^{3x}\cos x$

(g) $\dfrac{d^{2}x}{dt^{2}}+4x=\sin 2t$

(h)* $\dfrac{d^{2}y}{dx^{2}}-2\dfrac{dy}{dx}+10y=e^{x}\cos 3x$

3 Find general solutions of the following differential equations.

(a) $\dfrac{d^{2}x}{dt^{2}}+x=e^{-t}\cos 2t$

(b) $\dfrac{d^{2}y}{dx^{2}}-2\dfrac{dy}{dx}+50y=\sin x$

(c) $\dfrac{d^{2}x}{dt^{2}}+2\dfrac{dx}{dt}-15x=\cos 3t$

(d)* $\dfrac{d^{2}y}{dt^{2}}+6\dfrac{dy}{dt}+10y=e^{-3t}\sin t$

4 For each differential equation find the solution which satisfies the given conditions.

(a) $\dfrac{dy}{dx}+3y=10\cos x;\quad y=2$ when $x=0$

(b) $\dfrac{dx}{dt}+x=2e^{-t}\sin 2t;\quad x=0$ when $t=0$

(c) $\dfrac{d^{2}y}{dx^{2}}+4\dfrac{dy}{dx}+5y=4(\cos x+\sin x);\quad y=0$ and $\dfrac{dy}{dx}=2$ when $x=0$

(d)* $\dfrac{d^{2}x}{dt^{2}}-2p\dfrac{dx}{dt}+(p^{2}+q^{2})x=e^{pt}\cos qt;\quad x=a$ and $\dfrac{dx}{dt}=bq$ when $t=0$

Miscellaneous exercise 8

For the notation in Questions 9 and 10, see Miscellaneous exercise 3.

1 Find general solutions for the following differential equations in real form.

(a) $\dfrac{d^{2}y}{dx^{2}}+4y=0$

(b) $\dfrac{d^{2}x}{dt^{2}}+2\dfrac{dx}{dt}+50x=0$

(c) $\dfrac{d^{2}y}{dx^{2}}+6\dfrac{dy}{dx}+25y=10e^{-x}$

(d) $\dfrac{d^{2}u}{dt^{2}}-4\dfrac{du}{dt}+20u=100t$

(e) $\dfrac{d^{2}x}{dt^{2}}+8\dfrac{dx}{dt}+25x=\sin 5t$

2 Solve the differential equations with the given conditions.

(a) $\dfrac{d^2y}{dx^2} + 2\dfrac{dy}{dx} + 5y = 0,$ $y = 0$ and $\dfrac{dy}{dx} = 1$ when $x = 0$

(b) $\dfrac{d^2u}{dt^2} + 2\dfrac{du}{dt} + 2u = 5\sin t,$ $u = 1$ and $\dfrac{du}{dt} = 2$ when $t = 0$

(c) $\dfrac{d^2x}{dt^2} + 4x = \cos 2t,$ $x = 0$ and $\dfrac{dx}{dt} = 1$ when $t = 0$

3 By expressing $p\cos bt + q\sin bt$ as the real part of $(p - q\,\mathrm{i})e^{bti}$, find

(a) $\displaystyle\int e^{at}(p\cos bt + q\sin bt)\,dt,$ (b) $\displaystyle\int t(p\cos bt + q\sin bt)\,dt.$

4 Sketch the graph of $f(t) = e^{-at}\sin t$ for $t \geqslant 0$, where a is a positive constant. If u_n denotes $\displaystyle\int_{n\pi}^{(n+1)\pi} e^{-at}\sin t\,dt$, show that $u_0, u_1, u_2, \ldots$ is a geometric sequence. Find

(a) $\displaystyle\int_0^\infty e^{-at}\sin t\,dt,$ (b) $\displaystyle\int_0^\infty e^{-at}|\sin t|\,dt.$

5 A damped oscillation is modelled, for $t \geqslant 0$, by the differential equation $\dfrac{d^2x}{dt^2} + 2\dfrac{dx}{dt} + 4x = 0$. Find the solution for which $x = 0$ and $\dfrac{dx}{dt} = U$ when $t = 0$.

Find the value of t corresponding to the first stationary value of x.   (OCR)

6 A light spring is lying at rest on a smooth horizontal table. One end is fixed and a particle is attached to the other end. The particle is set in motion and subsequently the extension x of the spring satisfies the differential equation $\dfrac{d^2x}{dt^2} + 4k\dfrac{dx}{dt} + 8k^2x = 8kV$, where t is the time from the start of the motion and k and V are positive constants. Find the general solution. Given that $x = 0$ and $\dfrac{dx}{dt} = 0$ when $t = 0$, find x in terms of t, k and V. Deduce that, as $t \to \infty$, the extension of the spring approaches a constant value. State this value.   (OCR)

7 The differential equation governing the current I amps in an electric circuit containing a resistor of R ohms, a capacitor of C farads and an applied electromotive force of E volts, all in series, is $R\dfrac{dI}{dt} + \dfrac{I}{C} = \dfrac{dE}{dt}$ where R and C are constants and t is time. Initially the current is monitored with $E = E_0$ provided by a battery, and subsequently with $E = E_0\sin\omega t$, provided by a generator. Find the solution of the differential equation in each of the cases

(a) $E = E_0$, a constant, and initially $I = I_0$;

(b) $E = E_0\sin\omega t$, where both E_0 and ω are constants, and initially $I = 0$.   (MEI)

8 A reservoir supplies a large city. At time t days the level of the water above a fixed mark is x metres, where x and t are related by $\dfrac{d^2x}{dt^2} + 2\dfrac{dx}{dt} + 2x = 30\cos 3t - 35\sin 3t$. When $t = 0$, $x = 2$ and the water level is rising at a rate of 14 metres per day.

(a) Find x in terms of t.

(b) Show that, after a long time, the difference between the highest and lowest water levels is approximately 10 metres.   (OCR)

9 Show that the differential equation $\ddot{x} + 2\dot{x} + 10x = 16\cos\omega t$ has a particular integral of the form $A\cos\omega t + B\sin\omega t$, where $A^2 + B^2 = \dfrac{256}{(10 - \omega^2)^2 + 4\omega^2}$.

The differential equation models the motion of an oscillating machine part. Explain why the particular integral gives a description of the steady state motion. Deduce that the oscillation is in resonance (that is, has maximum amplitude) when $\omega = 2\sqrt{2}$.   (OCR)

10 In a simulation, a piece of machinery is subjected to vibrations of the form $a\sin\omega t$ to test the behaviour of one of the components. Different values of ω are used in different tests. The component is not subject to any damping. The displacement, x cm, of the component can be modelled by $\ddot{x} + 196x = 2\sin\omega t$, where t is the time in seconds.

(a) Find the complementary function.

(b) In the case $\omega \neq 14$, find a particular integral of the form $\lambda\sin\omega t + \mu\cos\omega t$, where λ and μ are to be found in terms of ω. Hence write down the general solution of the differential equation.

(c) In the case $\omega = 14$, why will a particular integral of the form given in (b) not satisfy the differential equation? In this case, find the particular integral and hence write down the general solution of the differential equation. Find the solution satisfying $\dot{x} = x = 0$ when $t = 0$. Describe the nature of the oscillations.   (MEI)

9 Groups

This chapter introduces and develops the idea of a group. When you have completed it, you should

- know the axioms for a group
- know how to decide whether a given structure is, or is not, a group
- be able to use algebraic methods to prove simple properties of groups
- know what is meant by the order of a group
- recognise some types of groups.

9.1 Mathematical structure

What are the similarities and differences between the multiplication of matrices and the multiplication of real numbers? How are complex numbers under multiplication equivalent to certain kinds of matrices under multiplication? And what is the connection between the composition of certain functions and the symmetries of a rectangle? The idea of a 'group' gives some answers to questions like these.

The value of the idea of a group is that, if you can show that certain structures, such as those described in the previous paragraph, satisfy the same properties, and you can prove theorems and results using these properties, then all the structures with these properties will obey the theorems and have corresponding results. It is thus time-saving and thought-saving to catalogue structures in this way.

The word 'structure' has now been used several times, but it is not clear precisely what is meant by a structure. It will be helpful to start by introducing some notation and expanding on the idea of a set.

9.2 Set notation

You have met already the abbreviations $\mathbb{N}$, $\mathbb{Z}$ and $\mathbb{R}$ for the natural numbers, integers and real numbers respectively. The symbols $\mathbb{C}$ and $\mathbb{Q}$ will be used for the complex numbers and the rational numbers (fractions, including integers, which are fractions with denominator 1) respectively. It is useful to introduce two other pieces of notation in conjunction with $\mathbb{R}, \mathbb{Z}, \mathbb{C}$ and $\mathbb{Q}$: the notation $\mathbb{R} - \{0\}$ is used to mean the real numbers except 0; similar notations apply with $\mathbb{Z}, \mathbb{C}$ and $\mathbb{Q}$. The superscript $+$ on $\mathbb{R}$, that is $\mathbb{R}^+$, means the positive real numbers; similarly with $\mathbb{Z}^+$ and $\mathbb{Q}^+$. Finally, $\mathbb{R}_0^+$ means the positive real numbers together with 0; similarly for $\mathbb{Z}_0^+$ and $\mathbb{Q}_0^+$.

> Recall that positive and negative have no meaning with complex numbers. That is why there is no symbol $\mathbb{C}^+$ or $\mathbb{C}_0^+$. Note also that $\mathbb{Z}^+$ is the same as $\mathbb{N}$.

The members of a set are often called its **elements**.

When you need to consider other sets, the braces notation is used, either with a list or with an explanation. Here are some examples.

The elements of the set $\{0, 2, 4, 6, 8\}$ are the numbers 0, 2, 4, 6 and 8.

The set $\left\{1, x, x^2, \ldots, x^n\right\}$ consists of the integer powers of x from 0 to n inclusive. If there is any doubt about the nature of n you could write this as $\{x^r : r \in \mathbb{Z}, 0 \leqslant r \leqslant n\}$, where the quantity before the colon tells you the nature of what is in the set, and what follows the colon makes the description more precise.

The set $\{x \in \mathbb{R} : 0 \leqslant x \leqslant 1\}$ is the set of real numbers lying from 0 to 1. Similarly $\{z \in \mathbb{C} : |z| = 1\}$ means the set of complex numbers with modulus 1.

9.3   Binary operations

Each of the structures mentioned in Section 9.1 had, in addition to the set of elements, an operation: for example, real numbers and the operation of multiplication.

Multiplication of real numbers is an example of a **binary operation**; another binary operation is the dot product $\mathbf{a} \cdot \mathbf{b}$ of two vectors $\mathbf{a}$ and $\mathbf{b}$.

> A binary operation $\circ$ on a set S is a rule which assigns to each ordered pair of elements x, y in S exactly one element denoted by $x \circ y$.

> The binary operation $\circ$ is often pronounced 'blob'!

Notice that multiplication, addition and subtraction are binary operations on $\mathbb{Z}$. On the other hand division is not, since $x \div 0$ has no meaning. Multiplication, addition and subtraction are binary operations on $\mathbb{R}$, $\mathbb{C}$ and $\mathbb{Q}$, and division is a binary operation on $\mathbb{R} - \{0\}$, $\mathbb{C} - \{0\}$ and $\mathbb{Q} - \{0\}$.

> In some books, $\mathbb{R}^*$ or $\mathbb{R} \setminus \{0\}$ are used instead of $\mathbb{R} - \{0\}$.

In the definition of binary operation, notice that $x \circ y$ does not have to be an element of the set S. For example, the scalar product of two vectors is not a vector. However, in cases where the binary operation on S always gives a result which is in the set S, the operation is said to be **closed** within the set.

> In some books, the term 'binary operation' is used to mean a closed binary operation.

Example 9.3.1
Decide which of the following operations on the given sets are binary operations. For those which are binary operations, say whether or not they are closed.

(a) $\mathbb{N}$, where $a \circ b$ means $a - b$

(b) $\mathbb{N}$, where $a \circ b$ means the lowest common multiple (lcm) of a and b

(c) $\mathbb{R}$, where $a \circ b$ means the greater of a and b

(d) $\mathbb{R}$, where $a \circ b = \dfrac{a+b}{1-ab}$

(e) $\mathbb{Z}$, where $a \circ b$ means a

(a) A binary operation. Since, for example, $1 - 2$ is not defined in $\mathbb{N}$, the operation is not closed.

(b) A binary operation. The lowest common multiple (lcm) of two positive integers a and b is always defined. As the lcm is a positive integer, the operation is closed.

(c) A binary operation. The greater of a and b is defined, except when $a = b$ when it is understood that $a \circ b$ is equal to either a or b. It is closed since the result is in $\mathbb{R}$.

(d) Not a binary operation, since you cannot calculate $1 \circ 1$.

(e) A binary operation. As a is in $\mathbb{Z}$ the result $a \circ b = a$ is also in $\mathbb{Z}$, so the binary operation is closed.

In Example 9.3.1 operations (b) and (c), the order in which a and b are written does not matter since $a \circ b = b \circ a$, but in operations (a) and (e) the order does matter.

> A binary operation $\circ$ on a set S is **commutative** if $a \circ b = b \circ a$ for all $a, b \in S$; otherwise it is **not commutative**.

Important examples of non-commutative binary operations are

- division on $\mathbb{R} - \{0\}$; a counterexample is $2 \div 1 = 2$ and $1 \div 2 = \frac{1}{2}$
- subtraction on $\mathbb{R}$; a counterexample is $3 - 2 = 1$ and $2 - 3 = -1$
- the multiplication of square matrices; a counterexample is $\begin{pmatrix} 1 & 0 \\ 1 & 0 \end{pmatrix} \begin{pmatrix} 0 & 1 \\ 0 & 1 \end{pmatrix} = \begin{pmatrix} 0 & 1 \\ 0 & 1 \end{pmatrix}$ and

$$\begin{pmatrix} 0 & 1 \\ 0 & 1 \end{pmatrix} \begin{pmatrix} 1 & 0 \\ 1 & 0 \end{pmatrix} = \begin{pmatrix} 1 & 0 \\ 1 & 0 \end{pmatrix}.$$

When you have expressions of the form $(a \circ b) \circ c$ and $a \circ (b \circ c)$ where $\circ$ is a binary operation and $a, b, c \in S$, it may or may not be true that $(a \circ b) \circ c = a \circ (b \circ c)$. For example, for the binary operation $+$ on $\mathbb{R}$, you can say that $(a + b) + c = a + (b + c)$, but for the binary operation $-$ on $\mathbb{R}$, the counterexample $(4 - 2) - 1 = 1$ and $4 - (2 - 1) = 3$ shows that in general, $(a - b) - c \neq a - (b - c)$.

> A binary operation $\circ$ on a set S is **associative** if $(a \circ b) \circ c = a \circ (b \circ c)$ for all $a, b, c \in S$; otherwise it is **not associative**.

When a binary operation is associative, you may leave out the brackets and write $a \circ b \circ c$, since both ways of evaluating it give the same answer.

Example 9.3.2

Say whether or not the following closed binary operations are commutative and associative.

(a) $\mathbb{N}$: multiplication

(b) Matrices of the form $\begin{pmatrix} x & x \\ 0 & 0 \end{pmatrix}$, where $x \in \mathbb{R}$: matrix multiplication

(c) Vectors in three dimensions: vector product

(d) $\mathbb{Z}$: the operation $a \circ b$ defined as $a + b - ab$

    (a) For natural numbers $ab = ba$ and $(ab)c = a(bc)$, so the operation is commutative and associative.

    (b) $\begin{pmatrix} x & x \\ 0 & 0 \end{pmatrix} \begin{pmatrix} y & y \\ 0 & 0 \end{pmatrix} = \begin{pmatrix} xy & xy \\ 0 & 0 \end{pmatrix}$ and $\begin{pmatrix} y & y \\ 0 & 0 \end{pmatrix} \begin{pmatrix} x & x \\ 0 & 0 \end{pmatrix} = \begin{pmatrix} yx & yx \\ 0 & 0 \end{pmatrix}$. As $x, y \in \mathbb{R}$,

        $xy = yx$, and so $\begin{pmatrix} x & x \\ 0 & 0 \end{pmatrix} \begin{pmatrix} y & y \\ 0 & 0 \end{pmatrix} = \begin{pmatrix} y & y \\ 0 & 0 \end{pmatrix} \begin{pmatrix} x & x \\ 0 & 0 \end{pmatrix}$. Thus the operation is

        commutative. Since matrix multiplication is associative, this operation is associative.

    (c) Since $\mathbf{i} \times \mathbf{j} = \mathbf{k}$ and $\mathbf{j} \times \mathbf{i} = -\mathbf{k}$, the operation is not commutative. Since $(\mathbf{i} \times \mathbf{j}) \times \mathbf{j} = \mathbf{k} \times \mathbf{j} = -\mathbf{i}$ and $\mathbf{i} \times (\mathbf{j} \times \mathbf{j}) = \mathbf{i} \times \mathbf{0} = \mathbf{0}$, the operation is not associative.

    (d) $a \circ b = a + b - ab = b + a - ba = b \circ a$ so the operation is commutative.

$$(a \circ b) \circ c = (a + b - ab) \circ c$$
$$= (a + b - ab) + c - (a + b - ab)c$$
$$= a + b - ab + c - ac - bc + abc$$
and $a \circ (b \circ c) = a \circ (b + c - bc)$
$$= a + (b + c - bc) - a(b + c - bc)$$
$$= a + b + c - bc - ab - ac + abc.$$

    As these expressions are equal, the operation is associative.

You can also define binary operations for sets which have only a finite number of elements.

You can use a combination table to show the details of a closed binary operation on a small set. Table 9.1 shows the result of 'last digit arithmetic' on $\{2, 4, 6, 8\}$. For example, $2 \times 8 = 16$ has last digit 6, so $2 \circ 8 = 6$. This is shown in the shaded cell in Table 9.1. Stated formally, the binary operation $\circ$ on the set $\{2, 4, 6, 8\}$ given by $a \circ b$ is the remainder after the product ab is divided by 10.

	Second number			
∘	2	4	6	8
2	4	8	2	6
4	8	6	4	2
6	2	4	6	8
8	6	2	8	4

First number

Table 9.1

A binary operation can actually be *defined* by a combination table. For example, Table 9.2 defines a binary operation ∘ on the set $\{a, b, c\}$.

∘	a	b	c
a	b	a	c
b	a	c	b
c	b	b	a

Table 9.2

You can see immediately that ∘ is a binary operation, and also that it is closed, because Table 9.2 shows the result of every possible combination of two members of the set.

You can also tell quickly from a table if a binary operation is commutative by looking for symmetry about the leading diagonal. Table 9.2 is not symmetrical since $c \circ a = b$ and $a \circ c = c$ and therefore the operation is not commutative.

Without detailed checking you can't tell from a table whether or not the binary operation is associative. To find out it is usually easier to exploit some other knowledge about the table.

Exercise 9A

1 Decide which of the following operations are binary operations on the given sets. If an operation is not a binary operation, give one reason. For those which are binary operations, check whether they are closed, commutative and associative.

(a) − on $\mathbb{Z}^+$

(b) matrix multiplication on 2×2 matrices

(c) ∘ on $\mathbb{Z}^+$, where $a \circ b = a^b$

(d) ∘ on $\mathbb{R}$, where $a \circ b = |a - b|$

(e) ∘ on $\mathbb{R}$, where $a \circ b = 0$ for all $a, b \in \mathbb{R}$

(f) ∘ on 2×2 matrices where $\mathbf{A} \circ \mathbf{B} = \mathbf{AB}^{-1}$ for all $\mathbf{A}$ and $\mathbf{B}$.

(g) ∘ on $\mathbb{R}$, where $a \circ b = b$ for all $a, b \in \mathbb{R}$

(h) ∘ on $\mathbb{R}^+$, where $a \circ b = a^b$

(i) ∘ on $\{1, 3, 7, 9\}$, where $a \circ b$ is the remainder when $a \times b$ is divided by 10

(j) ∘ on $\mathbb{R}$, where $a \circ b$ is the smallest number greater than $a + b$

9.4   Identity elements

The numbers 0 and 1 in $\mathbb{R}$ are very special. When the operation is addition, the number 0 has the property that

$$a + 0 = 0 + a = a$$

for every number a in $\mathbb{R}$.

Similarly, when the operation is multiplication, the number 1 has the property that

$$a \times 1 = 1 \times a = a$$

for every number a in $\mathbb{R} - \{0\}$.

In each of these examples you have a set S that is closed under a binary operation $\circ$ and an element, often denoted by e, with the property that $a \circ e = e \circ a = a$ for all members of the set S. This element e is called an **identity element** for the set S with the operation $\circ$.

A set with a closed binary operation need not have an identity element.

Example 9.4.1
Show that the set $\mathbb{Z}$ with the operation of subtraction does not have an identity element.

The element 0 is the only element with the property that $a - 0 = a$ for every $a \in \mathbb{Z}$, but as $0 - a = -a$, 0 is not an identity element for $\mathbb{Z}$ under subtraction.

Example 9.4.2
Find the identity element in $\mathbb{R} - \{1\}$ with the binary operation $a \circ b = a + b - ab$.

$$a \circ e = a \quad \Leftrightarrow \quad a + e - ea = a \quad \Leftrightarrow \quad e - ea = 0 \quad \Leftrightarrow \quad e(1 - a) = 0.$$

For this to be true for all a in $\mathbb{R} - \{1\}$, you need $e = 0$.

As $a \circ b = b \circ a$, there is no need to check separately that $e \circ a = a$.

9.5   Inverse elements

Consider again the two numbers discussed at the beginning of Section 9.4, 0 and 1 in $\mathbb{R}$.

For each number $a \in \mathbb{R}$, there exists a number $(-a) \in \mathbb{R}$ such that

$$(-a) + a = a + (-a) = 0.$$

For each number $a \in \mathbb{R} - \{0\}$, there exists a number $a^{-1} \in \mathbb{R} - \{0\}$ such that

$$a^{-1} \times a = a \times a^{-1} = 1.$$

In ordinary algebraic notation these statements look quite different, but $\mathbb{R}$ and $\mathbb{R} - \{0\}$ are both examples of a set S closed under a binary operation $\circ$, with an identity element e. The two statements mean that for each element a in S there exists an element b with the property that $a \circ b = b \circ a = e$. This element b is called an **inverse** of a.

Example 9.5.1
Find an inverse of a in $\mathbb{R} - \{1\}$ with the binary operation $a \circ b = a + b - ab$.

In Example 9.4.2, it was shown that the identity element is 0.

$$b \circ a = e \quad \Leftrightarrow \quad b + a - ba = 0 \quad \Leftrightarrow \quad b = \frac{a}{a-1}$$

so, as $a \neq 1$, $\dfrac{a}{a-1}$ is an inverse of a.

As $a \circ b = b \circ a$, there is no need to check separately that $a \circ b = e$.

Summarising the discussion in this and the previous section gives the following:

> Let S be a set with a closed binary operation $\circ$.
>
> If there exists an element $e \in G$ such that, for all $a \in G$, $e \circ a = a \circ e = a$, then e is an **identity element** for S with the operation $\circ$.
>
> If for each element $a \in S$, there exists an element $b \in S$ such that $b \circ a = a \circ b = e$, where e is an identity element for S, then b is called an **inverse** of a in S with the operation $\circ$.

Exercise 9B

1 In each of the following combination tables, identify the products $s \circ t$, $t \circ s$, $(p \circ q) \circ s$ and $p \circ (q \circ t)$, find the identity element and the inverse of s. Find also the solution for the equations $x \circ t = s$ and $u \circ y = t$.

(a)

	p	q	r	s	t	u
p	q	r	p	t	u	s
q	r	p	q	u	s	t
r	p	q	r	s	t	u
s	u	t	s	r	p	q
t	s	u	t	q	r	p
u	t	s	u	p	q	r

(b)

	p	u	s	r	q	t
p	r	t	q	p	u	s
u	q	s	r	u	t	p
s	t	r	u	s	p	q
r	p	u	s	r	q	t
q	s	p	t	q	r	u
t	u	q	p	t	s	r

2 In each part of this question a set with a closed binary operation is given. Find the identity element, if it exists, and if it does exist, find the inverse of a general element a, if it exists.

(a) Vectors with 3 components: vector product

(b) 2×2 matrices: matrix multiplication   (c) $\mathbb{C}$: multiplication

(d) $\mathbb{R}$: $\circ$ where $a \circ b = |a - b|$ (e) $\mathbb{R}$: $\circ$ where $a \circ b = b$ for all $a, b \in \mathbb{R}$

(f) The set of matrices of the form $\begin{pmatrix} x & x \\ 0 & 0 \end{pmatrix}$, where $x \in \mathbb{R} - \{0\}$: matrix multiplication

(g) $\{2, 4, 6, 8\}$: $\circ$ where $a \circ b$ is the remainder when $a \times b$ is divided by 10

(h) $\{0, 2, 4, 6, 8\}$: $\circ$ where $a \circ b$ is the remainder when $a + b$ is divided by 10

(i) $\{1, 3, 7, 9\}$: $\circ$ where $a \circ b$ is the remainder when $a \times b$ is divided by 10

9.6   Groups

You have now seen that sets with binary operations can be distinguished by various properties: the operations may or may not be closed or associative, and the sets may or may not have identity and inverse elements. Sets with binary operations which are associative and have identity and inverse elements are especially important.

> A set G, with a binary operation $\circ$, is called a **group** if it has four properties, called **axioms**.
>
> 1 **Closure**: $a \circ b \in G$ for all $a, b \in G$; that is, the operation is closed.
>
> 2 **Associativity**: $a \circ (b \circ c) = (a \circ b) \circ c$ for all $a, b, c \in G$; that is, the binary operation is associative.
>
> 3 **Identity**: there exists an identity element $e \in G$ such that for all $a \in G, e \circ a = a \circ e = a$.
>
> 4 **Inverse**: for each element $a \in G$, there exists an inverse element $b \in G$ such that $b \circ a = a \circ b = e$.
>
> The group G with binary operation $\circ$ is denoted by $(G, \circ)$.

Notice that a group operation need not be commutative.

It is an important fact that there is only one element $e \in G$ with the property that for all $a \in G, e \circ a = a \circ e = a$. Once you know that there is only one such element, you can call it *the* identity element for $(G, \circ)$. Similarly, given an element $a \in G$, there is only one inverse element $b \in G$ such that $b \circ a = a \circ b = e$, so you can talk about *the* inverse of a. The notation a^{-1} is used for the inverse of a.

These facts about the uniqueness of the identity and the uniqueness of the inverse for each element are proved at end of the section. Assume them for now.

Groups may have a finite or an infinite number of elements. Examples of infinite groups are $(\mathbb{Z}, +)$, $(\mathbb{R} - \{0\}, \times)$ and $(\{z \in \mathbb{C} : |z| = 1\}, \times)$. Example 9.6.1 shows a finite group.

> The number of elements in a group is called its **order**.
>
> If a group has an infinite number of elements, it is said to have **infinite order**.

To prove that a set with an infinite number of elements is a group, you cannot use arguments based on tables.

Example 9.6.1
Prove that the set $\{1, i, -1, -i\}$ with the operation of multiplication is a group.

For a set as small as this, it is often easiest to show that the binary operation is closed by constructing a table. Table 9.3 shows the results.

×	1	i	−1	−i
1	1	i	−1	−i
i	i	−1	−i	1
−1	−1	−i	1	i
−i	−i	1	i	−1

Table 9.3

There are four properties to establish, namely the four properties of the group.

1 **Closure**: The table shows that the operation of multiplication is closed since every possible product is a member of the set $\{1, i, -1, -i\}$.

2 **Associativity**: Multiplication of complex numbers is associative, so multiplication of these elements is associative.

3 **Identity**: The element 1 is the identity element, since $1 \times z = z \times 1 = z$ for every complex number z.

4 **Inverse**: The inverses of $1, -1, i$ and $-i$ are $1, -1, -i$ and i respectively, so every element has an inverse which is in the set $\{1, i, -1, -i\}$.

Therefore $\{1, i, -1, -i\}$ with the operation of multiplication is a group.

The row corresponding to the identity element is the same as the row of 'column labels' at the top of the table; the column corresponding to the identity element is the same as the column of 'row labels' at the left of the table.

You may have noticed that each element of the group in Table 9.3 appears just once in every row and once in every column. This is necessary for a group.

Theorem In a group table, each element appears just once in every row.

In the following argument, a very brief justification is given for each step by referring to one of the group axioms.

Proof The elements which appear in a row are those of the form $a \circ x$ where a is fixed and x ranges over the elements of the group. Suppose that two elements in a row are the same. Then $a \circ x = a \circ y$ for some x and y, with $x \neq y$. Therefore

$$
\begin{aligned}
a \circ x = a \circ y \quad &\Rightarrow \quad a^{-1} \circ (a \circ x) = a^{-1} \circ (a \circ y) && \text{(inverse } a^{-1} \text{ exists)} \\
&\Rightarrow \quad (a^{-1} \circ a) \circ x = (a^{-1} \circ a) \circ y && \text{(associative property)} \\
&\Rightarrow \quad e \circ x = e \circ y && \text{(property of inverse)} \\
&\Rightarrow \quad x = y. && \text{(property of identity)}
\end{aligned}
$$

This is a contradiction, so no element appears more than once in each row.

If there are n elements in the group, then there are n elements in the row of the group table, which, by the previous argument, must all be different. Therefore each element appears just once in each row.

The proof for columns is left to you in Exercise 9C Question 4.

This theorem has no meaning for infinite groups, because you can't draw a table, but the cancelling argument that

$$a \circ x = a \circ y \quad \Rightarrow \quad x = y$$

is valid for infinite groups.

Suppose that a and b are known and that you want to solve the equation $a \circ x = b$ for x.

$$
\begin{aligned}
a \circ x = b \quad &\Leftrightarrow \quad a^{-1} \circ (a \circ x) = a^{-1} \circ b &&\text{(inverse } a^{-1} \text{ exists)}\\
&\Leftrightarrow \quad (a^{-1} \circ a) \circ x = a^{-1} \circ b &&\text{(associative property)}\\
&\Leftrightarrow \quad e \circ x = a^{-1} \circ b &&\text{(property of inverse)}\\
&\Leftrightarrow \quad x = a^{-1} \circ b. &&\text{(property of identity)}
\end{aligned}
$$

There are corresponding results if the order of a and x is reversed:

$$x \circ a = y \circ a \quad \Rightarrow \quad x = y \quad \text{and} \quad x \circ a = b \quad \Leftrightarrow \quad x = b \circ a^{-1}.$$

In a finite group, each element appears exactly once in each row and each column of the group table.

For any group, $a \circ x = a \circ y \quad \Rightarrow \quad x = y$ and $x \circ a = y \circ a \quad \Rightarrow \quad x = y$.

This is called the **cancellation law**.

For any group, $a \circ x = b \quad \Leftrightarrow \quad x = a^{-1} \circ b$ and $x \circ a = b \quad \Leftrightarrow \quad x = b \circ a^{-1}$.

An $n \times n$ table in which each element occurs just once in each row and each column is called a **Latin square** and is used in the design of statistical experiments. A group table is always a Latin square, but the reverse is not true. See Exercise 9C Question 2.

Example 9.6.2

Prove that the set of non-singular 2×2 matrices with the operation of matrix multiplication is a group.

The matrices must be non-singular so that inverse matrices exist.

1 **Closure**: The product of two non-singular 2×2 matrices $\mathbf{M}$ and $\mathbf{N}$ is a 2×2 matrix $\mathbf{MN}$. Since $\mathbf{M}$ and $\mathbf{N}$ are non-singular, $\det \mathbf{M} \neq 0$ and $\det \mathbf{N} \neq 0$, and since $\det \mathbf{MN} = \det \mathbf{M} \det \mathbf{N}$ (FP1 Exercise 5F Question 8), $\det \mathbf{MN} \neq 0$, so $\mathbf{MN}$ is non-singular. The operation of matrix multiplication is therefore closed.

2 **Associativity**: Since matrix multiplication is associative (FP1 Section 3.3) the group operation is associative.

3 **Identity**: The 2×2 identity matrix $\mathbf{I}$ is non-singular and is a member of the set. It has the property that for any matrix $\mathbf{M}$ in the set $\mathbf{IM} = \mathbf{MI} = \mathbf{M}$.

4 **Inverse**: If $\mathbf{M}$ is non-singular, then $\mathbf{M}^{-1}$ exists and is non-singular, so there exists an element in the set such that $\mathbf{M}^{-1}\mathbf{M} = \mathbf{MM}^{-1} = \mathbf{I}$.

Therefore the set of non-singular 2×2 matrices with the operation of matrix multiplication is a group.

There is an important difference between the groups in Examples 9.6.1 and 9.6.2. In Example 9.6.1 the binary operation is commutative, while in 9.62 it is not.

> In a group $(G, \circ)$, if $a \circ b = b \circ a$ for all $a, b \in G$, the group $(G, \circ)$ is said to be **commutative** or **abelian**.

> The word 'abelian' is in honour of the Norwegian mathematician Niels Abel.

The next example gives you practice in carrying out calculations in a group. Index notation, which is defined in Chapter 10, is used informally, so that $a^2 = a \circ a$, and so on.

Example 9.6.3

Let $(G, \circ)$ be a group in which $a^3 = e$, $b^2 = e$ and $a \circ b = b \circ a^2$.
Show that $b \circ (a^2 \circ b) = a$, $b \circ a = a^2 \circ b$, and simplify the product $(a \circ b)^2$.

Note that, as $a^3 = e$, $a^{-1} = a^2$, and as $b^2 = e$, $b^{-1} = b$.

$$
\begin{aligned}
b \circ (a^2 \circ b) &= b \circ a \circ (a \circ b) && \text{(associative property)} \\
&= b \circ a \circ (b \circ a^2) && \text{(since } a \circ b = b \circ a^2 \text{)} \\
&= b \circ (a \circ b) \circ a^2 && \text{(associative property)} \\
&= b \circ (b \circ a^2) \circ a^2 && \text{(since } a \circ b = b \circ a^2 \text{)} \\
&= b^2 \circ a^4 && \text{(associative property)} \\
&= a. && \text{(since } a^3 = e \text{ and } b^2 = e \text{)}
\end{aligned}
$$

Since $b \circ (a^2 \circ b) = a$,

$$
\begin{aligned}
b \circ a &= b \circ (b \circ a^2 \circ b) && (b \circ (a^2 \circ b) = a \text{ from the first part}) \\
&= b^2 \circ a^2 \circ b && \text{(associative property)} \\
&= e \circ a^2 \circ b && \text{(since } b^2 = e \text{)} \\
&= a^2 \circ b. && (e \text{ is the identity)}
\end{aligned}
$$

Notice the strategy: in the first case, the bs were moved steadily across the expression from right to left using the given result $a \circ b = b \circ a^2$ until the results $a^3 = e$, $b^2 = e$ could be used; the second case was simpler, but only because the first part had already been proved.

Now

$$(a \circ b)^2 = (a \circ b) \circ (a \circ b) \qquad \text{(definition of } (a \circ b)^2)$$
$$= a \circ (b \circ a) \circ b \qquad \text{(associative property)}$$
$$= a \circ (a^2 \circ b) \circ b \qquad (b \circ a = a^2 \circ b \text{ from the second part)}$$
$$= a^3 \circ b^2 \qquad \text{(associative property)}$$
$$= e \circ e \qquad \text{(since } a^3 = e \text{ and } b^2 = e)$$
$$= e. \qquad \text{(} e \text{ is the identity)}$$

Here are some important algebraic results about groups and inverses. These results will be used continually in the sections which follow.

Theorem   A group $(G, \circ)$ has the following properties.

(a) The identity element for a group $(G, \circ)$ is unique.

(b) For any $a \in G$, the inverse of a is unique.

(c) For $a, b \in G$, if $a \circ b = e$, then $a = b^{-1}$ and $b = a^{-1}$ and $b \circ a = e$.

(d) For $a, b \in G$, $(a \circ b)^{-1} = b^{-1} \circ a^{-1}$.

(e) For $a \in G$, $(a^{-1})^{-1} = a$.

One strategy for showing that an element is unique is to suppose that there are two such elements, and then to prove that they must be the same.

Proof   (a) Suppose that there are two identity elements, e and f.

Since e is an identity, $e \circ a = a$ for any a.

Putting $a = f$, gives, $e \circ f = f$.

Since f is an identity, $a \circ f = a$.

Putting $a = e$, gives $e \circ f = e$.

Therefore $f = e$, and the identity element for a group is unique.

(b) Suppose that a has two inverses, b and c.

Then $a \circ b = e$ and $c \circ a = e$.

So

$$c = c \circ e \qquad \text{(} e \text{ is the identity)}$$
$$= c \circ (a \circ b) \qquad \text{(since } a \circ b = e)$$
$$= (c \circ a) \circ b \qquad \text{(associative property)},$$
$$= e \circ b \qquad \text{(since } c \circ a = e)$$
$$= b, \qquad \text{(} e \text{ is the identity)}$$

and the inverse of a is unique.

(c) To prove $a = b^{-1}$, multiply $a \circ b = e$ on the right by b^{-1}. Then

$$
\begin{aligned}
a \circ b = e \quad &\Rightarrow \quad (a \circ b) \circ b^{-1} = e \circ b^{-1} && \text{(associative \& identity properties)} \\
&\Rightarrow \quad a \circ (b \circ b^{-1}) = b^{-1} && \text{(associative property)} \\
&\Rightarrow \quad a \circ e = b^{-1} && \text{(since } b \circ b^{-1} = e) \\
&\Rightarrow \quad a = b^{-1}. && \text{(}e\text{ is the identity)}
\end{aligned}
$$

The proof of the second part is similar. Then

$$b \circ a = b \circ b^{-1} = e.$$

(d) The proof involves showing that $(a \circ b) \circ (b^{-1} \circ a^{-1})$ is e, and using part (c).

$$
\begin{aligned}
(a \circ b) \circ (b^{-1} \circ a^{-1}) &= a \circ (b \circ (b^{-1} \circ a^{-1})) && \text{(associative property)} \\
&= a \circ ((b \circ b^{-1}) \circ a^{-1}) && \text{(associative property)} \\
&= a \circ (e \circ a^{-1}) && \text{(since } b \cup b^{-1} = e) \\
&= a \circ a^{-1} && \text{(}e\text{ is the identity)} \\
&= e. && \text{(since } a \circ a^{-1} = e)
\end{aligned}
$$

Then, using part (c), $(a \circ b)^{-1} = b^{-1} \circ a^{-1}$.

(e) Since $a \circ a^{-1} = e$, using part (c) with $b = a^{-1}$, $(a^{-1})^{-1} = a$.

Exercise 9C

1 Which of the following sets with the given operations are not groups? Give what you believe to be the simplest reason why each is not a group.

(a) $\mathbb{N}$, under addition.

(b) $\mathbb{Q}^+$, under multiplication.

(c) $\{1, 2, 3, 4, 5\}$, where $a \circ b$ is the remainder after ab is divided by 6.

(d) $\{1, 2, 3, 4, 5, 6\}$, where $a \circ b$ is the remainder after ab is divided by 7.

(e) $\{1, 2, 3, 4, 5, 6\}$, where $a \circ b$ is the remainder after $a + b$ is divided by 6.

(f) $\{0, 1, 2, 3, 4, 5\}$, where $a \circ b$ is the remainder after $a + b$ is divided by 6.

(g) $\{1, 3, 5, 7, 9\}$, where $a \circ b$ is the remainder after ab is divided by 10.

(h) Rational numbers of the form $\dfrac{m}{2^n}$, where $m, n \in \mathbb{Z}$, under addition.

(i) Rational numbers of the form $\dfrac{m}{2^n}$, where $m, n \in \mathbb{Z}$, under multiplication.

(j) Numbers of the form 2^n, $n \in \mathbb{Z}$, under multiplication.

(k) Matrices of the form $\begin{pmatrix} a & -b \\ b & a \end{pmatrix}$, where $a, b \in \mathbb{R}$, $a^2 + b^2 \neq 0$ under matrix multiplication.

(l) Even integers under addition.

2 Show that this table is not a group table.

	e	a	b	c
e	e	a	c	b
a	a	c	b	e
b	c	b	e	a
c	b	e	a	c

3 Let the following functions be defined for the domain $x \in \mathbb{R} - \{0, 1\}$.

$$\text{i} : x \mapsto x \qquad \text{p} : x \mapsto 1 - x \qquad \text{q} : x \mapsto \frac{1}{x} \qquad \text{r} : x \mapsto \frac{1}{1 - x}$$

Show that these functions, together with two more functions which you should find, form a group under composition of functions.

4 Prove that in a finite group table, each element appears just once in every column.

5 Prove that $(\mathbb{Z} - \{0\}, \times)$ is not a group.

6 Prove that the set of nth roots of unity (see Section 6.2) forms a group under multiplication.

7 Show that functions of the form $f(x) = ax + b$, where $a, b \in \mathbb{R}$ and $a \neq 0$, form a group under the operation of composition of functions. What is the inverse of $x \mapsto ax + b$?

8 Let $(G, \circ)$ be a group in which $a^4 = e$, $b^2 = e$ and $a \circ b = b \circ a^3$. Show that $b \circ a = a^3 \circ b$, $b \circ (a^2 \circ b) = a^2$, and simplify the product $(a \circ b) \circ (a^2 \circ b)$.

9* Consider the set of number pairs (a, b) where $a, b \in \mathbb{R}$ and a and b are not both zero. The rule for combining the number pairs is $(a, b) \circ (c, d) = (ad + bc, bd - ac)$. Show that this set with this operation is a group.

10* Let $(G, \circ)$ and $(H, \bullet)$ be groups, and consider the set (g, h) where $g \in G$ and $h \in H$. Let a binary operation $\times$ be defined by $(g_1, h_1) \times (g_2, h_2) = (g_1 \circ g_2, h_1 \bullet h_2)$. Show that this set with this operation is a group.

9.7   Modular arithmetic and addition

Modular arithmetic is a kind of 'arithmetic with remainders'. When you divide a natural number by n, the remainder is one of the numbers $0, 1, 2, \ldots, n - 1$. So consider the set $\mathbb{Z}_n = \{0, 1, 2, \ldots, n - 1\}$ with the following rule for combining the elements:

$a \oplus b$ is the remainder when $a + b$ is divided by n.

1   Closure: As the remainder after division by n belongs to $\mathbb{Z}_n$, the operation is closed.

2 Associativity: Suppose that $a + b = nr + x$, where $x \in \mathbb{Z}_n$, and $x + c = ns + y$, where $y \in \mathbb{Z}_n$. Then $x = a \oplus b$, and $y = x \oplus c = (a \oplus b) \oplus c$.

Now $(a + b) + c = (nr + x) + c = nr + (x + c) = nr + (ns + y) = (nr + ns) + y$
$$= n(r + s) + y,$$

so $y = (a \oplus b) \oplus c$ is the remainder when $(a + b) + c$ is divided by n.

Similarly, $a \oplus (b \oplus c)$ is the remainder when $a + (b + c)$ is divided by n.

But $(a + b) + c = a + (b + c)$, so $(a \oplus b) \oplus c = a \oplus (b \oplus c)$.

3 Identity: The number 0 acts as the identity since $a \oplus 0 = 0 \oplus a = a$ for all $a \in \mathbb{Z}_n$.

4 Inverse: If $a = 0$, consider 0. Then $0 \oplus 0 = 0$, so 0 is the inverse of 0.
Now consider $a \neq 0$, where $a \in \mathbb{Z}_n$. Consider $n - a$. As $n > n - a > 0, n - a \in \mathbb{Z}_n$; and $(n - a) \oplus a = ((n - a) + a) - n = 0$ and $a \oplus (n - a) = (a + (n - a)) - n = 0$. Therefore $n - a$ is the inverse of a.

Therefore $\mathbb{Z}_n$ with this rule is a group. The group is called $(\mathbb{Z}_n, +)$, the group of **integers modulo n (mod n) under addition**, and the operation is sometimes written as $+ \, (\text{mod } n)$.

Notice that, now that the basic properties of modular arithmetic have been established, there is no need to go on using the 'ringed' addition sign. You can use the ordinary addition sign without ambiguity.

> The word 'modulo' has nothing to do with the word 'modulus'.

Table 9.4 is a group table for $(\mathbb{Z}_4, +)$

+	0	1	2	3
0	0	1	2	3
1	1	2	3	0
2	2	3	0	1
3	3	0	1	2

Table 9.4

9.8 Modular arithmetic and multiplication

You can also do modular arithmetic with multiplication, making the definition

$a \otimes b$ is the remainder when ab is divided by n.

However, there are two important differences between multiplication and addition.

- The number 0 has the property that $0 \times a = a \times 0 = 0$ for all $a \in \mathbb{Z}_n$. It follows that $(\mathbb{Z}_n, \otimes)$ cannot be a group, since 0 does not have an inverse. So it is best to consider $\mathbb{Z}_n - \{0\}$, that is the set $\{1, 2, \ldots, n - 1\}$.

- If n is not prime, then $(\mathbb{Z}_n - \{0\}, \otimes)$ is not closed. For example, in $\mathbb{Z}_6$, $2 \otimes 3 = 0$ which is not in $\mathbb{Z}_6 - \{0\}$. So you can only get a group if n is a prime number.

So consider the set $\mathbb{Z}_p - \{0\} = \{1, 2, \ldots, p-1\}$, where p is a prime number.

1   Closure: Since the remainder after division by p belongs to $\mathbb{Z}_p - \{0\}$, the operation is closed. Note that the remainder cannot be 0 because that would mean that $ab = xp$ and as the right side is divisible by p, the left side is also divisible by p. But $0 < a, b \leqslant p-1$ so this is impossible.

2   Associativity: Suppose that $ab = pr + x$, where $x \in \mathbb{Z}_p - \{0\}$, and $xc = ps + y$ where $y \in \mathbb{Z}_p - \{0\}$. Then $x = a \otimes b$, and $y = x \otimes c = (a \otimes b) \otimes c$.

Now

$$
\begin{aligned}
(ab)c &= (pr + x)c \\
&= (pr)c + (xc) \\
&= p(rc) + (ps + y) \\
&= (p(rc) + ps) + y \\
&= p(rc + s) + y,
\end{aligned}
$$

so $y = (a \otimes b) \otimes c$ is the remainder when $(ab)c$ is divided by p.

Similarly, $a \otimes (b \otimes c)$ is the remainder when $a(bc)$ is divided by p.

But $(ab)c = a(bc)$, so $(a \otimes b) \otimes c = a \otimes (b \otimes c)$.

3   Identity: The number 1 acts as the identity since $a \otimes 1 = 1 \otimes a = a$ for all $a \in \mathbb{Z}_p - \{0\}$.

4   Inverse: For $a \in \mathbb{Z}_n$, consider the elements $\{1 \otimes a, 2 \otimes a, \ldots, (p-1) \otimes a\}$. These elements are all different, since if two of them, say $r \otimes a$ and $s \otimes a$, are equal, then $r \otimes a$ and $s \otimes a$ have the same remainder on division by p. Suppose that $ra = kp + x$ and $sa = lp + x$ where k and l are integers and $x \in \mathbb{Z}_p - \{0\}$. Then

$$
\begin{aligned}
ra - kp &= sa - lp, \\
\text{so}\quad ra - sa &= lp - kp,
\end{aligned}
$$

that is,

$$
(r - s)\,a = (l - k)\,p.
$$

Now p divides the right side; so p divides the left side, and must divide either a or $r - s$.

But $a \in \mathbb{Z}_p - \{0\}$, so p does not divide a; and $-(p-1) \leqslant r - s \leqslant p-1$, so the only possibility is that $r - s = 0$, or $r = s$.

So no two of the set $\{1 \otimes a, 2 \otimes a, \ldots, (p-1) \otimes a\}$ are equal.

As they are all different, and there are $p-1$ of them, one of them must be 1.

Suppose that $b \otimes a = 1$.

Then $a \otimes b = 1$, from the definition of $\otimes$, so b is the inverse of a.

The proof that the inverse exists is interesting because it does not actually produce the inverse of each element. It only shows that each element must have an inverse.

So $\mathbb{Z}_p - \{0\}$ with this rule is a group which is called $(\mathbb{Z}_p - \{0\}, \times)$, the group of **non-zero integers modulo p (mod p) under multiplication**. In order to distinguish this operation from ordinary multiplication, it is sometimes written as $\times \pmod{n}$.

Notice that, as for addition, the multiplication sign rather than the 'ringed' multiplication sign is used. Table 9.5 shows $(\mathbb{Z}_5 - \{0\}, \times)$.

$\times$	1	2	3	4
1	1	2	3	4
2	2	4	1	3
3	3	1	4	2
4	4	3	2	1

Table 9.5

From Table 9.5, the inverse of 3 is 2, and vice versa. But if you had to find the inverse of 7 in $(\mathbb{Z}_{59} - \{0\}, \times)$, it would not be so easy.

Example 9.8.1
Find the inverse of 5 in $(\mathbb{Z}_{11} - \{0\}, \times)$.

$2 \times 5 = 10, \ 3 \times 5 = 4, \ 4 \times 5 = 9, \ 5 \times 5 = 3, \ 6 \times 5 = 8, \ 7 \times 5 = 2, \ 8 \times 5 = 7, \ 9 \times 5 = 1.$

Therefore the inverse of 5 is 9.

You can often use brute force in this way to find inverses in small groups.

Note that in Example 9.8.1, if you want inverses of other elements, things get progressively easier. You now know that the inverse of 5 is 9, so the inverse of 9 is 5. But since $3 = 5 \times 5$,

$$3^{-1} = (5 \times 5)^{-1} = 5^{-1} \times 5^{-1} = 9 \times 9 = 4,$$

so $4^{-1} = 3$.

If you want 2^{-1}, you need now try only 2, 6, 7, 8 and 10. Once you spot $2^{-1} = 6$, you can deduce from $6 \times 5 = 8$ that

$$8^{-1} = (6 \times 5)^{-1} = 5^{-1} \times 6^{-1} = 9 \times 2 = 7.$$

This leaves 10 as its own inverse.

Example 9.8.2

Construct a combination table for the numbers 1, 5, 7, 11, 13, 17 when combined under the operation $\times$ (mod 18). Show that these numbers with this operation form a group, and write down the inverse of each element.

The combination table is shown in Table 9.6.

$\times$ (mod 18)	1	5	7	11	13	17
1	1	5	7	11	13	17
5	5	7	17	1	11	13
7	7	17	13	5	1	11
11	11	1	5	13	17	7
13	13	11	1	17	7	5
17	17	13	11	7	5	1

Table 9.6

The numbers form a group, because:

- the table shows that the operation is a closed binary operation;
- the operation is associative, because ordinary multiplication is associative;
- the identity is 1;
- each element has an inverse. The inverses of 1, 5, 7, 11, 13 and 17 are respectively, 1, 11, 13, 5, 7 and 17.

It is true, but won't be proved here, that the integers which are less than n and have no factors in common with n form a group under the operation $\times$ (mod n).

Exercise 9D

1 Write out the group table for $(\mathbb{Z}_5, +)$, and write down the inverse of 2. Solve the equations $x + 2 = 1$ and $4 + y = 2$.

2 Write out a group table for $(\mathbb{Z}_7 - \{0\}, \times)$. Write down the inverses of 3 and 4.

3 Write out a table of operations for $(Z_6 - \{0\}, \times)$. Give one reason why $(\mathbb{Z}_6 - \{0\}, \times)$ is not a group. Give a reason why $(\mathbb{Z}_q - \{0\}, \times)$ is not a group if q is not prime.

4 Construct a combination table for the integers $\{1, 2, 4, 7, 8, 11, 13, 14\}$ under the operation $\times$ (mod 15). Use your table to solve the equation $13x = 8$ (mod 15).

5 Solve the equation $13x = 17$ using the operation $\times$ (mod 20).

6 Calculate 7×9 and 4×15 in $(\mathbb{Z}_{59} - \{0\}, \times)$. Use your answers to find the inverses of

(a) 4,   (b) 7,   (c) 28,   (d) 49.

7 Construct a combination table for the numbers $\{0, 1, 2, 3, 4\}$ under the operation $\oplus$ where $a \oplus b = (a + b + 2) \pmod 5$, and verify that it is a group table. Write down the identity element and the inverse of each element.

9.9 A group of symmetries

Let **E** be the equilateral triangle ABC shown in Fig. 9.7, and let the lines x, y and z and the points 1, 2 and 3 be fixed in the plane.

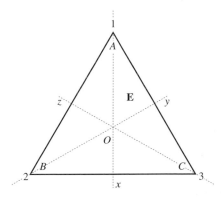

Fig. 9.7

Define the following transformations of the plane containing **E**.

- X is 'reflect in the line x'.
- Y is 'reflect in the line y'.
- Z is 'reflect in the line z'.
- R is 'rotate by $\frac{2}{3}\pi$ anticlockwise about O'.
- S is 'rotate by $\frac{4}{3}\pi$ anticlockwise about O'
- I is 'do nothing'.

Each of these transformations of the plane leaves the triangle where it is now, although it may change the positions of the vertices which make up the triangle **E**. This kind of transformation is called a **symmetry** of **E**.

You can describe the transformation X by writing

$$\begin{pmatrix} 1 & 2 & 3 \\ A & B & C \end{pmatrix} \xrightarrow{X} \begin{pmatrix} 1 & 2 & 3 \\ A & C & B \end{pmatrix}$$

where the notation in the first bracket shows that A started in position 1, B in position 2 and C in position 3, and after the transformation by X, A is still in position 1, B is now in position 3 and C is in position 2.

To combine operations use the rule 'followed by', that is the rule for combining functions (C3 Section 2.4).

The transformation RX (X followed by R) is

$$\begin{pmatrix} 1 & 2 & 3 \\ A & B & C \end{pmatrix} \xrightarrow{X} \begin{pmatrix} 1 & 2 & 3 \\ A & C & B \end{pmatrix} \xrightarrow{R} \begin{pmatrix} 1 & 2 & 3 \\ B & A & C \end{pmatrix}$$

which is the same as transformation Z. Thus $RX = Z$. Similarly $SR = I$.

You can make up Table 9.8, which shows how each of the transformations I, R, S, X, Y and Z combines with the others, using the rule 'followed by'. The result is always one of I, R, S, X, Y and Z, so 'followed by' is a binary operation on the set $\{I, R, S, X, Y, Z\}$.

In Table 9.8, the result $RX = Z$ is shown by going along the row containing R and down the column containing X.

		First operation performed					
		I	R	S	X	Y	Z
	I	I	R	S	X	Y	Z
Second	R	R	S	I	Z	X	Y
operation	S	S	I	R	Y	Z	X
performed	X	X	Y	Z	I	R	S
	Y	Y	Z	X	S	I	R
	Z	Z	X	Y	R	S	I

Table 9.8

As 'followed by' is the rule of combination of functions, it is associative.

The transformation I is the identity element.

Each element has an inverse. The inverses of I, R, S, X, Y and Z are respectively I, S, R, X, Y and Z.

So the set $\{I, R, S, X, Y, Z\}$ and the operation 'followed by' is a group. It is called the **dihedral group of the triangle** and is given the symbol D_3. Similar groups are defined for all regular polygons: the symbol for the dihedral group of the n-sided polygon is D_n.

The word 'dihedral' means having or being contained by two plane faces.

Exercise 9E

1 Write out the group table for the symmetries of a non-square rectangle.

2 In the group D_3 in Table 9.8 find the elements R^{-1} and X^{-1}. Calculate the products RAR^{-1} and XAX^{-1} when $A = I, R, S, X, Y$ and Z in turn.

   Solve for A the equation $RAX = Y$.

3 Write out the group table for D_4, the dihedral group of the square. (Keep this group table for use with future exercises.)

(Let R be an anticlockwise quarter-turn about the origin, and use the notation R^2 and R^3 for the other rotations. Let H and V be reflections in the x- and y-axes, and L and M be reflections in the lines $y = -x$ and $y = x$. Put the operations in the order, $I, R, R^2, R^3, H, L, V, M$. Your table should then match the one given in the answers.)

4 In D_4, see Question 3, solve for A the equation $RAV = H$.

Miscellaneous exercise 9

1 Write out a group table in which the only elements are e, a, b.

2 Let $(G, \circ)$ be a group with eight elements $\{e, a, a^2, a^3, b, a \circ b, a^2 \circ b, a^3 \circ b\}$ in which $a^4 = e$, $b^2 = a^2$ and $a^3 \circ b = b \circ a$. Show that $(a \circ b)^2 = a^2$, $(a^3 \circ b) \circ (a \circ b) = e$. Write out the group table for $(G, \circ)$.

3 The set S consists of the eight elements $9^1, 9^2, \ldots, 9^8$ where the operation is multiplication modulo 64. Determine each of the elements of S as an integer between 0 and 63.

Under multiplication modulo 64, the set S forms a group G with identity 1. Write down the inverses of each of the remaining elements of G.

A group in which each element x can be written as a power of a particular element g of the group is said to be a cyclic group; and such an element g is called a generator of the group. Write down all the possible generators of G.

4 Construct the composition table for $(S, \circ)$, where the binary operation $\circ$ is defined on the set $S = \{0, 1, 2, 3, 4, 5, 6\}$ by $x \circ y = x + y - xy$ modulo 7.

One of the elements of S is removed to form a set S' of order 6, such that $(S', \circ)$ forms a group. State which element is to be deleted, and prove that $(S', \circ)$ is a group.

5 Show that the Latin square below is not a group table.

	e	a	b	c	d
e	e	a	b	c	d
a	a	b	c	d	e
b	b	e	d	a	c
c	c	d	e	b	a
d	d	c	a	e	b

6 The binary operation $*$ is defined on the set $\mathbb{R}$ of all real numbers by

$$x * y = x + y + 1 \qquad \text{for all } x, y \text{ in } \mathbb{R},$$

where $+$ denotes the usual addition of real numbers. Show that $\mathbb{R}$ is a group under $*$.

(OCR)

7 Try constructing a table for a group of order 4 in which the elements are called e, a, b and c and are written in that order along the top row. Show that there are five such tables.

8 A binary operation * is defined on the set $\mathbb{Q} - \{0\}$ of non-zero rational numbers as follows:

$$x*y = xy \quad \text{if } x > 0,$$
$$x*y = \frac{x}{y} \quad \text{if } x < 0.$$

Prove that $(\mathbb{Q} - \{0\}, *)$ is a non-commutative group.   (OCR)

9 The operation * is defined on the set $S = \{x \in \mathbb{R} : x \neq \pm 1\}$ by $a*b = \dfrac{a+b}{1+ab}$ for a, $b \in S$.

(a) Determine the identity element of S under *.

(b) For each $a \in S$, describe the inverse element a^{-1} of a.

(c) Prove that * is associative on S.

(d) Prove that S, under the operation *, does not form a group.   (OCR)

10 Subgroups

This chapter extends the study of groups by investigating groups within other groups. When you have completed it, you should know

- what is meant by the order of an element
- what is meant by a cyclic group, and how to show that a group is, or is not, cyclic
- what a subgroup is, and how to test for a subgroup
- that the order of a subgroup divides the order of the group
- that the order of an element divides the order of the group
- that all groups of prime order are cyclic.

10.1 Notation

It can be tedious to use the notation $(G, \circ)$ for a group, and it is quite usual to leave out the symbol for the operation and to use multiplicative notation. From now on, provided there is no ambiguity, the symbol G will be used for a group and ab will be used instead of $a \circ b$.

However, in some groups, such as $\mathbb{Z}$, the operation is addition, and then it is usual to retain the $+$ sign. It is a convention that, whenever additive notation is used, the group is commutative. If multiplicative notation is used, the group may be either commutative or not commutative.

Here is an example of a proof in the new notation.

Example 10.1.1
Let G be a group in which every element is its own inverse. Prove that G is commutative.

> Let $a, b \in G$. Then $ab \in G$. As $ab \in G$, it is its own inverse so $(ab)^{-1} = ab$. Therefore $b^{-1} a^{-1} = ab$, and as $a^{-1} = a$ and $b^{-1} = b$, $ba = ab$. So G is commutative.

10.2 Powers of elements

In Example 10.6.3, you saw that when you multiply an element a of a group G by itself, you obtain aa, which is written as a^2. This leads to the following definition.

> Let a be an element of a group G. If n is a positive integer, then
>
> $$a^n = \overbrace{aa\ldots a}^{n \text{ times}} \qquad \text{and} \qquad a^{-n} = \overbrace{a^{-1}a^{-1}\ldots a^{-1}}^{n \text{ times}}.$$
>
> The power a^0 is defined to be e.

Many of the usual index rules are satisfied for all integers $m, n \in \mathbb{Z}$, but they require proof. Here are two examples of such proofs. If you wish, you may omit them, and assume the results of the next blue box.

Example 10.2.1

Show that $a^m a^n = a^{m+n}$ when m is a positive integer and n is a negative integer.

Let $n = -N$, so that N is positive. Then $a^m a^{-N} = \overbrace{aa \ldots a}^{m\ \text{times}}\, \overbrace{a^{-1} a^{-1} \ldots a^{-1}}^{N\ \text{times}}$.

Case 1 Suppose that $m > N$. Then

$$a^m a^{-N} = \overbrace{aa \ldots a}^{m\ \text{times}}\, \overbrace{a^{-1}\, a^{-1} \ldots a^{-1}}^{N\ \text{times}} = \overbrace{aa \ldots a}^{(m-N)\ \text{times}} = \overbrace{aa \ldots a}^{(m+n)\ \text{times}} = a^{m+n}.$$

Case 2 Suppose that $m = N$. Then

$$a^m a^{-N} = \overbrace{aa \ldots a}^{m\ \text{times}}\, \overbrace{a^{-1} a^{-1} \ldots a^{-1}}^{m\ \text{times}} = e = a^0 = a^{m-N} = a^{m+n}.$$

Case 3 Suppose that $m < N$. Then

$$a^m a^{-N} = \overbrace{aa \ldots a}^{m\ \text{times}}\, \overbrace{a^{-1} a^{-1} \ldots a^{-1}}^{N\ \text{times}} = \overbrace{a^{-1} a^{-1} \ldots a^{-1}}^{(N-m)\ \text{times}} = a^{-(N-m)} = a^{m-N} = a^{m+n}.$$

Therefore, in all cases, $a^m a^n = a^{m+n}$ when m is a positive integer and n is a negative integer.

Example 10.2.2

Show that $a^{-m} = (a^m)^{-1} = (a^{-1})^m$ when m is a positive integer.

From Case 2 above, $a^m a^{-m} = e$, so a^{-m} is the inverse of a^m, that is $a^{-m} = (a^m)^{-1}$.

By definition, $\overbrace{a^{-1} a^{-1} \ldots a^{-1}}^{m\ \text{times}} = a^{-m}$; but $\overbrace{a^{-1} a^{-1} \ldots a^{-1}}^{m\ \text{times}} = (a^{-1})^m$. So $a^{-m} = (a^{-1})^m$.

Therefore $a^{-m} = (a^m)^{-1} = (a^{-1})^m$ when m is a positive integer.

There are a number of possible results like this. They are summarised by:

In a group G, $a^m a^n = a^{m+n}$, $(a^m)^n = a^{mn}$, $a^{-m} = (a^m)^{-1} = (a^{-1})^m$,
where m and $n \in \mathbb{Z}$.

In general $(ab)^m \neq a^m b^m$, unless the group G is commutative.

It is clear that in a finite group the powers of an element cannot all be different from each other. For example, in $(\mathbb{Z}_7 - \{0\}, \times)$,

$$2^2 = 4, \quad 2^3 = 2 \times 4 = 1, \quad 2^4 = 2 \times 1 = 2, \quad \text{and so on.}$$

In D_3 (which you met in Section 9.9), $R^2 = S$, $R^3 = RS = I$, $R^4 = R$,   and so on.

Theorem   Let a be an element of a finite group G. Then the powers of a cannot all be different, and there is a smallest positive integer k such that $a^k = e$.

Proof   Consider the set of all possible powers of a. There are infinitely many of them, and all of them are elements of G. Since G is finite they cannot all be different. Let r and s be two positive integers, with $r < s$, such that $a^r = a^s$. Then

$$a^{s-r} = a^s a^{-r} = a^r a^{-r} = e.$$

Therefore there is at least one positive power, $s - r$, of a which gives the identity element. Let k be the smallest of these powers, so that $a^k = e$.

There is always a smallest power. See FP1 Example 6.3.5.

Let a be an element of a group G. Then a is said to have **finite order** if $a^n = e$ for some positive integer n. The least such n is called the **order** of a.

If no such n exists, the element a has **infinite order**.

'Order' is used quite differently here from its use in the context of 'order of a group'. Some books use the word 'period' instead of 'order' in this context.

Note that, from the definition, in any group the order of the identity e is 1.

Example 10.2.3
Find the orders of the elements of
(a) $(\mathbb{Z}_7 - \{0\}, \times)$,　　(b) D_3.

(a)　The orders of the elements of $(\mathbb{Z}_7 - \{0\}, \times)$ can be worked out systematically:

The element 1 has order 1.

As $2^1 = 2$,　$2^2 = 4$,　$2^3 = 1$, the order of 2 is 3.

As $3^1 = 3$,　$3^2 = 2$,　$3^3 = 6$,　$3^4 = 4$,　$3^5 = 5$,　$3^6 = 1$, the order of 3 is 6.

As $4^1 = 4$,　$4^2 = 2$,　$4^3 = 1$, the order of 4 is 3.

As $5^1 = 5$,　$5^2 = 4$,　$5^3 = 6$,　$5^4 = 2$,　$5^5 = 3$,　$5^6 = 1$, the order of 5 is 6.

As $6^1 = 6$,　$6^2 = 1$, the order of 6 is 2.

(b)　Using Table 9.8, reproduced here as Table 10.1, the orders of I, X, Y and Z are respectively 1, 2, 2 and 2. Since $R^2 = S$ and $R^3 = RS = I$, the order of R is 3. Finally $S^2 = R$ and $S^3 = SR = I$, so the order of S is 3.

		First operation performed					
		I	R	S	X	Y	Z
	I	I	R	S	X	Y	Z
Second	R	R	S	I	Z	X	Y
operation	S	S	I	R	Y	Z	X
performed	X	X	Y	Z	I	R	S
	Y	Y	Z	X	S	I	R
	Z	Z	X	Y	R	S	I

Table 10.1

Example 10.2.4

In $(\mathbb{R} - \{0\}, \times)$, give an element of

(a) finite order greater than 1,   (b) infinite order.

(a) As an element a of finite order has to satisfy the equation $a^n = 1$ and belong to $\mathbb{R} - \{0\}$, the only possibilities are 1 and -1. Since 1 has order 1 and -1 has order 2, the only example is -1.

(b) The element 2 has infinite order since $2^n \neq 1$ for any positive integer n.

10.3 Cyclic groups

If G is a group, it is sometimes the case that G consists entirely of the powers of a single element. In this case the group is said to be **generated** by this element.

An example of a finite group of this type is the group of symmetries of an object such as the Manx symbol in Fig. 10.2.

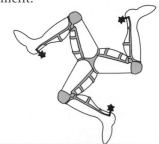

This group consists of the set $\{I, R, R^2\}$, where R is a rotation of $\frac{2}{3}\pi$, together with the operation 'followed by'. Note that R^2, which is equivalent to a rotation of $-\frac{2}{3}\pi$, is also a generator.

Groups like this are called **cyclic groups**. In the definition of a cyclic group which follows, recall that from the definition of the powers of an element a, $a^0 = e$.

Fig. 10.2

> Let G be a group. If there is an element $a \in G$ such that every element of G has the form a^n for $n \in \mathbb{Z}$, then G is called a **cyclic** group. The element a is called a **generator** for G. The notation $G = \langle a \rangle$ is used to show that G is generated by a.

If you can find an element of a group whose order is equal to the order of the group, then it follows that the group is cyclic. One way of showing that a group is not cyclic is to find the order of each element and show that none of them is the order of a group. But there may be simpler ways of showing that a group is not cyclic; for example, if a group is not commutative, it can't be cyclic, because all cyclic groups are commutative. (See Exercise 10B Question 6.)

Example 10.3.1

Show that the groups $(\mathbb{Z}_7, +)$ and $(\mathbb{Z}_7 - \{0\}, \times)$ are cyclic groups.

> To show that $(\mathbb{Z}_7, +)$ is cyclic, you need to interpret the multiplicative notation of the definition of cyclic groups so that you can apply it to a group which uses additive notation.

In $(\mathbb{Z}_7, +)$, 1 is a generator because $1 + 1 = 2$, $1 + 1 + 1 = 3$, $1 + 1 + 1 + 1 = 4$, $1 + 1 + 1 + 1 + 1 = 5$, $1 + 1 + 1 + 1 + 1 + 1 = 6$ and $1 + 1 + 1 + 1 + 1 + 1 + 1 = 0$.

In $(\mathbb{Z}_7 - \{0\}, \times)$, 3 is a generator. See Example 10.2.3(a).

Example 10.3.2
Show that $(\mathbb{Z}, +)$ is a cyclic group.

> If an element a is a generator, the group consists of the set of elements
> $\{\ldots, a^{-3}, a^{-2}, a^{-1}, e, a, a^2, a^3, \ldots\}$.

When $a = 1$, $a^2 = 1 + 1 = 2$, $a^3 = 1 + 1 + 1 = 3$ etc., and $a^{-1} = -1$, $a^{-2} = (-1) + (-1) = -2$ etc.

Therefore 1 is a generator for $(\mathbb{Z}, +)$, and so $(\mathbb{Z}, +)$ is a cyclic group.

> Note that -1 is also a generator for $(\mathbb{Z}, +)$.

Example 10.3.3
Show that the group $(\mathbb{Q}^+, \times)$ is not a cyclic group.

> Notice first that 1 is not a generator, since all its powers are 1, and that -1 is not a generator since all its powers are 1 or -1.
>
> Suppose now that x is a generator, where $x \neq 1$ or -1. Then $x^n = -1$ for some value of n, so $|x^n| = |-1| = 1$, giving $|x|^n = 1$. But $x \neq 1$ or -1, so this is a contradiction. So $(\mathbb{Q}^+, \times)$ is not a cyclic group.

Exercise 10A

1 Find the powers of 5 in the group G consisting of the elements 1, 2, 4, 5, 7, 8 where $a \circ b$ is the remainder when ab is divided by 9. How many distinct powers of 5 are there?

2 Find the orders of the elements in the groups
   (a) $(\mathbb{Z}_6, +)$,   (b) $(\mathbb{Z}_{11} - \{0\}, \times)$,   (c) D_4. (See Exercise 9E Question 3.)

   Keep your answer to part (c) for Exercise 10B Question 1.

3 Find all the elements of order 2 in the group of symmetries of a non-square rectangle. (See Exercise 9E Question 1.)

4 Find all the elements of order 4 in the group $(\mathbb{C} - \{0\}, \times)$. How many elements of $(\mathbb{C} - \{0\}, \times)$ have order 3?

5 In $(\mathbb{Q} - \{0\}, \times)$, write down all the elements of finite order.

6 Given that the set of non-singular matrices with the operation of matrix multiplication forms a group, show the number of elements of order 2 is infinite.

7 Is the group in Question 1 a cyclic group? Give a reason for your answer.

8 The set $2\mathbb{Z}$ is the set of even integers. Prove that $(2\mathbb{Z}, +)$ is a cyclic group. (You may assume that $(2\mathbb{Z}, +)$ is a group.)

9 The tables below show two groups: one is cyclic and one is not. Identify which is which, find all the generators of the cyclic group, and prove that the other group is not cyclic.

	e	a	b	c
e	e	a	b	c
a	a	e	c	b
b	b	c	e	a
c	c	b	a	e

	e	a	b	c
e	e	a	b	c
a	a	b	c	e
b	b	c	e	a
c	c	e	a	b

10 Prove that the groups $(\mathbb{Z}_5, +)$ and $(\mathbb{Z}_6, +)$ are cyclic, and find all their generators.

10.4 Subgroups

Look again at Table 9.8 for the group D_3, reprinted as Table 10.3 with the title D_3 in the top left corner. Part of the table is shaded; as $S = R^2$, this is the group $\{I, R, R^2\}$ of Fig. 10.2.

D_3	I	R	S	X	Y	Z
I	I	R	S	X	Y	Z
R	R	S	I	Z	X	Y
S	S	I	R	Y	Z	X
X	X	Y	Z	I	R	S
Y	Y	Z	X	S	I	R
Z	Z	X	Y	R	S	I

Table 10.3

The set $\{I, R, S\}$ with the operation 'followed by' is a smaller group inside the whole group; this is called a **subgroup** of D_3.

If you re-draw the table with the elements in the order $\{I, X, R, S, Y, Z\}$ you would find that there is also a small group $\{I, X\}$ in the top left corner. So $\{I, X\}$ is another subgroup of D_3. So too are $\{I, Y\}$ and $\{I, Z\}$.

In addition to these subgroups of D_3, the identity group $\{I\}$, and the whole group $\{I, R, S, X, Y, Z\}$ are also regarded as subgroups of D_3. The subgroups $\{I\}$ and D_3 are called trivial subgroups of D_3. The remaining subgroups are called proper subgroups of D_3.

> If H is a subset of a group G with operation $\circ$, such that H is a group with operation $\circ$, then H is a **subgroup** of G.
>
> Every group G has two **trivial** subgroups, $\{e\}$ and G itself.
>
> Subgroups of G other than $\{e\}$ and G are called **proper** subgroups.

Example 10.4.1

Explain why $(\mathbb{Q} - \{0\}, \times)$ is not a subgroup of $(\mathbb{Q}, +)$.

Although $\mathbb{Q} - \{0\}$ is a subset of $\mathbb{Q}$, the operations in the two groups are different, so $(\mathbb{Q} - \{0\}, \times)$ is not a subgroup of $(\mathbb{Q}, +)$.

Example 10.4.2

Find all the subgroups of $(\mathbb{Z}_6, +)$, saying which are proper subgroups.

The subgroups are $\{0\}$, $\{0, 3\}$, $\{0, 2, 4, 6\}$ and $\mathbb{Z}_6$ itself. Of these the proper subgroups are $\{0, 3\}$ and $\{0, 2, 4, 6\}$ with the operation of addition modulo 6.

Example 10.4.3

Find a finite proper subgroup and an infinite proper subgroup of $(\mathbb{C} - \{0\}, \times)$.

A finite proper subgroup is $\{1, -1\}$. An infinite proper subgroup is $\{\mathbb{R} - \{0\}, \times\}$.

Theorem   Let G be a group, and let H be a subset of G. Then H is a subgroup of G if

- $a \in H$ and $b \in H$ $\Rightarrow$ $ab \in H$
- $e \in H$

and

- $a \in H$ $\Rightarrow$ $a^{-1} \in H$.

Proof   If $a \in H$ and $b \in H \Rightarrow ab \in H$, then the operation of G is closed in H.

Suppose that $a, b, c \in H$. Then, since H is a subset of G, a, b, $c \in G$. But the group operation in G is associative, so $(ab)c = a(bc)$. Therefore the operation is associative in H.

Since $ea = ae = a$ for each $a \in G$, it is true for each $a \in H$.

For $a \in H$, and hence $a^{-1} \in H$, $a^{-1}a = aa^{-1} = e$ because a^{-1} is the inverse of a in G.

Therefore H is a subgroup of G.

Example 10.4.4

Verify that $(\mathbb{Z}_0^+, +)$, which satisfies the first two conditions of the theorem but not the third, is not a subgroup of $(\mathbb{Z}, +)$.

Since $-1 \notin \mathbb{Z}_0^+$, the element 1 in $\mathbb{Z}_0^+$ has no inverse, so $(\mathbb{Z}_0^+, +)$ is not a group and therefore is not a subgroup of $(\mathbb{Z}, +)$.

Example 10.4.5

Prove that $H = \{12x + 21y : x, y \in \mathbb{Z}\}$ is a subgroup of $(\mathbb{Z}, +)$.

As x and y are integers, $12x + 21y$ is an integer, so H is a subset of $\mathbb{Z}$.

If $p, q \in H$, then $p = 12x_1 + 21y_1$ and $q = 12x_2 + 21y_2$ for integers x_1, y_1, x_2 and y_2. So $p + q = (12x_1 + 21y_1) + (12x_2 + 21y_2) = 12(x_1 + x_2) + 21(y_1 + y_2)$ where $x_1 + x_2$ and $y_1 + y_2$ are integers. Therefore $p + q \in H$.

Since $0 = 12 \times 0 + 21 \times 0$, and 0 is an integer, $0 \in H$.

If $p = 12x_1 + 21y_1 \in H$, then $-p = -(12x_1 + 21y_1) = 12(-x_1) + 21(-y_1)$. As $-x_1$ and $-y_1$ are integers, $12(-x_1) + 21(-y_1)$ is also an integer, so $-p \in H$. Also $(-p) + p = p + (-p) = 0$ so $-p$ is the inverse of p. Therefore the inverse of p is a member of H.

Therefore H is a subgroup of G.

What is the subgroup in Example 10.4.5? Notice first that any factor of both 12 and 21 divides $12x + 21y$, so the highest common factor of 12 and 21, namely 3, divides every member of H.

If you take $x = 2$ and $y = -1$, you find that $2 \times 12 + (-1) \times 21 = 3$ is a member of H, so H consists of all multiples of 3.

This argument can be generalised to show that for positive integers a and b, $H = \{ax + by : x, \, y \in \mathbb{Z}\}$ is a subgroup of $(\mathbb{Z}, +)$, and consists of multiples of the highest common factor of a and b.

Subgroups of a finite group

For a finite group G it is usually easy to check from a table whether a subset H is a subgroup. You need only check that the operation on the subset H is closed. For example, in Table 10.3, once you have seen that $\{I, R, S\}$ is closed, you do not need to check the other group properties. This is summarised in the following theorem.

Theorem   Let G be a group, and let H be a finite subset of G. Then H is a subgroup of G if $a \in H$ and $b \in H \Rightarrow ab \in H$.

The theorem earlier in this section proved that any subset H (not necessarily finite) of G which satisfies

- $a \in H$ and $b \in H$ $\Rightarrow$ $ab \in H$
- $e \in H$

and

- $a \in H$ $\Rightarrow$ $a^{-1} \in H$

is a subgroup. So what remains to be proved is that the first condition, which is given, together with the fact that the set H is finite is sufficient to prove the second and third conditions.

Proof   If, in the statement '$a \in H$ and $b \in H \Rightarrow ab \in H$', you put a, a^2, a^3, ... in turn instead of b, you find that $a^2 \in H$, $a^3 \in H$, $a^4 \in H$ for all positive powers of a. Using the theorem in Section 10.2, let the order of a be k, so $a^k = e$, and $e \in H$.

Now consider a^{k-1}. Since $a^{k-1} a = a^k = e$, a^{k-1} is the inverse of a. But $a^{k-1} \in H$, so $a^{-1} \in H$.

By the previous theorem, H is a subgroup of G.

10.5 The subgroup generated by an element

In D_3 the set of powers of R is $\{R, R^2 = S, R^3 = I\}$, that is $\{R, S, I\}$, and you saw in Section 10.4 that this is a subgroup of D_3.

Similarly, in $(\mathbb{Z}_7 - \{0\}, \times)$, the powers of 2 are $\{2, 2^2 = 4, 2^3 = 1\}$, that is $\{2, 4, 1\}$, which is a subgroup of $(\mathbb{Z}_7 - \{0\}, \times)$.

Also, in $(\mathbb{Q}, \times)$, the powers of 2, $\{\ldots, 2^{-s}, \ldots, 2^{-1}, 1, 2, \ldots, 2^r, \ldots\}$, form a subgroup.

In fact, the set of powers of an element is always a subgroup.

Theorem   Let a be an element of a group G. Then the set of all powers of a, $H = \{a^n : n \in \mathbb{Z}\}$ is a subgroup of G.

> **Proof**   If $p, q \in H$, then $p = a^r$ and $q = a^s$ for integers r and s. Then $pq = a^r a^s = a^{r+s}$, and since $r + s$ is an integer, $pq \in H$.
>
> Since 0 is an integer, $a^0 \in H$. And since $a^0 = e$ by definition, $e \in H$.
>
> If $p \in H$, then $p = a^r$ for an integer r. Therefore $-r$ is an integer, and so $a^{-r} \in H$. But $a^{-r} a^r = a^{r-r} = e$, so a^{-r} is the inverse of p, and belongs to H.
>
> Therefore $H = \{a^n : n \in \mathbb{Z}\}$ is a subgroup of G.

This proof applies to both finite and infinite groups.

The subgroup H of a group G defined by $H = \{a^n : n \in \mathbb{Z}\}$ is said to be the subgroup **generated** by a.

If an element a has infinite order, then the group generated by a is $\{\ldots, a^{-2}, a^{-1}, e, a, a^2, \ldots\}$, and is infinite.

If an element a has finite order n, then the group generated by a is $\{e, a, a^2, \ldots, a^{n-1}\}$. The order of the subgroup generated by a is then the same as the order of a.

Notice that the subgroup generated by an element is a cyclic subgroup, and that the order of the cyclic subgroup is the same as the order of the generating element.

Exercise 10B

1 (a) Find the orders of the elements of the group D_4 (see Exercise 10A Question 2(c)).

   (b) Find the cyclic subgroups of D_4.

   (c) Find two proper non-cyclic subgroups of D_4.

2 Find all the subgroups of (a) $(\mathbb{Z}_4, +)$ and (b) $(\mathbb{Z}_5, +)$.

3 Find a finite subgroup, apart from $\{1\}$, of the group $(\mathbb{R} - \{0\}, \times)$.

4 Prove that the set $(\{\ldots, -3n, -2n, -n, 0, n, 2n, 3n, \ldots\}, +)$, where $n \in \mathbb{N}$, is a cyclic group.

5 Show that the group of functions $\{x \mapsto ax, a \in \mathbb{R}, a \neq 0\}$ is a subgroup of the group $\{x \mapsto ax + b : a, b \in \mathbb{R}, a \neq 0\}$ under the operation of composition of functions.

6 Prove that if G is cyclic it is commutative.

7 Let G be a group, and let g be a fixed element of G. Prove that the set of elements which commute with g, that is $H = \{x \in G : gx = xg\}$ is a subgroup of G. Identify the subgroup H for the following groups and elements.

(a) G is D_3 and g is R. (b) G is D_3 and g is X.

(c) G is the set of 2×2 matrices under multiplication and g is $\begin{pmatrix} 1 & 1 \\ 0 & 1 \end{pmatrix}$.

(d) G is Q_4 (see Question 8) and g is q. (e) G is A_4 (see Question 9) and g is x.

8 Find all the subgroups of the quaternion group denoted by Q_4, shown in the table. Keep a note of their orders for the next section.

Q_4	e	a	b	c	p	q	r	s
e	e	a	b	c	p	q	r	s
a	a	b	c	e	s	p	q	r
b	b	c	e	a	r	s	p	q
c	c	e	a	b	q	r	s	p
p	p	q	r	s	b	c	e	a
q	q	r	s	p	a	b	c	e
r	r	s	p	q	e	a	b	c
s	s	p	q	r	c	e	a	b

9* The group A_4 of rotational symmetries of the regular tetrahedron has order 12 and is shown in the table below. Find all the subgroups, and make a note of their orders for the next section. Check that A_4 has no subgroup of order 6.

A_4	e	a	b	c	x	y	z	t	p	q	r	s
e	e	a	b	c	x	y	z	t	p	q	r	s
a	a	e	c	b	z	t	x	y	s	r	q	p
b	b	c	e	a	t	z	y	x	q	p	s	r
c	c	b	a	e	y	x	t	z	r	s	p	q
x	x	t	y	z	p	s	q	r	e	c	a	b
y	y	z	x	t	r	q	s	p	c	e	b	a
z	z	y	t	x	s	p	r	q	a	b	e	c
t	t	x	z	y	q	r	p	s	b	a	c	e
p	p	r	s	q	e	b	c	a	x	z	t	y
q	q	s	r	p	b	e	a	c	t	y	x	z
r	r	p	q	s	c	a	e	b	y	t	z	x
s	s	q	p	r	a	c	b	e	z	x	y	t

10.6   Lagrange's theorem

If you look back at some of the results of Exercise 10B in which you found subgroups of finite groups, and at the examples before Exercise 10B, you find that

- the subgroups of D_3, which has order 6, have orders 1, 2, 3 and 6;
- the subgroups of $(\mathbb{Z}_4, +)$, which has order 4, have orders 1, 2 and 4;
- the subgroups of $(\mathbb{Z}_5, +)$, which has order 5, have orders 1 and 5;
- the subgroups of D_4, which has order 8, have orders 1, 2, 4 and 8;
- the subgroups of Q_4, which has order 8, have orders 1, 2, 4 and 8;
- the subgroups of A_4, which has order 12, have orders 1, 2, 3, 4 and 12.

You have enough evidence to conjecture that, for finite groups, the order of a subgroup divides the order of the group. This result is called Lagrange's theorem, after Joseph-Louis Lagrange who lived from 1736 to 1813.

> **Lagrange's theorem**   The order of a subgroup of a finite group G divides the order of G.

Lagrange's theorem is proved in Section 10.7.

Lagrange's theorem has a number of immediate consequences, called **corollaries**.

Corollary 1   The order of an element of a finite group G divides the order of G.

The order of an element a is equal to the order of the subgroup generated by a. By Lagrange's theorem, the order of a divides the order of the group.

Corollary 2   A group of prime order has no proper subgroups.

If the order of a group G is a prime number, p, by Lagrange's theorem the only possible subgroups will have orders 1 and p. But these subgroups will be the trivial subgroups consisting of the identity only and the whole group. Therefore there are no proper subgroups.

Corollary 3   Every group G of prime order p is cyclic.

Consider an element $a \in G$ other than the identity. As the order of a divides p, and a is not the identity, the order of a must be p itself. Therefore a is a generator for G, and G is cyclic.

It is tempting to think that the converse of Lagrange's theorem might be true, that if the order of a finite group G has a factor n, then there is a subgroup of G with order n; but this is actually false. A_4, the group with 12 elements in Exercise 10B Question 9, has no subgroup of order 6.

Exercise 10C

1 Use Lagrange's theorem to state the possible orders of subgroups of a group of order 24.

2 Explain why a group of order 15 cannot have a subgroup of order 10.

3 G is a finite cyclic group of order pq, where p and q are prime. What are the possible orders of subgroups of G?

4 Prove that the order of a finite group with at least two elements but no proper subgroups is prime.

10.7* Proof of Lagrange's theorem

You may, if you wish, omit this section.

Let H be a subgroup of a finite group G. The idea of the proof of Lagrange's theorem is to show that the elements of the finite group G can be parcelled up into separate packages, called cosets, one of which is the subgroup H itself. It will turn out that all these packages have the same number of elements as H. Lagrange's theorem then follows easily.

If $a \in G$, then the set $Ha = \{ha : h \in H\}$ is called a **right coset** of H in G.

Example 10.7.1
Find the right cosets of the subgroup $\{I, X\}$ in D_3.

To find the right cosets, write out part of the group table of D_3 with the elements of the subgroup $\{I, X\}$ in the top places in the left column.

	I	R	S	X	Y	Z
I	I	R	S	X	Y	Z
X	X	Y	Z	I	R	S

Table 10.4

Each column of the table is a right coset of the subgroup $\{I, X\}$ in D_3. To see that this is true, notice that the first column consists of the subgroup multiplied on the right by I; the second column consists of the elements $IR = R$ and $XR = Y$, that is the elements I and X of the subgroup $\{I, X\}$ multiplied on the right by R; and so on.

Recall that, as the order in which the elements of a set are written is irrelevant, the set $\{I, X\}$ is the same as the set $\{X, I\}$. Similarly $\{R, Y\} = \{Y, R\}$ and $\{S, Z\} = \{Z, S\}$. There are three distinct right cosets: $\{I, X\}$, $\{R, Y\}$ and $\{S, Z\}$.

Notice that the elements of the group are divided equally among three cosets.

Example 10.7.2

The group Q_4, called the *quaternion group*, is shown in the table below. Find the right cosets of the subgroups $H_1 = \{e, b\}$ and $H_2 = \{e, a, b, c\}$.

Q_4	e	a	b	c	p	q	r	s
e	e	a	b	c	p	q	r	s
a	a	b	c	e	s	p	q	r
b	b	c	e	a	r	s	p	q
c	c	e	a	b	q	r	s	p
p	p	q	r	s	b	c	e	a
q	q	r	s	p	a	b	c	e
r	r	s	p	q	e	a	b	c
s	s	p	q	r	c	e	a	b

Table 10.5

Proceed as in Example 10.7.1, and write out just those rows of the group table for Q_4 which contain the elements of the subgroup in the column on the left.

	e	a	b	c	p	q	r	s
e	e	a	b	c	p	q	r	s
b	b	c	e	a	r	s	p	q

Table 10.6

The right cosets of H_1 are $\{e, b\}$, $\{a, c\}$, $\{p, r\}$ and $\{q, s\}$.

Working in the same way with the subgroup $H_2 = \{e, a, b, c\}$ gives the following table.

	e	a	b	c	p	q	r	s
e	e	a	b	c	p	q	r	s
a	a	b	c	e	s	p	q	r
b	b	c	e	a	r	s	p	q
c	c	e	a	b	q	r	s	p

Table 10.7

The right cosets of H_2 are $\{e, a, b, c\}$ and $\{p, q, r, s\}$

Notice that, for both H_1 and H_2, the order of the subgroup multiplied by the number of cosets gives the order of the group.

Lagrange's theorem follows from the three parts of the following mini-theorem.

Mini-theorem   Let H be a subgroup of a finite group G. Then:

(a) any two right cosets of H in G are either identical or have no elements in common;

(b) all the right cosets of H in G have the same number of elements;

(c) every element of G is in some right coset of H in G.

> **Proof**   (a) Let a and b be elements of G. Then there are two cases. Either b belongs to Ha, or it does not.
>
> **Case 1** b belongs to Ha. Then $b = ha$ for some $h \in H$. Let x be any element of Hb. Then $x = h_1 b = h_1 ha = h_2 a$, where $h_2 \in H$, since H is a subgroup. But $h_2 a \in Ha$, so $x \in Ha$, and all the elements of Hb are members of Ha.
>
> **Case 2** b does not belong to Ha. Then no element of Hb belongs to Ha, since if $h_1 b = h_2 a$, then $b = h_1^{-1} h_2 a = h_3\, a$ where $h_3 \in H$, a contradiction.
>
> So either all elements of Hb are in Ha or no elements of Hb are in Ha. Now notice the symmetrical roles of a and b, in the sense that you could also prove that either all elements of Ha are in Hb or no elements of Ha are in Hb. Thus any two right cosets of H in G are either identical or have no elements in common.
>
> (b) G is finite, so H is finite. Let H have n elements, $H = \{h_1, h_2, \ldots, h_n\}$. Then the elements of Ha are $\{h_1 a, h_2 a, \ldots, h_n a\}$. No two of these are the same, since if $h_r a = h_s a$ then $h_r = h_s$ by the cancellation law; so Ha also has n elements. Therefore every right coset of H has n elements.
>
> (c) Let a be any element of G. Then the coset Ha contains a because $e \in H$ and you can write $a = ea$.

All the bricks are now to hand to prove Lagrange's theorem.

Lagrange's theorem   Let H be a subgroup of a finite group G. Then the order of H divides the order of G.

> **Proof**   Let G and H have orders m and n respectively. Then by mini-theorem (b), each right coset of H has exactly n elements. By mini-theorem (a), any two of the right cosets either are identical or have no elements in common. Suppose that there are d distinct cosets. These d cosets therefore account for nd elements of the group G. But part (c) of the mini-theorem states that every element of the group is in some coset, so these nd elements account for all the elements of the group. Thus $nd = m$, so n divides m.
>
> Therefore the order of H divides the order of G.

Exercise 10D*

1 Find the right cosets of the subgroups $\{I, R, S\}$, $\{I\}$ and D_3 itself in the group D_3.

2 Find the right cosets of $\{0, 3\}$ in $(\mathbb{Z}_6, +)$. (You will have to use additive notation.)

3 The table in Exercise 10B Question 9 shows the group A_4, the symmetry group of the tetrahedron. Find the right cosets of

(a) $H_1 = \{e, a, b, c\}$, (b) the subgroup H_2 generated by x.

4 Find the right cosets of the subgroup $\{0, \pm 3, \pm 6, \ldots\}$ of the group $(\mathbb{Z}, +)$.

Miscellaneous exercise 10

1 Let G be a commutative group. Prove that the set of elements of order 2, together with the identity element, that is $H = \{a \in G : a^2 = e\}$, is a subgroup of G.

2 G is a commutative group, and $H = \{x \in G : x^3 = e\}$. Prove that H is a subgroup of G.

3 Let G be a commutative group. Prove that the set of elements of finite order, $H = \{a \in G : a^n = e, \text{ some } n\}$, is a subgroup of G.

4 You are given that the set $\{1, 2, 3, \ldots, 12\}$ forms a group G under multiplication modulo 13. A subgroup with n elements is said to have order n. Find, or explain why none exists, a subgroup of G with order

(a) 2, (b) 3, (c) 5. (OCR)

5 The functions i(x), a(x), b(x), c(x) are defined for all $x \neq 0$, $x \neq 1$ by

$$\text{i}(x) = x, \quad \text{a}(x) = \frac{1}{x}, \quad \text{b}(x) = 1 - x \quad \text{and} \quad \text{c}(x) = \frac{1}{1 - x}.$$

The operation $\otimes$ is defined as the composition of functions: that is,

$$(\text{p} \otimes \text{q})(x) = \text{pq}(x) = \text{p}\{\text{q}(x)\}.$$

(a) Show that the set of functions {i, a, b, c} is not closed under $\otimes$, and find two further functions d(x) and e(x) such that {i, a, b, c, d, e} is closed under $\otimes$.

(b) Copy and complete the composition table for the set $G = $ {i, a, b, c, d, e}, under $\otimes$.

$\otimes$	i	a	b	c	d	e
i	i	a	b	c	d	e
a	a	i		b		
b	b		i			
c	c		a		i	
d	d			i		a
e	e	c			i	

(c) Hence show that $(G, \otimes)$ forms a group. (You may assume that the composition of functions is associative.)

(d) Find whether G is a commutative group, giving reasons.

(e) Find whether G is a cyclic group, giving reasons.

(f) Write down all the subgroups of G. (OCR)

6 The law of composition * is defined by $a * b = a + b - 2$ where a and b are numbers in arithmetic modulo 6.

(a) Show that the set $\{0, 1, 2, 3, 4, 5\}$ forms a group G under * in arithmetic modulo 6.

(b) Find all the subgroups of G.

7 The set $\{a, b, c, d\}$ under the binary operation * forms a group G of order 4 with the following operation table.

	a	b	c	d
a	d	a	b	c
b	a	b	c	d
c	b	c	d	a
d	c	d	a	b

(a) Find the order of each element of G.

(b) Write down a proper subgroup of G.   (OCR)

8 Show that the matrices $\begin{pmatrix} a & b \\ c & d \end{pmatrix}$, where $ad \neq bc$, form a group G under matrix multiplication.

Show that the following subsets of G form subgroups of G.

(a) $\begin{pmatrix} a & b \\ 0 & 1 \end{pmatrix}$ (b) $\begin{pmatrix} 1 & b \\ 0 & 1 \end{pmatrix}$ (c) $\begin{pmatrix} a & 0 \\ 0 & 1 \end{pmatrix}$ $(a \neq 0)$

(d) Find a proper subgroup of (a) which contains (b) as a proper subgroup.

(e) Find a subgroup of G of order 4.

9 (a) The elements a, b and c are elements of a non-commutative group G. Prove that $(abc)^{-1} = c^{-1} b^{-1} a^{-1}$.

(b) A group H contains distinct elements x, y and e, where e is the identity element. Given that $xy = y^2 x$, prove that $xy \neq yx$.   (OCR)

10* Let H and K be finite subgroups of a finite group G, and let the orders of H and K be relatively prime; that is, they have no common factors apart from 1. Prove that the only element common to H and K is the identity element.

11 Isomorphisms of groups

This chapter is about groups that are identical to each other as regards their structure. When you have completed it, you should know

- what is meant by isomorphic groups or an isomorphism between groups
- all the different (non-isomorphic) groups with orders up to seven.

11.1 What are isomorphic groups?

The word 'isomorphic' means 'equal in form'. When the word is applied to a pair of groups it means that the groups are structurally the same as each other.

For example, consider the groups $(\mathbb{Z}_4, +)$ and $(\{1, i, -1, -i\}, \times)$ in Tables 11.1 and 11.2.

+	0	1	2	3
0	0	1	2	3
1	1	2	3	0
2	2	3	0	1
3	3	0	1	2

Table 11.1

×	1	i	-1	-i
1	1	i	-1	-i
i	i	-1	-i	1
-1	-1	-i	1	i
-i	-i	1	i	-1

Table 11.2

You can see that these tables, apart from their labelling, are identical. The symbol 1 appears in Table 11.2 in every place that the symbol 0 appears in Table 11.1. Similarly i appears in place of 1, -1 appears in place of 2 and $-i$ in place of 3.

Groups with tables that are related in this way are said to be **isomorphic** to each other. In applying this statement, however, you need to take care. Table 11.3 shows the group $(\{2, 4, 6, 8\}, \times \,(\text{mod}\,10))$.

×(mod 10)	2	4	6	8
2	4	8	2	6
4	8	6	4	2
6	2	4	6	8
8	6	2	8	4

Table 11.3

×(mod 10)	6	2	4	8
6	6	2	4	8
2	2	4	8	6
4	4	8	6	2
8	8	6	2	4

Table 11.4

You might think that the group defined by this table is not isomorphic to $(\mathbb{Z}_4, +)$, but in fact, it is. The group identity is 6, so try rearranging the elements as in Table 11.4, so that they are in the order 6, 2, 4, 8, with the group identity first. You can now see, by comparing Table 11.4 with Table 11.1, that the group *is* isomorphic to $(\mathbb{Z}_4, +)$.

So tables can be helpful for detecting isomorphisms between small groups, but you must not be misled by the way the elements are arranged in the table. For larger groups, tables are cumbersome to use. For infinite groups, tables cannot be used at all.

However, you can use tables to develop a general definition of isomorphism of groups G and H. The important idea is that to every $a \in G$ in Table 11.5, there corresponds an $A \in H$ in Table 11.6. Moreover, if an element x in G is the product of two elements a and b, that is $x = ab$, an X must appear in the corresponding position in H, as the product of the image of a and the image of b, that is $X = AB$.

G	b
a	x

Table 11.5

H	B
A	X

Table 11.6

The language of the previous paragraph should remind you of the language of functions in C3 Chapter 2. To go further it is necessary to widen the definition of function from the one that you met in C3.

11.2   Another look at functions

In C3, all the functions that you met had domain $\mathbb{R}$, or a subset of $\mathbb{R}$, and the result $f(x)$ of a function f operating on a real number x was always a real number.

It is possible for the domain to be any set. For the purposes of this chapter, the domain will be the elements of a group.

In addition to the domain there is a 'target set', which includes the elements $f(x)$, where x is an element of the domain. The element $f(x)$ is called the **image** of x. The set of images $f(x)$ is called the **range** of the function f. The range need not be the same as the target set, but in this context in the book it will always be the same.

In general, if a function f has domain A and a target set B, you denote this by $f : A \rightarrow B$.

The meaning of one–one is almost exactly what it was in C3 Section 2.7. That is, a function f defined for some domain D is **one–one** if, for each y in the range of f, there is only one element $x \in D$ such that $y = f(x)$.

Looking again at Tables 11.5 and 11.6, and the paragraph above them, you can define a function $f : G \rightarrow H$, such that $f(a) = A$, $f(b) = B$ and $f(x) = X$. The condition that $X = AB$, can now be written as $f(x) = f(a)f(b)$, and since $x = ab$, it follows that $f(ab) = f(a)f(b)$.

11.3   A definition of isomorphism

In addition to the condition that $f(ab) = f(a)f(b)$ you would also expect isomorphic finite groups to have the same order. You can make sure that this happens by imposing two conditions: by allowing no spare elements in H which are not the images of elements in G, that is, the range of f is H; and by requiring that different elements of G be sent to different elements of H, that is, f is one–one. Summarising:

> Two groups $(G, \circ)$ and $(H, \bullet)$ are **isomorphic** if there exists a function $f : G \to H$ such that
>
> - the range of f is H
> - f is one–one
> - $f(a \circ b) = f(a) \bullet f(b)$ for all $a, b \in G$.
>
> The function $f : G \to H$ is called an **isomorphism**.

The definition looks oddly asymmetrical between the two groups G and H, but it isn't really. If you write $f^{-1} = F$, the definition could be reversed in terms of F by writing $F : H \to G$, with $F(A \bullet B) = F(A)F(B) = a \circ b$.

It is usual to drop the group operation symbols $\circ$ and $\bullet$, and to use multiplicative notation for both groups. Then $f(a \circ b) = f(a) \bullet f(b)$ becomes $f(ab) = f(a)f(b)$.

It is comforting that many of the things that you would expect to be true about isomorphic groups are indeed true. Here are three important examples.

Theorem   If $f : G \to H$ is an isomorphism of G and H, and e is the identity in G, then $f(e)$ is the identity in H. If $a \in G$, then $f(a^{-1})$ is the inverse of $f(a)$ in H.

> You must expect to use the relation $f(ab) = f(a)f(b)$ in this proof.

Proof   Let e be the identity in G.

If $a \in G$, then

$$f(e)f(a) = f(ea) \qquad \text{(using } f(ab) = f(a)f(b)\text{)}$$
$$= f(a) \qquad (e \text{ is the identity in } G)$$

and

$$f(a)f(e) = f(ae) \qquad \text{(using } f(ab) - f(a)f(b)\text{)}.$$
$$= f(a) \qquad (e \text{ is the identity in } G)$$

Therefore $f(e)f(a) = f(a)f(e) = f(e)$, so $f(e)$ is the identity in H. Call it e_H.

To prove that $f(a^{-1})$ is the inverse of $f(a)$, you must prove that

$$f(a^{-1})f(a) = f(a)f(a^{-1}) = e_H.$$

Starting with $f(a^{-1})f(a)$, you find that

$$f(a^{-1})f(a) = f(a^{-1}a) \qquad \text{(using } f(ab) = f(a)f(b)\text{)}$$
$$= f(e) \qquad (\text{as } a^{-1}a = e)$$
$$= e_H \qquad \text{(already proved)}.$$

Similarly, $f(a)f(a^{-1}) = e_H$, so $f(a)f(a^{-1}) = f(aa^{-1}) = f(e) = e_H$ and the theorem is proved.

Theorem   If f : $G \to H$ is an isomorphism of G and H, the order of the element $a \in G$ is the same as the order of f(a) $\in H$.

Proof   Let n be the order of a. Then n is the smallest positive integer such that $a^n = e$. Consider

$$
\begin{aligned}
(f(a))^n &= \overbrace{f(a)f(a)\ldots f(a)}^{n \text{ of these}} &&\text{(By definition of } n\text{th power)}\\
&= f(aa\ldots a) &&\text{(Using } f(ab)= f(a)f(b))\\
&= f(a^n) &&\text{(By definition of } n\text{th power)}\\
&= f(e) &&\text{(the order of } a \text{ is } n)\\
&= e_H
\end{aligned}
$$

But is n the least positive integer such that $(f(a))^n = e_H$?

Suppose that the order of f(a) is m where $m < n$. Then $(f(a))^m = e_H$.

As $f(a^m) = (f(a))^m = e_H$, there are two elements, a^n and a^m, with image e_H. But $a^n \neq a^m$, since $a^n = e$ and n is the smallest positive integer such that $a^n = e$ and $m < n$. This contradicts the fact that the isomorphism f : $G \to H$ is one–one. Therefore the order of $a \in G$ is the same as the order of f(a) $\in H$.

This theorem is particularly useful for proving that two groups are not isomorphic. Just look at the elements of each group and find their orders. If they don't match, the groups are not isomorphic.

> It is interesting that the converse of this result is false. You can have two groups G and H of the same size and set up a function f : $G \to H$ such that the range of f is H and f is one–one and that elements of G and their images in H have the same orders, but G and H are not isomorphic. The simplest example has order 16. (See *The Fascination of Groups* by F J Budden, Cambridge University Press, 1972 where on page 291 Q17.01 and the answer on page 569 show that two groups each have 1 element of order 1, 3 of order 2 and 12 of order 4.

Example 11.3.1
Prove that $(\mathbb{Z}_6, +)$ is not isomorphic to D_3.

The elements 0, 1, 2, 3, 4, 5 $\in \mathbb{Z}_6$ have orders 1, 6, 3, 2, 3, 6 respectively.

The elements I, R, R^2, X, Y, $Z \in D_3$ have orders 1, 3, 3, 2, 2, 2 respectively.

Therefore the groups are not isomorphic.

Example 11.3.2
Prove that $(\mathbb{R}, +)$ is not isomorphic to $(\mathbb{C} - \{0\}, \times)$.

The only element of finite order in $(\mathbb{R}, +)$ is 0, which has order 1. In $(\mathbb{C} - \{0\}, \times)$ the element -1 has order 2. Therefore the groups are not isomorphic.

Theorem   (a) Every infinite cyclic group is isomorphic to $(\mathbb{Z}, +)$.

(b) Every finite cyclic group of order n is isomorphic to $(\mathbb{Z}_n, +)$.

> To prove that two groups are isomorphic, produce a function from the first group to the second, and show that the function is an isomorphism.

Proof   For both parts (a) and (b), the method is to take a generator a of the cyclic group G, and to define a function $f : \mathbb{Z} \to G$ or $f : \mathbb{Z}_n \to G$ such that $f(r) = a^r$. Then every element of G is the image of some element of $\mathbb{Z}$ or $\mathbb{Z}_n$, so that the range of f is G.

(a) **Infinite case**   To prove that f is one–one, suppose that $f(r) = f(s)$ with $r > s$. Then $a^r = a^s$, so $a^{r-s} = e$ for $r - s \neq 0$. But this contradicts the fact that G is an infinite cyclic group. Therefore f is one–one.

To prove that $f(r + s) = f(r)f(s)$, consider first $f(r + s) = a^{r+s}$. But $a^{r+s} = a^r a^s = f(r)f(s)$, so $f : \mathbb{Z} \to G$ is an isomorphism.

(b) **Finite case**   Let the order of G be n.

Define $f : \mathbb{Z}_n \to G$ by $f(r) = a^r$ for $0 \leqslant r < n$.

To prove that f is one–one, suppose that $f(r) = f(s)$ with $r > s$. Then $a^r = a^s$, so $a^{r-s} = e$. But as $0 \leqslant s < r < n$, so $0 < r - s < n$, which contradicts the fact that n is the order of G. Therefore f is one–one.

Finally, to prove that $f(r + s) = f(r)f(s)$ there are two cases to consider. Notice first that $0 \leqslant r + s < 2n$, so that either $0 \leqslant r + s < n$ or $n \leqslant r + s < 2n$.

If $0 \leqslant r + s < n$, then $f(r + s) = a^{r+s} = a^r a^s = f(r)f(s)$.

However, if $n \leqslant r + s < 2n$, then the sum of r and s in $\mathbb{Z}_n$ is $r + s - n$, so

$$f(r + s) = f(r + s - n) = a^{r+s-n} = a^r a^s e = a^r a^s = f(r)f(s).$$

Therefore $f : \mathbb{Z} \to G$ is an isomorphism.

This theorem says that cyclic groups of a given order are isomorphic. This is sometimes stated as, 'there is only one cyclic group of a given order, up to isomorphism'.

Example 11.3.3

Prove that the following groups are isomorphic to each other.

(a) Rotational symmetries of a Catherine wheel with 10 spokes.

(b) $(\mathbb{Z}_{11} - \{0\}, \times)$

(c) $(\mathbb{Z}_{10}, +)$

(d) 10th roots of unity under multiplication.

The groups are all cyclic. Possible generators are (a) rotation through $\frac{1}{5}\pi$, (b) 2, (c) 1, (d) $\exp(\frac{1}{5}\pi\, i)$. The groups all have 10 elements, so they are isomorphic.

Exercise 11

1 Show that the group $(\{1, -1\}, \times)$ is isomorphic to $(\mathbb{Z}_2, +)$.

2 Use the function $f(x) = e^x$ to show that $(\mathbb{R}, +)$ is isomorphic to $(\mathbb{R}^+, \times)$.

3 Show that $(\mathbb{Z}_{13} - \{0\}, \times (\mathrm{mod}\ 13))$ is isomorphic to $(\mathbb{Z}_{12}, +)$.

4 Prove that the group of even integers under addition is isomorphic to the group of integers under addition.

5 Prove that $(\mathbb{R} - \{0\}, \times)$ is not isomorphic to $(\mathbb{C} - \{0\}, \times)$.

6 Let g be a fixed element of the group G. Prove that $f : G \to G$ defined by $f(a) = g^{-1}ag$ is an isomorphism from G to itself.

11.4 Group generators

You met the idea of a group generator in the context of cyclic groups in Section 10.3. However, you can extend the idea to non-cyclic groups.

Consider the group of symmetries of a rectangle which is not a square (see Exercise 9E Question 1). The individual symmetries are the identity e, the reflections a and b in the axes of symmetry, and the rotation of $180°$ about the centre, which you can obtain by carrying out either first a then b or first b then a. In fact, you can describe this group by saying that it is generated by a and b given that $a^2 = b^2 = e$ and $ab = ba$. You can then simplify any expression in a and b, such as bab^2aba^2 by moving all the b terms to the left using the relation $ab = ba$ to get b^4a^4. Using $a^2 = b^2 = e$ simplifies this to e.

Similarly, the group D_3, described in Table 9.8, is generated by R and X. Notice first that $S = R^2$, $Y = XR$, $Z = XS = XR^2$ and $R^3 = X^2 = I$, so that every element can be written in terms of R and X. But notice also that the two equations $XR = Y$ and $R^2X = SX = Y$ give the relation $XR = R^2X$ between R and X.

These relations are sufficient to carry out any calculations within the group.

Now consider XR^2.

$$XR^2 = (XR)R = (R^2X)R = R^2(XR) = R^2(R^2X) = R^4X = RX.$$

You can construct a table for D_3 using only R and X. The entries shown in Table 11.7 are easy to supply. The other entries come from calculations such as

$$(XR)(XR^2) = X(RX)R^2 = X(XR^2)R^2 = X^2R^4 = R,$$

and $(R^2)(XR) = (R^2X)R = (XR)R = XR^2,$

in which the terms in X are progressively moved to the left using the given relation $XR = R^2X$ and the relation $RX = XR^2$, which was derived from it. Try filling in the rest of the table for yourself.

	I	R	R^2	X	XR	XR^2
I	I	R	R^2	X	XR	XR^2
R	R	R^2	I			
R^2	R^2	I	R			
X	X	XR	XR^2	I		
XR	XR	XR^2	X		I	
XR^2	XR^2	X	XR			I

Table 11.7

Thus the group D_3 is generated by R and X where $R^3 = X^2 = I$ and $XR = R^2 X$.

In the next section, the idea of generators will be used extensively.

11.5 Classifying groups of order up to 7

The only group of order 1 is the group consisting of the identity element only.

As every group of prime order is cyclic (see Section 10.6) the only groups of orders 2, 3, 5 and 7 are cyclic.

This leaves groups of orders 4 and 6. They need a much more detailed treatment.

Groups of order 4

Let G be a group of order 4. As the orders of the elements must divide the order of the group, all the elements of G, other than the identity, have order 4 or 2.

If there is an element of order 4, the group G is cyclic, and is isomorphic to $(\mathbb{Z}_4, +)$.

If there is no element of order 4, all the elements other than the identity have order 2.

Now an element of order 2 is its own inverse; that is, $a^2 = e \Leftrightarrow a = a^{-1}$. Recall from Example 10.1.1 that a group in which every element is its own inverse is commutative.

Let a and b be two distinct non-identity elements of G, and consider the element ba.

As the group is commutative, $ba = ab$.

At this stage the group table shown in Table 11.8 is incomplete.

The element ba in Table 11.8, shown shaded, cannot be b or e because b and e are already in the same row. And it cannot be a since a is in the same column. So ba is distinct from the other elements, and $G = \{e, a, b, ba\}$.

Complete the table for yourself using similar arguments. You should end up with Table 11.9.

	e	a	b
e	e	a	b
a	a	e	
b	b		e

Table 11.8

This group is called the *four-group* or occasionally the *Klein four-group*. It is denoted by V after the German word *vier* meaning 'four'. It is isomorphic to the group of symmetries of the rectangle. See Exercise 9E Question 1.

	e	a	b	ba
e	e	a	b	ba
a	a	e	ba	b
b	b	ba	e	a
ba	ba	b	a	e

Table 11.9

There are thus two, and only two, distinct groups of order 4, the cyclic group $(\mathbb{Z}_4, +)$, and V. Every group of order 4 is isomorphic to one of them.

In Miscellaneous exercise 9 Question 7 you showed that there are five possible group tables. In fact, all the groups defined by these tables are isomorphic either to $(\mathbb{Z}_4, +)$ or to V.

Groups of order 6

Let G be a group of order 6. As the orders of the elements must divide the order of the group, all the elements of G, other than the identity, have order 6, 3 or 2.

If there is an element of order 6, the group G is cyclic, and is isomorphic to $(\mathbb{Z}_6, +)$.

If there is no element of order 6, suppose that there is an element a of order 3. Then the group includes the elements e, a and a^2, and there must be another element b such that $b \neq a$, a^2 or a^3. Thus the elements of G are $\{e, a, a^2, b, ba, ba^2\}$. It is easy to check that none of these six elements can be equal to one another. At this stage the incomplete group table appears as in Table 11.10.

	e	a	a^2	b	ba	ba^2
e	e	a	a^2	b	ba	ba^2
a	a	a^2	e			
a^2	a^2	e	a			
b	b	ba	ba^2			
ba	ba	ba^2	b			
ba^2	ba^2	b	ba			

Table 11.10

Now consider b^2. It is in the same row as b, ba and ba^2, so it can't be any of them. This leaves only $b^2 = a$, $b^2 = a^2$ or $b^2 = e$ as possibilities.

Suppose first that $b^2 = a$. Then $b^3 = b(b^2) = ba$, $b^4 = b(b^3) = b(ba) = b^2a = a^2$, $b^5 = b(b^4) = ba^2$ and $b^6 = b(b^5) = b(ba^2) = b^2a^2 = aa^2 = a^3 = e$. As these powers of b are all different, the order of b would be 6, contrary to hypothesis.

A similar argument shows that if $b^2 = a^2$, the order of b would also be 6. Try it!

Therefore $b^2 = e$.

Now consider the product ab. It is in the same row as a, a^2 and e and in the same column as b, so it can't be any of them. That leaves two cases, $ab = ba$ and $ab = ba^2$.

Suppose $ab = ba$ and consider the various powers of ab:

$$(ab)^2 = abab = a(ba)b = aabb = a^2b^2 = a^2e = a^2,$$
$$(ab)^3 = (ab)^2ab = a^2ab = a^3b = b, \qquad (ab)^4 = (ab)^2(ab)^2 = a^2a^2 = a,$$
$$(ab)^5 = (ab)^3(ab)^2 = ba^2, \qquad (ab)^6 = (ab)^2(ab)^4 = a^2a = a^3 = e.$$

So the order of ab is 6, contrary to hypothesis. Thus $ab \neq ba$.

If $ab = ba^2$, you can construct a table, using computations such as

$$(ba^2)(ba) = ba^2ba = ba(ab)a = baba^2a = bab = bba^2 = a^2;$$
$$(ba)(ba^2) = baba^2 = b(ab)a^2 = bba^2a^2 = b^2a^4 = a.$$

Complete the table for yourself. You should get the result shown in Table 11.11.

	e	a	a^2	b	ba	ba^2
e	e	a	a^2	b	ba	ba^2
a	a	a^2	e	ba^2	b	ba
a^2	a^2	e	a	ba	ba^2	b
b	b	ba	ba^2	e	a	a^2
ba	ba	ba^2	b	a^2	e	a
ba^2	ba^2	b	ba	a	a^2	e

Table 11.11

Comparing Table 11.11 with the completed version of Table 11.7, you can easily see that this group is isomorphic to the group D_3.

Suppose now that G has no elements of order 6 or of order 3. Then all the elements other than the identity have order 2, and the group is commutative (see Example 10.1.1).

Then, if a and b are two distinct, non-identity elements in G, the argument goes precisely as for the non-cyclic group of order 4: G contains e, a, b and ba, but there are no more products of a and b with results distinct from these. But $\{e, a, b, ab\}$ is V, a group of order 4 and, by Lagrange's theorem, a group of order 6 cannot have a subgroup of order 4. So the supposition that all the elements have order 2 leads to a contradiction.

Therefore the only distinct groups of order 6 are $(\mathbb{Z}_6, +)$ and D_3. Every group of order 6 is isomorphic to one or the other of them.

> The groups of order up to and including 7 are
>
> $(\mathbb{Z}_2, +)$ of order 2, $\quad (\mathbb{Z}_3, +)$ of order 3, $\qquad (\mathbb{Z}_4, +)$ and V of order 4,
>
> $(\mathbb{Z}_5, +)$ of order 5, $\quad (\mathbb{Z}_6, +)$ and D_3 of order 6, $\quad (\mathbb{Z}_7, +)$ of order 7.

Miscellaneous exercise 11

1 The set $\{2, 4, 6, 8\}$ forms a group G under multiplication modulo 10.

  (a) Write down the operation table for G.

  (b) State the identity element and the inverse of each element in G.

The set $\{1, i, -1, -i\}$, where $i^2 = -1$, forms a group H under multiplication of complex numbers.

  (c) Determine whether or not G and H are isomorphic, giving a reason for your answer. (OCR)

2 A group D, of order 8, has the operation table shown below.

	e	a	b	b^2	b^3	ab	ab^2	ab^3
e	e	a	b	b^2	b^3	ab	ab^2	ab^3
a	a	e	ab	ab^2	ab^3	b	b^2	b^3
b	b	ab^3	b^2	b^3	e	a	ab	ab^2
b^2	b^2	ab^2	b^3	e	b	ab^3	a	ab
b^3	b^3	ab	e	b	b^2	ab^2	ab^3	a
ab	ab	b^3	ab^2	ab^3	a	e	b	b^2
ab^2	ab^2	b^2	ab^3	a	ab	b^3	e	b
ab^3	ab^3	b	a	ab	ab^2	b^2	b^3	e

  (a) Find the orders of the eight elements of D.

  (b) Write down the number of subgroups of order 2.

  (c) Find two subgroups of order 4.

  (d) Give a reason why there is no subgroup of order 6.

  (e) Explain how you can tell that the group D is not isomorphic to the group M, in which the elements $\{1, 3, 7, 9, 11, 13, 17, 19\}$ are combined by multiplication modulo 20. (OCR)

3 (a) The set S consists of the eight elements 9^1, 9^2, ..., 9^8 written in arithmetic modulo 64. Determine each of the elements of S as an integer between 0 and 63.

    Under multiplication modulo 64, the set S forms a group G, with identity 1. Write down the orders of each of the remaining elements of G.

    Write down all the possible generators for G, and list all the subgroups of G.

  (b) The group H consists of the set $\{1, 9, 31, 39, 41, 49, 71, 79\}$ under multiplication modulo 80. Determine, with justification, whether G and H are isomorphic. (OCR)

4 The set $S = \{1, 2, p, q, 7, 8\}$ with the operation of multiplication modulo 9 forms a group G.

  (a) By considering the closure of G, find the integers p and q where $0 < p < q < 9$.

  (b) State the inverse of each element of G, and write down all the subgroups of G.

  (c) Given that $\omega = \cos \frac{1}{3}\pi + i\sin \frac{1}{3}\pi$, and H is the group $\{\omega, \omega^2, \omega^3, \omega^4, \omega^5, \omega^6\}$ under multiplication of complex numbers, find with reasons whether G and H are isomorphic.   (OCR)

5 (a) Prove that the set $\{1, 3, 5, 9, 11, 13\}$ together with the operation of multiplication modulo 14 forms a group G. (You may assume that the operation is associative.)

      List all the subgroups of G with fewer than three elements.

  (b) The group of symmetry transformations of the equilateral triangle under the operation of composition is H. Describe geometrically the six elements of H.

  (c) Determine, with reasons, whether G and H are isomorphic.

      Find a subgroup of G with three elements. Is it isomorphic to a subgroup of H?   (OCR)

6 Prove that the set $\{1, 2, 4, 7, 8, k, 13, 14\}$ together with the operation multiplication modulo 15 forms a group G, provided k takes one particular value. State this value of k. (You may assume that the operation is associative, but the other axioms for a group must be clearly verified.)

If H is a subgroup of G of order n, use Lagrange's theorem to find all the possible values of n.

Find three subgroups of order 4, each containing the elements 1 and 4, and prove that exactly two of them are isomorphic.   (OCR)

7 Given that the multiplication of complex numbers is associative, show that the set $\{1, -1, i, -i\}$ forms a group G under multiplication of complex numbers.

Prove also that the set $\{1, 7, 18, 24\}$ under multiplication modulo 25 forms a group H.

Determine, with reasons, whether G and H are isomorphic.   (OCR)

8 The elements of the group G_n are the number 1 and the integers between 1 and n which have no factor in common with n; for example, the elements of G_4 are 1, 3. The operation of the group is multiplication modulo n. Write out the tables of G_5, G_8, G_{10} and G_{12}.

State which groups are isomorphic, giving your reasons.   (OCR)

9 (a) The law of composition $*$ is defined by $a*b = a+b-ab$. Given that a, b and c are real numbers, prove that $a*(b*c) = (a*b)*c$.

(b) The law of composition $\circ$ is defined by $a \circ b = a+b-ab$ evaluated modulo 7 so that $2 \circ 4 = 5$ for example.

Copy and complete the combination table for the set $\{0, 2, 3, 4, 5, 6\}$ with law of composition $\circ$.

$\circ$	0	2	3	4	5	6
0	0	2	3	4	5	6
2	2	0	6	5	4	3

(c) Prove that the set $\{0, 2, 3, 4, 5, 6\}$ forms a group G under $\circ$.

(d) Determine, with reasons, whether G is isomorphic to the group of rotations of the regular hexagon.   (OCR)

Revision exercise 4

1 A set $H = \{g, h, i, j, k, m\}$ has a binary operation with composition table

	g	h	i	j	k	m
g	j	m	g	k	h	i
h	m	i	h	g	j	k
i	g	h	i	j	k	m
j	k	g	j	m	i	h
k	h	j	k	i	m	g
m	i	k	m	h	g	j

Explain carefully why H is not a group. (MEI)

2 A non-abelian group G consists of eight 2×2 matrices, and the binary operation is matrix multiplication. The eight distinct elements of G can be written as $G = \{\mathbf{I}, \mathbf{A}, \mathbf{A}^2, \mathbf{A}^3, \mathbf{B}, \mathbf{AB}, \mathbf{A}^2\mathbf{B}, \mathbf{A}^3\mathbf{B}\}$, where $\mathbf{I}$ is the identity matrix and $\mathbf{A}, \mathbf{B}$ are 2×2 matrices such that $\mathbf{A}^4 = \mathbf{I}$, $\mathbf{B}^2 = \mathbf{I}$ and $\mathbf{BA} = \mathbf{A}^3\mathbf{B}$.

(a) Show that $(\mathbf{A}^2\mathbf{B})(\mathbf{AB}) = \mathbf{A}$ and $(\mathbf{AB})(\mathbf{A}^2\mathbf{B}) = \mathbf{A}^3$.

(b) Evaluate the products (i) $(\mathbf{AB})\mathbf{A}$, (ii) $(\mathbf{AB})(\mathbf{AB})$, (iii) $\mathbf{B}(\mathbf{A}^2)$.

(c) Find the order of each element of G.

(d) Show that $\{\mathbf{I}, \mathbf{A}^2, \mathbf{B}, \mathbf{A}^2\mathbf{B}\}$ is a subgroup of G.

(e) Find the other two subgroups of G which have order 4.

(f) For each of the three subgroups of order 4, state whether or not it is a cyclic subgroup. (MEI)

3 (a) Show that the set $\{2, 4, 6, 8\}$ forms a group G_1 under multiplication modulo 10.

(b) The functions $\{e, f, g, h\}$ are defined for real values of x $(x \neq 1)$, and

$$e(x) = x, \ f(x) = 2 - x, \ g(x) = \frac{x - 2}{x - 1}.$$

The set of functions $\{e, f, g, h\}$ forms a group G_2 under composition of functions so that $f * g$ is the function h, where $h(x) = f(g(x))$. Show that $g * g = e$ and that $f * g = g * f$. Copy the table and use the fact that G_2 is a group to complete it.

$*$	e	f	g	h
e	e	f	g	h
f	f		h	
g	g	h	e	
h	h			

(c) Determine, with reasons, whether G_1 and G_2 are isomorphic. (OCR)

4 Use de Moivre's theorem to calculate the value of $(1 - 2i)^{20}$. (OCR)

5 (a) By writing $2\cos\theta = z + z^{-1}$, where $z = \cos\theta + i\sin\theta$, prove that

$$32\cos^6\theta = \cos 6\theta + 6\cos 4\theta + 15\cos 2\theta + 10.$$

(b) Evaluate exactly $\displaystyle\int_0^{\frac{1}{4}\pi} \cos^6\theta \, d\theta$. (OCR)

6 (a) An infinite series is given by $z - z^2 + z^3 - z^4 + \cdots + (-1)^{n+1} z^n + \cdots$.

   (i) Assuming that the series converges, find an expression for its sum.

   (ii) Given that $z = \frac{1}{4}(\cos\theta + i\sin\theta)$, explain why the above series converges for all values of θ, with $-\pi < \theta < \pi$.

(b) By using de Moivre's theorem, or otherwise, prove that the sum of the infinite series

$$\frac{\sin\theta}{4} - \frac{\sin 2\theta}{4^2} + \frac{\sin 3\theta}{4^3} - \frac{\sin 4\theta}{4^4} + \cdots + (-1)^{n+1}\frac{\sin n\theta}{4^n} + \cdots$$

is $\dfrac{4\sin\theta}{17 + 8\cos\theta}$.

7 You are given that $w = 1 - e^{i\theta}\cos\theta$, where $0 < \theta < \frac{1}{2}\pi$.

(a) Express $e^{ik\theta}$ and $e^{-ik\theta}$ in the form $a + bi$, and show that $w = -ie^{-i\theta}\sin\theta$.

   Series C and S are defined by

$$C = \cos\theta\cos\theta + \cos 2\theta\cos^2\theta + \cos 3\theta\cos^3\theta + \cdots + \cos n\theta\cos^n\theta,$$
$$S = \sin\theta\cos\theta + \sin 2\theta\cos^2\theta + \sin 3\theta\cos^3\theta + \cdots + \sin n\theta\cos^n\theta.$$

(b) Show that $C + iS$ is a geometric series, and write down the sum of this series.

(c) Using the results in part (a), or otherwise, show that $C = \dfrac{\sin n\theta\cos^{n+1}\theta}{\sin\theta}$, and find a similar expression for S. (MEI, adapted)

8 (a) The set $\{2, 4, 6, 8\}$, together with the operation of multiplication modulo 10, forms a group G.

   (i) Construct a combination table for G.

   (ii) State the inverse of each element of G.

(b) Transformations **I, P, Q, R** in the xy-plane are represented by the matrices

$$\begin{pmatrix} 1 & 0 \\ 0 & 1 \end{pmatrix}, \quad \begin{pmatrix} -1 & 0 \\ 0 & 1 \end{pmatrix}, \quad \begin{pmatrix} 1 & 0 \\ 0 & -1 \end{pmatrix}, \quad \begin{pmatrix} -1 & 0 \\ 0 & -1 \end{pmatrix},$$

respectively.

   Describe briefly the geometric effect of each of the transformations **P, Q, R**.

   The set $\{$**I, P, Q, R**$\}$ forms a group H under the operation of composition of transformations.

(c) State, with a reason, whether or not the two groups G and H are isomorphic. (OCR)

9 (a) Find an approximation to a fourth root of $40 + 9i$. Show your working in full, and give your answer in the form $a + bi$, where a and b are correct to 3 decimal places.

(b) Let $a + bi = z$. Express the other fourth roots of $40 + 9i$ in terms of z. (OCR)

10 Show that the set of all matrices of the form $\begin{pmatrix} 1-n & n \\ -n & 1+n \end{pmatrix}$ where n is an integer

(positive, negative, zero), forms a group G under the operation of matrix multiplication. (You may assume that matrix multiplication is associative.)

The subset of G which consists of those elements for which n is an even integer (positive, negative, zero) is denoted by H. Determine whether or not H is a subgroup of G, justifying your answer. (OCR)

11 The set $G = \{e, a, a^2, a^3, b, ab, a^2b, a^3b\}$ is a multiplicative group of order 8 such that $a^4 = e$, $a^2 = b^2$, $ba = a^3b$.

(a) Show that the order of the element ab is 4.

(b) Show that $ba^2 = a^2b$ and that $ba^3 = ab$.

(c) Find three subgroups of G of order 4. (OCR)

12 The set $\{2, 4, 6, 8\}$ forms a group G under multiplication modulo 10.

(a) Write down the operation table for G.

(b) State the identity element and the inverse of each element in G.

The set $\{1, i, -1, -i\}$, where $i^2 = -1$, forms a group H, under multiplication of complex numbers. (OCR)

(c) Determine whether or not G and H are isomorphic, giving a reason for your answer.

13 (a) Prove that $(z^n - e^{i\theta})(z^n - e^{-i\theta}) \equiv z^{2n} - 2z^n \cos\theta + 1$.

(b) Hence, or otherwise, find the roots of the equation $z^6 - z^3\sqrt{2} + 1 = 0$, giving your answers exactly in polar form. (OCR)

14 (a) Use de Moivre's theorem to prove that
$$\sin 7\theta \equiv 7\sin\theta - 56\sin^3\theta + 112\sin^5\theta - 64\sin^7\theta.$$

(b) Hence, or otherwise, prove that the only real solutions of the equation $\sin 7\theta \equiv 7\sin\theta$ are given by $\theta = n\pi$, where n is an integer. (OCR)

15 (a) Write $x^3 - 1$ and $x^3 + 1$ as products of real factors.

(b) Write $z^3 - 1$ and $z^3 + 1$ as products of complex factors.

(c) Solve the equations $x^6 - 1 = 0$, $x^6 + 1 = 0$ and $x^{12} - 1 = 0$ in real numbers, and illustrate your answers with graphs of $y = x^6 - 1$, $y = x^6 + 1$ and $y = x^{12} - 1$.

(d) Solve the equations $z^6 - 1 = 0$, $z^6 + 1 = 0$ and $z^{12} - 1 = 0$ in complex numbers, and illustrate your answers using Argand diagrams.

Practice examination 1 for FP3

Time 1 hour 30 minutes

Answer all the questions.

You are permitted to use a graphic calculator in this paper.

1 (i) Show, by using the substitution $u = x + y$, that the differential equation
$$\frac{dy}{dx} = \frac{x+y}{1-x-y} \text{ may be reduced to the form } \frac{du}{dx} = \frac{1}{1-u}.$$ [3]

   (ii) Hence find the general solution of $\dfrac{dy}{dx} = \dfrac{x+y}{1-x-y}$. [3]

2 Two planes have equations $x + 2y - z = 3$ and $2x - z = 0$.

   (i) Find the acute angle between the planes, giving your answer correct to the nearest degree. [3]

   (ii) Find a vector parallel to the line of intersection of these planes. [2]

   (iii) Find, in the form $\dfrac{x-a}{p} = \dfrac{y-b}{q} = \dfrac{z-c}{r}$, the equation of this line of intersection. [3]

3 (i) Solve the equation $z^3 = i$. [4]

   (ii) Hence find the possible values for the argument of a complex number w which is such that $w^3 = i(w^*)^3$. [4]

4 (i) A group has order 12. What are the possible orders of proper subgroups of this group? [1]

   (ii) A group C of order 12 has elements $\{0, 1, 2, 3, 4, 5, 6, 7, 8, 9, 10, 11\}$ and the group operation is addition modulo 12.

   (a) For each of the possible orders in your answer to part (i), identify a subgroup of C having that order. [4]

   (b) State all the elements of C which have order 12. [3]

5 G is a multiplicative group with identity element e, and a is a fixed element of G for which $axa = x^{-1}$ for all elements $x \in G$. Prove that

   (i) $a = a^{-1}$, [2]

   (ii) $ax = (ax)^{-1}$ for all $x \in G$, [2]

   (iii) $x = x^{-1}$ for all $x \in G$, [2]

   (iv) $xy = yx$ for all $x, y \in G$. [3]

6 (i) Show that $1 - e^{i\theta} = -2ie^{\frac{1}{2}i\theta} \sin\frac{1}{2}\theta$.   [2]

   (ii) State the sum of the series $1 + e^{i\theta} + e^{2i\theta} + \cdots + e^{(n-1)i\theta}$.   [2]

   (iii) Using the result in part (i), or otherwise, show that this sum may be expressed in the

   form $\dfrac{i\left(e^{-\frac{1}{2}i\theta} - e^{(n-\frac{1}{2})i\theta}\right)}{2\sin\frac{1}{2}\theta}$.   [3]

   (iv) Hence show that $1 + \cos\theta + \cos 2\theta + \cdots + \cos(n-1)\theta = \frac{1}{2}\left(1 + \dfrac{\sin\left(n-\frac{1}{2}\right)\theta}{\sin\frac{1}{2}\theta}\right)$.   [3]

7 The variables x and y are related by the differential equation $\dfrac{d^2 y}{dx^2} + 4\dfrac{dy}{dx} + 4y = 1$.

   (i) Find the general solution for y in terms of x.   [4]

   (ii) For the particular solution for which $y = 0$ and $\dfrac{dy}{dx} = 1$ when $x = 0$,

      (a) find the value of x for which $\dfrac{dy}{dx} = 0$,   [5]

      (b) sketch the graph of y against x, for $x \geqslant 0$.   [2]

8 The equations of a plane p and a line l are $\mathbf{r} = \begin{pmatrix} 1 \\ 3 \\ 2 \end{pmatrix} + \lambda \begin{pmatrix} a \\ 2 \\ -1 \end{pmatrix} + \mu \begin{pmatrix} 1 \\ 1 \\ 0 \end{pmatrix}$ and

   $\mathbf{r} = \begin{pmatrix} 3 \\ a+1 \\ 1 \end{pmatrix} + t \begin{pmatrix} -1 \\ 1 \\ 2 \end{pmatrix}$, respectively, where a is a constant and λ, μ, t are parameters.

   (i) Write down a set of three simultaneous equations satisfied by λ, μ and t if l and p have a point in common.   [1]

   (ii) By considering an appropriate determinant, or otherwise, show that l and p have a unique point of intersection for all values of a except $a = 3$.   [3]

   (iii) For the case $a = 0$, verify that l is perpendicular to p, and find the position vector of the point of intersection of l and p.   [5]

   (iv) For the case $a = 3$, determine the geometrical relationship between l and p.   [3]

Practice examination 2 for FP3

Time 1 hour 30 minutes

Answer all the questions.

You are permitted to use a graphic calculator in this paper.

1 The skew lines l_1 and l_2 have equations as follows.

$$l_1: \quad \mathbf{r} = \begin{pmatrix} 1 \\ -1 \\ -3 \end{pmatrix} + \lambda \begin{pmatrix} 1 \\ -1 \\ 2 \end{pmatrix}, \qquad l_2: \quad \mathbf{r} = \begin{pmatrix} 6 \\ 2 \\ 2 \end{pmatrix} + \mu \begin{pmatrix} 2 \\ 0 \\ -1 \end{pmatrix}.$$

(i) Find a vector in the direction of the common perpendicular to l_1 and l_2. [2]

(ii) Calculate the shortest distance between l_1 and l_2. [4]

2 The variables x and y are related by the differential equation $\dfrac{dy}{dx} + y \tan x = \sec x$, for $-\frac{1}{2}\pi < x < \frac{1}{2}\pi$.

(i) Show that an integrating factor for the differential equation is $\sec x$. [2]

(ii) Given that $y = 1$ when $x = 0$, find the value of x for which $y = 0$. [5]

3 G is a multiplicative group with identity element e. Given that G is commutative, prove that the set of all elements x for which $x = x^{-1}$ forms a subgroup of G. (You should make clear where in your proof you use the fact that G is commutative.) [7]

4 (i) Use de Moivre's theorem to find expressions for $\cos 5\theta$ and $\sin 5\theta$, each in terms of both $\cos\theta$ and $\sin\theta$, and deduce that $\tan 5\theta = \dfrac{5\tan\theta - 10\tan^3\theta + \tan^5\theta}{1 - 10\tan^2\theta + 5\tan^4\theta}$. [5]

(ii) Hence show that $5\tan^4\left(\frac{1}{10}\pi\right) - 10\tan^2\left(\frac{1}{10}\pi\right) + 1 = 0$, and deduce the exact value of $\tan\left(\frac{1}{10}\pi\right)$. [5]

5 (i) It is given that the following set of six matrices, under the operation of matrix multiplication, forms a group G:

$$\mathbf{A} = \begin{pmatrix} 1 & 0 \\ 0 & 1 \end{pmatrix}, \ \mathbf{B} = \begin{pmatrix} 0 & 1 \\ 1 & 0 \end{pmatrix}, \ \mathbf{C} = \begin{pmatrix} 0 & -1 \\ 1 & -1 \end{pmatrix}, \ \mathbf{D} = \begin{pmatrix} -1 & 0 \\ -1 & 1 \end{pmatrix}, \ \mathbf{E} = \begin{pmatrix} 1 & -1 \\ 0 & -1 \end{pmatrix}, \ \mathbf{F} = \begin{pmatrix} -1 & 1 \\ -1 & 0 \end{pmatrix}.$$

(a) State the identity element, and the inverse of $\mathbf{C}$. [2]

(b) State the order of each element in G. [3]

(c) Identify all the proper subgroups of G. [3]

(ii) The group H consists of the six complex numbers $e^{\frac{1}{3}k\pi i}$ for $k = 0, 1, 2, 3, 4, 5$, under the operation of multiplication of complex numbers. State with a reason whether or not G and H are isomorphic. [2]

6 Let $z = e^{i\theta}$.

(i) Give expressions involving trigonometrical functions for $z^n + \dfrac{1}{z^n}$ and $z^n - \dfrac{1}{z^n}$, where n is a positive integer. [3]

(ii) By considering $\left(z + \dfrac{1}{z}\right)^4 \left(z - \dfrac{1}{z}\right)^2$, show that

$$\cos^4 \theta \sin^2 \theta = \tfrac{1}{32}(2 + \cos 2\theta - 2\cos 4\theta - \cos 6\theta).$$ [7]

7 (i) Find the values of the constants a and b for which $at + be^{-t}$ is a particular integral for the differential equation $\dfrac{d^2 x}{dt^2} + 2\dfrac{dx}{dt} = 1 - e^{-t}$. [3]

(ii) Find the solution of the differential equation, given that x and $\dfrac{dx}{dt}$ are both zero when $t = 0$. [6]

(iii) For the solution in part (ii), state the values to which $\dfrac{dx}{dt}$ and $\dfrac{d^2 x}{dt^2}$ tend as $t \to \infty$. [2]

8 The plane p passes through the point with position vector $\mathbf{a}$, and a vector normal to p is $\mathbf{n}$.

(i) Explain, with the aid of a sketch, why the equation of p may be expressed as $(\mathbf{r} - \mathbf{a}) \cdot \mathbf{n} = 0$. [3]

Suppose now that $\mathbf{n}$ is a unit vector.

(ii) Show that, if $\mathbf{n}$ is directed from the origin O towards p, the perpendicular distance from O to p is $\mathbf{a} \cdot \mathbf{n}$. [3]

(iii) Show that the position vector of the foot of the perpendicular from O to p is $(\mathbf{a} \cdot \mathbf{n})\mathbf{n}$ whether $\mathbf{n}$ is directed from O towards p or away from p. [3]

(iv) The point B has position vector $\mathbf{b}$. Find an expression for the position vector of the foot of the perpendicular from B to p. [2]

Answers to Further Pure 2

1 Differentiating inverse trigonometric functions

Exercise 1A (page 7)

1 (a) $\dfrac{2}{1+4x^2}$　　(b) $\dfrac{1}{\sqrt{9-x^2}}$

　(c) $\tan^{-1}x + \dfrac{x}{1+x^2}$　(d) $\dfrac{2\sin^{-1}x}{\sqrt{1-x^2}}$

　(e) $\dfrac{1}{2\sqrt{x(1-x)}}$　(f) $\dfrac{3\sqrt{x}}{2(1+x^3)}$

　(g) $\dfrac{-1}{\sqrt{1-x^2}}$ if $x>0$, $\dfrac{1}{\sqrt{1-x^2}}$ if $x<0$

2 $(1,\,1-\pi)$

3 $-1 \leqslant x \leqslant 1$; $(\pm 0.8, \pm 1.218)$;
　$-1.218 \leqslant f(x) \leqslant 1.218$

4 $-1 \leqslant x \leqslant 1$; $(\pm 0.6, \pm 0.426)$;
　$-1.283 \leqslant f(x) \leqslant 1.283$

5 $-\frac{1}{16}\pi(4-\pi)$

6 $\frac{1}{54}\pi^3$

Exercise 1B (page 11)

1 (a) $\frac{1}{3}\pi$　　(b) $\frac{1}{20}\pi$　　(c) 0.260

　(d) $\frac{1}{18}\pi\sqrt{3}$　(e) $\frac{1}{4}\pi$　　(f) 0.284

2 (a) $\frac{1}{4}\pi$　　(b) $\frac{1}{6}\pi$　　(c) $\frac{1}{10}\pi$

3 (a) $\frac{1}{2}\pi$　　(b) π　　(c) $\frac{1}{3}\pi$

4 (a) $\frac{1}{6}\tan^{-1}\frac{2}{3}x + k$　(b) $\frac{1}{3}\sin^{-1}\frac{3}{2}x + k$

　(c) $\frac{1}{2}\sin^{-1}2x + k$　(d) $\frac{1}{3}\tan^{-1}3x + k$

　(e) $\dfrac{1}{\sqrt{6}}\tan^{-1}\left(\sqrt{\dfrac{3}{2}}\,x\right) + k$

　(f) $\dfrac{1}{\sqrt{5}}\sin^{-1}\left(\dfrac{\sqrt{5}}{2}x\right) + k$

5 (a) $\tan^{-1}(x+1) + k$　(b) $\frac{1}{2}\tan^{-1}\dfrac{x+3}{2} + k$

　(c) $\frac{1}{8}\tan^{-1}\dfrac{2x-3}{4} + k$　(d) $\sin^{-1}\dfrac{x+2}{3} + k$

　(e) $\frac{1}{3}\sin^{-1}\left(x-\frac{1}{3}\right) + k$　(f) $\sin^{-1}\dfrac{x-5}{5} + k$

6 (a) 0.0761　(b) 0.0405　(c) 0.0804
　(d) 0.105　　(e) 0.390　　(f) 0.283
　(g) 1.57　　(h) 1.57　　(i) 0.524.

7 $\dfrac{1}{ab}\tan^{-1}\dfrac{bx}{a} + k$

Exercise 1C (page 16)

1 (a) $\frac{2}{3}\pi$　(b) $\frac{1}{3}\pi$　(c) $\frac{1}{4}\pi$　(d) $-\frac{1}{6}\pi$

2 (a) $\dfrac{1}{|x|\sqrt{9x^2-1}}$　(b) $-\dfrac{1}{1+x^2}$

　(c) $\dfrac{1}{x^2-2x+2}$　(d) -1　(e) $-\dfrac{1}{1+x^2}$

　(f) $\dfrac{1}{x^2+1}$ if $x>0$, $-\dfrac{1}{x^2+1}$ if $x<0$

3 $\frac{1}{3}\pi$

4 (a) $\frac{1}{2}\pi - a$　　(b) b

5 (a) $x^2 + y^2 = x^2y^2$　(b) $xy = 1$
　(c) $x^2y^2 + 1 = y^2$

6 (a) 1　　(b) 0

　$\dfrac{1}{1+x^2}$

7 $\dfrac{2}{1+x^2}$

8 (a) $\tan^{-1}\frac{5}{12}$　(b) $\tan^{-1}\frac{120}{119}$　(c) $\tan^{-1}\frac{1}{239}$

Miscellaneous exercise 1 (page 17)

1 0.284; 0.292, an overestimate

2 (a) $\dfrac{2(1-2x\tan^{-1}x)}{(1+x^2)^2}$

　(b) $\dfrac{2(\sqrt{1-x^2} + x\sin^{-1}x)}{(1-x^2)^{\frac{3}{2}}}$

3 $y = 2\sin\left(x + \frac{1}{6}\pi\right)$. (But note that this is only valid for $-\frac{2}{3}\pi \leqslant x \leqslant \frac{1}{3}\pi$, the interval round $(0, 1)$ for which $\dfrac{dy}{dx} \geqslant 0$. For $x > \frac{1}{3}\pi$, the differential equation is satisfied by $y = 2$; and for $x < -\frac{2}{3}\pi$, it is satisfied by $y = -2$.)

4 $y = \tan\left(x + \frac{1}{4}\pi - 2\right)$; $(0, -2.69)$, $(1.21, 0)$

5 $y = \frac{1}{2}x - \frac{1}{2}\sqrt{3(4-x^2)}$. (But note that this equation is only valid for $-1 \leqslant x < 2$, the interval round $(1, -1)$ for which $\dfrac{dy}{dx} \geqslant 0$. When $x = -1$, $y = -2$, and for $-2 < x < -1$ the differential equation is satisfied by $y = -2$.)

6 $\sin^{-1}\frac{1}{2}s$, which $\to \frac{1}{2}\pi$ as $s \to 2$

7 $\frac{1}{2}\pi\tan^{-1}\frac{1}{2}r$, which $\to \frac{1}{4}\pi^2$ as $r \to \infty$

8 $(0.786, 0.666)$; $0.618, -1.62$

9 $x\sin^{-1}x + \sqrt{1-x^2} + k$

11 $\frac{1}{4}\sqrt{3} - \frac{1}{12}\pi$

2 Rational functions

Exercise 2A (page 25)

1 (a) $\dfrac{1}{x-1} + \dfrac{1}{x^2+1}$

 (b) $\dfrac{x+2}{x^2+1} - \dfrac{1}{x}$

 (c) $\dfrac{1}{x+3} + \dfrac{x-2}{x^2+3}$

 (d) $\dfrac{2x+3}{x^2+25} - \dfrac{1}{2x-1}$

 (e) $\dfrac{x-1}{x^2+9} - \dfrac{2}{3x+2}$

 (f) $\dfrac{1}{x+2} + \dfrac{x-2}{x^2+4}$

2 (a) $A=2,\ B=2,\ C=-1$

 (b) $A=1,\ B=-2,\ C=3$

 (c) $A=3,\ B=-4,\ C=3$

 (d) $A=-1,\ B=1,\ C=-2$

3 (a) $\dfrac{1}{2x+3} + \dfrac{2x-3}{4x^2+9}$ (b) $\dfrac{1}{2+x} - \dfrac{1+x}{2+x^2}$

4 (a) $2\ln 2$ (b) 0

 (c) $\frac{13}{2}\ln 2 - \frac{3}{2}\ln 13$

 (d) $2\ln 2 - \ln 3 - \tan^{-1}\frac{1}{3}$

5 (a) $-1-x^2$ (b) $-x+4x^2$

 (c) $5-6x-7x^2$ (d) $\frac{5}{6} - \frac{13}{36}x - \frac{19}{216}x^2$

6 $\dfrac{x+2}{x^2+1} - \dfrac{2}{(x+1)^2},\ \dfrac{4}{(x+1)^3} + \dfrac{1-4x-x^2}{x^2+1}$

Exercise 2B (page 32)

1 (a) $2 - \dfrac{1}{x+1} + \dfrac{2}{x-1}$

 (b) $1 - \dfrac{2}{x+3} + \dfrac{1}{x-2}$

 (c) $1 - \dfrac{2}{3-x} + \dfrac{2}{1-2x}$

 (d) $3 - \dfrac{1}{x+2} + \dfrac{4}{2x-1}$

 (e) $2x - 1 + \dfrac{3}{x+1} + \dfrac{3}{2x-1}$

 (f) $x + 2 - \dfrac{1}{3+x} - \dfrac{1}{1+x}$

 (g) $8x^2 + 2 + \dfrac{1}{2x-1} - \dfrac{1}{2x+1}$

 (h) $x^2 - x - 1 - \dfrac{1}{x+3} - \dfrac{4}{2x-3}$

 (i) $x + \dfrac{1}{x} - \dfrac{2x}{1+x^2}$

2 (a) $1 + 2\ln\frac{3}{2}$ (b) $2 + \ln\frac{3}{2}$

 (c) $3 + \ln 6$ (d) $2 - \ln 2 - \frac{1}{4}\pi$

3 (a) $2x + 4 - \dfrac{1}{x^2+1} + \dfrac{1}{(x-1)^2} + \dfrac{4}{x-1}$

 (b) $3 - \dfrac{2(2x+1)}{x^2+2} + \dfrac{3}{(x+1)^2} - \dfrac{2}{x+1}$

 (c) $3 + \dfrac{2(4x+1)}{2x^2+1} - \dfrac{15}{(2x+1)^2} - \dfrac{14}{2x+1}$

4 $1 - \dfrac{3}{2x^2+3} - \dfrac{1}{(x+1)^2},\ \dfrac{12x}{(2x^2+3)^2} + \dfrac{2}{(x+1)^3}$

Miscellaneous exercise 2 (page 32)

1 (a) $\dfrac{1}{x^2} + \dfrac{2}{x} + \dfrac{2}{1-x}$

 (b) $2 - x - \dfrac{2}{x+2} + \dfrac{1}{x^2+2}$

2 (a) $A=-1,\ B=1,\ C=1$

 (b) $a=\frac{1}{2},\ b=-\frac{1}{2}$

3 (a) $A=1,\ B=4,\ C=2$

4 (a) $\dfrac{1}{x-3} - \dfrac{1}{x-1}$,

  $\dfrac{1}{(x-3)^2} - \dfrac{1}{x-3} + \dfrac{1}{(x-1)^2} + \dfrac{1}{x-1}$

 (c) $\left(\frac{25}{48} - \ln\frac{3}{2}\right)\pi$

5 $\frac{1}{2}\ln\frac{2}{3}$

6 $3\frac{1}{2} - 3\ln 2$

7 $\frac{3}{2}\ln 3 - \ln 2 - \frac{1}{2}$

8 (a) $a=2$ (b) $\frac{5}{8} + \ln 2$

9 $A=-1,\ B=1;\ 1-4x+6x^2$

3 Maclaurin series

Exercise 3A (page 39)

1 (a) $1 + \frac{3}{2}x + \frac{3}{8}x^2 - \frac{1}{16}x^3$

 (b) $1 + \frac{3}{2}x + \frac{15}{8}x^2 + \frac{35}{16}x^3$

 (c) $1 - 6x + 24x^2 - 80x^3$

 (d) $1 + \frac{1}{2}x^2$

2 (a) $x - \frac{1}{6}x^3 + \frac{1}{120}x^5$

 (b) $2x - \frac{4}{3}x^3 + \frac{4}{15}x^5$

 (c) $1 + x + \frac{1}{2}x^2 + \frac{1}{6}x^3 + \frac{1}{24}x^4$

 (d) $1 - 3x + \frac{9}{2}x^2 - \frac{9}{2}x^3 + \frac{27}{8}x^4$

 (e) x^2

 (f) $1 - x^2$

 (g) $-x - \frac{1}{2}x^2 - \frac{1}{3}x^3 - \frac{1}{4}x^4$

 (h) $1 + x + \frac{3}{2}x^2 + \frac{5}{2}x^3$

 (i) $1 - \frac{1}{2}x^2 + \frac{1}{8}x^4$

 (j) $x^2 - \frac{1}{2}x^4$

3 $1,\ \frac{1}{2}$

4 $1,\ \frac{1}{2}$

5 $\frac{1}{2},\ -\frac{1}{24}$

6 $1 + mx + \dfrac{m(m-1)}{2} x^2 + \dfrac{m(m-1)(m-2)}{6} x^3$
$+ \dfrac{m(m-1)(m-2)(m-3)}{24} x^4$

Exercise 3B (page 42)

1 (a) 1.6487   (b) 0.8415   (c) 0.9655
(d) 0.9397   (e) −0.0513   (f) 0.8109
(g) −0.9900

2 $2x + \frac{2}{3}x^3 + \frac{2}{5}x^5 + \cdots + \dfrac{2}{2r+1} x^{2r+1} + \cdots,$
$-1 < x < 1$; 1.099; $x = 2$ is outside interval of validity $-1 < x \leqslant 1$

3 $-\frac{1}{3}x^3 + \frac{1}{30}x^5 \, ; -\frac{1}{3}$

4 (a) 2   (b) $\frac{1}{2}$ (c) 1   (d) $-\frac{1}{2}$

6 1, 2; the second, which uses a value of x closer to 0

7 4×10^{-4}, 7×10^{-10}. For any value of x, the error in using $p_n(x)$ for $\cos x$ becomes very small if n is large, suggesting that the expansion is valid for all real numbers.

Exercise 3C (page 48)

1 (a) $1 + 3x + \frac{3}{2}x^2 - \frac{1}{2}x^3 + \frac{3}{8}x^4$
(b) $1 - 2x + 2x^2 - \frac{4}{3}x^3 + \frac{2}{3}x^4$
(c) x^3 (d) x^3

2 (a) $1 + 3x + \frac{9}{2}x^2 + \cdots + \dfrac{3^r}{r!} x^r + \cdots, \quad \mathbb{R}$
(b) $1 - \frac{1}{8}x^2 + \frac{1}{384}x^4 - \cdots + \dfrac{(-1)^r}{2^{2r} \times (2r)!} x^{2r}$
$+ \cdots, \quad \mathbb{R}$
(c) $x - \frac{1}{6}x^2 + \frac{1}{120}x^3 - \cdots + \dfrac{(-1)^{r-1}}{(2r-1)!} x^r + \cdots,$
positive $\mathbb{R}$
(d) $-x - \frac{1}{2}x^2 - \frac{1}{3}x^3 - \cdots - \dfrac{1}{r}x^r - \cdots,$
$-1 \leqslant x < 1$
(e) $2x - 2x^2 + \frac{8}{3}x^3 - \cdots + \dfrac{(-1)^{r-1}2^r}{r}x^r$
$+ \cdots, -\frac{1}{2} < x \leqslant \frac{1}{2}$
(f) $e + ex + \frac{1}{2}ex^2 + \cdots + \dfrac{e}{r!}x^r + \cdots, \quad \mathbb{R}$
(g) $1 - x^2 + \frac{1}{3}x^4 + \cdots + \dfrac{(-1)^r 2^{2r-1}}{(2r)!} x^{2r}$
$+ \cdots, \quad \mathbb{R}$
(h) $1 + \dfrac{1}{e}x - \dfrac{1}{2e^2}x^2 + \cdots + \dfrac{(-1)^{r-1}}{re^r}x^r$
$+ \cdots, -e < x \leqslant e$
(i) $\cos 1 - (\sin 1)x - (\frac{1}{2}\cos 1)x^2 + \cdots$
$+ \dfrac{(-1)^r \cos 1}{(2r)!}x^{2r} + \dfrac{(-1)^{r+1}\sin 1}{(2r+1)!}x^{2r+1}$
$+ \cdots, \quad \mathbb{R}$

3 (a) $x - x^2 + \frac{1}{3}x^3$
(b) $1 - \frac{1}{2}x - \frac{5}{8}x^2 + \frac{3}{16}x^3 + \frac{25}{384}x^4$

(c) $1 + \frac{1}{2}x^2 - \frac{1}{3}x^3 + \frac{3}{8}x^4$
(d) $x + \frac{3}{2}x^2 + \frac{1}{3}x^3 - \frac{1}{12}x^4$
(e) $3x - \frac{21}{2}x^2 + 24x^3 - \frac{205}{4}x^4$
(f) $-6x^2 - 6x^3 + x^4$

4 (a) $e + 2ex + 3ex^2 + \frac{10}{3}ex^3 + \frac{19}{6}ex^4$
(b) $e + \frac{1}{2}ex + \frac{1}{48}ex^3 - \frac{5}{384}ex^4$
(c) $1 - \frac{1}{2}x^2 + \frac{5}{24}x^4$
(d) $\sin 1 - (\frac{1}{2}\cos 1)x^2 + \frac{1}{24}(\cos 1 - 3\sin 1)x^4$
(e) $1 + \frac{1}{2}x^2 + \frac{5}{24}x^4$
(f) $1 + \frac{1}{2}x^2 - \frac{1}{12}x^4$
(g) $x + \frac{1}{3}x^3$
(h) $\ln 2 + \frac{1}{2}x + \frac{1}{8}x^2 - \frac{1}{192}x^4$
(i) $1 + x + \frac{1}{2}x^2 + \frac{1}{2}x^3 + \frac{3}{8}x^4$

5 (a) e^{x^2}
(b) $\frac{1}{2}(e^x + e^{-x})$
(c) $\begin{cases} \frac{1}{2}(e^{\sqrt{x}} + e^{-\sqrt{x}}) & \text{if } x \geqslant 0, \\ \cos(\sqrt{-x}) & \text{if } x < 0. \end{cases}$

6 $g'(0)h(0) + g(0)h'(0),$
$g''(0)h(0) + 2g'(0)h'(0) + g(0)h''(0)$

Exercise 3D (page 50)

1 $x + \frac{1}{6}x^3 + \frac{3}{40}x^5 + \cdots$
$+ \dfrac{3 \times 5 \times 7 \times \cdots \times (2r-1)}{(2r+1) \times r! \times 2^r} x^{2r+1} + \cdots,$
$\frac{1}{2}\pi - x - \frac{1}{6}x^3 - \frac{3}{40}x^5 - \cdots$; 3.1416

2 3.141 59

3 $x - \frac{1}{18}x^3 + \frac{1}{600}x^5 - \cdots$
$+ \dfrac{(-1)^r}{(2r+1) \times (2r+1)!} x^{2r+1} + \cdots$

4 $x + \frac{1}{4}x^2 + \frac{1}{18}x^3 + \cdots + \dfrac{1}{r \times r!} x^r + \cdots$; 0.570

5 $\frac{1}{3}\theta + \frac{2}{81}\theta^3$; 0.82 radians

6 $(-1)^n \displaystyle\int_0^x \dfrac{u^n}{1+u}\, du$ (a positive error means that the approximation is too small)

7 6

Miscellaneous exercise 3 (page 51)

1 $1 + 6x + 22x^2$

2 $-\dfrac{\sin x}{1 + \cos x}, \ -\dfrac{1}{1 + \cos x}, \ -\dfrac{\sin x}{(1 + \cos x)^2},$
$-\dfrac{2 - \cos x}{(1 + \cos x)^2}$; $\ln 2 - \frac{1}{4}x^2 - \frac{1}{96}x^4$

3 $\frac{1}{2}(1 + \cos 2x); \ 1 - x^2 + \frac{1}{3}x^4 - \frac{2}{45}x^6$

4 $\ln 3 + \frac{1}{3}x - \frac{1}{18}x^2$

5 $-\frac{1}{4}$

6 $\frac{1}{2}, \frac{1}{2}$

7 10

8 3, 2, −1

9 $1 + x + \frac{1}{2}x^2$

10 $\frac{1}{9}$; 0.223 137

11 $r\left(\theta - \frac{1}{24}\theta^3 + \frac{1}{1920}\theta^5\right)$, $r\left(2\theta - \frac{1}{3}\theta^3 + \frac{1}{60}\theta^5\right)$;
$2r\theta - \frac{1}{240}r\theta^5$, error $\frac{1}{240}r\theta^5$;
0.016%; $\frac{1}{6}r(8a - b)$

12 $2x + \frac{4}{3}x^3 + \frac{12}{5}x^5 + \frac{40}{7}x^7$

13 e is an irrational number.

4 Hyperbolic functions

Exercise 4A (page 58)

1 (a) 3.762...   (b) 11.548...
   (c) 7.610...   (d) $\frac{4}{3}$
   (e) −1.935...   (f) e
   (g) 0.135...   (h) $\frac{17}{8}$

2 (a) cosh A (b) sinh 2
   (c) cosh 2   (d) −1
   (e) 2 cosh A cosh B (f) e^{2x}
   (g) sinh 3   (h) −cosh($x − y$)

3 In parts (a) and (d), replace cos by cosh and sin by sinh.
   (b) $2 \sinh x \sinh y \equiv$
      $\cosh(x + y) - \cosh(x - y)$
   (c) $\sinh 3x \equiv 3 \sinh x + 4 \sinh^3 x$

4 (a) e^u or e^{-u} (b) $-e^u$ or e^{-u}
   (c) $\cosh u \pm 1$
   (d) $\frac{\sinh u}{\cosh u}$ or $-\frac{\cosh u}{\sinh u}$

6 (a) $2(\cosh x - \sinh x)$ (b) $2|\sinh x|$
   (c) $\dfrac{1}{2 \cosh x}$ (d) $\dfrac{\cosh \frac{1}{2}x}{\sinh \frac{1}{2}x}$

7 (a) $\dfrac{1}{4 - x^2} + \dfrac{2}{x(4 - x^2)}$; $\mathbb{R} - \{-2, 0, 2\}$
   (b) $\dfrac{1 + x^2}{(1 - x^2)^2} + \dfrac{-2x}{(1 - x^2)^2}$; $\mathbb{R} - \{-1, 1\}$
   (c) $\frac{1}{2} + \dfrac{1 - e^x}{2(1 + e^x)}$; $\mathbb{R}$
   (d) $\dfrac{2}{4 - \sinh^2 x} + \dfrac{-\sinh x}{4 - \sinh^2 x}$;
      $\mathbb{R} - \{-\sinh^{-1} 2, \sinh^{-1} 2\}$
   (e) $\sec x + (-\tan x)$; $\{x \in \mathbb{R}; x \neq (n + \frac{1}{2})\pi\}$
   (f) $\dfrac{2(x^2 - 3)}{(x^2 - 1)(x^2 - 4)} + \dfrac{x(x^2 - 5)}{(x^2 - 1)(x^2 - 4)}$;
      $\mathbb{R} - \{-2, -1, 1, 2\}$
   (g) $\dfrac{-2(x^2 + 3)}{x^4 + 3x^2 + 4} + \dfrac{x(x^2 - 1)}{x^4 + 3x^2 + 4}$; $\mathbb{R}$
   (h) Even function

Exercise 4B (page 60)

1 (a) 4 sinh 4x (b) 5 cosh 5x
   (c) cosh 2x (d) 2 sinh x cosh x
   (e) $\dfrac{\sinh x}{2\sqrt{\cosh x}}$ (f) 1
   (g) $-\dfrac{\cosh x + 2 \sinh x}{(\sinh x + 2 \cosh x)^2}$
   (h) $\dfrac{x \cosh x - 2 \sinh x}{(x + \cosh x)^2}$
   (i) $\dfrac{2 \cos x \sinh x}{(\cos x + \sinh x)^2}$
   (j) e^{2x}

2 In parts (b) and (c) replace cos by cosh and sin by sinh
   (a) $\dfrac{d}{dx} \cosh^2 x = \sinh 2x$
   (d) $\displaystyle\int \sinh^2 u\,du = \frac{1}{2}(\sinh u \, \cosh u - u) + k$

3 (a) $\frac{1}{3} \cosh 3x + k$
   (b) $\frac{1}{4} \cosh 2x + k$
   (c) $\frac{1}{2}(\sinh x \cosh x + x) + k$
   (d) $x \cosh x - \sinh x + k$
   (e) $\frac{1}{2}\left(x^2 + \frac{1}{2}\right) \sinh 2x - \frac{1}{2}x \cosh 2x + k$
   (f) $\frac{1}{4}e^{2x} + \frac{1}{2}x + k$

4 (a) 6.82   (b) 1.76   (c) 8.46
   (d) 5.82   (e) 19.6   (f) 0.541

5 $2.5 \ln 2 - 1.5 \approx 0.233$

6 $\frac{1}{2}\pi(4 + \sinh 4) \approx 49.2$

7 $\frac{1}{10} \cosh 5x - \frac{1}{2} \cosh x + k$

8 (a) 1.543 08   (b) 74

9 (a) $1 + 2x^2 + \frac{2}{3}x^4 + \frac{4}{45}x^6 + \cdots$
      $+ \dfrac{2^{2r}}{(2r)!} x^{2r} + \cdots$
   (b) $x^2 + \frac{1}{3}x^4 + \frac{2}{45}x^6 + \cdots + \dfrac{2^{2r-1}}{(2r)!}x^{2r} + \cdots$
   (c) $1 + \frac{3}{2}x^2 + \frac{7}{8}x^4 + \frac{61}{240}x^6 + \cdots$
      $+ \dfrac{(3^{2r} + 3)}{4 \times (2r)!}x^{2r} + \cdots$
   (d) $x^4 + \frac{2}{3}x^6 + \cdots + \dfrac{2^{4r-3} - 2^{2r-1}}{(2r)!}x^{2r} + \cdots$

Exercise 4C (page 64)

1 (a) $\frac{13}{5}$ $\pm\frac{12}{5}$ $\pm\frac{12}{13}$ $\frac{5}{13}$
   (b) 3 $2\sqrt{2}$ $\frac{2}{3}\sqrt{2}$ $\frac{1}{3}$
   (c) $\frac{2}{3}\sqrt{3}$ $\frac{1}{3}\sqrt{3}$ $\frac{1}{2}$ $\frac{1}{2}\sqrt{3}$
   (d) $\frac{5}{4}$ $\pm\frac{3}{4}$ $\pm\frac{3}{5}$ $\frac{4}{5}$

2 (a) $\frac{4}{5}$ (b) $\frac{5}{13}$ (c) $-\frac{4}{3}$ (d) $\frac{25}{24}$

3 $\coth^2 x - 1 \equiv \operatorname{cosech}^2 x$

4 (b) all real numbers except 0
  (c) $-\operatorname{cosech} x \coth x$

5 (b) $f(x) < -1$ and $f(x) > 1$
  (c) $-\operatorname{cosech}^2 x$

6 (a) $-\tanh x$　　　(b) $\operatorname{cosech} x$
  (c) $-\operatorname{cosech} x(\coth^2 x + \operatorname{cosech}^2 x)$
  (d) $-2\operatorname{sech}^2 x \tanh x$　　(e) $2\operatorname{sech}^2 x \tanh x$
  (f) $\frac{1}{2}\operatorname{sech} x$

8 (a) $\ln(\sinh x) + k$　(b) $\tanh x + k$
  (c) $-\operatorname{cosech} x + k$

9 (a) $\ln(\cosh x) + k$
  (b) $x - \tanh x + k$
  (c) $\ln(\cosh x) - \frac{1}{2}\tanh^2 x + k$
  (d) $x - \tanh x - \frac{1}{3}\tanh^3 x + k$

Exercise 4D (page 69)

1 (a) $0.693\ldots$　　　(b) $1.443\ldots$
  (c) $-0.255\ldots$　　(d) $-0.652\ldots$

2 (a) $\frac{4}{5}$　(b) 5　　(c) $\frac{3}{5}$　(d) $\frac{4}{3}$

3 (a) $4\sqrt{3}$　(b) $\frac{1}{2}$　　(c) $\frac{1}{4}\sqrt{2}$　(d) $\frac{1}{3}\sqrt{3}$
  (e) $\frac{1}{2}(\sqrt{5}-1)$　　　(f) $\frac{5}{4}$

4 $\sinh^{-1} x = \ln(x + \sqrt{1+x^2})$; $x - \sqrt{1+x^2}$ is
  negative, so $\ln(x - \sqrt{1+x^2})$ does not exist.
  $\cosh^{-1} x = \ln(x + \sqrt{x^2-1})$; note that
  $x - \sqrt{x^2-1} = (x + \sqrt{x^2-1})^{-1}$, so
  $\ln(x - \sqrt{x^2-1}) = -\cosh^{-1} x$.

7 (a) $\dfrac{1}{2\sqrt{x(1+x)}}$
  (b) $\dfrac{1}{\sqrt{1+x^2}}$ if $x > 0$, $-\dfrac{1}{\sqrt{1+x^2}}$ if $x < 0$
  (c) $-\dfrac{1}{2x}$

9 $\operatorname{cosech}^{-1} x = \sinh^{-1}\dfrac{1}{x}$,
  $\coth^{-1} x = \tanh^{-1}\dfrac{1}{x}$
  $\operatorname{sech}^{-1} x$:
  (a) $0 < x \leqslant 1$, $\operatorname{sech}^{-1} x \geqslant 0$
  (c) $-\dfrac{1}{x\sqrt{1-x^2}}$　　(d) $\ln\dfrac{1+\sqrt{1-x^2}}{x}$
  $\operatorname{cosech}^{-1} x$:
  (a) $\mathbb{R}$ except 0, $\mathbb{R}$ except 0
  (c) $-\dfrac{1}{|x|\sqrt{x^2+1}}$　　(d) $\ln\left(\dfrac{1}{x} + \dfrac{\sqrt{x^2+1}}{|x|}\right)$
  $\coth^{-1} x$:
  (a) $x < -1$ and $x > 1$, $\mathbb{R}$ except 0
  (c) $-\dfrac{1}{x^2-1}$　　(d) $\frac{1}{2}\ln\dfrac{x+1}{x-1}$

10 (a) $\ln(1+\sqrt{2})$　　(b) $\ln 2$
  (c) $\ln\dfrac{3+\sqrt{10}}{1+\sqrt{2}}$　　(d) $\ln(4-\sqrt{7})$
  (e) $\ln\dfrac{2(1+\sqrt{2})}{1+\sqrt{5}}$　　(f) $\frac{1}{3}\ln\dfrac{7+\sqrt{40}}{4+\sqrt{7}}$

11 (a) $x\tanh^{-1} x + \frac{1}{2}\ln(1-x^2) + k$
  (b) $x\sinh^{-1} x - \sqrt{1+x^2} + k$

12 (a) $-\cosh^{-1}(\sec x)$　(b) $-\cosh^{-1}(\sec x)$

13 $x - \frac{1}{6}x^3 + \frac{3}{40}x^5 - \cdots$
  $+ (-1)^r \dfrac{1 \times 3 \times 5 \times \cdots \times (2r-1)}{(2r+1) \times 2^r \times r!} x^{2r+1} + \cdots$

14 $-\cosh^{-1}(-x) + k$, $\ln(2+\sqrt{3})$

Exercise 4E (page 73)

1 (a) $\frac{1}{12}\tan^{-1}\left(\frac{4}{3}e^x\right) + k$
  (b) $-\frac{1}{12}\tanh^{-1}\left(\frac{4}{3}e^x\right) + k$

2 (a) $\ln 3$　　　　　(b) 0, $\ln\frac{7}{5}$
  (c) No solution　　(d) $\ln 2$, $\ln\frac{2}{7}$

3 (a) $\dfrac{2}{3-e^x} + k$　　(b) $\ln\left|\dfrac{5e^x-7}{e^x-1}\right| + k$
  (c) $\frac{1}{5}\ln\dfrac{3e^x+13}{e^x+1} + k$　(d) $\frac{1}{12}\ln\left|\dfrac{e^x-2}{7e^x-2}\right| + k$

4 (a) $3\cosh(x-\alpha)$, $\alpha = \ln 3$
  (b) $\sqrt{35}\cosh(x-\alpha)$, $\alpha = \frac{1}{2}\ln\frac{7}{5}$
  (c) $-\sqrt{39}\cosh(x-\alpha)$, $\alpha = \frac{1}{2}\ln\frac{13}{3}$
  (d) $4\sqrt{7}\cosh(x+\alpha)$, $\alpha = \frac{1}{2}\ln\frac{7}{4}$

5 $-\frac{1}{2}\pi < u < \frac{1}{2}\pi$; $\sec u$, $\sin u$; $\sec u$, $\operatorname{sech} t$;
  (a) $\sinh^{-1}(\tan u) + k$
  (b) $\tan^{-1}(\sinh t) + k$
  $2\tan^{-1}(e^t) = \tan^{-1}(\sinh t) + \frac{1}{2}\pi$

Miscellaneous exercise 4 (page 74)

1 $\left(\pm\ln(1+\sqrt{2}), \frac{1}{2}\sqrt{2}\right)$

2 $2\tan^{-1}(1+\sqrt{2}) - \frac{1}{2}\ln 2 - \frac{1}{2}\pi = \frac{1}{4}\pi - \frac{1}{2}\ln 2$

3 $\left(\sinh^{-1}\lambda, \sqrt{1+\lambda^2}\right)$

7 $\frac{1}{3}\ln(6+\sqrt{37})$

9 (a) $\dfrac{1}{a}\tanh^{-1}\dfrac{x}{a} + k$　　(b) $\dfrac{1}{2a}\ln\dfrac{a+x}{a-x} + k$

10 $y = \operatorname{sech} x$ (because $2\pi > \frac{1}{2}\pi^2$)

11 (b) 12　　　　　(c) $\ln 2$, $\ln\frac{2}{9}$
  (d) $\frac{1}{6}\tan^{-1}\left(\frac{3}{2}e^x\right) + k$

12 If $a > 1$, $\dfrac{1}{\sqrt{a^2-1}}\ln\left|\dfrac{e^x\sqrt{a+1}-\sqrt{a-1}}{e^x\sqrt{a+1}+\sqrt{a-1}}\right| + k$
  If $a = 1$, $-e^{-x} + k$
  If $-1 < a < 1$,
  $\dfrac{2}{\sqrt{1-a^2}}\tan^{-1}\left(e^x\sqrt{\dfrac{1+a}{1-a}}\right) + k$

If $a = -1$, $e^x + k$

If $a < -1$,

$$\frac{1}{\sqrt{a^2 - 1}} \ln \left| \frac{\sqrt{1-a} + e^x\sqrt{-1-a}}{\sqrt{1-a} - e^x\sqrt{-1-a}} \right| + k$$

13 $1 - \frac{1}{6} x^4 + \frac{1}{2520} x^8 - \cdots + (-1)^r \frac{4^r}{(4r)!} x^{4r} + \cdots$

14 (a) $\frac{1}{4} \sinh 3x - \frac{3}{4} \sinh x$

   (b) $\frac{1}{8} \cosh 4x + \frac{1}{2} \cosh 2x + \frac{3}{8}$

   (c) $\frac{1}{32} \cosh 6x - \frac{3}{16} \cosh 4x + \frac{15}{32} \cosh 2x - \frac{5}{16}$

   (d) $\frac{1}{16} \cosh 5x + \frac{1}{16} \cosh 3x - \frac{1}{8} \cosh x$

15 $16 \cosh^5 x - 20 \cosh^3 x + 5 \cosh x$

   (a) $16 \sinh^5 x + 20 \sinh^3 x + 5 \sinh x$

   (b) $32 \cosh^6 x - 48 \cosh^4 x + 18 \cosh^2 x - 1$

5 Graphs of rational functions

Exercise 5A (page 81)

1 (a) $x = 0$, $y = 0$ (b) $x = 1$, $y = 0$
   (c) $x = -2$, $y = 0$ (d) $x = \frac{1}{2}$, $y = 0$
   (e) $x = 0$, $y = 1$ (f) $x = -1$, $y = 3$
   (g) $x = -2$, $y = 4$ (h) $x = \frac{1}{2}$, $y = 3$
   (i) $x = 0$, $y = 1$ (j) $x = 0$, $y = 1$
   (k) $x = 1$, $y = 1$ (l) $x = -2$, $y = 3$

2 (a) $x = 0$, $y = x$ (b) $x = 0$, $y = x + 1$
   (c) $x = 1$, $y = 3x - 2$ (d) $x = 2$, $y = x - 3$
   (e) $x = 0$, $y = x$ (f) $x = 1$, $y = x - 1$
   (g) $x - 2$, $y - x + 1$ (h) $x - 1$, $y = 2x - 1$
   (i) $x = -\frac{1}{2}$, $y = 1 - x$

3 (a) $(-2, -4)$ maximum, $(2, 4)$ minimum
   (b) $(-2, -2)$ maximum, $(0, 2)$ minimum
   (c) $\left(-\frac{3}{4}, -5\right)$ maximum, $\left(-\frac{1}{4}, 3\right)$ minimum

4 (a) $x = 0$, $y = x$; $(-1, 0)$, $(1, 0)$; no maxima or minima
   (b) $x = 0$, $y = x$; curve does not cross either axis; $(1, 2)$ minimum, $(-1, -2)$ maximum
   (c) $x = 0$, $y = 2x + 3$; $\left(\frac{1}{4}(-3 \pm \sqrt{5}), 0\right)$; $\left(-\frac{1}{2}, 1\right)$ maximum, $\left(\frac{1}{2}, 5\right)$ minimum
   (d) $x = \frac{1}{2}$, $y = x - 1$; $(0, 0)$, $\left(\frac{3}{2}, 0\right)$; no maxima or minima
   (e) $x = 1$, $y = 9x + 4$; $(0, 3)$, $\left(\frac{1}{18}(5 \pm \sqrt{133}), 0\right)$; $\left(\frac{2}{3}, 7\right)$ maximum, $\left(\frac{4}{3}, 19\right)$ minimum
   (f) $x = \frac{1}{2}$, $y = x + \frac{1}{2}$; $(0, 0)$; $(1, 2)$ minimum, $(0, 0)$ maximum

5 8

6 $x = a$, $y = a + x$

7 $p = a^2$, $q = 2ab$, $r \neq b^2$

Exercise 5B (page 87)

1 (a) $x = 0$, $x = 2$, $y = 0$; $(1, -1)$ maximum
   (b) $x = 0$, $x = 2$, $y = 0$; no maxima or minima
   (c) $x = 0$, $x = 2$, $y = 1$; $(1, 0)$ maximum
   (d) $x = 1$, $y = x$; $(0, -1)$ maximum, $(2, 3)$ minimum
   (e) $x = -2$, $x = 2$, $y = 1$; $(0, 0)$ maximum
   (f) $x = -2$, $x = 2$, $y = 0$; no maxima or minima
   (g) $x = -2$, $x = 2$, $y = 0$; no maxima or minima
   (h) $x = -2$, $x = 2$, $y = 0$; $\left(0, -\frac{1}{4}\right)$ maximum

2 (a) $x = 0$, $y = 0$; no maxima or minima
   (b) $x = 0$, $y = 0$; $\left(2, \frac{1}{4}\right)$ maximum
   (c) $x = 1$, $y = 0$; no maxima or minima
   (d) $x = 1$, $y = 0$; $\left(-1, -\frac{1}{4}\right)$ minimum

3 (a) $y = 0$; $(0, 1)$ maximum
   (b) $y = 0$; $\left(-2, -\frac{1}{2}\right)$ minimum, $\left(0, \frac{1}{2}\right)$ maximum
   (c) $y = 0$; $\left(-1, \frac{1}{2}\right)$ maximum, $\left(1, -\frac{1}{2}\right)$ minimum
   (d) $y = 0$; $\left(-2, -\frac{1}{3}\right)$ minimum, $(0, 1)$ maximum

4 (a) $y = 1$; $\left(0, \frac{2}{3}\right)$; $(-2, 2)$ maximum, $\left(1, \frac{1}{2}\right)$ minimum
   (b) $x = 1$, $y = 1$; $(0, 0)$; $(0, 0)$ minimum
   (c) $x = 1$, $y = 1$; $(0, -1)$, $(-1, 0)$; no maxima or minima
   (d) $y = 1$; $(0, -1)$, $(-1, 0)$, $(1, 0)$; $(0, -1)$ minimum

5 -5, $x = 1$

Exercise 5C (page 90)

3 (a) $y \geqslant -\frac{1}{8}$ (b) No restrictions
   (c) No restrictions

5 $0 < k < 3$

Miscellaneous exercise 5 (page 90)

1 $x = -1$, $y = x + 1$

2 $x < -2$ or $x > 2$; $x = -2$, $x = 2$, $y = 0$

3 $-\frac{1}{4}$, $\frac{1}{4}$; $y = 0$

4 No stationary values; $x = -2$, $x = 2$, $y = 0$

5 -1 minimum, $\frac{1}{7}$ maximum

6 $p < -1$

7 $y = x + a - b$; if $a = 2b$ the equation of the curve reduces to the straight line $y = x + b$.

8 For example,

(a) $y = -\dfrac{1}{x+2}$ (b) $y = 4 - \dfrac{1}{x-3}$

(c) $y = 1 + \dfrac{x}{x^2-1}$ (d) $y = \dfrac{2x^2}{x^2-1}$

9 (a) $(-\sqrt{2}, 0), (\sqrt{2}, 0), (0, -\frac{1}{2})$

(b) $x = 2,\ y = 1$

(c) $(1, -1)$

11 (a) $(-\frac{1}{2}, 0),\ x = 1$ (b) $(-2, -1)$

12 (a) $(4-k)^2 \geqslant 4(4-k)$

(b) $(-2, 0), (0, 4)$

13 (c) $(-a, 0)$

6 Polar coordinates

Exercise 6A (page 95)

2 (a) $(0, 10)$ (b) $(-\sqrt{3}, 1)$

(c) $(-2\sqrt{2}, -2\sqrt{2})$ (d) $(-3, -3\sqrt{3})$

(e) $(-5, 0)$ (f) $(-1.248\ldots, 2.727\ldots)$

3 (a) $(3, \pi)$

(b) $(13, 0.394\ldots)$

(c) (i) $(2\sqrt{2}, 1\frac{3}{4}\pi)$ (ii) $(2\sqrt{2}, -\frac{1}{4}\pi)$

(d) (i) $(4, 1\frac{1}{2}\pi)$ (ii) $(4, -\frac{1}{2}\pi)$

(e) (i) $(5, 4.068\ldots)$ (ii) $(5, -2.214\ldots)$

(f) $(2, \frac{2}{3}\pi)$

4 $\sqrt{19}$

5 (a) $\left(r\cos\frac{1}{2}(\beta-\alpha), \frac{1}{2}(\alpha+\beta)\right)$

(b) $\left(-r\cos\frac{1}{2}(\beta-\alpha), \frac{1}{2}(\alpha+\beta) \pm \pi\right)$

6 $(4, \frac{5}{6}\pi)$

7 $(2\sqrt{2}, \frac{5}{12}\pi)$, $(2, \frac{2}{3}\pi)$, or $(2\sqrt{2}, -\frac{1}{12}\pi)$, $(2, -\frac{1}{3}\pi)$

8 $(5\sqrt{3}, \frac{1}{6}\pi)$, $(5\sqrt{3}, \frac{1}{2}\pi)$

Exercise 6B (page 97)

3 It is a spiral.

Exercise 6C (page 99)

3 Yes

4 Symmetrical about the lines for $n = 0, 2$ and 4.

Exercise 6D (page 102)

2 (a) (ii) $0, \pi^2$ (iii) $\theta = 0$ (iv) $\theta = 0$

(b) (ii) $0, 2$ (iii) $\theta = -\frac{1}{4}\pi, \frac{3}{4}\pi$

(iv) $\theta = \pm\frac{1}{4}\pi$

(c) (ii) Least value $\frac{1}{3}$; no greatest value

(iii) The curve does not pass through the pole.

(iv) $\theta = 0$ (or π)

(d) (ii) $0, 2$ (iii) $\theta = \frac{1}{2}\pi$ (iv) $\theta = \frac{1}{2}\pi$

(e) (ii) $0, 3\frac{1}{8}$ (iii) $\theta = -\frac{1}{2}\pi$ (iv) $\theta = \frac{1}{2}\pi$,

(f) (ii) $0, 2\frac{1}{4}$ (iii) $\theta = -\pi$ (iv) $\theta = 0$

(g) (ii) $0, 10$ (iii) $\theta = 0.927$

(iv) $\theta = 0.927$

(h) (ii) $0, 2$ (other turning values are minima of 0.728 at ±1.15 and maxima of 1.27 at ±1.99)

(iii) $\theta = \pi$ (iv) $\theta = 0$

Exercise 6E (page 104)

1 (a) $x^2 + y^2 = 2y$

(b) $(x^2 + y^2)^3 = a^2(x^2 - y^2)^2$ for $x > 0$

(c) $y = a$ (d) $8x^2 + 8x + 9y^2 = 16$

2 (a) $r^2 = 2\operatorname{cosec} 2\theta$ for $0 < \theta < \frac{1}{2}\pi$

(b) $r = 2$

(c) $r = 2(\cos\theta + \sin\theta)$ for $-\frac{1}{4}\pi < \theta < \frac{3}{4}\pi$

(d) $r = a(\sec\theta + \operatorname{cosec}\theta)$ for $0 < \theta < \frac{1}{2}\pi$

Exercise 6F (page 107)

1 (a) $\frac{1}{4}(e^{2\pi} - 1)$ (b) $\frac{1}{5}\pi^5$

(c) $\pi a^2 + 2\pi^2 ab + \frac{4}{3}\pi^3 b^2$ (d) $\frac{1}{8}(\pi + 2)a^2$

(e) $2ab + \frac{1}{4}\pi(2a^2 + b^2)$

2 $\frac{1}{2}a^2$

3 $\frac{1}{2}\pi$

5 $\frac{1}{2}\pi a^2$

Exercise 6G (page 113)

4 Simple closed curve if $k \geqslant 1$; convex if $k \geqslant 2$, dented if $1 < k < 2$, cusp if $k = 1$. Integral represents area enclosed. Closed curve with two loops if $0 < k < 1$. Integral represents sum of areas of loops. Circle if $k = 0$. Integral represents twice the area enclosed.

5 $\frac{1}{4}\pi$ if n is odd, $\frac{1}{2}\pi$ if n is even

6 Through $(2a, 0)$ perpendicular to the initial line

7 (b) $\theta = \pi$ (c) $\theta = 0$ (d) $\theta = \pm\frac{1}{3}\pi$; for $k = -2$, area $= \sqrt{3} + \frac{4}{3}\pi - 4\ln(2 + \sqrt{3})$

8 $\frac{1}{2}(4 - \pi)a^2$

Miscellaneous exercise 6 (page 114)

1 (a) 7   (b) $10\sqrt{3}$

3 (a) $(x^2 + y^2)^2 = x^3$ (b) $y^2 = x^2(x - 1)$

4 $r = \sec^2\theta + \operatorname{cosec}^2\theta$

5 (a) $\frac{5}{16}\pi$ (b) $\left(\frac{3}{4}\sqrt{3}, -\frac{1}{6}\pi\right)$

6 $OCQ,\ CQP$

7 $r = a(\cos\theta - \sin\theta)$;
$r = \sqrt{2}a\cos\theta$, $x^2 + y^2 = \sqrt{2}ax$

8 $r^2 \cos 2\theta = a^2$; $2xy = a^2$

9 $\dfrac{(x+4)^2}{25} + \dfrac{y^2}{9} = 1$

10 $x^2 + y^2 = x^{\frac{4}{3}}$

11 $\frac{1}{3}\pi$, $\frac{1}{2}\pi$, $\frac{2}{3}\pi$; $\alpha = \frac{1}{3}\pi$,
$f(\theta) = \frac{1}{2}(\cos 3\theta + 2\cos\theta)^2$; $\frac{5}{6}\pi + \frac{3}{4}\sqrt{3}$

12 $\frac{1}{2}(4 - \pi)a^2$

13 $\frac{8}{3}\sqrt{2}$

14 $-\frac{1}{8}$, $\cos^{-1}\left(-\frac{1}{4}\right)$

Revision exercise 1 (page 117)

1 $1 - 2x^2 + \frac{2}{3}x^4$, $1 + x - \frac{3}{2}x^2$

2 $2 + \frac{3}{4}\pi$

3 (a) $\dfrac{x}{x^2+4} - \dfrac{1}{x+2}$ (b) $-\frac{1}{2}\ln 2$

5 $x = 2$, $x = -1$, $y = 3$

6 (a) $1 + ax + \frac{1}{2}a^2 x^2$
(b) $1 + (a - b)x + \left(\frac{1}{2}a^2 - ab\right)x^2$
(c) $a = 2$, $b = 2$ or $a = -2$, $b = -2$

7 (a) $-\frac{1}{4}\pi$, $\frac{1}{4}\pi$ (b) $\frac{1}{2}\pi$

8 (b) $\ln(3 \pm \sqrt{8})$

9 (a) $\dfrac{1}{a}\cos y$ (b) $\dfrac{a}{\sqrt{1 - a^2 x^2}}$
(c) $\frac{1}{3}\sin^{-1} 3x + k$ (d) $\frac{1}{24}\sqrt{3} + \frac{1}{36}\pi$

10 (a) $2 - 9x^2$, $-3x - \frac{9}{2}x^2$
(b) $2 + 6x + 18x^2$

11 (b) $(-1, -1)$, minimum; $\left(\frac{1}{2}, 2\right)$, maximum
(c) $\dfrac{1}{\sqrt{2}}\tan^{-1}\sqrt{2} + \ln 3$

12 (a) $r = 2$, when $\theta = \frac{1}{4}\pi$, $\frac{5}{4}\pi$
(b) Because $r = 0$ when $\theta = \frac{3}{4}\pi$
(c) $\frac{3}{4}\pi$ (d) $(x^2 + y^2)^{\frac{3}{2}} = (x + y)^2$

13 (b) $\ln 2 + 3\tan^{-1} 2 - 3\tan^{-1} 3$

14 $\ln \frac{2}{3}$, $\ln 2$

15 (a) 0.1155 (b) 0.1163

16 (a) $\dfrac{a}{a^2 + x^2}$, $\tan^{-1}\dfrac{x}{a}$ (b) $\frac{1}{4}\pi$

17 $0 \leqslant x \leqslant 1$; 1.791

18 $-\frac{1}{3}$, $\frac{3}{2}$, $-\frac{5}{12}$, $\frac{1}{12}$; $\cdots + \frac{1}{432}x^6$, $\cdots - \frac{1}{288}x^6$,
second is better; $0.995\,004\,169$, $0.995\,004\,163$,
$0.995\,004\,165$

19 (c) $10 + \frac{9}{2}\ln 3$

20 0, $-\ln 3$

21 (a) $\dfrac{1}{\sqrt{4 - x^2}}$ (b) $-\dfrac{2}{x\sqrt{4 - x^2}}$;
$3\sin^{-1}\left(\dfrac{x}{2}\right) - \cosh^{-1}\left(\dfrac{2}{x}\right) + k$

22 (a) $1 + 2x^2 + \frac{5}{3}x^4$ (b) $\frac{255}{32}$

23 (b) $\ln 3 + \frac{3}{4}x - \frac{45}{128}x^2$

24 $x + \frac{1}{6}x^3 + \frac{1}{120}x^5$; $\frac{1}{3}\sinh\frac{3}{2}$

7   Series and integrals

Exercise 7A (page 124)

1 (a) 4.5, 3.5; 4.1, 3.9; exact value 4
(b) $8.156\,25$, $5.906\,25$; 7.455, 6.555;
exact value 7
(c) $5.146\ldots$, $4.146\ldots$; $4.911\ldots$, $4.411\ldots$;
$4.790\ldots$, $4.540\ldots$; exact value $4\frac{2}{3}$
(d) $\frac{3}{4}\pi$, $\frac{1}{4}\pi$; $\frac{2}{3}\pi$, $\frac{1}{3}\pi$; exact value $\frac{1}{2}\pi$
(e) 14, 6; 11.06, 10.26; exact value $10\frac{2}{3}$

2 (a) 48.08π, 28.88π; 42.92π, 33.32π;
40.43π, 35.63π; exact value 38π
(b) 1.75π, 1.25π; 1.6π, 1.4π; 1.55π, 1.45π;
exact value 1.5π
(c) 9π, 6π; 8.25π, 6.75π; 7.8π, 7.2π;
exact value 7.5π
(d) $4.386\,56\pi$, $3.186\,56\pi$; $4.046\,66\pi$,
$3.446\,66\pi$; exact value $3\frac{11}{15}\pi$
(e) $0.749\ldots\pi$, $0.549\ldots\pi$; $0.710\ldots\pi$,
$0.610\ldots\pi$; exact value $\frac{2}{3}\pi$

3 (b) $\displaystyle\sum_{r=1}^{9}(r + \ln r)$
$< \displaystyle\int_{1}^{10}(x + \ln x)\,dx < \sum_{r=2}^{10}(r + \ln r)$
$9 + \ln 10$
(c) $\frac{1}{10}(9 + \ln 10)$

Exercise 7B (page 131)

2 (a) 4243, 4246
(b) 30.69, 30.18
(c) 57.29, 56.29
(d) $0.007\,854$, $0.007\,803$

3 (a) $\dfrac{(n + m - 1)(n - m + 1)}{2(m - 1)^2 n^2}$,
$\dfrac{(n + m + 1)(n - m + 1)}{2m^2(n + 1)^2}$
(b) $\frac{1}{6}\ln\dfrac{1 + 2n^3}{1 + 2(m - 1)^3}$, $\frac{1}{6}\ln\dfrac{1 + 2(n + 1)^3}{1 + 2m^3}$
(c) $\dfrac{(n + 1)^{n+1}}{(m + 1)^{m+1}}e^{-(n-m)}$, $\dfrac{n^n}{m^m}e^{-(n-m)}$

4 (b) $\frac{3}{4}(9^{\frac{4}{3}} - 1)$

(c) $\frac{3}{4}(201^{\frac{4}{3}} - 101^{\frac{4}{3}})$, $\frac{3}{4}(200^{\frac{4}{3}} - 100^{\frac{4}{3}})$

6 (c) $\cosh^{-1}(2n + 1)$

Miscellaneous exercise 7 (page 132)

2 $4h + 14h^3$; 30; 0.445

3 $\sqrt{17} + \sqrt{26} + \sqrt{37}$

5 (c) $\frac{1}{2}((\ln(n + 1))^2 - (\ln 4)^2)$

8 Approximations and errors

In this chapter your answers may differ from those given by 1 or 2 in the last decimal place. This will usually depend on whether or not you have rounded intermediate values in the calculations. Don't spend time trying to get an exact match between your answers and those given if they are close enough to indicate that you have used a correct procedure.

Exercise 8A (page 139)

1 1.892 60, 1.897 33, 1.894 32; −0.004 51, 0.002 89, −0.001 84, 0.001 17; −0.641, −0.637, −0.636; 2 cos 1.895 49 = −0.638

2 0.592 73, 0.590 43, 0.589 71, 0.589 49, 0.589 42, 0.589 40, 0.589 39, 0.589 39; $k = 7$; −0.010 61, −0.003 34, −0.001 04, −0.000 32, −0.000 10; 0.315, 0.311, 0.308, 0.312; F′(α) ≈ 0.312; 9×10^{-8}

3 2.314 59, 2.312 77, 2.313 00, 2.312 97; 0.012 97, −0.001 62, 0.000 20, −0.000 03; −0.125, −0.123, −0.150; F′(α) ≈ −0.125

4 If $F(x) = \frac{1}{3}(1 - x^3)$, −0.1225 < F′(x) < −0.09 at the root; 0.322 185

5 If $F(x) = \sqrt[5]{10 - x}$, −0.0364... < F′(x) < −0.0360... at the root; 1.533 01

6 (b) F_1, F_3 for smaller root, F_2, F_4 for larger

(c) F_3 for smaller root, F_2 for larger

(d) 1.585 79, 4.414 21

(f) About 23, 14, 14, 37

7 (b) F_1 does not converge to either root, F_2 gives the lower, F_3 the higher, F_4 both.

(c) F_4 (with minus sign), F_3

(d) −6.123 11, 2.123 11

(f) About 14, 14, 14 (lower), over 200 (higher), the last answer is only of theoretical interest.

8 F_3, F_4, F_3; −2.8820, −0.2235, 3.1055

9 F_2, F_3, F_3; −3.7093, −1.1939, 0.9032

10 (a) 4.107 24 (b) 3.355 30 (c) 0.514 93

(d) 0.765 01 (e) 0.703 29 (f) 1.660 80

12 (a) $1 + 2x + 2x^2 + \frac{8}{3}x^3$

(b) $3 + \frac{1}{6}x - \frac{1}{216}x^2 + \frac{1}{3888}x^3$

(c) $2 + 2\sqrt{3}x + 7x^2 + \frac{23}{3}\sqrt{3}x^3$

(d) $\frac{1}{6}\pi + \frac{2}{3}\sqrt{3}x + \frac{2}{9}\sqrt{3}x^2 + \frac{8}{27}\sqrt{3}x^3$

Exercise 8B (page 142)

1 (a) 0.652 92 to 5 significant figures

(b) 0.739 085 to 6 significant figures

(c) 2.302 775 64 to 9 significant figures

(d) 1.146 to 4 significant figures

1.146 193 to 7 significant figures

Exercise 8C (page 148)

1 2.152, 2.095 927 808, 2.037 691 319, 2.005 736 088, 2.000 131 800, 2.000 000 007; −0.152, −0.095 927 808, −0.037 691 319, −0.005 736 088, −0.000 131 800, −0.000 000 007 compared with predicted −0.16, −0.092 416, −0.036 808 577, −0.005 682 542, −0.000 131 611, −0.000 000 007

2 $\alpha = 2$; 2.026 446 281, 2.000 515 456, 2.000 000 199, 2.000 000 000; −0.026 446 281, −0.000 515 456, −0.000 000 199 compared with predicted −0.03, −0.000 524 554, −0.000 000 199

4 0.347 296 355; errors -2.7×10^{-3}, -2.9×10^{-6}, 0

1.532 088 886; errors 3.2×10^{-2}, -1.2×10^{-3}, -1.8×10^{-6}, 0

−1.879 385 241; errors 2.1×10^{-2}, 3.1×10^{-4}, 7.1×10^{-8}, 0

5 (a) 0.426 302 751; errors 2.6×10^{-2}, -1.1×10^{-3}, -1.9×10^{-6}, 0

(b) 0.739 085 133; errors -1.1×10^{-2}, -2.6×10^{-5}, 0

6 $x_{r+1} = \frac{1}{3}\left(2x_r + \dfrac{N}{x_r^2}\right)$; 2.154 434 690

7 $x_{r+1} = \frac{1}{m}\left((m - 1)x_r + \dfrac{N}{x_r^{m-1}}\right)$; 1.974 350 486

Miscellaneous exercise 8 (page 149)

1 $k \approx -0.176$; $0.531\,39$

2 (a) $4, 1, 0.25, 0.0625; \left(\frac{1}{4}\right)^{r-1}$
  (b) $4, -2, 1\ -0.5; \left(-\frac{1}{2}\right)^{r-2}$
  (c) x_r diverges; it is negative with a large modulus.
  (d) x_r diverges; it is alternately positive and negative with a large modulus.
  (e) x_r takes the values 0 and 8 alternately.

3 (a) 2 roots: $4.541\,381$, $-1.541\,381$
  (b) 3 roots: $-4.592\,253$, $0.250\,789$, $4.341\,465$
  (c) 2 roots: $1.611\,793$, $3.820\,704$
  (d) 2 roots: $-0.815\,553$, $1.429\,612$
  (e) 3 roots: $-1.534\,645$, $1.612\,756$, $4.010\,988$
  (f) 1 root: $2.219\,107$

4 (c) Not convergent for $k = 2$; convergent to $2.153\,292$ for $k = -1$.

5 (b) $2.107\,086$ (c) First iteration

6 $k \approx 0.5265$; $0.703\,290\,66$

7 (a) $0.714\,556\,38$
  (b) $0.876\,726\,22$
  (c) $0.111\,832\,56$, $3.577\,152\,06$

9 The Newton–Raphson method

In this chapter your answers may differ from those given by 1 or 2 in the last decimal place. This will usually depend on whether or not you have rounded intermediate values in the calculations. Don't spend time trying to get an exact match between your answers and those given if they are close enough to indicate that you have used a correct procedure.

Exercise 9A (page 156)

1 $y - f(x_0) = f'(x_0)(x - x_0)$

2 (a) 0.8080 (b) 0.5869 (c) 3.7944

3 (a) 2.4973, accurate to 4 decimal places
  (b) 2.5051, accurate to 4 decimal places
  (c) 0.6417, accurate to 4 decimal places
  (d) -1.0920, accurate to only 3 decimal places

4 $n\pi + \dfrac{(-1)^n}{n\pi}$

5 (a) With $x_0 = 2.43$, $2.429\,7811$ to 7 decimal places; $2.429\,781\,066$ to 9 decimal places
  (b) With $x_0 = 1.62$, $1.621\,35$ to 5 decimal places; $1.621\,347\,946$ to 9 decimal places
  (c) With $x_0 = 2.2$, $2.197\,45$ to 5 decimal places; $2.197\,451\,757$ to 9 decimal places

Exercise 9B (page 162)

1 (a) Error $\approx -9.9 \times 10^{-6}$, 3.1958 to 4 decimal places
  (b) Error $\approx 1.7 \times 10^{-3}$, 2.2 to 1 decimal place
  (c) Error $\approx -4.6 \times 10^{-6}$, $1.503\,34$ to 5 decimal places
  (d) Error $\approx -5.5 \times 10^{-5}$, 3.7687 to 4 decimal places

2 (a) $0.824\,132\,312$ (b) $1.234\,762\,161$
  (c) $0.588\,532\,744$

4 (a) $0.689\,139\,46$ (b) $0.772\,882\,96$
  (c) $0.510\,973\,43$ (d) $1.199\,678\,64$

5 2.79 m

6 -3.0×10^{-3}, -2.0×10^{-5}, -1.0×10^{-9}, -2.7×10^{-18}; $\dfrac{e_{r+1}}{e_r^2} \approx -2.66, -2.60, -2.53$;
  $\dfrac{-f''(\alpha)}{2f'(\alpha)} \approx -2.60$

Exercise 9C (page 164)

1 $0.684\,124\,319$, $-2.059\,142\,445$

2 $-0.297\,632\,210$, $-2.070\,275\,995$

3 $9.126\,123\,78$

4 $4.390\,977\,87$, $-9.999\,997\,73$

5 $1.150\,584\,967$

6 $2.219\,107\,149$

Miscellaneous exercise 9 (page 164)

1 3.686

2 0.739

3 1.986

4 3.327

5 4.026

6 (a) $(0, 1)$, $(\pm2.982\,87, 0.101\,04)$
  (b) $(0, 1)$, $(1.109\,14, 0,445\,43)$, $(3.698\,15, -0.849\,08)$
  (c) $(1.434\,55, 2.952\,22)$, $(-0.593\,32, -0.208\,86)$

7 $(\pm1.199\,68, \pm0.662\,74)$

8 (a) $\dfrac{\pi}{1+a}$
  (b) $p = \dfrac{1}{4n^2\pi^2}$, $q = \dfrac{1}{(2n+1)^2\pi^2}$

9 (b) $x_{r+1} = x_r - \dfrac{\tan x_r - 2x_r}{\sec^2 x_r - 2}$
  (c) Converges with $x_0 = 1.1$
  (e) It might diverge, or it might converge to one of the other roots.

10 $0.132\,86$

11 $0.3314 + 0.4712i$

12 $1.229 + 0.726i$
    (more accurately $1.228 + 0.726i$)

10 Integration using trigonometric functions

Exercise 10A (page 166)

2 For example, in part (e)

$$\int \cot x \, dx$$

$$= \begin{cases} \ln(\sin x) & \text{if } 2n\pi < x < (2n+1)\pi, \\ \ln(-\sin x) & \text{if } (2n+1)\pi < x < (2n+2)\pi. \end{cases}$$

In either case, $\int \cot x \, dx = \ln(|\sin x|)$, if $x \neq \mathbf{r}\pi$.

Exercise 10B (page 175)

1 (a) $-\cot x - x + k$
   (b) $\frac{1}{2}\tan^2 x + \ln|\cos x| + k$
   (c) $\frac{1}{3}\tan^3 x - \tan x + x + k$

2 (a) $\frac{2}{3}(\sin x)^{\frac{3}{2}} + k$
   (b) $\frac{1}{3}\sin^3 x - \frac{1}{5}\sin^5 x + k$
   (c) $-\cos x + \frac{2}{3}\cos^3 x - \frac{1}{5}\cos^5 x + k$
   (d) $-\operatorname{cosec}\theta - \sin\theta + k$
   (e) $-\ln|\cos\theta - \sin\theta| + k$
   (f) $\ln|1 + \tan t| + k$

3 1, $\cos^2\theta$, $1 + \sin 2\theta$
   (a) $2\tan\theta - 2\sec\theta - \theta + k$
   (b) $\tan\theta + \sec\theta + k$
   (c) $\sin\theta - \cos\theta - \frac{2}{3}\cos^3\theta + \frac{2}{3}\sin^3\theta + k$

4 (a) $-x\cot x + \ln|\sin x| + k$
   (b) $-\cos x \ln(\sin x) + \ln\left(\tan\frac{1}{2}x\right) + \cos x + k$
   (c) $\tan x \ln(\sec x) - \tan x + x + k$

5 (a) $\frac{1}{2}e^\theta(\cos\theta + \sin\theta) + k$
   (b) $\frac{1}{5}e^\theta(\sin 2\theta - 2\cos 2\theta) + k$
   (c) $e^{\theta\cos\alpha}\cos(\theta\sin\alpha - \alpha) + k$

6 x, $\ln|\cos x + \sin x|$;
   $\frac{1}{2}(x + \ln|\cos x + \sin x|) + k$,
   $\frac{1}{2}(x - \ln|\cos x + \sin x|) + k$
   (a) $\frac{1}{4}\pi$ (b) $\frac{1}{2}\ln 2$

7 0.8, 0.6

8 $\frac{1}{3}$ or 3

9 (a) 0.6436 or 2.2143
   (b) -2.2143 or 1.1760
   (c) -1.1760 or 0.9273

10 (a), (b) $61.9°$, $180°$ (c) $61.9°$
    Because $t = \tan\frac{1}{2}x$ is undefined when $x = 180°$.

11 (a) $\ln\left|\dfrac{1 + 2\tan\frac{1}{2}x}{2 - \tan\frac{1}{2}x}\right| + k$

    (b) $\ln\left|\dfrac{1 + \tan\frac{1}{2}x}{1 - \tan\frac{1}{2}x}\right| + k$

    (c) $\frac{1}{5}\ln\left|\dfrac{3 + \tan\frac{1}{2}x}{2 - \tan\frac{1}{2}x}\right| + k$

12 In some of these questions more than one method is possible, and you may get answers which look different from those printed. As a check, plot the graph of your answer minus the printed answer; this should be constant.
    (a) $-x\cot x + \ln|\sin x| - \frac{1}{2}x^2 + k$
    (b) $-\cot\frac{1}{2}t - t + k$
    (c) $\ln\left|\dfrac{\sin\theta}{1 - \sin\theta}\right| + k$
    (d) $\sin x(\ln(\sin x) - 1) + k$
    (e) $-\frac{1}{2}\ln|\cos\theta - \sin\theta| - \frac{1}{2}\theta + k$
    (f) $-\frac{1}{3}\cot^3 x + \cot x + x + k$
    (g) $-\ln|1 + \cos t| + k$
    (h) $\frac{1}{13}(\ln|5\tan\frac{1}{2}\theta - 1| - \ln|\tan\frac{1}{2}\theta + 5|) + k$
    (i) $\frac{1}{2}(\ln(\sec u))^2 + k$
    (j) $\frac{1}{2}x - \frac{1}{2}\ln|\sin x + \cos x| + k$

13 (b) $x\tan x + \ln|\cos x| - \frac{1}{2}x^2 + k$

Exercise 10C (page 183)

1 (a) $\frac{1}{3}\pi - \frac{1}{2}\sqrt{3}$ (b) $\frac{1}{8}\pi\sqrt{2} + \frac{1}{2}\sqrt{2} - 1$
   (c) $\frac{1}{36}\pi\sqrt{3}$ (d) $\frac{1}{24}\pi$

2 (a) $\sinh^{-1} x + k$ (b) $\cosh^{-1}\frac{1}{3}x + k$
   (c) $\frac{1}{3}\sinh^{-1} 3x + k$

3 (a) $\frac{1}{2}(\ln 2)^2$ (b) $\frac{13}{5}\ln 2 - \ln 5$
   (c) $\frac{3}{4}\ln 2 - \frac{1}{4}$ (d) $\frac{1}{2}(\ln 2)^2 + \frac{15}{32}\ln 2 - \frac{9}{64}$

4 (a) $\dfrac{\sqrt{x^2 - 25}}{25x} + k$

    (b) $\frac{1}{2}x\sqrt{4x^2 - 1} - \frac{1}{4}\cosh^{-1} 2x + k$
    (c) $\frac{1}{4}x - \frac{5}{8}\tan^{-1}\frac{2}{5}x + k$
    (d) $\frac{1}{8}(x(1 + 2x^2)\sqrt{1 + x^2} - \sinh^{-1} x) + k$

    (e) $\sinh^{-1}\frac{1}{3}x - \dfrac{\sqrt{9 + x^2}}{x} + k$
    (f) $\sqrt{x(1 + x)} - \sinh^{-1}\sqrt{x} + k$
    (g) $\sqrt{x(x - 1)} - \cosh^{-1}\sqrt{x} + k$

Miscellaneous exercise 10 (page 183)

1 $\frac{2}{5}\sin^5 x + k$

3 $\frac{4}{3}\pi + \frac{1}{2}\sqrt{3}$

4 $2\sqrt{2}\left(\cos\frac{1}{2}x - \frac{2}{3}\cos^3\frac{1}{2}x\right) + k$

5 $\frac{1}{2}\ln\frac{3}{2}$

6 $\sin^{-1}\frac{1}{5}(x+3) + k$

7 $\tan^{-1}(x-3) + k$

9 $\frac{1}{64}x^2 - \frac{1}{36}y^2 = 1$;

$x = 4\left(\frac{1}{t}+t\right)$, $y = 3\left(\frac{1}{t}-t\right)$;

$4(1-p^2)y = 3(1+p^2)x - 48p$;

$(10, 4\frac{1}{2})$

10 $y^2 = 4x^2 + 4x\sin 2x + 2\cos 2x + 1$

12 0.185; minimum

13 (a) $\frac{1}{4}\pi$ (b) $\frac{1}{3}\pi$ (c) $\frac{1}{18}\sqrt{3}\pi$

(d) $\frac{1}{24}\pi$ (e) $\frac{3}{16}\pi$ (f) $\frac{2}{3}\sqrt{3}-1$

(g) $\ln(2+\sqrt{3})$ (h) $\frac{1}{6}\pi$ (i) $\frac{1}{2}(\pi-2)$

(j) $(1-\frac{1}{2}\sqrt{2})\ln(1+\sqrt{2})$

14 $\frac{2}{3}\pi - \ln(2+\sqrt{3})$

15 $\pi^2 - 2\pi$

17 (a) $\frac{1}{2}\sqrt{2}\ln\left(\sec\left(X+\frac{1}{4}\pi\right) + \tan\left(X+\frac{1}{4}\pi\right)\right)$

$- \frac{1}{2}\sqrt{2}\ln(1+\sqrt{2})$; $\displaystyle\int_0^{\frac{1}{4}}$ does not exist

(b) $\frac{1}{2}\tan\left(X+\frac{1}{4}\pi\right) - \frac{1}{2}$

(c) $A = 2 - 2\sqrt{1-\frac{1}{4}\pi} = 1.073...$,

$B = \frac{1}{2}\pi = 1.570...$

11 Reduction formulae

Exercise 11A (page 190)

1 $\frac{1}{8}(15 - e^2)$

2 $I_n = 2x^n e^{\frac{1}{2}x} - 2nI_{n-1}$;

$(2x^3 - 12x^2 + 48x - 96)e^{\frac{1}{2}x} + k$

3 $\frac{1}{27}x^3(9(\ln x)^3 - 9(\ln x)^2 + 6\ln x - 2) + k$

4 (a) $\ln\cosh x - \frac{1}{2}\tanh^2 x - \frac{1}{4}\tanh^4 x + k$

(b) $x - \tanh x - \frac{1}{3}\tanh^3 x - \frac{1}{5}\tanh^5 x + k$

5 $I_n = \dfrac{1}{n-1} - I_{n-2}$, $n > 1$

(a) $\frac{5}{12} - \frac{1}{2}\ln 2$ (b) $\frac{1}{4}\pi - \frac{76}{105}$

6 $9e - 24$

7 $I_n = nI_{n-1} - 1$, $n > 0$; $120e - 326$

8 $C_n = -nS_{n-1}$, $n > 0$; $S_n = \pi^n + nC_{n-1}$, $n > 0$

$\pi(\pi^4 - 20\pi^2 + 120)$

10 $S_n = \cosh 1 - nC_{n-1}$; 0.1621

Exercise 11B (page 194)

1 $\frac{388}{2835}$

2 (a) $nI_n = 2^{-n}\sqrt{3} + (n-1)I_{n-2}$; $\frac{3}{32}\sqrt{3} + \frac{5}{48}\pi$

(b) $nI_n = \dfrac{3^{n-1}\times 5}{4^n} - (n-1)I_{n-2}$;

$\frac{3}{8}\ln 2 - \frac{225}{1024}$

3 (b) $I_0 = 1$ (c) $\frac{1}{2}\sqrt{2}$

(d) (i) $\frac{96}{35}$ (ii) $\frac{7}{8}\sqrt{2} + \frac{3}{8}\sinh^{-1}1$

(iii) $\frac{1}{4} + \frac{3}{32}\pi$

4 (b) $\frac{1}{24}(8x^2 - 10x + 15)\sqrt{x(1+x)}$

$- \frac{5}{8}\sinh^{-1}\sqrt{x} + k'$

5 $8(n-1)I_n = 3^{-(n-1)} + (2n-3)I_{n-1}$

(a) $\frac{17}{1152} + \frac{3}{512}\ln 3$ (b) $\frac{7}{1080}\sqrt{3}$

6 $n > \frac{1}{2}$

(a) $\dfrac{(2n-3)(2n-5)\cdots 1}{(2n-2)(2n-4)\cdots 2} \times \dfrac{\pi}{2}$

(b) $\dfrac{(2n-3)(2n-5)\cdots 2}{(2n-2)(2n-4)\cdots 3}$

7 $n > 1$; $e^{\frac{1}{2}\pi}$ $1, \frac{1}{2}(e^{\frac{1}{2}\pi} - 1), \frac{2}{5}e^{\frac{1}{2}\pi} - \frac{3}{5}$,

$\frac{3}{10}e^{\frac{1}{2}\pi} - \frac{2}{5}$

8 $\frac{1942}{35}$

9 $\frac{1}{2}\sec x\tan x + \frac{1}{2}\ln(|\sec x + \tan x|) + k$,

$\frac{1}{3}\sec^2 x\tan x + \frac{2}{3}\tan x + k$,

$\frac{1}{4}\sec^3 x\tan x + \frac{3}{8}\sec x\tan x$

$+ \frac{3}{8}\ln(|\sec x + \tan x|) + k$

Miscellaneous exercise 11 (page 195)

2 (b) $\frac{3}{4}\pi^2 - 6$

3 $\frac{3}{16}\pi$, $\frac{8}{15}$

5 0.8814, 0.4142; $n > 1$; 0.127, 0.108

6 (b) $\frac{35}{128}\pi$

7 $10\sqrt{e}$ 16; $\dfrac{1}{n+1}$

9 $I_n = 0$ for odd n, $I_n = (n-1)(n-3)\dots 1$ for even n

10 Valid for all n except 0, but no useful special cases are known except for negative integral n.

11 (a) $\frac{128}{109\,395}$ (b) $\frac{128}{230\,945}$ (c) $\frac{35}{131\,072}\pi$

12 $2(n-1)I_{m,n} = (m-1)I_{m-2,n-1}$ for

$1 < m < 2n - 1$

(a) $\frac{1}{120}a^{-6}$ (b) $\frac{1}{5}a^{-2}$

13 $I_n = I_{n-1} - \dfrac{x^n}{n!}e^{-x}$

12   The graph of $y^2 = f(x)$

Exercise 12 (page 203)

6   $(0, 0)$, $(4, 32)$; $(4, 4\sqrt{2})$, $(4, -4\sqrt{2})$, $\pm\sqrt{6}$

7   10, $(-1, 0)$

8   (e)

9   (c)

10   $(2, 1)$, $(3, 0)$, $(4, 1)$

13

$(-3, 1)$, $(-3, -1)$, $(2, \sqrt{5})$, $(2, -\sqrt{5})$

17   There are two branches at the origin, with gradients $\pm\frac{1}{3}\sqrt{3}$.

Miscellaneous exercise 12 (page 205)

2   (a)   (b)

3   (a) has $y = 0$ at $(0, 0)$ and $(-b, 0)$; gradients at these points are 0 and b^2.

   (b) has $y = 0$ at the same points; gradients at these points are $\pm\sqrt{b}$ and '∞'.

5   (a)

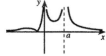

   (b)

7   (a) $x = \pm a$, $y = 0$; $\left(0, -\dfrac{1}{a^2}\right)$

   (b) $x = \pm a$, $y = 0$; $\left(0, \dfrac{1}{a^2}\right)$

   (c) $x = \pm a$, $y = 0$

8   $\left(1, \pm\frac{1}{2}\sqrt{2}\right)$

9   (a)   (b)

Revision exercise 2 (page 207)

1   $3 - \sqrt{3}$

2   (b) 1.92

4   $\ln\frac{13}{9}$, $\ln\frac{1}{3}$

5   (b) $\frac{16}{105}$

6   (a)

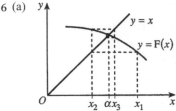

   (b) (ii) is suitable and (i) is not. The gradients at $x = 3$ of (i) and (ii) are respectively $-\frac{27}{2}$ and $-\dfrac{1}{3 \times 34^{\frac{2}{3}}}$, so the second satisfies the condition $-1 < F'(x) < 0$ near $x = 3$, and the first does not.

7   (b) $9e - 24$

8   (a) $\dfrac{4(20 - 8x - x^2)}{(x + 4)^2}$, $(-10, 100)$, $(2, 4)$

   (b) $x = -4$, $y = 36 - 4x - \dfrac{144}{x + 4}$, $y = 36 - 4x$

   (d) $(-10, 10)$, $(-10, -10)$, $(2, 2)$, $(2, -2)$; $(0, 0)$, $(5, 0)$

9   (b)

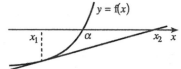

   (c) 1.01

11   (a) $\frac{8}{27}\sqrt{3} - \frac{2}{3} + \frac{1}{12}\pi$ (b) $2(\sqrt{2} - 1)$

   (c) $\frac{1}{4}\pi - \frac{1}{32}\pi^2 - \frac{1}{2}\ln 2$ (d) $\frac{3}{25}(e^{\frac{2}{3}\pi} - 1)$

12   0.53 ; $f'(0) = 0$, so $\dfrac{f(0)}{f'(0)}$ can't be evaluated

13   $\frac{4}{3}\pi - 2\sqrt{3}$

14   (b) $f'(x_1) \approx \dfrac{f(x_0) - f(x_1)}{x_0 - x_1}$ (c) $0.739\,085$

   (e) There is no need to find an expression for $f'(x)$; after a few iterations the numerator and denominator both become small, so rounding errors become significant and restrict the accuracy that can be achieved.

16   (a) $\displaystyle\int_{m+1}^{n+1} \dfrac{1}{x^3}\,dx$

17   (c) $x_{r+1} = 3e^{-\frac{1}{2}x_r}$ converges, $x_{r+1} = \ln\left(\dfrac{9}{x_r^2}\right)$ diverges

   (d) Converges to $1.4517\ldots$

18 (a) $x = 1$, $y = 1$

19 (a) About 16
   (b) 0.439 743 552, 0.447 441 908
      0.441 649 054; 0.441 136 388
   (d) 0.444 216 503, 0.444 134 786
      [$X = 0.444\ 130\ 23$ correct to 8 decimal
      places]

Practice examinations

Practice examination 1 for FP2 (page 211)

1 (i) $\dfrac{1+x}{1-x}$, $y = -1$
   (ii)

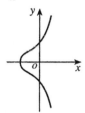

2 (i) $\dfrac{1}{\sqrt{2}}\left(1 + x - \dfrac{x^2}{2} - \dfrac{x^3}{6} + \dfrac{x^4}{24}\right)$
   (ii) 0.001 51

3 (ii)

   (iii) $2a^2$

5 (i) $\dfrac{1}{x-2} - \dfrac{1}{x+2} + \dfrac{1}{x^2+1}$
   (ii) $\tfrac{1}{4}\pi - \ln 3$

6 (i)

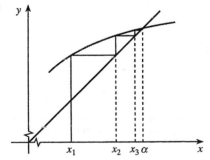

   (ii) $\dfrac{1}{2+\alpha} \approx 0.3$
   (iii) 9
   (iv) $x_{10} \approx 1.146\ 188\ 2$

7 (v) $\tfrac{1}{2}\ln 3$

Practice examination 2 for FP2 (page 213)

2 1

5 (i) $\tfrac{1}{4}a^2(\pi + 2)$
   (ii) $x^2 + y^2 = a(x + y)$
   (iii)

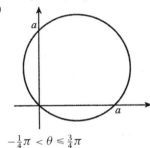

   $-\tfrac{1}{4}\pi < \theta \leqslant \tfrac{3}{4}\pi$

6 (iii) $I_0 = 1$

7 (i) $x = a$, $y = x + a$
   (iii) $(0, 0)$, $(2a, 4a)$
   (iv)

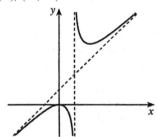

8 (ii) $e_{n+1} \approx 0.2e_n$
   (iii) 2.1339, 2.1323
   (iv)

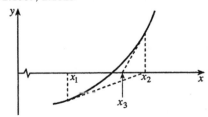

Answers to Further Pure 3

1 First order differential equations

Exercise 1A (page 224)

1 (a) $y = \frac{1}{3}x^2 + \frac{k}{x}$ (b) $x = (t+k)\operatorname{cosec} t$

   (c) $y = -\frac{1}{2x} + kx$ (d) $u = (2x+k)e^{-x^2}$

2 (a) $y = \frac{x-1}{x^2}$ (b) $y = \operatorname{cosec} x$

   (c) $y = \frac{x^2+3}{4\sqrt{x}}$

3 (a) $u = \frac{1}{3}x + \frac{k}{x^2}$ (b) $y = k\sec x - \cos x$

   (c) $x = ke^{4t} - \frac{1}{2}e^{2t}$ (d) $y = kx^3 - x^2$

   (e) $y = (t+k)\cos t$ (f) $y = \cos x + k\cot x$

4 (a) $y = 3x - 1 + ke^{-3x}$ with
     $k = -1, 0, 1, 2, 3$

   (b) $y = \frac{1}{4}x^2 + \frac{k}{x^2}$ with
     $k = -\frac{1}{4}, \frac{3}{4}, \frac{7}{4}, -4, 0, 4$

   (c) $y = \sec x + k\cos x$ with
     $k = -3, -2, -1, 0, 1$

   (d) $y = kx^3 - x$ with $k = 2, 1, 0, 0, 1, 2$

5 $y = x(1 - \ln x)$

6 $\frac{dx}{dt} = -0.1x, \quad \frac{dy}{dt} = 0.1x - 0.2y;$
   $x = 50e^{-0.1t}, \quad y = 50(e^{-0.1t} - e^{-0.2t});$
   $12\frac{1}{2}$ litres, after 6.93 hours

7 $\frac{dx}{dt} = c(a + b\sin ct - x)$

9 $y = 2x + kx^2$; gradient positive within the
   acute angles between $y = x$ and the y-axis,
   negative within the obtuse angles

10 $y = \frac{k}{x} - \frac{1}{x^2}$; solution curves bend upwards
   above $y = \frac{2}{x^2}$, bend downwards below.

Exercise 1B (page 233)

1 $y = ke^{\frac{x}{y}}$

2 $y^2 = x(x+k)$

3 $y = \frac{x}{x^2 + k}$

4 $y = \frac{(x-1)^2}{4x}$

5 $q = -\frac{1}{2}; \; y = \frac{1}{\sqrt{x^2(1+kx^2)}}$

6 $y = \sqrt[3]{16x^3 - \frac{3}{2}x}$

7 (a) $y = \dfrac{1}{\sqrt{x^2 + x + \frac{1}{2} + ke^{2x}}}$

   (b) $y = (x - 2 + ke^{-\frac{1}{2}x})^2$

8 $x^2 + y^2 = ky$; circle through O with centre on
   the y-axis

9 $y = x + \dfrac{1}{x^2 + k}$

10 $m = 2, \; a = 2; \; y = 2x^2 + \dfrac{1}{x+k}$

Miscellaneous exercise 1 (page 234)

1 $s = (\frac{1}{2}t^2 + k)e^{3t}$

2 $y = \frac{1}{5}x + \frac{k}{x^4}; \; y = \frac{1}{5}\left(x + \frac{4}{x^4}\right)$

3 $y = (\frac{1}{2}x^2 + k)e^{x^3}; \; y = (\frac{1}{2}x^2 + 1)e^{x^3}$

4 $y = 10(x + 2)e^{-x^2}$

5 $y = 1 - x\cot x + k\operatorname{cosec} x;$
   $y = 1 - x\cot x - \operatorname{cosec} x$

6 $y = \frac{1}{x}(1 + ke^{-x}); \; y = \frac{1}{x}(1 + e^{1-x})$

7 $y = \dfrac{k - \sin^{-1} x}{\sqrt{1 - x^2}}; \; y = \dfrac{\cos^{-1} x}{\sqrt{1 - x^2}}$

8 $\ln x; \; y = \frac{1}{2}\left(\ln x + \dfrac{1}{\ln x}\right)$

9 $y = 2\tan^{-1}(x - k) - x$

10 $y = \sqrt{x^2 - x + \frac{1}{2} + ke^{-2x}}$

11 $(y + 2x)(y - x)^2 = 2$

12 (b) $y = \dfrac{\sin x}{\cos x + k}$ (c) $0, 1$

13 $y = -x - \frac{1}{4} - \frac{3}{4}e^{4(x-1)}$

14 $V = 5t - 80 + 80e^{-0.05t}; t = 216$

15 $V = \dfrac{1}{\alpha + \beta}(e^{\beta t} - e^{-\alpha t})$

16 (a) $y = x^2 - 2x + 2$
   (b) $y = x^2 - 2x + 2 + (A - 2)e^{-x}$

17 (c) $P(x) = x - 1$

18 $y = \dfrac{(1 + x^2)^{\frac{3}{2}}}{3x^2} + \dfrac{k}{x^2}; \; y = \dfrac{(1 + x^2)^{\frac{3}{2}} + 3 - 2\sqrt{2}}{3x^2};$
   y becomes very large;
   $y \approx \dfrac{c}{x^2} + \frac{1}{2} + \frac{1}{8}x^2$ (writing $c = \frac{1}{3} + k$);
   $y = \dfrac{(1 + x^2)^{\frac{3}{2}} - 1}{3x^2}$; other solutions exist
   for $x < 0$, but these do not cross over
   to $x > 0$.

19 $Y = -\dfrac{1}{X^2}\cos X + \dfrac{2}{X^3}\sin X + \dfrac{2}{X^4}\cos X + \dfrac{k}{X^4}$;

$Y \to \frac{1}{4}$ (with $k = -2$)

20 (b) (i) $y = \dfrac{1}{k}(2 - e^{-kx})\sin x$

(ii) $y = -\dfrac{1}{k}e^{-kx}\sin x$;

(i) approximates to a periodic oscillation for large x, (ii) tends to zero

(c) $y = (x + k)\sin x$, oscillates unboundedly for large x

21 (a) $E = \dfrac{2G}{1 + 4k^2}(\cos\theta - 2k\sin\theta) + ce^{-2k\theta}$

(b) $\cos\alpha + 2k\sin\alpha$
$= e^{2k(\alpha+\beta)}(\cos\beta - 2k\sin\beta)$

22 (a) 1, 2

(b) $\dfrac{dy}{dx} = u + x\dfrac{du}{dx}$

(d) $y_0(y - x) = (y - 2x)^2$, solutions lie in half-plane $y - x > 0$

23 (a) $y = \dfrac{3}{x^3}$

(b) $z = \frac{1}{2}x^3 + kx$, $y = \dfrac{\frac{3}{2}x^2 + k}{x^3(\frac{1}{2}x^2 + k)}$

(c) $k = 0$ gives $y = \dfrac{3}{x^3}$, $k \to \infty$ gives $y = \dfrac{1}{x^3}$

(d) solutions with $k \geqslant 0$

24 $\int e^{x^2}\,dx$ can't be found algebraically;
$f'''(x) = -4f'(x) - 2xf''(x)$; $1 + x - x^2 - \frac{2}{3}x^3$

2 Lines and planes

Your answers may differ in form from those given

Exercise 2A (page 245)

1 (a) $\mathbf{r} = \begin{pmatrix} 1 \\ 2 \\ 3 \end{pmatrix} + t\begin{pmatrix} 0 \\ 1 \\ 2 \end{pmatrix}$ (b) $\mathbf{r} = t\begin{pmatrix} 0 \\ 0 \\ 1 \end{pmatrix}$

(c) $\mathbf{r} = \begin{pmatrix} 2 \\ -1 \\ 1 \end{pmatrix} + t\begin{pmatrix} 3 \\ -1 \\ 1 \end{pmatrix}$

(d) $\mathbf{r} = \begin{pmatrix} 3 \\ 0 \\ 2 \end{pmatrix} + t\begin{pmatrix} 4 \\ -2 \\ 3 \end{pmatrix}$

2 (a) $\mathbf{r} = \begin{pmatrix} 2 \\ -1 \\ 2 \end{pmatrix} + t\begin{pmatrix} 1 \\ 0 \\ 2 \end{pmatrix}$

(b) $\mathbf{r} = \begin{pmatrix} 1 \\ 2 \\ 2 \end{pmatrix} + t\begin{pmatrix} 1 \\ -4 \\ 0 \end{pmatrix}$

(c) $\mathbf{r} = \begin{pmatrix} 3 \\ 1 \\ 4 \end{pmatrix} + t\begin{pmatrix} -4 \\ 1 \\ -1 \end{pmatrix}$

3 They all represent the same straight line.

4 The point lies on line (a) only.

5 Set (a) lies on a straight line, but not set (b).

6 (a) $(-3, 1, 5)$ (b) $(3, -5, 4)$

7 (a) $\dfrac{x - 2}{1} = \dfrac{y + 4}{-1} = \dfrac{z - 1}{2}$

(b) $x = 1$, $\dfrac{y - 5}{1} = \dfrac{z}{-2}$ (c) $\dfrac{x}{1} = \dfrac{y}{3} = \dfrac{z - 1}{2}$

8 (a) $(7, 0, 3)$ (b) No point of intersection
(c) No point of intersection

9 $\frac{16}{21}$

10 $(1, 2, 4)$

11 $(-2, -8, 3)$

Exercise 2B (page 258)

1 (a) $\mathbf{r} = s\begin{pmatrix} 1 \\ 0 \\ 0 \end{pmatrix} + t\begin{pmatrix} 0 \\ 1 \\ 0 \end{pmatrix}$

(b) $\mathbf{r} = \begin{pmatrix} 1 \\ -1 \\ 0 \end{pmatrix} + s\begin{pmatrix} -1 \\ 2 \\ -1 \end{pmatrix} + t\begin{pmatrix} -2 \\ 1 \\ 1 \end{pmatrix}$

(c) $\mathbf{r} = \begin{pmatrix} 1 \\ 2 \\ 3 \end{pmatrix} + s\begin{pmatrix} 1 \\ -3 \\ -1 \end{pmatrix} + t\begin{pmatrix} 2 \\ -1 \\ -4 \end{pmatrix}$

(d) $\mathbf{r} = \begin{pmatrix} 4 \\ -1 \\ 2 \end{pmatrix} + s\begin{pmatrix} -4 \\ 1 \\ 1 \end{pmatrix} + t\begin{pmatrix} -5 \\ 3 \\ -2 \end{pmatrix}$

2 (a) $\mathbf{r} = \begin{pmatrix} 1 \\ -3 \\ 0 \end{pmatrix} + t\begin{pmatrix} 2 \\ 4 \\ 1 \end{pmatrix}$ or
$\mathbf{r} = \mathbf{i} - 3\mathbf{j} + t(2\mathbf{i} + 4\mathbf{j} + \mathbf{k})$

(b) $\mathbf{r} = \begin{pmatrix} \frac{1}{2} \\ 0 \\ 0 \end{pmatrix} + t\begin{pmatrix} -1 \\ \frac{7}{3} \\ \frac{1}{5} \end{pmatrix}$ or
$\mathbf{r} = \frac{1}{2}\mathbf{i} + t(-\mathbf{i} + \frac{7}{3}\mathbf{j} + \frac{1}{5}\mathbf{k})$

(c) $\mathbf{r} = \begin{pmatrix} 0 \\ 0 \\ 0 \end{pmatrix} + t\begin{pmatrix} \frac{1}{2} \\ \frac{1}{3} \\ \frac{1}{4} \end{pmatrix}$ or $\mathbf{r} = t(\frac{1}{2}\mathbf{i} + \frac{1}{3}\mathbf{j} + \frac{1}{4}\mathbf{k})$

3 (a) $x - 1 = \dfrac{y}{-2} = \dfrac{z + 2}{-1}$

(b) Not possible

(c) Not possible

4 (a) $(1, 4, -3)$ (b) $(11, -1, 2)$ (c) $(8, -2, -8)$

5 $(-1, -1, -1)$

6 $5x - 8y + 4z = 1$

7 $2x - y - z = 4$

8 $\mathbf{i} - 4\mathbf{j} - 7\mathbf{k}, \quad x - 4y - 7z = 23$

9 $x + y + z = -3$

10 (a) $z = 0$ (b) $x + y + z = 0$
   (c) $11x + 2y + 5z = 30$
   (d) $5x + 13y + 7z = 21$

11 There are many possibilities. Two are $(2, 0, 0)$ and $(0, 0, 1)$.

12 (b) 1

13 $(0, 0, 0)$, 7

14 1

16 $5x + y + 7z = 0$

17 $\mathbf{r} = \begin{pmatrix} 4 \\ 2 \\ -1 \end{pmatrix} + t \begin{pmatrix} 3 \\ 4 \\ -1 \end{pmatrix}$

18 $53°$

Miscellaneous exercise 2 (page 260)

1 $(-4, 4, -4)$

2 It does not lie on the line.

3 $61.9°$

4 $8x + 3y + 4z = -11$

5 (a) $\begin{pmatrix} -6 \\ 5 \\ 13 \end{pmatrix}$ (b) $\mathbf{r} = \begin{pmatrix} 1 \\ 2 \\ -3 \end{pmatrix} + t \begin{pmatrix} -6 \\ 5 \\ 13 \end{pmatrix}$

6 (a) $63.1°$ (b) $\mathbf{r} = \begin{pmatrix} 0 \\ -2 \\ 8 \end{pmatrix} + t \begin{pmatrix} 3 \\ 2 \\ -7 \end{pmatrix}$

7 $k = 3; \quad x = 2 - 2t, \quad y = t, \quad z = 1 - 5t$
The solution may be written in vector form
as $\mathbf{r} = \begin{pmatrix} 2 \\ 0 \\ 1 \end{pmatrix} + t \begin{pmatrix} -2 \\ 1 \\ -5 \end{pmatrix}$ which represents the
line of intersection of the three planes whose
cartesian equations are given.

8 (a) $(5, 1, -1)$ is a point on the line, so the
position vector of $(5, 1, -1)$ is suitable for
a. The vector $2\mathbf{i} - 3\mathbf{j} + \mathbf{k}$ is normal to the
plane, and therefore lies along the line,
and so is a suitable choice for **b**.
  (b) (i) $69°$ or $111°$

9 (a) $\mathbf{r} = 2\mathbf{i} + \mathbf{j} - \mathbf{k} + t(\mathbf{i} - \mathbf{j})$
    $\mathbf{r} = 5\mathbf{i} - 2\mathbf{j} - \mathbf{k} + t(\mathbf{j} + 2\mathbf{k})$
  (c) $71.6°$ or $108.4°$
  (e) $2x + 2y - z = 7$

10 (a) $24°$ (b) $-3\mathbf{i} + 7\mathbf{j} + \mathbf{k}$ (c) $\frac{1}{2}\sqrt{30}$

11 (a) $(3, 4, 1)$ (c) $(5, 4, -3)$
   (d) $\mathbf{r} = 3\mathbf{i} + 4\mathbf{j} + \mathbf{k} + t(2\mathbf{i} - 4\mathbf{k})$

12 $a = 2; \quad \dfrac{x - 2}{9} = \dfrac{y - 1}{-7} = \dfrac{z - (-2)}{13}$

3 Linear differential equations

Exercise 3A (page 266)

1 (a) First, non-linear
  (b) Second, linear
  (c) Second, linear
  (d) First, linear
  (e) Second, non-linear
  (f) First, non-linear

2 (a) $x\dfrac{dy}{dx} = 2y + (x - 2)e^x$

  (b) $\dfrac{d^2 y}{dx^2} = 0$

  (c) $\dfrac{d^2 x}{dt^2} + 4x = 0$

  (d) $x^2\dfrac{d^2 y}{dx^2} + x\dfrac{dy}{dx} - y = 0$

5 (a) $x = \sin t + A; \ \sin t, \ A$
  (b) $y = -\ln|x| + Ax + B; \ -\ln|x|, \ Ax + B$
  (c) $y \sin x = x + A; \ x \operatorname{cosec} x, \ A \operatorname{cosec} x$
  (d) $y = -\cos x + A \sin x; \ -\cos x, \ A \sin x$
  (e) $y = x + A \ln|x| + B; \ x, \ A \ln|x| + B$
  (f) $y = \dfrac{1}{2x^2} + \dfrac{A}{x} + B; \ \dfrac{1}{2x^2}, \ \dfrac{A}{x} + B$

6 (a) $Ae^{3x}, -e^x; \ y = Ae^{3x} - e^x$
  (b) $\dfrac{A}{x}, x^3; \ y = \dfrac{A}{x} + x^3$
  (c) $Ae^{-x} + B, \ e^{-2x}; \ y = Ae^{-x} + B + e^{-2x}$

7 $A = -1, \ B = 1$

Exercise 3B (page 272)

1 (a) $y = Ae^{3x} + Be^x$ (b) $y = Ae^x + Be^{-4x}$
  (c) $x = Ae^{-3t} + Be^{-4t}$ (d) $x = (At + B)e^{-6t}$
  (e) $u = A + Be^{-6x}$ (f) $y = (At + B)e^{\frac{1}{2}t}$

2 (a) $y = 2e^{-x} - e^{-2x}$ (b) $u = 2e^{-6t}$
  (c) $x = \frac{1}{2}(e^{3t} - e^{-3t})$ (d) $z = \dfrac{1}{1 - e^2}(e^{2y} - e^2)$
  (e) $z = (1 - t)e^{-3t}$ (f) $y = \frac{1}{2}(3e^{2x} - e^{4x})$

3 (a) Ae^{-2x} (b) Ae^{3x}
  (c) $Ae^{-x} + Be^{-4x}$ (d) $Ae^{-\frac{1}{3}t} + Be^{-t}$
  (e) $A + Be^{-t}$ (f) $(A + Bx)e^{2x}$

Exercise 3C (page 275)

1 (a) $2e^{3x}$ (b) -2 (c) $2x - 4$
  (d) $\frac{1}{5}e^{-2t}$ (e) $-te^{-t}$ (f) $2x + 3$

2 (a) $y = Ae^{2x} + Be^{-2x} - 3x$
  (b) $x = Ae^{-\frac{1}{2}t} + Be^{-t} + e^t$
  (c) $x = Ae^{-\frac{1}{2}t} + (B - 6t)e^{-t}$
  (d) $z = 2x + A + Be^{-3x}$
  (e) $x = Ae^t + Be^{-t} - 2\cos t$
  (f) $y = (\frac{1}{2}x^2 + Ax + B)e^x$

3 (a) $y = e^x - e^{3x} + 2$
  (b) $x = e^{-2t} + 2e^{-\frac{1}{2}t} - \cos t$
  (c) $y = (2 - x)e^x$
  (d) $y = e^{-3t} - 2\sin t - \cos t$
  (e) $u = (\frac{1}{2}x^2 - x + 1)e^{-x}$
  (f) $y = \frac{1}{2}x\sinh x$

4 $y = \dfrac{A}{x} + Bx - 1$

5 $k = \frac{1}{2}, 1; \ y = x^3 + A\sqrt{x} + Bx$

Miscellaneous exercise 3 (page 276)

1 $y = 3\cos 2x - 4\sin 2x + Ae^{-x} + Be^{4x}$,
  $y = 3\cos 2x - 4\sin 2x - 3e^{-x}$

2 (a) $\dfrac{d^2y}{dx^2} + \dfrac{dy}{dx} - 2y = 3\cos x - 9\sin x$
  (b) $\dfrac{d^2y}{dx^2} - 4\dfrac{dy}{dx} + 3y = 2 - 8x + 3x^2$
  (c) $\dfrac{d^2y}{dx^2} - 4y = 4e^{2x}$
  (d) $\dfrac{d^2y}{dx^2} + \dfrac{dy}{dx} = 2$
  (e) $\dfrac{d^2y}{dx^2} - 2\dfrac{dy}{dx} + y = 2e^x$
  (f) $\dfrac{d^2y}{dx^2} - 9y = 2\cosh 3x + 12x\sinh 3x$

3 (a) $y = Ae^{-x} + Be^{-2x} + x - 1$
  (b) $y = e^{-2x} - e^{-x} + x - 1; \ \ln 4$

4 (a) $y = (1 - x)e^{-x}$
  (b) $y = (x^2 - 1)e^x$
  (c) $y = (x + 1)\cosh x$

5 (a) $x = 2e^t - 3e^{-t} - 5t$
  (b) $x = e^{2t} + e^{-2t} - 2\cos t$
  (c) $x = e^{2t} - e^{-2t} + 2te^{2t}$

6 $y = Ax^3 + 2x^2 + Bx$

7 $u(x) = x^2; \ y = \frac{1}{12}x^3 + \dfrac{A}{x} + B; \ \dfrac{A}{x} + B, \ \frac{1}{12}x^3$

8 (a) $\to 0, \ \dot{x} = 0$ when $t = \frac{1}{4}\ln\frac{5}{3}$
  (b) $\to \infty$
  (c) $\to -\infty, x = 0$ when $t = 1, \dot{x} = 0$ when $t = \frac{1}{2}$
  (d) $\to -\infty, \ x = 0$ when $t = \frac{1}{5}\ln 6$
  (e) $\to 0, \ \dot{x} = 0$ when $t = \frac{2}{35}$

9 (a) $\to 0$ if $\alpha < 0, \to \infty$ if $0 < \alpha \leqslant c$,
      $\to -\infty$ if $\alpha > 0$ and $c < \alpha$
  (b) If $\alpha > c, x = 0$ when $t = \dfrac{1}{\alpha - c}$

(c) If $0 < c < \alpha, \ \alpha < 0 \leqslant c$ or $c < \alpha < 0$,
    $\dot{x} = 0$ when $t = \dfrac{c}{\alpha(\alpha - c)}$

10 (a) $\to 0$ if $\alpha < 0, \ \to 1 - \dfrac{c}{\beta}$ if $\alpha = 0$,
       $\to \infty$ if $\alpha > 0$ and $\beta < c$,
       $\to -\infty$ if $\alpha > 0$ and $\beta > c$;
       if $\alpha > 0$ and $\beta = c, \to \infty$ if $c > 0$,
       $\to 1$ if $c = 0, \ \to 0$ if $c < 0$
   (b) If $\beta > c, x = 0$ when $t = \dfrac{1}{\alpha - \beta}\ln\dfrac{\alpha - c}{\beta - c}$
   (c) If $\beta > c > 0$, or if $\alpha > 0$ and $\beta < c < 0$,
       or if $\alpha < 0$ and $c > 0$, or if $c < \beta < \alpha < 0$,
       $\dot{x} = 0$ when $t = \dfrac{1}{\alpha - \beta}\ln\dfrac{\beta(\alpha - c)}{\alpha(\beta - c)}$

11 $K = \dfrac{V_0 n}{\sqrt{\left(\dfrac{1}{C} - Ln^2\right)^2 + R^2 n^2}}$

4 The vector product

Exercise 4A (page 283)

1 (a) $-\mathbf{j}$ (b) $\mathbf{0}$ (c) $\mathbf{k}$
  (d) $\mathbf{0}$ (e) $-\mathbf{i}$ (f) $\mathbf{i}$
  (g) $\mathbf{0}$ (h) -1 (i) $\mathbf{j}$

2 (a) $\begin{pmatrix} -13 \\ -4 \\ 7 \end{pmatrix}$ (b) $\begin{pmatrix} -5 \\ -1 \\ 7 \end{pmatrix}$ (c) $\begin{pmatrix} -9 \\ -10 \\ -2 \end{pmatrix}$

  (d) $\begin{pmatrix} 0 \\ 8 \\ 4 \end{pmatrix}$ (e) $\begin{pmatrix} 0 \\ 0 \\ 1 \end{pmatrix}$ (f) $\begin{pmatrix} -2 \\ -2 \\ 1 \end{pmatrix}$

3 (a) $-2\mathbf{j} + 2\mathbf{k}$ (b) $\mathbf{i} + \mathbf{j} + \mathbf{k}$
  (c) $12\mathbf{i} - 10\mathbf{j} - 9\mathbf{k}$ (d) $2\mathbf{i} + 2\mathbf{j} + 3\mathbf{k}$
  (e) $-4\mathbf{j} - 5\mathbf{k}$ (f) $3\mathbf{i} - 42\mathbf{j} - 22\mathbf{k}$

4 $\frac{1}{2}\sqrt{122}$

Exercise 4B (page 286)

1 $x - 2y + z = 0$

2 $8\mathbf{i} - 2\mathbf{j} + 3\mathbf{k}, \ 8x - 2y + 3z = 19$

3 (a) $4x + y + 11z = 37$ (b) $x + y + z = 0$
  (c) $3x - 8y + 7z = 4$ (d) $x - y = -1$

4 They lie in the plane $5x + y = 10$.

5 $\dfrac{x + 7}{33} = \dfrac{y - 3}{-9} = z$

6 $\mathbf{r} = \begin{pmatrix} 4 \\ 2 \\ -3 \end{pmatrix} + t\begin{pmatrix} 2 \\ 3 \\ -4 \end{pmatrix}$

7 $2x + y - z = 0$

8 $5x - y + 7z = 20$

9 $5x - y + 3z = 12$

Exercise 4C (page 290)

1 (a) $\mathbf{r} = \mathbf{i} - 2\mathbf{j} + t(\mathbf{i} + 2\mathbf{j} - \mathbf{k})$
   $\mathbf{r} = 4\mathbf{i} - 4\mathbf{j} - 4\mathbf{k} + t(2\mathbf{i} + 3\mathbf{j} - \mathbf{k})$
   (b) $\mathbf{i} - \mathbf{j} - \mathbf{k}$
   (c) $\mathbf{r} = \mathbf{i} - 2\mathbf{j} + \alpha(\mathbf{i} + 2\mathbf{j} - \mathbf{k})$ gives a fixed point on the first line, and the $s(\mathbf{i} - \mathbf{j} - \mathbf{k})$ is perpendicular to it. Now choose α and s so that this point lies on the line $\mathbf{r} = 4\mathbf{i} - 4\mathbf{j} - 4\mathbf{k} + t(2\mathbf{i} + 3\mathbf{j} - \mathbf{k})$.
   (d) 2, 3, $(6, -1, -5)$
   (e) $3\sqrt{3}$

2 $\mathbf{r} = \begin{pmatrix} 1 \\ 1 \\ 1 \end{pmatrix} + t \begin{pmatrix} -5 \\ 2 \\ 3 \end{pmatrix}$

3 (a) $x = y$
   (b) $\begin{pmatrix} 1 \\ 1 \\ -2 \end{pmatrix}$ (c) $\left(-\frac{1}{3}, -\frac{1}{3}, \frac{2}{3}\right)$

4 3

5 (a) $\mathbf{r} = \begin{pmatrix} 0 \\ -3 \\ 0 \end{pmatrix} + t \begin{pmatrix} 1 \\ 1 \\ -1 \end{pmatrix}$ (b) $\mathbf{r} = t \begin{pmatrix} 1 \\ -2 \\ 1 \end{pmatrix}$

6 If l_1 and l_2 are parallel, then algebraically, the vector product $\mathbf{n} = 0$, so that both $|(\mathbf{a}_2 - \mathbf{a}_1) \cdot \mathbf{n}|$ and $|\mathbf{n}|$ are equal to 0 and geometrically, there is no longer a unique direction perpendicular to both of them.

Miscellaneous exercise 4 (page 291)

1 (a) $\begin{pmatrix} 2 \\ 7 \\ 5 \end{pmatrix}$ (b) $\begin{pmatrix} 14 \\ -13 \\ 23 \end{pmatrix}$ (c) $\begin{pmatrix} 0 \\ -3 \\ 0 \end{pmatrix}$

2 (a) $-6\mathbf{j}$ (b) $-10\mathbf{i} + 5\mathbf{j}$ (c) $\mathbf{0}$

3 $2x - 3y - 8z = 28$

5 $3x - 2y - z = 16$

6 (a) $64°$
   (b) $\mathbf{r} = (\mathbf{i} + \mathbf{j} + \mathbf{k}) + t(2\mathbf{i} - 5\mathbf{j} - 6\mathbf{k})$

7 (a) $\dfrac{39}{\sqrt{35}}$ (b) $5x - y + 3z = 39$

8 $2x + 2y + x = 11$

9 (a) $3\mathbf{i} - 2\mathbf{j} + 6\mathbf{k}$ (b) $\frac{29}{7}$

10 $\dfrac{2}{\sqrt{17}}$

11 (a) $\begin{pmatrix} 1 \\ -2 \\ 2 \end{pmatrix}, \begin{pmatrix} -2 \\ -3 \\ 5 \end{pmatrix}$ (b) $\frac{1}{2}\sqrt{146}$

12 (a) $\mathbf{r} = \begin{pmatrix} 2 \\ -1 \\ 1 \end{pmatrix} + t \begin{pmatrix} -1 \\ 3 \\ -4 \end{pmatrix}$,
   $\mathbf{r} = \begin{pmatrix} 1 \\ -1 \\ 1 \end{pmatrix} + t \begin{pmatrix} 0 \\ -3 \\ 4 \end{pmatrix}$
   (b) $(1, 2, -3)$ (c) $\cos^{-1} \dfrac{5}{\sqrt{26}}$
   (d) $\begin{pmatrix} 0 \\ 4 \\ 3 \end{pmatrix}$

13 (a) $\begin{pmatrix} 7 \\ 4 \\ 1 \end{pmatrix}$
   (b) (i) $\mathbf{r} \cdot \begin{pmatrix} 7 \\ 4 \\ 1 \end{pmatrix} = 14$ (ii) $\frac{1}{2}\sqrt{66}$

14 (a) $\dfrac{1}{\sqrt{6}} \begin{pmatrix} 1 \\ -1 \\ 2 \end{pmatrix}$ (b) $\sqrt{6}$

15 (a) 3
   (b) $\begin{pmatrix} -17 \\ -10 \\ 14 \end{pmatrix}$ (c) $\dfrac{21}{\sqrt{65}}$

16 (a) $\begin{pmatrix} 9 \\ -11 \\ -3 \end{pmatrix}$
   (b) $\mathbf{r} = \begin{pmatrix} 8 \\ -7 \\ 4 \end{pmatrix} + t \begin{pmatrix} 1 \\ 4 \\ -1 \end{pmatrix}$
   (c) $\frac{1}{9} \begin{pmatrix} 8 \\ -1 \\ 4 \end{pmatrix}$ (d) $\frac{71}{9}$

17 (a) $\begin{pmatrix} 7 \\ -7 \\ 14 \end{pmatrix}$
   (b) $(11, 6, -2)$
   (c) $x - y + 2z - 1 = 0$
   (d) $11x - 5y - 8z - 107 = 0$

18 $\left| \dfrac{(\mathbf{a} - \mathbf{c}) \cdot (\mathbf{b} \times \mathbf{d})}{|\mathbf{b} \times \mathbf{d}|} \right|$

5 Complex numbers in polar form

Exercise 5A (page 296)

1 (a) $1 + \sqrt{3}i$ (b) $-5\sqrt{2} + 5\sqrt{2}i$
   (c) $0 - 5i$ (d) $-3 + 0i$
   (e) $-4.16 + 9.09i$ (f) $-0.99 - 0.14i$

2 $r(\cos\theta + i\sin\theta)$ where

(a) $r = 5,\ \theta = 0$ (b) $r = 2,\ \theta = \frac{1}{2}\pi$

(c) $r = 10,\ \theta = \pi$ (d) $r = 1,\ \theta = -\frac{1}{2}\pi$

(e) $r = 2,\ \theta = \frac{1}{6}\pi$ (f) $r = 2,\ \theta = -\frac{1}{3}\pi$

(g) $r = 2.83,\ \theta = \frac{3}{4}\pi$ (h) $r = 2,\ \theta = -\frac{3}{4}\pi$

(i) $r = 13,\ \theta = 0.39$ (j) $r = 5,\ \theta = -0.64$

(k) $r = 2.24,\ \theta = 2.03$ (l) $r = 3.61,\ \theta = -2.16$

Exercise 5B (page 299)

1 $r(\cos\theta + i\sin\theta)$, where

(a) $r = 2,\ \theta = \frac{7}{12}\pi$ (b) $r = 2,\ \theta = \frac{1}{12}\pi$

(c) $r = \frac{1}{2},\ \theta = -\frac{1}{12}\pi$ (d) $r = 8,\ \theta = -\frac{1}{2}\pi$

(e) $r = 2,\ \theta = \frac{5}{6}\pi$ (f) $r = \frac{1}{4},\ \theta = -\frac{11}{12}\pi$

(g) $r = 4,\ \theta = \frac{2}{3}\pi$ (h) $r = 16,\ \theta = \frac{1}{3}\pi$

(i) $r = 8,\ \theta = 0$ (j) $r = 1,\ \theta = \frac{11}{12}\pi$

(k) $r = 2,\ \theta = -\frac{1}{3}\pi$ (l) $r = 2,\ \theta = \frac{1}{12}\pi$

(m) $r = 2,\ \theta = -\frac{1}{12}\pi$ (n) $r = 4,\ \theta = \frac{1}{3}\pi$

(o) $r = 1,\ \theta = -\frac{1}{4}\pi$ (p) $r = 1,\ \theta = -\frac{1}{3}\pi$

(q) $r = 1,\ \theta = -\frac{1}{3}\pi$ (r) $r = 2,\ \theta = -\frac{1}{6}\pi$

2 $2\left(\cos\frac{4}{5}\pi + i\sin\frac{4}{5}\pi\right)$

5 (a) $-\frac{2}{3}\pi$ (b) -2 (c) $\frac{1}{3}\pi$

(d) $\frac{1}{3}\pi$ (e) $-\frac{1}{3}\pi$ (f) $\frac{4}{5}\pi$

(g) $\frac{1}{14}\pi$ (h) $\frac{3}{14}\pi$ (i) $-\frac{3}{8}\pi$

6 (a) $\cos\theta - i\sin\theta$ (b) $\cos\theta - i\sin\theta$

(c) $r(\cos\theta - i\sin\theta)$ (d) $\frac{1}{r}(\cos\theta - i\sin\theta)$

7 $2\left(\cos\frac{1}{3}\pi + i\sin\frac{1}{3}\pi\right)$,

$\sqrt{2}\left(\cos\left(-\frac{1}{4}\pi\right) + i\sin\left(-\frac{1}{4}\pi\right)\right);\ -\sqrt{3} + i$

8 (a) $-11 - 2i$ (b) $-122 - 597i$

(c) $0.0028 + 0.0096i$

9 (a) $-\frac{1}{6}\pi$ (b) $\frac{1}{6}\pi$ (c) $\frac{1}{3}\pi$ (d) $\frac{1}{3}\pi$

Exercise 5C (page 304)

1 (a) $\pm2\left(\cos\frac{1}{5}\pi + i\sin\frac{1}{5}\pi\right)$

(b) $\pm3\left(\cos\frac{2}{7}\pi - i\sin\frac{2}{7}\pi\right)$

(c) $\pm(1 - i)$ (d) $\pm(2 + 5i)$

(e) $\pm(1.098... + 0.455...i)$

(f) $\pm(3 - 2i)$

2 (a) $\pm(2 + 2\sqrt{3})i$

(b) $\pm(\sqrt{3} + i),\ \pm(1 - \sqrt{3}i)$

3 (a) $1e^{\frac{1}{2}\pi i}$ (b) $3e^{\pi i}$ (c) $4e^{-\frac{1}{2}\pi i}$

(d) $\sqrt{2}e^{\frac{1}{4}\pi i}$ (e) $2e^{-\frac{5}{6}\pi i}$ (f) $\sec\phi\, e^{\phi i}$

5 (a) $e^{\frac{1}{3}\pi i},\ e^{-\frac{2}{3}\pi i}$ (b) $\pm\sqrt{e}(\cos 1 + i\sin 1)$

6 $i\tan y$

10 $e^{\cos\theta},\ \sin\theta$

11 (a) $e^{0.805+0.464i}$ (b) $e^{1.417-1.326i}$

(c) $e^{1.151-2.820i}$

Any integer multiple of $2\pi i$ can be added to the index without changing the value.

12 $e^z - e^{z^*}$ is imaginary, $e^z \div e^{z^*}$ has modulus 1.

Exercise 5D (page 312)

1 $-2 + 4i,\ 4 + 2i$

2 $(3 + 2\sqrt{3}) + (3\sqrt{3} - 2)i,$

$-(2\sqrt{3} - 3) - (3\sqrt{3} + 2)i$

3 $5 + 3i,\ -3 - i$

4 $(4 + 2\sqrt{3}) + (3\sqrt{3} - 1)i$

8 (a) $8 + 4i$ (b) $6 + 3i$

(c) $\frac{51}{16}(2 + i)$ (d) $\frac{16}{5}(2 + i)$

9 (a) $12 + 4i$ (b) $10(1 + i)$

(c) $\frac{15}{2}(1 + i)$ (d) $8(1 + i)$

10 $\frac{1}{5}(1 + 7i)$

11 $\frac{8}{13}(1 - 5i)$

12 (a) $\frac{1}{2}\pi$ (b) $-\frac{1}{2}\pi$ (c) $-\frac{1}{2}\pi$

13 The semicircle in the first quadrant of the circle with 3 and 4i at ends of a diameter

14 The line segment AB

15 The part of the circle with centre -1 passing through i and $-i$ for which the real part is negative

Miscellaneous exercise 5 (page 314)

1 (a) $\sec\alpha$ (b) $4\sec\alpha$ (c) $\frac{1}{2}\pi - \alpha$

(d) $\frac{2}{5}\pi - \alpha$

2 $5,\ -0.927;$ (a) $\frac{5}{3}$ (b) 0.120

3 (a) $\sec\theta,\ \theta$ (b) $-\sec\theta,\ \theta - \pi$

(c) $-\sec\theta,\ \theta - \pi$ (d) $\sec\theta,\ \theta - 2\pi$

4 (a) $2\sin\theta,\ \theta - \frac{1}{2}\pi$ (b) $-2\sin\theta,\ \theta + \frac{1}{2}\pi$

5 $r = \sqrt{8 - 4\sqrt{3}},\ \theta = \frac{7}{12}\pi;$

$r = \sqrt{8 - 2\sqrt{6} - 2\sqrt{2}},\ \theta = \frac{17}{24}\pi;$

$r = \sqrt{8 - 4\sqrt{2}},\ \theta = \frac{5}{8}\pi$

6 $2\sin(\alpha + \beta)\cos(\alpha - \beta),$

$-2\sin(\alpha + \beta)\sin(\alpha - \beta)$

7 (a) $2\cos\frac{1}{2}\theta,\ \frac{1}{2}\theta$ (b) $2\sin\frac{1}{2}\theta,\ \frac{1}{2}\pi + \frac{1}{2}\theta$

(c) $\frac{1}{2}\pi$

If U, V represent 1 and -1, then

$VZ = 2\cos\frac{1}{2}\theta,\ UZ = 2\sin\frac{1}{2}\theta;\ \overrightarrow{VZ}$ and $\overrightarrow{UZ}$ make angles $\frac{1}{2}\theta$ and $\frac{1}{2}\pi + \frac{1}{2}\theta$ with the real axis, angle $V\hat{Z}U = \frac{1}{2}\pi$.

(a) unchanged   (b) $-2\sin\frac{1}{2}\theta,\ \frac{1}{2}\pi - \frac{1}{2}\theta$

(c) $-\frac{1}{2}\pi$

9 (b) $s^* = -\lambda i t^*$ (c) $ac + bd = 0$

10 $r = b + i(q - b)$, $s = a + i(r - a)$,
$t = b + i(s - b)$

12 $(1 - i)a + ic$, $(1 + i)b - ic$,
$\frac{1}{2}(a + b) + \frac{1}{2}(b - a)i$; M is the third vertex of
an isosceles right-angled triangle having AB
as hypotenuse.

13 $3 - 3i$, $5 + 3i$, $4i$, -2

15 (a) (i) Line through A parallel to OB
        (ii) Line AB
        (iii) Circle having AB as diameter

Revision exercise 3 (page 317)

1 $7(6i + 2j + 3k)$

2 (a) $\frac{1}{2}\sqrt{1563}$

(b) $\mathbf{r} \cdot \left(\frac{-35}{\sqrt{1563}}\mathbf{i} - \frac{17}{\sqrt{1563}}\mathbf{j} - \frac{7}{\sqrt{1563}}\mathbf{k} \right) = \frac{137}{\sqrt{1563}}$

3 $\frac{22}{\sqrt{38}}$

4 $y = \frac{1}{2}(x^2 - 1 + e^{-x^2})$

5 (a) (i) $Ae^{2x} + Be^x$ (ii) $x^2 - 2x$
   (b) (i) $Ae^x + B$ (ii) e^{2x}
   (c) (i) $Ae^x + Be^{4x}$ (ii) $\sin 2x + 2\cos 2x$

6 (a) (i) $1, 0$ (ii) $1, \pi$ (iii) $1, 0$
      (iv) $1, \pi$ (v) $1, 2\theta$ (vi) $1, 2\theta - 2\pi$
      (vii) $1, 2\theta$ (viii) $1, 2\theta + 2\pi$
   (b) (i) $2, 0$ (ii) 0, undefined (iii) $2, 0$
      (iv) 0, undefined   (v) $2\cos\theta, \theta$
      (vi) $-2\cos\theta, \theta - \pi$ (vii) $2\cos\theta, \theta$
      (viii) $-2\cos\theta, \theta + \pi$

7 $y = -2e^{-x}$

8 $y = 2x + x^2$

9 $2x - 2y + z = 3$ (a) 4 (b) 7.76

10 (b) $\cos 2\beta + i \sin 2\beta$
   (e) If angle $APB = \frac{1}{4}\pi$, P lies on a circle
       centre C, radius $\sqrt{2}$.

11 (a) $y = 0$, $y = x$ (b) $y = \frac{cx^2}{cx - 1}$

   (c) $y = \frac{x^2}{x + k}$, equivalent by taking $k = -\frac{1}{c}$

   (d) $y = x + \frac{1}{c} + \frac{1}{c(cx - 1)}$ has asymptotes
       $x = \frac{1}{c}$ and $y = x + \frac{1}{c}$, stationary points at
       $(0, 0)$ and $\left(\frac{2}{c}, \frac{4}{c} \right)$, approximates to
       $y = -cx^2$ near $x = 0$.

   (e) From the differential equation, $\frac{dy}{dx} = 0$
       when $y(2x - y) = 0$.
   (f) Bends upwards when $y > 0$, downwards
       when $y < 0$.

12 (a) 22 (b) $12i - 15j - 9k$
      2.27

13 $3i + 4j + k$, $3x - 2y - 2z = -1$

14 (b) $3i + 4j - 5k$ (c) 6

6   De Moivre's theorem

Exercise 6A (page 326)

1 (a) 16 (b) $-\frac{1}{512}$ (c) $\frac{1 + i}{\sqrt{2}}$
   (d) -1 (e) $-i$
   (f) $(8.98 - 4.40i) \times 10^{29}$ (g) $1.57 - 1.10i$
   (h) $-0.692 - 0.722i$

2 (a) 2, negative   (b) none
   (c) 5, positive   (d) 3, negative
   (e) 6, negative   (f) none
   (g) 4, negative   (h) none

3 (a) ± 1, $\pm i$, $\frac{\pm 1 \pm i}{\sqrt{2}}$ (the $\pm$ signs are
       independent of each other)
   (b) $1, 0.623 \pm 0.782i$, $-0.223 \pm 0.975i$,
       $-0.901 \pm 0.434i$

4 (a) $\pm i$ (b) -1, $\exp(\pm \frac{1}{3}\pi i)$
   (c) $\exp(\pm \frac{1}{4}\pi i)$, $\exp(\pm \frac{3}{4}\pi i)$
   (d) -1, $\exp(\pm \frac{1}{5}\pi i)$, $\exp(\pm \frac{3}{5}\pi i)$
   (e) $\exp(\pm \frac{1}{6}\pi i)$, $\pm i$, $\exp(\pm \frac{5}{6}\pi i)$
   $\exp\left(\frac{r\pi i}{n} \right)$ for $r = \pm 1, \pm 3, \dots, \pm(n - 1)$
   if n is even, -1 and $\exp\left(\frac{r\pi i}{n} \right)$ for
   $r = \pm 1, \pm 3, \dots \pm(n - 2)$ if n is odd

Exercise 6B (page 328)

1 (a) ω^2 (b) 1 (c) $-\omega$ (d) -1
   (e) -3ω (f) 3 (g) ω^2 (h) ω

2 (a) 1 (b) ω (c) $-\omega^4$ (d) 5

4 $3x, 3y, 3z$; $x = 2$, $y = -\frac{1}{3} + \frac{1}{3}\omega$, $z = -\frac{2}{3} - \frac{1}{3}\omega$

5 (a) $a^2 - ab + b^2$
   (b) $a^4 - a^3b + a^2b^2 - ab^3 + b^4$

6 $\beta = \alpha^2$, $\gamma = \alpha^3$, $\delta = \alpha^4$
   (a) 1 (b) -1 (c) 1
   (d) 2 (e) -1

7 $y = -c\omega^2 - a\omega$, $z = -a\omega^2 - b\omega$;
   $a + b\omega^2 + c\omega$, $b + c\omega^2 + a\omega$, $c + a\omega^2 + b\omega$

Exercise 6C (page 334)

1 (a) $-i$, $\pm \frac{1}{2}\sqrt{3} + \frac{1}{2}i$
   (b) $\pm(\sqrt{3} - i)$, $\pm(1 + \sqrt{3}i)$
   (c) $\pm 2i$, $\pm \sqrt{3} \pm i$

2 (a) $\pm(0.924 - 0.383i)$, $\pm(0.383 + 0.924i)$

(b) $-1 - i$, $1.397 + 0.221i$, $0.221 + 1.397i$
   $-1.260 + 0.642i$, $0.642 - 1.260i$

(c) $4.547 + 2.080i$, $-4.075 + 2.898i$,
   $-0.472 - 4.978i$

3 (a) $(z^2 - \sqrt{2}z + 1)(z^2 + \sqrt{2}z + 1)$

(b) $(z - \sqrt{2})(z + \sqrt{2})(z^2 + 2)$
   $\times (z^2 - 2z + 2)(z^2 + 2z + 2)$

(c) $(z^2 - z + 1)(z^2 + z + 1)$

(d) $\left(z^2 - 2z\cos\frac{1}{9}\pi + 1\right) \times \left(z^2 - 2z\cos\frac{5}{9}\pi + 1\right)$
   $\times \left(z^2 - 2z\cos\frac{7}{9}\pi + 1\right)$

4 Answers are $\exp(k\pi i)$ for the stated values of k.

(a) Both $\pm\frac{1}{3}$, 1

(b) (i) $\frac{1}{2}$ (ii) $\pm\frac{1}{2}$

(c) (i) $-\frac{1}{4}$, $\frac{3}{4}$ (ii) $\pm\frac{1}{4}$, $\pm\frac{3}{4}$

(d) (i) $\frac{3}{8}$, $-\frac{5}{8}$

(ii) $\frac{1}{24}$, $\frac{3}{8}$, $\frac{17}{24}$, $-\frac{7}{24}$, $-\frac{5}{8}$, $-\frac{23}{24}$;
   $(z^p)^{\frac{1}{q}}$ always has q distinct values; $\left(z^{\frac{1}{q}}\right)^p$
   has q distinct values if p and q have no
   common factors, otherwise it has $\dfrac{q}{h}$
   distinct values where h is the highest
   common factor of p and q.

7 (a) 2   (b) n

Miscellaneous exercise 6 (page 334)

1 $\sqrt{2}\exp\left(\frac{1}{4}\pi i\right)$, $2\sqrt{2}\exp\left(\frac{3}{4}\pi i\right)$;
   $\sqrt{2}\exp\left(\frac{11}{12}\pi i\right)$, $\sqrt{2}\exp\left(-\frac{5}{12}\pi i\right)$;
   $\sqrt{2}\exp\left(-\frac{11}{12}\pi i\right)$, $\sqrt{2}\exp\left(-\frac{1}{4}\pi i\right)$,
   $\sqrt{2}\exp\left(\frac{5}{12}\pi i\right)$

2 $8e^{\frac{1}{2}\pi i}$; $-2i$, $\pm\sqrt{3} + i$;
   $1 - 3\sqrt{3}i$, $1 - \sqrt{3}i$, $-2 - 2\sqrt{3}i$

3 $\exp\left(\dfrac{(2r + 1)\pi}{n}i\right)$ for $r = 0, 1, 2, \ldots, n - 1$

4 $\pm 1 \pm i$; $-1 \pm 2i$, $\frac{1}{5}(-1 \pm 2i)$

5 $2e^{\pi i}(= -2)$, $2e^{\pm\frac{1}{3}\pi i}$, $2e^{\pm\frac{3}{5}\pi i}$; $\pm\frac{1}{10}\pi$, $\pm\frac{3}{10}\pi$

9 $3(\omega - \omega^2)$, $\dfrac{1}{3}\begin{pmatrix} 1 & 1 & 1 \\ 1 & \omega & \omega^2 \\ 1 & \omega^2 & \omega \end{pmatrix}$

10 $b = \omega^2 a$, $c = \omega a$

7 Further trigonometry

Exercise 7A (page 344)

1 (a) $3s - 4s^3$

(b) $16s^5 - 20s^3 + 5s$

(c) $32c^6 - 48c^4 + 18c^2 - 1$

(d) $2cs(16s^4 - 16s^2 + 3)$

(e) $256c^9 - 576c^7 + 432c^5 - 120c^3 + 9c$

(f) $256s^9 - 576s^7 + 432s^5 - 120s^3 + 9s$

2 (a) $\dfrac{4t - 4t^3}{1 - 6t^2 + t^4}$

(b) $\dfrac{7t - 35t^3 + 21t^5 - t^7}{1 - 21t^2 + 35t^4 - 7t^6}$

(c) $\dfrac{8t - 56t^3 + 56t^5 - 8t^7}{1 - 28t^2 + 70t^4 - 28t^6 + t^8}$

3 $16c^4 - 16c^2 + 3 = 0$; $\frac{1}{2}\sqrt{3} = \cos\frac{1}{6}\pi$,
   $\frac{1}{2} = \cos\frac{1}{3}\pi$, $-\frac{1}{2} = \cos\frac{2}{3}\pi$, $-\frac{1}{2}\sqrt{3} = \cos\frac{5}{6}\pi$

4 $cs(16s^4 - 16s^2 + 3) = 0$; $0 = \sin 0$,
   $\pm\frac{1}{2} = \sin\left(\pm\frac{1}{6}\pi\right)$, $\pm\frac{1}{2}\sqrt{3} = \sin\left(\pm\frac{1}{3}\pi\right)$,
   $0 = \cos\frac{1}{2}\pi$

5 $8s^4 - 8s^2 + 1 = 0$; $\frac{1}{2}\sqrt{2 - \sqrt{2}}$

6 $\tan\frac{5}{16}\pi$, $-\tan\frac{3}{16}\pi$, $-\tan\frac{7}{16}\pi$;
   $\sqrt{4 + 2\sqrt{2}} - \sqrt{2} - 1$

8 0, $-\frac{3}{4}$, $\frac{1}{8}$

9 $32s^5 - 40s^3 + 10s - 1 = 0$;
   $\sin\frac{1}{30}\pi$, $\sin\frac{1}{6}\pi$, $\sin\frac{13}{30}\pi$, $-\sin\frac{7}{30}\pi$, $-\sin\frac{11}{30}\pi$;
   $2s - 1$

10 $8c^3 - 6c + 1 = 0$; $\frac{1}{8}$

11 $t^7 - 21t^5 + 35t^3 - 7t = 0$, with roots
   $\tan\frac{1}{7}r\pi$ for $r \in \mathbb{Z}$, $-3 \leqslant r \leqslant 3$;
   $u^3 - 21u^2 + 35u - 7 = 0$
   (a) 21   (b) $\sqrt{7}$

12 (a) 1.047, -0.946, -0.101
   (b) 2.529, -2.361, -0.167

13 $k = 2$, $a = -\frac{1}{2}$;
   1.827, 1.338, -0.209, -1, -1.956

Exercise 7B (page 346)

1 (a) $\frac{1}{4}(\cos 3\theta + 3\cos\theta)$

(b) $\frac{1}{8}(\cos 4\theta - 4\cos 2\theta + 3)$

(c) $\frac{1}{32}(\cos 6\theta + 6\cos 4\theta + 15\cos 2\theta + 10)$

(d) $\frac{1}{64}(-\sin 7\theta + 7\sin 5\theta - 21\sin 3\theta + 35\sin\theta)$

(e) $\frac{1}{16}(-\sin 5\theta + \sin 3\theta + 2\sin\theta)$

(f) $\frac{1}{64}(\cos 7\theta - \cos 5\theta - 3\cos 3\theta + 3\cos\theta)$

2 (a) $\frac{1}{32}\sin 4\theta + \frac{1}{4}\sin 2\theta + \frac{3}{8}\theta + k$

(b) $\frac{1}{12}\cos 3\theta - \frac{3}{4}\cos\theta + k$

(c) $-\frac{1}{80}\sin 5\theta - \frac{1}{48}\sin 3\theta + \frac{1}{8}\sin\theta + k$

3 (a) $\frac{3}{32}\pi - \frac{1}{4}$ (b) $\frac{35}{256}\pi$ (c) $\frac{1}{16}\pi$

Exercise 7C (page 351)

2   $-\dfrac{\sin 20\theta}{2\cos\theta}$, $\dfrac{1-\cos 20\theta}{2\cos\theta}$

3   $\dfrac{\cos(\alpha+\frac{1}{2}(n-1)\theta)\sin\frac{1}{2}n\theta}{\sin\frac{1}{2}\theta}$; terms are the projection of a regular n-gon on a line.

4   (a) $\dfrac{9\sin\theta}{10+6\cos\theta}$

   (b) $e^{-\cos\theta}\sin(\sin\theta)$

   (c) $\sin^n\theta\cos n\theta$, $\sin^n\theta\sin n\theta$,
       $-\sin^n\theta\cos n\theta$, $-\sin^n\theta\sin n\theta$

5   (a) $0.28+0.96i$ (b) $1.01+0.69i$
   (c) $-2.95+3.19i$ (d) $0.82+0.54i$

6   $\dfrac{\beta}{n}\cos\dfrac{(n\mp1)\beta}{2n}\sin\frac{1}{2}\beta\Big/\sin\dfrac{\beta}{2n}$; $\to\sin\beta$

Exercise 7D (page 356)

1   (a) $4C^3-3C$
   (b) $4S^3+3S$
   (c) $16C^5-20C^3+5C$
   (d) $64S^7+112S^5+56S^3+7S$
   (e) $8CS(16S^6+24S^4+10S^2+1)$

2   (a) 2.951
   (b) 3.625
   (c) 0.760
   (d) -4.107
   (e) 3.233, 0.423, -3.656

3   $x=e^u$ (a) $\frac{1}{4}(\cosh 3u+3\cosh u)$
   (b) $\frac{1}{8}(\cosh 4u-4\cosh 2u+3)$
   (c) $\frac{1}{32}(\cosh 6u+6\cosh 4u+15\cosh 2u+10)$
   (d) $\frac{1}{64}(\sinh 7u-7\sinh 5u+21\sinh 3u$
       $-35\sinh u)$
   (e) $\frac{1}{16}(\sinh 5u-\sinh 3u-2\sinh u)$
   (f) $\frac{1}{64}(\cosh 7u-\cosh 5u-3\cosh 3u$
       $+3\cosh u)$

4   (a) $\frac{1}{32}\sinh 4u+\frac{1}{4}\sinh 2u+\frac{3}{8}u+k$
   (b) $\frac{1}{12}\cosh 3u-\frac{3}{4}\cosh u+k$
   (c) $\frac{1}{80}\sinh 5u+\frac{1}{48}\sinh 3u+\frac{1}{8}\sinh u+k$

5   $\dfrac{9\sinh u}{10+6\cosh u}$, $|u|<\ln 3$

6   $\sinh^n u\cosh nu$ for n even,
   $-\sinh^n u\sinh nu$ for n odd

Miscellaneous exercise 7 (page 356)

5   $(0,1)$, $\left(\pm\sqrt{\dfrac{5+\sqrt5}{8}},\dfrac{\sqrt5-1}{4}\right)$,

   $\left(\pm\sqrt{\dfrac{5-\sqrt5}{8}},\dfrac{-1-\sqrt5}{4}\right)$

6   $64s^7-112s^5+56s^3-7s-1=0$; roots
   $s=1$ and $s=\sin\frac{3}{14}\pi,-\sin\frac{1}{14}\pi,-\sin\frac{5}{14}\pi$
   (all repeated)

7   $8c^3+4c^2-4c-1=0$; 0.623 490,
   $-0.222\,521$, $-0.900\,969$

8   $\frac{1}{16},-\frac{1}{32},-\frac{1}{16},\frac{1}{32}$

9   $\frac{5}{32}\pi a^2$

10   $\frac{35}{128}\pi^2$

11   $\dfrac{z(1-z^8)}{1-z}$; $-2i\sin\frac{1}{2}\theta e^{\frac{1}{2}\theta i}$; $\dfrac{\sin 4\theta\cos\frac{9}{2}\theta}{\sin\frac{1}{2}\theta}$

12   $\dfrac{2\cos\theta+1}{5+4\cos\theta}$, $\dfrac{2\sin\theta}{5+4\cos\theta}$

13   $\pm(1\pm\sqrt3)$; $2\sqrt2\cos 15°$, $2\sqrt2\cos 105°$,
    $2\sqrt2\cos 75°$, $2\sqrt2\cos 165°$; $\dfrac{\sqrt3+1}{2\sqrt2}$

14   $\frac{1}{3}(\exp z+\exp(\omega z)+\exp(\omega^2 z))$;
    $\dfrac{1}{3}\displaystyle\sum_{r=0}^{2}\exp\left(\cos\left(\theta+\tfrac{2}{3}r\pi\right)\right)\cos\left(\sin\left(\theta+\tfrac{2}{3}r\pi\right)\right)$

15   1.041 691 47, 1.008 333 609, 1.001 388 891

16   $-\frac{2}{3}$

8   Calculus with complex numbers

Exercise 8A (page 362)

1   (a) $e^{-2x}(A\cos 6x+B\sin 6x)$
   (b) $A+Be^{-4x}$
   (c) $A\cos 2x+B\sin 2x$
   (d) $Ae^{-10x}+Be^{4x}$
   (e) $e^{2t}(A\cos t+B\sin t)$ (f) $Ae^{-5t}+Be^t$

2   (a) $y=e^{-2x}(A\sin x+B\cos x)$
   (b) $y=e^{3x}(A\sin 4x+B\cos 4x)$
   (c) $x=A\sin 3t+B\cos 3t+\frac{2}{5}e^{-t}$
   (d) $u=e^{-t}(A\sin t+B\cos t)+\frac{1}{2}(t-1)$

3   (a) $y=e^{2x}\cos 2x$
   (b) $x=e^{-2t}(2\sin 3t+\cos 3t)$
   (c) $u=(t-1)^2+e^{-t}(\sin t-\cos t)$
   (d) $x=e^{-t}(1+\sin 3t)$

Exercise 8B (page 366)

1   (a) $\frac{1}{5}e^{2x}(2\cos x+\sin x)+k$
   (b) $\frac{1}{17}e^x(\sin 4x-4\cos 4x)+k$
   (c) $\frac{1}{5}e^{-x}(2\sin 2x-\cos 2x)+k$
   (d) $-\frac{1}{25}e^{-4x}(4\sin 3x+3\cos 3x)+k$
   (e) $\frac{1}{169}e^{2x}((26x+5)\cos 3x$
       $+(39x-12)\sin 3x)+k$
   (f) $\frac{1}{2}e^{-x}(\sin 3x-\cos 3x)+k$

2 (a) $y = 2\cos t + \sin t$

(b) $y = \frac{1}{2}e^t \sin 2t$

(c) $x = -\frac{1}{113}(7\sin 2t + 8\cos 2t)$

(d) $u = \frac{1}{10}(\sin t - 3\cos t)$

(e) $u = -\frac{1}{2}(\cos x + \sin x)$

(f) $y = -e^{3x}\cos x$

(g) $x = -\frac{1}{4}t\cos 2t$

(h) $y = \frac{1}{6}xe^x \sin 3x$

3 (a) $x = A\sin t + B\cos t$
$\quad - \frac{1}{10}e^{-t}(2\sin 2t + \cos 2t)$

(b) $y = e^x(A\sin 7x + B\cos 7x)$
$\quad + \frac{1}{2405}(49\sin x + 2\cos x)$

(c) $x = Ae^{3t} + Be^{-5t} + \frac{1}{102}(\sin 3t - 4\cos 3t)$

(d) $y = e^{-3t}\left(A\sin t + (B - \frac{1}{2}t)\cos t\right)$

4 (a) $y = \sin x + 3\cos x - e^{-3x}$

(b) $x = 2e^{-t}\sin^2 t$

(c) $y = (1 + e^{-2x})\sin x$

(d) $x = e^{pt}\left(\left(b - \frac{ap}{q} + \frac{t}{2q}\right)\sin qt + a\cos qt\right)$

Miscellaneous exercise 8 (page 366)

1 (a) $y = A\cos 2x + B\sin 2x$

(b) $x = e^{-t}(A\cos 7t + B\sin 7t)$

(c) $y = e^{-3x}(A\cos 4x + B\sin 4x) + \frac{1}{2}e^{-x}$

(d) $u = e^{2t}(A\cos 4t + B\sin 4t) + 5t + 1$

(e) $x = e^{-1t}(A\cos 3t + B\sin 3t) - \frac{1}{40}\cos 5t$

2 (a) $y = \frac{1}{2}e^{-x}\sin 2x$

(b) $u = e^{-t}(3\cos t + 4\sin t) + \sin t - 2\cos t$

(c) $x = \frac{1}{4}(2 + t)\sin 2t$

3 (a) $\dfrac{e^{at}}{a^2 + b^2}\left(\begin{array}{c}(ap - bq)\cos bt \\ + (aq + bp)\sin bt\end{array}\right) + k$

(b) $\dfrac{t}{b}(p\sin bt - q\cos bt)$
$\quad + \dfrac{1}{b^2}(p\cos bt + q\sin bt) + k$

4 (a) $\dfrac{1}{a^2 + 1}$

(b) $\dfrac{1}{a^2 + 1} \times \dfrac{1 + e^{-\pi a}}{1 - e^{-\pi a}}$

5 $\dfrac{U}{\sqrt{3}} e^{-t}\sin(\sqrt{3}t);\ \dfrac{\pi}{3\sqrt{3}}$

6 $x = \dfrac{V}{k} + e^{-2kt}(A\cos 2kt + B\sin 2kt);$
$\quad x = \dfrac{V}{k}(1 - e^{-2kt}(\cos 2kt + \sin 2kt)); \to \dfrac{V}{k}$

7 (a) $I = I_0 e^{-t/RC}$

(b) $I = \dfrac{E_0 C\omega}{1 + R^2C^2\omega^2}(\cos \omega t$
$\quad + RC\omega\sin \omega t - e^{-t/RC})$

8 (a) $5\sin 3t + e^{-t}(\sin t + 2\cos t)$

9 Since the complementary function has a factor e^{-t}, which $\to 0$ as $t \to \infty$, for large values of t the solution of the differential equation can be approximated by the particular integral.

10 (a) $A\sin 14t + B\cos 14t$

(b) $\dfrac{2}{196 - \omega^2}\sin \omega t,$
$\quad x = \dfrac{2}{196 - \omega^2}\sin \omega t + A\sin 14t + B\cos 14t$

(c) $x = A\sin 14t + B\cos 14t - \frac{1}{14}t\cos 14t;$
$\quad x = \frac{1}{196}\sin 14t - \frac{1}{14}t\cos 14t;$ oscillation whose amplitude increases without limit.

9 Groups

Exercise 9A (page 373)

1 (a) Binary operation: not closed; not commutative; not associative

(b) Binary operation: closed; not commutative; associative

(c) Binary operation: closed; not commutative; not associative

(d) Binary operation: closed; commutative; not associative

(e) Binary operation: closed; commutative; associative

(f) Not a binary operation as $\mathbf{B}^{-1}$ does not exist for all 2×2 matrices.

(g) Binary operation: closed; not commutative; associative

(h) Binary operation: closed; not commutative; not associative

(i) Binary operation: closed; commutative; associative

(j) Not a binary operation as there is no smallest number greater than $a + b$

Exercise 9B (page 375)

1 (a) $s \circ t = p,\ t \circ s = q,\ (p \circ q) \circ s = s,$
$\quad p \circ (q \circ t) = t;\ r,\ s;\ q,\ p$

(b) $s \circ t = q,\ t \circ s = p,\ (p \circ q) \circ s = r,$
$\quad p \circ (q \circ t) = t;\ r,\ u;\ p,\ q$

2 (a) No identity

(b) Identity I; no general inverse

(c) Identity $1 + 0i$; no general inverse, e.g. 0

(d) No identity

(e) No identity

(f) Identity $\begin{pmatrix} 1 & 1 \\ 0 & 0 \end{pmatrix}$; inverse $\begin{pmatrix} x^{-1} & x^{-1} \\ 0 & 0 \end{pmatrix}$

(g) Identity 6; inverses of 2, 4, 6 and 8 are 8, 4, 6 and 2.

(h) Identity 0; inverses of 0, 2, 4, 6 and 8 are 0, 8, 6, 4 and 2.

(i) Identity 1; inverses of 1, 3, 7 and 9 are 1, 7, 3 and 9.

Exercise 9C (page 381)

1 (a) Not a group; no identity element.
  (c) Not a group; 2 has no inverse.
  (e) Not a group; not closed.
  (g) Not a group; 5 has no inverse.
  (i) Not a group; 0 has no inverse.
  All the rest are groups.

2 There is no identity element.

3 $x \mapsto \dfrac{x-1}{x}, \ x \mapsto \dfrac{x}{x-1}$

7 $x \mapsto a^{-1}(x-b)$

8 a^3

Exercise 9D (page 386)

1

	0	1	2	3	4
0	0	1	2	3	4
1	1	2	3	4	0
2	2	3	4	0	1
3	3	4	0	1	2
4	4	0	1	2	3

The inverse of 2 is 3. $x = 4$; $y = 3$

2

	1	2	3	4	5	6
1	1	2	3	4	5	6
2	2	4	6	1	3	5
3	3	6	2	5	1	4
4	4	1	5	2	6	3
5	5	3	1	6	4	2
6	6	5	4	3	2	1

The inverse of 3 is 5, and the inverse of 4 is 2.

3

	1	2	3	4	5
1	1	2	3	4	5
2	2	4		2	4
3	3		3		3
4	4	2		4	2
5	5	4	3	2	1

The operation is not closed as 2×3 is not in the set. If q is not prime, then $q = mn$ for some $q = m, n \in (\mathbb{Z}_q - \{0\}, \times)$; $mn = q \notin (\mathbb{Z}_q - \{0\}, \times)$, so the operation is not closed.

4

	1	2	4	7	8	11	13	14
1	1	2	4	7	8	11	13	14
2	2	4	8	14	1	7	11	13
4	4	8	1	13	2	14	7	11
7	7	14	13	4	11	2	1	8
8	8	1	2	11	4	13	14	7
11	11	7	14	2	13	1	8	4
13	13	11	7	1	14	8	4	2
14	14	13	11	8	7	4	2	1

11

5 9

6 4, 1; (a) 15   (b) 17   (c) 19   (d) 53

7

	0	1	2	3	4
0	2	3	4	0	1
1	3	4	0	1	2
2	4	0	1	2	3
3	0	1	2	3	4
4	1	2	3	4	0

The identity is 3, and the inverses of 0, 1, 2, 3 and 4 are 1, 0, 4, 3 and 2 respectively.

Exercise 9E (page 388)

1

	I	X	Y	H
I	I	X	Y	H
X	X	I	H	Y
Y	Y	H	I	X
H	H	Y	X	I

where X and Y are reflections in the x- and y-axes, and H is a half-turn.

2 S and X; for RAR^{-1} the elements are I, R, S, Y, X and Z and for XAX^{-1} they are I, S, R, X, Z and Y. $A = R$

3 D_4

	I	R	R^2	R^3	H	L	V	M
I	I	R	R^2	R^3	H	L	V	M
R	R	R^2	R^3	I	M	H	L	V
R^2	R^2	R^3	I	R	V	M	H	L
R^3	R^3	I	R	R^2	L	V	M	H
H	H	L	V	M	I	R	R^2	R^3
L	L	V	M	H	R^3	I	R	R^2
V	V	M	H	L	R^2	R^3	I	R
M	M	H	L	V	R	R^2	R^3	I

4 R

Miscellaneous exercise 9 (page 389)

1

	e	a	b
e	e	a	b
a	a	b	e
b	b	e	a

2 In the table $a^2 \circ b$ is written as $a^2 b$, etc. The right half of the table is below the left half.

	e	a	a^2	a^3
e	e	a	a^2	a^3
a	a	a^2	a^3	e
a^2	a^2	a^3	e	a
a^3	a^3	e	a	a^2
b	b	$a^3 b$	$a^2 b$	ab
ab	ab	b	$a^3 b$	$a^2 b$
$a^2 b$	$a^2 b$	ab	b	$a^3 b$
$a^3 b$	$a^3 b$	$a^2 b$	ab	b

	b	ab	$a^2 b$	$a^3 b$
e	b	ab	$a^2 b$	$a^3 b$
a	ab	$a^2 b$	$a^3 b$	b
a^2	$a^2 b$	$a^3 b$	b	ab
a^3	$a^3 b$	b	ab	$a^2 b$
b	a^2	a	e	a^3
ab	a^3	a^2	a	e
$a^2 b$	e	a^3	a^2	a
$a^3 b$	a	e	a^3	a^2

3 1, 9, 17, 25, 33, 41, 49, 57; inverses of 9 etc. are 57, 49, 41, 33, 25, 17, 9; 9, 57, 25 and 41 are generators.

4

	0	1	2	3	4	5	6
0	0	1	2	3	4	5	6
1	1	1	1	1	1	1	1
2	2	1	0	6	5	4	3
3	3	1	6	4	2	0	5
4	4	1	5	2	6	3	0
5	5	1	4	0	3	6	2
6	6	1	3	5	0	2	4

Delete the element 1.

5 $(bb)b \neq b(bb)$, so the operation is not associative.

9 (a) 0   (b) $-a$
(d) There is a problem with closure when $ab = -1$, so $2^*\left(-\frac{1}{2}\right) \notin S$.

10 Subgroups

Exercise 10A (page 395)

1 $5^1 = 5$, $5^2 = 7$, $5^3 = 8$, $5^4 = 4$, $5^5 = 2$, $5^1 = 1$; there are six distinct powers.

2 (a) The orders of 0, 1, 2, 3, 4, 5 are 1, 6, 3, 2, 3, 6.
(b) The orders of 1, 2, 3, 4, 5, 6, 7, 8, 9, 10 are 1, 10, 5, 5, 5, 10, 10, 10, 5, 2.
(c) The orders of I, R, R², R³, H, L, V, M, are 1, 4, 2, 4, 2, 2, 2, 2.

3 X, Y, H

4 i, $-$i; 2

5 1, -1

6 For example, any matrix of the form $\begin{pmatrix} 1 & k \\ 0 & -1 \end{pmatrix}$ where $k \in \mathbb{N}$ has order 2.

7 Yes; 5 is a generator.

8 2 and -2 are both generators.

9 The first is not cyclic, since $a^2 = b^2 = c^2 = e$; the second is cyclic, with a and c as generators.

10 1, 2, 3 and 4 are generators of $(\mathbb{Z}_5, +)$; 1 and 5 are generators of $(\mathbb{Z}_6, +)$.

Exercise 10B (page 399)

1 (a) The orders of 1, R, R², R³, H, L, V, M are 1, 4, 2, 4, 2, 2, 2, 2.
(b) $\{I\}, \{I, R^2\}, \{I, H\}, \{I, L\}, \{I, V\}, \{I, M\},$ $\{I, R, R^2, R^3\}$
(c) $\{I, H, R^2, V\}, \{I, L, R^2, M\}$

2 (a) $(\{0\}, +), (\{0, 2\}, +), (\mathbb{Z}_4, +)$
(b) $(\{0\}, +), (\mathbb{Z}_5, +)$

3 $\{1, -1\}$

7 (a) $\{I, R, S\}$ (b) $\{I, X\}$
(c) $\left\{ \begin{pmatrix} a & b \\ 0 & a \end{pmatrix} : a, b \in \mathbb{R} \right\}$
(d) $\{e, b, q, s\}$ (e) $\{e, x, p\}$

8 $\{e\}, \{e, b\}, \{e, a, b, c\}, \{e, p, b, r\}, \{e, q, b, s\},$ Q_4

9 $\{e\}, \{e, a\}, \{e, b\}, \{e, c\}, \{e, x, p\}, \{e, y, q\},$ $\{e, z, r\}, \{e, t, s\}, \{e, a, b, c\}, A_4$

Exercise 10C (page 402)

1 1, 2, 3, 4, 6, 8, 12, 24

2 As 10 is not a factor of 15, Lagrange's theorem shows that a group of order 15 cannot have a subgroup of order 10.

3 1, p, q and pq

Exercise 10D (page 404)

1 $\{I, R, S\}$, $\{X, Y, Z\}$;
$\{I\}$, $\{R\}$, $\{S\}$, $\{X\}$, $\{Y\}$, $\{Z\}$; D_3

2 $\{0, 3\}$, $\{1, 4\}$, $\{2, 5\}$

3 (a) $\{e, a, b, c\}$, $\{x, y, z, t\}$, $\{p, q, r, s\}$
(b) $\{e, x, p\}$, $\{a, t, r\}$, $\{b, y, s\}$, $\{c, z, q\}$

4 $\{0, \pm 3, \pm 6, \ldots\}$, $\{\ldots, -2, 1, 4, \ldots\}$,
$\{\ldots, -1, 2, 5, \ldots\}$

Miscellaneous exercise 10 (page 405)

4 (a) $\{1, 12\}$ (b) $\{1, 3, 9\}$
(c) By Lagrange's theorem, the order of a subgroup divides the order of a group. As 5 does not divide 12, there is no subgroup of order 5.

5 (a) $(b \otimes c)(x) = 1 - \dfrac{1}{1-x} = \dfrac{1-x-1}{1-x} = \dfrac{x}{x-1}$
$d(x) = \dfrac{x-1}{x}$; $e(x) = \dfrac{x}{x-1}$

(b)

G	i	a	b	c	d	e
i	i	a	b	c	d	e
a	a	i	c	b	e	d
b	b	d	i	e	a	c
c	c	e	a	d	i	b
d	d	b	e	i	c	a
e	e	c	d	a	b	i

(d) Not commutative as $d \otimes a = b$ and $a \otimes d = e$.
(e) Not cyclic since it is not commutative.
(f) $\{i\}$, $\{i, a\}$, $\{i, b\}$, $\{i, e\}$, $\{i, c, d\}$, G

6 (b) $\{2\}$, $\{2, 5\}$, $\{2, 4, 0\}$, G

7 (a) a, 4; b, 1; c, 4; d, 2
(b) $\{b, d\}$

8 (d) $\begin{pmatrix} \pm 1 & b \\ 0 & 1 \end{pmatrix}$

(e) $\left\{ \begin{pmatrix} 1 & 0 \\ 0 & 1 \end{pmatrix}, \begin{pmatrix} 0 & -1 \\ 1 & 0 \end{pmatrix}, \begin{pmatrix} -1 & 0 \\ 0 & -1 \end{pmatrix}, \begin{pmatrix} 0 & 1 \\ -1 & 0 \end{pmatrix} \right\}$
This is the subgroup generated by a rotation of $\frac{1}{2}\pi$ anticlockwise about the origin.

11 Isomorphisms of groups

Exercise 11 (page 412)

3 2 is a generator of $(\mathbb{Z}_{13} - \{0\}, \times (\bmod 13))$.
Define a function $f : \mathbb{Z}_{13} \to \mathbb{Z}_{12}$ by the rule $f(2^n) = n$ and show that it is an isomorphism.

Miscellaneous exercise 11 (page 416)

1 (a)

	2	4	6	8
2	4	8	2	6
4	8	6	4	2
6	2	4	6	8
8	6	2	8	4

(b) 6; $2^{-1} = 8$, $4^{-1} = 4$, $6^{-1} = 6$, $8^{-1} = 2$
(c) Both groups are cyclic with generators 2 and i respectively, so they are isomorphic.

2 (a) The orders of e, a, b, b^2, b^3, ab, ab^2, ab^3 are 1, 2, 4, 2, 4, 2, 2, 3.
(b) 4
(c) $\{e, b, b^2, b^3\}$ and $\{e, ab, b^2, ab^3\}$
(d) By Lagrange's theorem the order of a subgroup of a finite group divides the order of the group. As 6 does not divide 8, there is no subgroup of order 6.
(e) M is commutative and D is not, $ab \neq ba$.

3 (a) 9, 17, 25, 33, 41, 49, 57, 1
The orders are 8, 4, 8, 2, 8, 4, 8, 1 respectively.
The possible generators are 9, 25, 41, 57.
The subgroups are $\{1\}$, $\{1, 33\}$, $\{1, 17, 33, 49\}$, G.
(b) G contains a generator, so it is cyclic. Every element of H apart from the identity has order 2, so H is not cyclic. Therefore G and H are not isomorphic.

4 (a) $p = 4$, $q = 5$
(b) 1 and 8 are self-inverse; the other inverses occur in pairs, 2, 5 and 4, 7; $\{1\}$, $\{1, 8\}$, $\{1, 4, 7\}$, G.
(c) The order of the element 2 of G is 6, so G is cyclic. $\omega \in H$ has order 6, so H is cyclic.
Therefore G and H are isomorphic.

5 (a) $\{1\}$, $\{1, 13\}$

(b) The elements are the rotations of $\frac{2}{3}\pi$, $\frac{4}{3}\pi$ and 0 about the centre of the triangle, together with reflections in the lines of symmetry.

(c) G and H are not isomorphic; $\{1, 9, 11\}$ is a subgroup of G which is isomorphic to the subgroup of rotations of H.

6 $k = 11$. The possible values of n are 1, 2, 4 and 8. $\{1, 4, 7, 13\}$, $\{1, 2, 4, 8\}$ and $\{1, 4, 11, 14\}$. The orders of the elements in these groups are 1, 2, 4, 4 and 1, 4, 2, 4 and 1, 2, 2, 2. The first two groups both have generators, and are therefore cyclic and isomorphic. The third group does not have a generator, and is not isomorphic to the other two.

7 The orders of the elements $\{1, -1, i, -i\}$ are 1, 2, 4, 4. The orders of the elements $\{1, 7, 18, 24\}$ are 1, 4, 4, 2. Both groups have generators, and are therefore both cyclic and isomorphic.

8

G_5	1	2	3	4
1	1	2	3	4
2	2	4	1	3
3	3	1	4	2
4	4	3	2	1

G_8	1	3	5	7
1	1	3	5	7
3	3	1	7	5
5	5	7	1	3
7	7	5	3	1

G_{10}	1	3	7	9
1	1	3	7	9
3	3	9	1	7
7	7	1	9	3
9	9	7	3	1

G_{12}	1	5	7	11
1	1	5	7	11
5	5	1	11	7
7	7	11	1	5
11	11	7	5	1

There are only two groups of order 4, up to isomorphism, the cyclic group $\mathbb{Z}_4$ and the four-group V. The groups G_5 and G_{10} have generators 2 and 3 respectively, so they are cyclic and isomorphic to $\mathbb{Z}_4$. The elements of G_8 and G_{12}, apart from the identity elements, all have order 2, so these groups are not cyclic, and are isomorphic to the four-group V.

9 (b)

	0	2	3	4	5	6
0	0	2	3	4	5	6
2	2	0	6	5	4	3
3	3	6	4	2	0	5
4	4	5	2	6	3	0
5	5	4	0	3	6	2
6	6	3	5	0	2	4

(d) 3 is a generator G, so G is a cyclic group. The group of rotations of the regular hexagon has an element (rotation of angle $\frac{1}{3}\pi$) of order 6 and is therefore cyclic. Therefore the groups are isomorphic.

Revision exercise 4 (page 419)

1 The binary operation is not associative. For example, $g(gh) = gm = i$, $(gg)h = jh = g$.

2 (b) (i) **B**   (ii) **I**   (iii) $\mathbf{A^2B}$

(c) **I** has order 1;
$\mathbf{A^2}$, **B**, **AB**, $\mathbf{A^2B}$, $\mathbf{A^3B}$ have order 2;
A, $\mathbf{A^3}$ have order 4.

(e) $\left\{\mathbf{I, A^2, AB, A^3B}\right\}$, $\left\{\mathbf{I, A, A^2, A^3}\right\}$

(f) $\left\{\mathbf{I, A, A^2, A^3}\right\}$ is cyclic; the others are not.

3 (b)

	e	f	g	h
e	e	f	g	h
f	f	e	h	g
g	g	h	e	f
h	h	g	f	e

(c) In G_1, the order of 2 is 4, so G_1 is cyclic. In G_2, the order of each of the non-identity elements is 2, so G_2 is not cyclic. They are therefore not isomorphic.

4 $-9\,653\,287 + 1\,476\,984i$

5 (b) $\frac{1}{192}(44 + 15\pi)$

6 (a) (i) $\dfrac{z}{1+z}$

(ii) The series is a geometric progression, and the modulus of the common ratio is $\frac{1}{4}$, which is less than 1.

7 (a) $\cos k\theta + i\sin k\theta, \cos k\theta - i\sin k\theta$

(b) $\dfrac{e^{i\theta}\cos\theta(1 - e^{ni\theta}\cos^n\theta)}{1 - e^{i\theta}\cos\theta}$

(c) $\dfrac{\cos\theta(1 - \cos n\theta\cos^n\theta)}{\sin\theta}$

8 (a) (i)

×(mod 10)	2	4	6	8
2	4	8	2	6
4	8	6	4	2
6	2	4	6	8
8	6	2	8	4

(ii) $2^{-1} = 8,\ 4^{-1} = 4,\ 6^{-1} = 6,\ 8^{-1} = 2$

(b) **P** reflects in the y-axis,
   Q reflects in the x-axis,
   R rotates through π about the origin.

(c) No; G is cyclic (generator 2), but H is not.

9 (a) One possibility is $2.527 + 0.140i$.

(b) $zi, -zi, -z$

10 Yes, it is a subgroup.

$$M_{2n}M_{2p} = \begin{pmatrix} 1-2n & 2n \\ -2n & 1+2n \end{pmatrix}\begin{pmatrix} 1-2p & 2p \\ -2p & 1+2p \end{pmatrix}$$

$$= \begin{pmatrix} 1-2(n+p) & 2(n+p) \\ -2(n+p) & 1+2(n+p) \end{pmatrix}$$

$$= M_{2n+2p} \in H$$

$M_0 \in H$

$$M_{2n}^{-1} = \begin{pmatrix} 1-2n & 2n \\ -2n & 1+2n \end{pmatrix}^{-1} = \begin{pmatrix} 1+2n & -2n \\ 2n & 1-2n \end{pmatrix}$$

$$= \begin{pmatrix} 1-(-2n) & (-2n) \\ -(-2n) & 1+(-2n) \end{pmatrix} = M_{-2n} \in H$$

The result follows from the theorem in Section 10.4.

11 (c) $\{e, a, a^2, a^3\}, \{e, a^2, ab, a^3b\},$
   $\{e, a^2, b, a^2b\}$

12 (a)

×(mod 10)	2	4	6	8
2	4	8	2	6
4	8	6	4	2
6	2	4	6	8
8	6	2	8	4

(b) The identity element is 6, and the inverses of 2, 4, 6 and 8 are 8, 4, 6 and 2 respectively.

(c) In G the order of 2 is 4 so G is cyclic. In H the order of i is 4, so H is cyclic. As the groups G and H are both of order 4 and cyclic, they are isomorphic.

13 (b) $\cos\theta + i\sin\theta$ where $\theta = \frac{1}{12}\pi, \frac{3}{4}\pi, \frac{17}{12}\pi,$
   $-\frac{1}{12}\pi, -\frac{3}{4}\pi, -\frac{17}{12}\pi$

15 (a) $(x-1)(x^2+x+1), (x+1)(x^2-x+1)$

(b) $(z-1)(z+\frac{1}{2}+\frac{1}{2}\sqrt{3}i)(z+\frac{1}{2}-\frac{1}{2}\sqrt{3}i),$
   $(z+1)(z-\frac{1}{2}+\frac{1}{2}\sqrt{3}i)(z-\frac{1}{2}-\frac{1}{2}\sqrt{3}i)$

(c) $-1, 1$; no roots; $-1, 1$

(d) $\pm 1, \pm\frac{1}{2}\pm\frac{1}{2}\sqrt{3}i; \pm i, \pm\frac{1}{2}\sqrt{3}\pm\frac{1}{2}i;$
   $\pm 1, \pm i, \pm\frac{1}{2}\pm\frac{1}{2}\sqrt{3}i, \pm\frac{1}{2}\sqrt{3}\pm\frac{1}{2}i$ (where the $\pm$ signs are independent of each other)

Practice examinations

Practice examination 1 for FP3 (page 422)

1 (ii) $y = \frac{1}{2}(x+y)^2 + k$

2 (i) $57°$

   (ii) $\begin{pmatrix} 2 \\ 1 \\ 4 \end{pmatrix}$

(iii) $\dfrac{x-1}{2} = \dfrac{y-2}{1} = \dfrac{z-2}{4}$ is one possibility.

3 (i) $e^{\frac{1}{6}\pi i}, e^{\frac{5}{6}\pi i}, e^{-\frac{1}{2}\pi i}$

   (ii) $-\frac{11}{12}\pi, -\frac{7}{12}\pi, -\frac{1}{4}\pi, \frac{1}{12}\pi, \frac{5}{12}\pi, \frac{3}{4}\pi$

4 (i) 2, 3, 4, 6

   (ii) (a) $\{0, 6\}, \{0, 4, 8\}, \{0, 3, 6, 9\},$
      $\{0, 2, 4, 6, 8, 10\}$

   (b) 1, 5, 7, 11

5 Here is a sketch of the solution.

   (i) Put $x = e$. Then $a^2 = e$ leads to $a = a^{-1}$.

   (ii) $axa = x^{-1} \Rightarrow ax = x^{-1}a^{-1} = (ax)^{-1}$

   (iii) Since $axa = x^{-1}$ is true for all $x \in G$ it is true for $a^{-1}x$, since $a^{-1}x \in G$.

   (iv) $xy = (xy)^{-1} = y^{-1}x^{-1} = yx$

6 (ii) $\dfrac{1 - e^{ni\theta}}{1 - e^{i\theta}}$

7 (i) $y = \frac{1}{4} + (Ax + B)e^{-2x}$

   (ii) (a) $x = 1$

   (b)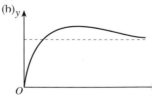

8 (i) $a\lambda + \mu + t = 2, 2\lambda + \mu - t = a - 2,$
   $\lambda + 2t = 1$

   (iii) $\begin{pmatrix} 2 \\ 2 \\ 3 \end{pmatrix}$

   (iv) l lies in p.

Practice examination 2 for FP3 (page 424)

1 (i) $\begin{pmatrix} 1 \\ 5 \\ 2 \end{pmatrix}$ (ii) $\sqrt{30}$

2 (ii) $-\frac{1}{4}\pi$

4 (i) $\cos^5\theta - 10\cos^3\theta\sin^2\theta + 5\cos\theta\sin^4\theta$,
   $5\cos^4\theta\sin\theta - 10\cos^2\theta\sin^3\theta + \sin^5\theta$

   (ii) $\sqrt{1 - \frac{2}{5}\sqrt{5}}$

5 (i) (a) Identity is **A**, $\mathbf{C}^{-1} = \mathbf{F}$

      (b) Element: **A B C D E F**
          Order: 1 2 3 2 2 3

      (c) $\{\mathbf{A}, \mathbf{B}\}$, $\{\mathbf{A}, \mathbf{D}\}$, $\{\mathbf{A}, \mathbf{E}\}$, $\{\mathbf{A}, \mathbf{C}, \mathbf{F}\}$

   (ii) Not isomorphic; e.g. H has an element of
        order 6 but G does not.

6 (i) $2\cos n\theta$, $2\mathrm{i}\sin n\theta$

7 (i) $a = \frac{1}{2}$, $b = 1$

   (ii) $x = \frac{1}{2}t + \mathrm{e}^{-t} - \frac{3}{4} - \frac{1}{4}\mathrm{e}^{-2t}$ (iii) $\frac{1}{2}$, 0

8 (i)

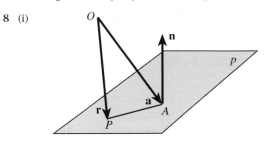

   $\overrightarrow{AP} = \mathbf{r} - \mathbf{a}$ lies in p and is thus
   perpendicular to $\mathbf{n}$.

   (iv) $\mathbf{b} + \{(\mathbf{a} - \mathbf{b}) \cdot \mathbf{n}\}\,\mathbf{n}$

Index